PORTABLE UTOPIA

At Greenock, for
NEW YORK,
The very fine A. I. American Ship
ELIZA,
Capt. GEO. F. DE LAROCHE,
Burthen 500 tons,

Coppered fastened, and newly coppered will positively be despatched for the above port on the 20th May.

This ship has excellent accommodations in Cabin and Steerage, her height between decks being Seven feet, and Passengers will be taken on moderate terms.

Apply in Greenock to the Captain, or Messrs. Thomson and Buchanan; here to

JOHN CREE
27, *Wilson Street.*

Glasgow, 28th April, 1830.

PORTABLE UTOPIA

GLASGOW AND THE UNITED STATES 1820–1920

with a comprehensive biographical list of the
Scots and Americans who created the connection

BERNARD ASPINWALL

ABERDEEN UNIVERSITY PRESS

First published 1984
Aberdeen University Press
A member of the Pergamon Group

The publisher acknowledges subsidy from
the Scottish Arts Council towards
the publication of this volume

British Library Cataloguing in Publication Data
Aspinwall, Bernard
    Portable utopia
    1. United States—Social conditions   2. Glasgow
    (Strathclyde)—Relations (general) with United States
    I. Title
    973.8   HN59.2

ISBN 0 08 028447 7

PRINTED IN GREAT BRITAIN
THE UNIVERSITY PRESS
ABERDEEN

To
Nancy   Richard
Judith
Mark   Timothy

Contents

Illustrations

Advertisement for Emigration from Glasgow aboard the *Eliza*, 28
April 1830   *Frontispiece*

between pages 126 and 127

1   Frontispiece of Temperance Tract by Revd Theodore L Cuyler, who
    visited Glasgow several times to aid temperance campaigns
2   Glasgow after Temperance Poll. The results of the 1920 prohibition
    poll in Glasgow
3   Propaganda in Sauchiehall Street during the prohibition campaign
4   Anti-prohibition poster used in Glasgow prohibition campaign
5   Anti-prohibition poster: 'Pussyfoot' William E Johnson, a prohibi-
    tionist who visited Glasgow
6   Frontispiece of Temperance Tract by Revd T DeWitt Talmage. The
    author is seen congratulating William Collins, the Lord Provost of
    Glasgow, publisher and temperance activist

Acknowledgements

This book had its origins in a seminar paper which I wrote for Professor O O Winther at Indiana University in 1961. The subject of Scottish immigration to the Pacific Northwest and other parts of the United States continued to fascinate me after I came to Glasgow in 1965 and on several visits to America since 1970.

In writing this book I am grateful to a large number of people. In particular I wish to thank the staffs of the libraries and various manuscript collections for their kindness and cooperation which even extended to running me to the airport on one occasion in California. For permission to publish material in their collections I thank the following archivists and institutions: Charles G Palm, the Hoover Institution, Stanford University; the Chicago Circle Campus, University of Illinois; Kenneth A Lorf, the Butler Library, Columbia University; Alan Seaburg, Andover-Harvard Theological Library, Cambridge, Mass.; Rodney G Dennis, the Houghton Library, Harvard; Josephine L Harper, the State Historical Society of Wisconsin, Madison, Wisconsin; Kathleen A Major, the American Antiquarian Society, Worcester, Mass; Donald Anderle, Associate Director for Special Collections, Rare Books and Manuscripts Division, The New York Public Library, Astor, Lenox and Tilden Foundations; Mary Jo Pugh of the University of Michigan; Mary Ann Bamberger, the University of Illinois at Chicago; the Toledo-Lucas County Public Library; Patrick M Cadell, Keeper, National Library of Scotland Department of Manuscripts, Edinburgh. I also thank Professor W Turrentine Jackson, University of California at Davis; Professor Daniel J Walkowitz and the University of Illinois Press and the American Economic History Review for permission to publish material. I am especially grateful to Professor Fred Buchanan of the University of Utah for his helpful discussions and permission to use his unpublished dissertation; to Dr Andrew Gibb, Glasgow, for a copy of an unpublished essay; to Professor Ian B Cowan of the Scottish Historical Review for permission to use material previously printed there; to the librarian and staff of the Manuscript Collections, Library of Congress whose delightful charm, humour and help have been unmatched over some ten years.

At home I am grateful to Mr Henry Heaney, the Librarian and Keeper of the Hunterian Books and Manuscripts, and the superb staff of Glasgow University Library, the National Library of Scotland and the Mitchell Library, Glasgow. In particular, Mr Joseph Fisher, and his long suffering colleagues in the Glasgow Room, Anne Escott and Hamish Whyte, proved unfailingly patient and generous of their time in translating the mysteries of the city to a benighted Lancashire lad.

Many people were generous in their help beyond the purely academic. I am particularly grateful to the Revd Alexei Michaelenko of Washington

DC; Dr Zdzislaw Chlewinski, Lublin, Poland; Professors Thomas Ganschow, Roland Di Franco, Vincent P De Santis, Philip Gleason, Jay P Dolan, William Berge, Kerney M Adams; Dr Bob and Judith Moran among many generous Americans. At home I am especially grateful to Dr John and Carol McCaffrey; Dr Gavin and Robin White; James and Dr Irene Armstrong; and Dr John Durkan for similar encouragement. Geoffrey B A M Finlayson kindly helped with the revision of a chapter at a late stage. To those students in my special subject, The Progressive Era in America, during the last twelve years I am grateful for their Glaswegian humour and criticism.

To Ian McClenaghen of the Royal Bank of Scotland my indebtedness is great in every way. Likewise the hospitality of Sister Hilda and the community of St Charles' Carstairs provided the peace to write. I owe an especial debt to Professors Esmond Wright, W R Brock, and Keith G Robbins for their support at various stages. I also acknowledge the very kind grants in aid from the University of Glasgow, the Carnegie Trust and the British Academy. Thanks are due also to Mr Colin MacLean of Aberdeen University Press for his gentle prodding and patience; to Marjorie Leith for her genial and efficient guidance through the press; to the long suffering typists of this work, Mrs Irene Barr and Mrs Aileen Henderson. Finally, I owe more than anything to my parents for their help in every way.

Introduction

The connections between Glasgow and the United States have been attracting increasing interest in recent years. Professor Andrew Hook's pioneering study, Tom Devine's meticulous account of the Tobacco Lords as well as the more recent studies by William R Brock and others have begun to focus attention on this important and neglected transatlantic link.[1] The connections were vast, varied and continuous throughout the eighteenth and early nineteenth centuries, but during the period 1820 to 1920 they were even more substantial.

Scottish shipping interest in America stemmed from the seventeenth century when Glasgow shipowners had offered to ship out vagrants, dissenters and prisoners from the various civil conflicts. Awareness of America had been stimulated through the eighteenth century by visits from Americans seeking funds for colleges and Indian missions or merely publicising lands available to Scottish emigrants. In the nineteenth century the traffic was dominated by three major companies; the Allan Line 1819; Anchor Line 1837; Donaldson Line from 1879, though the Cunard to Canada and the ill-fated Glasgow and New York Steamship Company also operated. There were links with every major American port. So that by the end of the century it was claimed to be possible to sail to America every single day of the year.[2] That availability was stimulated by various other economic interests. Glasgow, after all, was the workshop of the world.

Glasgow was probably the greatest of all nineteenth-century cities. I stress the nineteenth century, for that was when the city grew, developed and flourished—at an American pace. It was, as Horace Greeley, the New York editor, observed, 'more American than any city I have seen in Europe. Half of Pittsburgh spliced on to half of Philadelphia would make a city like Glasgow'.[3] Any study of the link between Glasgow and America raises important questions about the nature of Scottish society in the past two centuries: its openness to opportunity, its dynamism and its failing. The inevitable conclusion is that there was a common transatlantic culture in which Glasgow played an important, even at times a decisive role. The weakening of the link has been bound up with a loss of faith in and by Glasgow itself. The city flourished only so long as that confidence in the individual, race or group persisted.

Between 1820 and 1920 two industrialised urban democratic societies shared similar attitudes in economics, religion and social issues. Glasgow, confident in itself and its ability to cope with any challenge, provided material and intellectual direction to American development. When the economic base deteriorated, the loss was far more psychological than material. An essential ingredient was lost: it was the dream of the Great Society defined by Lyndon Johnson in 1965 as 'a place where the city of man serves not only the needs of the body and the demands of commerce

[1] Notes begin on p. 189.

xi

but the desire for beauty and hunger for community. . . . It is a place where men are more concerned with the quality of their goals than the quantity of their goods.'

The commercial element was undoubtedly present in the transatlantic culture of the nineteenth century but it was part of a larger package that was also religious and ethical. In combining Christian sense of duty, economic interest and enlightened benevolence, Scottish immigrants into America made a vital contribution to the national sense of identity: they organised and justified the spirit of expectant capitalism, and they contributed a deep sense of national mission. Democratic, economic and religious expectations could, they believed, be realised in and through the United States.

Two national characteristics in the developing United States were also two aspects of the nineteenth century utopian vision: these were benevolence and progress. Benevolence, it was thought, would hasten the advent of the millenium. A humanitarian virtue, benevolence was in line with the traditional Christian values and with the ideal of civic service: it provided a leadership role for the newer entrepreneurial groups emerging on both sides of the Atlantic. Through the humanising social conditions a more harmonious society would inevitably evolve. A belief in progress, the second characteristic, let people place their faith in the continued expansion of scientific knowledge, in economic growth and in an increasingly democratic and more social order. Progress assumed an ever-improving, ever-expanding and increasingly efficient society: whatever the setbacks, evolution towards the fulfilment of higher ideals, and the ascent of man to ultimate perfection, were guaranteed.[4]

Both Scotland and America had sustained these millenarian expectations from the sixteenth and seventeenth centuries.[5] Both countries looked upon themselves as 'redeemer nations' with a providential mission. By the nineteenth century a more sophisticated and somewhat secularised version prevailed: in this respect Glasgow was prominent. In the west of Scotland, visionaries abounded, from Edward Irving through Thomas Lake Harris to some brands of revolutionary socialism. Such visionaries expected the almost immediate realisation of their dream. The main stream, more restrained, nevertheless retained a utopian vision.[6] The west of Scotland, like the United States, was permeated by a dynamic millenarianism which was an intrinsic element in religious, intellectual and practical life. Scottish education embraced all three elements and enhanced the expectation of the millenium.[7] The expansion of the English-speaking world through the United States and the British Empire—in population, territory and wealth—justified the most sanguine expectations. Everywhere democracy and Protestantism seemed to be in the ascendancy and autocratic Catholicism was in full retreat. The triumph of the well-to-do entrepreneurial evangelical elements seemed at hand. Within the Atlantic world, Glasgow as the Second City of the British Empire embodied that confidence. The Scottish contribution to America was funnelled through Glasgow, which exported educational entrepreneurial and engineering expertise within an ethical and religious framework which was peculiarly Scottish.

The Scottish condition was essentially a religious one. In Scotland there were many conflicting and contradictory theological traditions: many went with the immigrants to the United States and were refought in the New World. Few debates have generated so much heat as religious controversy has done among Scots: Glasgow was no exception. To describe the ramifications and subtleties of religion in Scotland and among immigrants in America in the eighteenth and nineteenth centuries is far beyond the scope of this work: but there is an obvious and persistent undercurrent of religious enthusiasm in the matters discussed in the following pages. Both the Scottish and the American sense of national identity was moral and religious: this sustained many in the urban centre of Glasgow or in the United States. Whatever forces drove the Scots forth, they could find solace in some providential plan for individual, national and universal regeneration. They had been and still were a chosen people.

Numerous ministers, inspired to become missionaries in the new settlements of America after their training in Glasgow and Edinburgh, crossed the Atlantic. Their vast contribution may be gauged from the names which appear in the biographical listing at the end of this book. They and many who accompanied them injected into their communities a sense of moral earnestness, a longing for individual and social salvation. That injection, with its respect for honest toil and endeavour, with honesty and integrity rewarded within a moral consensus, proved advantageous. Slavery, intemperance, ignorance and inefficient civic administration were all threats to the ethical social ideal. Glasgow and those associated with her in America were to be pre-eminent in countering such threats to a thriving democratic entrepreneurial order. There were on the way many reverses, but a firm religious conviction sustained them in their belief in the inevitability of their triumph.

Scotland and America had seemed threatened in several ways in the late eighteenth and early nineteenth centuries. The impact of the American and French Revolutions, as well as the growing population concentrated in cities, undermined the old cohesive social order. The rapid influx of peoples displaced from the land into Glasgow or into the United States, often from very different cultural traditions, posed problems. The millenium might, it was feared, be thwarted or postponed: the forward movement of benevolence and progress might be checked. As a result evangelical activity generated a vigorous response. It sought to protect the moral freedom of the individual from the tyranny of the majority in the America of Jacksonian democracy and in the Scotland of the first Reform Act. The individual converted to a thorough Christian commitment would, in association with likeminded people, create and sustain a moral vision through public pressure and public law. While checking the excesses of demagoguery such people would stress the moral responsibility of the individual and the sovereignty of God. The implication was that men of talent and virtue formed a natural moral aristocracy who would uplift the less able and vicious to a more advanced stage of civilisation. The Glasgow entrepreneur, the evangelical and the Jeffersonian American, though perhaps sharing few convictions, could agree on that emphasis.[8]

Two men closely associated with Glasgow, Dr David Bogue and Revd

David Brown, wrote influential books envisaging the establishment of the Kingdom of God on earth. Dr David Bogue, the Scottish founder of the London Missionary Society and close friend of Revd Greville Ewing, a Glasgow Independent minister, received an honorary doctorate from Yale in 1815. In his view the establishment of permanent peace and missionary enterprise would usher in the millenium. Revd David Brown, formerly assistant to Edward Irving in London, spent fourteen years (1843–57) at St James', Glasgow. During that time he wrote *Christ's Second Coming,* in which he envisaged the end of institutions which enslaved man. Individual failings might persist but all lands and nations would be united in one faith and one lord:[9] the process was already under way. The dissemination of that spirit, and of education and of improvement would hasten the millenium. The views of these two men, reprinted and widely read in the United States, reinforced similar American sentiments.

In the Atlantic world the area of freedom was expanding. The forces and agencies which enslaved man by limiting his ability to make free, informed moral choices were losing their power. The older political structures crumbled to make way for more democratic approaches. The old state churches came under attack: in America they were disestablished, while the Church of Scotland was split by the Disruption. Drunkenness came under attack as but another form of slavery: so too did illiteracy. Black slavery was the worst example of man's enslavement to the will of another: a slave could not make any free moral choices. While this was a moral crusade, there was also an economic need to remove the barriers to greater efficiency and social advance. A growing industrial nation could not be created from an ignorant, uneducated, drunken population subject to the whim of privilege, prescription or Popery. An incompetent, inefficient people lacking independence and initiative could achieve neither economic success nor spiritual salvation.[10]

The individual disciplined by industry, frugality and piety would, it was argued, achieve integrity: he could achieve personal economic success and spiritual development. In turn he would transform his group, his community and ultimately his nation. The locality was the microcosm of the whole nation.[11] Small local successes gave meaning to the individual, a role and status and a sense of responsibility in a fluid mobile society. A thriving cohesive local community could transform the nation. Such thinking paralleled the prevailing evolutionary ideas of race and of social classes: through proper stewardship, both could ascent to the highest ideals of man. The acquisition of the right values was vital to the process. Will-power, self-confidence, energy and initiative, all these stemmed from a belief. Whatever hindered the triumph of such ideals had to be destroyed. It was a moral and economic necessity.

This shared value system on both sides of the Atlantic contributed to the sense of Scottish–American solidarity. Reason following upon revelation established God's law in reality.[12] As a result the voluntary organisations of the Protestant evangelical revival harnessed the aroused millenial energies to practical ends. Staffed by clergymen from voluntary religious bodies, by entrepreneurs and by the aristocracy of labour, they set the tone of society, established codes of respectability and stabilised the idea of success. By establishing organisations opposed to slavery, drink, Popery and illiteracy, these elements sought to ease the way of progress and the advent of the millenium. In moral terms these evils prevented the triumph of pure religion. In economic terms they prevented the emergence of the able, talented individual. The elimination of these evils, these artificial barriers, would ensure the greatest possible happiness of the greatest possible number. The regenerated individual served the common good and so transformed society.

The Scottish contribution to the regeneration of America was considerable. By no means all emigrants were highly moral or highly motivated but sufficient numbers of ministers, teachers, managers, skilled artisans and entrepreneurs carried strong and elevated convictions with them to contribute decisively to the formation of American national identity. Scotland in general contributed expertise and personnel, but within that contribution Glasgow's part was preeminent. Church, college and industry were but different aspects of the same cultural package. Together they embodied and inculcated a sense of civic service.

This almost chivalric ideal was widely accepted in the land of Scott and among his admirers in America, but this ideal seemed to many to be somewhat mediaeval, aristocratic and romantic, laying emphasis upon a continuing hierarchical state.[13] Americans might respect this, but they were far more at ease with the social democratic vision of Burns, through whose vision the ordinary daily experience of the common man was elevated and given dignity. Scott was a man of southeast Scotland, Burns of the southwest, which Glasgow dominated. Glasgow, a democratic, mercantile and mobile city, was in so many respects consonant with, and in so many ways contributed to the American experience. Fluid and dynamic, Glasgow seemed a contemporary exponent of the best values of the old world. The Scottish connection with the United States was wide and rich, but Glasgow in particular gave practical and businesslike expression to those qualities which would promote the Kingdom, the millenium, the triumph of the industrious and the respectable. In and through Glasgow was to be seen a utopia; the utopia was portable, indeed exportable.

Glasgow, far more than Edinburgh, was akin to the nineteenth-century American city. Glasgow's development was nineteenth-century. Its leadership, like that of American cities, was self-made. Its assumptions, its democratic social habits and its lack of snobbery added greatly to its appeal for Americans, not a few of whom indulged their ethnic pride in admiring Glasgow and its varied successes. Not a few Glaswegians and emigrants from the west of Scotland succeeded within the United States in church, college or commerce. America in turn influenced Glasgow's religious thinking, her political outlook and her business practices, leading them all in a more liberal, democratic and efficient direction. Together these influences established a social democratic framework. The individual, his community and nation had to be free from restraints of an immoral character. A free, evangelised, sober and educated people would seek out injustice and vice. In time these attitudes were to be applied in ever-increasing areas by still more logical, extreme or thoroughgoing individuals. Americans and their Glasgow associates would campaign for women's equality, for a more intelligent appreciation of health and diet, for freer, undogmatic religion—ranging from Unitarianism through Universalism to Spiritualism—and for the poor.

What had begun as a drive for individual voluntary self improvement would eventually give way to demands for greater state intervention. Perhaps the state had been won to their moral outlook. More pertinently, it may be argued, the individual could not begin to assume his moral responsibility if he was an unequal competitor from birth. Already by the late nineteenth century an increased social awareness among churchmen and businessmen had given rise to new initiatives.[14] The chivalric civic ideal resulted in public service: the neighbourhood and the municipality were means of moral improvement. The monopoly of power, whether in Westminster or in corrupt American city government, in massive concentrations of capital whether in land or in industry, was immoral and inefficient. Such monopoly encouraged vice and crime. It forced the public to pay excessive sums for building land and for vital commodities like gas or transport. Even the industrious poor were denied reasonable housing, fair rents and wages and in consequence became incapable of making proper moral choices. Monopoly, it was believed, by removing decision making from local participation and control, lowered the moral leadership and awareness of the locality. Remote bureaucratised decision makers were eroding local moral fibre. Power had to be in the hands of the local 'good' men, who were known for their righteousness, philanthropy and entrepreneurial success. Unlike the financiers of their time, they made their wealth by the sweat of their brow. The civic achievements of Glasgow around 1900 highlighted that fact. Successful moral, civic and business enterprises set the city apart. Far more than any other British city, Glasgow seemed to have established a thriving philanthropic polity. Pre-eminent among Scottish cities, Glasgow embodied the essential Scottish virtues, the attributes which Americans had needed over the previous century. The pilgrimage to Glasgow's civic shrines was a recognition of the longstanding and substantial contribution to American success.

Glasgow as seen by American visitors within the broader Scottish context generally showed the triumph of their kind of people. Just as they were concerned to improve America, so their Glasgow counterparts were deeply committed to various moral reforms. Accordingly their pictures of Glasgow, as we shall see, showed considerable success against a background of poverty and sin—and sometimes an element of ethnic Irish inferiority. The visitors tended to see poor women as prostitutes and drunken because the visitors' own moral and, in some cases, socialist preconceptions made them assume this. Glasgow as a centre of moral crusade was welcomed, and its failings were seen in stark contrast. In some cases Americans were observing problems identical to their own. In others they were reasserting the superior quality of the New over the Old World: even so, Scotland remained peculiarly attractive and Glasgow particularly akin to the American character.

The years 1820 to 1920 coincided with the buoyant optimistic faith and economic supremacy of the Clyde. The Second City of the British Empire presided over a thriving industrial area. Coal, iron, steel and shipbuilding took off where tobacco and textiles left off. The city grew at an American pace: 'scarcely has the Chicago of the western world displayed a more marvellous growth'.[15] Glasgow was in many respects a boom town, a frontier town, a metropolis of meteoric growth. It had absorbed vast numbers of immigrants from the Highlands and Ireland, as well as Italians, Poles, and Jews from southern and eastern Europe. At the same time the city had managed to impose order, discipline and a sense of community upon a fluid—to some Americans seemingly uncontrollable—urban industrial society. The fact that major work appeared to have been undertaken by men who had risen to eminence and wealth through their own efforts, through merit rather than privilege, through philanthropy and public service, made the city particularly interesting to concerned Americans. They faced similar problems at home which they had to confront without the benefit of an urban tradition. They had to establish a moral consensus among a polyglot population by inculcating thrift, sobriety and a civic culture. Equally, Americans followed the critical spirit of Glasgow in education, the advancement of women and radical criticism of monopoly capitalism. Glasgow was an inspiration and a measure for Americans.

Glasgow seemed to have found a means by which the worst excesses of wealth and poverty might be contained. Whether or not these initiatives were mere palliatives, as socialist critics would suggest, they highlight fears of class conflict or, perhaps, they highlight the collapse of the old cohesive community amid economic changes. The success of Glasgow also seemed to be a religious success in that the culture was permeated with a religious sense of duty and obligation. Religious groups managed, through voluntary associations and then through the municipal government, to achieve desirable social ends—the destruction of appalling rookeries and the prohibition of drink on municipal property. A city could actually be a force for good. In American thought, all too often it was Babylon. Glasgow brought American civic thinking into the twentieth century.

The close connection between Glasgow and the United States is a remarkable story. It has existed in a very intimate way for almost three hundred years. My purpose is to suggest that between 1820 and 1920 that relationship had a peculiar intensity, far stronger than before or since. During that period Glasgow and America found certain common interests and pursuits from which each derived substantial advantages. Those qualities went far beyond mere economic interest or selfish concern. Glasgow and the United States were members of a very tightly knit family, held together by economic interests but even more by common cultural assumptions. They shared an antipathy towards arrogance and snobbery— anything, in short, which seemed privileged or devoid of personal merit or social utility. That critical, even captious, spirit was a necessary component in the modernisation of American society, a process to which Glaswegians greatly contributed. They provided intellectual, industrial and commercial skills. They exported their valued qualities to a developing nation. They supplied the know-how and moral discipline, the education necessary to produce a future leadership, the philosophy and theology to sustain a work ethic vital to industrial development and innovation.

With like-minded friends in America and Scotland, these individuals mounted an effective campaign against various brakes on social progress: ignorance, the subjection of women, the abuse of drink, the evils of slavery, the corrupt inefficiency of municipal government. These ills and others were their targets since these prevented the amelioration of the ordinary man, his intellectual, economic and social advancement. At the same time as this common alliance was promoting the rapid industrialisation and commercialisation of American life, it retained a critical spirit towards that society. Monopoly, exploitation and discrimination were not ignored. The Scottish sense of solidarity remained strong: within America it was a critical sense of solidarity. Trade union and radical leadership in the latter period demonstrated the continuity of a Scottish vision of an ideal society at home and in America. Each could reinforce the other. They did this until around 1920.

The strength and intensity of that connection continued unabated until around 1920. Since then a form of communication has continued although lacking that economic substance of earlier days. Significantly the characters who come to mind in more recent times are Stan Laurel, the movie comedian; James Reston, the renowned *New York Times* reporter; John Grierson, the doyen of film documentary; R D Laing, the analyst and guru of the 'sixties. All were born or brought up or educated in Glasgow and district. All were, generally, specialists in the business of communication. They were communicating interpretations of facets of human behaviour. It was perhaps a vestige of that older connection which had communicated a comprehensive, cohesive almost homogeneous view. Now the communication continues but in a diverse and pluralist way.

I have tried to outline this Scottish republic of the mind. Chapter One seeks to demonstrate the formative consolidation and effect of a common cultural outlook between Scotland and America. In this Introduction I have tried to demonstrate the pre-eminence of Glasgow in that rich connection. Chapter Two examines the educational contribution; Chapter Three the feminine republic of the Atlantic; Chapter Four the crusade against drink; Chapter Five the municipal example of Glasgow to America. Finally I try to assess the results of this close association and its subsequent decline. I have paid relatively little attention to the transatlantic crusade against slavery, a story which has been well told elsewhere by George Shepperson, Duncan Rice and others. It was an important element in the alliance.

The story is one of close personal associations, common religious and economic pursuits within an Atlantic community. In the century under discussion there was almost a family atmosphere: goodwill, understanding and some disagreements but always within a certain framework. That relationship stemmed from a long-established tradition, through immigration, religion, education and politics. To these issues we will now turn.

Chapter One

The Common Culture

Inspiration, Immigration, Industry

'The Scottish Whigs', wrote the emigrant novelist, William Brownlee, 'achieved in their nation what the patriots of every nation will achieve in the day they rise to vindicate their rights. Theirs is the proud honour of having struck the first blow, as the van of patriotic hosts who will overthrow tyranny; and give liberty to the world.'[1] With this sense of manifest destiny in bringing reinforcement to civil and religious liberty in the growing American nation, Scots were especially welcome. As Neal Dow, the Maine entrepreneur and prohibitionist, wrote of one Scottish visitor: he was 'a downright hearty Scotsman; a capital specimen of their race and blood, so heroic in many a field, so true and tenacious in church and council. May the race never be fewer; the blood cannot be purer. Of all immigrants to our country the Scotch are always the most welcome. They bring us muscle and brain and tried skill and trustworthiness in many of our great industries of which they are managers of the most successful ones.'[2] So pervasive was this view that almost thirty years later, a one-time Lord Provost of Glasgow, Sir Samuel Chisholm, was able to tell a New York audience that the strength of Presbyterianism and the democratic spirit was attributable to Scotland: 'the ever coming Scot has assimilated and is assimilating the American people'.[3] But Sir Samuel was exaggerating his own religious heritage for most Scottish religious and social groups contributed to the creation and regulation of an ethical democracy. Scots seemed to be everywhere. As David Macrae of Gourock observed, 'I begin to think that either the world was very small or Scotland very large.'[4] America, as Andrew Carnegie saw 'would have been a poor show had it not been for the Scotch'.[5] It would have been all the poorer had it not been for Glasgow.

Scottish ethnic self assertion confirmed—and contributed to—American social, political and religious attitudes to produce a confident belief in progress. In celebrating their ethnic success, Scots were celebrating America. They were constructing and identifying with American nationality.

As a black child is reported by David Macrae to have said: 'We know the Scotch who have emigrated to this country are all sober and steady; they do not take a conspicuous part in politics: nor do they seem inclined to usurp political power. Politeness seems to be a very general and attractive characteristic in them as a class amongst us.'[6] The typical Scottish immigrant to America went with a stable consistent character. Reinforced in America it became 'a social character whose conformity is insured by their tendency to acquire early in life an internalised set of goals'.[7] Though

1

Scottish emigrants retained a strong affection for their homeland, they did not develop that intense nationalism like Polish, German, Italian, nor above all, Irish immigrants. Unlike these groups, Scots could not easily identify an alien oppressor: they saw only aristocratic (industrial or Anglicised) privileged groups of their own kind at home. For that and other reasons, Scots tended to develop a portable, almost messianic vision which was appropriate to their role in the expanding English-speaking world of the last century.[8] In a developing expanding economy, their education and technical skills gave them considerable advantages. In a fluid American society, their opportunities for self-improvement and self-fulfilment were vast and rewarding. America represented the realisation of those potentialities denied them at home by privilege in its various guises. The United States was Scotland realised beyond the seas. Accustomed at home to hard relentless toil on unrewarding land and to heavy industrial work, Scots came highly motivated with a sense of religious crusade, duty and the work ethic: like Robert Burns, they were universal men. Disciplined through education, religion and hardship, they arrived with a well regulated internal moral mechanism. Sometimes they had been able to save the fare through adherence to temperance principles. With these qualities they were well equipped as the shock troops of modernisation.[9] In effect they confirmed Weber's thesis regarding capitalism and protestantism: Scots in general accepted the benign operation of natural law in economics, they depended upon the possession of certain qualities—thrift, the post-ponement of immediate gratification, industriousness and 'being frank and honest with oneself about affairs'.[10] Elected by God to be his stewards and to work to multiply his glory in every way, Scots were well placed in this and the other world. Their virtues were equally acceptable in this world as in the next.[11]

Sober, thrifty Scottish immigrants who were prepared to work hard would, according to many contemporary commentators, inevitably prosper. 'The gospel of wealth', declared Andrew Carnegie, 'but echoes Christ's words'.[12] Self-disciplined service would bring its just reward. American entrepreneurs urged intending Glasgow immigrants to develop acceptable habits and secure good references so as to have access to better opportunities upon arrival in America.

Scottish emigrants to America were thus committed to the realisation of an efficient moral social order. In general they held an alternative vision, one which they could invoke consistently throughout the period to 1920 as we shall see, in order to criticise the existing order and to evolve more purposefully toward a providential order in America. Their cultural 'package' gave them this insight. That Scottish outlook enabled them to champion capitalist enterprise *and* to sustain labour union critics. In both cases their Protestant ethic railed against privilege and monopoly. Andrew Carnegie, the millionaire son of a Scottish Chartist, is a case in point. His famous letter of December 1868 shows that heritage emerging: 'To continue much longer overwhelmed by business cares and with most of my thoughts wholly upon the way to make money in the shortest time, must wholly degrade me beyond the hope of permanent recovery.[13] That paradoxical approach worked until technology undermined the old work ethic and mass immigration eroded the cultural base and status of the Scots as a group.

The reordering coincided with the changing Scottish perception of America.[14] In the early days of the United States, Scots saw America as the work of an enlightened and Christian providence. In removing religious, class and educational barriers to individual self improvement, America seemed to be an ideal, peaceful, democratic state. A reformed Scotland might achieve similar goals. Her failure to do so allowed America to become a useful myth, an escape valve and the hope of the future, whatever the disappointments at home. Though Scottish conservatives migh have carped at American democracy, they must have realised that emigration to America provided a guarantee of domestic stability. By the 1880s the consolidation of big business, the conflicts with labour and the erosion of Scottish skill and status was dimming the attractions of America. By the close of the First World War, the decline of Scottish industry and the emergence of Soviet Russia made other models somewhat more attractive. The persistent 'Red Scare' and the Depression reinforced that view of dry America. In so far as America provided a dream world, Hollywood was to be that.[15] Though Scots might recognise the American contribution in Second World War and after, the old strong identification was much weakened. Continued economic decline at home, McCarthyism in America and the weakening of ethnic ties all contributed.[16] No matter how radical American emigres might seem to Scottish conservatives, their dream was to be realised along similar 'conservative' social lines in America. In fact Scots were neither radical nor reactionary but consistent. In a sense Albert Brisbane, the Fourierist American, was not far wrong in believing a brand new idea was not easily hammered into a Scottish head.[17] Scots reasoned from Common Sense tradition, from experience and for an organic evolutionary view. They did not radically alter their position though massive social changes took place around them. Sufficiently flexible, they had an internal, resilient moral sense which could cope with varied challenges. Theirs was a republic of the mind which gave no hostages to fortune. They did not identify with fixed positions, fixed hierarchies or static social orders. Their essential convictions, their belief in Providence, Protestantism and Progress remained secure and readily evolved satisfactory responses to the changing circumstances.[18] In a very important sense, Scots were the engineers of American social and political progress.

The Scots undoubtedly contributed talent and skill to the developing country. But they were also pugnacious and aggressive. If they placed great store on the church and the schoolhouse, 'these fortresses against ignorance and the devil paralleled a chain of blockhouses and forts against the French and Indian. The Scots were as eager to fight one as another.'[19] Even in the earliest days of the American revolution, Ezra Stiles, the president of Yale College found Scots too ready to place a liberal gloss on their pugnacity: 'The policy of Scotland and all the governmental Ideas of the Body of that people are abhorrent to all Ideas of civil liberty and are full of tyrannical superiorities and subordinations.'[20] He had detected that evangelistic fervour, which George S Pryde felt verged on 'self-righteousness and intolerance'.[21] That was the strength and weakness of Scotland.

Why did Scots emigrate? The reasons, predictably, were many and varied. Certain pressures and attractions might be more apparent at one time, and others later. From the earliest days of British colonisation, there had been Scottish interest in the new settlements. Captain John Mason, the founder of New Hampshire, had published a pamphlet in Edinburgh in 1620 encouraging settlement in North America. Four years later, Sir William Alexander, a promoter of the Newfoundland colonies and associated with New England interests, published his Encouragement to Colonies, while the following year Sir Robert Gordon of Lochinvar published his tract dedicated to the 'undertakers in the plantations of New Scotland in America'.[22] As early as 1638, John Burnett of Aberdeen was trading with Virginia.[23] With the growth of the American trade, particularly in tobacco, with the pressure on land at home and the prospect of better land in America, interest greatly increased.[24]

In the late eighteenth century, the consolidation of landowning into a few hands, the increasingly unrepresentative and unresponsive parliamentary system as seen from Scotland, and the lack of prospects in Scotland made the prospect of America increasingly attractive. Though allegedly fifty times more wealthy than the English 40 shillings freeholder, the Scottish tenant was unable to vote: 'In fact the lower classes of the people in North Briton who pay a great proportion of all the taxes imposed on the nation, are as really without representation in parliament as the British colonies in North America'.[25]

The farmer, even though efficient and improving, reaped no benefit from his efforts. Only the landowner gained the profits.[26] The traditional attachment of the individual to his local community was being eroded: he was unable to secure social justice or political voice. The middle and lower classes were being neglected to the detriment of the long-term good of Scotland. It was claimed that the merchants and talented men of business were leaving in great numbers to go to America. Naturally with a literate public, ample publicity and available ships to America, considerable numbers were forming themselves into companies to emigrate.[27] Earlier emigrants were sending letters back home encouraging migration: 'North America is the best poor man's country in the world for the price of grain there is very low and the price of labour very high'.[28] The landless forced into town and mechanics faced with high costs through the monopoly of land-ownership readily took themselves to America.[29]Significantly the minister of Govan also lamented the lack of adequate educational and religious provision for the nation: knowledge was for an elite and even then not appropriate to a commercial society. The quality of individual and civic life deteriorated. In a freer American atmosphere such higher aspirations might be fulfilled.[30]

The evangelical revivals of the eighteenth century, the Second Awakening and the later revivals through the nineteenth century stimulated interest in the United States. The constant traffic of ministers in either direction made the knowledge of the other side commonplace.[31] The availability of ships was a further encouragement and the formation of emigration societies in small communities in hard times was common. The fears of political persecution, unemployment and a desire for a freer atmosphere also contributed to the decision to leave in the 1790s and following the Napoleonic Wars. In the political repression of the 1790s many men sought the freer atmosphere of America—men like Alexander Wilson, the Paisley poet, and John Maclean, of Glasgow University. The lack of opportunity, of adequate religious and educational provision in a commercial society further encouraged departure. The whole process might be seen as a providential means for the greater happiness of mankind.[32] With Scottish education geared to produce 'an agreeable, a respectable and a useful member of society' the emigrant was well equipped to advance himself.[33] Rural emigrants were numerous but many factory workers also left to better their lot. The pace at which they left is debatable but the flow was continuous over the period.

In the last quarter of the eighteenth century about 25,000 Scots left mainly from the highlands and islands. They and the Scots Irish generally were to enjoy better conditions than at home. The knowledge of that success, the visits of Americans (including Witherspoon) to the West of Scotland, fluctuating economic conditions, and the slow pace of political change at home made America all the more attractive.

The overall impression remains that agricultural districts were gradually losing population inexorably over the hundred years to 1870.[34] That economic improvement in America was considerable seems undeniable, though the consequences of that flight upon the communities left behind seems to have been disastrous. In the late nineteenth century the Scottish Land Restoration League was to emerge as a belated response.

The emigration traffic grew rapidly in the early nineteenth century. The organisation of several emigration societies with several hundred members in the aftermath of the Napoleonic wars set the pace. Though the emigrants mainly went to Canada, the idea of emigration caught the popular imagination. 'Amero-mania' spread rapidly.[35] Passenger companies followed with regular services. In 1840, the Cunard company was established with the backing of George Burns in Glasgow and the Glasgow-born David MacIver for its service between Liverpool, Halifax and Boston.[36] Other lines provided a direct service. Tod and McGregor, the Clyde shipbuilders, launched *The City of Glasgow* in 1850 to work a direct route to New York under the auspices of the Glasgow and New York Steamship Company. On its second voyage it set up a record time of twelve days five hours for the crossing. The company proved short-lived and the ship was sold to the Inman Lines. Others proved far more successful.[37]

The Allan Line had served Canada from 1819. From 1856 it served New York; from 1871 Baltimore; from 1872, briefly, New Orleans; from 1884 Philadelphia. Eventually in 1915 the company was absorbed by the Canadian Pacific Company. The Anchor Line began its service to New York in 1856 and soon held a virtual monopoly on the route. Some twenty years later the company claimed a daily service throughout the year to New York. With the declining Scottish traffic in the late nineteenth century, the line looked to other routes. It developed a Scandinavian connection through Leith to Glasgow and New York in 1869–71. It opened an Italian immigrant route from southern Italy to New York in 1869 and then later developed a direct Naples–New York connection. In 1870 the line carried 25,000 passengers between Glasgow and New York: 23,000 significantly were steerage class. In 1890 19,000 passengers went direct from Naples to New York. The company was heavily involved in the immigrant traffic until restrictive American legislation after the First World War effectively brought it to an end. The company also entered the cattle and meat trade, shipping the first live cattle in 1872, and three years later made the first ever shipment of refrigerated meat.

Another company, the Donaldson Line, which had entered the American passenger market with services to Portland, Maine in 1879, and later to Baltimore, also joined the meat trade. The frequency of passenger services from Glasgow was remarkable and at its peak unmatched, but changing traffic patterns in the years before 1914, heavy wartime shipping losses in the First and Second World Wars, takeovers and failures led to the end of service by 1966.[38] With shipbuilders on the Clyde laying down numerous liners for other North Atlantic companies, Glasgow was peculiarly America conscious.

Americans were similarly aware of Glasgow. As early as 1872, the Anchor Line was offering cheap package tours to American tourists. Their 3000 agents in America could offer Scottish tours with a week in Ireland, London and Paris in turn for $475.[39] The new affluent Americans merely followed in the steps of many of their countrymen. Pleasure could be overlaid with a sense of duty in visiting the social democratic shrine of Burns, attending a temperance or evangelical congress and inspecting the moral grandeur of Glasgow's municipal government. To many it was a return to the land of their imagination if not of their ancestors.

Glasgow graduates not only emigrated but also became significant commentators on the United States. These analysts form a respectable tradition. Frances Wright, the Dundee radical with Glasgow connections produced her important book, *View of Society and Manners in America*. Two years later, the Glasgow graduate J M Duncan wrote a comprehensive account which was printed on the Columbiad printing machine of the Glasgow University, the only such American machine in Britain. A host of others followed. In the 1850s Andrew Bannatyne, a member of a well known Glasgow legal firm abandoned a career in Scottish law for one in New York commercial law during which he wrote an interesting little work on United States government.[40] Lord Bryce, the author of the magisterial *The American Commonwealth* lived in the city, attended the university and then went off on his brilliant career. In more recent times Sir Denis Brogan, the phenomenally erudite and prolific academic, followed in that tradition. In the last twenty years the last two Professors of Modern History, Esmond Wright and William R Brock, have been distinguished scholars in American history. Glasgow is unmatched in Europe in this respect.

The many later travel books on America written by Scots show writers moving within a world of Scots, better fed, clothed, housed and greatly improved on their native land. It seems to be a world of numerous friends and acquaintances who have moved en masse to America from Glasgow, Paisley, Ayrshire or wherever. The same Presbyterian church services with local Scottish-born ministers served their flock who were working in similar industries as those at home. More might be in white collar jobs compared with recent immigrants from other lands who were working in textiles or mining. Such books spread reassurance, encouragement and confidence among those contemplating emigration. They also suggested areas where the Scots' skills might be most welcome among ethnic kin. When that knowledge was reinforced by numerous American visitors to Scotland—politicians, writers or more popularly preachers—the break would not seem so dramatic compared with other lands. The Atlantic was progressively shrinking through the century so that seasonal migration or hard times in either direction might encourage transatlantic traffic. America was not so much a foreign land as an upmarket Scotland or idealised Scotland.

The stream of visitors who passed back and forth across the Atlantic further increased mutual interest, disseminated knowledge of each other's country and served to strengthen certain prejudices. Though the vast majority of travel books were very favourable in their reported impressions, critical comment abounded. The prominence of certain topics suggests what the writers valued in their host country and at home. Scotland invariably impressed visitors with the beauty of its moral ideas and its scenery: it appalled them by its drinking and dirt. The American educator, Emma Willard, epitomised that spirit on her visit to Edinburgh: 'The very graves of some of the fathers of my mind, who here reposed, awaken feelings, which I have never experienced on a similar occasion—except it might be visiting the tomb of Washington—and convince me of what I have never thought before that I cherish a more intimate affection for the Scottish than the English writers.'[41] If Scots were intellectual they were undoubtedly 'the most moral churchgoing people in the world'.[42] Visitors were consistently astonished throughout the nineteenth century at the throngs who poured onto the streets to attend church on the sabbath. Churches were invariably packed on sabbaths, sabbaths observed with old time New England rigour and with sermons, as in the case of Thomas Chalmers, of New England quality. On her visit to Scotland in 1886, Jane Addams found the crush getting into church suffocating.[43] Glasgow, an earlier visitor declared, 'is the first place in Europe where we have found what may be properly called an American Sabbath—for nowhere I believe, is the Christian Sabbath observed as it is in the United States'.[44] The streets were deserted as people poured into church for three services every Sunday.[45] But while they were the greatest churchgoers, they were, according to a Southern visitor, the greatest whisky drinkers in the world.[46]

The beauty of Scottish scenery was breathtaking to these tourists. Almost without exception, even with pouring rain and packed travelling conditions, the impact was overwhelming.[47] Edinburgh invariably enlivened the account of the most jaundiced observer. It exceeded the wildest expectations of some, was unequalled in Europe in beauty, and was known as if the visitor were a returning exile.[48] The usual pattern was to visit Abbotsford, Melrose and the Borders: the accounts are uniformly admiring. Others with social democratic notions paid homage to the Burns country.[49] It afforded an opportunity to snipe at English snobbery: the English failure to admire Burns showed 'that genius is more appreciated in America than anywhere else'.[50] Shorn of class consciousness, the Scot had more than abundant common sense, that rare quality so valued in America.[51] The redoubtable blue stocking and feminist, Margaret Fuller Ossoli, summed up the feeling on top of Ben Lomond: 'I had my grand solitude, my Ossianic visions and the pleasure of sustaining myself.'[52] The moral grandeur and scenic beauty were balanced by some horrendous sights.[53]

Glasgow to many writers appeared a city of two classes, the haves and have-nots. To those of an evangelical mind, the leading citizens were heroically labouring to uplift the masses, from their drunkenness, vice and ignorance. The self-made men and those aspiring to respectability were by their exemplary efforts forwarding the Kingdom. Against the prevailing evils they were inculcating the correct moral values which would promote self-help and social advance. Americans of a similar outlook could feel great affinity with them and their social activism: they had the same enemies. Significantly they described the poor in highly charged moral terms: ill-clad women necessarily were morally evil. How could they be otherwise in failing socially to become upwardly mobile and in failing personally to be respectable like their observers? Such writers were hardly criticising the existing social order but rather the immorality of some elements within it. In general they were applauding their Glasgow hosts for their efforts to improve it. In effect they were observing these elements in Glasgow which had yet to evolve morally, intellectually, religiously, and perhaps racially up the scale. Like some groups at home in America, these people had to be trained and disciplined. The reformer almost saw them as a separate species, for whom and to whom things were done for their benefit: morally incapable or incurable, they were not in any sense equal members of the community, they were not responsible members of the society. Only later would radical critics question that view of poverty.

The general poverty, squalor and drunkenness nonetheless outraged Americans: 'The streets seemed to be full of men, women and children of the lowest class—filthy, ragged and idle.'[54] In highlighting the failings of Scottish society, they were highlighting the achievements of America: its wealth, self-improvement and sobriety. They may also have been compensating for intellectual and, in some cases, moral shortcomings at home. Significantly, R R Gurley, the agent for the American Colonisation Society, a body dedicated to the repatriation of freed slaves to Africa, found abolitionist Scotland somewhat hypocritical. The huts of the highland peasantry were far worse than any negro slave cabin. It was a view that radical and conservative critics of Harriet Beecher Stowe's *Uncle Tom's Cabin* would develop further: 'Would that half the sympathy and eloquence now expended in Scotland in behalf of American slaves were directed to her wretched and perishing poor'.[55]

Glasgow as an industrial city attracted particular interest. Huge factories and their remarkable weaving machinery were tourist attractions especially

for those who saw industry, Christian moral disciplines and social advance
as part of the same process.[56] Some examined industrial techniques as well.
Zacharaiah Allen, the Rhode Island entrepreneur is a case in point. A mill
owner with a model village, Allenton, which had the first reservoir in
America used for hydraulic purposes, he had wider interests than mere idle
curiosity. He saw technical innovation as much as social vision. The
Scottish model villages and their imaginative use of water power, for
instance at Catrine in Ayrshire, had obvious attractions. That form of
power eliminated the need for mining and other industrial developments;
the American idyllic dream might remain secure. New Lanark was even
more acceptable in that respect.[57] It was morally well ordered, efficient and
free from poverty.

The general poverty of Scottish life comes through clearly in most
travellers' accounts. The 'miserable huts' of Glencoe, the 'large and dirty
town of Hamilton', 'the unprogressive villages' of the highlands, the 'dull
and dirty old town' of Inverness, the 'pitiable sights of Glasgow,' the dirt of
Dumfries, Ayr, and Dundee recur in the various authors.[58] Such critics
might have been predisposed to assail aristocratic landowners, the urban
industrial threat to their idyllic American dream, and the limited political
franchise, but there was a certain puritan streak in relation to drink and
affluence. Loretta J Post worried that tourists in Oban 'introduce luxurious
notions among a people who have heretofore been satisfied to live on
oatmeal cakes and porridge all year round'. Even so the fact of poverty was
inescapable.

Edinburgh and Glasgow shocked with their slums. On seeing the
Canongate in Edinburgh, Margaret Fuller wrote 'were ever people so
villainously dirty?'[59] The Saltmarket area of Glasgow was something of a
tourist attraction. Several visitors accompanied the chief constable on his
inspection of the district and were happily appalled.[60] Later it would be an
object of great admiration as a result of the civic housing reforms. In
particularly the sight of masses of drunken women, especially in Glasgow,
horrified Americans. Sinclair Torsney claimed that he had never seen so
many drunks and ill-looking prostitutes as in the city.[61] Prostitutes paraded
openly, it was claimed, free from any police supervision: women 'bare
footed, coarsely clad and . . . of the very lowest order of womankind'
crowded parts of the city.[62] Radical and socialist visitors around the First
World War found that the horrors persisted. The Americans, Margaret
Sanger, the birth control propagandist, and Emma Goldman, the anarchist,
were predictably appalled at the conditions of women under capitalism: the
drunken women and children on Saturday night were a severe indictment of
bourgeois reformism.[63]

Visitors invariably found Glasgow wrapped in a dense smog. The
darkness permanently hung over the city: Bret Harte, the novelist and
American consul in Glasgow found it 'like living in a dark cellar.'[64] He was
a scathing critic: 'I cannot get acclimated. I cannot help feeling that I am
living by gaslight in a damp cellar with an occasional whiff from a drain,
from a coal heap, from a mouldy potato bin, and from a dirty washtub.
That is Glasgow to *me*, and that is all it has ever been since I have been

here.'[65] Even the people were unattractive: 'I could not stand the dull vulgar ostentation of the few people I met, who were mostly retired merchants. I knew only one family and in this country of classes and divisions, they wanted me to take sides and participate in their prejudices, so I presently fell back in my seclusion.'[66] Coming from California he was unable to adjust to contemporary industry.

Other impressions of Scotland were somewhat more favourable. Edinburgh impressed while the Trossachs was 'the land of chivalry, of tragedy, of romance and of song.'[67] In that light the Trossachs exercised considerable impact through the writings of Sir Walter Scott on the Southern imagination with its penchant for romanticism.[68] Even Glasgow surprised many visitors with its considerable beauty. The president of Wesleyan University delighted in its beautiful light sandstone architecture, delightful wide streets and the statues to civic heroes in George Square.[69] Unlike Edinburgh, Glasgow was celebrating the contemporary social romanticism of the self made man.

Most Americans felt at home in Scotland. The people seemed welcoming, warm and far removed from the stuffy English: they were far more democratic and uninhibited. The Scots, according to the editor of the *Springfield Republican,* 'are very nice people, both sensible and good-natured, who make you feel at home among them just as the English, unless you have a hatful of introductions, make you feel that you are not at home and several other nations I could name make you wish you were at home'.[70] Lady visitors felt respected and treated as human beings, unlike in England.[71] Nathaniel Carter found his Scottish lady companions 'handsome, friendly, intelligent and always agreeable, manifesting less fondness for show and more simplicity of manners than their southern neighbours.'[72] One or two, like Herman Melville, were less charitable: he was appalled by the 'women—faces like cattle'.[73] They were perhaps the same beaten, degraded and humanly destroyed wretches of poor women his fellow Americans found around Edinburgh and Glasgow: 'There are drunken brawling men and women, idiots, cripples, loathesomely scarred people, prostitutes attired in gaudily striped petticoats or skirts, dirty, crying children, and among all, the decent poor, struggling against misery and crime for bread to enable them to stay longer in the misery and to endure more of it.'[74] These were but the failures, it seemed, in a thriving bustling and prosperous commercial and industrial land. The huge sprawling shipyards, factories lighting the night sky and crowded thoroughfares were evidence of better lives.[75] Only one book reflected a bitter bad-tempered attitude, the rest were enthusiastic admirers.[76] Scots were warm, hospitable and welcoming people.[77] Their manners, cities and intelligence were finer than England.[78] Their newspapers were like American newspapers; their hotels were like American hotels. The St Enoch and Cockburn hotels in Glasgow were like home: one with all American facilities and the other managed by a lady from Louisiana.[79] With such strong affinities, the Scot would 'always find a hearty welcome in the land of the setting sun'.[80]

How did Scottish visitors fare in America? They like their American counterparts frequently found much to reinforce their prejudices. The vast majority found their countrymen flourishing in comfort and affluence as a result of their own endeavours. Everywhere in Vermont, Maine, New York or California the emigrants had prospered.[81] In travelling through the country, Scottish visitors invariably met large numbers of their country-men, old friends, relatives or members of their old congregations in Scotland.[82] America was hardly foreign in any real sense.

In some surprising ways, it was. Visitors were delighted at the accessibility of the American president. President Jackson, however, proved ignorant and uncouth: Martin Van Buren was 'urbanity and frankness of manner.'[83] Thomas Hamilton found that 'no man of high principles can enter American political life': significantly he only admired the conservatives Edward Livingston and John Calhoun.[84] A somewhat less virulent critic of America than other contemporary English visitors, Hamilton was merely expressing his conservative social views. Scottish radicals underwent a similar transformation in their American experience. The educational reformer George Lewis returned, he claimed, cured of political meddling.[85] The temperance lecturer and former Chartist, John Dawson Burn, returned from three years among the American workers utterly opposed to universal suffrage. He was equally hostile to social engineering by mixing the classes in school 'under the idea of social equality entertained by the most worthless members of society'.[86] The sons of radicals, Andrew Carnegie and Allan Pinkerton, both emigrated and enjoyed astonishing success as an industrial entrepreneur and as head of a detective agency which specialised in breaking industrial unions.[87] They, like many of their compatriots, were able to succeed with their native Scottish qualities in a land which, they found, highly valued these virtues. Glasgow visitors to America invariably found, as suggested earlier, that their fellow Glaswegians were wonderfully prosperous. Their entrepreneurial and craft skills were generally channelled into economic activity rather than abortive political agitation. Their native Scottish radicalism seemed unnecessary in America: their aspirations were a conservative norm. Scotland and America seemed one and the same:

> Sobriety, love of work and perseverance in both; the same attachment to religion, mingled with more caution in Sanders and more enterprise in Jonathan. Both are inhabitants of a poor country and both have become by habits of steady industry and frugality. Both send forth a large portion of their population to participate in the wealth of more favoured regions. The Scot, however never loses his attachment to his native land. It has probably been to him a rugged nurse yet wander where he will, its heathy mountains are ever present to his imagination and he thinks of the bleak moorland cottage in which he grew from infancy to manhood, as a spot encircled by a halo of light and beauty. Whenever fortune smiles on him he returns to his native village and the drama of his life closes where it commenced.[88]

These highly prized virtues, according to Scottish visitors, stemmed from his home experience which demanded 'sober habits and well directed industry' and gave him advantages in America.[89] His strong religious sense also contributed to his purposeful drive to economic success here and to salvation in the hereafter. Whether explained by terror, a sense of duty or ambition, that quality made him well equipped for self-improvement in America.

Some Scottish observers were doubtful that America could continue to satisfy the expectation of élite Scottish emigrants:

> The bulk of the emigrant population then must long consist of wealthy peasants dressed in home spun clothes, cultivating their own ground with their own hands and living in simple plenty. For the higher ranks this continent affords no refuge; and scarcely for any in the middling classes who do not stand at the bottom of the scale. The exclusion from social intercourse, the distance from church, the want of any opportunity of attaining the higher branches of education, must also operate strongly with those accustomed to the accommodations and elegances of European life.[90]

The writer, predictably from Edinburgh, was at best merely questioning the vitality of the American democracy and failing to appreciate the dynamism of the 'wealthy peasants' with their remarkable ability to create a new culture, new forms of churches and new colleges and universities. It was an achievement carried through with the aid of Scottish middle class values of simplicity, thrift and godliness. Popular religion, popular education and the idea of bread earned by the sweat of each individual's brow showed the essentially democratic nature of the American enterprise.

Alexander Graham Dunlop, the son of the Scottish temperance reformer, John Dunlop, was very impressed by early Chicago: it seemed well built, regular and had good wide streets. Even more agreeable, Chicago took pride in music and flowers, sure signs of civilisation and refinement. Milwaukee seemed pretty; Detroit clean and well supplied with good hotels; Cairo, Illinois a miserable place. Overall he left well pleased and charmed by the rapid progress and substantial advances of civilisation. The ladies might generally be plain and young men hardworking—even when idle— but America had great potential. But above all he was very aware of American antipathy to all things English.[91] A Scot might well feel at home.

The connections between Glasgow and America were thus reinforced by the numerous visitors on each side. Throughout the century a steady stream of impressions issued from the press. Glasgow invariably appeared as the most American city in Europe: 'Every part of Glasgow shows life and energy and industry.'[92] The American poet William Cullen Bryant found Glasgow in 1845 like 'one continuous building site increasing with a rapidity almost equal to New York'.[93] The Clyde seemed like one continuous ship-yard: it was an industrial city which never slept.[94] A United States government commissioner of the tariff found the city filled with 'lots of enterprise, lots of pluck, lots of 'go-aheadness', lots of manufacturing and lots of business'.[95]

The beauty of Glasgow itself also deeply impressed many American visitors. Far from the grim picture presented in most accounts already mentioned, contemporaries found the industrial city a delight. Some stressed the ugly face of the city but many more responded favourably to the more positive aspects of a manysided city. The virtues of a new, self-made meritocracy were there for all to see. Mrs E A Forbes believed that she had 'never seen so beautiful a city'.[96] The clean wide streets, handsome statues in George Square, and the abundance of fine church buildings struck many observers.[97] Glasgow had by some happy chance managed to combine rapid industrialisation and growth with splendid harmonious building developments.[98] Throughout the century visitors noted the fine houses and regular planned appearance of the city: 'The splendid ranges of hewn stone dwelling houses and spacious streets and squares of the city of Glasgow, cannot fail to excite the admiration of the stranger.'[99] Thirty years later, the visitors were very impressed by the recent West End developments and Kelvingrove Park.[100] Order, regularity and planning stood in marked contrast to the American experience: 'The houses and streets are elegant, the parks well laid out and finely cared for, the streets wide and clean and the whole city having an elegance for which I was wholly unprepared.'[101] Grace Greenwood reinforced that view: 'Glasgow for a manufacturing town, makes a very handsome appearance. Many of the public buildings are of a fine style of architecture; and the planted squares, those fresh breathing spaces off the crowded business streets are truly beautiful.'[102] To the imaginative son of the architect of the Capitol buildings, the high chimney of the chemical works, Tennant's stalk, rivalled 'the Pyramids or Strasbourg Cathedral' and even those who were but moderately impressed felt a strong similarity between Paris and the city with the bridges over the Clyde.[103]

The University of Glasgow also received much attention and not a few compliments. The president of Wesleyan University was 'charmed with his visit'. Its many visitors included Herman Melville.[104] Though most found the old and new university buildings splendid, George Buckham, who probably wrote the sourest book of Scottish travels, found the new buildings 'the most repulsive pile I ever beheld'.[105] Glasgow did however demonstrate to American observers that 'a commercial and manufacturing city can possess a great and flourishing institution of learning'.[106] Through Glasgow rather than German universities, Tappan may have been influenced in his idea of the university as a service to the state and closely articulating with the life of the people at Michigan, and through him other state universities like Wisconsin and elsewhere.[107]

Whatever the derivation of that influence, the move of the university to the west end of the city was understandable in view of American opinions of the new housing there. Nathaniel Hawthorne, the novelist, thought it 'the stateliest of cities' and 'a noble city'.[108] Glasgow, as Hawthorne and others thought, had superb shops, particularly in Buchanan Street, which excelled those of London.[109] But the houses of the West End 'are the finest erections and command especial notice. They excel in many cases the much extolled palaces of the fashionable quarter of London, and are both pretty and clean externally.'[110] New buildings and 'improving' seemed the hallmark of city.[111]

Americans might identify Glasgow with their native cities, Baltimore, New York, Philadelphia and even New Orleans: the Broomielaw was compared to the levee at New Orleans.[112] In feeling at home they were again identifying with success, self help and civic control by the better elements.

At the same time they could still be shocked and horrified by the poverty and drunkenness they encountered: the unregenerate and the alien were the same on both sides of the Atlantic. Drink and churchgoing seemed both to be furious pastimes.[113] The sight of crowds of drunken men and women was a commonplace observation by most travellers. The filth and squalor of the older, poorer section of the city oppressed many: Hawthorne believed the children were unwashed from birth.[114] Even a hardened clergyman from Hartford, Connecticut, claimed that he had never seen such drinking even at home: the only relief was that the two worst were English gentry.[115]

That feature constantly recurs through many of the travel books; an antipathy to English hauteur, snobbery and ignorance:[116] The genuine warmth and unrestrained welcome of Scottish hosts was thought to be the norm though on occasion the hotelier could be singularly surly and filthy.[117] Even these disappointments did not dispel the affection for Scotland over England. Even the appalling filth of the Glasgow slums still seemed to produce far superior characters to those of England: 'The inhabitants are friendly and intelligent, but cautious and distrustful. They are active and industrious and keep their streets free from beggars, so much so as to cause the stranger who has visited England to notice the fact.'[118] Nathaniel Hawthorne likewise might be outraged by the filth, smell and drunkenness but in his opinion with all these afflictions 'they are better looking people than the English (and this is true of all classes) more intelligent of aspect with more regular features'.[119] As a later New England observer wrote 'the Scottish paupers look more like American paupers than others in the British Kingdom'. In every way and at every level Americans felt at home in Glasgow.

Scots felt much at home in America where 'all pretensions to importance are disregarded without being canvassed as they might be in Europe.'[120] The prospect of adequate education was attractive. The schools in existence even before the labours of William Russell and his friends, are geared to the education of the poorer classes: they were allegedly not élite schools. Their existence was also attractive to well educated Scots for the opportunity to teach. Some like Ayrshire-born John Regan in Illinois seized the opportunity and settled down to a far more comfortable if arduous existence than at home.[121]

A fair number of immigrants did not go directly to America. Some seem to have gone to Canada or Nova Scotia and then moved into the United States. Others, like those encountered by the Paisley weaver, Alexander Mackay, may have been more common. After leaving home at fourteen he spent two years as a waiter at the Athol Arms, Dunkeld, four more in Glasgow, seven years as a steward on the Belfast-Glasgow ferry with two years as a traveller for a Belfast distillery before he eventually had enough capital to go to Ohio.[122] He had every reason to hope that, like Mr Greig, a Scots emigrant of forty years standing, he might have 'a ducal palace' through honest effort and endeavour.[123] The Edinburgh and Glasgow educational reformer, Hugo Reid, envisaged emigration as a means of working class improvement—though perhaps at the cost of loosening moral restraint and violent crimes.[124]

Scottish emigrants who were prepared to work hard, to be sober and thrifty would inevitably prosper in America according to most contemporary commentators. In 1837, Edward Delavan, the successful New York businessman and temperance advocate, visited Glasgow and urged intending immigrants to join teetotal associations. In that way they would develop acceptable habits, good references and access to better opportunities.[125] Provided that the immigrant was prepared to be 'regardless of preconceived ideas of his own dignity' he would succeed.[126] The developing cities offered excellent opportunities. St Louis wanted 'not idle clerks and lazy shopkeepers but hardworking industrious men who mean to succeed'.[127] Out there lay 'a boundless inheritance in the west . . . waiting our younger unsettled but aspiring sons who complain there is no room for them in our Scotland'.[128] In the west 'no occupation was considered derogatory and in fact everyone was too occupied with his own affairs to trouble himself in the smallest degree about his neighbour. . . . Every kind of business custom and employment was solicited with an importunity little known in old countries, where the course of all such things is so well worn and channelled that it is not easily directed. But here the field was open and everyone was striving for what seemed to be within the reach of all—a foremost rank in his own sphere. To keep one's place in the crowd required an unremitted exercise of the same vigour and clarity which were necessary to obtain it; and many a man though possessed of qualities which would have enabled him to distinguish himself in the quiet routine of life in old countries was crowded out of his place by a multitude of competitors.'[129] As Patrick Shirreff of East Lothian saw, the Scot was well groomed to succeed in such an atmosphere. He had had a practical education, unlike the English with their classics which 'often converts weak minds into polished nothings without adding to the usefulness of men'.[130] Free from class and status considerations, from élite cultural attitudes and from atrophying religious or nationalist influences, the Scot could enter freely into this competitive world without distraction. He was single-minded in pursuit of his objective.

The sense of religious solidarity gave an added dimension of security and harmony. The religious links were well established in the eighteenth century. Glasgow had supplied ministers to the colonies in fair numbers. As early as 1717 several Glasgow graduates were labouring in Pennsylvania. One of the later graduates, Francis P Alison was to educate many ministers in his training school as well as three signatories of the Declaration of Independence.[131] The American revivals, in turn, had been readily imported into Scotland. The success of George Whitefield in the Colonies had been relayed to the west of Scotland by letters from emigrants, by family connections and by Whitefield himself. Revd William McCulloch, of Cambuslang, married to the daughter of Glasgow's Lord Provost, cousin to the acting governor, Dinwiddie of Virginia, had wished to be a missionary in America. His son had spent some time there. He and his friends were receptive to the ideas of Jonathan Edwards while Revd John Gillies regularly corresponded with New England ministers. McCulloch's *The Weekly History* became the first religious periodical in Scotland: it was devoted to disseminating news of revivalist success. These revivals were to continue down to the present.[132]

The Second Great Awakening was conveyed by ministers in correspondence and on visits in the early nineteenth century. That movement was an
effective means of reaching the unchurched masses. As Perry Miller has
shown, it was a means of asserting the unity of American culture in pressing
danger of disintegration. This remarkable combination of patriotism and
piety, humiliation and exertion, repentance and reform organised the
American people for their providential future. They were a chosen people
dedicated to the future. That optimistic confidence found echoes in
Glasgow.[133] John Dunmore Lang, the future evangelical zealot for Australian
education was influenced by Revd John Mason of New York in Greenock.
Mason visited Scotland on a number of occasions and was well known in
religious circles. Ashahel Nettleton, a leading figure in the Connecticut
awakening preached in Ralph Wardlaw's Glasgow church. David Naismith,
the Scottish city missioner, visited the redoubtable Tappan brothers of New
York and assisted in setting up missions to the poor. William Barnes of
Philadelphia visited Glasgow as did the Baptist president of Brown
University, Francis Wayland. The president of Amherst, Herman Humphrey,
came to instruct his Glasgow hearers in the glories of the American revival.
Lyman Beecher's sermons were reprinted in the city as a host of lesser figures
descended on the unchurched.[134] Among them Lydia Sigourney, the poet of
the revival, came to write an inspirational poem on the Necropolis. Travel
books invariably highlighted that sermon in stone as well as the statue of
Knox. Romanticism and tradition were united in maudlin fashion.

The need for a warm personal reassuring faith intensified amid the rapid
social and economic changes in the Glasgow region. Zeal for a new
community was common to most faiths, secular and religious: an ethical,
utopian vision was abroad. The influence of the writings of William
Grandison Finney, the American revivalist was pervasive. The young
Glasgow graduate and theological student, Fergus Ferguson, and eight
fellow students at the Glasgow Theological Academy were expelled for their
unorthodox 'American' views. David Livingstone's brother went off to
study at Oberlin College, where Finney taught at the centre of evangelical
ideas. Few seemed untouched.[135] A further series of revivals ensued from
1858 to 1860 on the eve of the American Civil War. Phoebe Palmer arrived
from America to enjoy success among sympathetic Glasgow audiences.
Finney himself also came to London where he worked with the former
Kilmarnock minister, John Campbell. A former member of Greville
Ewing's Congregational church in Glasgow had written the life of David
Naismith. From there Finney toured the east coast of Scotland but his fears
of being involved in sectarian quarrels prevented him from coming to the
Evangelical Union church in Glasgow. Twelve months later the American,
Edward Payson Hammond, drove himself to total exhaustion in his three
months in the city.[136] Such were the precursors of the several visits of
Moody and Sankey to Scotland. Their tumultuous success was to transform
the religious scene. In this respect Glasgow and America were one.

Revivals were part and parcel of the American voluntary tradition in
religion. Though not always meeting with the approval of the clergy of the
established Church of Scotland, they did prove invaluable in disciplining an

increasingly democratic, fluid industrial and commercial society. In giving rise to individual identity, releasing new organisational skills, the revivals boosted self confidence, self help and a sense of America as a peculiar nation under God. In the Atlantic world, that become the Scottish-American people under God. It provided a base for a civil religion. It was a way of life:

> They have not to acquire a taste for revivals; their difficulty would be to destroy it. They are mostly the children of revivals; their churches have been mostly raised or nourished in revivals; their whole history and that of their country is the history of revivals.[137]

The voluntarist American churches, unlike the established Church of Scotland, were able to respond successfully to the urban challenge. The flourishing voluntary benevolent societies and the well observed sabbath were evidence enough.

Not all Scots were uncritical admirers of American religious zeal. Revd John G Lorimer of Glasgow found evidence that Americans were un-churched. The success of voluntarism was a myth. In Ohio, he claimed, there were only eleven ministers, seven of whom were merely itinerants. The sabbath was largely ignored: Popery and Unitarianism flourished as did intemperance and slavery. His was a lonely voice among much Scottish praise.

These tides of millenarian enthusiasm in the wake of the French Revolution had great impact in the Atlantic world. Social changes further contributed to that sense of eager anticipation. The West of Scotland seems to have remarkable parallels with New York's 'Burned Over' district in producing millenial notions. In 1785 an Ayrshire woman had claimed to be a female prophet. Edward Irving, the assistant to Thomas Chalmers in Glasgow, developed his own apocalyptic vision of the imminent return of Christ, against a background of prophesying and speaking in tongues at Roseneath and Port Glasgow in 1830. The Revd James 'Shepherd' Smith, a Glasgow graduate aware of these influences, predicted a universal millenium: 'If Christianity were truly established . . . it would put an end to private capital, to private monopolies, to private ambition, to distinctions of rank, to unequal distribution of wealth, to ruinous competitions among manufacturers, to swindling, to adulteration of goods, to quackery and imposition of every description'.[138]

Scottish Methodism had some association with these developments. Its growth and enthusiasm coincided with the American Awakening. Thomas Coke, the Welsh Methodist bishop, crossed the Atlantic at least eight times organising, preaching and sustaining his brethren. In 1797 he revisited Glasgow in the course of his duties and reacted critically to the Scottish religious condition:

> There was a time when *Scotland* was the glory of all the Churches; but that time is passed. Speculative knowledge is the all in all among the generality of Professors; whilst the Infidels who compose a considerable part of the nation beholding nothing in religion but a bare profession—nothing of that image of God, which is the only desirable thing in the universe—fly naturally to Deism for a refuge from

hypocrisy. And who can be surprised? For what sensible man in the world can believe that God would give his only begotten Son to die upon the Cross, in order to make us *orthodox*?[139]

Those observations again indicated the need for a more enthusiastic approach to faith. There was a reaction against the reason of the Enlightenment and the aridity of Calvinism. A more hopeful optimistic view gained ground. Man could be saved through God's grace and his own repentance. By kindling that faith and stimulating good works, the American Second Great Awakening, coincided with a more democratic path to heaven, emphasising the individual sense of sin and salvation. It enabled men to wage war against the world, the flesh, the devil and their political opponents.[140] In every way self awareness and confidence were encouraged in a dynamic positive way. Others found the evangelical mixture a heady brew. David Nasmith or Naismith (1799–1839) emerged in the early nineteenth century as a dynamic secretary of some twenty-three religious associations in Glasgow. The Glasgow of Professor Stevenson Macgill and Thomas Chalmers naturally stressed the social aspects of Christian practice. The founder of the city mission movement, Nasmith sought a united evangelical approach to the poor. Concentrating on individual moral regeneration, he was responsible for the first Young Men's Association for Prayer and Religious Improvement. Not only did he spread his ideas through Britain but he took them on an extensive tour to some fifty towns in the United States and Canada in 1830. In contact with the Tappan brothers and other evangelicals he returned to further evangelical success in Britain before his untimely death in 1839.[141]

Nasmith's Young Men's Association was to run a parallel course to the Young Men's Christian Association which was introduced into Glasgow in 1848. They eventually united in 1877 and thereafter the American connection strengthened. The general secretary of the Glasgow Association visited the United States, corresponded with and attended international conferences with leading American workers. The dynamic American leader of the movement, John R Mott, visited Glasgow on several occasions to stimulate Christian missionary enterprise, to consolidate a sense of international co-operation and unity in a world of common assumptions. His visits in 1894, 1905 and 1910 won warm support from Glasgow University staff, students and city ministers. In 1914 his visit proved a disaster: war had destroyed that slender brotherhood.[142]

The several visits of Dwight L Moody and Ira Sankey to Glasgow marked a watershed in religious revivalism in the late nineteenth century.[143] Their first visit in 1874 lasted three months and was marked by massive interest and attention. Their second lasted even longer from September 1882 to April 1883. Great activity, new churches and enthusiastic services followed. The moral uplift of the masses became central.

Thomas Chalmers and his efforts to improve the lot of the urban poor attracted American interest. His preaching brought over many Americans to examine his ideas. He enjoyed enormous vogue in America: his sermons were described as 'super-excellent' by one university president.[144] Those who heard him preach were initially bewildered by his deep Scottish accent but once adjusted they enjoyed his performance immensely: 'Dr Chalmers repeatedly spoke with his characteristic fulness and power. He has none of the gracefulness of the practised orator and his countenance is heavy until irradiated by his subject. The mind triumphs over matter and makes the broad Scotch a pliant vehicle eloquent with thought.'[145] Even more interesting, an American visitor heard Chalmers preach on behalf of the Roman Catholic Free School in 1825. Nathaniel Carter had to secure a seat more than an hour before the service and he was borne along in a 'vortex' to the church in Albion Street. Though unimpressive in appearance and speaking with his heavy accent, Chalmers won his hearer with a remarkable display:

> Dr Chalmers has none of the graces of oratory, either as regards his elocution or his gestures. Both of these are positively bad. The effect of his preaching arises from the vigour of his thought, boldness of conception, and earnestness of manner. He throws himself forward as if he would pitch headlong from the pulpit; he clenches his white pocket handkerchief firmly in his fist, and brings down his hand, as if smiting someone at his feet: this gesture is uniform, answering fully to what Hamlet calls 'sawing the air', and nothing but the conviction that it is wholly involuntary can reconcile it to the hearer: the orator seems convulsed with the throes of thought, and the grandeur of his periods, rolling out one after another in rapid succession, leaves the mind little time for dwelling on minor considerations.
>
> His manner approaches very nearly to what our country would call methodistical. For some minutes he continues to kindle gradually, and the tones of his voice grow louder and louder, till he fairly thunders. As he ascends these climaxes of all that is sublime in imagery, or violent in gesture, the listener sits astounded at the bolts which are falling around him. The audience are silent as death, and 'the boldest holds his breath for a time'. Then comes a respite—a break in which the language of the speaker is in an undertone, so low as to be scarcely audible. I cannot illustrate his manner better than by comparing him to a torrent of his native hills, which at one time rushes impetuously down its rugged bed, and then glides away in a deep and silent current.[146]

William Ellery Channing, the Unitarian, was searching for some principle of social union. He had visited Britain in 1823 and returned inspired to preach a moral revolution. Corresponding with William Burns of Saltcoats, author of *The New Era of Christianity*, Channing wanted to apply Christian principles to social and political institutions as a means of forwarding the Kingdom here.[147] Hedderwick, the Glasgow printer who had himself spent some time in America, printed the first complete edition of Channing's works in the world.[148] Even before that he had been in correspondence with Channing, in contact with the American reform circles associated with William Rathbone of Liverpool, and visited by several prominent American Unitarians. In addition Captain Fullarton of Ayrshire and Mr Fyfe, a Glasgow businessman, had visited Channing in Boston.[149] Unfortunately, Hedderwick ran into difficulties when in the midst of his marketing operation. A rival publisher, Richard Griffin of Glasgow, brought out a cheap single volume edition of Channing's works. In the ensuing legal battle Hedderwick lost considerable money.[150] The case merely demonstrates the popularity of Channing in Glasgow and the West of Scotland. Griffin had printed some 2000 copies of the works while Hedderwick had reported steady sales of his more expensive multi-volume edition. Channing's *Essay on Self Culture*, as well as those on the Labouring classes and temperance, had substantial sales: his *Address on Temperance*, published in cheap form for the Glasgow Temperance Society, soon ran to over 3000 copies. His *Address on the Present Age* reached a similar figure.[151]

From the earliest days of the Unitarian movement in Glasgow the transatlantic element had existed. In the eighteenth century, English Unitarians had attended the University of Glasgow. In the aftermath of the trial, conviction and transportation of the Dundee Unitarian minister, Thomas Fysshe Palmer in the Treason Trials, his assistant, William Christie, served in Glasgow for a year before emigrating to America where he settled near the English radical exile, Joseph Priestley, in Pennsylvania.[152] In 1812, the cultivated James Yates, a graduate of Glasgow University, settled down to form a permanent congregation. That effort involved him in a lengthy pamphlet war with Revd Dr Ralph Wardlaw, the Independent Glasgow congregationalist minister. Later Yates left for Birmingham before he began a very productive scholarly life. His successor was George Harris who ministered for some sixteen years to 1841. Both Yates and Harris were drawn into contact with visiting American reformers, in particular Joseph Tuckerman.[153]

Four prominent American Unitarians came to Glasgow: Ezra Stiles Gannet; Charles Brooks, Benjamin Bussey Thatcher and Joseph Tuckerman. Gannet, a Harvard graduate, married the daughter of president Ezra Stiles of Yale and acted as assistant to W E Channing. He was to be largely responsible for the organisation of the American Unitarian Association in 1835 as well as the assistant editor of the *Christian Register*. He, like most visitors, heard Chalmers preach, passed similar comments on his style but noted the strong similarities to Channing.[154] Brooks, clergyman and educator, had spent two years in Germany examining the Prussian education system before he returned to America to campaign vigorously for state teacher training colleges. He addressed the state legislatures of New Hampshire, Vermont, Maine and New Jersey as well as public gatherings in Rhode Island and Pennsylvania. He then spent four years in Europe from 1839, but failing eyesight prevented him carrying through his promising career.[155] Thatcher came in 1837 after recently abandoning the editorship of his paper *The Colonisationist* which supported the Liberian settlement for freed slaves in Africa. A successful lawyer, he remained a firm supporter of the scheme although forced to give up his paper.[156] Brooks and Thatcher would seem to have had other reasons than religion to visit Glasgow: Brooks to examine the educational experiments and Thatcher possibly, to bolster his ideas in the wake of the defeat of Revd Robert Breckenridge at the hands of the Glasgow abolitionists.[157]

Joseph Tuckerman was born in Boston, the son of a merchant, where after Harvard he became a minister. After urban pastoral experience and a visit to Europe in 1816, he decided to dedicate himself to the Association for Religious Improvement among the Poor under Channing's inspiration. Increasingly he was drawn under the influence of Thomas Chalmers and Patrick Colquhoun, in his efforts to secure the moral and material improvement of the poor. Colquhoun was a former Virginia merchant, later Lord Provost of Glasgow, who subsequently went to London where he laid the foundations for an effective police force and wrote several important tracts on social problems. The inculcation of morality, regular habits and foresight into the poorer elements of society was a necessary prelude to self improvement.[158] Amelioration demanded personal contact, especially home visiting, an idea Tuckerman borrowed from his Catholic friends.[159] Central to that general improvement was temperance which he urged upon the Boston mechanics. In 1833–4, Tuckerman visited Glasgow again. In the reforming Unitarian circles of Britain, among the ladies were Harriet Martineau, the American traveller and Joanna Baillie, the poet and playwright. Joanna Baillie's father was minister at Bothwell when she was born in 1762. He subsequently became minister in Hamilton and then briefly in 1776 Professor of Divinity at Glasgow University, before his death two years later. Though wealthy she began to write and moved to London where she enjoyed numerous literary connections.[160] She and Tuckerman soon developed a strong mutual respect and concern for the uplifting of society. His visit to Glasgow further impressed him with the accomplishments of the city in responding to poverty and founding various philanthropic institutions.

Tuckerman also spent some time with William Smith, the veteran Unitarian MP who had recently retired from the House of Commons after forty-eight years service. Smith had played a leading role in the Scottish Fisheries Society, and was well acquainted with Robert Owen.[161] After touring Ireland, Tuckerman arrived in Glasgow to be appalled by the sight of a poor woman giving a glass of whisky to each of her children. After that initial impression, he was delighted by the various philanthropic institutions he visited and the hospitality of the Lord Provost, Robert Graham, of Dugald Bannatyne, the liberal Chamber of Commerce friend of America, and of Mr Harris, the Unitarian minister.[162] After visiting the Glasgow bridewell, interviewing the gentlemen responsible for the children's reformatory, he gathered up various annual reports for further study at home. Warmly admiring Scottish virtue and education beyond any in Europe, he was struck by the civic comfort and wealth of Glasgow. He was appalled by the Saltmarket area but still more by the intense religious bigotry between Protestant ministers in the face of that poverty, a feature which also distressed the Quaker abolitionists, the Motts, on their visit a few years later.[163]

If Unitarianism was a featherbed for failing Christians, other groups were equally anxious to cut through dead traditions and dogmas to establish a new initiative. Alexander Campbell, the Ulster born founder of the Disciples of Christ, had spent some time at Glasgow University under Professor Jardine of Moral Philosophy before he emigrated to America. There he established an extreme form of Baptist faith which sought to draw all Christians together by returning to the primitive church. In asserting the essential unity in basic fundamentals of the faith and ignoring diversity of opinions in other areas, he hoped to inaugurate the millenium. By emphasising the democratic nature of the church, freed from formal and even educated leadership, at least initially, he envisaged an active involved church.[164] With his brother he built a thriving movement in America, debated with Robert Owen and returned to Scotland to gather further converts in the 1840s. The Disciples of Christ had begun their mission.

Glasgow Universalism emerged in the late eighteenth century. Neil Douglas (1750–1823) a Glasgow graduate from Argyll, had become a Relief Synod minister in the East of Scotland. There he came into contact with the Edinburgh Universalists, became a convert and returned to preach his new faith in Greenock. He then went to Glasgow and preached in the hall of the Andersonian University. Acquitted on a charge of sedition in 1817, he continued to preach until his death when he was succeeded by a member of his congregation, William Worrall.[165]

Worrall began to correspond with the American Universalists, Thomas Jefferson Sawyer of Clinton New York, and Stephen R Smith of Buffalo and Philadelphia. They were to organise the body in America and conduct itinerant proselytising campaigns in the early days.[166] Unfortunately with the death of Worrall in 1838 the congregation declined and a missionary Abel C Smith of Philadelphia, was unable to revitalise it. Later P H Waddell, who was training for the Church of Scotland ministry, adopted Universalist ideas and began a church in Glasgow known as 'The Church of the Future'.[167]

The struggling Universalist congregation agreed to merge with this new body but the scheme foundered when Waddell returned to the Church of Scotland.

James Ure Mitchell (1833–1905) then played a dominant role in revitalising the small body. A former assistant preacher in Glasgow he helped to build up Universalist congregations through central Scotland. He re-established closer links with the United States through J S Cantwell, an American Universalist on holiday in Scotland. He returned to appeal for funds to the Universalist General Convention in 1872. The following year Mitchell himself went to America to attend the General Convention in Washington DC and he also persuaded a member of his congregation, Donald Fraser (1850–1925) to study for the ministry in America. Fraser was to remain there for forty years.[168] Ure Mitchell's son was also to serve in America.

Following Mitchell's visit, the American Universalists decided to send a missionary to Scotland. Caroline Soule arrived in 1875. A teacher and poet, she had travelled through the United States on behalf of the Universalist missions. She began a new congregation in Glasgow at St Paul's Pitt Street in 1879 where she remained three years where she was visited by an American Universalist, Sullivan H McCollester.[169] After another American from Utica, New York had briefly served in Glasgow, Soule returned from 1887 until her retirement in 1892. She remained in Glasgow until her death in 1903, taking an interest in temperance, vegetarianism and spiritualism. The congregation went into decline and disappears from the Glasgow directory after 1894.

To meet these and other threats, more orthodox Americans came to Glasgow in the eighteenth and nineteenth centuries seeking funds for their educational and missionary enterprises. Revd Samuel Davies had enjoyed a very profitable tour of Scotland, with Glasgow particularly generous in support of the New Jersey College, later Princeton.[170] A dozen years later, Revd Nathaniel Whitaker of Norwich, Connecticut raised £2500 in Scotland for the Baptist College, Rhode Island, later Brown University. He was accompanied by the first American Indian minister ever to visit Britain, Revd Samson Occum. A Mohican, he preached on behalf of further missions to his people.[171] Other Indians came in the nineteenth century. They found a ready patron in an illegitimate son of the Duke of Sussex, Augustus d'Este, who had Lanarkshire connections. One of his protegés was overwhelmed by the beauty of the Clyde and another sought help when his tribe was forcibly removed from its traditional lands in 1841.[172] Another fascinating character with Glasgow business connections, Sir William Drummond Stewart held the American Indian in great esteem. Not only did he take the American artist, Alfred Jacob Miller, with him on his 1837 trip to the west to capture a fast disappearing civilisation, he wrote two novels in which the Indian was highly extolled.[173] In his novels, *Altowan* and *Edward Warren,* he gave full rein to his romantic admiration for the American Indian, his noble grandeur and true liberty.[174] He literally brought back the American wilderness: buffalo, cranes, saplings and plants. On his way to Glasgow with his touring Indians, the American artist, George Catlin, admired the collection.[175] Colonel Cody would bring others in 1891. Hollywood would continue that interest.

Glasgow concern for the underprivileged in America persisted. In 1841 two emissaries, Revd John Keep and William Dawes, arrived to solicit funds for Oberlin College.[176] Founded by those who sought the immediate emancipation of slaves in America, the college was an integrated institution from the beginning.

Glasgow had a long anti-slavery tradition and with the end of slavery in the British dominions turned its attention to America. Revd Ralph Wardlaw, the Congregationalist, played a leading role in the formation of a renewed Glasgow abolitionist society. A regular correspondent of Revd Leonard Woods of Andover, he shared similar evangelical views. Some American visitors even thought they looked identical.[177] That organisation and its Edinburgh counterpart were very active in the years preceding the Disruption. The dissension which then ensued weakened the movement though Glasgow continued to show great sympathy with the American black. In 1833 Revd Remond was warmly welcomed in his campaign against the conservative American Colonisation Society. The renowned freed slave, Frederick Douglass, came to address Glasgow audiences on a number of occasions. Though enjoying the personal friendship of many Glaswegians, he had few illusions about the appalling drunkenness which prevailed. That, however, might have been a very effective way of criticising white society in the most polite way. William Wells Brown, also a freed slave, visited the city several times. The Cleveland black leader, John P Green, was entertained on his visit in 1892 by the aged William Smeal, the Quaker tea merchant and abolitionist.[178] Finally the energetic black intellectual, W E B DuBois came to the city in the course of a bicycling holiday: significantly, Booker T Washington, the more compromising leader merely passed by in the train en route to visit Andrew Carnegie. That difference summarised the two differing philosophies of the two men, one seeking acceptance as an equal as a right and the other prepared to win that acceptance in more gradual ways.[179]

Swedenborgian interest also crossed the Atlantic. As we shall see there was a distinct contribution to the educational revolution. Revd J F Potts of the Glasgow New Church exchanged pulpits with the minister of Providence, Rhode Island in 1877 where he encountered members of his congregation who had emigrated.[180] The most fascinating link was Thomas Lake Harris. An Englishman by birth, he had emigrated as a child to America where he had followed a chequered career, becoming in turn a Universalist minister, a spiritualist and then a Swedenborgian minister.[181] Around 1859 he came to Glasgow promoting his Brotherhood of the New Life. Returning to America he began a model community of celibates which attracted the remarkable Scottish eccentric Laurence Oliphant.[182] Incorporating many of the communitarian notions of the period, the members shared all their property, the field work and a form of spiritual life. The community discovered a remarkable facility for wine making and moved from New York state to Santa Rosa, California. Soon large shipments of wine were being sent to Britain. Meanwhile Oliphant fell out with Harris over his property and broke with the community. Following the death of his wife, he married the spiritualist, Rosamund Dale Owen, grand-daughter of Robert Owen, and began to develop his scheme for the recolonisation of Palestine by the Jews. His idea was to build a model community at Haifa but he died before he could achieve that dream. Harris had attempted to unite the spiritual and temporal in his earlier work. He had experimented with community living in Virginia and after its failure had attempted to give practical social application to Christian ethics: heart and intellect had to be united. That would be achieved only in an American setting with a model community. Santa Rosa with its eventual 1700 acres for farm, vineyards, hotel and coffee shop as well as a printing press would be the 'pivotal centre' of this new dispensation. Neither communistic nor materialistic, Harris sought to liberate the divine essence of each member through song, dance and special forms of breathing to evoke the 'electro-vital form'. Such an eclectic philosophy touched on most contemporary advanced thought.[183]

Harris continued this work in California. In 1891 he produced a remarkable theo-socialist work, *The New Republic*. Its sexual mysticism envisaged the regeneration of man: 'Man is only in his real manhood as he is socialised through all his powers: the more of him, the more of humane worthfulness in his fellow men: his being becomes the household workroom of the organising deity.'[184] That outlook seemingly appealed to some early Glasgow socialists. In 1885 his close disciple, A A Cuthbert, had returned to Britain and begun publishing works about Harris, who already had some Scottish followers in California.[185] Richard McCully, a Glasgow spiritualist, discussed Harris's ideas in the Glasgow spiritualist magazine, *Light and*

Life, (1 May 1886) and the journal reported a visit by A A Cuthbert to the city.[186] The publication of Mrs Oliphant's *Life of Laurence Oliphant* produced much annoyance among Harris's friends.[187] A Glasgow supporter, C W Pearce, a fire insurance manager, wrote to the Glasgow *Evening Citizen* attacking the book as a gross slander on Harris.[188] The Glasgow spiritualists continued to discuss the work of Harris and shortly afterwards McCully published an exposition of his ideas.[189]

C W Pearce and his wife Bella, an early supporter of Glasgow socialism, began a new business as California wine importers.[190] Pearce also published a massive edition of Harris's works.[191] Mrs Pearce meanwhile visited Harris in America and Harris determined to revisit Glasgow. He arrived to stay with the Pearce family at Nithsdale, Maitland Avenue, Langside, a site ironically now occupied by co-ownership apartments. Harris and his third wife, the wealthy heiress of a New York municipal reformer, settled down to a splendid time: 'Fountaingrove seems nearer to Glasgow than to New York.'[192] The Pearces knew the leading figures in the local community, especially the more advanced thinkers, and the Harrises felt ever more at home, even contemplating settling in Glasgow. His ideas found a very responsive audience. Working men showed some interest as did some of the local spiritualist group, though they withdrew an invitation to have him address them. A succession of visitors came to visit Harris, including Caroline Soule, the retired American Universalist missionary to Glasgow. Sight-seeing and the beauty of Queens Park eventually palled and the Harrises left after three months.[193]

After Harris's death in 1906, Bella Pearce was drawn into contact with another of Harris's associates, the poet Felix Markham. He was renowned for his poem 'The Man With The Rake'. In 1910 she visited Mrs Harris and Markham in America and continued to correspond with him for many years. She sent him and later, George Lawton, the biographer of Harris, all the papers which she had not lost in removing house. Her daughter-in-law sent the rest in 1930.[194]

The Harris connection casts interesting light on the general reform endeavours, the drive towards greater social unity and cohesion, as well as on the early socialists. Given the non-sectarian, liberating spirituality of Harris, his concept of the duality of every person, and of God as male and female, and his sexual notions he might be seen as a radical. In his rejection of existing institutions and mores he certainly was. His extreme position gives some insight into the ferment of religious and reform thought around the turn of the century. Like many other Scottish-American links it combined spirituality, economic interest and social amelioration. In that respect it was part of a larger tradition.

Glasgow Theosophists enjoyed friendships with several American figures. Centred in four middle class areas of the city, the organisation entertained Mrs Besant on several occasions in its search for universal brotherhood and social reconstruction. Membership grew markedly in the years preceding the First World War from 126 in 1910 to 358 by June 1912. Dr Anna Shaw, the American suffragist, doctor and preacher, gave at least one address to the society. Once again the search for community and cohesion beyond the traditional limited boundaries was apparent.[195]

Mormon emigration from Glasgow forms a much neglected subject. As early as 1839 Mormon missionaries were active in Glasgow. In December Alexander Wright, a Banffshire man who had emigrated to Canada joined the Mormons in their Kirtland home in Ohio. He then came to Scotland proselytising in Glasgow, Aberdeen and Edinburgh, and then spending October 1840 to May 1841 in Paisley. After further missionary work up north he returned to America with a party of seventeen family relatives, travelling up the Mississippi to Nauvoo, Illinois.[196] With Wright in Glasgow came Samuel Mulliner, a Scot from Haddington who had likewise been converted in America.[197] Their preaching in Paisley district seems to have grown quickly: 'The poor are in as great bondage as the children of Israel in Egypt.'[198] Converts were made in Johnstone, Bridge of Weir, Paisley, and preaching begun in Kilbarchan. A large hall with seating for over 400 was rented as was a Universalist church for use as a schoolroom. By the time a conference was held in Paisley in May 1840 there were officials and sixty members. Two more American missionaries came to aid their brethren— Orson Pratt and Reuben Hedlock. By June there were more than 100 members. Encouraged, they took the large hall at the Andersonian University. By the third week attendances had trebled to over 300.[199] Two months later the first formal branch of the church was established in Glasgow with 193 members. The following month the first emigrants from Glasgow and Paisley left.[200]

The Mormon growth continued in the face of the opposition of clergy and mob violence, as in Kilpatrick. Strict rules were applied to members and those who refused to comply were quickly cut off from the church. There was a steady stream of converts to Zion in America. In March 1849, fifty-seven were reported as having departed.[201] In 1847 at Maybole a mob of some 300 attacked the missionaries.[202] Among the first missionaries was Brigham Young who was to place the church on a firm footing in America.

TABLE 1   Dec. 1844 membership in the west of Scotland

Glasgow	568	Kilmarnock	86
Airdrie	104	Kilbirnie	82
Auchenairn	26	Knightswood	31
Ayr	31	Lanark	67
Balfron	12	Maybole	26
Bridge of Weir	26	Paisley	93
Campsie	39	Renfrew	16
Dalry	71	Rutherglen	41
Girvan	26	Stewarton	21
Greenock	77	Thornliebank	52
Holytown	85	Tollcross	83
Irvine	45	Vale of Leven	36
Johnstone	38		

Total membership 1782

The Mormon numbers remained fairly low because of frequent excommunication of ill-disciplined members, the lapse of some and the continuous
trickle of others to Utah. In some years emigration was far greater than in
others. In 1857 152 left, in 1867 4 over six months, in 1872 55, in 1874 135,
in 1876 63, in 1878 43, in 1881 170, in 1887 48. Though their numbers were
relatively small their impact was considerable in that they epitomised that
ideal moral realised community. Between 1840 and 1900 over 9000 Scots
joined the Mormons and some 3000 emigrated to America.[203]

TABLE 2   Glasgow Conference membership figures

1849	1782	1860	747
1850	2063	1861	808
1851	—	1862	841
1852	2030	1863	700
1853	1637	1864	719
1854	1540	1865	689
1855	1170	1866	642
1856	916	1867	660
1857	741	1868	831
1858	783	1869	1018*
1859	731	1887	344
			members

* Glasgow Conference now incorporated the whole of Scotland

If the Mormons were the most outstanding attempt at group migration,
there were others. The experiments of Robert Owen in New Lanark and at
New Harmony are perhaps the best known. The New Lanark village
attracted American entrepreneurs and philanthropists and provided the
inspiration for several American industrial and educational experiments.
Owen went to the United States to supervise his model settlement and to
publicise his ideas, enterprises in which he was greatly aided by his Glasgow
born son, Robert Dale Owen, the Ayrshire emigrant William Maclure and
Francis Wright. The schoolmaster from New Lanark went over to teach in
New Harmony but the community soon foundered. It remained as an
inspiration to working class radicals in the eastern seaboard.[204]

Others like the Mauchline Chartist, John Alexander, unsuccessfully tried
to build a model community in Texas. With the collapse of the experiment
he returned to Britain. In Wisconsin, a community named Glasgow sprang
up with many immigrants from the West of Scotland in 1859. They had
come after working in various parts of America and settled down to a happy
prosperous life: a frugal, contented and thrifty people who 'never made any
trouble in the community, always keeping the Sabbath and anything else
they could lay their hands on'.[205] The Scottish miners' leader, Alexander
McDonald, a Glasgow graduate, considered establishing a co-operative
community in Eastern Kentucky but though co-operation was in vogue the
scheme foundered. In 1867 Colonel Richard Hinton, the Washington
correspondent of the *Boston Weekly Voice* visited Glasgow at the start of

his projected three months tour of British co-operatives. Early the following year he returned to eulogise the achievements in improving the lot of the British working classes in trade union and middle class journals like the *North American Review*. He was to make a second trip five years later.[206] The dream persisted. George Jacob Holyoake, the former secularist missionary in Glasgow, vigorously encouraged his Glasgow friends in co-operative emigration schemes. Little seems to have come of them.[207] The Kilmarnock-born, Revd John Kerr, the Congregational minister of Forres, sought to establish a temperance colony in Minnesota. Under the auspices of the state government and the local railway company he secured lands but failed to attract many settlers. Even that small-scale effort soon collapsed in the wake of severe winters and hot dry summers. It destroyed the illusion that Minnesota was the 'sanitorium' of the west. Scottish emigrants would have to come to terms with the city.[208] Scottish Catholics shared in these Atlantic connections. In the eighteenth century the Scottish bishops had assisted highlanders to emigrate to British North America.[209] In the wake of the massive Irish influx into the West of Scotland, the Vicar Apostolic of the Western District, Dr John Murdoch, had sent his coadjutor Bishop Smith and Revd Mr Gray to America to solicit funds for the district. Their appeal took them to New York, Philadelphia and Boston.[210] A sprinkling of Catholic priests went to America and presumably a fair number of nuns also, but that is not yet documented. Most were Irish-born priests who served in the West of Scotland for a period before they moved on. Most went during the heyday of European immigration into America between 1880 and 1920. Revd Jeremiah Bric served in Ohio for eleven years until 1886; Revd William J Cullen in Minnesota from 1881–5; Revd Michael Collins spent over thirty years in Texas and Revd Patrick Daly over forty years in New York; Revd Thomas Dunne served in Illinois. Others went earlier and several subsequently. There were even two American-born clergy who served in the West of Scotland.[211]

There were also close relations between the leading laymen on both sides. Orestes A Brownson, the convert controversialist and editor of *Brownson's Quarterly Review* was in correspondence with Robert Monteith, the Scottish convert son of a phenomenally wealthy Glasgow family.[212] In his Russophobe campaign, Monteith was anxious to recruit Brownson's aid at the time of the Crimean War. Brownson an American nationalist and dependent on Irish Catholic support, refused to endorse Monteith's moral crusade although he did publish his views.[213]

The Glasgow Catholic immigrant most in the public eye was undoubtedly Bishop Richard Gilmour, the second Bishop of Cleveland, 1872–91. Born in Glasgow of staunch Presbyterian parents, he was taken to Nova Scotia at the age of four, then to Schuykill county, Pennsylvania. There he took the temperance pledge from a Catholic priest before he joined the church to study for the priesthood.[214] After ordination, he served in Cincinnati where he restored to peace the ethnically divided Catholic community, built a model school and taught himself. In addition he wrote a large number of books for children: illustrated Bible histories, hymnals, readers and primers which remained standard texts in American Catholic schools for forty years. Discipline, temperance and education were his recipe for a vital Catholic body.

On his appointment to the diocese of Cleveland, he immediately set out to establish a Catholic schools system, introduced the *Catholic Universe* to counteract the Irish nationalist *Celtic Index,* and established the Catholic Central Association to defend Catholic rights.[215] To unite his polyglot ethnic flock he embarked upon a vigorous Romanisation policy, condemning the Irish Land League, stoutly opposing any German influences or any other element which might seek to divide the Catholic community. Amid the vastly increasing industries and population of his area, that seemed a natural and necessary response. Cleveland, for example, trebled her population during his episcopacy to reach 263,000 by 1890. With increasing numbers of immigrants from southern and eastern Europe, the local population was estimated to be around one third Catholic. To meet the needs of these new arrivals, Gilmour recruited numerous religious orders to teach, to nurse and to succour in various ways. In fourteen years he built thirty-five churches. Such demands took their toll and Gilmour, partly for recruiting and partly for health, spent several periods in Europe. He returned to Scotland on at least three occasions—1875, 1882, 1885— where he enjoyed the close friendship of Revd Joseph Hannan, brother of Revd Edward, founder of Hibernian F C Throughout he never lost his Scottish accent nor his close affection for his homeland.[216]

He was a supporter of the rights of labour but had reservations about the Knights of Labour organisation. Under the leadership of the Catholic Terence Powderly, it had become the first major successful labour organisation in American history. Many thousands of Catholics were members but the Catholic hierarchy were divided about the society. Some called for condemnation but Gilmour, though hostile to radicalism, was opposed. In the event he played at best an ambivalent role in the controversy among the bishops. The organisation was not condemned as a secret society but by then it was a spent force. Though not reactionary, Gilmour was cautiously seeking to safeguard the interests of his flock and his church.[217]

Other secular clergy also served in America. Revd. Ambrose Graham of St Mary's, Irvine, after building a new school and a new church for his flock left for Cleveland, Ohio in 1888. A year later, Revd Van Der Hyde, a curate at St Mary's, left to serve in New Orleans. The religious orders also served in this apostolate. The Benedictines of Fort Augustus sent members of their community to Washington DC to establish a monastery. But the most interesting was the attempted foundation of a Catholic colony in Florida.[218]

That initiative drew together a number of strands. The general interest in Florida as the last wilderness to be settled had grown in the 1880s. The general emphasis upon health in immigration schemes markedly increased in the period: the west, California and Florida focused on this concern. The Scottish and Irish Land Leagues harked back to the small settlements in the country. In the wake of Irish famine in 1880, Catholic Colonisation schemes flourished on the western prairies. Though they were to fail they seem to have been a hopeful antidote to the moral and physical evils of the city. Glasgow Catholics were extremely well informed on American Catholic developments by regular 'letters from America', by visits of American priests and the Irish nationalist connection. Catholic social

initiatives in the United States were closely followed whether on the grand
scale of Catholic University and the McGlynn case or rescue homes for
children.[219] The idea of settling orphan children in Canada and America was
growing under the inspiration of Mgr James Nugent of Liverpool. He had
been closely involved in immigration schemes for many years and had
toured America.[220] There was also the frequent tours of American shows
and circuses.[221] The Catholic community was very conscious of the United
States.

At this point the wide-ranging opportunist, J S Tait, appeared. A minor
popular novelist, a land speculator and valuer, Tait was a Scot who had
been deeply involved in the Scottish-American cattle boom.[222] Even in his
The Cattlefields of the Far West, he was already extolling the attractions of
Florida before he wrote his *Emigration By Colony For the Middle Classes,*
(Edinburgh 1885). It was emigration for a better class of folk. Florida for
fifteen years had been seeking to attract emigrants through a special
commissioner, European visits and promotions, but without success.[223] Tait
established the Florida Land and Mortgage Company in 1883 with an office
in Edinburgh. He hoped to capitalise on the popular interest aroused by
articles in the *Times* and *Edinburgh Courant*.[224] He wanted to recruit
between 50 and 150 families for his colonies schemes.

These proposals appealed to some elements in the Catholic community.
Dr Patrick Letters, the district surgeon of Dundee and Revd James Browne
of Arbroath responded and put their proposals to the Glasgow *Catholic
Observer's* readers.[225] They proposed to set up colonies with 250 families
exclusively Catholic with 40 acres each. Numerous inquiries poured into
them. Dr Letters claimed to have put the whole issue before Bishop John
Moore of St Augustine, Florida. Now he was the only supporter in the
American hierarchy of Revd Edward McGlynn, the fervent supporter of
Henry George, and later provided him with a refuge. At the same time,
within his diocese, Bishop Moore had a Catholic colonisation project. A
former chief justice of Arizona, E F Dunne, had selected 50,000 acres with
Moore's approval for a Catholic colony.[226] In the event, a number of
colonists did leave Glasgow in 1885 but were disappointed to find only flat
sandy soil. Most soon left and the colony collapsed.[227] The failure of the
colony proved the end of such Catholic interest. It coincided with the end of
the Scottish careers of the two Catholic promoters. Tait turned to other
interests in publishing where he proved even more unsuccessful.[228] His firm
went bankrupt in a few years. The Florida Company folded and was
eventually wound up in 1908.

A steady trickle of radicals from the Glasgow region went across the
Atlantic from the 1790s to the days of the Chartists. In seeking freedom
from political persecution, their careers suggest that they fulfilled these
ambitions in greater political and economic success than would have been
possible at home.[229] In 1794, John Craig, son of Professor John Millar, felt
obliged to seek political asylum in America. Unfortunately he died soon
after he arrived. In his escape he was not alone. The Glasgow graduate John

Maclean, a leading chemist, similarly found refuge in America, became the first Professor of Chemistry in American history, and exercised decisive influence upon Benjamin Silliman, the father of American chemistry at Princeton.[230] As we have seen, John Wilson, the Paisley poet and ornithologist, likewise fled to build a new reputation assisted by several fellow countrymen in Philadelphia. Grant Thorburn, later the subject of a novel by John Galt, prospered immensely in the new land and returned home for a visit in 1833 to defend the achievements of American democracy.[231]

Chartists also took diplomatic leave of absence in the 1840s. Ray Boston lists seven leading figures from the West of Scotland in his study.[232] All seem to have prospered far more in America than ever would have been possible at home. Some, like Allan Pinkerton and the son of William Carnegie, were to become rather conservative men—or perhaps merely fulfilling their acquisitive natures in a more open, less stratified society than Britain.[233] Until late in the nineteenth century, America was the land of radical dreams. Then American monopoly capital began to change the image.[234] The co-operation between the labour movements in Scotland and the United States began to strengthen. The Knights of Labour, the first effective national union recruited members in Scotland, most spectacularly in Saltcoats.[235] Terence Powderly was to visit Glasgow later as commissioner of immigration when his organisation had effectively collapsed.[236] As we shall see, Keir Hardie and American Labour leaders knew each other's countries very well in the early twentieth century. Solidarity in a common culture continued in other ways.

From the earliest days of American industrialisation, some Glasgow immigrants evidently went over 'on the tramp', moving from place to place in search of better opportunities. Some were disappointed and returned but those who remained generally prospered.[237] Weavers and other skilled workers were in demand in the United States. Scots who were experienced in crafts at home could do well there.

The Scottish textile industry spearheaded the industrial revolution at home as the new factory machinery spawned new technology, in iron, chemicals, engineering, and entrepreneurial skills. If factories proliferated in the squalid industrial cities of England, in Scotland there were many more instances of model villages where factories were established under the benevolent despotism of their owners. Robert Owen's New Lanark, Smith's at Deanston and several others were markedly different from their English counterparts. Ideally they were provided with model housing, schools, church, libraries and other institutions of self-improvement in either a drink-free or carefully controlled licensed environment. Well kept houses, strict discipline and sobriety were their essential characteristics. In short, the Scottish textile industry was a model to the world.

The structure, technology and skilled manpower of this industry were attractive to Americans. Anxious to develop their own textile industry free from the frequent fluctuations and interruptions caused by the various European wars from 1789 to 1815, the Americans were eager to acquire Scottish expertise. Unfortunately British law forbade the export of machinery and the emigration of skilled artisans. American entrepreneurs sought to evade these restrictions by bringing over experienced Scottish craftsmen, employing industrial spies or by going on tours of British factories themselves. Even before the stimulus provided by Eli Whitney's cotton gin in 1793, and the arrival of Samuel Slater in America with some of the British textile industry's technical secrets in 1790, Americans were attempting to recruit Scottish technicians. The Pennsylvania Society for the Encouragement of Manufactures, established in 1787, unsuccessfully tried to secure cotton manufacturing information from a Scot, John Barber. Significantly almost 20 per cent of textile workers who had emigrated to America in 1773–6 were located in the Philadelphia area. A few years later, in 1792, John Douglas, a Scots machinist, was offering plans of a gig mill and a slubbing billy to a group of merchants but was persuaded to return to Britain by the British consul before he could establish himself in Pennsylvania. In 1816, misgivings about the large investment which might be required prevented a Scot, Gilmore, from introducing a model loom into American factory production. The following year, however, Scottish looms were introduced into Rhode Island and began to spread throughout most of New England. They gradually superseded the Waltham loom which had been introduced earlier, in the model American textile town of that name. The town had been intended to be an ideal moral centre of industry. That and also the model town of Lowell seem to have been influenced more by model Scottish textile towns than American historians have prepared to credit.

The impact of New Lanark upon American entrepreneurs was considerable. Both at Lowell and other locations they intimated the ideal of Owen. As William Gregg, the Southern factory master, said: 'A cotton factory should not be located in a city where it would be impossible to control the moral habits of the operatives and to keep up a steady efficient and cheap working force.'[238] Free from the overcrowding of squalid manufacturing towns, the sober, educated and moral workman would be the backbone of the nation.

Nathan Appleton, the textile entrepreneur had spent much time in Britain and in 1810–11 went on a tour of model Scottish mill towns including New Lanark, probably Deanston and others around Edinburgh and Paisley.[239] Suitably impressed, he returned to begin the construction of the textile town of Lowell. Scots and other British weavers were already established in early American mills: many Scottish mechanics became industrial manufacturers. According to Caroline F Ware, 'Nearly every company reveals the important role of the skilled foreigners'.[240] New Ipswich, New Hampshire, was a Scottish weaving settlement though by 1877 Scottish weavers were an exception in that locality. Other areas utilised Scottish workers to teach their skills to their workers. By 1860 Scots seemed to be dominant in the managerial and clerical sections of many factories.[241] The lack of a skilled experienced workforce, high rates of pay and the availability of other well-paid jobs contributed to a high turnover rate in the American mill workforce.[242] Aware of their value, ready to strike to enforce demands for even higher wages and better conditions, Scots gradually became less attractive to employers. In an effort to stabilise their workforce, employers had actively recruited in Scotland. In 1853, an agent for the Hadley Falls mills secured some 82 woman weavers while in 1853–7 an agent for the Lyman mills was recruiting in Glasgow.[243] Another agent for the Holyoke mills secured 67 women for his sponsors. Their success in paying off their transatlantic fare, buying new clothes and shoes within a few months confirmed the roseate views in emigrant letters home to other workers.[244] The later emigrants sometimes proved less reliable in the fulfilment of obligations. Some women deserted in New York en route to the New England mills. Employers responded with heavier deductions from wages. That and the deportations of some women as public charges may have contributed to later difficulties in recruitment. In 1865 Holyoke mills could only secure 200 women from Scotland although then needed 1000.[245]

The Amoskeag Mills, Manchester, New Hampshire were more successful. They were desperately short of experienced specialised weavers in the years immediately following the Civil War but their efforts to recruit labour in North America proved unsuccessful. They then turned to Scotland and began to recruit accomplished weavers from Glasgow to improve and expand gingham production. In 1868, some fifty women and children were brought over on security of character references, and guaranteed repayment of passages with a promissory note from a Glasgow friend against the fulfilment of the contract. Though Glasgow employers had already lost many weavers to America in this way and were concerned at American competition for labour, they still gave references. The success of the first wave encouraged further recruitment. Two years later another fifty went out and were admirable employees. Some went with some knowledge of America from friends who had already emigrated, or simply to improve themselves. The company agent claimed that he could have secured far more employees. In 1870 he claimed to have 112 available in addition to the forty he had already signed up. He also gave introductions to many others who were interested in emigrating, and some went out to America. Whether the employees fulfilled their obligations or (as with some 14 per cent) they did not, they had reaced America in a form of assisted passage.[246] Though further efforts at recruitment were to continue, employers began to look at Belgium and to new machinery to replace their skilled Scottish workers. By 1881 Scotland was no longer supplying mill workers.[247]

New technology, the increasing availability of cheap unskilled immigrant workers and the maturing of the American industry meant less dependence upon Scottish labour. By the late nineteenth century Scottish workers went to America with their employers; Scottish manufacturers, apprehensive about American tariffs, had became internationalised. As early as 1850 Coats of Paisley had established plants in Pawtucket while the Glasgow Linen Company had an almost entirely Scottish workforce at Grafton, Massachusetts. Following the 1890 tariffs, Kerrs of Paisley moved their mill to Fall River with their workforce. Workers received about double the Scottish wage so they were satisfied. At the same time the Cumnock brothers rose to prominence as major figures in the textile field: two of the three had been born and bred in Glasgow.[248] Their role was perhaps indicative of the upward social mobility of the Scots not merely within the textile industry but in the larger American world. Some expressed considerable reservations about the prospects in America. The departure of industrious, sober artisans from Scotland left a gap at home into which unintelligent, disorderly, ill-disciplined, uncivilised Irish poured.[249] As early as 1829, an Edinburgh authority was suggesting that the golden opportunities had passed:

To earn simple plenty by a life of labour is all that America now offers.[250]

Though openings remained for clergymen, the professions were over-crowded.

The bulk of the emigrant population then must long consist of wealthy peasants dressed in home spun clothes, cultivating their own ground with their own hands and living in simple plenty. For the higher ranks this continent affords no refuge; and scarcely for any in the middling classes who do not stand at the bottom of the scale. The exclusion from social intercourse, the distance from church, the want of any opportunity of attaining the higher branches of education, must operate strongly with those accustomed to the accumulations and elegances of European life.[251]

That is an Englishman's view, and to some extent it explains the success of Glaswegians in America. The migration of the less fortunate if highly motivated people was in marked contrast to the pretentious English who bewailed their lot and the shortcomings of their hosts with boring frequency.

The promise of better wages, conditions and prospects in America, together with more democratic institutions and universal suffrage, was consistently offered to intending emigrants.[252] With a voluntary church, the settler could set his own sights and improve himself and the prospects for his family.

Urbanisation, increased purchasing power among the populace and new forms of enterprise, consolidating producer, distributor, wholesaler and retailer into one company became the norm. Scots with their penchant for dry goods were well placed. Scotland and America contributed to the somewhat neglected retailing revolution. By the later nineteenth century, popular shopkeeping began to develop. Thomas Lipton, the Glasgow provision merchant, soon built up a chain of 245 shops providing cheap food and one tenth of the tea trade.[253] He would become famous in the transatlantic world for his yachts and competitions. But he was sympto-matic of deeper social and organisational changes which were taking place. For some time ideas of the modern department store had been taking shape in Britain, as in Andersons of Glasgow and elsewhere, but Bon Marché of Paris was to revolutionise the retail trade. By gathering all merchandise under one roof in various departments, that store inspired many others like Wanamaker of Philadelphia and Macy's of New York.[254] Enterprising individuals flourished who were astute enough to realise the new democratic nature of merchandising, the subtle status shifts and potential of free access to a wide range of departments without sales pressure. Needless to say several Glasgow-trained dry goods merchants were to the fore in America. The fortunes of Scottish immigrants have a bearing on the current discussion of American social mobility and 'success'.[255] Carnegie obviously fulfils the wildest dreams of avarice in his surge from rags to riches, though for most emigrant Scots the improvement was less spectacular—but in many instances still remarkable. The three Donahoe brothers who emigrated from the east end of Glasgow as poor immigrants, went to California and made a spectacular fortune in San Francisco with the first iron works, the first railway engines, the first ironclad ships, and investments in hotels and railways. They even had a town named after them.[256]

The department store seems to have been a favourite route to wealth. Several emigrants learned their entrepreneurial skills in Glasgow, while one Glaswegian saw American success in this area and returned to found his own department store: William Wilson and the Coloseum.[257] Samuel Wanamaker and his predecessors in the wholesaling trade who had then developed into department stores were well known in Scotland. They were frequent visitors and appear to have had fair business links with Scotland.[258]

St Louis provided the opportunity for two Scottish entrepreneurs to rise to considerable wealth. David Nicholson, 1814–80, was born in poverty in Fowlis Wester, Perthshire. After working in Glasgow and Oban merchant houses, he emigrated to Canada where working as a carpenter he moved on to Pennsylvania, Chicago and then to St Louis in 1835. Eight years later he began his own business, importing high quality goods, new commodities and 'more than any other man in St Louis trade' educated his customers to superior quality.[259] By 1870, he had a five-storey store which employed fifty assistants. At the same time he ventured in to real estate with considerable success, erecting the Temple Buildings at 5th Avenue and Walnut Street and also Nicholson Place. A staunch presbyterian he frequently returned to Scotland. Dugald Crawford established his store in 1866 which developed into one of the largest dry goods stores in America. From a start with $2000 capital he had in 1880 a capital of $10,000,000 and a turnover of $35,000,000. Crawford was born in Argyllshire, 1830, served an apprenticeship in a Glasgow dry goods shop, went to Dublin and then returned to the Glasgow firm of Arthur and Company, the largest wholesale and retail dry goods firm in Britain. In 1856 he went to Canada before moving to St Louis in 1864. Crawford was also president of the Congregational Missionary society, of the Caledonian Society of St Louis, trustee of Drury College and a leading figure in various mercantile organisations.[260]

More substantial Scottish interest in the west came later with the development of the cattle industry.[261] The completion of the transcontinental railroads, the invention of refrigeration, and large-scale companies catering to mass European markets encouraged considerable Scottish investment in American cattle companies. These funds and their headquarters were centred mainly in Dundee and Edinburgh although Glasgow and Aberdeen had a very small interest. Between 1879 and 1888 at least 33 British registered companies were investing in cattle ranching.[262]

Though Glasgow participated in the cattle and meat import trade, her investments were usually in mining companies, fruit and cotton adventures. They invariably failed within a few years.[263] A Glasgow lawyer R L Brown, emigrated to Austin, Texas in 1883 and two years later became the agent for the Scottish American Mortgage Company, a major investor in western land schemes. With two brothers in the cotton trade in Galveston and Waco, he enjoyed a very successful career until his death in 1910. William MacKenzie of Dunscore, Dumfries became involved in the investment enthusiasm and made some fourteen trips across the Atlantic before his death. Amid his many concerns he managed to write *A History of the United States.*[264] R B Cunninghame Graham also went out west to Texas before he returned to take up radical causes. His experience with intolerant American treatment was to contribute to his later anti-American prejudices.[265] Others were to transmit other more acceptable liberal attitudes.

Glasgow contributed mightily to the psychology of the Atlantic world. It was a severely practical utilitarian attitude which that literary hostess of many Americans in Edinburgh recognised: 'You will observe that though we of the intellectual city profess to be, and perhaps are, better bred and more refined, our western friends are better informed, than any set of merely commercial people in the world.'[266]

The fur trade provided many opportunities to adventurous men. Among them was Ramsay Crooks of Greenock. Emigrating to Canada at sixteen he entered the fur trade and moved to St Louis a few years later. After working for major fur companies during which he made a trip to the Pacific, Crooks entered John Jacob Astor's American Fur Company in 1817 and became the virtual head of the company's western operations.[267] Eventually he became president of the company before his death in 1859. Another Scot, Kenneth McKenzie of Ross-shire, a relative of the famous explorer Alexander McKenzie, after working with Canadian companies became president of the Columbia Fur Company which amalgamated with the American Fur Company in 1827. He then set up trading posts in the remotest regions and developed a thriving business until discredited by building an illegal distillery in Indian territory. Forced to withdraw to Europe, he later returned to found a very successful liquor business before he died in 1861. Several other Scots were prominent in the fur trade: as one observer said 'These Scots boys were ideal types for the fur trade service. Having the basis of classical education, the Shorter Catechism and the Westminster Confession of Faith for sheet anchors, they carried their unbending principles with them in their careers. What they may have lacked in exuberance of spirits they made up in loyalty and moral qualities.'[268]

The trade flourished until European fashions began to change as new materials like silk became popular. The other way of life associated with the buffalo also changed. The animal was the basis of the Indian way of life, providing clothing, tents, tools and food. That society was under threat from American expansion and the increasing demand for buffalo hides. In 1840, 47,000 were shipped through St Louis. Eight years later the American

Fur Company had sent 110,000 throughout the world. About this time arrived one of the most remarkable characters, Sir William Drummond Stewart. The younger son of the Laird of Murthly Castle, Perthshire, he had few connections with Glasgow beyond business and taking a Mackintosh rubber boat out west on his adventures. But he cannot be ignored. Born in 1795, he had joined the army at an early age, served with distinction in the Napoleonic wars and retired on half pay. After his brother inherited the family estates, Sir William went to America in 1832. He subsequently enjoyed a series of remarkable trips through the west, attending the annual fur traders' rendezvous and meeting the legendary figures of the west, like Jim Bridger. In the course of his absence he inherited the estates. By then Sir William had made the acquaintance of Alfred Jacob Miller the artist whom he took on his expedition to the west to record the fast-disappearing civilisation. He was recording the noble savage for posterity. He was to capture that fading life by returning with buffalo, birds, plants and other items to Perthshire. Some he gave to the Breadalbane estates where Queen Victoria greatly admired them. Stewart wrote two fascinating, largely autobiographical novels, *Altowan* and *Edward Warren* which captured the romanticism of the west for posterity.[269] He rhapsodised over the west, the charm and beauty of the Indian peoples. His last visit to the west was in 1843. He never forgot the simpler grandeur of the tribal tradition far superior to the destructive restrictions of English society. A man stood on his own intrinsic merits, not on birth and servility. With those convictions he looked forward to the United States and the mighty race, the fusion of all mankind.[270] He returned to manage his estate, enjoy the affection of his tenantry, return to the Catholic faith of his ancestors and rebuild the chapel of St Anthony at Murthly with lavish pictures by Miller. He also entertained American visitors including the artist, Henry Inman, who died before he could illustrate *Altowan*. His Indian servant, Antoine, proved a local character, prone to bouts of heavy drinking before he finally disappeared back in America. Sir William Drummond Stewart proved the attractions of America to Scots at every level of appreciation.[271]

There were substantial interconnections in natural history. Alexander Wilson, the Paisley poet and ornithologist, as we have seen emigrated in the 1790s. His radical poetry and his disdain for the contemporary establishment in church and state forced his withdrawal to America in 1794. After working as a teacher for a spell in Frankfort, Pennsylvania 'a settlement of canting, preaching and praying and snivelling, ignorant Presbyterians' he moved to another post with hopes of returning to Scotland. He met Tom Paine and Thomas Jefferson who were more of his kidney, as well as the botanist Bartram. Resuming his nature interest, he began to publish his *American Ornithology* in 1808, the first serious study of American birds in their natural abodes and from observation.[272] Engraved and printed by fellow Scots, the work was a major scholarly contribution.

During his travels, Wilson met John James Audubon in his Louisville shop. Almost twenty years later the renowned naturalist was to visit

Glasgow in the course of his British tour. His fellow ornithologist Charles Waterton bore him a life long loathing. Waterton had married Anne Mary Edmonstone of Cardross Park, Dumbarton who died shortly after giving birth to their only child in 1830. His sisters in law were to remain his constant companions. Some years before his marriage Waterton had visited the United States en route to his *Wanderings in South America,* a decision inspired by his reading Wilson's work. In Philadelphia he met George Ord who was to correspond for forty years on politics and nature. Though a great admirer of American achievements, Waterton like others before and since returned somewhat more conservative and cautious about universal suffrage.[273] With his interest in conservation Waterton forms an interesting link with his fellow Catholic, Sir William Drummond Stewart.

David Douglas who had worked with Professor Sir William Hooker of Glasgow in the Botanic Gardens made an important collection of specimens on his trip to California in 1823. He then returned again and spent several years in the Pacific Northwest and California. Unfortunately he was to die in a tragic hunting accident in Hawaii.[274] He and Hugo Reid of Cardross were two of the first Scots to penetrate to California. Born in 1810, Reid had studied at Cambridge University before he went to settle in southern California in 1831 with an earlier Cardross emigrant, James McKinley. Together they ran a thriving hide and household business. After his marriage to a local Catholic Indian lady, Reid built up an extensive landholding, begun a school and treated the local Indian population with a respect unusual in those days. When California was acquired by the United States, Reid attended the state constitutional convention where he championed the foundation of a public school system, the protection of the Indians and the abolition of slavery. So pronounced was his stance on the Indian question that he became the model for Helen Holman Jackson's *Ramona*, a novel in which the injustice practised towards the Indian was attacked. In real life Reid unfortunately contracted tuberculosis and died in 1852 before he was able to accomplish much.[275]

Reid was one of a handful of Scots who settled in California before 1840.[276] Three doctors, a shipowner, a packer and a blacksmith were but a prelude to the flood of immigrants drawn by the discovery of gold in 1849. Among this flow were the three Donahoe brothers.

The case of the three Donahues, sometimes Donahoes, Peter (1822–85), Michael (1817–84) and James (died 1863) is worth discussing at length. Neglected in recent studies of San Francisco, they deserve attention since they challenge several stereotypes about the nature of the Scottish immigration and its Catholic component.[277] Born in Glasgow of Irish parents, Michael emigrated with an uncle to New York in 1831. Peter worked two years in a Glasgow mill before he went out in 1833 with his mother. Two years later father emigrated. All three boys served apprenticeships in Thomas Rogers, locomotive builders, Paterson, New Jersey, in moulding, machining and foundry work. Following the death of the mother, the boys scattered. James, a sickly fellow, went to Alabama, sailed the West Indies and then lost his newly acquired ship. Michael went from the Union Iron Works to sea and then moved to Cincinnati in 1844. After serving in the First Ohio Volunteers during the Mexican-American war he established a foundry to repair US navy vessels on the Rio Grande. With the discovery of gold he made a remarkable journey across country to California. There he met up again with Peter. He had helped build a gunboat for the Peruvian navy. He sailed round the Horn in the first steam vessel ever to round the Horn. He remained in Peru two years. He then repaired and supervised a vessel en route to the gold rush. On arrival in San Francisco he had some $6000. Peter and his brother Michael then opened a foundry after six unsuccessful months prospecting. Manufacturing stoves and shovels was lucrative work. James joined them in 1851–2 in the Union Iron Foundry, named after the works in the East. In 1852 Peter secured the franchise for gas in San Francisco. Later it was alleged to pay between 60 and 90 cents on every dollar. Shortly afterwards James retired from the business and Michael went east.

Peter Donahoe now went from strength to strength. He ran a steamship company between San Francisco and Sacramento, built the first steam engine for a US naval vessel on the west coast; the first quartz mill in California; the first printing press there; assembled the first prefabricated ironclad on the west coast; built the first locomotive in California and introduced the first street railway to San Francisco. The president of the Omnibus Railroad company for twenty years, he became a director of the Hibernia Savings and Loan Society and the First National Gold Bank. Meanwhile he built the San Francisco and San Jose railway, owned one third of its stock and eventually sold out to the Southern Pacific in 1870 for around $3.5 million. The railroad even had a town named after him in Sonoma county, where he built a carriage works.[278] A generous benefactor, he redecorated St Mary's Church Glasgow on a trip back to Europe, as well as giving to various charitable institutions in California.[279] At his death his will required all bequests to be paid in gold coin.

Michael Donahoe, a millionaire also, bought a foundry in Davenport, Iowa and quickly made it the largest in the state.[280] Building steam engines, and agricultural machinery he played a major role in the organisation of the Davenport and St Paul Railroad. Then after serving as mayor for two terms he refused a third and went on a year's tour of Europe. He returned to undertake the construction of a vast modern waterworks for the city, allegedly the best in America. A charitable respected man, at his death he was described as 'a citizen who did as much if not more to advance her in growth and prosperity than any other resident that ever lived here'. By his deathbed his niece, Baroness von Schraeder stood. From the slums of Glasgow to millionaire and aristocratic family was a remarkable step.

The Donahoes never employed Chinese labour, whether for reasons of social justice or racial antipathy is unclear; Peter Donahoe was the only major local employer not to be attacked by the 'Sand Lot' orators in the late nineteenth century. These working men banded together to oppose the employment of Chinese whom they claimed were prepared to accept lower pay and poorer conditions from their Protestant employers.[281]

The policy must have assisted Robert Forsyth, a Lanarkshire immigrant who served an apprenticeship with Randolph Elder in Glasgow before he went on to become president of the Union Iron Works Company.[282] An even more colourful character was Andrew Smith Hallidie, the London-born son of Dumfriesshire parents who developed the San Francisco cable railways, the Mechanics Institution and the San Francisco Public Library.[283]

Another mechanical innovator, Alexander Winton built the first motor car in the United States. A Clyde trained marine engineer, he had established himself in Cleveland as a bicycle manufacturer. Soon he began to build motor cars which carried the motto, 'He wears the crown of excellence.' Marketing them with imaginative publicity stunts like the first trans-America run and a record breaking trip from Cleveland to New York, Winton seemed to justify his claim. Ambitiously trying to defeat European rivals abroad and Ford at home in competitions, he failed. Henry Ford's victory over him was to bring him great backing and led to the foundation of the Ford Motor Company. Winton continued the automobile business with increasing interest in marine engines until 1925. Shortly afterwards his company was absorbed by General Motors.[284]

In contributing to increasing mobility of Americans, Winton was to help to destroy the old Scottish ideal of a cohesive community. The car changed habits irrevocably by the 'twenties. Religion, social customs and pursuits altered. People defined themselves by what they did in their leisure time rather than by what they laboured at. The shift was momentous and decisive.[285]

Contacts between American and Scottish manufactures were close. The three Brownlee brothers from Carluke began their timber firm in New Orleans where they processed trees from settlers' clearings in the early nine-teenth century. Templetons' Glasgow factory provided the carpets for the Abraham Lincoln White House. Whisky played an ever increasing role in the export trade until Prohibition put an end to legal importation. From 7700 gallons in 1855 exports rose to ten million gallons by 1913 and after the repeal of Prohibition boomed to reach 33 million gallons by 1968.[286]

Singers, the American cycle and sewing machine manufacturers came to Glasgow in 1855. The establishment of the new plant at Clydebank came through the prompting of a Scot, George Ross McKenzie who later rose to be president of the company. Cheapness, productivity, docility of labour and access to markets contributed to the success of the enterprise. In 1885 *The Engineer* described the factory as 'probably the finest monument that this age has produced'.[287] Glasgow transmitted and received the new technology. Perhaps it was the second city of the Empire in size but in creative talent it was unmatched. In making and doing Glasgow had no rival in the Atlantic world. From the earliest times merchants had succeeded in America, her immigrants had—even the least promising—and she had maintained a liberal, entrepreneurial mentality.[288] In Ohio, for example, the Glasgow Port Washington Iron and Coal Company bought several thousand acres after the Civil War and developed two blast furnaces at Hanging Rock. To man this Scottish technique all the company officers were brought over from Scotland.[289]

Professor John Pringle Nichol and his family provide an excellent example of the transmission of ideas through and by Glasgow. The professor of Astronomy at Glasgow University, Nichol married Elizabeth Jane Pease, daughter of the Quaker Darlington banker. Already active in abolitionist work through her friends the Motts and William Lloyd Garrison, Mrs Nichol was drawn into the Glasgow liberal milieu. European nationalist leaders like Kossuth and Mazzini visited their home as did American abolitionists like Parker Pillsbury and Levi Coffin. John Pringle Nichol had begun a lecture tour of the United States but had been recalled by the university though not before he had made the acquaintance of many leading Americans. His son, John Nichol, one of the brilliant Oxford group which included T H Green, the political philosopher, John Bryce, the author of *The American Commonwealth,* and Dicey, the constitutional historian. Professor of English Literature at Glasgow University, 1862–89, Nichol wrote the first comprehensive study of American literature: 'Our scholars know more about Babylon than Chicago.'[290] He himself toured the United States in 1865, staying with Longfellow for several days and introducing several other Glaswegians to his American contacts including a former pupil who edited the New York *Athenaeum,* a short lived cultural journal. Throughout he maintained his close correspondence with Longfellow sending his verses and plays to him for assessment and criticism. His home, filled with 'wise thought and elevated sentiment', welcomed William Morris in due course.[291] The Nichols had sent John Nichol's earliest writings in the Glasgow University album to William Lloyd Garrison, the uncompromising American abolitionist. While John Pringle Nichol was in contact with leading American intellectuals, his wife was already closely acquainted with the leading American abolitionists, the Motts, Grimké sisters and Elizabeth Cady Stanton.[292]

That liberal innovative community of intellect and action overcame whatever drawbacks Glasgow had—'little nature within thirty miles and no art within 300'—and showed itself far more likely and imaginative than English cities.[293] In that it proved its 'American' character as a 'go-ahead' city. Thriving, bustling and unassuming Glasgow was a natural inspiration to Americans who sought some European inspiration. It had a long standing democratic tradition unique in Europe. It was a successful industrial and commercial centre and it had educational leadership.

The literary associations, as Andrew Hook has shown, were considerable in the early period. Thomas Campbell, the poet, had studied under Professor John Millar, the liberal whose son emigrated to America. Campbell toyed with the idea of emigrating to America where he had many relatives.[294] Ralph Waldo Emerson, Hawthorne and Melville all visited the city. Bret Harte was the American consul for a time in the 1880s. The novelists G W Cable and Charles M Sheldon, author of the best seller, *In His Steps,* also briefly visited the city early in the twentieth century.[295] The kailyard novelists enjoyed enormous popularity in the United States: S R Crockett and Ian MacLaren sold well, presumably among immigrants. MacLaren was to die in America while on tour.

Sporting connections were predictably very close especially in association football. With the growth of the sport in the late nineteenth century, emigrants naturally took the game with them. Fall River and Pawtucket,

Massachusetts had teams which played occasional fixtures with predominantly Scottish sides from Canada. The Detroit soccer team was founded by a Scot and included the McKendrick brothers from Greenock Morton F. C. in their earliest side.[296] Other cities had teams. Chicago Thistle, and Chicago Colhours were entirely Scottish sides while other Chicago teams had large Scottish elements. There were also teams in Pittsburgh, St Louis, Denver, San Francisco, Seattle, Tacoma, New York and Philadelphia. Predictably the Scottish Illinois mining centre of Braidwood boasted a team.[297] In addition there were strong teams in Joliet, Streator and elsewhere with a Scottish presence. Football had become a form of cultural and community endeavour on both sides of the Atlantic for in 1891–2 an American team came to Scotland on tour. It came without the approval of the American Association and its performance on tour was unsuccessful, marked by a series of defeats.[298] As early as 1884 the enthusiasts were dreaming of matches between the United States and Scotland.[299]

There were even dark associations in the connection. Madeleine Smith, the lady who had been the centre of the most celebrated trial in the nineteenth century died in New York while Oscar Slater had to be brought back from there to face his trial. In short the ramifications of the transatlantic connection are endless.

So far we have largely overlooked the Presbyterian links: they were the norm as the dominant faith of the dominant group. The Protestant connection in the nineteenth century was mainly in practical evangelical works, abolitionism; temperance; education and revivalism. In all these areas there was considerable co-operation. Ministers as in the eighteenth century continued to emigrate to labour in the United States.[300] They were expanding the base which had been established in previous years. Their activism was the result, the renewed evangelicalism, the need to inculcate some sense of responsibility into the new democracy which had few traditions of control and restraint, and the fears of unacceptable philosophies: atheism, Unitarianism and Catholicism. They might subvert the promise of the American Protestant democracy. American Protestants therefore had to be up and doing to capture the culture for the future. Scottish immigrants and their descendants were peculiarly equipped for this providential role. A Paisley immigrant, Hugh Maxwell, the son of a tallow chandler provides a good illustration. A leading Whig lawyer of New York he eloquently toasted the Scottish parochial schools as 'the cheapest defence, the best of treasures and the highest glory of nations'. They were the 'bloodless triumphs of Caledonia.'[301] Morality diffused by education, trade and peace would bring harmony under the aegis of Scotland. To that prospect we shall now turn.

Chapter Two

Exporting the Democratic Intellect
Education for Development

'Scotland' wrote Henry Barnard, 'furnishes a valuable example of the reformatory and preservative power of a judicious system of common schools.'[1] Strangely, American historians have largely ignored the Scottish contribution to educational development in the nineteenth century. The revisionist historians of education have ultimately remained staunchly nationalist in their interpretations. Even Professor Andrew Hook in his useful *Scotland and America, 1750–1835* gives inadequate recognition to the importance of Scottish popular educational ideas.[2] In general the earlier work of Nisbet at Dickinson, Witherspoon, and later McCosh at Princeton has been acknowledged, but they are seen as exceptional individual cases.[3] In fact they were part of a larger, widely diffused and effective Scottish influence upon all levels of education in the United States. Scottish educators, theorists and organisers laid the foundations, and just as firmly erected the framework within which educational progress might take place. Even the theories of Pestalozzi were largely mediated through Scots, who created the conditions of an educational revolution, provided its officers, and then its administrators to carry it through to fruition.

Why should Scotland have had such an impact upon American education? The obvious explanation is the ethnic link between Scotland and many thousands of settlers and their descendants. There were numerous Scots-born or trained ministers, lawyers and doctors. There were many Scottish teachers: Elizabeth Cady Stanton had a Scottish nurse and then a Glasgow graduate as her teacher.[4] Robert Owen brought over Mr Applegarth from New Lanark to teach in New Harmony. The educational innovator, Robert Cunningham brought over Mr Dunn of Edinburgh to teach in his model school in Easton, Pennsylvania. The strong Presbyterian religious democratic outlook found a ready response on both sides of the Atlantic. Scottish literary influences through Walter Scott and the lesser figures like Joanna Baillie and Mrs Anne Grant of Laggan were also substantial.[5] The trading links with Glasgow were generally flourishing in tobacco, cotton and immigrants. Scottish dynamism seemed essentially American.

So indeed it was. As Henry F May has suggested, 'the only acceptable European teachers for the early builders of nineteenth-century American official culture were the Common Sense philosophers of Scotland'.[6] It was a philosophy admirably fitted to American needs: 'It was neither anti-scientific nor obscurantist, never cynical, and it opend no doors to intellectual or moral chaos.'[7] As such it was hardly static though an antidote

43

to democratic excesses. From Witherspoon onwards, moral philosophy, drawn largely from imported Scottish works, had assumed an increasingly important role in the curricula of American colleges and universities. The reason was clear. In an increasingly urban, democratic society, confronted by ever more divergent theologies and ideologies, moral philosophy provided a common ground for an emerging liberal evangelical Protestantism, for an underlying desire for moral and spiritual consensus and for a national identity. Such an eclectic philosophy could offer cohesion to a fragmented society. The Common Sense philosophy as popularly understood was sufficiently flexible to blend moderate evangelical Calvinism with elements of the Enlightenment, English empiricism, romantic sentimentalism and middle class moralism. It was particularly acceptable as the old moral restraints crumbled under the pressure of urban growth, the demise of church establishments and the rise of political demagoguery. In attempting to recreate a coherent organic community bound by an enveloping web of shared moral and social values, the advocates of the Common Sense philosophy sought to re-enact the cohesive moral order of the village in the city.

Moral philosophy had to perform the same function in a new democratic society as that performed by custom, tradition and coercive institutions in Europe: as Edward Everett said, 'What is done in other countries by *gens d'armes* and horse-guards must here be done by public sentiment or not at all.'[8] As part of the shift from external to internal regulatory mechanisms upon the individual, it provided and implemented moral values to guide and direct men. As an activist philosophy it was appropriate to a developing economy. To educators like Wayland, Everett, Bowen and Horace Mann, moral philosophy would counteract possible social and political anarchy. If, as Thomas Reid wrote, 'The law of God is written in man's heart,' then the individual had an internal voice of virtue, 'conscience', which would dominate all mental and moral judgements in his system of morality.[9] In this rationale of capitalism and the protection of property, the moral philosophers would persuade the property holders to adopt the moral attitudes and socially stabilising mores designed by the moral philosophers. Salvation was thus transposed from theological to social grounds and a new class of moral guardians was empowered to enforce a newly created moral code.

Economic values and the neo-puritan standards extolled by the nineteenth century Protestant evangelical coincided, as Tyrell suggests, 'to create Weber's Protestant ethic'.[10] The family as the basic unit of society with its strong sense of hierarchy and order received considerable emphasis. That in turn sharpened the focus upon the child as the future of the nation and as the means of influencing the family unit.

This Americanised Protestantism and Protestantised America was to be a society permeated by religious purpose and directed towards the establishment of the Kingdom of God in America. Apart from the secularist blasts from Maclure and Fanny Wright, the Protestant Commonwealth was generally accepted. This millenarian perfectionist and nationalist ideal was dependent upon individual and social regeneration. In such an efficient enterprising society, informed by moral checks on poverty, wealth would, it was anticipated, be easily accessible to all. W E Channing, like Thomas Chalmers, saw that 'the chief evils of poverty are moral in their origin and character'.[11] In the absence of legal regulation, voluntary moral welfare organisations were established as disciplinary institutions. Such bodies might also serve as harmonious class encounters. This emphasis upon social homogeneity was to find its more effective expression in education. Puritanism and education were strongest in the same areas of America. As the Revd Robert Baird observed, 'Two things are ever considered as indispensable alike to temporal and to spiritual and eternal welfare—a church and a school house.'[12] The little red school house was a potent myth and reality.

Scottish Moral Philosophy served as the vehicle, Scottish educational institutions as the models, and Scotsmen as the purveyors of this ideal to the United States. That is not to discount other influences nor to exclude the impact of Prussian, French or Lancasterian educational ideas upon America. Neither is this to argue in support of conspiratorial Machiavellian influences upon the formative stages of American education. It is merely to suggest that those with wealth and power were naturally inclined to uphold the virtues of a society they valued and in which they had succeeded.

The Common Sense philosophy sustained a theory of education.[13] If the moral sentiments had their spontaneous origins in the individual, then the liberation of that spirit of moral self-awareness must be given priority. In that process, self awareness became social awareness. A sense of duty and obligation would naturally lead the individual to disinterested benevolence.[14] The instructed, self-restrained by experience, necessity and consensus, would be the naturally desirable citizen: conscientious, deferential and hard working. The morals of this community would be safeguarded by the individual conscience. That conversion, amid the decline of the church and the family, would have to be accomplished through education.[15] Just as the desired qualities were to be liberated from within rather than enforced from without, so the external method of learning by rote the external or dead language of the classics was to be replaced by a new pedagogy and a new emphasis upon science and understanding. Implied in that approach was a social revolution, a critique of aristocratic artificiality against the vibrant vitality of common experience, an outlook which might blend with social romanticism in the early nineteenth century. Even within the sciences, there was a Scottish preference for a certain emphasis on applied geometry rather than upon abstract analytical geometry: external nature conformed to internal human intuition. Imposed government and dead tradition, it suggested, should be replaced in a democracy by freedom within a popular moral consensus and practical interest within education itself.

From this Common Sense philosophy three educational attitudes emerged. The conservationist line of Stow, Cunningham and their American counterparts; the universal idealists, non-sectarian though with a decidedly Protestant bias like Horace Mann; and the radical deists around William Maclure and Fanny Wright who demanded educational reform as part of a total reorganisation and restructuring of society. Like all

American enterprises, these views were loudly advertised, marketed and demonstrated to potential consumers in the competitive marketplace.

Scottish superiority in education was affirmed in several ways: the availability of philosophical works of pedagogy; the Scottish-born educators who emigrated; and the American visitors who returned home determined to imitate the best features of Scottish schools on their return. Considerable Scottish educational capital had been sunk in America in the eighteenth century: Princeton and the University of Pennsylvania, as we have seen, were examples.[16] The educational activities of numerous Scottish and Scottish-trained lawyers, doctors and ministers were widespread. The educational writings and practical experiments of Andrew Bell and Patrick Colquhoun were well known in the early nineteenth century.[17] Bell, a St Andrews graduate, had spent several years in Virginia before his ordination as an Episcopalian priest. After spending nine years in India, he developed the Madras system of education, under which the more advanced pupils aided the learning of the younger. Though he generously bequeathed money to Scottish universities to foster his ideas, the system did not take root in Scotland. Colquhoun had similarly spent several years in Virginia before he returned home to become Lord Provost of Glasgow on two occasions. He then went to London in 1789 where he became largely responsible for the policing of the capital. A strong advocate of the extension of education, he stressed the moral, economic and spiritual value of reducing the cost of the poor law and generally improving the lot of the needy. But both men were essentially conservative in their approach, a point illustrated by Bell's *A Sketch of a national institution for training up the children of the poor in the principles of our holy religion and in habits of useful industry* and Colquhoun's *New and Appropriate System of Education for the Labouring People* (1806).

These initiatives, nevertheless, together with those of John Abercrombie, Henry Brougham, Thomas Dick, Professor Jardine, but above all, George Combe, exercised considerable influence. In his *Constitution of Man*, Combe emphasised the superior moral and intellectual faculties which might be best developed in harmony with physical and organic laws.[18] In short, Scottish writers demonstrated unity and cohesion, the very qualities which were particularly appropriate to the new nation. Education was at once a stabilising and a nationalising force.

In the early nineteenth century, America may have witnessed the first ethnic revival within the nation. For Scots were invariably to the fore in celebrating the wisdom, validity and practicality of their group and their tradition. Within Scotland herself Scots were rediscovering or even inventing their past. For instance, in the west of Scotland the erection of the Knox memorial inspired by Stevenson Macgill, the historical works of McCrie on Knox and Melville, and the biographies of Covenanters were an indication of that awareness, helped on by Sir Walter Scott.[19] The religious revivals were a similar harking-back to those old traditions. Scots at home in general were enjoying a somewhat higher standard of living than ever before and a nostalgia for a world passing away. In America emigrant Scots were discovering, as were later generations of immigrants, that the homeland's values could perform useful service in the new land. From such sympathies, a sense of community and cohesive purpose might emerge. It was at once a celebration of the older Scottish culture and a solution to present difficulties.

Christian and Freethinker alike might agree on several points. To each the United States presented a unique challenge and opportunity. In a country of voluntary Christian churches, as state established churches were dismantled, the teacher was a vital element in inculcating and sustaining traditional values. In stressing the values of sobriety, regularity and self discipline, the work ethic might sustain the existing social order. To the Freethinker, education provided an excellent opportunity to eliminate Old World superstitions and build a truly democratic, utilitarian society. Frances Wright and William Maclure, the inheritors of the Scottish enlightenment, felt education was the key to a world democracy of progress and intelligence: 'Our liberties will never be secure for they will never be understood until you have a national system of education.'[20] It was opportune 'to turn our churches into halls of science; our schools into schools of knowledge, our privileged colleges into state institutions for all the youth of the land. Time to arrest our speculations respecting unseen worlds and inconceivable systems and address our inquiries to the improvement of our human condition.'[21] To Jacksonian America, Robert Dale Owen's vision of education as *the* means of enabling the toiling masses to seize economic opportunities was peculiarly attractive.[22]

New methods of education appealed to many interests in the United States. Those who wished to secure a more enlightened view of man; the social conservatives, who wished to bolster social and political stability; the evangelical Protestant anxious to secure the future of his version of America; the reformer who saw education as a means to general consciousness-raising and social amelioration; the entrepreneur who perhaps envisaged a more malleable, efficient and docile workforce; and the mechanic who saw education as the open sesame to his own personal advancement. Education, then, was a central issue.[23]

Christian and Freethinker were both engaged in the same enterprise: they sought to ease the friction of personal and social adjustment to the new order. In their deepest convictions they were antipathetic towards the growth of cities. To both groups cities seemed the centres of vice, crime and the unpredictable passions of the untutored masses: both were also lamenting the real and prospective loss of their control in cities. Each wished to capture the future, whether seen in terms of culture or the soul. Each wanted the new order to accept its persuasion: conversion was everything. And both zealously pursued that end.

The upshot was compromise: the Enlightenment was baptised. But the central point was well made: the individual had to be given the opportunity to develop himself to the fullest possible extent. In so doing they were demonstrating a conviction—and the absence of any feasible institutions to meet the social crisis.[24] The pulpit, law and press were the only available means in a democratic society. The illiteracy of the masses cut them off from the desirable printed message; the location of the churches and the lack of conviction among the masses further removed such influences; and the law was either ineffectually enforced or counter productive. The law enforcement agencies were too few and frequently too remote to uphold the desirable morality. The individual had to be informed, educated or even indoctrinated in his own sense of moral responsibility. He had to believe that he was making his own moral, informed judgements. Only in that way could effective self-discipline and social order be maintained. The problem was how to convey, communicate or awaken that moral sense within the individual.

The traditional methods were clearly ineffective. In the face of the shock of poverty in America and the growth of towns and cities, new techniques which might offer short cuts to success were vital.[25] Either religion or reason alone was inadequate. Religion alone would become bogged down in interminable doctrinal disputes which merely further fragmented the cohesive power of faith. Reason alone, as the French Revolution showed, injured rather than improved man. Some new approach incorporating the cultural capital of Christianity and the new insights of reason had to be employed. Utility was the yardstick. It would work to produce the greatest happiness of the greatest number in the shortest possible time, it was confidently anticipated. New techniques, better-trained and informed teachers, were necessary. But which techniques? How were teachers to be formed and recruited? Where were successful examples and models available? Were 'the production of a just disposition, virtuous habits and a rational self-governing character' adequate? Scotland provided the obvious answer. Language, custom and mentality ensured that. Scotland was New England in Europe.[26]

Education was the touchstone of American progress. In the eighteenth century Scotland had made considerable and decisive contributions to the foundation, development and consolidation of American universities, that is, in the provision of leadership, organisers and staff for the professions. But in the nineteenth century the extension of democracy logically demanded an extension of, and a somewhat changed emphasis within, American education. It meant the upgrading of existing institutions and the opening of new areas of educational opportunity. To improve university standards, to maintain and extend the knowledge necessary to a flourishing democracy meant improving the existing infant schools, the foundation of new colleges for the professional training of teachers and an emphasis upon 'relevant' studies rather than gentlemanly culture. As centres of academic and moral excellence universities were to send out missionaries for the upbuilding of the American identity and community. But if America was a democracy, then education, self-improvement and social salvation had to be freely available not only to all classes of children but to all classes of men and women through lyceums, mechanics' institutes and local voluntary bodies. To each of these areas Glasgow made an important contribution.

However such intentions might be described in retrospect, there were several different approaches to education. To the confident Whiggish mind, education was a worthy preparation for the sacred exercise of the suffrage. In that light the *Edinburgh Review* praised American efforts: 'The universal diffusion of education has rendered the terms, mob, or rabble, inapplicable even in the dregs of her citizens in the Northern States: and fits them for enjoying without abusing the freeest institutions.'[27] To more guarded elements, that smacked of enthusiasm. *Blackwoods* and David Stow had reservations.[28] An aristocracy must set the tone: inherited wealth and rank allowed virtue, decency and honour to flourish in a stable society. But to working-class radicals and their friends, both fell short of their expectations. The worker had an inherent right to education, free and freely available. In America, as we shall see, similar groups with similar motivations existed.

The older, more established groups and families in church and state in America wished to maintain their position as the moral guardians of society. Others wanted to represent American democratic institutions as efficient models to the world. The American working man, like his British counterpart, wanted a school system freely available and free from any taint of pauperism or charity. By placing the children of rich and poor in one school, America showed what might be accomplished. In effect, British radicals were admiring a Scottish export model which was efficiently operating in the American market. Like much else about America, until the late nineteenth century it was very appealing. Like much else, the image might be far more beguiling than the reality. But these divergent views were united in the educational crusade.

The motives of these promoting educational improvement were widely varying. America was building a new nation and sought education as a binding force. At the same time, that might allow older established groups and individuals to maintain their status role and set the tone of society by asserting their standards of education, as their political influences and economic interests declined. In other words, they might control the lower orders in a form of social engineering and control the entry to 'respectability'. Others sought to diffuse the knowledge of Christianity and secular learning for the better organisation and functioning of urban commercial life and labour. That utilitarian outlook, with the emphasis upon practical skills rather than intellectual dreams, might create a different informing role for the emerging voluntary churches: conscience, law and order were the key words. The family was the essence of stability in that scheme of things. In particular, woman had an especial function to communicate her inherent virtues of domesticity to her children, the future of the nation, and by her effective training to curb and correct the vices of the future society.[29] In so far as the traditional family was unable or unwilling to continue that providential task, education had to supplement or even initiate its young charges into the mobile urban scene. An orderly, disciplined citizenry depended upon expert tuition through professionally trained teachers imbued with high moral purpose. The school house was but one of many institutions which were necessary to provide a framework within which the novel democratic body might develop.[30] That might appear manipulative of the workers, the artisans and mechanics, but the genuine desire to uplift them was present. It was, perhaps, part of an early American ethnic reassertion by the Scots and Scots-Irish of their cultural inheritance and its

American quality. The drive for greater educational achievement was nationalist, revivalist, enlightened, democratic, utilitarian and ethical. It was also arguably a form of class or cultural 'imperialism' and possibly, to modern eyes, a form of sexism, Whatever it was, American society would be quite different as a result.

The position of American Protestantism had been eroded in the early nineteenth century.[31] The dismantling of state established churches, the abolition of religious restrictions on state officeholders and the fragmentation of Protestantism into numerous new sects caused serious misgivings. At the same time there was something of a revolution among the clergy. The lack of a formal parish system, as in Scotland, created particular problems. Allied to clerical mobility, short stays in charges and socio-economic changes, the intellectual revolution altered the pattern of clerical recruitment. Increasingly poor but pious youths were recruited through scholarships to newly-established colleges for a more systematised training for their churches. Clergy became more job-oriented than congregation-oriented.[32] That concern for the future pre-eminence of New England encouraged lay-Protestant participation in new social reform initiatives as a means allegedly of proving the continued moral pre-eminence of their region.[33] Education naturally was a central concern in such considerations. As Robert Cunningham said, 'The schools are the pillars of the church.' An earlier commentator had said, 'The *schools* are the pillars of the republic.'[34] In the Protestant commonwealth, that idea was normal and natural.

Education fulfilled the same role in America as that fulfilled by customs, traditions and coercive institutions in more traditional European nations. The evangelical emphasis upon the heart meant that disinterested moral vehemence and sacrificial devotion to a good cause were essential to good character. To some critics that idealistic rhetoric obscured the class basis of some educational reforms. The sense of shame had to be awakened and installed to maintain the moral hegemony of the élite by playing upon ingrained habits of deference through voluntarist means rather than by legal coercion of a formal establishment of religion. In seeking new supports for the community these individuals avowed their own class aspirations and found a meaning or role in voluntary effort. That success was elusive: the American Sunday School Union reported a Scottish teacher in 1847 as saying, 'Our object has always been to reach the masses but we cannot get to them.' The drive was on to secure harmonious class encounters through children's institutions, with pervasive discipline and routine, and shame as a primary disciplinary device. Civic, local and national ideals were utilised as an awesome authority in this context. Its purpose was to foster a new social type attuned to and responsive to the drifting demands of urban living. With the stress upon social homogeneity, an organic community was created by an enveloping web of shared moral and social values. Education, then, was a remedy for the faltering influence of the family and church. At the same time American youth had to be trained for its providential mission in civilising the West: 'Our Heavenly Father has made us an epistle to other lands.' America was a form of democratic theocracy: 'The Christian citizen of an evangelised nation may regard his country as an abode of the Church and love his country the more without loving the kingdom of God the less; the more he is a patriot, the more he is a Christian.[35]

The profession of teaching demanded certain new skills and techniques. To attract new entrants training should be readily accessible, either through grants in aid or through a centralised government scheme. Upon completion of training, an adequate salary and house should be provided, partly to recognise the value and quality of the new teacher, partly to exert a certain social pressure for gratitude for the teacher, and partly to place a former relatively low-status person in a significant position within the local community, where he might exercise moral leadership, encourages others to imitate his social rise and give roots to the locality.[36]

The new skills were largely psychological. The teacher had to recognise the individuality of the child and through the judicious use of classroom and playground pressures channel its inclinations into acceptable patterns of social thought and behaviour. Authentic personal moral conduct naturally followed, without the need for physical punishment. Pestalozzi, his Scottish followers and imitators like Robert Dale Owen, David Stow and A J D Dorsey were agreed on that point. The pupils' interest was to be stimulated by the teacher in imaginative ways so that natural curiosity, once aroused, demanded continuous fulfilment. The teacher was the key to the system. The quality, character and training of the teacher produced a leader, preacher and enforcer of moral truth and community peace. The individual was realised within a community in a process which 'saved' the child and influenced the parents. For the child took his recently-acquired moral insights and social aspirations into his home: the family unit was uplifted. It was, so many believed, an effective short cut to the moral regeneration of society. A democratic society merely needed a teacher rather than an army or bureaucracy. It was liberal, cheap and hopefully successful within the old Protestant tradition. As such, that Scottish education appealed to Americans. It exuded confidence, optimism and Protestantism.

As already suggested, there was an audience for Scottish ideas in the United States. For example, Isabella Marshall Graham, 1742–1814, from Lanarkshire who had spent some time in America and had returned to run a ladies' school in Edinburgh, was encouraged by Witherspoon to establish a similar institution in New York.[37] With Charles Wilkes, she was to play a leading role in the New York Free School movement as well as in the numerous philanthropic enterprises which flourished in the city. Significantly, her funeral sermon was preached by the Revd John M Mason, the son of an emigrant Scottish minister of the Scottish Church in New York. Francis Jeffrey of the *Edinburgh Review* married an American and was to play a part in extending Scottish interests still further. A succession of American investigators came, saw and adapted Scottish experience for use at home. John Griscom came in 1819; Cogswell in 1821; Lowell, of cotton town fame, in 1837–8; Alexander D Bache in 1837–8, as well as a host of lesser-known characters who often published reports of their visits and so spread Scottish influences.[38]

Glasgow, as the port of entry or departure, naturally attracted attention. Some Americans were of Scottish ancestry, with ethnic religious sympathies. Some were correspondents of Scottish academics and educators. Robert Owen and New Lanark naturally gained a reputation. His schemes of education and the educational writings of his son, Robert Dale Owen, made the village an obligatory duty call.[39] What his visitors were studying was Pestalozzianism in action. For though an educational historian has claimed that Pestalozzianism was absent and irrelevant in Scotland, its practice was quite widespread.[40] For many reformers, though expressing their abhorrence of sin, were also betraying a certain antipathy to a more democratic order by identifying the urban poor with 'unhallowed passion'. They had to defend morality and class interests. Others saw Pestalozzi as more positive and liberating.

The introduction of Pestalozzianism into Scotland in the early nineteenth century took many varied avenues but it was largely funnelled through Glasgow to America. Mrs Elizabeth Hamilton, in her educational writings, reflected Pestalozzian ideas.[41] Her brother, significantly, served in India and many of her ideas were devoted to the effective communication of Christian morality to the heathen at home and abroad. Questioning the validity of Bell and Lancasterian methods, she advocated the joyful recognition of Providential sentiments of the heart in the child. Early training in morality inspired a sense of filial duty, Divine obedience to government of the good and the acceptance of a loving God. Superior ladies might inspire such ideals among poor children. Far from being unnecessary in Scotland, Pestalozzian ideas were welcomed: 'God is the God of my heart, the God of the brain is a chimera.'[42] (The Mayos said, 'God is the God of order.'[43]) In keeping with the romanticism which was largely Scottish in origins, these ideas were taken, digested and propagated by Pestalozzi's Scottish adherents. Through Robert Dale Owen and the four sons of Professor Charles Badham of Glasgow University that link was given physical content: all were educated at Yverdun. The several Scottish experiments in the early nineteenth century coincided with or were influenced by such notions. Hamilton, Wood, Pillans and Stow shared a similar outlook. Morality and social order now took precedence over faith and eternal salvation. The aboriginal Christian lay in the individual conscience: he would emerge naturally in time. It also coincided with the Scottish Common Sense philosophy.

The work of Thomas Chalmers in Glasgow was decisive in awakening Christian conscience to urban deprivation.[44] His sermons and writings, as suggested earlier, had a great impact on Americans. As a minister in Glasgow he showed imaginative Christian responses to the terrible conditions. American leaders like William Ellery Channing readily admitted their debt to him in formulating the American civic conscience. Not surprisingly David Stow, one of his elders, was to demonstrate the efficacy of education in meeting those problems.

As already indicated, there were, then, three educational attitudes: the conservationist approach of Stow, Cunningham and their American counterparts; the non-sectarian efficiency of Horace Mann and his American friends; and the radical deist or universalist brotherhood of reason around William Maclure and Fanny Wright.

William Maclure (1763–1840) of Ayr was a disturbing, if not decisive, influence upon many comfortable educational assumptions.[45] Though educated at the local Ayr school, Maclure was essentially a free, self-educated spirit who generally rejected the formal schooling of his day in favour of natural history. To that extent he was in the mould of other Scottish-Americans like Ord, Charles Waterton and Wilson. But Maclure was central to many other areas: Owenism and science of the popular humanitarian variety. With his scepticism he was a challenge to the prevailing smugness of some Christians: he forced a positive, constructive response. Natural science had to be reconciled with Christian tradition, a feasible exercise within the Scottish tradition. At the same time he continued his optimistic views of the enlightenment in his interest in phrenology. He subsidised the publication of *Crania Americans* by his friend and biographer, S G Morton, who was later to exhibit his collection before the Glasgow Phrenological Society.[46] Maclure carried his faith in nature into temperance, pure food and drink, into natural health and country communal living, away from the vices of the cities. With his links with French radicalism and Babeuf in particular, he provides a link with the latter vegetarian and millenarian elements at the end of the nineteenth century. In all these areas the deist utopia could be realised only through innovative schemes of education.

The advancement of that scientific knowledge in the United States was associated with Glasgow. William Maclure was an indefatigable geological surveyor of the country, a ready supporter of scientific institutions with money, books and specimens. Closely associated with Benjamin Silliman, he was largely responsible for the formation and success of the Philadelphia Academy, over which he presided for twenty-two years. In addition, he was largely responsible for the introduction of Pestalozzianism into the United States. He had spent some years with Pestalozzi at Hofwyl and tried unsuccessfully to persuade him to emigrate to America. He did, however, persuade two Pestalozzians to go: Francis J N Neef who wrote the first pedagogical work in English published in the United States, and Gerard Troost, a professor of mineralogy. Silliman himself, educated by John Maclean of Glasgow at Princeton, visited Glasgow in 1805 and returned to become the father of American chemistry. But Maclure was far more influential in advancing popular education in America:

I have been endeavouring for some twenty years to change the education of children, and stumbled by accident about eighteen years ago on the school of Pestalozzi in Switzerland, which subserved the useful purpose that I had formed to myself of a rational education. I have been ever since doing something toward propagating and improving the scheme, and the success in the fruits are more than I expected, . . . but have not been able to penetrate deep into the crust of prejudices which is early interwoven with our self love, so as to make the greatest part of mankind jealous and inveterate enemies of any system that gives knowledge on cheaper terms than they themselves paid for it: though I have little doubt that in time some such system will generally prevail in our country where the power being in the hands of the people, . . . renders a diffusion of knowledge, necessary to the support of freedom, and of course the necessity of an almost equal division of property and knowledge, which the advantages given to those who can afford to send their sons to colleges very naturally counteracts.[47]

Maclure influenced Owen's sons in the direction of geology. New Harmony became a centre of geological studies until the foundation of the Smithsonian Institution: the bill, significantly, for this centre was introduced in congress by Robert Dale Owen. Its library was notable, while Maclure left provision for 160 libraries in his will, which must have had some impact on a land previously bereft of many such institutions.

Maclure wanted to break free from European reaction and establish an American education. His views coincided with those of the American workingmen's party in the major cities of the eastern seaboard, Boston, New York and Philadelphia. The lack of free education, they believed, effectively excluded them from economic opportunity. But more than most working men, he identified several vested interests which were opposed to popular education and the social revolution they represented.[48]

Maclure wished to extend the benefits of education to the largest possible audience; through free schools 'the highest political perfection that any people have yet arrived at'.[49] In pursuing that objective, simplicity was not merely rational but the most effective means of elevating the mass of mankind: 'When we abandon utility as the scale of value, we are adrift on the sea of caprice, fancy and whimsy without either rudder or compass.'[50] American education should be guided by simple republican virtue. New techniques of teaching without corporal punishment would effect great improvements: 'As much real and useful knowledge might be learned in a month as is now in years by the ancient absurd method of education, copied from the ages of barbarity, tending to confuse and puzzle the understandings by fanciful creations of the imagination and to enslave their independence by schemes of terror and punishments beyond the limits of probability.'[51] The other checks to vast advances were the clergy, professors and belles lettres. The clergy had a vested interest in perpetuating ignorance. Professors had a vested interest 'in the difficulty and complexity they can introduce into their lessons'. In contemporary literature 'the flowers of rhetoric and declamation only serve to disguise the truth and puzzle those who attempt to convert it into common sense'.[52] Education through Pestalozzian methods, the elimination of family pride, the provision of healthy foods, pure water and recreation would enable man to make real progress.

To that end Maclure enthusiastically supported New Harmony. Not only did he provide money and a substantial library, but he also secured Pestalozzian teachers for the scheme, Madame Fretageot and Philquepal d'Arusmont.[53] He also encouraged other scientists like the geologist Thomas Say and the naturalist Charles Alexandre Le Sueur to join the enterprise. Research, innovative teaching methods and manual labour combined to produce a flourishing educational community. The whole regime was marked by utilitarianism: 'These sheets will contain observations on the possibility of improving practical education by separating the useful from the ornamental, and thereby reducing the labour and fatigue of instructing youth, and we will endeavour to prove that children can educate, clothe and feed themselves by their own labour when judiciously applied to produce articles of real value.'[54] Maclure wanted an American education suited to American needs.

Phiquepal d'Arusmont married Fanny Wright during the New Harmony experiment.[55] She followed in the Maclure mould. Born in Dundee to a radical printer, she had stayed in Glasgow with her distant relative, Professor Mylne, had free rein in Professor Muirhead's American books, and spent some time with Professor John Millar's daughter-in-law before going to America. She came with excellent liberal credentials to New Harmony in 1825. Her efforts to establish a community at Nashoba, Tennessee and free her slaves proved less successful. But she travelled the country lecturing and writing on behalf of her ideal society in which education loomed large. She had high hopes of American schools:

> The better half of education in the Old World consists of unlearning. We have to unlearn when we come from the nursery, to unlearn when we come from the school and often to continue unlearning through life and to quit the scene at last without having rid ourselves of half the false notions which have been implanted in our young minds. All this is saved here.[56]

She therefore supported the campaign for free schools in America. For her the key measure was, 'NATIONAL, RATIONAL, REPUBLICAN EDUCATION: FREE FOR ALL AT THE EXPENSE OF ALL: CONDUCTED UNDER THE GUARDIANSHIP OF THE STATE, AND FOR THE HONOUR, THE HAPPINESS, THE VIRTUE OF THE STATE.'[57]

With her associate, Robert Dale Owen, she publicised the ideal. For Owen, born in Charlotte Street, Glasgow, had written his *Outline of the System of Education at New Lanark,* (Glasgow 1824), in which he sought to direct children to an intelligent appreciation of real objects through conversation and play rather than the stultifying influence of books.[58] The free, uninhibited education conducted with sympathetic happiness made New Lanark a model to many Americans. But that sympathy was dissipated, to a considerable degree, by the advanced social and sexual views of Wright and Owen, particularly his *Moral Physiology* (1830). Law, religion and education, unfortunately, were the relics of the dark ages. To sustain the new vision a rational and national form of education was required. Liberty might then be secure. *The* problem for America was the provision of a free, equal, universal and republican education. As Fanny Wright wrote to the radical freethinker, Richard Carlile on 16 October 1829: 'We have succeeded in starting the public mind in the great northern cities, Boston, New York and Philadelphia, on a plan of national education, equal, protective and republican. This is the point of union and has already [been] made the turning point of an election in Philadelphia'.[59]

To contemporaries such ultra-democratic views expressed by Freethinkers were unacceptable. Education, yes, but deism, no: the social, political and religious implications were too horrendous to contemplate.

Conservatism developed a reformist face. The fear of the unregulated passions might be seen as shorthand for cultural or class control. Whatever the interpretation, the problem was considerable, as the stormy events in many American cities demonstrated, with major riots against abolitionists and Catholics in the 1830s and 1840s. The problem was there. In 1817, it was claimed, less than half the population of New York possessed a Bible, while in 1830 only about half the population attended any service on the Sabbath. Part of the problem may have been the intense competition between religious sects and the lack of any traditional parochial structure: the strength of that parish element in Roman Catholicism may have appeared as even more ominous in consequence. There were no localised Protestant ecclesiastical districts as in Scotland. To a degree voluntary bodies to support various desirable objectives, the suppression of vice, temperance and the like may have been organisational efforts. Education was an even more obvious effort in that direction: an attempt to build an integrated community. By 1840, 47,209 common schools had 1.8 million on their rolls, with almost half a million given free education. It was little short of an educational and ecclesiastical revolution. Education, according to Baird, began orthodox spiritual influence.[60]

In this endeavour for better common schools, America naturally looked to Glasgow. Tradition, religion, commerce and friendships encouraged a close interest in Glasgow educational initiatives. David Stow, one of Chalmers' elders, had begun his educational career by establishing Sunday Schools for the deprived children in the slum areas.[61] Experience showed the ineffectiveness of one-day-a-week schooling in morality and so he was led into the more systematic educational plans. Love, proper example and proper environment were seen as the final determinants of the child's glorious destiny here and in the hereafter. To that end Stow and his friends established the Glasgow Infant School Society in 1826, after ten years' work among poor children. The Revd David Welsh, later Professor of Church History at the University of Edinburgh and later in the Free Church College there, was secretary and Mr Caughie was appointed teacher. That Glasgow example stimulated James Simpson to found a similar body in Edinburgh and the Revd Mr Wilderspin to come north to lecture and to learn. Stow himself published his *Physical and Moral Training* (1832) and his *Training System* (1835). At the same time the infant department was developed, with a juvenile school. In 1836 the Glasgow Education Society took over the school, promoted a lecture series which resulted in the foundation of the first teacher training college in Britain (1837) under the son of Dr McCrie, the biographer of Knox. He died shortly aferwards, to be replaced by the Revd Dr Robert Cunningham, to whom we shall return.

The attraction of this innovative regime was immense. Glasgow's model infant school impressed American educators on their visits. The use of objects, teaching gallery and illustrations were, perhaps, not original, but the use of the playground was. Under skilled supervision, moral principles of social utility and happiness were inculcated in a very relaxed, playful atmosphere, through singing and through a daily different Bible reading. Such stories were designed to elevate the feelings, excite patriotism and repress evil tendencies. Free from corporal punishment, competitive emulation in class, and taught to dress tidily and in cleanliness, the children, without any formal effort, learned to read. Like Owen and Horace Mann, Stow seems to have preferred emotional maturity to over-taxing intellectual exercises which might provoke insanity.[62] The heart, then preceded the intellect. Moral and physical attainments were not sacrificed on the narrow altar of intellect. It was an approach in keeping with contemporary medical wisdom and evangelical mentality. Not surprisingly Stow's school provided many teachers for overseas work and for missions to the inner cities. It was a missionary enterprise.

The Glasgow experiment was a response to tradition and to secular challenge. Glasgow had long-established Sunday Schools. In 1775, Revd Dr John Burns had launched them in Glasgow and further efforts followed until a permanent Sunday School Union was established in 1837.[63] Significantly, Burns' two sons, John and James, exemplify the missionary endeavour and the identity of secular enterprise with religious uplift. John Burns was the first professor of surgery in the University of Glasgow who, besides writing his important *Observations on Abortion* (1806) and *The Principles of Midwifery* (editions 1814–37), wrote several moral treatises including *The Principles of Christian Philosophy* (1828). James was an extremely successful entrepreneur, who was to be a founder of the Cunard Line, while giving generously of his time and money to various philanthropic endeavours. From an early date the family had been closely involved with Chalmers' efforts to ameliorate the lot of the poor. In a very real sense the family illustrates the professionalisation of philanthropy and the nature of the secular professions. Sense and sensibility could handle the evils of urban development.

Revd Dr Stevenson Macgill, Professor of Divinity in Glasgow University, was a supporter of moral education as part of a general strategy of improvement.[64] In particular he saw that as long as children were placed in industrial employment at a very early stage in life they would have little chance to acquire an adequate education to undertake their Christian social duties cheerfully. In conjunction with those proposals he advocated and helped carry through new hospitals, an asylum, and a magdalene institution, while later his ideas for a juvenile reformatory and a school of industry were put into effect.

His efforts in the General Assembly of the Church of Scotland to promote urban education, though recognised, yielded few immediate results. His success in securing the erection of the Knox memorial in Glasgow Necropolis was a rallying point for the slumbering spirit of the Reformation, a cry for an ethnic revival far more profound than the romanticism of Scott. Presbyterians had to be up and doing in their contemporary society. That awareness might be related to the contemporary political unrest and the well publicised activities of Robert Owen at New Lanark. His model village and educational experiments attracted the interest and visits of Americans, including Mr Lowell of the model mill town in America, John Griscom, the New York Quaker philanthropist, and Emma Willard, the educator. All were suitably impressed, though some like

George Ticknor were dismayed by Owen's tiresome talk and attempts at indoctrination.[65] But Owen's scepticism and radical social ideas did not detract from the insight provided by his school. That might be adapted for use in America.

Stow sought to teach the child through observation, description and classification. In that way 'the inner world of the conscious intellectual being' would be opened to the conception of power, cause and effect and 'its inference of the Deity'.[66] As in America, the lower orders were considered ill disciplined, weak-willed, and perhaps more enmeshed in original sin and ignorance than their betters. The idea was to educate children as good republicans, save the individual child and the nation. Cohesion, harmony, tractability were the results. Revisionist historians might see such enterprises as 'conspiratorial' or social engineering but the reformers were clearly seeking to sustain the idealism of the past in a new inchoate society.

Some reformers evaded the difficult question of religious instruction by emphasising 'consensus' Christianity rather than doctrine in education.[67] According to a revisionist view, education was sold to manufacturers as character-training. The problem is whether the reformers actually believed that or whether they were merely seeking to place men of substance and influence behind their efforts. At the same time by producing the gentleman teacher, the process was revolutionising not merely the profession but also inculcating certain desirable characteristics into their charges.

Both secular and religious drives to extend educational opportunities had several objectives: to save the child now, secure the future stability of the nation, awaken the parents to their personal responsibilities for the child and themselves, and so to generate a new moral climate. Education was the precursor for the total transformation of society, *the* reform of reforms. Individual and intensely personal, education was authentic rather than an alien-imposed rule on authority and so was all the more potent. Without accepting education as bourgeois intrusive engineering, there was a very considerable element of fear, genuine concern and the need for an intelligent, literate workforce in the expanding commercial world.[68] But overriding that concern was a revitalised Christian desire to save souls which cannot be overestimated. It was a major factor.

Education, then, was part of the total reform programme: 'WE ARE NOT A MORALLY EDUCATED PEOPLE.'[69] If religion were rooted in reality and authenticity, then the higher morality would permeate the social and political order. Whatever the external appearances, the respectable classes were as indifferent as the working classes. The former showed their lack of social responsibility in their blood sports and bloody penal code, while both classes were intemperate. With a more planned economy, greater leisure and more relevant education, the workers might be elevated through the dissemination of useful knowledge.

To achieve that purpose all sections of the Scottish community, including even Catholics, were to be trained in the values desirable in the new social order. Stow's associate, Revd David Welsh addressed them in a handbill:

Infant schools are intended for the reception of children from the age of two to that of six years with a view to imbuing their minds with the knowledge of religious truths of training them up in habits of obedience and good order, and of giving them such elementary instruction, as will enable them to enter into parochial and other schools. The plan of communicating religious truth is by the narratives, the precepts and plainest pronouncements of scripture.[70]

But these protestations did not assuage Glasgow Catholic suspicions, though Edinburgh Catholics shared in a similar experiment. Even so, by 1834 the Catholic School Society, which was run by a joint board of Catholics and Protestants, had raised funds and managed the schools since 1817 for some 20,000 children: some 1200 a year were given free schooling and free books.[71] In Glasgow Protestant businessmen and ministers had readily supported the undertaking though latterly as Kirkman Finlay complained, their interest had declined. In Edinburgh and Liverpool, the Catholic Thomas Wyse, MP supported these cooperative schemes with Vatican support, but aggressive Protestantism and Irish ethnicity seem to have killed the experiment. The need to establish a moral consensus within education was not lost on American observers.

As Professor Knox, the renowned anatomist, finding Glasgow unresponsive to his lecture, said of the city 'material interests, shopocracy and a fervid Calvinism overshadowed all other considerations'.[72] It wanted straight forward practical results—so did Americans. The difficulties which confronted Americans in the early nineteenth century are well exemplified by J G Cogswell. A teacher, and later librarian of what was to become New York Public Library, he spent some five years in Europe (1815–20). With Edward Everett and George Ticknor, he studied and travelled in Germany where he became acquainted with Goethe. In 1819, he was in Edinburgh with George Ticknor. Education naturally was on the agenda. In two articles he wrote for *Blackwood's Magazine,* Cogswell gives an excellent insight into the mind of the educational reformer.

Education for Cogswell failed on several counts. 'The literary character of a nation depends upon the few, not upon the diffusion of it among the many.' The New Englander received 'a great deal too much (education) to leave him contented with his lot and place in life'. Such men demanded relevant forms of education: 'Life is a round of practical duties.' Cultivation in the broadest sense was absent: 'Man is still a ferocious animal and consequently dangerous in proportion to the number of herd . . . intellectually and morally savage at the same time as powerful as a perfect knowledge of all the artificial means of increasing physical strength can make him'.[73] America needed a powerful antidote, a prophylactic cultural injection to forestall this fever.

But how? Inadequate college teachers, uncultivated, underpaid and overworked, inadequately instructed their charges amid poor libraries and scanty equipment. America had a mere 150,000 books in libraries for her 10 million inhabitants. Only the Logan library in Philadelphia was impressive. Bereft of first class classical training and ill disciplined from childhood, students passed their time drinking and smoking in their excessive unsupervised leisure. A degree merely indicated three or four years residence, without any examination. Although medical schools were the equal of Britain's, legal training was pitiful. The profession which attracted the best talent and provided a passport to political life gave little insight into the philosophy or form of law and government.

The clergy were largely ill-equipped for their mission: only 2000 of the 5000 ministers in the country had received any formal training, and nearly half of these were in New England. South and west of the Chesapeake river, 200 trained ministers faced 4 million souls. Even in New England, the itinerant evangelical preacher was eroding the old ministerial tradition. Few cared to enter an illpaid, unrecognised and arduous profession: only 1 in 5 Harvard graduates entered the church. Too often under the influence of Unitarianism, sermons had become exegetical exercises rather than sources of inspiration and guidance. The head ruled the heart: sectarian strife produced innumerable controversies. But Massachusetts and Connecticut had 'still respectable, for the most part, well instructed clergy but the residue of the land is a prey to delusion'.[74] Although in recent years theology had vastly improved at Princeton, Andover and Harvard, and although Maclure, Wilson and Hossack had advanced American science, scientific pursuits were in their infancy. The danger of ignorance, the mob, despotism, Catholicism and Unitarianism were clear. The old order was passing and Scottish help was needed. In that conflict the infant school would be the battleground.

George Jardine, Professor of Logic in Glasgow University from 1774 to 1827, wrote an influential work *Outlines of Philosophical Education* (1818 and 1825) in which he insisted on the vital importance of the sciences over classics, the practical over the esoteric, the cultivation of the total character of the student in contrast to the limited narrow specialist.[75] The main aim of education was to make the pupil think for himself rather than impose some cultural trappings upon his unwilling mind. That entailed observation and understanding of practical realities, the nature and property of materials and analysis rather than theory which was clearly communicated to others. Implied was an education which instilled a philosophy of history, political economy and eloquence. It was a process which demanded great skills on the part of the teacher to effect any significant improvement among his students. To carry such a burden he had to be a lively, professionally-trained man. A former pupil of Adam Smith, Jardine had been a colleague of Professors Thomas Reid and John Millar. He had also taught Francis Jeffrey, John Gibson Lockhart and Sir William Hamilton. Jardine might speak with some authority on the teacher as a key to the educational revolution. Understanding the ability to think for oneself and to develop a philosophy of life within a 'democratic' teaching system was very attractive to the Americans.

Jardine was voicing the Scottish solution. It was implicit in the philosophy of Common Sense but it had been given effect in educational writings in the early nineteenth century. John Wood of Edinburgh had begun his educational activity in the wake of the riots of 1812. For him education was directed towards 'regularity, order and business' among the lower orders, whose assent had to be won through imaginative textbooks and excellent teachers: 'He must be the very life and soul of the system.'[76]

Sheriff Wood's school naturally attracted American interest but so, too, did Edinburgh High School under James Pillans, later Professor of Humanity in the University of Edinburgh. He sought to arouse public interest in schooling. By eliminating corporal punishment, providing suitable textbooks and well-trained teachers, Pillans hoped to improve standards dramatically: 'A course of lectures on principles and practices of teaching continued for four or five months . . . could not fail to diffuse correct notions and improved methods over the country.'[77] Such hopes were related to John Abercrombie's philosophy. Reason and moral principle were identical.[78] Christian truth and the philosophy of moral feelings were unassailable. Significantly, a doctor, Abercrombie, was reinforcing the contemporary medical idea that too early intellectual demands upon the child bred insanity and related difficulties. It was a view which secularist and Christian shared, but though understanding replaced rote, the heart assumed primacy over the intellect. Some might say they were integrated. It also curbed reason alone and gave a somewhat conservative, even anti-intellectual, tone to the ideas of some educations. In harmony with romanticism, contemporary medical science and religious needs, it offered the prospect of a new profession with a sense of mission, national and providential. It gave power, influence and self esteem to the individual teacher. He was a copartner in the regeneration of society.

Jardine had been well publicised in America through the *New York Academician*. It was published by Albert and John W Picket between 1818 and 1820 who were partners in a private school and in the management of the Incorporated Society of New York Teachers. But such publicity perhaps indicated the poverty of many schools for children and the inadequate quality of the teachers:

> The multitude of teachers at least in some states are made up of thriftless of every grade, too lazy to work, too poor to live without it, and much more fit to be peddling wooden nutmets, or making hickory hams, than to undertake the task of training the youth of a nation to the knowledge and love of their duty as citizens and men.[79]

In short there was enthusiasm but inadequate personnel to carry through an educational revolution. For teachers might be nasty, brutish and their tenure short. They might teach in winter months and follow other trades in summer whilst low salaries and competition for the better teachers between settlements further eroded stability of residence. In other areas the refusal of townships to impose heavier taxes upon themselves encouraged the more able to seek opportunities elsewhere. Standards and expectations accordingly varied markedly.

Among Jardine's students was William Russell from Ayrshire, who was to play a major role in early public education in America. After attending Glasgow University for a time, without graduating, Russell went out to

Georgia to seek some relief for his ill health in 1817. After returning to Glasgow, he again went out to Georgia in 1818. Having spent some time as a tutor in Judge Berrien's household, he opened a private school in Savannah, married and then migrated northwards with his New England bride. Russell began to develop his ideas about the professionalisation of teaching from his school in New Haven. He was particularly anxious to improve the quality of teachers, their potential and expertise: to extend useful knowledge through the lyceum movement, with which he was associated: to produce new 'relevant' textbooks: to hold summer and autumn schools for teachers to inculcate more knowledge, better classroom skills, elocution and so forth.

In 1823 he published his *Suggestion on Education* in which he urged a teachers training institute in Connecticut, the first in the United States, though the idea had been mooted earlier in 1816 and 1823.[81] In 1826 he was to become the editor of the first educational journal in the English speaking world, the *American Journal of Education,* a post in which he continued until 1830.[82] Later he was to establish with A Bronson Alcott, the renowned transcendentalist brother of an influential educationalist, a school at Germantown, near Philadelphia. Though the experiment proved short lived, its authors later believed their advanced educational notions had been generally accepted by 1860. That was a momentous relationship for, as Alcott said, no man except W E Channing gave him 'greater pleasure in conversation or offered more cordial sympathy'. Russell for his part recalled in 1862 the 'pleasures of earlier days and their hopeful purposes, some of which we are begining to realise, if not in person, in proxy'.[83] Russell, then, in association with a galaxy of Boston talent, was in close contact with the most formative influences in America.[84] Horace Mann was deeply impressed by him, as was his former student, Francis Parkman, the renowned historian. But through Henry Barnard's close friendship he was even more influential in numerous enterprises and activities.

Russell like Noah Webster believed that morality and religion could be spread through popular biographies of American heroes: 'The education of youth is an employment of more consequence than making laws and preaching the gospel because it lays the foundation on which both law and gospel rest for sources.'[85] In 1829 Russell gave an address at the inaugural meeting of the American Institute of Instruction in Boston together with Ticknor, Woodridge and May. Like many others he saw education as *the* reform: 'Intelligence enters the poor man's dwelling in the person of his own child and brings docility and peace and happiness along with it.'[86] The healthy pursuit of recreation in school playgrounds and its extension beyond into the larger world brought moral and social improvement. Adopting some of Combe's notions and Stow's techniques, Russell wrote widely on educational methods, produced some of the earliest children's schoolbooks in America and so contributed to the formation of the new nation. One of his methods was to stimulate local patriotism and intense interest in the locality in the new nation, to impose some solidity in a fluid changing local population:

A narrow feeling of exclusive preference for home scenes and mere local information is no proper fruit of education, but an early and enlightened attachment to local associations while it forms a distinctive basis of social character in communities is in no respect incompatible with that enlarged and liberal regard to the national interest and relations which should ever distinguish the citizens of the United States. Local preference may be justly cherished without incurring the faults of local prejudice.[87]

In that process the citizen would acquire an interest and loyalty which would make him more effective, better equipped and more rooted in his society. As his friend Henry Barnard saw, Scottish identity once acquired was never abandoned: it was a moral, intellectual and democratic condition. Wherever Scots travelled they always retained a fondness for the old country and the values bound up with that affection, and would often return to pass their last days in the land of their birth. To those who were moving out from New England the message was clear. Education was an excellent antidote to radicalism and a guarantee of further social and political stability. Not surprisingly, many of the American school advocates were drawn from old Federalists, rather conservative Whig sympathisers, or New Englanders who were shocked by the Dorr rebellion in Rhode Island, or staunch evangelically-minded clergy.

To some extent that explains the character of American colleges as strongholds of Protestant piety in the period to 1860. Revd. Francis Wayland of Brown University is perhaps indicative. A conservative evangelical friend of William Russell he replaced the previous Unitarian president, imposed stricter moral controls and showed the similarities with Scotland in his writings *Elements of Moral Science* (1835), *Political Economy* (1837) and *Intellectual Philosophy* (1857). These three showed the same moral, economic and intellectual concerns as in Scotland: the purity of heart preceded doctrinal differences. Inspired by Scottish commonsense philosophy America was ennobling the ordinary, the prosaic and the simple individual life rather than celebrating the noble.[88] With his interest in infant schools, it suggests that college presidents were not only concerned in the cultural crusade but also sought to upgrade the standard and quality of their students and so ultimately improve their own prestige and the potential of the nation. John Maclean, later president of Princeton University, was a strong supporter of improved popular schooling in New Jersey. The son of a Glasgow graduate who had established the first chair of chemistry in America in 1795, he was significantly a very conservative Calvinist and a firm supporter of the American Colonisation Society, an organisation committed to the resettlement of freed slaves in Africa. It was a position he maintained long after the American Civil War. Other educational supporters who favoured that body included Henry Barnard while Wayland wrote a scriptural tract in support of slavery. For the black represented irrevocable change against which they were struggling in many other areas with enlightened results. Assimilation and absorption was feasible for whites but not for blacks. The integrated society, with the best intentions, looked backwards to an older idealised white Protestant conformist society.

In a sense these elements confirmed de Tocqueville's view that Americans were free to conform. The individual was submerged in the community's standards. That mentality is also evident in the widespread reissue of William McGavin's *The Protestant,* a highly charged anti-Catholic polemic in America as well as his *Sunday School lessons,* or Robert Baird the American missionary and author of *Religion the United States of America* (1844), with a very wide Scottish circulation, who was also a friend of popular education in New Jersey.[89] That is not to suggest that the educational reformers were bigoted but that American culture naturally, understandably and predictably had a Protestant bias.

Russell was the secretary of the American Institute of Instruction which was both a learned society and a pressure group. For Russell it seemed more like an audience for his views. With George Combe he believed in eliciting ideas from the mind rather than inculcating—or too obviously inculcating—desirable attitudes upon the child. To him, like Stow, the school was a microcosm of a society for the suppression of vice, a means of generating respect for each other, curbing excesses of behaviour and enlightening the pupil largely through his own experience. Education in this sense was a form of self help. It was a training for that adult self culture so much admired by W E Channing. That aspect of self help and involvement of the recipient and his parents was further demonstrated by the small contributions towards the cost of education which Russell felt was an important psychological feature of his scheme. For example in Scotland it eliminated truancy. Like his American colleagues he was glad to see many Scottish works readily available in cheap popular series, like John Abercrombie's writings, or Combe's *Physiological and Moral Management of Infancy.*[90]

Russell also sought to enlist American women into the teaching profession. They were his embodiment of national virtue with a special supportive role in the male dominated world of education. Although liberal enough to envisage the teaching profession for women like Emma Willard and Catherine Beecher, Russell saw their role as reinforcing in more subtle domestic ways the moral attitudes of Protestant tradition. As his friend Wayland argued woman's sphere of duty lay *within* the family, man's lay *without.*

Teachers for Russell were a new priesthood who would transform American society: 'Let teachers make themselves what they ought to be, truly instructors of society. . . . A high intellectual and moral character is ensured to a community in which teachers are competent to the great task if rightly developing and directed the power of the mind.' Taught by observation, description and classification within a happy atmosphere the child's 'inner world of conscious intellectual being' would be opened up to the perception of power the recognition of cause and effect and 'its inference of the Deity'.[91] In short such scientific ideas elicited from the mind confirmed the child's religious intuition. Russell envisaged a future within a moral Christian democracy, in which all faculties of the individual and all groups in the community advanced proportion.[92] That message was beamed through personal contacts, through his numerous textbooks, articles and large gatherings either in Lyceums or teachers' institutes. Russell was firing an educational broadside at the children, in methods and textbooks: at teachers through demands for improved standards: at parents through appeals to their aspirations for their children and themselves: at public opinion through papers and pamphlets. He was involved at every level.

Russell made a major contribution to the growing sense of a providential and popular American mission. The rejection of European continental backwardness in intellect, social organisations and religion intensified in the early nineteenth century. In his *The American Common School Reader* with John Goldsbury, Russell asked of Washington and Franklin 'What other two men, whose lives belong to the eighteenth century of Christendom, have left a deeper impression of themselves upon the age in which they lived, and upon all after time?'[93] This divinisation, as one recent historian has seen it, was decisive in building up the ideal American, brave, charitable, industrious, religious, courteous and a paragon of the domestic virtues. Practicality took precedence over intellectual concerns. After the Bible, school textbooks have been seen as the most influential elements in forming the desirable national virtues. Opposed to the luxurious idle life of court or plantation, as well as the vices of the mob or untutored democracy of the west, these works imposed a secular ethic of puritanism upon those who lacked restraints by intensifying the concern with individual morality. Under the guise of religion and a belief in man's capacity for good, they promulgated the providential unique American mission. In the process the old New England groups found themselves again and extended their ideals to the rest of the nation. The innumerable editions of Russell's various readers must have significantly contributed to that end.

A reviewer in the *Common School Journal* believed Russell's *A Selection of Easy Reading Lessons with Introductory Exercises in Articulation for Children* was excellent: 'the best book in its purpose that can be found in the language.'[94] The reader 'feels the freshness of early days pervading the spirit and its sensibilities gushing at the eyes'. Russell, abandoning the hitherto dull formal style of children's writers, made simplicity the means of winning 'heart and habit'. Russell 'by the selection of pieces tending to cherish sentiments of love truth and piety . . . by avoiding low subjects, low characters and low forms of expression' established the norms of good taste. The same journal endorsed Russell's stress upon elocution and technique: 'There is no mistake so fatal to the proper education and training of youth, as the practical error of imagining that because a man possesses knowledge therefore he will be able to communicate it. The knowledge of a Newton or a Bacon would avail little, without a proper mode of communication.'[95]

Russell's many textbooks and teaching aids serve to emphasise the importance of the Scottish contribution to early common school education. For example John Abercrombie's *Inquiries Concerning the Intellectual Powers* (Edinburgh 1830) and his *The Philosophy of Moral Feeling* (Edinburgh 1833) were both reprinted in New York for Harper's School District library series.[96] In addition educational journals gave considerable coverage to the annual reports of the Glasgow Education Society. In short books confirmed the stable and gave the transient some mobile ideals, a sense of philosophical, moral if not geographical roots.[97] At the same time Russell's advocacy of teachers' associations and institutes gave a sense of professional identity, encouragement and reassurance in what necessarily must have been a trying task. Russell's close friend, Henry Barnard, greatly extended the scope and influence of Scottish ideas in the common school system.[98] A Yale graduate, Barnard had been a staunch supporter of the American Colonisation Society and the American Peace Society before he took up his interest in education. He made a study of European education which he later published as secretary to the Board of School Commissioners of Connecticut in the *First Annual Report* in 1839. In Connecticut with the help of Russell he sought to extend the effectiveness of the common school system. In the campaign he maintained the Chalmers principle that education should be readily available but with a small charge to sustain parental interest and so encourage attendance. That was hardly surprising in that Barnard had actively sponsored Combe's American lecture tour in 1839–40. But in addition to political and lecture campaigns, Barnard also produced the *American Journal of Education* from 1855 in an attempt to promote new ideas for the new professionals. In that periodical many articles with a distinct Scottish flavour appeared including some by Russell himself, David Stow, J Morrison of the Glasgow Free Church, and his own on 'Object Teaching'.[99]

Barnard as secretary of the Connecticut school board proposed considerable improvements. He aimed his campaign at two targets: better teachers and better schools. To secure the first he wanted normal schools for training, teachers' institutes to provide up-to-date methods and to improve salaries and conditions for the new professionals. Better school buildings and facilities, improved textbooks and improved supervison under state superintendents supported by public taxes would ensure that standards were maintained and improved.[100]

In that campaign Russell readily assisted, not merely in Connecticut but also in Rhode Island and Massachusetts.[101] He vigorously pursued his work in teachers' institutes throughout New England. Though rarely in good health, Russell held institutes over several months most years. In 1848 for example he was twice in Rockingham county, twice at Taunton and Middlesborough, Portsmouth, Reeds Ferry, New Hampshire as well as teaching classes at Brown University and private classes elsewhere. President Wayland of Brown, as an author and the first president of the American Institute of Instructors, was deeply committed to free public education. Russell also taught at Harvard, Andover, Union Theological College and elsewhere. But he seems to have supported the annual teachers' institutes in Rhode Island which were held in each county so that the common school and the teacher were given a very strong base and local identity. Even the role of such institutes which were largely pressure group rallies did not end for Russell with the establishment of normal schools. In constant correspondence with Henry Barnard whom he zealously encouraged, Russell campaigned for normal schools in New Hampshire, attended the opening of the Merrimack normal school and ran institutes with Krusi, son of Pestalozzi's coadjutor, at

Lancaster, Massachusetts. In tirelessly supporting Barnard's preoccupation with efficiency, professionalisation and precision, Russell helped with what might be considered refresher courses and improved methods conferences. But by the 1850s Russell's two to four week courses had given way to five day meetings. The institutes were a form of revival agency to regenerate the old moral drive, sense of ministry and professionalism. A more formal structure was gradually superseding them and eroding their need. It was a measure of Russell's successful support.

Russell was also deeply involved in the educational journals of his day. He was editor of the first English language journal entirely devoted to education, *The American Journal of Education,* established in 1826.[102] In it the wonder of Glasgow schools and mechanics institutes were highly publicised. In 1832 he again went to Philadelphia where perhaps he may already have encountered Robert Vaux and the Philadelphia Society for the Promotion of Public Schools (1827). Vaux, a Quaker, was president of the Board of Philadelphia Schools 1818–31, a prison reformer, and a promoter of temperance and savings banks. At any rate Russell helped with an innovative school at Germanstown with Alcott. While there he ran the short-lived *Journal of Instruction* 1 January–15 March 1832 for the association of Philadelphia teachers. Later he contributed to the *New England Journal of Education,* Barnard's *American Journal of Education* and presumably others like Barnard's *Connecticut Common School Journal* (1838–66) and Mann's *Boston Common School Journal* (1842–8). These and similar journals which proliferated in the 1830s and 1840s would funnel ideas similar to those of Russell to the wider public.

The crusaders for the expansion and improvement of American common schools were many and varied in their backgrounds, outlook and intentions. Among those associated with Russell were idealists, social romantics and even transcendentalists with whom he might be numbered. There were evangelicals seeking for more effective salvation of souls through educational mission, professionals who sought to upgrade the quality and expertise of teachers, and also writers and administrators who might embark on a respected and valued career in the fluid social order. Social conservatives like Cogswell sought to protect their status, tradition and interests. Women, though subservient by modern feminist standards, had opportunities in writing and teaching. Russell was an exceptional one-man support team in himself.

The second point to be made is the close network of relationships, personal and familiar, which sustained this educational enterprise around Russell. One contact led naturally into a network of similarly motivated people. Many of these young men had studied at Yale under the presidency of Timothy Dwight (1752–1817). The grandson of Jonathan Edwards and a graduate of Yale, he followed Scottish philosophy. Practical and common-sensical, he had a utilitarian view of happiness through 'a system of duties'. Under him Yale, according to Benjamin Silliman, became 'a little temple; prayer and praise seem to be the delight of the greater part of the students, while those who are still unfeeling are awed with respectful silence'.[103] Federalist in political sympathies, Dwight sent forth many students, particularly Moses Stuart (1780–1852), who with Leonard Woods (1774–1854) was to present a more intellectual historical appreciation and understanding of orthodox Christian views. These and others were well read and published in Glasgow and America. But for our purposes here they regenerated that moral missionary enthusiasm which was to guide many researchers and teachers in the nineteenth century. Russell and his kind were able to capitalise upon that mood. The revivalist influence of Yale and Andover seems to have been considerable. President Timothy Dwight of Yale, his protégé, Revd Moses Stuart of New Haven, Leonard Woods of Andover, Asahel Nettleton and Lyman Beecher and their like directed American religious interests towards more active demonstrations of their faith. That renewed Christian commitment gave rise to new missionary and outreach enterprises, voluntary bodies dedicated to moral, humanitarian reforms and the extension of the Protestant gospel territory. Education was one of those concerns. Lyman Beecher's daughter, Catherine (1800–78) sister of Henry Ward and Edward, was a vigorous supporter of women's education, particularly emphasising their domestic role and formative influences on the child and the new republic. Lucy Ann Reed, who taught in Beecher's school, married William Channing Woodbridge (1794–1845), the cousin of William Ellery Channing. A Yale graduate, he relinquished the idea of becoming a missionary to join Revd Thomas Gallaudet, a graduate of both Yale and Andover, in his Hartford Asylum for the Education and instruction of the Deaf and Dumb. Ill health forced him to travel in Europe and he returned to write his influential innovative *Universal Geography* to which Emma Willard contributed. Enthusiastic for women's education, she visited Glasgow and was associated with Russell. Woodbridge later became part editor of the *American Annals of Education*. He was also a relative of A Bronson Alcott whose five pupils at one time included Russell's four children and one black. Russell worked with Alcott and Elizabeth Peabody in his schools. They both wrote extensively on the philosophy of education: Alcott on *The principles and methods of infant Instruction* (1830) and *The Doctrine and Discipline of Human Culture* (1836) and Peabody wrote on her school experiences while under Russell's influence. Alcott's sister was married to the abolitionist Samuel J May of Brooklyn who later became the second principal of the first Massachusetts Normal School in 1842. Her cousin, W A Alcott, also wrote widely on education and then took up food reform with another relative, W Sylvester Graham, *the* food reformer, the grandson of a Glasgow graduate minister and his minister son: significantly both ministers had remained in their charges forty years, indicating the stability which was passing.[104]

Harriet Beecher, the author of *Uncle Tom's Cabin,* and sister of Catherine, married another educational reformer, Calvin Stowe. He was educated at Bowdoin, Andover and Dartmouth before migrating westward to Ohio. Following his marriage he came to Scotland as part of his investigation of public educational provision in Europe. His *Report on Elementary Instruction of Europe* (1839) was placed in every school district in the state of Ohio and reprinted for use in several others including Massachusetts and Pennsylvania.

There was also a Unitarian network with which Russell was associated through William Ellery Channing on both sides of the Atlantic. For Channing was renowned in Britain with the Rathbones of Liverpool, Lady Noel Byron and Joanna Baillie, the daughter of a Glasgow Professor, as well as with the Glasgow Unitarians like Hedderwick and William Burns. In Boston he was associated with Benjamin Tuckerman, Orestes Brownson, Horace Mann, Orville Dewey and others who were connected with Glasgow in various ways. Through the Rathbones, Channing was able to introduce Dorothea Dix, the asylum reformer, to a British audience while Rathbone introduced George Combe to Channing and the wider American audience. Elizabeth Peabody was amanuensis to Channing for some nine years and taught with Alcott in the Boston Temple School. Her sister, Sophia, married that failed teacher, Nathaniel Hawthorne, and her other sister, May, married Horace Mann. In later life she was to lecture at Alcott's Concord School of Philosophy alongside the Scot, Thomas Davidson, of whom we will treat later.

In effect there was a reform mafia or freemasonry which enabled ideas to spread rapidly through close-knit groups to take effect. The gospel of education was spread through a network of ministers, teachers and philosophers but also by familial groups and close friends. It was as if one relationship opened all other connections, to complete a circuit of knowledge.

On the Glasgow side there was a similar related network of education-minded families and groups.[105] Dugald Bannatyne, the founder of the Glasgow Chamber of Commerce was a cousin of Dugald Stewart, the philosopher. Andrew Bannatyne, his elder son, married the daughter of Professor James Millar and the grand-daugher of Professor John Millar, the Whig sympathiser and thinker. His daughter had married Professor James Mylne, a sympathiser with Professor George Jardine and a relative of Frances Wright. Thomas Hamilton (1789–1842), the novelist and American traveller and brother of Sir William Hamilton, (1788–1856) the Common-sense philosopher, graduated from Glasgow University where his father had been the Professor of Botany. Stevenson MacGill (1765–1840) a former tutor to the Earl of Buchan, an American sympathiser, was Professor of Divinity, while Sir William Hooker had won an international reputation for his botanical studies and field work before he went south to found Kew Gardens as a national institution in 1841. Another migrant south was Professor Thomas Graham of the Andersonian University renowned for his work on the diffusion of gases who became Professor in London University from 1837–55. The Andersonian University also had Revd Ralph Wardlaw and several prominent city businessmen as trustees. Education flowed through a system of religious intellectual and business connections within a tightly knit community.

George Ticknor, the educator and author, twice visited Scotland in 1819 and 1838. On the second occasion he stayed with Robert Monteith at Carstairs but on the first he had been accompanied by J G Cogswell, as already noted, and accordingly gained some insight into Scottish education in New Lanark and Edinburgh.[106] Though renowned for his Spanish scholarship as a Professor at Harvard, for our purposes his importance in the foundation of Boston Public Library in 1852 is even more significant. For his father had founded the Boston School Board with which he was closely associated. He was to lend his name to new initiatives in Boston education. Russell in 1826 worked with Professor Ticknor to promote infant schools in Boston. Over several months they worked with a group of some fifty like-minded people in Ticknor's home. They hoped to draw up some scheme of schooling together with a suitable library of works on education whilst Russell was to act as agent for the society. But significantly many of the major figures in the educational crusade had been Whigs and somewhat opposed to social and political reform movements, like Barnard and Mann. As a recent historian has observed, before 1850 there was 'an ambiguous sense of professionalisation which made morality and peda-gogical technology mutually reinforcing'.[107] Russell allegedly was a trans-cendentalist, believing in the unity and coherence of mental life with the duties of man: they were based upon natural science rather than revealed religion and metaphysics.

Russell literally formed a circle of educational innovators. In his *American Journal of Education*, Russell published *Letter on Early Education addressed to J P Greaves* by Pestalozzi, London 1829. It was the first work of Pestalozzi in English. James Pierrepoint Greaves had worked with Pestalozzi at Yverdun for four years and subsequently taught at the Universities of Basel and Tubingen.[108] In 1825 Greaves returned to Britain and founded the London Infant School Society. As its secretary he published several books on educating children. Greaves was drawn into contact with two men associated with Glasgow: James Eliamet 'Shepherd' Smith and Alexander Campbell. Smith was a Universalist minister in Glasgow who published a translation of Saint-Simon's *New Christianity* in 1834, and was involved in several communitarian experiments. Alexander Campbell who was to be Greaves biographer had been a member of the Orbiston community before working as a missionary for Robert Owen's Society of Rational Religion. Also associated with this group was F F Badham, one of three sons of a Glasgow professor, all three had been educated at Yverdun by Pestalozzi. Greaves was drawn into correspondence with A Bronson Alcott who came to Britain and worked at Ham Common School. It had been named Alcott House after Alcott's Temple School in Boston. Alcott was to take back three members of the staff to America in the hope that 'on a survey of the present civilised world Providence seems to have ordained the United States of America more especially New England as the field wherein this idea (of a New Eden) is to be realised in actual experience'.[109]

Phrenology exercised far more influence in the transatlantic world than most historians have realised.[110] Originating from Dr Franz Joseph Gall of Vienna, phrenology in its simplest form suggested a strong correlation between the mind of man and the shape of his head. The brain as the organ of the mind shaped the skull and so each mental attribute of the mind was clearly visible. Mental, physical and spiritual capacities were interrelated and man could control his own development. Gall's disciple, Johnann Gaspar

Spurzheim, spread his master's views through Scotland during his seven months in Edinburgh in 1817 where George Combe was among his converts. Several Americans fell under phrenological influences when they studied medicine under Gall and Spurzheim in Paris. The most renowned was Dr Charles Caldwell of Transylvania University, Kentucky who then became an enthusiastic advocate of the new science in America. Dr Robert MacNish of Glasgow was also converted there.[111] To educationalists it seemed to offer a liberating, scientific and effective short cut to popular education and mass amelioration. Given the 'right' influences and environment, the child properly appreciated and trained in harmony with nature would develop physically mentally and spiritually as a wholly integrated human being. Balanced, well adjusted and carrying nothing to excess, the future adult would ensure the orderly progress of democratic government.

The links between American and Glasgow phrenologists was considerable. In 1829 Spurzheim had lectured in Glasgow to large audiences of the respectable and to specialised gatherings of medical men including Samuel Wilderspin the educationist. Nearly a decade later Dr Jonathan Barber, a teacher of elocution at Harvard came to address the Glasgow Phrenological Society.[112] At the same time both groups published and widely circulated works by each other on both sides of the Atlantic. Dr Amariah Brigham who had accompanied Spurzheim on his tour of Connection penal, mental and deaf and dumb institutions wrote *Remarks on the Influence of Mental Cultivation on Health* (1832). It was edited and republished in Glasgow by Dr Robert MacNish and James Simpson in 1836. MacNish had graduated from Glasgow University and studied in Paris with Gall and Spurzheim. A local literary celebrity, he had written his influential *Anatomy of Drunkeness* (1827) and a similar work on dreams. A correspondent of Revd Dr Sprague of Albany, New York, the editor of *Annals of the American Pulpit,* MacNish, a staunch opponent of Catholic Emancipation, received an honorary doctorate from Hamilton College through his influence. Like his friend, James Simpson, MacNish had many of his works published in America. Together they contributed to the growing awareness of the need for education.[113]

Rejecting the stern rigidity of Calvinism, the phrenologists demanded a proper education in harmony with nature which would simultaneously develop the physical, intellectual and moral nature of man. With that corrected method the world would be regenerated anew. Samuel Gridley Howe and other leading New Englanders were deeply impressed. Howe, the corresponding secretary of the Boston Phrenological Society, and Joseph Tuckerman who was closely associated with Spurzheim were to visit Glasgow. Some, like writers in the *American Annals of Education,* were well disposed towards the ideas but uneasy about the apparent dangers to religion. Their conviction that phrenology was essentially atheist, materialist and determinist was borne out by its advocacy by Abner Kneeland and Robert Dale Owen, but Scottish phrenologists were less uneasy. Phrenology merely bore out their Christian convictions. Extreme evangelicals like Alexander Campbell, the Glasgow born founder of the Disciples of Christ, remained adamantly hostile.[114]

The influence of George Combe was considerable. In particular he exercised great power upon James Simpson, 1781–1853, the advocate son of three generations of ministers, who was deeply interested in education.[115] A friend of Sir Walter Scott, Simpson played a leading role in the founding of the *Phrenological Journal* in 1823 and maintained his interest until the demise of the periodical in 1847. As chairman of the Edinburgh Infant School Society, he worked ceaselessly to promote improved standards of education as a means of regenerating society. In books, pamphlets and lectures in Scotland and England, he tirelessly spread Combe's ideas. He gave two series of lectures in Liverpool and Manchester as well as addressing several thousand working men. Associated with Thomas Wyse MP, he vigorously supported moral though non-sectarian education: 'EDUCATION TO EMBRACE ALL SECTS, OR NO EDUCATION.'[116] The plan met severe difficulties in Glasgow but success in Edinburgh. Well acquainted with the *American Journal of Education,* he showed B W Richards, the Mayor of Philadelphia and chairman of Girard College, round the various schools of Edinburgh and exchanged views with Francis Lieber on education.[117] For him, 'The political reform is *external,* the moral is *intrinsic,* above all party spirit as it is, is necessary to the stability and efficiency of the political.'[118] The need was to develop all faculties in harmony: physical, intellectual, moral for the general happiness of all. The net result would be a temperate, healthy, cohesive moral society. To that end Simpson eagerly supported mechanics institutes and workers educational bodies like the Glasgow Caledonia Pottery Mechanics Institute and publicised the excellent work of two men whom he greatly admired: Robert Cunningham and Alexander J Dorsey.[119]

Cunningham and Dorsey put into practice many of the ideas advocated by Combe and Simpson. Robert Cunningham had been born in Galloway, educated at Edinburgh University and entered the teaching profession which was then taking shape.[120] Possibly he was the Scottish 'R C' who accompanied the New York Quaker philanthropist John Griscom back home. Griscom had meticulously examined Glasgow and Edinburgh schools as well as meeting Professor Mylne of Glasgow before returning home determined to establish a school along Scottish lines. However that may be, Cunningham served as a house governor at George Watson's, Edinburgh, for some five years before he established his own institution. In this innovative school, he began cutting down on the study of the classics and introduced greater emphasis upon language, natural history, natural philosophy and chemistry. He also began to produce the first suitable children's textbooks on mathematics. His venture proved successful, growing from 60 to 220 pupils in the first year. It was a tribute to his new teaching methods. In remedying the defects of existing schools, he tried to introduce a more intelligent appreciation and understanding of Latin through his new methods rather than rote learning. Following Pestalozzi and Mayo, he used objects in lessons to stimulate greater powers of observation, perception and precision of language. Likewise in geography and arithmetic he succeeded with his pupils to win glowing tributes from the leading intellectual business and professional classes of the city. As a sympathiser with Combe, he won considerable favour and esteem with visiting Americans like A D Bache and others. Indeed so successful was he, that Lafayette College, Easton, Pennsylvania, invited him to take a post and organise the educational training of their students.

In 1838, Cunningham went to settle in Easton. Cunningham was to teach the theory and practice of education whilst William Dunn, another Edinburgh model school teacher would introduce a model school into the college. To broadcast the plan, Cunningham and Revd Professor Junkin began *The Educator* which gave prominence to the various Glasgow experiments in infant and normal schools. As the *Connecticut School Journal* reported, they would demonstrate 'the very best plans now practiced in Europe and in this country'.[121] Cunningham wanted to establish teaching as a profession. The American people would have to pay better salaries to attract worthwhile dedicated teachers, even provide them with a house and a garden as in Scotland. The schools were the best guarantee of the continuation of free democratic institutions and religion: 'The schools were the nursery of the Church.'[122] After travelling through Ohio, New Jersey and New York observing and giving some lectures, Cunningham was convinced that the cheapest and most efficient way of expanding the educational profession in Pennsylvania was to attach a model school to each of the eight major colleges in the state: graduates might then as in Scotland readily enter the profession. It was a scheme which echoed James Pillans' proposals for Scottish education. In addition he urged that two female seminaries be established. In this way some 200 graduates might speedily be recruited. Even more radical students should be given grants so that the talented poor might be encouraged to devote themselves to teaching. Their example, zeal and success aided by good salaries and conditions would permeate society. Local attachments, continuity of position and sense of mission meant the teacher was an agent of stability and an advertisement for individual achievement and respect within the existing order of society.[123]

After two years' effort, Cunningham was somewhat disappointed at the slow pace of development. A nationwide campaign to attract students to the normal schools failed: a paltry three pupils applied for admission.[124] In addition, Cunningham at the request of the Philadelphia public school controllers investigated the city schools. Appalled by the poor quality of monitors, poor attendance and small enrolments under the Lancasterian system, he called for a drastic reorganisation of the schools. There was no immediate effect although several years later Alexander Dallas Bache reassured him by sending the Report on the Organisation of a High School for Girls and a Seminary for Female Teachers. Some improvement had taken place. But that came too late for Cunningham. When the opportunity arose to succeed to the principalship of the new Glasgow teacher training institution he seized it. Even so his ideas were still widely disseminated throughout the United States since George Combe added to the account of his travels a considerable appendix on Cunningham and the Glasgow teacher training institute.[125] In addition, Cunningham returned on two occasions to America and maintained a correspondence with Henry

Barnard, the architect of the American teaching system in the last century. With the Disruption in 1843, Cunningham, though he had never held a charge since his ordination almost twenty years before, joined the Free Church. Ordained to Polmont, near Falkirk, he opened a school at his home which proved extremely successful. After aiding various Free Church educational groups, he retired to Edinburgh until 1859 when he returned to live in Stranraer where he died in 1883. As the *Connecticut Common School Journal* had stated in 1842, 'his views were greatly in advance of public opinion and liberality'.[126]

It is perhaps significant that Horace Mann visited Glasgow, in the aftermath of Cunningham's work.[127] Encouraged by William Ellery Channing, Mann arrived with Samuel Gridley Howe and his wife then on their honeymoon. After visiting Scottish schools, with Samuel and Julia Ward Howe (the authoress of the Battle Hymn of the Republic), Mann declared 'the most active and lively schools I have ever seen in the United States must be regarded as dormitories, if compared with the fervid life of Scottish schools: and by the side of theirs, our pupils would seem to be hibernating animals just emerging from their torpid states and as yet but half conscious of life and faculties'.[128] Though deeply impressed by the facilities for teacher training at Dundas Vale, Glasgow and elsewhere, Mann nevertheless felt that overall there was far too much rote learning and too little comprehension. But by 1843 matters had changed with the Disruption in Scotland and the beginnings of Manifest Destiny in America. In the previous decade Glasgow educational experiments had attracted considerable American interest and admiration. That spirit was best seen in Glasgow High School among the children of the more substantial citizens, and particularly in the teaching of Alexander J Dorsey.[129] Born at Haunchwood House, Nuneaton, he had been brought north by his father on the promise of a position of some consequence. But his patron reneged and his father's sporting character led him into various adventures, including apparently a coal business and coffee house which proved uniformly unsuccessful, before he died penniless in 1829. Dorsey, educated in both England and Scotland, was apprenticed to a Glasgow lawyer when he decided to enter Glasgow University in 1830. At the same time he appears to have begun teaching artisans on the south side of the city in order to meet his student fees. He seems to have been caught up in many of the optimistic intellectual currents of the day, accepting a somewhat optimistic theological view of man—perhaps under Owenite influence. Soon he had more than 300 pupils enrolled and his success encouraged further schools in the suburbs of Glasgow, but overwork took its toll. He went on a recuperative tour of Europe during which he visited the schools and other educational institutions of Prussia, Holland and France. Shortly after his return he was appointed teacher of English at Glasgow High School and began to formalise a department within the school, a radical innovation at the time.[130]

The town council who controlled the school had recently cut down the time allocated to classics to a mere two hours a day so that more time might be devoted to 'more useful and practical branches of education'.[131] For mathematics, science and physics had 'a direct relation to the commercial, manufacturing and engineering character of Glasgow'. In his English department, possibly the first in Britain, with the aid of an assistant, Dorsey taught nine classes of pupils whose ages ranged from four to twenty in 'useful knowledge of realities'.[132] By use of visual aids, anecdotes and original composition together with elocution, he stimulated interest in English literature and history. His aim was 'to implant a desire for scientific pursuits in after life'.[133] Inventiveness, creativity and intelligent appreciations of situations were essential in the new urban industrial society.

Dorsey extended his horizons—and his income—by going to the people. He had previously taught popular classes for ladies, evening and early morning classes as well as running a private school for ladies in Dunlop Street. He was also teaching at Croy Place Academy and taking in boarders as private students, including one from Trinidad and a Canadian. In addition, from 1836 his German wife gave private lessons.[134] But Dorsey came under the influence of James Simpson, the Edinburgh advocate who vigorously championed mechanics institutes. As a result of this phrenological influence, Dorsey abandoned corporal punishment, a regime which he confessed to have severely practised before 1834, and developed more inventive approaches to teaching. The effect was to massively increase his classes in the High School from a mere 11 in 1834 to 306 in 1839–40. For him education brought to fruition the religious and moral training of the home which were readily communicated through kindliness to a receptive audience rather than superficially and ineffectively imposed by threat of force. Sympathy eased the way of progress.

In that frame of mind, admired by Simpson and in correspondence with George Combe, Dorsey began to teach in various mechanics institutes which proliferated in Vale of Leven, Calton, Bridgeton and Mile End while his friend Simpson opened a well publicised institution at Murray's Caledonia Pottery works in Glasgow.[135] Dorsey also lectured in Forfar and Edinburgh on educational improvements. But under some pressure from the High School authorities for his alleged neglect of duties and his 'notions of physical, moral and intellectual education' he resigned as lecturer to the Calton, Mile End and Bridgeton Mechanics Institution.

Dorsey had established a reputation for himself. For a time he lived with a surgeon relative but his success enabled him to use his £500 a year salary to move from Regent Terrace to Kew Terrace and ultimately Dalbeth House. Both he and his first wife Ann, daughter of John Brook Samson of Berlin, considered emigrating to America. But Dorsey's developing interest in the Anderston Sanitary Association and the later foundation of the Glasgow Sanitary Association turned his attentions elsewhere. His second marriage to Lucy Georgina Irving, the daughter of the vicar of Ormesby, Yorkshire, seems to have encouraged his entrance to Corpus Christi Cambridge in 1846 and his ordination the following year when he established the church of St John, Anderston. It was significantly advertised as the church for the working class, though observers were sceptical. Enjoying some renown as a preacher Dorsey's ritualism proved too much for his bishop. Dogged by continuing ill health, he resigned from both his charge and the High School to settle in Madeira. There, after failing to establish a school for English children, he won recognition for his work in the cholera epidemic in 1854. After being decorated for his services, he continued to work in Madeira, returning to Cambridge in 1860 as the first lecturer in English history before going to the University of London as lecturer and then from 1884 to 1890 Professor of Elocution and Rhetoric. He died near Redcar in 1894.[136]

This remarkable man of varied talents attracted the attention of several influential American visitors like the Quaker abolitionists, the Motts, in 1840; Revd Robert J Breckinridge, the evangelical opponent of George Thompson; but above all, Alexander D Bache, the descendant of Franklin and recently appointed head of the new Girard College, Philadelphia in 1836–7.[137] Dorsey, an extremely cultivated man—he played the harp—was more than a very effective teacher. He was involved in many aspects of educational advancement. A willing supporter of David Stow and the Glasgow Infant School Society, he lectured to raise funds for that organisation and was to prove an extremely fascinating host to Bache, who was deeply impressed by his enthusiastic integrity. Bache, formerly professor of natural philosophy and chemistry at the University of Pennsylvania, was to return to America and spend some three years in the organisation of Philadelphia public schools. He was later to become superintendent of the United States Coast Survey, a regent of the Smithsonian and a vice president of the Sanitary Commission during the American Civil War. His large *Report of European Education,* which he published on his return, was to be extremely influential. Glasgow needless to say loomed large in that account but even more so in his private papers.

Dorsey brought Bache into contact with the phrenological wing of the educational reform movement. For he was an enthusiastic member of the Glasgow Phrenological Society, whose members included James Cleland, the renowned Glasgow statistician, Dr William Weir, surgeon at the Royal Infirmary and later lecturer in phrenology at the Andersonian University, Dr William Maxwell, the abolitionist and Dr Hunter of the anatomy department at the Andersonian university. But perhaps most significantly, the librarian and curator of the society was Revd David George Goyder.[138] Converted to Swedenborgianism by his brother Thomas, also a minister, Goyder had been closely associated with infant education in Bristol and Hackney before coming to Glasgow. He was very active in lecturing to mechanics institutes in Cowcaddens, Mile End, Calton, Bridgeton, Vale of Leven, Sunderland and Huddersfield. His brother, Thomas, had been president of the Norwich Mechanics Institute. Goyder was later to produce a *Phrenological Almanac* which circulated in the United States, leave Glasgow and become involved in the spiritualist—mesmerism and electro magnetism of the body—enthusiasms in the later nineteenth century. But in himself he indicates that thirst for unity and social harmony in a new form which pervaded the educational enterprise.

Dorsey, like Bache, was somewhat sceptical about the prevailing efforts at ethical education: 'To establish this excellency of conduct there ought to be religious instruction and moral training carried on as from infancy at home and at school. But was it so? Moral training at home was sadly neglected.'[139] The result was that parents, unwilling to give adequate personal, financial or moral support to the school expected it to correct 'to correct rude boisterous habits from years of ill regulated feelings'. The mother in particular had to be awakened to her responsibility in home training, a perennial theme in contemporary America: 'Until every child, rich or poor, passed through a rational infant school, not an intellectual forcing house: and until the educator was raised from his present shackled and despised conditions to his proper status in society as the equal of the clergyman, the physician and other professional men.' Significantly Dorsey was to be a leading figure in the formation of the Educational Institute of Scotland. Combe lavishly praised Dorsey's educational initiative while his success seems to have encouraged the foundation of the Glasgow Western Academy, whose prospectus emphasised the formation of character, absence of corporal punishment and its commitment to the whole education of soul, mind and body. In large measure it represented Pestalozzian ideals in practice: 'A pupil educated . . . in harmony with his own nature feels an interest in his studies unknown to those who are subject to an unnatural process.'[140] For Dorsey Christianity in its principles, ceremonies and social concerns appealed to the soul, mind and body. The individual and society were reconciled.

Bache spent several weeks in Glasgow in December 1836 and January 1837.[141] After examining the Irish educational system, he arrived with letters of introduction from William Rathbone of Liverpool to Andrew Bannatyne and Dorsey. Bache was concerned with every area of education, infants, mechanics, high school and university. In the process he met ministers, businessmen, reformers and some fellow Americans. In some ways he was an American answer to Mrs Trollope for he found Mr Neilson, the Gas Works entrepreneur and supporter of popular education, 'a common sort of man in his manners' and Hugo Reid, a lecturer at the Mechanics Institute, 'somewhat uncouth and conceited'[142] though that impression subsided when Reid was found to be intelligent. Bache dined with Mr Ledbetter, the president of the Mechanics Institute and businessman and councillor, John Cleland the statistician, the Wardlaw family, but above all with David Stow whom he had decidedly wished to meet.[143] In his diary Bache seems to have some reservations about the moral training system expounded by Stow as somewhat restricted, particularly the heavy emphasis on bible training which constituted one third or a quarter of the teaching. Stow also stressed singing as an essential ingredient of his system: it made a lasting impression on the children and guided them in their recreation out of doors. On visiting the schools in the Saltmarket under Mr Caughie, he was impressed by the superiority of the children in intellect, dress and cleanliness to those of Liverpool, Belfast or Wilderspin in London. On a visit to the juvenile school in the absence of Mr Auld he was less impressed: 'I saw more of the untrained Adam and less of the new morally trained child.'[144] Mr McCrie of the Glasgow Education Society particularly impressed him with his German experience: 'His views are so much more liberal than those of the party who have charge of their schools that I fear there will soon be some difference of opinion if he is firm.'[145] That Roman Catholics also sent their teachers for training at the schools was very encouraging. Stow was uneasy about the lack of the scriptures as such in the schools and considered the extracts inadequate but necessary, to please the Catholics. Clearly an integrated community was a possibility even allowing for such tensions.

Bache also met the professors of Glasgow University, including Professor Mylne, but perhaps his sense of ruffled pride at their disregard for his position, their age and unprepossessing appearance reduced the impression. He did show considerable interest in the Andersonian Institution and the Mechanics Institution. At the latter he was agreeably surprised to find an American from the Franklin Institute had signed in the visitors book before him. Reid however explained to him that the institute did not attract the mechanics but rather the shopkeepers. A twelve hour day for workers made them more likely to go to the theatre or drink. The same picture was supposedly true in the suburban mechanics institutes. Even so some 200 attended a chemistry class. To Bache the story was similar to his Philadelphia experience with the Franklin Institute. He was delighted with Mr Murray's Caledonia pottery factory: 'This is a quiet young man, an enthusiast in his desire to improve the condition of his operatives, labouring under the disappointment of a favourite scheme for combining school, society and church in one establishment. The failure essentially being caused as represented to me by his throwing himself upon the high church party for aid in a new scheme and meeting there no support.'[146] Nevertheless Murray's factory held a school for his employees' children, a library and reading room, lecture hall and even a Sunday sermon on the premises: 'This is his own *mutuum in parvo* and is supported by voluntary subscriptions of his own men.'[147] After further visits to manufacturers, attending the Peel dinner, and meeting Revd George Lewis, author of *Scotland A Half Educated Nation,* Bache left Dorsey and Glasgow with great regret. For Dorsey had accompanied him on many visits and entertained him frequently. Not surprisingly in Edinburgh, beside visiting the major schools, Bache spent much time with James Simpson, the advocate, educator and phrenologist. Together they visited the Edinburgh Infant school though Simpson proved 'an everlasting talker'.[148] Professor Pillans disappointed: 'Poor man he seems to have lost all spirit and reminds me of a sick chicken in appearance and demeanor.' Sherriff Wood and his school likewise did: 'Mr. Wood's manner is quite abrupt and coarse at times, and there is considerable admixture of kindness, it struck me in general as harsh. The rapidity and sternness mixed with occasional unbending has obviously been imitated by Mr. Thompson' (*sic,* the principal). With less imagination and poorer facilities like no playground, it did not compare with Stow's school. Apart from the Chambers brothers, Bache enjoyed the company of the Combe brothers, He however differed strongly from George Combe in theology and seems to have had misgivings about Simpson's idea of excluding proselytising religion from schools and his proposals to include anatomy, physiology and hygiene in the curriculum. The Scottish emphasis on science and utilitarian subjects to the detriment of classics was most striking. Even more striking was that Bache travelled back to America with none other than George Combe.

Bache returned to develop his interest in education. In May 1840 he succeeded the philanthropist John Griscom as president of the National Convention of the Friends of Education.[149] That body was the outcrop of the American lyceum movement which had increasingly become a pressure group in the interest of the common school and was to become in time a professional educators' lobby. Glasgow had taught its pupil well. For that body linked up with another Glasgow educational initiative.

The influence of Chalmers and the increasing conviction that education would solve social problems by enabling people to help themselves was further demonstrated in Henry Brougham's inaugural rectorial address at Glasgow University in 1825. It was a speech which was to inspire many Americans:

> No man of science needs fear to see the day when scientific excellence shall be too vulgar a commodity to bear a high price. The more widely knowledge is spread the more will they be prized whose happy lot it is to extend its bounds by discovering new truths or multiplying its uses by inventing new modes of applying it in practice.[150]

Glasgow graduates might elevate the quality of society by their 'bright example to other nations in a path yet untrodden by taking the lead of his fellow citizens—not in frivolous amusements, not in the degrading pursuits of the ambitious vulgar—but in the truly noble task of enlightening the mass of his countrymen . . . theirs will be the delight—theirs the triumph—who can trace the remote effects of their enlightened benevolence in the improved condition of their species and exult in the reflection, thus the prodigious change they now survey, with eyes that age and sorrow can make dim no more—of knowledge become pure—virtue sharing in the dominion—superstition trampled under foot—tyranny driven from the world—are the fruits, precious though costly and though late reaped, yet long enduring, of all the hardship and all the hazards they encountered here below.'[151] Evangelical zeal and enlightened liberality were united in a holy endeavour to uplift the masses. Common sense and community needs were one.

Glasgow was an appropriate setting for the speech. The city had played a pioneering role in popular adult education: the foundation of the Andersonian University in 1796 together with George Birkbeck's early involvement in the classes for working men, were initially free.[152] In later years the working men had taken matters into their own hands and established their own institutions in 1821.[153] Supported by benevolent employers, like the merchant and town councillor Ledbetter and Neilson of the Glasgow Gas Company, the Mechanics Institute flourished under Andrew Ure. With its emphasis upon useful scientific knowledge, its example spread with Birkbeck himself to London, to the founding of the Society for the Diffusion of Useful Knowledge and the University of London. Glasgow proved an inspiration to similar institutions in the west and rest of Scotland. American visitors were invariably impressed by the institution and sent back glowing reports of its success.

The American Lyceum was largely modelled on the Glasgow experience and established with the enthusiastic assistance of William Russell.[154] *The American Journal of Education* had printed considerable information about the Glasgow Mechanics Institute which Dr George Birkbeck had pioneered in Glasgow and which John Ure had expanded and improved with the aid of Glasgow businessmen. Further publicity followed Henry Brougham's efforts in London and his inaugural lecture as Rector of Glasgow University in 1825. The idea of diffusing useful knowledge among the masses was greatly encouraged by the Glasgow poet, Thomas Campbell, who was instrumental in the foundation of London University.

William Russell's friend, Josiah Holbrook persistently publicised the virtues of popular lyceum education.[155] Initially he hoped to diffuse popular knowledge within a good moral and political climate and so cheaply elevate Americans and aid the improvement of common schools. By 1829 Holbrook believed that lyceums would perform some eleven important functions: improve conversation; direct amusements to intelligent temperance ends; cheaply promote the intellectual and religious quality of the community; encourage the foundation and greater use of libraries; provide a seminary informal for teachers; benefit academies particularly of ladies; improve the character of local district schools; promote local history and local map-making; undertake local agricultural and geological surveys; and aid the state to gather a collection of minerals for the understanding and development of industry in the state.

The movement spread through the country.[156] Significantly John Latrobe, Abbot Lawrence and Mr Lowell who had all visited Glasgow were prominent in the early efforts. Professor John Nichol went to lecture in Lynn, Massachusetts lyceum in 1849 while Emerson lectured in Glasgow. Russell was very active in the foundation of the Boston Society for the Diffusion of Useful Knowledge and the Boston Lyceum. Russell also helped Holbrook to establish similar bodies in Pennsylvania from 1834. The education reformers in New Jersey, having suffered a setback in their efforts in 1831, founded a state lyceum at Princeton and used it to promote improved schooling throughout the state. With the foundation of a national lyceum association in 1831, Russell's friends, like the Unitarian Revd Orville Dewey and Professor W R Johnson, the educational historian, contributed to its publications. Another Glasgow admirer, John Griscom, the New York Quaker philanthropist, was its president for many years. Though Holbrook continued to build up support for the organisation within America and Scotland in a scheme of universal lyceums, the heyday was over in the 1840s. Its real importance lay in the fact that it created a climate favourable to the advancement of the common schools. In 1839 the American lyceum called for a national convention on public schools which met the following year under the presidency of Dr Alexander Dallas Bache, the head of Girard College, Philadelphia. It was the beginning of the divorce betweeen the public and the professionals in education.

Alexander Dallas Bache cast a very critical eye over the University of Glasgow. He was surprised, as was Francis Wayland of Brown University, that the University did not have a formal gathering for prayer. After meeting the principal and being introduced to some of the professors, Bache was given the 1826 report on Scottish Universities, a calendar and a copy of Cleland's Statistics. He attended some lectures which did not impress him: of Professor Meikleham of Natural Philosophy he wrote: 'I have never seen so old a gentleman so embarrassed, so diffident I should say if he were younger.'[157] At a second lecture the professor was even more embarrassed as the students were unable to solve the problem posed and did not seem to understand at all. Bache was however very impressed with Sir William Hooker and Professor Graham but equally surprised at the children of thirteen attending lectures in university. After attending the Peel celebrations Bache was clearly irritated at what he considered his less than adequate treatment. Wayland on the other hand was very impressed at the simplicity and successful training of large numbers of students particularly from modest homes unlike Oxbridge: 'when I reflect that this expenditure [at Oxbridge], if otherwise appropriated, would have given to Great Britain twenty universities instead of two'[158] he felt for the underprivileged poor. Above all, the kindness and courtesy of his Glasgow university hosts was most marked, as they explained the system of education to him.

A Glasgow visitor to American universities had a good impression. John M Duncan believed that American universities would prove better in any comparison with Glasgow. Glasgow students were admitted too young, 'exposed to the vice and allurements of a populous city' without supervision or any effort to form their moral character.[159] If the length of terms seemed less in Glasgow, a mere six as against nine months, in America, standards perhaps less exacting in Glasgow, the fees and expenses were far lower in Glasgow. With more competitive emulation in classes, Glasgow with Professor Jardine had considerable credit but at least Yale seemed to combine the best of English and Scottish universities.

Education narrowly construed was not the only concern of American visitors and reformers.[160] They were curious about the other forms of education; the asylum. David Rothman has demonstrated the proliferation of institutions dedicated to the reform and rehabilitation of their deviants or clients as part of an attempt to establish models for society. The properly conducted institution embodied the desirable principles of society. Asylums for the blind, deaf and indigent; juvenile reformatories; prisons; all such institutions prepared their residents for the larger world by acting as agents of stability. Containment and contentment were almost interchangeable concepts. Without going so far as some recent American revisionist historians and portraying the whole exercise as a form of 'intrusive' bourgeois regulation, there was undoubtedly an ambivalent, paradoxical mixture of cultural imperialism, concern and compassion.

To that outlook Glasgow contributed in the theory and practice of poverty and penal programmes. Chalmers is already known for his contribution but Patrick Colquhoun, former Virginia merchant and Lord Provost of Glasgow migrated to London where he wrote his *Treatise on Indigence* (1806). Though mainly concerned with the problems of poor law administration, he envisaged education as an excellent means of eliminating poverty by inculcating provident habits, temperance and social deference.

The essential conservative bias was obvious: 'science and learning if universally diffused would speedily overturn the best constituted government on earth. In contriving social efficiency, the poor as 'more orderly servants and better labourers, mechanics and handicrafts' would be checked in their profligacy, their propensity to join trade and political associations and remain away from the large unhealthy towns.[161] The state through the legislature 'the efficient guardian of the poor' would prevent human and material waste through education for the right social order.

America, as de Tocqueville and others would suggest, was renowned for her innovative penal methods.[162] But American historians have been reluctant to recognise the importance of Glasgow's bridewell under Mr Brebner as the most important efficient unit in Europe. Dr Stevenson Macgill had written his humanitarian *Thoughts on Prison* (1809). About the time Elizabeth Fry visited Glasgow, the city reformed its prison, so that Sir William Crawford, the British prison authority who visited America for a parliamentary commission, claimed that Glasgow had erected her model five years before the much vaunted Philadelphia prison.[163] Benjamin Tuckerman, Robert Breckinridge and I. MacClellan all visited the Glasgow and Edinburgh bridewell in their travels. J J Gurney found it exemplary in every way. Humanity and cheapness went together so successfully that the *Phrenological Journal* in 1827, in praising the Glasgow institution, looked forward to the day when 'all criminals may be regarded as patients'.[164] Brebner went even further by urging the institution of a special juvenile reformatory in 1829. Eddy, the New York Quaker merchant and philanthropist, closely followed Scottish social initiatives. John Griscom, another Quaker philanthropist of New York, besides inspecting educational establishments returned deeply impressed by the Glasgow bridewell as the finest and most efficient in the kingdom. If the Americans discovered the asylum during this period, it might be argued that it was largely a Scottish import.

But it must be admitted that American investigative tourists found Edinburgh prison impressive too: 'The construction and police of the penitentiary exceed anything of the kind I have seen in Europe'.[165] Visitors also went to see Glasgow's various asylums for the blind, deaf, the juvenile delinquent and the various refuges. Bache was impressed if a little daunted by the uncouthness of some Glaswegian reformers. R W McGavock in 1854 found these institutions particularly impressive especially those for the elderly.[166] Not surprisingly J M Duncan, a Glasgow graduate, reported that the New York orphanage was run by a Glaswegian and his wife.[167] Apart from the poor effort in lunatic asylum care, which appalled Dorothea Dix, the record was remarkable.[168] Custodial corrective reform and return to society as a model of new found virtue was the ideal. In principle it seemed to work.

There was a scientific base, a utilitarian bias which appealed to Americans. The object lesson expressed the Common Sense Philosophy and a scientific outlook. To understand the tangible and real, rather than the abstract, naturally encouraged scientific pursuits. Observation analysis and the integration of impressions into some greater whole was almost second nature.[169] Wilson the Paisley poet had spent his youth in natural observation to produce ultimately his great work on American ornithology. William Maclure a keen practical man undertook the first geological surveys of many areas. It may not be without significance that Bache was to become the United States surveyor general of coasts. Benjamin Silliman, a student of James Maclean the first professor of chemistry, came to Scotland and visited Glasgow to return to popularise literature and encourage Josiah Holbrook to embark on his popular educational career. One of Sir William Hooker's assistants, David Douglas, was to go to America to collect botanical specimens in 1823. The following year he returned to spend three years in the Canadian west and California. He then spent two further years in San Francisco sending back large numbers of specimens to the Royal Horticultural Society before going to Hawaii where he died in an accident. That scientific bias under Lord Kelvin was to grow in influence in America as we shall see, but the pattern was set.

By the 1840s and 1850s America seemed less interested in the early stages of education for children in other lands. That was partly attributable to the growth of American nationality, an American literature and an American schools system in most states. A free school system was established with organised districts, boards and state supervision. The principle of a freely accessible education at the basic level was firmly established as necessary and just. Though questions of religious teaching created difficulties, the system was extended to more states. Essentially the revolution had been quietly accomplished with Scottish assistance.

Americans and Glaswegians could recognise each other in education. Thomas Hamilton in New England found exactly the same principles in education as at home. He admired the school established by John Griscom in New York without corporal punishment as essentially Scottish. To Orville Dewey, the Ohio educator, the similarities between New England and Scotland were astonishing in their achievements and lack of recognition: 'A people in both instances, virtuous, religious, almost beyond example—carrying popular education to a point of improvement almost unexampled in the world till the Prussian system appeared and furnishing far more than their respective quotas to the noblest literature in their respective countries—would seem to have deserved more respect than has been awarded to Scotland or New England.'[170] With minimal resources but massive commitment, ingenuity and imagination the achievements had been considerable. Not every one agreed. John D Burn, the former Chartist turned temperance reformer, considered that American schools had encouraged foolish notions of social equality 'entertained by the most worthless members of society'. But his was a lonely voice. A sense of national identity and entrepreneurial ability if not social harmony had been established. Attention was now shifting to the higher levels of education. America needed universities to direct the nation's rich resources to effective ends—economic, social and personal. Once again, as we shall see, Glasgow provided not merely ideas but also personnel of no mean calibre.

The continuity of Scottish involvement in American education was apparent in the later nineteenth century. In January 1868 A Bronson Alcott sent William Russell a copy of the *Journal of Speculative Philosophy* which Thomas Davidson, 'a countryman of yours' had produced. Davidson, an Aberdeen university graduate, had been born in the northeast and emigrated to America. He was to greatly influence William Torrey Harris, the first national commissioner of education in the United States. Davidson first knew him as superintendent of schools in St Louis, and a firm close relationship developed.

In a larger way through libraries, Glasgow also contributed aid. The first librarian of what came to be the library of Congress was from the west of Scotland, whilst the Macmillan family from the area also built up a considerable publishing house in New York from after the Civil War.

The continuity of Scottish connections with Princeton was maintained by the appointment of James McCosh as president. He forms the link with the later civic progressive mentality which dominated American life around the early twentieth century. A Glasgow and Edinburgh graduate, McCosh had studied under Chalmers: his class ticket is one of the most interesting items in the McCosh papers. As J David Hoeveler has shown in his fine study of McCosh, there was a neo-puritan strain in his character which reconciled the enlightenment and evangelicalism. Hutcheson, Reid and Dugald Stewart were his Scottish philosophical mentors. They encouraged 'the will to believe', showed the moral and spiritual nature of man and inspired moral activity. That and Chalmers' influence made him disgusted with the squalor of Glasgow slums: 'The Glasgow professors may not have been directly responsible for the growing wickedness: but there was nothing in their teaching, moral or theological, adequate to the task of purifying the pollution coagulating all around them.'[172]

That outlook governed his views at Princeton. At Glasgow University he had been disappointed at the gap between the university and religion, and had found piety and intellect with Revd David Welsh in practical Christian activity. He therefore sought to integrate religion and what later would be called 'the forward movement'. Hardly radical but aware of contemporary intellectual developments, McCosh sought to bridge the gap between higher education and religion. Both inspired a higher sense of duty and social responsibility. Through a growing understanding of life, religion was positively enhanced. In virtually every area of life was a tendency 'to rise to higher states'. For him the university was to be permeated by an informal Christian spirit. To that end he brought Moody and Sankey to Princeton in 1876 to promote a firm revival. An inspirational university experience was to lay the broad philosophical and intellectual basis for the rules and standards which govern professions. Utility and Christianity were somehow combined in this apostolate of civic amelioration and service. That was the legacy of Scottish educational influence.

Glasgow had assisted what might have been described as a shopkeeper's millenium. The loss of control, status, self esteem of many influential groups and families had been repaired. As with the Mechanics Institutions in Britain, 'The object of this general diffusion of knowledge is not to make men discontented with their lot—to make the peasant yearn to become an artizan or the artizan dream of the honours and riches of a profession—but to give the means of content to those who for the most part, must necessarily remain in that position which requires great self denial and great endurance.'[173] Or as another British observer said of them and their lectures on political economy, 'By such means they not only keep up a system devoted to the aggrandisement of wealth, but they pervert the minds of the rising generation.'[174] Notions of radical reconstruction of society were contained and the masses integrated into an ideology of great expectations.

Chapter Three

Gentle Persuasion

The Influence of Women

The influence of American feminist reformers on Glasgow and of Glasgow on the course of American feminism is a largely neglected field of study. That neglect can be explained in various ways. To some extent the good respectable ladies endorsed causes like temperance and prohibition which are unfashionable in our day. They were often part of an Anglo-Saxon Protestant cultural consensus which as we have seen was confident in its unassailed dominance in the nineteenth century. That is no longer the case. Their enthusiastic confidence in the progresses of mankind through education and good will was rudely destroyed in the First World War. The almost religious enthusiasm with which they disseminated their humanitarian concern throughout the world was checked. That expansive frame of mind gave way in the 'twenties and later to more withdrawn, inward looking self-concern. Armed ideologies and protective tariffs replaced these open, optimistic feminine views. Now in the aftermath of the women's liberation, perhaps male historians, in particular, should pay some more gentlemanly attention to these neglected ladies.

The American lady visitors to Glasgow fall into five main interest groups: anti-slavery advocates; woman suffragists; social settlement workers; temperance crusaders; and radical social and political militants. To each of these diverse groups Glasgow provided a warm welcome. It seemed like an American city: even the city plan had an American grid-like appearance. With their similar ethnic and intellectual background within a shared religious sentiment, Americans could feel very much at home. Filled with and ably administered by self made men, Glasgow seemed more democratic, less aristrocratic; more reassuring and less warped by affectations of superiority than othe areas of Britain. As Emma Willard, the educator, observed in conversation, Scotsmen made a woman feel like a human being rather than an ornament. The apparently fluid nature of Glasgow society paralleled American urban experience; the dominance of a middle class, imbued with a strong democratic religious, or perhaps, a strong religious democratic sense, was right and fitting. Even the university was actively involved in urban life: Professor Edward Caird for example, was an enthusiastic supporter of higher education for women. It was not remote or aloof.

Glasgow was a living, vibrant organism. This European industrial city state reassured the emergent commercial and industrial power of America, just as America's achievements bolstered Glasgow's social democratic impulses.

Women on both sides of the Atlantic had been very involved in the new popular education movement in the early nineteenth century.[1] To Joanna Baillie, the literary daughter of the Glasgow professor of divinity, to Fanny Wright, the niece of another, and to Elizabeth Pease who was to marry another, education was part of a general strategy for infusing society with a new moral purpose. Joanna Baillie encouraging the social experiments of Benjamin Tuckerman, and Elizabeth Hamilton spreading Pestalozzian ideas, or Mrs Laggan supporting American hopes of cultivation, were important transmitters of culture in the Atlantic world.[2] To nineteenth-century American ladies who arguably lived in an English cultural province, Glasgow as a vibrant provincial 'capital' had special appeal. It combined the mediaeval ideal of the city state with the romanticism of Scott and with the most advanced engineering and industrial skills of the day. That held irresistible appeal to American feminists.

The Glasgow connection demonstrated the tension within American reformers. The majority sought to promote family stability. An educated, morally informed womanhood might exercise untold influence for social stability through her family and through her children, the future of the nation. They naturally campaigned against drink, war and slavery and demanded the enfranchisement of women. With the strong religious overtone these crusades were eminently respectable, yet at the same time they were strongly feminist. As the radical Charlotte Perkins Gilman argued, war, drunkenness, wage and chattel enslavement were essentially male creations. Woman suffrage meant a purer, healthier and more harmonious society. By the early twentieth century it meant the protection of the woman and child worker in the interests of national social efficiency. In general these reformers were more concerned with the humane ethical operation of the existing social system rather than any radical reconstruction.

The minority of feminine reformers were somewhat different. To the two main exponents, Frances Wright and the Nichols, a new sexual mentality was needed. Rather than the limited contemporary prudish treatment of sex, they wanted a forthright honest appreciation of the nature of sex. Frances Wright, an epicurean, wanted the right of the woman to say 'yes' well established whilst the Nichols wanted the right to say 'no' recognised. Both wanted the woman to be responsible for her own body and both arrived at that conclusion by a different path. For Wright, in association with Robert Dale Owen, published materials on contraception in *The Free Inquirer*. The discussion they produced in America was further developed by Owen's *Moral Physiology*.[3] A new view of sexual relations meant education, and a reconstructed economic order. All men and women would be equal within the just society. Their views were to remain influential through the late nineteenth century. Attacks on planned parenthood and abortion increased. Beginning with the New York law of 1829 and culminating in the Comstock laws in 1873 when Congress passed a law against 'any article or thing designed or intended for the prevention of conception or procuring an abortion', moralists and professional medicine united against these ideas. Mrs Woodhull and her associates, including G F

Train the entrepreneur who had failed to win Glasgow Corporation approval for his electric tramways, continued the campaign.[4] Scottish visitors to New York found abortion freely available and advertised in the newspapers. One of the involved in these activities, Rose Witcop, was to be closely associated with Guy Aldred the Glasgow anarchist. Sexual radicalism and social radicalism were closely associated.

Mary Gove and Thomas Low Nichols were two remarkable figures in the women's amelioration campaign. Mary Gove Nichols, a New Englander, had been deeply involved in the American health reform movement from the 1830s. She was the first woman to publicly lecture to women on physiology in Boston in 1837. After her unhappy marriage she became even more committed to the cause to 'scientific' diet, water cure and to sex education. She then met Thomas Low Nichols whom she married and together they formed their own health establishment in New York. Moving west to Ohio they formed a model community before they were converted to Catholicism. Both had been interested in the spiritualist craze which swept New York and they remained dedicated to notions of spiritual communication and cure throughout the rest of their lives which from 1861 were passed in Britain. Their numerous books, pamphlets and leaflets on sexual health and hygiene enjoyed a wide circulation which was reinforced by their health establishment Malvern and by lecture tours. In addition Nichols also founded a shortlived journal in Glasgow. His ideas of diet and hygiene appealed to temperance advocates. His vegetarianism appealed to moral reformers. In total he and his wife were advocates of scientific paths towards respectability. Abstinence from sex, meat, tobacco and other stimulants; the use of cheap nourishing foods, natural foods including one of the earliest breakfast cereals; regular exercise and fresh air were all part of a respectable well ordered life.

In many ways the Nichols represented a compromise between the American extremes of Mormon polygamy and Shaker total abstinence from sex. They illustrated the social changes which had occurred: women had an institutionalised sphere. With an increasingly demanding role in the nurture of children women found sympathy, compassion and a structured way of life in health crusades. In the absence of adequately trained doctors in America, faced with the heroic idea of medicine by an all-male profession, women naturally found attractions in the Nichols prescription. In an age of excessive child-bearing, Nichols plea for self control, sublimation and responsibility offered benefits to the woman. She had rights. Her husband had responsibilities and duties towards her as a person rather than a sexual object. By preparing suitable 'moral' foods for the husband's diet the woman could contain the lustful male. Improved education, especially in sexual matters, was vital: 'For the sake of the race I ask that it be done for the woman what can be done, for it is our awful truth that fools are the mothers of fools.' In the process, while perhaps not offering liberation in the modern sense, Nichols showed a means of respectability: restraint, education and consideration. Woman could contribute to the sense of middle-class respectability and provide a model for others to follow, including her own children. In a somewhat compassionate view of marriage, sexual restraint uplifted the poor from poverty, provided savings, more sophisticated interest, and concerns with a higher ideal. Sex and lower urges were sublimated and channelled into constructive and economically productive ends.

The feminist antipathy to the prevailing male-dominated world found expression in other ways. Mrs Nichols with her health reforms; Mrs Soule, the American Universalist preacher and missionary, and Emma Hardinge, the spiritualist were also advocating forms of denying male dominance. The Nichols approach indicted the unsympathetic male medical profession. Only when Mrs Elizabeth Blackwell, the first American woman doctor, returned to her native Britain did the medical profession begin to feel a little embarrassed.[5] Her father had been a religious dissenter in Bristol devoted to the abolition of slavery, to temperance and equal rights. She had come under Scottish influence when Thomas Chalmers stayed a few days in their home, and she recalled that her earliest memories included Revd Henry Craik, the Scottish evangelist and the lectures of Fanny Wright. After years of struggle she qualified as a doctor and began to preach *The Religion of Health*.[6] The influence of the earlier phrenologists and writers were apparent: health 'depends on all the laws of our complex nature; it applies to the mind as well as the body. A deteriorating influence which proceeds from within is more to be dreaded than one that comes from without.'[7] Health was simply morality and competence. The health of the educated woman was the key to the nation. Significantly in the wake of the municipal enfranchisement of women she was urging 'a more decided educational effort . . . to show our voters how the town council really represented in modern days much of the practical action of the church in past ages, and that it ought really to present the Theocratic idea—i.e. government by the Highest Good'.[8] Her views held appeal in Glasgow. She often spent her holidays at Kilmun in her declining years and came to know many locals, eventually dying and being buried there.[9]

Emma Hardinge likewise was born in England but emigrated to America.[10] An accomplished child pianist, she had gone on the stage and then moved to New York in 1855. In the process she became a spiritualist of some considerable renown, associated with Garrison, Robert Dale Owen and others. Politically she was also active on behalf of Abraham Lincoln in California. After the Civil War she made two visits to Britain and then in 1867 came to Scotland.[11] She came to Glasgow under the auspices of the Glasgow Spiritualist association and gave several addresses. Whatever the validity of her claims, she was rejecting the traditional male-dominated Christian church and experiencing personal status, freedom and respect in her own right as a person. Several Theosophists from America also came over to Glasgow Miss Shaw, presumably the suffragist leader, and Mrs Armour, the temperance lecturer.[12] Miss Shaw was a doctor *and* a preacher. The radical implications were clear.[13]

The two attitudes associated women doctors, women ministers and what might be loosely termed anti-male crusades against drink war and sexual demands. Given the vote and a truly independent sense of identity, women would transform the unjust male-dominated society. How effective were these campaigns?

Harriet Beecher Stowe was the most renowned visitor of the mid nineteenth century. In 1852 she published *Uncle Tom's Cabin.* Within eight months more than a million copies were sold. Stage and musical version quickly followed. She had become an overnight celebrity. By appealing to sentimental humanity, Mr Stowe had awakened more support for the abolitionist cause. The new Glasgow anti-slavery association had invited her to come to Britain as a token of their appreciation. Glasgow had a long tradition of support for the abolition of slavery, and her reception was rapturous and exhausting. Everywhere she found 'earnest eager friendly faces ever so many'. She received delegations from all over Scotland and from Ireland. She was taken round the sights of Glasgow, down the Clyde to Helensburgh and to tea with some 2000 guests: as she wrote, 'I could not help wondering if old mother Scotland had put 2,000 teaspoonfuls (*sic*) for the company and one for the pot as in our good Yankee custom.' Little wonder she was worn out.[14]

Her visit made abolition somewhat more respectable and popular. By associating with the great and titled aristocracy of Britain she made her cause acceptable. But to the industrial workers and displaced Highlanders, Mrs Stowe and her crusade were merely diversions from pressing social evils at home. A Scots weaver who had worked on a southern plantation believed that factory conditions in Scotland were far worse. Her praise of the Highland Clearances as 'a sublime example of progress' drew down the wrath of many, including Donald McLeod, a Sutherlandshire stonemason. Strongly opposed to slavery, he bitterly attacked the support of the Duchess of Sutherland for the Stowe visit: 'the shortest process of civilisation in the history of nations . . . the whole interior of the county of Sutherland . . . in eight years converted to the solitary wilderness.'[15]

If her visit exposed the social tensions within Scottish society, Mrs Stowe also showed the divisions within the Glasgow abolitionists. She did not meet the Garrisonians like William Smeal but she met the more conservative gradualists like Revd Ralph Wardlaw and Bailie William P Paton, her host. Thereafter, she seemed to spend her time with the high and mighty outside the main abolitionist groups in Britain. Her visit merely highlighted awareness of defects at home and abroad.

Earlier in 1840, the American Quakers, Lucretia Mott and her husband, attended the World Anti-Slavery Convention in London. Unfortunately attempts to seat women at the gathering were defeated.[16] Some twenty-four Glasgow delegates were in attendance including William Smeal, the Quaker tea merchant and editor of *The Friend,* who was deeply suspicious of the American Hicksite Quaker visitors. After this rebuff the Motts went up to Glasgow where they were welcomed by the local Unitarian minister, Revd George Harris, who gave them the use of his church for a meeting since they had been disowned by Smeal and his fellow Glasgow Quakers.[17]

The Motts stayed up three flights on Argyll street and were astonished by the height of Glasgow Building. They were amazed by the activity, large numbers of people walking, the scarcity of servants, and the sight of women both drawing heavy wheelbarrows and carrying heavy burdens on their backs.[18] They walked through the Necropolis and were appalled by the crowded poor in Rotten Row. After visiting George Combe in Edinburgh, the Motts then went on a tour through the Trossachs and Loch Lomond. On their return to Glasgow they attended an anti-slavery meeting but the women were voted down from speaking. With George Harris and Hedderwick, the Unitarian printer, they established good relations as well as with Mr D'Orsey, the master at the High School (see above). At the continued meeting of the anti-slavery society, the local Chartists took over, and Lucretia Mott was impressed 'that they could be heard to speak for their own poor'.[19] Later when they met Revd Patrick Brewster of Paisley they were very impressed by the moral force of his Chartism. The Motts were clearly identified with the Garrisonian wing of the American abolitionist movement. The visit to Glasgow of Garrison himself, Elizabeth Cady Stanton and the fund raisers for Oberlin College further contributed to the growing tension with the Glasgow Emancipation Society. The more conservative wing was being pressurised by the more radical members like George Gallie who produced John A Collins' *Right and Wrong among the Abolitionists of the United States* in 1841. Collins had come over as a representative of the Garrison wing of the abolitionist movement. The Garrison faction saw the abolitionist crusade as part of a larger reconstruction of society.[20] The more limited strategy was associated with the Tappan brothers of New York. Strongly evangelical, they concentrated all their energies on slavery as *the* evil. Anything which alienated potential support to them seemed irresponsible. As Duncan Rice has shown, these complex divisions were imported into the Scottish anti-slavery camp. As in America, dissension led to formal division and in Scotland to eclipse. Collins then came to spread the Garrison version of abolitionism with rather mixed results until Miss Elizabeth Pease, the daugher of a Quaker banker from Darlington, gave him her full support.[21] She and the Motts were well acquainted and stood on the same firm principles.[22] Elizabeth Pease also knew the Grimke sisters and Elizabeth Cady Stanton, who were all redoubtable abolitionists so that she was able to bring an American feminist view to her Glasgow home, the Observatory, on her marriage.[23] One of the most active anti-slavery campaigners in Glasgow, she married Professor John Pringle Nichol of Glasgow as his second wife in 1853.[24] She was a woman suffragist, a sympathiser with Mazzini and Kossuth, and not unfavourably disposed towards radical Chartist demands: 'It appears to me that they ask nothing more than what accords with the grand principle of the natural equality of man—a principal (*sic*) alas! almost buried beneath the rubbish of the hereditary aristocracy and the farce of state religion—the natural consequences of which are the love of patronage in the *great,* power in the great—the domination of the few over the many and the destruction of the rights of the great mass of the people.' That reflected her close relationship with the radical abolitionists, William Lloyd Garrison and Wendell Phillips. She might have been writing as an American Jacksonian Democrat.

She brought radical abolitionism reinforcement in Glasgow. She had been active in anti-slavery work from the 1830s. The daughter of a wealthy philanthropist, her uncle Edward Pease was 'the father of railways' and her cousin the first Quaker MP, Mrs Nichol had played a leading role in developing British support for the radical abolitionists. Where Smeal and others had misgivings she had been positively encouraging: she had already written vigorous pamphlets supporting the immediate abolition of slavery. She strongly supported John Anderson Collins, the general agent of the Massachusetts Anti-slavery Society, in his radical tour of Britain. During his visit he met Robert Owen who seems to have converted him to even more radical views. In July 1841 he wrote to Elizabeth Pease that the slavery of the industrial working class had risen from 'out of the system of exchange by which one class of men can secure the fruits of the poor labourer without returning him an equivalent'.[25] With the later radical visitor Henry C Wright she also enjoyed a close relationship. She met Pringle at a water cure though he had also lectured in Darlington; after the marriage their home became a radical centre in Scotland. After her husband's death she went to Edinburgh and continued her activities. Significantly, her stepson Professor John Nichol, the first professor of English in the University of Glasgow, was to be one of the lights of liberalism, visit America and write the first comprehensive study of American literature.[26]

John Pringle Nichol had pursued a successful academic career at Aberdeen and Glasgow Universities. With a considerable reputation in astronomy he had been invited to America in 1847-8 where he gave two lectures at the Salem, Massachusetts, Lyceum among other places.[27] Associated with Edward Everett, the distinguished editor of the *North American Review,* governor of Massachusetts (1835-9) and then president of Harvard University (1846-9), Nichol had a very good insight into American life. As William Lloyd Garrison wrote to Elizabeth Pease, 'Surely Professor Nichol must have possessed the noblest qualities and soul to have excited in you such admiration and love.'[28] John Nichol grew up in a radical-liberal household with a strong American influence. Garrison and Frederick Douglass, the former slave, were close friends so that Nichol could introduce a former Glasgow student, Professor James Bryce, and Albert Dicey to the abolitionists.[29] He would later send letters of reference for Glasgow figures and for Emily Faithfull, the feminist editor of the Victoria Press.[30] In 1865 he visited America and after meeting with Garrison and Wendell Phillips, the radical abolitionists, he spent three days with Longfellow the poet. Garrison informed his step mother: 'He is so well pleased with what he has seen in America that he thinks of returning again with a view to lecturing on various subjects.'[31]

By the time Nichol's book appeared in 1882, American ladies had already made further sorties upon Glasgow. Nichol favoured the university extension movement, the democratisation of education. His colleague, Professor Edward Caird, actively supported higher education for women and the movement for female suffrage. Scottish women made two significant gains in 1881, with the passage of the Married Women's Property Act (Scotland) and the Municipal vote to the Women Householders of Scotland Act. To maintain the pressure for votes for women and Scottish National Demonstration of Women was held in St Andrew's Hall, Glasgow, on 3 November 1882. Among the guest speakers was Elizabeth Cady Stanton.[32] Elizabeth Cady Stanton was an outstanding figure in the movement of American woman suffrage. Born in New York State, she was nurtured by a Scottish nursemaid, reared on Scottish religion and letters at the hands of Revd Simon Hosack, a Glasgow graduate, minister of Johnstown for almost fifty years.[33] Imbued with the literary ideas of Scott, Burns and the philosophy of Dugald Stewart, she attended the 1840 World Anti-Slavery Convention in London. At that meeting, women were neither permitted to speak nor treated as equals. It was to be a turning point in Anglo-American feminist history. Stanton then travelled north to visit the Burns country and Abbotsford and to spend some twelve hours alone on Ben Nevis.[34] It was over forty years before she returned to Glasgow.

In the interim, she had established her reputation as a leading suffragist. In 1848 the Seneca Falls meeting in New York State demanding not merely equal suffrage but also social equality. Equality before the law, equal educational opportunity and sexual rights naturally followed: 'Man in his lust has regulated long enough this whole question of sexual intercourse.'[35] To Stanton, woman in marriage surrendered everything including the right to her own person.[36] Marriage increasingly to feminists seemed little more than legalised prostitution.[37] The later progressive reformers might take a similar view though they would emphasise the departure from traditional feminine roles.[38] Women according to this view were in need of greater protection, though the real motive allegedly was to impose certain controls on private and personal behaviour in an increasingly anonymous urban environment.[39] That may partly explain the concern but the result was to exercise control within and without the home over the male. It was part of another Scottish American revolution.

The argument is not so much about the difference between feminism and domesticity as a demand for a common equal moral standard for both sexes. The proliferation of prostitution together with a white slave traffic from Glasgow to America was a fact.[40] Traditional moral machinery seemed inadequate to the task. In mid-nineteenth century that coincided with the emergence of popular health notions.[41] As already suggested these ideas had considerable impact upon the temperance movement but to some feminists they had even greater appeal. By controlling the diet, the appetite for matters sexual might similarly be curtailed. Partly puritan, partly in self defence in view of the high mortality rates in child birth or the ruined health thereafter, the appeal was considerable.

The main American exponents of these notions came to Glasgow in mid century to spread them. Thomas Low and Mary Gove Nichols, as we have seen, were tremendous publicists in the cause. The Fowlers who had already produced their *Amativeness: or Evils and Remedies of Excessive and Perverted Sexuality* (New York 1848), a ferocious attack on matrimonial excesses, and who were to produce their 1052-page *Creative and Sexual Science* in 1870, allegedly rated 'next to their Bible' by 100,000 women, also came to lecture.[42] Even more significantly, the English-born Bible Christian, Revd William Metcalfe, MD came to Glasgow in 1856. A leading member of the American Physiological Association, an educator associated with William Alcott, and a water cure enthusiast, he addressed the ninth annual meeting of the Vegetarian Society in the city. His audience included Davie of Dunfermline and representatives from Paisley, Motherwell, Beith, Dumfries and Edinburgh. Having abstained from flesh meat for some forty-six years, thirty-nine in America, and with a family of vegetarians, he considered health and temperance in all things went together. These individuals were indicative of a silent revolution which was taking place within the home. However repressive and conservative some historians may consider the cult of domesticity, women were slowly being freed from excessive child bearing, from the deadly dangers of childbirth and the early onset of old age. Initially these changes would affect the more well-to-do wives and pave the way for their activity in temperance in the 1870s, their demands for greater educational opportunities at university level and for entry to the professions. The revolution within the marriage bed was perhaps more significant than generally believed.

By 1900, women were the centre of concern in a transatlantic debate over the future of the Anglo-Saxon world. Women themselves were concerned with their self-image amid the technical changes in an increasingly complex urban industrial world. To political and religious figures the home was the first and last bulwark of civilisation. They vigorously condemned divorce, contraception and anything remotely salacious. They toughened laws against abortion. Conservative thinkers and most women reformers could agree on idealised women uplifting the inhabitants of the home through her peculiar moral quality. Better-built homes in a pleasanter environment meant better, happier families and a more efficient society.[44] The passage of the Comstock Law 1873 which effectively barred contraceptive information and materials from the American mails also contributed to the suppression of anything remotely risqué. Historians often forget that leading progressive figures were associated with boards of censorship and prohibitionist committees: F C Howe and Revd Washington Gladden are but two cases in point.[45] The woman was the future. The debate was over the nature of that future.

The old roles and expectations were neither as predictable nor as acceptable as before to women. The decline in the birth rate in both countries was marked in the latter half of the nineteenth century. In Britain the annual rate dropped from 35.5 births per thousand in 1871 to 23.9 per thousand in 1913. In the United States the drop was from 25.6 per thousand in 1860 to 19.2 per thousand in 1890.[46] That change, as Daniel Scott Smith has persuasively argued, was central to opening up the choices available to the average woman.[47] The focusing of attention upon the married couple elevated the idea of conjugality in the family structure. The romantic cult of childhood may have encouraged the decline of fertility: the emphasis was now upon quality rather than quantity. Women were able to assign meaning to themselves and their work within or without the home. Though feminist historians have seen domesticity as the antithesis of the movement toward selfhood, in fact positive advances accrued through the cult of domesticity. Woman began to control her reproductive capacity: sexual restraint served the needs of the market place and self interest. From this form of sexual bartering women gained greater freedom. Change took place first within the family and then within the wider world. The wife and mother image merged into a person and citizen viewed as an integrated whole. The temperance and social purity movements were part of the assertion of the decisive role of the woman within the family and within the larger society. Both aspects had an anti-male element, a critique of the male double standards of the day. In the Atlantic Woman's world new views followed.

Self conscious woman may have become, but the society was increasingly concerned with the future of the race, the dominant class or cultural values and the nation.[48]

When Elizabeth Cady Stanton returned to Glasgow in 1882, the position of women was considerably altered. The Glasgow ladies, encouraged by the militant temperance women of Ohio, had followed their lead in organising the Scottish Women's Temperance Association prayer union. Mrs 'Mother' Stewart of Ohio together with Mrs Parker of Dundee, Miss Mary White, the secretary of the Glasgow Ladies Prayer Union, Miss Bryson, and an American missionary's wife, Mrs Boardman, brought the Glasgow ladies out of their drawing rooms into the political arena.[49] Travelling throughout Scotland, Mrs Stewart aroused ministers and still more ladies to temperance activity.

At the same time, women were beginning to enter American colleges and universities on equal terms and to found major female institutions like Bryn Mawr. Wellesey and others. Dilke's idea of a Greater Britain seemed to be coming a reality.[50] Professor Edward Caird of Glasgow University was encouraging the higher education of women and the movement for female suffrage. At the same time Scottish women made two significant gains in 1881 with the passage of the Married Women's Property Act (Scotland) and the grant of the municipal vote to Women Householders of Scotland Act. To celebrate and to maintain the pressure for full suffrage a Scottish National Demonstration was held in St Andrew's Halls Glasgow on 3 November 1882. Among the guest speakers was Mrs Elizabeth Cady Stanton.

The president of the National Woman's Suffrage Association, the somewhat more radical of the two major women's organisations in America, Mrs Stanton was an appropriate choice for the occasion. Flattered by the attentions of Professor Caird, and by her room in the best hotel in the city, she reported 'it was indeed a grand affair as far as the size of the audience went; but in our country we should not have considered the speaking up to the occasion. As you will wish to know what I did, I have only to say that I was complimented on having made the best speech of the evening; but it was by no means up to what I have often done. However, it was given smoothly and without notes. A Scotch lady and one from Ireland spoke lauding their respective countries and firing bombshells into English policy, to which the audience responded with wild enthusiasm. I was astonished, for in America you never hear such wholesale criticisms of England. When Mrs. Craigen said "England never conquered Scotland, we gave them a king" the audience just shouted, rose to their feet and waved their handkerchiefs all over the house, all those on the platform rising and waving and waving until their arms ached. I waved with the rest.'[51] It was the first time Mrs Stanton had ever spoken in public in the old world.

The return of Mother Stewart in 1891 and the advent of Frances Willard in 1893 further strengthened the woman's public commitment to temperance and related reforms (see below). But the most formidable lady visitor, Carry Nation,[52] came in 1908–9. Such was her impact that a railway engine which ran through the buffers at Queen Street Station, Glasgow, was nicknamed 'Carry Nation'.[53] She believed in direct action. She went beyond picketing the saloon like the Ohio ladies to invading the illegal bars. Her most famous exploit was in 1900 in Wichita, Kansas where she smashed a saloon to pieces with a hatchet. On arrival in Glasgow she declared that Scotland was far nearer hell than Kansas. Mobbed on her arrival at Queen Street station, she had to make her exit through the North British Hotel where she denounced a barmaid in forthright manner. *The Glasgow Herald* reported that at a meeting with the Glasgow magistrates, in the course of an argument, a cigar and cigarette case was hurled into the fire. In Paisley she told her audience that a mother might legitimately shoot a man supplying her son with drink. Her meeting in Glasgow predictably was marked by considerable disorder. Unabashed she went south to continue her wild foray in London.

Temperance and suffrage remained inextricably entwined. The Glasgow-born WCTU lecturer, Deborah Knox Livingstone from Bangor Maine, appeared many times in her native city between 1900 and 1920. In America besides her temperance activity she was a vigorous campaigner for woman suffrage. In 1915 her persuasive address to the West Virginian conference of the Methodist Episcopal Church helped the passage of a resolution favourable to woman suffrage. She also helpèd in New Hampshire campaigns. Her major effort, however, was in her home state of Maine. In 1916–17 she was the state organiser for the campaign to put pressure on the state legislature to secure voting rights for women. Encouraged by a personal message from President Woodrow Wilson, she threw herself wholeheartedly into the struggle. Some 500 meetings were held, often addressed by leading national figures like Mrs Carrie Catt an others. The clergy of all denominations each received three separate circulars. Some 1.5 million pieces of propaganda were distributed and Mrs Knox Livingstone herself gave 150 addresses, collected $4000 and travelled 20,000 miles. All to no avail: the measure was defeated by some 18,000 votes. Prejudice, the unfortunate militant image of some women and the failure to get out the rural vote, according to Mrs Knox Livingstone, ensured the result. Two years later although both houses of the state legislature approved the idea, the measure was defeated at the polls. Only the ratification of the nineteenth amendment to the federal constitution was to enfranchise women in Maine and throughout the United States in 1920.[54]

Scottish women were contributing to the formation of an international woman's suffrage movement.[55] Temperance women were again to the fore. In 1882 Mrs Parker of Dundee, president of the Scottish section of the British Women's Temperance Association, attended the first International Convention of Women in 1882. Four years later she addressed the New York

State Woman's Suffrage Association.[56] The gathering at the Chicago World's Fair, 1893, attracted further contracts and early in the twentieth century Miss Chrystal MacMillan, who raised the issue of woman suffrage before the House of Lords judiciary committee in 1908, attended the International Suffrage Alliance meetings in Amsterdam, 1908, London 1909, Stockholm 1911, Budapest 1913 and Geneva 1920. At the last one she was voted on to the board. Such occasions were invariably graced with a strong American delegation including leaders like Jane Addams and Charlotte Perkins Gilman.[57]

The social welfare reformers and social settlement workers were less obtrusive. In 1855, Dorothea Dix, the pioneer reformer on behalf of the mentally ill, visited Glasgow and other parts of Scotland.[58] Though very impressed by the excellent standard of public mental institutions, she was deeply distressed by the conditions prevailing in private institutions. Welcomed by Professor D Y Simpson of Edinburgh University, she exercised enormous influence in a short space of time. In less than a fortnight she was instrumental in the establishment of two government commissions to investigate mental health in Scotland generally, and to consider conditions in Musselburgh hospital in particular. Two American gentlemen subsequently came to assess the Scottish approach to mental health. E C Wines, a major American authority on institutional care, a member of New York Prison Discipline Association, was an innovator in his time in his wish to return prisoners and other confined persons to the community as soon as possible with suitable safeguards and supervision.[59] Like Frank B Sanborn, Massachusetts charity commissioner and literary man, Wines visited insane hospitals of Scotland and was particulary impressed by the cottage system of treatment.[60] If Cupar and Lenzie impressed them, Julia C Lathrop, the settlement house worker, did even more so. On a visit to Carstairs in 1898, she found the contrast with American experience marked. With Dr John Frazer, the commissioner in lunacy and Mr T W L Spence, the secretary to the commission, she found the cottages well furnished and well supervised. About a fifth of the total insane Scottish population were housed or boarded out in this humane and economical way. Above all the relative freedom and placidity of the patients in these surroundings was astonishing. America could well imitate them.[61] An integrated community with a moral oversight was the ideal.

The settlement house idea captured something of that flavour. Originating in Toynbee House, London, that example was followed in Glasgow and the United States.[62] Jane Addams, the renowned driving spirit of Hull House, Chicago, showed great interest in Glasgow.[63] On a tour in Europe in 1883 she had arrived, like so many visitors, in pouring rain. Her tour through Scotland proved rewarding if somewhat damp. At Loch Ness 'in the morning it rained as I never saw it rain before except two or three times in Scotland, since we have been here'.[64] The St Enoch Hotel, Glasgow, proved a pleasant surprise 'with an elevator, gas in the bedrooms, and a rocking chair, we felt we might be in the Palmer House'.[65] Glasgow with its necropolis and cathedral was also pleasing. With a visit to Alloway, Jane Addams completed her social democratic pilgrimage. For pleasure still had to have a higher purpose: 'It is certainly a delightful at the same time a vivid way to take in history.'[66] That idea was to reappear frequently in her late writings as part of her philosophy. She wanted a 'cathedral of humanity' which was 'capacious enough to house a fellowship of common purpose' and 'beautiful enough to persuade men to hold fast to the vision of human solidarity.'[67] The beauty and history of the locality, the sustaining sense of tradition and the community were to be important features of her thought. In a complex urban society, rootlessness seemed the major problem. Jane Addams felt a need to help people to realise an identity in harmony with their ethnic past and their contemporary condition.

The attitude reappeared several years later when Jane Addams had returned to Chicago and established Hull House. Her contacts with and research into the conditions of the poor made her realise the magnitude of the problem.[68] Her home town, Chicago, was in need of reform and a new direction. The diverse ethnic groups in the rapidly growing city needed some cohesive quality: as she wrote, 'a university settlement ought to be a stronghold of that rising municipal loyalty which is in some respect as noble as patriotism among the civic virtues'.[69] The civic concern gave rise to proposals for an international union of settlement houses. There had already been attempts to take Professors Henry Drummond and William Smart of Glasgow to a conference on settlement work.[70] F H Stead, brother of W T Stead, the editor of the *Review of Reviews* and a Glasgow graduate, wanted to establish an international union of settlement houses. Though little came of his proposal Jane Addams visited his Browning House settlement in London.[71] Glasgow obviously had some attraction. Armed with letters of introduction, she planned to visit Glasgow's municipal undertakings, housing and sanitation departments and hopefully, the Belvidere Hospital and Toynbee House settlement in Glasgow.[72] George Hooker of Chicago seems to have toured the Scottish settlement houses in 1894–5 and also to have met the old Glasgow Chartist and pacifist, Revd Arthur O'Neill, at the Birmingham settlement.[73] At the same time Jane Addams' colleague at Hull House, Ellen Gates Starr, gave her an introduction in Manchester. Charles Rowley, city councillor and reformer, who had strong Scottish connections, had entertained her during her visit to Manchester.[74] Whether settlements were religious or preferably neutral, Jane Addams believed they 'cast about social service and glamour of the moral picturesque'.[75] In regenerating society particularly at the neighbourhood level, settlements could exercise almost unlimited influence.[76] In the event the introductions were unnecessary. Miss Addams seized the unexpected opportunity to visit Count Tolstoy in Russia. The change of plan was sudden for she was already in Britain. Glasgow and Tolstoy were both for her expressions of the desire for social improvement.

The health and efficiency of the nation was a major preoccupation among the intelligentsia on both sides of the Atlantic. Arising from the settlement house enterprises were two main ideas. The first, with overtones of Protestant morality, fresh air fortnights for the underprivileged and the like developed a new nationalist gloss. It was essentially conservationist. Education, self discipline and health reform would safeguard the quality of future racial stock. Woman would be a major beneficiary of these reforms. Others sought a more radical re-ordering of the existing order through their experience in the settlement houses. Florence Kelley, the first English translator of Engels' *The Condition of the Working Class in England,* later factory inspector in Illinois and an organiser for the National Consumer's League, and Charlotte Perkins Gilman, a radical feminist, seem to have been launched on more radical views through their settlement house work.[77]

The combination of the spiritual and human aspects of Christianity, the local, national and universal ideals gave settlement houses their appeal. However limited their immediate impact on the neighbourhood might be, they were laboratories of social reform, largely organised and run by women. With their emphasis on good housekeeping, they used romantic, sociological and public pressures to force governments to take a more protective, interventionist role in the life of women and so in the whole community. Like many Progressive reformers, the ladies associated with the settlement houses wanted a controlled environment. Their work and researches led them to conclude that playgrounds, as in Scotland, were very desirable to eliminate street vices; that hygiene, which Jane Addams had intended to investigate in Glasgow, had to be legally enforced; that slum clearance on the Glasgow model had moral and social bonuses.[78] An education in democracy and a democratic education would bolster the family *and* society. The home, as one observer quoting St Bernard of Clairvaux observed, 'is there not to teach in the formal method of teaching, but to inspire, to encourage and to revive and renew'.[79] In that atmosphere of revived civic consciousness, woman could play a leading role.

Women were equipped for urban life and their new role. On the other hand they had to be kept in contact with that idealised past, the wonder of beauty and return to nature.[80] If women were to be protected in their works and educated for their future as mothers, new professionals and resilient individuals, they had to experience nature at first hand. The Girl Scouts of America were but one of several organisations devoted to that end.[81] Teachers, doctors, writers and clergymen all shared in this movement of uplift; the same names invariably appeared on all 'forward' movements.[82]

Mary MacArthur, the daughter of a Glasgow drapery family, had her interest in working conditions aroused through her father's shop assistants. She helped to found the British Women's Trade Union League, a body which was imitated in the United States. A vigorous campaigner against the sweated trades, she attended the American Women's Trade Union League conference in 1909 and gave a stirring address in the case for a minimum wage to such effect that the conference adopted 'legal minimum wage in the sweated trades' as part of its programme. She was to marry John Anderson, later MP for Sheffield Attercliffe, but both he and she were to die within a short time. Even so her contribution was considerable.[83]

Juliette Gordon Low, the foundress of the American Girl Scouts, spent several summers in Scotland laying the foundation for her work at home, Born in the South, she had toured Europe in 1882 but returned in 1884 to Scotland: 'The mountains of the Trossachs is enough (*sic*) to make one thank God for being alive and that there are such things on earth. Strange to say I had a patriotic feeling as if I was a Scot myself in some distant way.'[84] After an unhappy marriage to William Low of Leamington, Warwick, a multi-millionaire of Scottish descent, she began to cast around for some purposeful career. Most summers she spent in Scotland, visiting the 1901 Glasgow exhibition, touring or spending time in her house in Glen Lyon, Perthshire.[85] Glasgow appalled her: 'Glasgow is the most dismal place I ever saw. It is more like a cellar than anything I can think of. The Clyde with its wharves and traffic is decidedly the brightest spot: it all looks as if dug out of a tomb—only it has not enough dust and dirt to make it picturesque.'[86] In her many summers she came to know the local people very well, though some servants did enjoy themselves too readily at her expense. In particular she was concerned about the simple country girls who seemed ignorant of elementary nursing and so would bring up delicate children. Her Girl Scouts of America was a natural result.[87] She was in regular contact with Baden Powell, the founder of the Boy Scouts throughout 1911.[88] He visited her in Scotland and recommended Alex Paterson, *Across the Bridges,* the life of a slum boy: 'In parts it touches on women and gives first hand experiences of them and their needs.'[89] She was duly impressed, organised local Scottish girls on the estate and hoped to teach them enough to enable them to remain in the healthy countryside. Keeping chickens, carding and spinning wool for sale in London would provide the girls with skills, income and an antidote to urban life: it also had many similarities to the arts and crafts movement. Juliette Gordon Low then returned to Savannah where she began her work in earnest with the foundation of her American Girl Scouts. By the time of her death there were over 168,000 members.[90] Jane Addams and other 'uplifting' individuals supported her efforts meeting with her and other youth leaders at Hull House.[91] Like the Boys Brigade of William Alexander Smith of Glasgow[92] founded 'for the promotion of Christ's Kingdom among Boys, the promotion of habits of obedience, reverence, discipline, self-respect and all that tends to true Christian manliness', a movement had spread from Scotland and grown rapidly in America.[93]

Glasgow entertained some militant ladies. Charlotte Perkins Gilman[94] an American socialist came in 1896.[95] After an unhappy marriage she had launched out on her own. A lecturer and publicist she was best known for her incisive book *Women and Economics* which vigorously attacked the male-dominated socio-economic culture[96] On her arrival she tried three Glasgow hotels before she settled satisfactorily into Cranston's Weekly Temperance Hotel. She was entertained by the Glasiers and Keir Hardie while she impressed the correspondent of the *Labour Leader* by her charming smile.[97] She spoke at the Albion Halls, at the Labour Church, Miller Street and at the Brunswick Street Rooms, At her first meeting in the Albion Street, Halls, Miss Gilman, who had been advertised as the niece of Harriet Beecher Stowe, gave 'An American View of Socialism'. She appeared as 'a bright, racy speaker, full of shrewd commonsense and her address abounded with quaint touches of American humour . . . being a pleasant change from the usual monotony of the regulation "economic" Socialist speeches with which we are most favoured'.[98] Miss Gilman herself was also satisfied: 'A good house, good time—spoke pretty well.'[99]

During the rest of the week she was shown round Glasgow by 'a socialist councillor' and gave further talks. Her hosts, greatly impressed, invited her back the following Sunday to talk on 'The New Religion'. In the presence of Keir Hardie, she looked forward to the old religion divested of its priestcraft and superstitions. Six weeks later she returned to tour through Cambuslang, Paisley and Glasgow, preaching her modernist social religion. After speaking in Bridgeton Halls, she was somewhat disappointed: 'A week of foregone failure, hard work and heavy sledding in general. Pay $16.25. Stood it fairly well.'[100] Though she returned to Scotland in 1899 she does not seem to have visited Glasgow again.

More uncompromising feminists—and anarchists—came in her wake. Emma Goldman, the American anarchist, came on three occasions. Born in Lithuania she had emigrated to America via St Petersburgh in 1885.[101] About ten years later she returned to Scotland as a fully fledged anarchist, an ardent admirer of the Haymarket Martyrs, the radicals who had been executed following the death of a policeman in the Chicago disturbance of 1885[102] Then at the height of the Boer War she returned to Glasgow to attack British imperialism. Later in 1919, she was deported from the United States to Russia. Though initially an enthusiastic supporter of the Russian Revolution, she was bitterly hostile to the Bolshevik regime. Even so she refused to lecture to the Paisley branch of the Woman's Guild of Empire in 1925:

> I regret deeply not to be able to accept your invitation. All my life I have been against the iniquitous arrangements in society which raise one man to be a king, while compelling others to remain paupers for life. In other words, the conditions which make for differences among human beings.
>
> I do not happen to belong to the kind of revolutionists who proclaim that all good is the heritage of the poor and all the bad represents the characteristics of the rich. Indeed not. To me all human beings are alike in the sense that I want to reach their minds and their hearts. But on the other hand, the economic conditions of society today, unfortunately create barriers between those who produce the wealth of the world and those who make use of that wealth and since my sympathies are with those who toil, as against those who lead idle lives, I cannot very well speak under the auspices of any society which upholds the forces that make for social and economic inequality. . . . Having read your programme I am quite certain that your opposition to Bolshevism includes also your opposition to any theory which stands for fundamental change of a social and economic nature.[103]

Twelve years later she did return to Glasgow to lecture on the Spanish Civil War in opposition to Franco. She came under the auspices of Guy Aldred and the Anti-Parliamentary Federation to the City Hall, 14 February 1937.

On her visit at the turn of the century she had found the city one of great contrasts: 'Everybody was kind and friendly to me, but the city itself proved a nightmare, in some respects worse than London. On a Saturday night, returning home on the tramway, I counted seven children on the street, dirty and undernourished, staggering along with their mothers, all under the influence of drink.' To such critics, the achievements of municipal

government paled into insignificance.[104] Local socialist opinion endorsed
that view. The SLP writer W Paul believed that municipalisation was
merely a form of safe investment for the middle class in that the intellectuals
secured well paid posts in the administration and reinforced capitalism and
class rule.[105] That women gained little in the model municipality was the
stock in trade of the socialist *Forward*. Women were sacrificed to the
excesses of capitalism. In March 1911, the paper claimed that some 17,000
women were virtually prostitutes in the streets of Glasgow, one in twelve of
the age group fifteen to forty-five years of age.[106]

Another American lady visitor agreed with Emma Goldman's assessment
of Glasgow: Margaret Sanger, a nurse in New York City at the height of
European immigration at the turn of the century, became a member of the
Socialist Party. The daughter of an Irish-American immigrant who had
brought both Henry George and the free thinker Colonel Bob Ingersoll to
lecture to his Catholic community, before taking up socialism she followed
in that tradition.[107] Acquainted with the leading socialists of her day, from
'Big' Bill Haywood, the secretary-treasurer of the Industrial Workers of the
World, the most class-conscious American union movement, to Upton
Sinclair, the novelist, Miss Sanger began to contribute to the radical paper,
The Call. In particular she saw the dissemination of information on sex as
her primary socialist duty: she wrote articles entitled 'What Every Mother
Should Know' and 'What Every Girl Should Know'. In the process she
narrowly avoided infringing the Comstock Law which denied the mails to
offensive material.

In 1913 Mrs Sanger visited Glasgow to write a series of articles on twenty-
five years of municipal ownership:

> Socialists were talking about how everything there belonged to the people
> themselves and had earned their own way: banks, schools, parks, markets, art
> galleries, museums, laundries, bath houses, hospitals and tramways. The city was
> about to pay off the last debt on the transportation system, and this was being
> hailed as a great victory, a perfect example of what Socialism could do. It sounded
> big and fine, and I, too, was impressed. Certainly in Glasgow I thought I should
> find women walking hand in hand with men, and children happy and free.[108]

She found the city booming, ironically on war industries, and like so many
of her predecessors, wet.[109] Initially she was impressed by municipal
endeavours but on closer inspection she was very disappointed. The model
tenements were unimpressive, the streets filled with drunken women and
beggars. The poor were not helped except indirectly, if at all. Large families
could not rent municipal houses: the vaunted wash houses were inaccessible
to the poor because of the distance and the refusal of the tramways to carry
laundry baskets. The city officials seemed indifferent in a bureaucratic
manner: 'Oh, the women of Glasgow are all dirty and low. They're
hopeless. . . . It's their own fault.'[110] The municipal housing policy effectively limited accommodation to those with three children and beyond that
condemned families to slum dwellings. In short, the people seemed 'cold
and rigid, as dismal as their climate'.[111] After her horrifying experiences

Margaret Sanger even found Paris 'another Glasgow more like a provincial village than a great metropolis'.[112]

The result of her European tour was to give her a mission. She returned to the United States and began the National Birth Control League and a paper *The Woman Rebel,* in March 1914. She confidently believed that 'all America was Hyde Park corner as far as criticism and challenging thought were concerned'.[113] She was quickly disabused: *Woman Rebel* was barred from the mails and she was indicted on nine counts for violating federal statutes. Eventually she fled to Europe where she continued her campaign in favour of contraception. Later, she returned to America, fought her campaign in the courts and lost: she was given thirty days in the workhouse. In July 1920, under the auspices of Guy Aldred's Bakunin Communist group, she returned to Glasgow to lecture on 'Birth Control and the Workers' and 'Sex, Health and Wealth'.[114] In addition she held private meetings for women on four evenings a week. Aldred's Bakunin Press was to publish her *Family Limitation* in cheap popular form for adults of twenty-one and over. Her three-week tour of Scotland had proved markedly different from her previous visit:

> When I had been in Glasgow before I had encountered only officials but on this occasion I met the people in their homes and found them quite opposite to the stingy, tight-fisted, middle class stereotype. They were hospitable, generous, mentally alert, just as witty as the Irish and in much the same way, which rather surprised me.[115]

On 4 July 1920 Mrs Sanger addressed some 2000 working men. In the evening she addressed a socialist gathering which included an astonishingly large number of women. Her message was received in a moving way: 'Women who had never been on their feet before got up to tell dramatic, vivid, personal stories.'[116] Margaret Sanger had made her point on both sides of the Atlantic.[117]

Guy Aldred, her host, had American connections. His lady companion, Rose Witcop, an American anarchist, had been involved in the Victoria Woodhull movement in New York before coming to Britain. Generously funded by a benefactor, Aldred had been persuaded to move from London to Glasgow shortly before the First World War. On his arrival, he and Rose Witcop began *Spur,* a radical paper which was to replace *The Herald of Revolt.* Supported by American subscribers and occasionally bailed out by their donations—including a dollar from Emma Goldman—Aldred closely followed American events.[118] In correspondence with Goldman, Aldred publicised the numerous addresses and articles on the woman question by his associate, Rose Witcop and Margaret Sanger.[119] 'Women and War', 'Mothering Our Land' and 'Should Women Know?' were typical of the discussions on birth control, abortion and the proletarian struggle.[120]

Among the articles published by *The Herald of Revolt* and *Spur* were several by Voltairine de Cleyre, the American anarchist. Born in Michigan, 1866, educated in a convent school, she had become a socialist and following the execution of the Haymarket martyrs an anarchist.[121] In 1897 following the visit of a British anarchist, John Turner, to Philadelphia, she decided to visit Europe. In London she met many leading anarchists like Kropotkin while staying with the Turners. She also met Mrs Turner's brother, Thomas H Bell, a Scottish anarchist.[122] Shortly afterwards she went on a month's visit to Scotland: 'my pet place of all the earth.' . . . If I could make my living in Scotland, I'd never care to come back to America to live.' For Voltairine de Cleyre, Scotland was the 'sharpest ruggedest, wittiest place on earth—that's of the earth Ive seen—.'[123] 'Oh I love you all!'[124]

The reason for her enthusiasm for Scotland was the scenery, the very successful series of lectures she gave and the friendship of the Duffs. She stayed with the Duffs at 9 Carfin Street, Govanhill, Glasgow. Will Duff was a contributor to the London anarchist papers *Alarm* and *Freedom* as well as to the American *Free Society*. In addition he was also a distributor for the controversial short-lived journal *Adult*.[125] A close friend of Kropotkin, for whom he saved a copy of his own *In Russian and French Prisons* when Tsarists agents bought up and destroyed the whole edition in 1887, Duff also knew William Morris, Goldman and other radicals.[126] A very widely read working man, Duff had two sons, who were conscientious objectors during the First World War and who both suffered imprisonment and harsh treatment from which one eventually died.[127] Will Duff published an account of her tour in Scotland in *Freedom* (November 1897) and again acted as her host on her second visit in 1903. He also published her *The Gods and the People* as a pamphlet in 1898, and continued to correspond with her until her death in 1912. Her visits undoubtedly contributed to the revival of anarchist sentiment in the west of Scotland. The arrival George Barrett from London and John Paton from Aberdeen gave rise to the Glasgow anarchist group: much of their literature came from America.[128] They might gather on Sundays in the fruit market hired by the Rationalists to hear anarchists like John Turner or other freethinkers and later Aldred would come north to begin his own campaign. Soon they had more than fifty members.

The transatlantic links persisted through the First World War. Emma Goldman gave moral support to Aldred and to his supporter, Rose Witcop, who took over the editorship of *The Spur* when he was imprisoned for his anti-war efforts.[129] The growing militancy of labour, the shop stewards movement and the Russian Revolution gave rise to left wing optimism. In the aftermath of the war another American lady, Crystal Eastman, came to observe, these developments. The daughter of two ministers, her mother the first woman ordained Congregationalist minister in New York State, Crystal was born in 1881.[130] 'A superb creature' according to a contemporary socialist, she was the 'perfect American woman': wherever you met her 'she was the most intelligent woman in the room'[131] Educated at Vassar, with degrees in sociology and law from Columbia and New York University, she was, with Max, her brother, the first Trotskyite in America, the proprietor of the *Liberator*. She had served on the New York State commission on industrial accidents, employers liability and unemployment, 1909, and was a regular transatlantic commuter.[132] She arrived in 1919.

After attending the Labour Party conference in Southport, where she met David Kirkwood, she travelled north to draw an incisive view of Glasgow Labour leadership.[133] Arthur MacManus she found 'the most able intellectually of the group I met in Glasgow, but I think he is a little too bitter and scornful to make a great leader. He thinks Glasgow should have started the revolution in January'.[134] He frequently failed like many left wingers to identify himself with the movement: 'He is too given to using "you" instead of "we" in his speeches.'[135] Kirkwood seemed colourful but a sentimentalist; John MacLean had a 'loveable but unmanageable recklessness'.[136] She also met Emmanuel Shinwell and Willie Gallacher—with whom she discussed the shop stewards' movement. She was deeply impressed for she returned to lecture Americans on their lethargy. Following Gallacher's advice she believed America was the first place to have a revolution but the workers were totally unprepared for their historic role: they were fifty years behind their British counterparts.[137]

In effect she was indicating the gap between Scotland and America which had arisen by 1920. Different mentalities, different outlooks and different expectations, for whatever reasons, seemed to be apparent to the most casual observer. The various American feminist visitors had come to Glasgow and found what they wanted to find; encouragement, reassurance, sisterly religious and political support, the triumph of their sort of people, or the predictable failure of any form of society but their own peculiar brand. In that they followed in the steps of their men folk, as we shall see, though the nineteenth century. Tories and Liberals, radicals and reactionaries had found excellent proof of their established positions or prejudices in the United States. Glasgow performed a similar service for many American ladies, particularly around the turn of the century. Glasgow, well publicised in the American papers, was portrayed either as the New Jerusalem or the precursor of the Socialist state. American women might share these different attitudes but on one point they were agreed— they wanted equality within society, whether existing, adjusted or to come.

The American ladies during this period changed as to their social background. In the earliest period, they were invariably comfortably off ladies in search of a role, a humanitarian crusade to give purpose to a leisured existence. Later, from Jane Addams onwards they were more professionalised, as social workers, as nurses, as doctors and the like. To that extent, whatever the shortcomings which remained there had been a quiet revolution. To that change Glasgow had given encouragement, assistance and example. Glasgow had received similar aid from the United States. The Lease-Lend movement in ideas was in operation long before the Second World War gave economic expression to the idea.

The central problem was the city. The women's movement in all its diversity highlighted the city as a battleground. The nature, form and prospect of the city was a matter of debate. Woman would secure her social salvation within an increasingly urban society. Whether that social salvation was bourgeois, socialist or utopian, proletarian or progressive was the point.

Chapter Four

The Demon Drink

The Drift to Prohibition

Religion and education provided the essential links between Glasgow and the United States. Temperance reformers gave coherence and substance to these hopes and aspirations. A minister in 1892 condemned 'the publicans (who) were in fact licensed robbers, licensed murderers, wreckers of the city's peace and prosperity and ruiners of human souls'.[1] Samuel Chisholm, the councillor and later Lord Provost, who pushed forward the city housing improvements declared, 'If we wish Glasgow to be a model city, an ideal city, those public houses licensed at every street corner must be prohibited so that the benevolent and religious agencies may not be thwarted in their beneficient role.'[2] Even Labour councillors believed that but for drink housing reforms would be unnecessary.[3] More nationally known figures like Cunninghame Graham and Keir Hardie were firm supporters of temperance.[4]

Councillor Shinwell later believed that Labour voters would welcome prohibition. Neil Maclean declared: 'I would welcome the advent of prohibition. A sober people would soon make a free democracy.' The Red Clydesider, James Maxton, believed that 'any legislation bringing further restriction would not be felt as harsh, repressive legislation by any considerable section of the community'.[5] *Forward* declared, 'Alcohol is a hindrance to the realisation of the Co-operative Commonwealth.'[6]

The drive towards prohibition had three main stages; first, the growth of a public awareness of the issue; second, the evolution of organisations; and third the broadening of the appeal of the movement into many social reforms. Provincial pride also had a part in that the touring stars of the temperance world reassured their provincial audiences of their unique moral character and respectability. They almost gave approval to a form of cultural racialism among their listeners. Those occasions were demonstrations of self-appreciation and self-admiration as much as commitment to social improvement and reform. In that process many individuals were introduced into a political world, given training in oratorical and organisational skills, and in becoming concerned with wider social issues they contributed to the decline of the temperance movement. The alternative strategy of socialism had a certain immediacy. After 1917 it had an irresistible sense of triumph at the very time when prohibition became identified with an increasingly conservative American business civilisation. The interests of morality, social efficiency and cohesion were identified as one and the same. All men of good will could only join in that campaign for amelioration, improvement and control. That approach was a common transatlantic view. As Chisholm told the Pan Presbyterian Congress New York Council meeting in 1909, the persistence of Protestantism, Calvinism, Presbyterianism and 'the general democratic spirit suggests that the ever-coming Scot has assimilated and is assimilating the American people'.

Brian Harrison has portrayed the crusade against drink as part of a wide ranging movement.[7] The Temperance organisations provided socialising agencies in which aspiring young people taught themselves the principles of conduct in an achievement-oriented society. They provided the means of social mobility through the life styles of one's social superiors. In Scotland such organisations appealed to the militant provincial view of the metropolis, London and the South: Chisholm, for example, played a leading role in the revival of the Bannockburn anniversary. Latterly that antipathy to aristocratic dominance might lead to overt attacks upon the landed interest. If it was indicative of the tensions and strains within the late Victorian Liberal party, it was also expressive of that provincial, dissenting culture which demanded recognition in the larger society.

If public houses were centres of working-class culture, the onus was on the temperance reformers to provide alternative sources of sober entertainment to the saloon. If taking the pledge for total abstinence from all alcoholic beverages meant the complete abandonment of the local working-class society then an alternative inclusive culture had to be available. Savings schemes, self esteem and property ownership were admirable but the worker paid a psychological and social cost. Drink was associated with virility, stamina and other manly virtues. Some compensation and reassurance on that issue was needed. Ministers and priests could unite with their folk in a war on sin and so give themselves a relevant role and status: drink, it has been suggested, was an alternative form of worship or liturgy. Significantly many religious groups who had previously eschewed elaborate worship with organ music and similar aids to devotion developed a strong interest in revivalist warmth. Medals, regalia and a virtual temperance freemasonry contributed to a strong sense of loyalty and identity. Catholicism in the 1840s in Scotland underwent a similar transformation. More lavish decoration, liturgy and devotions in elaborate churches provided a sense of theatre, of belonging, and of social and spiritual well-being. The preachers of that day attacking drink had something of a superstar image. Their sermons and addresses were in a very real sense 'performances'. John B Gough for example comes readily to mind. Finally in the late nineteenth century women on both sides of the Atlantic would play an increasingly assertive and effective role in the movement. It gave them a sense of purpose and identity, a means of respectable public activity, and provided an opportunity to denigrate the man-made world which refused them basic civil and political rights. Temperance was a means of defending the traditional family whilst asserting feminine individuality. In a larger way it united individualism and authoritarianism. The early Victorian voluntarist view gave way to a more interventionist approach.

The transatlantic crusade gave practical effect to moral and educational aspirations. It meant organisations with strong religious overtones, opportunities for men of science and medicine, writers and newspaper editors, those seeking status and those defending it, woman suffragists and health advocates, specialised entrepreneurs and careerists. The movement, with regular local meeting and huge celebrity occasions, with national and international figures, was a way of life. The individual found reassurance in a larger world of like-minded crusaders: it was a permanent revival. That feeling gave rise to a strong peace wing as part of an almost millenarian vision. Prohibition ultimately was *the* reform and the means to larger reforms throughout the world.

The Scottish aversion to Westminster control, to allegedly remote, irresponsive and uncomprehending government had its counterpart in the United States. The rural reaction to the increasing cultural dominance of New York city with its urban commercial and later industrial problems— immigrants and the threat of an alien culture, an alien religion and alien customs—was part of an effort to sustain an independent cohesive moral identity in a fluid world. Such responses might be seen as defending true American patriotism or true Scottish nationalism, but they also revealed a darker aspect unattractive in a democratic society. They might chill liberals in their foreboding about the Ku-Klux-Klan in Main Street America or anti-Catholic bigotry in Scotland. Such sentiments might flourish and effectively control the perceived threats without the formality of legislation. Effective informal prejudice was far more successful than inadequately enforced laws, as de Tocqueville saw. From the 1830s on both sides of the Atlantic the old cultural dominance was restated in terms of humanitarian reform. At the same time that moral concern enabled new groups in the cities to assert their respectability within an aroused Protestantism. Social activism could transcend sectarian boundaries and, as the century progressed, the intellectual difficulties of religion.

That should not hide the extent of the poverty, squalor and drunkenness in early nineteenth-century Glasgow. The problem was real. In large cities, as John Dunlop saw, 'dissociation' contributed to the spread of social evils.[8] The urban masses were neither sober nor sabbatarians. The suppression of the drink traffic would regenerate the nation. As Dunlop told the Select Committee on Drunkenness in 1834, effective legislation would secure a moral, educational and political revolution:

> Judicious small endowments in the minor towns in Scotland for teachers of the moral and physical sciences; with a scale of moderate fees in part suited to the circumstances of the mechanics and operatives. The member for Dumbartonshire presented a petition upon this subject at my request. I have also been in use to suggest that boards might be appointed in various parts, with power to examine any candidate in reading, writing, arithmetic, such foreign languages as may be thought necessary, such knowledge of theology and philosophy as might be thought sufficient; and if the candidate be found qualified he might, on further certificate of character, receive a qualification to vote for members of Parliament. This would create a desire for solid education among operatives. Judicious gratuities to libraries might also be given.[9]

Temperance advocates envied the quality of democratic 'dry' life in

America with its excellent educational opportunities. Scotland seemed far behind in every respect.[10]

To discuss the Scottish temperance movement is far beyond the scope of this study but I would suggest that America consistently forced the pace among Scottish temperance reformers. The idea of temperance associations was largely imported from America as was the Protestant drive for political relevance. The passage of Catholic Emancipation in 1829, and the continued expansion of the franchise, meant that voluntary political pressure groups assumed increasing importance in the informal party structures of the day.[11] As a later Scottish reformer saw, 'conscious evolution if *socially localised* . . . becomes at once capable of effective action'.[12] Such informal unions of Protestant opinion might be the precursors of more formal reunions of churches. In general their members, like the American theologian Lyman Abbott, preferred order to liberty: the masses in America seemed adequately prepared for and disciplined in the exercise of their moral political responsibilities.[13] Enthusiasts tended to overlook the fact that the strength of temperance support lay in rural areas and not in the major cities.

The evangelical revival on both sides of the Atlantic had given rise to public concern about social order in the new urban centres. The evangelicals saw negro slavery and slavery to drink as the main social evils. In 1826 the American Temperance Society was formed. Its activities and those of the state societies were to have considerable impact in Scotland.[14] Their success coincided with and accompanied another resurgence of evangelical fervour in America which was closely followed in Scotland. On both sides of the Atlantic there was opposition to the unacceptable spirit of affluence in every sense.[15]

The ideal city of the reformers was a dry regime. At Rothesay, James Silk Buckingham conceived his model town free from drink—with parks, museums, libraries and recreational areas. Titus Salt of Saltaire and Richardson of Bessbrook, Ulster as well as many American towns shared that dream. In Maine and in Illinois some 600 townships enjoyed that potential future.[16] The Cadbury model housing at Bournville in a dry environment had similarities with the great dry estates of A. Cameron Corbett, MP, for Glasgow Tradeston. A veteran temperance campaigner, he had not only given Glasgow two huge country estates at Thornliebank and Lochgoilhead but also had dry estates in Scotland and Ilford: some 35,000 people lived in 7000 homes without a public house.[17] Early and late civic theorists considered drink the greatest barrier to social advance. It caused ill health and it prevented the achievement of the co-operative community.[18] America, with fewer vested interests, a more evangelical awareness and democratic spirit, seemed to be fulfilling that promise.

Temperance meant a reform of the individual character rather than a redistribution of wealth. To that extent its bias was essentially conservative. It was an antidote to the extremism of Jacksonian democracy in America and of radicalism in Britain. Sobriety, savings and education would equip the individual for real personal success in contemporary society. In the west of Scotland many of its leading advocates seemed upwardly mobile businessmen and artisans, together with the more independent churchmen: the established church of Scotland did not play a leading role in developing temperance organisations. Men already associated with voluntary churches and those desiring a more flexible imaginative approach to the urban apostolate were more likely to be numbered among the membership of temperance organisations.

Dr Leonard Woods of Andover had sent his friend, Dr Ralph Wardlaw, the independent Glasgow clergyman, the first annual reports of the American Temperance Society with other temperance literature.[19] But the first substantial effort came from John Dunlop of Greenock. A Glasgow graduate, he returned from a European visit determined to eliminate the evils of drink. Inspired by the American example he established the first temperance society in Scotland in 1829. It proved short lived but his example encouraged Miss Graham and Miss Allen to begin a similar body in Maryhill. Soon afterwards, following several visits to Glasgow by Dunlop, William Collins, the publisher, initiated the Scottish Temperance Society in 1830. Within a year there were 100 societies with 15,000 members in Scotland. Another admirer of the American example, Revd Professor John Edgar of Belfast, a total abstinence advocate, helped the movement spread through Britain. Henry Forbes, a Scot in business in Bradford, was converted to the cause in Glasgow and took the idea back to the West Riding. Collins himself was in London in 1831 contributing to the formation of the British and Foreign Temperance Society. The organisation had followed the American pattern.[20]

Propaganda followed from America. The annual reports of the American Temperance Society, the state societies, the formation of congressional societies and the general progress in America were closely studied in Glasgow temperance journals.[21] The writings of Sylvester Graham, later renowned as water-cure and vegetarian enthusiast, Dr Tuckerman, the Boston Unitarian reformer, and others were reprinted in the journal.[22] Even the technique of an annual day of temperance recollection for all societies throughout the area was adopted from America: 'Some such measure is needed to give new life and vigour to our operations.'[23] Rapid progress was being made in the United States as visitors reassured Scottish reformers: 'Several intelligent and decided American friends have visited this country during the present year who confirm the delightful news.'[24] After initial enthusiasm, dissension between the total abstinence elements and the 'moderates' contributed to a general decline in activity.

The more assertive element went over to the offensive. J S Buckingham returned in November 1834 to give several lectures, while Edward Morris and Joseph Swann contributed 120 lectures in twenty months.[25] The general decline, however, was only arrested by the arrival of John Finch of Liverpool in September 1836. In a series of lectures over two months, he uncompromisingly supported total abstinence from all intoxicants. In the next few years the moderates were largely won over to total abstinence.[26] That resolve was increasingly stiffened not only by American support but also by American physical presence.

The Glasgow Temperance Society had followed American example by

printing vast amounts of literature. In June 1830 140,000 publications had
been distributed and by August that figure doubled. These included 46,960
copies of Mr J Kittredge's speech at the second anniversary of the American
Temperance Society; 21,000 copies of another address by him; 27,000 of
Revd Dr Theodore Dwight's sermon on drunkenness; and 8700 copies of
Revd Dr Lyman Beecher's *Six Sermons on Intemperance*. Numerous other
editions were published by other local societies.[27] Considerable publicity
was given to the need for temperance references for intending immigrants to
the United States. Edward Cornelius Delavan, the founder of the New York
State Temperance Society, wrote several letters to the *Temperance Record*
on this issue.[28] In October 1833 his circular to emigrants was published. In
American society, a moral upright character had to be established by the
immigrant in the new community. That might be best accomplished by
keeping clear of all hostelries and dram shops. Even better, the immigrant
should join a temperance society before he left his native land and bring
that record of membership with him to America. Failing that, the ship
should form an immigrant temperance society en route with records of
membership. Finally the new arrival should immediately upon landing join
a temperance society so as to establish his credentials to respectability:
'These certificates will be of very great service to you in aiding you to find
employment in any part of America: unless indeed you prove by your
conduct, or by your appearance that you frequent dram shops in violation
of your agreement.'[29]

American example forced the pace. Advertisements for American temperance tracts appeared in Glasgow papers.[30] American sermons like those
of President Woods of Andover seminary, American literary propaganda
like the writings of Mrs Sigourney, and the personal appearances of
American temperance advocates hammered home the message. These pressures increased as the temperance movement faltered somewhat in the mid
thirties. More militant uncompromising leadership and attitudes emerged
following the visit of John Finch of Liverpool in September 1836. Temperance increasingly meant teetotalism. It was no longer adequate to
abstain from spiritous liquors: abstinence from all alcoholic beverages was
necessary. Even to retain them for the social use of guests at home was considered totally unacceptable. Moderation, far from bringing any immediate
tangible results, had merely fudged the issue in Scotland. Advocates of
more uncompromising attitudes gained an ascendancy in Scotland.

The visit of Edward C Delavan, the New York State temperance leader,
stiffened the Glasgow resolve. He had already sent over Revd Dr Hewitt to
sustain the drive. Revd Dr Herman Humphrey, President of Amherst, was
appalled by the lack of solid temperance opinions among Glasgow clergy:
distinguished popular preachers who were 'most read and admired in this
country were not members' of total abstinence societies.[31] While George
Thompson, the anti-slavery advocate, lectured on temperance a succession
of American temperance apostles poured into Britain to bolster the movement's sagging fortunes: Revd Robert Baird, missionary to Europe, in
1836; Revd Dr E N Kirk of Boston and Revd George B Cheever of Salem in
1837; Revd Dr Potter and Revd Dr Nathaniel Berman in 1839.[32] They

sought to consolidate the initial burst of enthusiasm into a solid base. That required demonstrable evidence: 'The only evidence of repentance in such a case is A CONTINUED COURSE OF ENTIRE ABSTINENCE FROM INTOXICATING DRINK OF EVERY KIND.'[33]

In 1839 at the annual general meeting of the temperance society, Delavan gave an account of American developments on total abstinence with a platform which included Joseph Livesey of Preston and J Dougall of Montreal. Later, following his tour of Europe, Delavan was given a formal reception in recognition of his personal commitment to the cause to which he had given some £10,000 up to that time.[34]

The following year a Mr Gordon came from America, as did the renowned British abolitionist George Thompson. In later years the reinforcements came in droves. Henry C Wright, the radical abolitionist and social reformer, came in 1844. The following year Revd George Lewis, the newspaper editor, educator and churchman, came to report on his American impressions. As early as 1846 Glaswegians were following the rhetorical exploits of John B Gough, the emigrant English orator in America, while they listened to addresses from the ex-slave Frederick Douglass and from James Buffom.[35] That impressive gathering also included the Chartist temperance orator, Henry Vincent. That year also marked the World's Temperance Convention in London. Several American delegates stimulated Scottish enthusiasm, men like Revd John Marsh, New York, Dr Mussey, Henry C Wright, Douglass and Buffom.[36] Another former slave, Revd Dr Pennington of New York, who had been active for about a decade in American temperance, came in 1850 as did the original Uncle Tom, Mr Henson.[37] The following year William Wells Brown, the renowned slave, and two other ex-slaves arrived.[38]

Enthusiasm for temperance led into other areas of uplift and social amelioration. Travel, holidays and temperance hotels were alternatives to a drink culture and also positive benefits available to temperance adherents. These hygeian interests provided an outlet from the sodden city and opportunities for the pleasurable spending of time, money and effort in healthy surroundings. They might bring greater personal satisfaction and fulfilment to the individual, make him a more amenable and productive member of the workforce, and provide new opportunities for businessmen in catering for the new leisured purchasing power. The capital, financial and social, previously wasted in drink and its disastrous social consequences of crime, vice and disease, might be channelled into productive, socially useful and even educational areas.

Hydropathic concerns were largely an American import. Sylvester Graham (1794–1851), the grandson of a Glasgow graduate and minister, had given effective expression to these health concerns in America. A temperance agent for the Pennsylvania society, he became increasingly preoccupied with physiological matters. Personal health reform was inextricably bound up with moral reform. With W A Alcott, the doctor and educator, Revd William Metcalfe, an English immigrant, Mary Gove, later Mrs Nichols and others, Graham under the influence of George Combe formulated a new approach towards temperance and health. Considering the health of vegetarian 'uncivilised' peoples, he was drawn to the astonishing conclusion: 'DISEASE IS NEVER THE LEGITIMATE RESULT OF THE OPERATION OF ANY OF OUR ORGANS . . . ALL MEDICINE AS SUCH IS IN ITSELF EVIL.'[39] The endemic epidemics of the first half of the nineteenth century persuaded Graham that only a vegetarian diet could safeguard man from such ills: epidemics were the natural consequence of the artificial unnatural life enforced by urban commercial society. A meatless society would be 'less violent, less ferocious and blood thirsty'.[40] Stimulants of any description were decidedly harmful: alcohol, tobacco, tea or coffee fell into this category. Only natural foods, natural whole meal bread and pure water were guaranteed safe—though in the state of sanitary science then the last seems doubtful. Regular exercises, bathing, singing and loose fitting clothing were essential aids to health.

Artificial constraints or treatments in health paralleled moral patterns: 'Whatever in food or drink, or any other bodily indulgence or habit, vitiates or impairs the sensorial power or the nervous system commensurately impairs the moral sense.'[41] That evil was further reflected in other areas: 'The more widely man has departed from the true civilisation the more largely have religious institutions and observances entered into the constitution of economy and civil government.'[42] Individual informed moral choices were vital to a democratic society.[43]

Such sentiments coincided with several Scottish elements. The puritan tradition of self denial and the rejection of artificiality looked with suspicion upon the complex, relatively affluent communities developing in and around Glasgow in the early nineteenth century: the old Calvinist restraint was giving way to more liberal theological views. The older simple village society was being submerged within a larger market economy: old moral, social and political authorities were increasingly called into question. The skilled craftsman or artisan might respond to some milder version of Graham's views: he was antipathetic to those forces which had resulted in his migration to the industrial factory discipline of the town, to a demanding employer and to competition from the unskilled, especially that of the Catholic Irish immigrant. Temperance enabled him to assert his moral superiority over those above or below him in the social scale. As an American idea which found echoes in Scottish Chartism, it might appear as progressive. American concern with cleanliness found an echo in the bath house and Turkish bath movements in Scotland: the ideas of some Chartists and David Urquhart, the Russophobe, seemed at one in this respect. The Graham code of sexual discipline might further appeal to traditional religious precepts and to those in pursuit of Victorian respectability.[44]

In this tradition the American phrenologists and physiologists, Lorenzo Fowler and Samuel Wells, arrived in 1861.[45] Their dietary and sexual ideas supported temperance and might be used in conjunction with the existing hydropathic institutions in Scotland. Mrs Lydia Fowler, health reformer, staunchly supported the British Women's Temperance Association of which her reformist daughter, Jessie, became honorary treasurer.[46] Their notions of feminine dress reforms, sexuality and temperance found echoes in Glasgow within a few years. The arrival of Thomas Low Nichols and his wife, Mary Gove Nichols gave these ideas greater currency. Largely through the personal interest of Hay Nisbet, the publisher of Jamaica Street, the Nichols reached a Scottish audience.

The Nichols were a remarkable couple. They came to Britain in 1861 after a chequered career as health, dress and sexual reformers. After considerable experience in the water-cure and spiritualist movements, the Nichols had become Roman Catholics in 1858. Their experiments in community living had led them through various phases to Rome.[47] He had arrived in Glasgow from America in the land of the second sight and his wife's ancestors. The strength of religious and temperance sentiment seems to have encouraged him to found *Nichol's Journal of Sanitary and Social Science* in Glasgow in 1873. The journal's radical views on property redistribution, wasteful competition and health, though short lived, provided a link with another American group whom we encountered earlier, Mrs Soule, and Mr and Mrs James Coates, who were settled in Glasgow. Coates was a contributor to temperance journals on health and a member of the Scottish Temperance League. With his health foods (he was an agent for Nichols' products), spiritualism and temperance concerns, he and his wife presented a thorough-going radical view of temperance: religion, health and society had to be rethought.[49]

The food reformers were an important element in temperance critiques of contemporary society. The proliferation of food reform restaurants in London encouraged the formation of a small but influential Vegetarian Society, the establishment of a Vegetarian restaurant, Eden, on Jamaica Street and attempts to curb drinking habits through radical changes in diet.[50] That in turn had links with the anti-vivisection movement, anti-vaccination campaigns and socialism.[51] Those in turn were connected with America.

The hygeian movement had several influential supporters in Scotland. The leading British authority on the system had converted Robert Simpson in Glasgow.[52] A *Hygeian Journal* was established, a series of lectures delivered by Revd Alexander Munro MD, and a hydro was established at Gilmorehill on the present site of Glasgow University. A congregational minister at Forres, Munro had studied at Glasgow and Aberdeen without graduating, received a medical degree from a New York college and established a hydro at Forres. In 1859 he began the *Aberdeen Water Cure Journal* which popularised the notions of Dr R T Trail, the leading New York authority on the water cure. Combining godliness and cleanliness, Munro won the admiration of the Ohio temperance pioneer, 'Mother' Stewart, and the first American woman doctor, Elizabeth Blackwell.[53] Munro not only wrote numerous articles on the subject but also operated hydropaths in other parts of Scotland. At Gilmorehill he seems to have worked with Dr Archibald Hunter of Glasgow. Numerous other hydropaths followed in Crieff, Bridge of Allan, Skelmorlie, Saltcoats and elsewhere.[54] Munro continued to preach the benefits of hydropathy, lecturing and holding consultations in the Glasgow area until shortly before his death.[55]

A hydropath had been established at Rothesay in 1843. It soon had accommodation for 200 people. In 1890 the establishment was taken over by Andrew Philp, a friend of Thomas Cook, the great traveller and temperance advocate. Philp had opened the first substantial temperance hotel in Britain, the Albion, in Edinburgh in 1861 and through his association with Cook and the temperance movement he had built up a substantial chain of grand hotels in Edinburgh, London, Rothesay, Dunblane and Glasgow. Among Americans these enjoyed an unrivalled reputation as temperance and efficiently run establishments.[56] The Glasgow hotel became a byword in the United States for its temperance, comfort and American manageress. It was known as 'the American House of Scotland, a new one and much like the hotels at home' and 'the American hotel of Glasgow'.[57]

America came to Glasgow. In the late nineteenth century American ideas and attitudes flowed across into the temperance crusade. Godliness, health and business went together. Temperance reformers might lease the grounds of the Gilmorehill hydropath for recreation. At the opening there were some 20,000 patrons. During the succeeding Saturdays, American entertainers appeared among the various field games and races.[58] Healthy recreation and good, well-prepared food went together. Thomas Corbett opened his first Great Western Cooking Depot in 1860. Within a few years there were 20 within the city and several in the adjoining burghs.[59] One could accommodate over 500 people. Soon additional facilities were provided, like newspapers and recreational and educational opportunities.[60] These ideas were taken up and developed in Leeds to become temperance refreshment rooms. The Liverpool British Workman Public House chain, a drink-free eating house with recreational facilities, spread to Glasgow. Soon there were more than a dozen branches in 1879 and still growing.[61]

Hygiene, health and temperance led to vegetarianism. The American ideas of scientific vegetarianism of Dr R T Trall had been popularised from the 1860s, through the *Dietetic Reformer*.[62] A small active group in Glasgow gave rise to the Scottish Food Reform Society in 1879. The writings of Thomas Low Nichols distributed through James Coates were closely studied. The *Social Reformer* carried several articles praising his ideas.[63] The success of Food Reform restaurants in London, one of which Robert Reid, a leading Glasgow temperance figure, returned from America to manage, was observed.[64] The need for proper teaching and understanding of human physiology was stressed by Nichols, Coates and their Scottish friends like Alexander Munro: pure food meant pure minds in healthy bodies.[65] Old teetotal vegetarians and hydropathic enthusiasts like John Davie agreed. Married to the daughter of Archibald Livingstone, Glasgow merchant and host to John B Gough in 1857, Davie endorsed these ideals.[66] John Fraser, the old Chartist long exiled in America, returned to die a teetotaller and vegetarian.[67]

In 1879 the Scottish Food Reform Society was established. A Food Reform Cookery School followed at Allison Street, Glasgow, under the direction of Anna Soule, the American Universalist missionary friend of the Coates.[68] Within a few months Coates and Mrs Soule were apparently addressing the sixty members of the Food Reform Society, a support they continued.[69] The annual meetings of the Food Reform Society were graced by the Lord Provost, Sir William Collins, and the movement persisted as an element in the Scottish social reform movement to the end of the First World War.[70]

Concern for health led to the formation of the Scottish Anti-Smoking Society along American lines in 1871.[71] Its chairman was the Glasgow timber merchant, James McNair, who had emigrated to New Zealand and then travelled extensively in America before settling back home. He was married to the daughter of John Anderson, the Glasgow merchant who was host to the American temperance delegates to the general assemblies and synods of 1872. Anderson's other daughter was married to Revd Dr Sinclair H Patterson, MD, of Bellgrove Presbyterian Church, Glasgow. He was to move to London and to become very active in the anti-vivisection campaign in close collaboration with Americans.[72] That in turn led to the rejection of vaccination as dangerous and impure.

Even allowing for these extreme positions, there was a considerable body of respectable medical opinion opposed to drink. Sir Benjamin W Richardson, educated at the Andersonian Institution and Edinburgh, was a nationally renowned figure; Dr Norman Kerr, a frequent platform speaker and prolific author, was a Glasgow graduate who had sailed the Atlantic with the Allan Line before settling in London; Revd Sinclair H Patterson MD was a regular lecturer and writer on physiology and temperance.[73]

A theme of compulsion was present from the earliest stages in the movement, but American pressures, example and uncompromising prohibitionist sentiment pushed the west of Scotland advocates further in a similar direction. Temperance increasingly meant militant prohibition views. At each stage America forced the pace. At a very early stage many Americans were total abstainers. In that sense the parallels with the anti-slavery movement are striking. The conflict between the immediate abolitionists and the gradual emancipationists was comparable to that between the immediate total prohibitionists of all traffic in alcoholic drinks and the more moderate gradualists who usually wanted restrictions, controls and limited licensing but not always total prohibition. By the 1850s, with the example of the Maine Law, Scottish temperance forces were drawn into association with the United Kingdom Alliance. In the later nineteenth century the efforts by the prohibitionist forces to infiltrate and persuade the Liberal party to take up the cause was comparable to similar efforts in the United States. Local option and local control became the main preoccupation on both sides of the Atlantic until the First World War. That policy had appeal to local rate-payers who could determine the quality of their own local area. It had strong parallels with the ideas of home rule for Scotland and Ireland as well as local state powers in the United States. It meant that in Scotland the rate-payer, not the masses, determined the issue: it might then appear as class, religious and ethnic cultural domination through legislation. Some elements were not averse to that idea. In Scotland and America it meant that certain groups determined the test for admission to 'respectability'. A pressure group was establishing the framework for the only acceptable notions of democracy. It was the very antithesis of pluralism. The parallel is perhaps closest with the south in America where a small politically manageable group could be relied upon to come to the 'right' decision. Unfortunately in the Scottish context it merely meant that the respectable areas remained dry and the wet areas remained untouched. The local control idea also had strong parallels with municipal initiative in demonstrating the benefits of certain forms of regulation and control—so it was believed. First the ward, then the city, then the nation for dry influence. At every stage enthusiastic Americans were ready, willing and frequently present to give their encouragement. That connection was dramatically demonstrated in the effort to export prohibition from the United States to Glasgow at the end of the First World War.

In the initial stages the Glasgow temperance movement had attracted a wide range of figures. Once the moral suasion fervour subsided and the fragmented activities were gathered around the Scottish Temperance League in 1844, several features were apparent. The leadership seemed closely connected either by family ties, area of origin, business or religious affiliation. The fact that many were newcomers to the city, men of new wealth and members of voluntary churches, may have intensified their moral earnestness and the drive towards respectability.

Saltcoats seemed to have provided a disproportionate number of leading men in the movement. Thomas Service of Saltcoats, 1807–80, had established himself in business at the age of eighteen in Glasgow.[74] A member of Dr Heugh's Secession church, he built up a thriving muslin business and a railway interest before retiring to Cranley, Carstairs, in 1870. His brother, William, was for many years treasurer of the Scottish Temperance League. His sister was married to Robert Smith of the City Line, another prominent temperance figure. President of the Glasgow Evangelistic Association, he warmly supported Moody and Sankey in their missions, and as an elder of Wellington Street UP church he built two mission halls in the city. His brother, George was a partner in his business and philanthropic enterprises. The wife of Thomas Service was a daughter of Alexander Allan, founder of the Allan Line. He and his family all came from Saltcoats.

Though never teetotallers, the Allans were staunch supporters with money and goodwill. They were also married into the temperance action. The five sons of the founder, Alexander Allan, were to spread the line around the Atlantic and South America: James Allan 1808–80 supported the league while his wife was a founder member of the British Women's Temperance Union in 1876. His brother, Alexander Allan, was married to the daughter of Robert Smith and took a keen interest in the Glasgow Evangelistic Union and the British Workman restaurants. With their brothers, Sir Hew in Canada and Andrew and Bryce in Liverpool, they all promoted the Allan Line Temperance Society. In time they were to absorb the City Line and become the largest shipping fleet in the world by 1892. Robert Simpson, 1807–87, born in Saltcoats, also came to Glasgow and built up a substantial drapery business at the corner of Argyle Street and Jamaica Street.[75] At thirty he had entered the University of Glasgow, then studied theology and followed his friend Revd Fergus Ferguson into the Evangelical Union. Similarly William Melvin, another activist, was a prosperous draper in the city.

Printing and publishing provided several leading men. William Collins, 1789–1853, and his son, Sir William Collins 1817–95, were extremely successful printers[76] who had built up a considerable trade in the early nineteenth century following their association with Thomas Chalmers and with the evangelical revival. George Gallie, the brother-in-law of the renowned city missionary, Revd David Naismith, was a steady supporter of temperance who enjoyed his printing and publishing. In both cases, many American tracts, sermons and works were reprinted in Glasgow.

Like some of the leading figures in the Scottish movement, they were predictably associated with Thomas Chalmers in Glasgow. William Collins and Robert Kettle, a deacon, were cases in point. They were following out a Christian civic sense of responsibility, the demand for social and individual salvation.[78] Others were apparently upwardly mobile characters who may have been thoroughly committed Christians but who were also able to use the temperance interest to develop (not necessarily advance, a loaded word) their careers. Two cases suggest as much. Baillie Torrens of Glasgow (1811–84)[79] was born in Edinburgh. He had joined a Glasgow firm of painters and decorators before he established his own business in Greenock. Following a brief visit to America, he returned to Glasgow as the head of Torrens and Husband. He was to be a leading light in supporting the United Kingdom Alliance and the beginning of the Scottish Permissive Bill and Temperance Association.

Other supporting figures in the temperance campaign were moderated radicals. In the 1840s the Scottish Temperance League Lecturers included the Chartists Henry Vincent and Robert Lowery.[80] The latter was to remain a popular lecturer until ill-health forced him to emigrate to Canada. Revd Thomas Adam, who was a friend of Audubon, the American naturalist, of Revd Edward Irving, the millenarian, and of William Cobbett, was a lifelong abstainer.[81] Similarly, Thomas Smith of Hamilton with his father had supported Cobbett and temperance before he emigrated to America in 1867 to join his brother-in-law, brothers and sisters in Cold Spring, New York.[82] He died shortly afterwards at thirty-seven. Temperance did provide an alternative career for some. James Browning White, a Good Templar and a miner, emigrated to America and then returned to become a full time agent for the Scottish Temperance League in the west of Scotland. James McNair, a former Roseneath wood merchant and speculative property developer, emigrated to New Zealand, travelled extensively in America and then returned to run a rehabilitative centre on the shores of Loch Fyne in 1860.[83]

Robert Reid, 1816–1908, a founder of the Scottish Temperance League, married Catherine Gibson of Morris, Illinois, emigrated to America in 1864, moved to Canada and then returned to Glasgow in 1871 before finally establishing a vegetarian restaurant in London.[84] His brother, Revd William Reid, was for many years vice-president of the Scottish Temperance League. Their mother was the daughter of William McGavin, the author of *The Protestant*, a famous anti-Catholic publication which had a continued influence in Scotland and America in the first half of the nineteenth century. His brother-in-law, John McGavin, Glasgow merchant, was a founder member and elder of Kent Road UP church in 1863. The minister

Revd Dr Joseph Brown, a Glasgow graduate, formerly minister in Dalkeith for almost thirty years, a vigorous teetotaller, gathered a formidable dry congregation around himself, including John Guthrie, Alexander MacDonald and Neil McNeil, the publisher. Brown, with relatives in America, closely followed developments there and presided at J B Gough's visit to Glasgow in 1879. Revd William M Taylor took that interest a stage further. Born in Kilwinning, he graduated from Glasgow University, entered the UP ministry and after brief service at Kilmaurs spent some seventeen years in Bootle. Invited to New York by his brother-in-law, he deputised for Revd Dr Storrs of the Pilgrims Church, Brooklyn for almost three months. In that time he won a reputation as a rival preacher to Henry Ward Beecher. Soon afterwards he was invited to the charge of the Broadway Tabernacle, New York. From there he claimed he exercised a far greater influence than in Great Britain. Like Revd J Newman Hall of Dublin, he had built up a great reputation as guest preacher at annual temperance gatherings in Glasgow before he settled in America.

There was a closely connected audience—almost an incestuous one—for transatlantic propaganda about temperance. Revd W M Taylor who settled in New York, was, according to a former Glaswegian, still preaching to his own countrymen.[85] On departing from Glasgow in 1873, Revd J M Earnshaw of Nebraska 'hoped to see the day when the united exertions of Scotland and America would place the cope-stone upon total abstinence'.[86] That was a likely prospect. What had been a co-operative venture became increasingly a very Scottish enterprise as many Scots, schooled in temperance, emigrated to the United States. Emigrants, as Robert Smith claimed in his farewell address to Robert Reid in 1864, were part of a working-class movement to spread the message of self help and self improvement through total abstinence.[87]

The figures for Scottish immigration into America are difficult to firmly establish. Scottish emigrants were generally considered part of the British exodus and many non-British emigrants travelled to America from Scottish ports just as many Scots left from English ports. Some indication of the continued close Scottish community can be gauged from the visits of several Scottish temperance advocates to the United States. In a literal sense they hardly seem to have experienced America but rather to have continued their Scottish experience on a larger stage. Travelling from a Scottish port on a Scottish ship, they toured through American Scottish communities meeting old friends, acquaintances and religious brothers. America was an idealised version of a happier, healthier more affluent and dry nation, peopled by happy families in solid substantial homes. Old Scottish values of thrift, sobriety and hard work were essential: 'A disappointment almost as great awaits those who come from the old country to America thinking that it is an El Dorado and land of certain and easy success. The difficulties here, especially to the workingman, are fewer, and his prospects, thank God, are larger, and brighter; but it is a balance of advantages and disadvantages after all. To seek the better we must leave much that is good behind.'[88] Forty years later, Sir Samuel Chisholm, the former Lord Provost of Glasgow, on a visit to America could rejoice that Protestantism, Presbyterianism and democracy were thriving amid the American culture, assimilated to Scottish ideals of temperance.[89]

There were temperance emigration schemes. One of the organisers, Revd Robert Kerr, an Independent Congregational minister at Forres, formerly of Caistor, Lincolnshire, had taken his charge in January 1867. A leading local temperance figure, he was a member of the Scottish Temperance League. In 1871 he resigned his pastorate and in association with James Miller, editor and publisher of the *Forres Gazette*, another temperance advocate, he promoted a temperance colony in Minnesota. After a lengthy tour of the area, he returned to Scotland in October 1872 and began to lecture on the benefits of emigration.[90] The rules of the temperance emigration society were advertised in the *League Journal*, 16 November 1872. Initially membership was to be 2s. 6d. but soon became 5s. with a pledge that members who settled in the colony would neither make, sell nor permit to be sold any intoxicating liquors. After some six months recruiting, Kerr had gathered 150 members from northern England and Scotland and he went to Washington to finalise the purchase of a tract 12×24 miles.[91] The first party, armed with two temperance references and their pledge, left Glasgow at the end of April 1873. Kerr and a group from England followed in May. They were the sort of reliable industrious immigrants the Northern Pacific Railroad wanted on its available lands.[92] They, like many American contemporaries, were expectant capitalists.

America was useful in creating a public opinion favourably disposed to temperance. American tracts, the example of American social and legislative change, especially in the Maine Law, and the continuous procession of American propagandists to the west of Scotland all helped to create the moral and social climate hostile to drinkers. The concern for moral and physical health expanded and reinforced the interests which had drawn the group to reform. Temperance organisations developed a full life, moral, active and socially useful. The tensions between moral suasion and legislation gradually subsided. Temperance Ohio accurately declared at a Scottish Temperance League breakfast: 'We are the two Christian nations of the earth.'[100] Several factors contributed to that good conceit of oneself. A succession of temperance crusaders, culminating in the successful initial visit of John B Gough, stiffened Scottish resolve. The enactment of Prohibition in Maine in 1851, followed by massive temperance legislation in twelve other states over the next four years, was a further stimulus to action. Only in 1856 were the opposition to successfully challenge the legality of some of the acts.[101] These American successes, well advertised by American visitors to Britain, encouraged the English teetotallers to establish the United Kingdom Alliance, a move paralleled by the formation of the Scottish Permissive Bill and Temperance Association.[102] In Scotland the Forbes-MacKenzie Act of 1853 restricted licences, enacted 11 p.m. closing on weekdays and the prohibition of liquor sales on Sunday except in hotels to bona fide travellers and residents. It was a firm base on which to build further restrictions.

The growing confidence reflected the consolidation of the temperance societies on a sound basis, the general economic improvement of the mid century and the apparently irresistible advance of liberal and democratic notions throughout the world. The spread of Anglo-Saxon culture, Christianity and commerce throughout the world was reassuring for Scots as their native land lost its old ways. As suggested earlier, compensations were found in the Atlantic alliance. As Revd Dr Edmond, a UP delegate to an American Presbyterian assembly in 1870, observed, their kind of folk were fulfilling a providential role: 'Presbyterianism, gathering largely into its pale the middle classes of the community, has vast opportunities for leavening the nation and is bravely girding itself to the task. We may learn not a little from its enterprise, and from the intercourse with its noble leaders. The interchange of brotherly fellowship which has recently begun, it is to be hoped may be maintained till the churches of this country, finding their way to home union, may begin to ask whether the Atlantic itself might not be overstepped in the wide federalisation, if not incorporation of a happy Pan-Presbyterianism, with a glad freeness of thought and action within the firm circle of a common faith and order.'[103]

Henry Ward Beecher could hardly have expressed it better. Apart from fear of the new centralised discipline of Catholicism after Vatican I, the moral liberal democrats of the Atlantic world were concerned by the challenge of the masses. They had to be disciplined for their own good, trained to the acquisition of education and wealth, and ultimately the responsible use of the franchise. The restrictions placed upon the freed blacks after 1865 and upon artisans in the 1867 Reform Act in Britain were acceptable to this moral caucus.[104]

Temperance was a central element in that strategy. Individual reform took precedence over social structural reform. But after 1870 temperance advocates were demanding much greater state intervention for moral social ends in an ever-widening array of concerns. Prohibition remained the ultimate objective but it only became a central issue once more in the 1890s. In the aftermath of short-lived victories as in Maine, the temperance leaders were educating new adherents, voters and churchmen in the ultimate necessity of prohibition. By the 1890s, health, housing, women's suffrage and other issues had been fully exploited without solving the ultimate problem of drunkenness. By then new scientific professional assessments of social evils were beginning and there was the alternative vision of the left. Temperance concerns were largely subsumed into the transatlantic progressive movement. In that atmosphere, the logic and purity of temperance ideas demanded prohibition: the outlook narrowed somewhat to a single minded pursuit of that objective. In that sense temperance failed but it had awakened public interest in many social ills. In educating public opinion it had made reform respectable.[105]

In the pre-Civil War period, the attack upon black slavery was bound up with that upon slavery to drink. In 1851, Revd Amos Dresser of Ohio lectured on 'War, Slavery and Intemperance' in Wardlaw's chapel, Glasgow. The link had already been well established by various tracts, by the lectures of the abolitionist George Thompson to the West of Scotland Temperance Union a decade earlier and lectures of William Lloyd

Garrison, Frederick Douglass and Mr Buffom in 1846.[106] Henry C Wright, the most radical abolitionist, peace advocate and water-cure advocate, likewise made the connection. The confidence of the temperance movement then greatly improved during the mid century. The passage of the Maine Law in America, making the state dry in 1851, the passage of the Forbes-MacKenzie Act in Scotland in 1853, which provided for Sunday closing and placed restrictions on hours and licences, and the visits of several American 'stars' gave added impetus for prohibition. In Glasgow, James Morton, a baker who later emigrated to Brooklyn, and his friends organised a meeting demanding the Maine Law for Scotland: 20,000 leaflets were printed extolling the virtues of that American legislation.[107] Robert MacKay, later secretary of the Scottish Permissive Bill and Temperance Association, similarly demonstrated in Aberdeen for the Maine Law. In England the United Kingdom Alliance resulted while in Scotland the Scottish Permissive Bill and Temperance Association began to take shape until its formal foundation in 1858.[109] The World's Temperance Convention in New York in 1853 showed its prohibitionist outlook: Neal Dow sought to make prohibition the only issue.[110] This growing sentiment might capitalise upon the Scottish revival of 1858–9.[111] Temperance now meant total abstinence, if not legally enforced prohibition. The newer leadership, self-made in a brief spell, were perhaps more assertive, aggressive and insecure than their predecessors: they were men in a hurry. They sought American aid.

In the decade preceding the American Civil War that aid already was forthcoming. In 1850 Revd Leonard Bacon, a renowed if somewhat socially conservative American churchman toured Scotland giving temperance lectures.[112] Two years later, Archibald Prentice, the former Manchester editor and Anti-Corn Law League protagonist, returned to his home area after an American visit to lecture on intemperance.[113] At the same time F W Kellogg, an American lecturer and later congressman, spent some five weeks in Scotland with such success that he returned to persuade John B Gough to come over and consolidate his efforts.[114] In 1860, Revd Dr Kerr, Professor of Church History in the UP Theological Seminary, Pittsburgh, with his colleague Revd Mr Harper of Xenia, Ohio, renewed his acquaintance with Revd David Macrae of Crossmyloof in Glasgow. They had previously met in Pittsburgh. The gathering was a demonstration of the goodwill, common interest and concern of Scottish-Americans in the progress of liberty and temperance.[115] These, however, paled into insignificance at the advent of Dow and Gough.

Neal Dow and John B Gough were the two major figures to visit Scotland in 1857–9. Neal Dow had won his considerable reputation in the campaign for prohibition in Maine. The Maine Law, as it was called, made the state the first dry state in the United States. 1851 was a major triumph. Dow had been born the son of a Quaker who had been prominent in drives for sabbatarianism, temperance and improved public morals. A Federalist rather than a Jacksonian, somewhat conservative rather than radical, Dow had considerable business interests in banking, mills and property. A member of the African Colonisation Society, he had rather conservative views on race, aliens and women.[116] In 1855 he became mayor of Portland with a strong prohibitionist platform but his political difficulties resulted in his defeat the following year. In 1857 he went on his first of three tours of Britain; April–November 1857; May 1866–November 1867; April 1873–May 1875. On each occasion he visited Glasgow.[117] His initial visit seems to have been something of a disappointment: he did not have the platform presence. The prohibitionists were paying homage to a pioneer (to their own sense of liberty, blood and tradition).[118] He was to be quickly outshone by John B Gough.

Gough had emigrated from Kent as a youth, fell into bad habits and drink. Saved from evil he had begun a temperance career.[119] After the successful tour of F W Kellogg in Britain, during 1852, Gough decided to undertake a visit at the invitation of the Scottish Temperance League and the British Temperance Association. Kellogg had spent five fruitful weeks in Scotland. Gough came somewhat apprehensively: 'The English and Scotch love argument; I cannot argue, for I want logic; I am no logician, I have no education. I can only tell them about what I believe to be the truth in my own way.'[120] As an American temperance observer noted, Gough 'in a simplicity and modesty promising nothing, in less than three minutes he struck in every heart and drew a tear from every eye'.[121] On his first appearance he won his audience. An observer claimed he was moving his audience, an audience such as he had never seen: 'He has made the cause somewhat fashionable and this is a great matter'.[122] Kilmarnock, Paisley and Edinburgh were overwhelmed. He had been decisive in the cause. On his second visit to Glasgow in September 1857 Gough became an even greater success. He was to travel backwards and forwards throughout Scotland, moving, converting and enthralling his audiences in their thousands.[123] Week after week the temperance press carried rave reviews of his performance and moving successes throughout the land.[124] The appeal and success never faltered on any of his numerous visits. Even on his last tour in 1879 he was still in great demand.[125] By then the Glasgow leadership had changed somewhat. Several old leaders still exerted influence but newer figures, who had risen rapidly to wealth and who were more eager to utilise popular political pressure to moral ends, were emerging.

In 1851 William Wells Brown, the former slave had addressed several meetings on temperance in the city with the former slaves Mr and Mrs William Crafts.[126] Wells returned some twenty-six years later as a delegate of the Independent Order of Templars. Once again he was enthusiastically welcomed, particularly by Revd George Gladstone who bitterly attacked the segregationist Good Templars in America. Gladstone, with Revd William Ross of Rothesay, was a regular visitor to Illinois, Boston and elsewhere: both shared strong views on racial equality and prohibition.[127] In 1878 Ross was again with Brown in Boston and the following year in Liverpool, Ross and Gladstone were the preachers and prayer leaders at the Good Templars World gathering.[128] Other blacks supported the campaign—Revd Dr Pennington in 1850, Mr Hanson, the original 'Uncle Tom', an American Indian, Mr Powell, Mr Anderson, an ex-slave, and many others.[129] On one occasion, however, tension crept in. Revd Mr Webster of Ontario, bitterly reproached the New York Temperance Society for expelling a coloured Glasgow graduate, Macune Smith, from the proceedings on account of his skin. That version was quickly denied by the following speaker. The original Christy minstrels, the Ohio minstrels, Albain's Coloured Opera Troupe and the later Fisk Jubilee Singers were utilised in the dry campaigns.[130]

If temperance ideas drew the lines of respectability for blacks, they did also for Catholics in the West of Scotland. Irish and other Catholic migrants into Glasgow were attracted to temperance by the work of several priests. The redoubtable Fr Peter Forbes, St Mary's Abercromby Street, organised temperance activities among his flock assisted by two laymen, Mr McEnteer from Liverpool, and Charles Bryson. In November 1839 they established a total abstinence society. Fr Forbes, distressed by the evils of drink in destroying the last vestiges of family stability in his poverty stricken flock, brought Fr Theobald Mathew to Glasgow. The Irish priest was welcomed by all shades of religious opinion to Glasgow. Tens of thousands took the pledge from him in the cattle market and the organisation flourished for several years. Fr James Enraght, an Irish priest, went further and consolidated good relations with Protestant temperance groups, organising joint rallies on Glasgow Green which included some 9000 Catholic pledges, addressing joint meetings with Protestants before Fr Mathew arrived. Like Fr Mathew, he also went to America, lecturing extensively on behalf of the cause.[131] The evident good relations do not seem to have survived the massive influx of poor Irish immigrants to Britain and America, the intensification of religious and political animosities from 1848 revolutions in Europe. The old prejudices were revived as poverty seemed identified with Catholicism: the larger social questions were not asked. Temperance in Catholic minds seemed identified with those who bigotedly indulged in petty persecution. The renegade priests, Gavazzi and Chiniquy, lectured on behalf of temperance whilst some temperance agents gave unequivocal anti-Catholic lectures, views which might be reflected in the pages of temperance journals and magazines.[132] That distance persisted until Archbishop Manning founded the League of the Cross which penetrated into Scotland largely through the work of Archbishop Eyre in Glasgow. That work and that of Bishop Ireland in Minnesota received favourable reports in the *League Journal*. Its paternalistic character, however, alienated many potential Catholic supporters.

The essential link between Catholics and Protestants on both sides of the Atlantic was a common crusade in support of so-called modernisation; the inculcation of sobriety, saving, discipline and adjustment within urban industrial society. Where those attitudes seem to flourish a common bond existed. When class, ethnic, sectarian or political self-consciousness took precedence that alliance collapsed. In crude terms the gap between Irish Catholic immigrants and their Protestant hosts on both sides of the Atlantic intensified at certain times in many areas on local, national or even international issues—for example, the 1848 revolutions or the Irish question from 1885. That should not obliterate the fact that some limited cooperation in the process of modernisation persisted.[133]

Theodore L Cuyler, a Princeton graduate, was converted to temperance by Fr Mathew in Glasgow. The pastor of a thriving Brooklyn church which refused membership to all connected with the drink traffic, Cuyler not only ministered to a fairly large Scottish congregation but also wrote regular columns for the *League Journal* as well as occasionally for the *Pictorial Tracts* series (see illustration). That influence was further reinforced by two further visits to Glasgow in 1872 and 1887. In that year Cuyler, accompanied by Revd J B Dunn, who had visited Glasgow some nineteen years earlier, and Revd Mr Wells of Chicago came as deputies to the synod and general assemblies of the Scottish Presbyterian churches. It was a dramatic gesture in support of temperance.[134] On his return Cuyler was meeting with James Morton, baker and a vigorous temperance worker who had emigrated from Glasgow in 1856 to Brooklyn. His regular letters to the *League Journal* maintained a close check on American developments.[135] He was almost a temperance Alistair Cooke with his interviews with Revd W M Taylor, Broadway Tabernacle, Theodore L Cuyler and Henry Ward Beecher.[136] Emphasising the common urban problems associated with drink, and the difficulty of arousing public concern, and complaining of the apathy of American clergy, Morton returned to renew personal contacts in Glasgow in 1870[137] Cuyler sent back reports to American papers about Glasgow temperance forces.[138]

Further indications of cross-fertilisation were the appearance of American religious bodies in the Glasgow area. The Christadelphians seem to have appeared in the mid seventies.[139] The Churches of Christ had appeared slightly earlier, seemingly developing from an already existing Baptist chapel on the Broomielaw.[140] This body, which originated in the preaching of a Glasgow graduate, Alexander Campbell, was in a sense a celebration of American providential destiny and mission.[141] By 1913 there were seven Churches of Christ in the Glasgow area together with thirty-eight Assemblies of the Christian Brethren.[142] With their temperance views they provided reinforcements for the existing church organisations. Some of their members were to become outstanding temperance leaders. John Adam, manager of the Pollokshaws Gas Company and member of the Church of Christ, played a very active role for over twenty years.[143] Mr H Eliot Tickle, who served as chairman of the Scottish Temperance League executive, and an elder in the Shawlands church, spent twenty years in Glasgow temperance activity to his death.[144] R D Craig of the Church of Christ, Renfrew, attended Ruskin College and returned to become the League agent in Dundee.[145]

The Good Templars were introduced into Scotland in 1868 from America. Brother T R Roberts, a Scottish emigrant, recruited Jabez Walker and thirty-nine others to establish the first lodge in Scotland. The regalia was perhaps an attempt to rejuvenate the flagging temperance fortunes. But within a few years Walker emigrated to California.[146] George Gladstone was perhaps the leading Glaswegian supporter and visited America to attend Good Templar meetings in Illinois in 1873. Such exchanges which brought Americans from Illinois, the Carolinas and the mid west further consolidated the trans-atlantic alliance.[147] That same year a large army of female

Good Templars descended upon Glasgow from America. Though many were drawn from the traditional east coast centres of temperance support, others came in considerable numbers from the mid west and even more significant was the prominence of women. These two new factors made an enormous impact upon temperance fortunes on both sides of the Atlantic. Respectability with respect for law and order in raw communities was an excellent argument.[148] Neal Dow, the veteran of the Maine Law, presided at the gathering.

Dow was hardly a stranger to the Glasgow platform. He had visited the city on at least two previous occasions. As early as 1857 he had come but failed to match up to Gough in his appearance or speaking: 'From Demosthenes to Ruskin great souls have been housed in what seemed to the outward eye inappropriate tabernacles.' In extolling the virtues of the Maine Law in enabling people to acquire property, modest comfort and self respect, Dow may have been on the defensive.[149] As the reporter wrote, 'Far away fowls have fine feathers.'[150] The church had to be mobilised on behalf of the cause in Scotland as in America.[151] American developments were closely followed.[152] In 1866 Dow again returned to Scotland—to Edinburgh, Glasgow and Greenock—but significantly his speeches went virtually unreported whilst his presence was used to bolster the local leadership like Revd George Gladstone, Revd J A Johnston of Springburn, and Neil McNeill.[153] Glaswegians saw that leadership and effective policing based on community support were needed for effective enforcement of prohibition as in Maine.[154] In 1873 Dow's visit to Kilmarnock passed virtually unnoticed.[155] It was as if temperance people were looking for new, younger, fresher approaches to the perennial problem.

There were several initiatives which received new impetus in the period after 1865. From 1841 Glasgow temperance organisations had organised excursions to various resorts in Scotland and south of the border. Thomas Cook allegedly copied these ideas in Leicester.[156] Train excursions had been arranged to London and even to the continent from Glasgow temperance headquarters in 1866.[157] Cheap fares were secured for travellers to the society's annual general meeting.[158] As soon as the American Civil War was over, Thomas Cook was offered specially conducted tours of America from Glasgow under his personal supervision.[159] Cook had already visited Robert Reid, the Glasgow advocate in Chicago, on his tour of America to see his old Leicester friends and explore the territory for tourism.[160]

Travel then helped to unite humanitarian concern, elevated experiences and the sheer pleasure of tourism amongst those who still laboured under their puritan heritage. Several Glasgow temperance leaders visited the United States and sent reports which might encourage further endeavours at home: they also brought news of old friends invariably doing well in the States, though whether from temperance principles, freer society or more opportunities was often unclear. Their reports may have stimulated further immigration from Scotland.

Robert Reid and his American wife went to settle with his father-in-law in Morris, Illinois in 1864.[161] Almost immediately he arrived in the area he was holding public meetings to promote teetotalism. At one he secured one

A NEW YEAR'S TRACT.

A NEW YEAR'S EPISTLE FROM AMERICA.
BY REV. THEODORE L. CUYLER, D.D. OF BROOKLYN, U.S.A.

1   Frontispiece of Temperance Tract by Revd Theodore L Cuyler, who visited Glasgow several times to aid temperance campaigns, reproduced by kind permission of Mitchell Library Collections, Glasgow

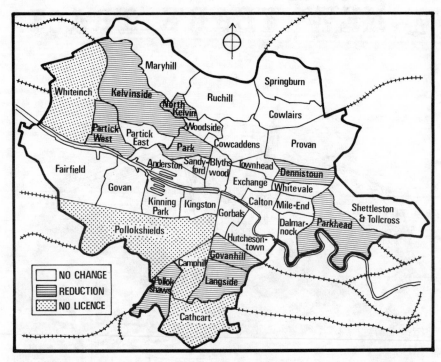

2   Glasgow after Temperance Poll. The results of the 1920 prohibition poll in
     Glasgow. *Source* Temperance Leader and League Journal 15 Nov 1920

3   Propaganda in Sauchiehall Street during the prohibition campaign, from
     Kenneth L Roberts, Why Europe Leaves Home (London 1920)

4 & 5   Anti-prohibition posters used in Glasgow prohibition campaign: 'Pussyfoot' William E Johnson, a prohibitionist who visited Glasgow, from Kenneth L Roberts, Why Europe Leaves Home (London 1920)

A NEW YEAR'S TRACT.

THE DARK PLOT.
BY REV. T. DE WITT TALMAGE, D.D., BROOKLYN.

6   Frontispiece of Temperance Tract by Revd T DeWitt Talmage. The author is seen congratulating William Collins, the Lord Provost of Glasgow, publisher and temperance activist, reproduced by kind permission of Mitchell Library Collections, Glasgow

hundred pledges.[162] But he was soon disappointed, whether by his impressions of poor temperance sentiment or his business is unclear.[163] Even so he continued to address meetings of Sons of Temperance and Good Templars though with increasing disenchantment: 'I do not anticipate any great result from their labours.'[164] Clearly the temperance sentiment was well established, but merely that and not a crusading endeavour; in the aftermath of the American Civil War, crusading was somewhat muted.

With the abolition of slavery in the United States, attention focused upon the issues of drink and woman suffrage. Sensitive Christian consciences in the transatlantic world worried about the subjection of man to drink and of woman to (drunken) man. In an increasingly fluid American society which was undergoing rapid industrialisation and urbanisation the need for the effective regulation, if not repression, of drink seemed all the more pressing. With the rapid influx of more cosmopolitan immigrant peoples from southern and eastern Europe, fears for the future of the social order, the stability of the family and American democracy increased. The old Protestant order was under threat. With the erosion of old status and power, the vulgar professionalisation of politics, and the need to compensate in moral superiority, drink became an important issue, temperance a symbol of respectability. American politics in the late nineteenth century, it has been suggested, was about such perceptions. It did not have issues as we would understand them. The churches on the defensive in the post-Darwinian world found temperance a means of demonstrating their relevance. It was part of the crusade to recapture the cities for the church. In that campaign women played an increasingly forceful role. Increasingly well educated, aware of their subjection to men, and leisured, women played a vital role in pushing through prohibition. As earlier legislation had failed because it was too far in advance of public opinion, later legislation gradually succeeded because women educated public opinion to the benefits of prohibition. The new social order allowed more women to pursue respectable moral campaigns: their radical demands were essentially devoted to conservationist ends. Prohibition with enfranchised women would stabilise and regenerate society. Similar notions flourished in Scotland. The same need to assert ethnic religious and social dominance might be seen in both countries. Invoking active women's participation was a means of gerrymandering a moral and eventually an electoral majority for your form of respectability. With the expansion of transatlantic steamship companies, improved comfort and shorter crossings, these complex motives could contribute to a more aggressive and more democratic prohibitionist movement.

Transatlantic opinions could be rapidly formulated. The rapid flow of people, information and journals to and fro across the Atlantic made the emotional and intellectual union a reality. International gatherings of prohibitionists were indicative of this new consensus. The Centennial Celebrations in Philadelphia in 1876 provided the beginning of the international women's movement. The Chicago, St Louis, Glasgow and New York World Fairs all gave opportunities for gatherings on temperance. In addition there were international conventions on Temperance in London in 1890, in

Edinburgh in 1900 and 1910 to coincide with the World Missionary Assembly. Delegates to international gatherings of the Order of Good Templars might join together in Liverpool, Glasgow, Chicago or New York. At all these gatherings Glaswegians freely exchanged their views with American prohibitionists. Revd George Gladstone invariably appeared on such occasions. Frequently he took delegates back with him to Glasgow to address rallies there. In 1900 he brought several American delegates to a conference in Edinburgh over to Glasgow: Mrs Stevenson of the Massachusetts WCTU, Mrs Boole of New York.[165] In Edinburgh he was associating with another Glasgow visitor, Charles M Sheldon the author of *In His Steps*, with Madame Demorest, New York, as well as Mrs Greenwood, Miss Marianne Framingham, Mrs F J Barnes and Anna Gordon from America.[166] In 1877 Gladstone met large numbers of Grand Templars from America, particularly the South in Liverpool. He himself attended some conventions in America as well. A prohibition international was a reality. Strategy, tactics and methods were discussed. Morale was boosted. There was a moral world majority whatever the position in the homeland.

The relative ease of transportation meant large numbers of American leaders could visit Scotland and many Scottish figures could tour America. In 1891 John M Stearns, President of the New York Temperance League and editor of the *National Temperance Advocate*, visited Glasgow.[167] Three years later the renowned reformed lawyer, J G Woolley, gave three lectures in Glasgow and others in Greenock and Paisley.[168] Returning to America, he was to edit the *New Voice*, a vigorous prohibitionist journal, run for president of the United States on the prohibition party ticket in 1900, and returned to Europe on three further occasions—1901, 1905 and 1921. In 1900 Joshua L Baily, the Quaker prohibitionist from Philadelphia, lectured in the Glasgow Christian Institute to a select audience which included Revd James Barr, later socialist MP.[169]

The newspaper and periodical press provided further consolidation of this view. Old established figures like Neal Dow of Maine and Theodore L Cuyler regularly contributed articles to the *League Journal*.[170] Cuyler was a frequent correspondent. W S Caine's travels in America and his interview with the Columbus Congregational minister and reformer, Washington Gladden, received good coverage. The visits of Guy Hayler and Joshua L Baily to Maine; the workings of prohibition and its uplifting effects in Kansas, Atlanta and elsewhere were thoroughly, glowingly reported.[171] Articles from the *New Voice* were reprinted and developments in America closely monitored. The campaigns of Carrie Nation, the Kansas 'smasher' were comprehensively examined, attitudes of American workers favourable to prohibition publicised. A former Glasgow Wesleyan minister who had emigrated in 1905 sent an article on the Liquor Traffic in America.[172] In this way reports gained credence from known correspondents. Visitors to Glasgow were established in their audience's mind before they arrived and the memory after their departure home was cultivated. A personal and political connection was forged in this way.

If Catholics were suspicious of their American and Glaswegian prohibitionists they might have been reassured by the eagerness with which Catholic endorsements of temperance and in a few isolated cases of the Anti-Saloon League were reported. The Catholics of Glenboig worked in close co-operation with Mr Thomas Dunnachie in furthering prohibitionist ideas, sharing holiday trips and promoting harmonious community relations.[173] The spread of temperance principles in the Glasgow archdiocese following Archbishop Eyre's urging of the League of the Cross was considerable. Bishop Maguire, his auxiliary, could report that 133 branches with 33,000 members had some 43 halls for meetings and entertainments. In America the news seemed even more encouraging, with bishops speaking out against the drink traffic. Bishop Watterson of Columbus, Ohio, refused to have officials of Catholic organisations men who were liquor dealers in any way.[174] Good will then might be used to political effect. In the case of Glasgow, that was dissipated in the First World War and immediately following. There had been a willingness to co-operate in social affairs. The question of Ireland, the growth of the Labour party support among the Glaswegian Catholics, and the growing irrelevance of the cosmetic reforms of the earlier town council proved too divisive.[175]

The religious revivalism, the awakened civic conscience and the general concern for the quality of future democratic life on both sides of the Atlantic became pronounced in the late nineteenth century. The massive influx of polyglot immigrants into the growing urban industrial centres of America and the advent of Germans, Jews, Italians, Poles and even more Irish into the west of Scotland about the same time heightened that concern. In a fluid social order, voluntary religious groups might seize the initiative and set the tone of life. Independent minded, staunchly democratic and usually successful entrepreneurs, their temperance concern reflected that background. Opposed to monopoly in church and state, they wanted a free society of like minded people dedicated to ameliorating the lot of the unfortunate through their own efforts. The removal of hindrances to the free play of moral influences—like the free play of honest competition in their business life—was central to social regeneration. The control, if not repression, of drink would safeguard social order, eliminate sources of corruption in social and political life, help to lower taxes and to benefit business through new patterns of the savings and expenditure of these new consumers. Better business meant better health, happier families—better clothed and better housed in a drink free environment.

The Scottish temperance forces embraced a wide social spectrum but the dynamic leadership now came from men with an almost indivisible moral business sense, who invariably had close affiliations with the United States. They in turn went over to the offensive as the moral suasion campaign proved slow and ineffective. They effectively captured the town council in Glasgow for temperance and they began to send leading local temperance figures to parliament to carry the campaign into Scottish law and ultimately to the wider world. Some came of engineering firms where presumably temperance made for better discipline, productivity, and fewer accidents. Others were drapers, a very large and significant group, wholesale tea, provisions and fruit merchants as well as ministers, usually from the UP church. Other groups were represented but overall these groups were the dominant and decisive forces. Accountants with a clear sense of social profit and loss were also prominent but some like John Mann were less doctrinaire than others.

The similar nature of post Civil War temperance activity can be seen in the American entrepreneur and philanthropist, John Wanamaker. Beginning as a British Woollen merchant in Philadelphia, he built up a thriving department store chain. Influenced by Revd Albert Barnes of the First Presbyterian Church of Philadelphia, a vigorous temperance preacher, Wanamaker originally required his staff to be teetotallers.[176] A regular Republican party supporter, he associated with Francis Murphy of the Blue Ribbon Army and J B Gough as well as the YMCA and similar religious institutions. He established a model Sunday School, 'Bethany' in Philadelphia which concerned itself with temperance, self improvement and other ameliorating activities. In pursuit of business and his studies of the co-operative commonwealth, he visited Britain many times. Among his cities of interest was Glasgow, and he was well known among temperance groups there. Total abstinence, business considerations and religion were virtually identical. Sobriety, productivity, savings and good consumers could transform society. The shopkeepers' millenium spanned the Atlantic.[177] The revivals of Moody and Sankey would crown that development.

Numerous Glaswegians went to the United States to contribute to the prohibitionist impulse in their turn. Easton, Ferguson, Craib and Mackay and many temperance supporters toured America for health or holidays, like Councillor John Breze in 1879 or Revd D D Robertson MA, a Glasgow graduate friend of Lord Overtoun.[178] Some returned to inform their congregations of their visits with special talks, like Revd Robert Hood, Glasgow graduate, minister of the Morisonian school and teacher.[179] Others reported their experiences in the *League Journal*, like the Dundee accountant, J C Robertson, who found nothing like Glasgow Saturday nights anywhere in America.[180] Other ministers spent frequent summer vacations in the United States. Revd W S Swanson of the Paisley Road FC seems to have spent six successive summers in America. Three were spent basking in the natural and moral superiority of the prohibitionist state of Maine and three in the Collegiate Church of New York 5th Avenue.[181] Revd A F Forrest made two lengthy visits. In 1906 he spent three months traversing the country even as far as Alaska, meeting his old congregation members and then in 1909 taking the opportunity as a delegate to the Pan Presbyterian congress in New York to retrace much of the same ground.[182]

Some Glaswegians took their prohibitionist sentiments with them when they settled permanently in the United States. A founder member of the Scottish Temperance League, W T Templeton emigrated around 1867.[183] Mathew MacDougall of Kilbarchan settled in New York, returned as American Consul in Dundee and died there in 1888.[184] Drapery allowed others to follow their convictions. Samuel Chisholm Blair after several years in the Glasgow trade emigrated to Iowa where he conscientiously maintained his firm prohibitionist convictions in regular letters home.[185] William Howat after several years in America returned to manage his father's Dumfries drapery business until he settled in Glasgow as agent for an American insurance company.[186] Samuel Todd of Fir Park Terrace emigrated to Chicago where he attended the funeral of Frances Willard.[187] Formerly a leading figure in the Third Ward Temperance Association and the Scottish Permissive Bill Association, he had been closely associated with the Glasgow Women's Temperance Prayer Meeting groups around Mrs Woyka, Miss White and Miss Wallace.

Some sought opportunities on both sides of the Atlantic. James Jamieson, woollen manufacturer from Ayr, seems to have spent two spells in America. On the first trip he travelled through Canada, Illinois and Kansas before returning via Maine and Neal Dow. He wrote to the *Social Reformer* praising the advanced state of American opinion on drink, the dry nature of social life and lack of drunks in his travels.[188] After returning home he seems to have returned for a further four years in Kansas before finally settling back in Ayr.[189] Business commuting and temperance activity were part of the same concern.

The close affinities of the home from home aspect are perhaps best demonstrated by the visit of Revd Dr Fergus Ferguson to America in 1874.[190] A well known teetotal advocate and supporter of the Scottish Permissive Bill Association, he was editor of the *Evangelical Reporter* for eighteen years. Ferguson was popular among English Congregationalists in Huddersfield, in Halifax and in Dr Parker's London church. Ostensibly he was going to attend the assembly of the Cumberland Presbyterian church in Missouri but the trip was something of a triumphant tour to old Scottish friends and acquaintances, clerical and lay. He renewed acquaintanceship with Henry Ward Beecher; Dr Talmage; Dr Cuyler and Mr Dunn of Boston who had visited Scotland in 1872, Frederick Douglass whom he had met in 1846 on the coach from Perth to Glasgow, and Dr John W M Taylor of the New York Broadway Tabernacle. The freshness of that friendship might have been maintained through Ferguson's regular contributions to the *Cumberland Presbyterian*. Even so he also met large numbers of former Glasgow parishioners scattered across the land. Welcomed in Jersey City by two former Glasgow EU members, he travelled to meet others in Philadelphia, Baltimore where Captain Logan of South Portland Street, Glasgow had won a reputation as a friend of the coloureds, to Washington DC, St Louis, Chicago, Milwaukee, Detroit and Pittsburg. In addition he noted former students of Morison like Revd Henry Melville in Union Town, Pennsylvania; Revd J M Campbell of Langholm, now in Streator, Illinois, and Revd Mr Craig, formerly of Bellgrove Street Congregational Church Glasgow in Detroit. The earlier visit of Revd George Gladstone to a temperance convention in Bloomington, Illinois, was well remembered. He himself gave several addresses including one on 'Scotland and the Scotch' in Springfield, Illinois, and one in support of the Ohio 'Whisky War' in Detroit. One of his old Blackfriars Street, Glasgow congregation, a Mrs Miller of Cincinnati, seems to have been active in the cause, only regretting that she had not been arrested in a recent campaign. But the message runs through the book, of continued Scottish success in a dry environment. An old friend had the finest plumbing business in Cincinnati, with a son an architect and another at Amherst; another from Thornhill had a large 'Hub and Spoke Works' in Louisville; John Aitken of Cumbernauld in his forty years had got himself a handsome home on 44th Street, a huge wholesale retail business on Broadway and was a pillar of the Presbyterian church. His American correspondents abound. All in all Ferguson travelled on the ship with Scots back and forth—including an ex-councillor from Glasgow and in effect never left his desirable version of Scotland.

The dry world was one of opportunity for improved individuals, upwardly mobile, anxious to prove their respectability, build an ideal moral American nation while remembering the hope of a similar democratic revolution at home in Scotland. After all, Ferguson found large numbers with relatives and friends back home whom they closely followed and remembered. Ferguson was but a personal embodiment of several thousand similar links, memories and folk cultural connections. It was something the temperance movement could capitalise upon. In America activity gave purpose, identity, respectability and entree to an ethnic religious cultural world and a form of reassurance that one had succeeded in self improvement. It was also part of a link with home. The frequent pulpit exchanges, temperance rallies and religious meetings reinforced that element. Pastorally temperance kept the group together as a religious ethnic entity and gave it an effective weapon, in a capitalist open society, for rapid advancement and acquisition. In Scotland, temperance also served to contribute to that sense of Scottish-American identity, that sense of achievement elsewhere if not at home, that encouragement to ever greater efforts in the Scottish campaign in the light of American success. That international dimension was essential to inject a sense of novelty, innovation and enthusiasm periodically into a movement which because of its single mindedness was subject to repetition, boredom and even disintegration. Once the initial point was conceded, all else followed in individual and social amelioration. The ability to discover new areas of concern, new techniques and new organisations was a vital ingredient. The proliferation of children's temperance societies, orders for adult males and women, insurance and savings schemes and a social round of teas and soirées gave the movement a cradle-to-grave dimension in which the basic point was unlikely to be questioned.

Revd Thomas Craib, a Congregational minister of Wardlaw Bellgrove Church, associated with the Scottish Temperance League, visited the United States in 1875. *The Advance and Congregational Miscellany* which he later edited published his impressions.[191] He saw little evidence of drinking in his travels but found considerable drunkenness, poverty and vice in major cities: vices were many but so too were the uplifting religious agencies. In Cincinnati he met ladies who took part in the recent 'Whisky War' and was greatly impressed by them and their results. He himself addressed numerous churches and meetings on the Scottish revival in the wake of Moody and Sankey and he was particularly anxious to promote temperance campaigns in Pittsburgh and Philadelphia. Happily to his Scottish eyes, drink was the besetting sin of the 'other' immigrants, the French, the Germans and the Irish. Scots invariably prospered in every undertaking whether in business, house or factory. He met John Wanamaker, the redoubtable Philadelphia clothier and philanthropist who had established the impressive Bethany Sunday School.[192] The success of Stewart's department store in New York, MacDonald in St Louis and the Scottish sympathiser, George H Stewart, the philanthropic banker, who was a frequent visitor to Scotland, demonstrated the power of temperance teaching. Like all things American it was practical: as Stuart said 'it is easier for an evangelist to labour in Scotland than America for there is a better backbone of theology with you than with us'.[193] The techniques of conversion and conviction were different, the result hopefully would be the same.

Robert MacKay, a former Chartist, editor of the *Social Reformer* single-handed from 1857 to 1877 when it merged with the *Scottish Reformer* which he then edited, visited the United States in 1893. His purpose was to attend the World Temperance Congress in conjunction with the Chicago World Fair. He seized the opportunity to visit various parts of the United States, including the dry states, and sent back numerous reports of his travels. His experiences were far more than simple reportage for they portray social attitudes which he envisaged would follow prohibition in Scotland. Like Revd David Macrae and Samuel Chisholm he had a strong Scottish nation-alist sense. To them drink was the fact which prevented 'Scotland reaching the van of nations'.[194] If Scotland could go dry like Kansas, she might experience 'a flow of prosperity and wealth, intellectual progress and moral advancement such as has no parallel in her otherwise brilliant history'.[195] Scottish visitors to American prohibition states constantly returned to that theme: Scotland lagged far behind American standards in every respect. Only self respect through prohibition could possibly help matters at home.

Not all ministers were convinced. Revd J F Potts, of the Swedenborgian Church, Glasgow, believed 'Americans keep their evils more out of sight than we do. I suspect that what is called the social evil prevails there, in secret, to a fearful extent, far more than it does in this country. America is the great stronghold of teetotalism but I greatly doubt that it is any the better for it. Mere teetotalism is but a washing of the outside of the cup and of the platter without regeneration; the evil will remain within and find some other outlet.'[196]

Scottish visitors did what they could to rekindle the old time zeal in various ways. In 1870, the UP Church sent Revd Dr Alexander MacLeod of Glasgow with Revd Dr Edmond of Islington as delegates to the Presbyterian church re-union assembly.[197] MacLeod in particular was impressed by American drys: 'Almost the last words I heard in the Scotia were the shrieks of a man in delirium tremens; and almost the first sounds I heard in the United States were the intelligent welcomes by speech and song of the friends of temperance.'[198] They travelled widely through the country: New York, Princeton, Philadelphia, Pittsburgh, where MacLeod was the guest of old Strathaven members who had greatly prospered there.[199] Edmond went to Buffalo, Detroit, Chicago, Milwaukee, while MacLeod went up into Wisconsin, St Paul, and back to Washington DC, where they met President Grant[200] at a cabinet meeting. There they also attended a Methodist Episcopalian church[201] where they preached.[202] They returned to

Jersey City where they lodged with old Scottish friends, Mr and Mrs Mathews, editor of the *Christian Worker*, and met Dr Ormiston.[203] After visiting Boston they returned to New York and heard Dr Green of Princeton preach.[204] MacLeod then rejoined his colleague after touring out west.[205] They returned to spread further the news of American Presbyterian advance to their Scottish brethren.

The intensity of that connection was maintained by other visitors in the temperance cause. George Easton, an agent or lecturer for the Scottish Temperance League, toured North America in 1873. He was merely following James Johnston of Springburn who toured mainly Canada in aid of the cause in 1872–3. A massive number of articles on his activities appeared in the *League Journal*, including reports on conditions in Detroit.[206] His church was later consecrated with Moody at the harmonium, and his successor as pastor was an American trained minister.

David Macrae who was a UP minister in Gourock embarked on a literary temperance career in America. He had won a prize for his tale of temperance, *George Harrington*. He had then become a popular reciter of his own works around the west of Scotland.[207] He went ostensibly as a delegate to the American Missionary Congress of the UP Missionary Society in New York:[208] 'If our American friends wished to hear the pure Doric they could not have a better expositor.' He believed Americans would give Scotland a lead in the campaign. He toured Canada and much of the United States giving readings.[209] He appeared with General O O Howard of the Freedmans Bureau in Washington DC and General Lee.[210] Reassured by the feeling that abstainers in America vastly outnumbered those in Scotland, Macrae found his compatriots succeeding everywhere, like Mr Williamson, Lincoln's former tutor who had entered the US Treasury office.[211] Beecher deeply impressed him. Ironically he said, 'If Henry Ward Beecher turned bad I should never believe anymore.'[212] He had the look of a brave strong man exulting in his strength, the look of one who is going to fight you and knows perfectly well that he will win, but means to let you off without too much punishment.' . . . 'He has lowered the level' of the American pulpit 'but increased its power. He has made it stoop to conquer.'[213] Macrae was drawn into the Beecher milieu, meeting Harriet Beecher Stowe and Catherine Beecher. In Boston he was with Wendell Phillips, Oliver Wendell Holmes, Longfellow and Horace Bushnell. Among others he also met the brother of A F Stoddard of Port Glasgow, a very old established family.[214] Back in New York he again consorted with Beecher, Dr Storrs, Bennet of the *New York Herald* and Mr Stewart, editor of the *Scottish-American Journal*.[215] In Philadelphia Macrae had an entrée to all Scottish-American society. He met Robert Dale Owen: 'an unmistakeable a Scotch accent as if he had only left Scotland the month before'.[216]

While Macrae's reports continued through the first half of 1869, George Easton the agent for the Scottish Temperance League had also begun to send back reports of his activities on tour in North America.[217] As one American told Easton, 'I don't smoke nor snuff and never vote the Democratic ticket. I am a firm believer in my own inimitable soap which I can assure you possesses the power of removing stains and filth of every description from anything and every quarter except from the mouth of a Democrat.'[218] After lecturing at the Tremont Temple in Boston, Easton visited Scottish friends in Boston, Lynn and Salem including the family where his daughter had spent some two or three years.[219] Thereafter followed a series of visits to relatives of Revd Dr Brown of Kent Road Church, old friends from Kilsyth, Vale of Leven, Langholm and Alva.[220] Travelling the thickly Scottish settlements of Canada, he went to Detroit, Chicago and Illinois where an emigrant from Roxburgh some twenty-nine years earlier had prospered massively. His son-in-law, a currier, had been settled in Boston for some years.[221] He returned home well satisfied that Scottish temperance could bear comparison with its American counterparts, as he told the United Workingmen's Society.[222] Neil McNeill, the chairman of the Board of Directors of the Scottish Temperance League, had also toured America about the same time and was welcomed back home at a meeting.[223] A returning Scot from Baltimore, Andrew Muirhead also addressed the gathering. Revd John Reid of America addressed a temperance gathering at Galatown in August 1870.[224] Revd W M Taylor was keeping members of the UP church and the Temperance League abreast of American developments.[225] American Christianity was 'bold, joyous, hopeful . . . but the general appeal of Christian life is practical. . . . The characteristic preaching is outspoken, direct and stimulating.'[226] The visit of Theodore L Cuyler with Revd Wells and J B Dunn in 1872 heightened awareness of the benefits of the future in America.[227] Significantly Revd Robert Kerr returned from Minnesota with plans for a dry colony on the Northern Pacific Railroad. But as noted earlier it did not prosper.[228]

The following year the visit of Moody and Sankey to Glasgow stirred a massive evangelical revival. It coincided with the awakening of a vigorous women's movement in support of temperance. Women had been active in the movement from the earliest days but they were becoming increasingly visible. In 1873 many American ladies had attended the Independent Order of Good Templars, meeting in Glasgow with their Glasgow sisters. Simeon B Chase, Pennsylvania, a prohibitionist candidate for governor, and his wife, Fanny Du Bois, a founder member of the WCTU, came over.[229] The following year the Ohio 'Whisky War' burst upon the scene. Ohio ladies demonstrated by direct action against public houses, holding prayer meetings, singing hymns and generally shaming saloon proprietors and their customers into temperance.[230] Mrs Catherine R MacCartney, Northwood, Logan County, Ohio appealed to the Ladies of Glasgow to follow the example of the Ohio Whisky War and begin similar campaigns in Glasgow, particularly against the Saltmarket area.[231] Glasgow zealots seized upon the example to call a meeting in April 1874.[232] Revd Fergus Ferguson, recently returned from America, presided over an audience in which middle-aged ladies dominated. Mrs Wilhelmina Woyka, a German lady of some twenty-three years standing in Glasgow, considered the Saltmarket area with some eighty-five drinking establishments far worse than anything in Germany. She and her supporters felt unable to take direct action as in America but they would pray at home and so began the Women's League of Prayer.[233] News from Ohio came with Revd Mr and Mrs J L MacCartney who were working with the Ayrshire emigrant, Mathew MacDougall, who returned as American consul in Dundee.[234] MacCartney was closely associated with Moody and Sankey. Against the background of the revival and the threat of Darwinism, it was reported in the League *Journal* that 'the infallible way to crowd a church was to announce a temperance sermon'.[235] Street parades 'like Sisters of Mercy', street praying and prayer meetings and even sit-ins were effective means of capturing the public imagination. In America, Protestants, Jews, Catholics and Unitarians were all co-operating, a point rammed home by the growing strength of the British Catholic temperance movement under Archbishop Manning.[236] The immediate expression of this newly mobilised women's movement was the opening of a British Workman's Public House in the Gallowgate directed towards the cultivation of the working classes. Alexander Allan of the shipping line presided and George S Weeks of New York played the harmonium for the accompanying Ladies' Temperance Prayer Meeting. Further encouraging news from Ohio came with two more visitors, Hon William Fox, a former Prime Minister in New Zealand, and Councillor Whittaker. The former had passed through Ohio and Maine en route to Glasgow and recounted his experiences to his Scottish audience.[237] Councillor Whittaker of Scarborough, a veteran temperance supporter, had just returned from some eight months in America and he was to spend two months working in Scotland for the Scottish Temperance League.[238] 'The women of America' he claimed 'were men.' Already known from his activities seven years earlier in Paisley, Whittaker had travelled through the States from Brooklyn to Boston and Chicago: everywhere the women were the backbone of the movement. The American churches, with staunch teetotal ministers, were far in advance of their British brothers. By appealing to a sense of national rivalry, he was hoping to spur his audience to even greater activity. Soon afterwards Whittaker was addressing meetings with J G Richardson, the proprietor of Bessbrook, the model dry town in Ulster, who had also returned from Ohio.[239] Some 6000 saloons had been forced to close during the Ohio campaign. Mrs Richardson also addressed the Scottish Temperance League on 'Womens Temperance Union of America and the late convention in Cincinnati'.[240] Women working in twos had worked wonders not only in Ohio but also in Brooklyn where 900 saloons were shut down within a year. She had addressed the women's gathering in America.[241]

In this climate temperance enthusiasm was reaching new heights. Municipal elections were now beginning to feel the pressure of the temperance lobby; the Glasgow City Improvement Trust passed resolutions against any licences on its lands.[242] Into Glasgow came 'Mother' Stewart of the Ohio Whisky War fame.[243] Invited by the Glasgow Ladies' Prayer Meeting group, she addressed rapturous audiences in Glasgow and throughout Scotland.[244] Accompanied by Mrs Woyka, she went to a grand meeting in Newcastle where British women were invited to join with the Womens Christian Temperance Union of America in the centennial celebrations in Philadelphia. At the International Conference on Temperance in Philadelphia, Scotland was represented by Mrs Parker of Dundee and by Robert Reid.[245] On her return Mrs Parker was to play a leading role in the formation of the British Women's Temperance Association.[246]

In America Revd Dr W M Taylor addressed the American National Temperance meeting in New York as chairman while Eli Johnson of Brooklyn lectured in some twenty Scottish towns and villages.[247] Other Americans worked at the Evangelical tent hall on Glasgow Green.[248] To add to the momentum John B. Gough returned to the city in 1878.[249] Professor Spence of Fisk University appeared at East Campbell Street UP Church in 1879.[250] Born in Huntly, Spence had gone to America, accepted a post at the University of Michigan and then joined the new black institution to build up its facilities and reputation. The tours of the Jubilee Singers were central to that growth.[251] Meanwhile Revd George Gladstone and Revd William Ross of Rothesay were mixing with many American delegates at the Liverpool Templars gathering; both were to be presiding officers of the Right Worthy Grand Lodge of the World.[252] The majority seemed to be coloured representatives from the south, including Bishop William Hillery of the African Methodist Episcopalian Church.[253] William Wells Brown and many American black delegates also attended the IOGT meeting in Glasgow in the summer of 1877.[254] A former slave, a Mr Anderson, also addressed the Glasgow Band of Hope.[255] The Chicago WCTU showed great interest in the Glasgow Women's Temperance Prayer Union.[256]

In Glasgow, the development of prohibition in Atlanta was closely followed—as perhaps more pertinent to Glasgow experience—than say Kansas.[257] Joseph Malins, an Englishman who had joined the Order of Good Templars in America, brought the movement into Britain. He was totally opposed to either the municipalisation of the drink traffic, which might have been accomplished in Britain, or state control such as attempted in some American states. Good management of public houses similarly was anathema to him. Some temperance leaders like Daniel Macaulay Stevenson in Glasgow were inclined to support the idea. But the hard-line groups were encouraged by American successes in prohibition.[258] Malins visited the United States and his reports were well publicised.[259] The *Glasgow Herald* likewise gave considerable coverage to the anti-saloon campaign through a special correspondent in America.[260] Malins returned home via the Anchor Line to Glasgow with Mr Archer of the Scottish Templars.[261]

Theodore Cuyler, an aged man, returned to give two sermons in Dunoon and Kirn while the guest of Alexander Allan the shipping magnate.[262] More significantly, women were emerging as driving forces in the movement. In the summer of 1889, Mrs Leavitt, the honorary secretary of the WCTU, with Miss White of Glasgow held six meetings in Edinburgh and six in Glasgow.[263] This world-travelled missionary of six years' standing revelled in her affinity to Scots wherever she had met them. She regretted that only five American states were prohibition but she was very confident that women suffrage would make all states dry.[264]

Though temperance propaganda might publicise the national waste of natural and human resources through the ravages of drink, abstinence did not always ensure long happy life. The younger brother of the Provost of Largs, W H Paton, formerly a bank clerk, had joined his other brother in a ranching operation in America but drowned in tragic circumstances.[265] An abstainer from childhood, William Mowat, son of a Glasgow JP was killed in San Francisco.[266] John McLean, the Roseneath postmaster, died on a visit to his son in Columbus Ohio.[267] There were several others who died visiting friends and relatives in America. Dr Peter Ferguson, son of a Glasgow temperance JP, died at Rosewell, New Mexico in 1898.[268] The transatlantic temperance links were found even among the dead.

Glasgow ladies were supported by American women in their activities. The Scottish *Temperance Journal* spread reports of constant American temperance advance in the passage of laws as in Washington DC and the territories,[269] the support of leading politicians and churchmen like Theodore Roosevelt and Cardinal Gibbons[270] and the welcome accorded Sir Samuel Chisholm in New York.[271] At the same time the emphasis on historical tradition as part of the psychological drive for reform, the deaths of long-standing Scottish and American leaders and the growing association with the American Anti-Saloon League seemed to make for a more militant, narrower approach. That might also be explained by the capture of the municipal power in Glasgow by temperance forces and the increasing social welfare interest of the Liberals and the growing Labour party which naturally reduced the areas of temperance concern: all might unite on particular issues.[272] There was, too, something of an increased preoccupation with sexual matters and drink. The Glasgow Vigilance Association, the reports of salacious crimes and advertisements in America made Glaswegians aware of similar concerns at home.[273] Once again the ministerial link was to the fore. Revd W J Dawson, a former Glasgow Methodist minister, sent an article on 'The Liquor Traffic in America' while Glasgow ministers with strong temperance views spent summers in America.[274] Revd A F Forrest of Renfield UF Church was a frequent visitor who travelled extensively to meet his former congregational members from Alaska to the East.[275] Revd. W S Swanson, Paisley Road UF Church, spent three successive summers in the Collegiate Church New York, 5th Avenue, with his friend Revd Dr Mackay.[276] At the same time the Scottish Temperance League was in correspondence with the Anti-Saloon League,[277] and being urged to follow its lead. Prohibition seemed increasingly attractive and necessary in Scotland as in America.[278] The success of this drive found ultimate expression in the 1913 Act. Under the terms of that legislation local option was firmly established, with stricter control of licenses and of opening hours, and the provision of regular polls of electors every three years. The first polls under this Temperance Act were taken in 1920.

That revivalist spirit seemed to coincide with the growth of the Kent Road UP Church in Glasgow. As Samuel Chisholm said, 'a man's parentage may give him a seat in the House of Lords but it is no passport to position in a radical congregation like that of Kent Road'.[279] That kirk epitomised the new modernising man who identified with temperance and still more with outright prohibition. In that tough-minded congregation Revd. Dr Joseph Brown D D, the minister for over thirty-five years, played an important role. Two of his five daughters married ministers of the UP church; one married John Colville MP, the steel magnate, another Dr W L Reid, MD, who lectured and toured the United States in the temperance cause as president of the Royal Faculty of Physicians and Surgeons.[280] With relatives in America, with Glasgow town councillors, with paper manufacturing interests and partners in the firm of Brown and Polson, cornflour producers, in his congregation, Brown was well placed to mobilise his congregation in support of prohibition. His members included the photographer Robert Annan whose firm had exposed the evils of the Salt-market slums. These were cleared largely through the driving force of Councillor Samuel Chisholm in the Civic Improvement Trust. Like his minister he also hailed from Dalkeith and was largely responsible for the dry character of all Glasgow Corporation property until recent times. As Lord Provost in 1900, Chisholm was interviewed for the New York *New Voice* by W E 'Pussyfoot' Johnson on the benefits of temperance and municipal enterprise. Together they were to campaign strenuously for prohibition in Scotland in 1920. Mrs Henderson, Chisholm's second wife, the widow of a shipping line owner, had travelled extensively in America before she again visited America in 1907 with Sir Samuel Chisholm. Another member of the congregation, ex-Bailie John L Selkirk, a founder member of the Scottish Permissive Bill and Temperance Association, was an admirer of American prohibition initiatives. For over thirty years he served as session clerk at Kent Road and served on the Glasgow town council for nine years, 1875–84. With directors of the Scottish Temperance League like William Johnston, men of substantial business interest like Chisholm, a wholesale grocer, well connected reforming ladies like his wife, the church was very much the prohibitionist party at prayer.

Chisholm shows how the Glasgow town council assumed an increasing temperance complexion in the last quarter of the nineteenth century. Well known and admired by F C Howe, the American civic reformer, Chisholm also highlights the knowledge and experience of America within the town council. A large number of councillors for reasons of business, health, holidays or temperance interest—or a combination of motives—had travelled extensively in the United States. They can hardly have been un-aware of the much vaunted benefits to business of American prohibitionist states. Glasgow town council was probably more knowledgeable about the United States than any other representative body in Great Britain. In America the demand for a pure civic morality gave rise to a movement of the respectable, the Mugwumps, and later the Progressives, to purify and cleanse the administration of large American cities, so in Glasgow there was a similar drive, as we shall see in detail later The present purpose is to suggest the temperance concerns brought the respectable into civic govern-ment, and their achievements in housing particularly were an inspiration to American reformers.

American experience and support for prohibition did not always coincide but there was a fair correlation. Councillor George MacFarlane, a partner in a South American merchant company, had begun his business in 1858 in Philadelphia. A son of the Free Church manse and an elder, he was a staunch temperance figure in support of Moody and Sankey. Ex-Bailie John L Selkirk, associated with Kent Road UP Church, served on the council from 1875 to 1884. An accountant, he was a founder member of the Scottish Permissive Bill and Temperance Association, a vice-president of the United Kingdom Alliance and latterly president of the Scottish Temperance League. America persuaded him of the strength of local option as a means of reform while another Kent Road member, ex-Bailie Ure, returned from an extensive American tour deeply impressed. A member of the temperance movement for over twenty years, tour councillor John Breze, a Glasgow graduate of Chilean birth, visited America for health reasons in 1879. Councillor John Davidson, a sausage manufacturer, travelled extensively in America with his two brothers, both UP ministers. Hugh Brechin, a well-established butcher, travelled extensively, particularly in the west, returned to join the council and served for almost twenty-five years with temperance sympathies. Daniel Macaulay Stevenson, later Lord Provost, and perhaps the most distinguished man ever to serve on the town council, toured America where he had a brother in Pennsylvania. Ex-Bailie John King, a former student of the Anderson Institution, had built up a thriving iron business in Shettleston. Widely travelled in the American prohibitionist states, he was active in religious and philanthropic enterprises while as chairman of the licensing court he seriously curtailed and suppressed many licenses in 1902. In 1894 some 40 of the 75 councillors were considered 'drys' as members or subscribers to the Scottish Permissive Bill and Temperance Association. Only 18 were opposed. Two years later, following the formation of the Progressive Union, a co-ordinating body of some 700 members from 250 organisations, the dry forces were even stronger with some 49 councillors. Glasgow potentially might be made safe for temperance and respectability.

There was some division within the local temperance forces. There were suggestions that public houses might be municipalised and the profits devoted to community good.[281] Such compromise was totally unacceptable to prohibitionists. There was also the Public House Trust idea, in England: businessmen would manage a well run, superior public house to secure a 4–5 per cent return and profits would be distributed to public beneficiaries. In Glasgow, D M Stevenson and John Mann, the accountant, established a Glasgow Public House Trust. These trusts, too, like Bishop Potter's similar experiment in New York met opposition in the temperance press.[282] Some American reformers like E R L Gould, a consistent admirer of Glasgow, might find the Gothenburg system attractive whereby the public benefited from careful control of the drinking vice of individuals. Though the American state dispensary system might have much in common with that scheme, where by the state monopolises the sale and profits for the public good of the drink traffic, the idea did not succeed.[283] Gould and his associates were more impressed by the Glasgow People's Palace as an excellent alternative to the saloon: 'The general idea is that the permanent collections to be formed should relate to the history and industries of the city, and that some space should be set apart for special sectional exhibitions to be held from time to time. . . . One element of originality in the way of municipal enterprises that can be claimed for this institution lies in the combination practically under one roof of a museum, picture gallery, winter garden and concert hall.[284] That was the work of the municipal authorities. In the meantime Gould, who seems to have known D M Stevenson fairly well, felt that the public house trust was an excellent interim solution. The provision of alternative attractions for recreation of the workers was urgent necessity: 'It reacts favourably upon family like and saves male members from the unfortunate or evil associations surrounding public house and cheap music hall entertainments. No class of persons stand in greater need of recreation than working people, yet to no other is so little available. The conditions of city life need to be vastly ameliorated in this and other ways before there can be an appreciable diminution of drinking.'[285] Stevenson and Gould represented the 'soft' temperance wing against the 'hard' repressive wing of Chisholm and the Anti-Saloon League.

In the period to 1920 the 'hard' wing were forcing the pace. In parliament the campaign had four leading figures between 1870 and 1920. The leading spokesman had been Peter Maclagan, MP for Linlithgowshire. A regular speaker at Glasgow rallies, he had substantial shale-oil interests on his estates in association with 'Paraffin' Young, a friend of the American Fabian journalist, Henry Demarest Lloyd, whose books were invariably severe condemnations of American capitalism. Subsequently, John P Wilson MP for Govan, had played a leading role. The owner of a tube manufacturing and brass foundry, Wilson had considerable interests in Montreal. He had toured the American prohibitionist states and returned impressed by the benefits of business in that 'robust, Christian and large-hearted charity'. Predictably he found Toronto and Philadelphia far more attractive in their like-mindedness, and Chicago with its rumbustuous ethnic diversity appalling.[286] R Hunter Craig, MP for Govan 1900–6, was another parliamentary supporter of the restriction and suppression of drink. A wholesale fruiterer with interests on both sides of the Atlantic, he was a director of both the Glasgow Chamber of Commerce and the Scottish Temperance League. These representatives were supported by A Cameron Corbett, later Lord Rowallan.[287] He had married Alice Polson of the Brown and Polson family. With a chequered party career, he was eventually raised to the House of Lords in 1911. Extraordinarily generous to the city of Glasgow, with the gifts of Thornliebank and Lochgoil estates, he won American admiration for his dry estates: 7000 homes with 35,000 people and no public houses.[288]

The connection between the pressure groups, local councillors and members of parliament was kept alive and well through an almost continuous injection of American enthusiasm. John B Gough returned to tour Scotland in 1878 and 1879. He appeared in Glasgow in October 1878 and returned in April and September the following year. The halls were packed to capacity on every occasion and the ideas were kept fresh by correspondence, articles and even renderings of his speeches later by local temperance talent.[289] With the return of Moody and Sankey in 1879 and 1884, evangelical fervour intensified. John M Stearns, president of the New York Temperance League and editor of the *National Temperance Advocate,* visited Glasgow in 1891. J G Woolley, a reformed alcoholic lawyer who later stood for the presidency of the United States on the

Prohibition party ticket, gave a series of addresses in Glasgow and Paisley. Joshua Baily, the Philadelphia Quaker, after investigating conditions under prohibition in Maine lectured in Glasgow.

In 1881, Francis Murphy and the Blue Ribbon Army came to Scotland. An Irish emigrant, Murphy had had a drinking problem until he was converted to total abstinence. He then became an evangelist for temperance, aided by John Wanamaker, the Philadelphia business philathropist. For over a year Mr Murphy campaigned in Scotland. More concerned with personal pledges than with legal prohibition he seems to have had a mixed reception in the west of Scotland. He had enjoyed considerable success in Forfarshire over some three months. In Forfar about one-third the population were alleged to have joined the Blue Ribbon Army: 3000 adults and 1600 juveniles. Forth, Aberdeen, Alloa, Dumfries and Paisley were similarly aroused. In Paisley with Bailie Torrens, he addressed a meeting of some 3000. Efforts to organise Glasgow failed, largely because the ministers refused to endorse the campaign. Perhaps Murphy overlapped with the Moody campaign. Whatever the reason, Murphy had to fend for himself with minimal local aid. Bailie Torrens, assisted by only ex-Bailie Pinkerton who has his own Free Gospel Church, Charlotte Street, allowed Murphy church facilities. Even vast audiences at the Trades Hall, Glassford Street, failed to impress the local churchmen and Murphy abandoned his campaign after securing some 1600 pledges. In Edinburgh he enjoyed enormous success but the Blue Ribbon Army seems to have had limited lasting appeal north of the border.[290]

Theodore L Cuyler, who made a fleeting visit in 1889, was but one of many links.[291] Numerous ministers from America gave their accounts of prohibition while former Glasgow residents returned to recount their experiences in America to their old temperance associates.[292]

American ladies also contributed to the movement. Mrs Mary Leavitt, the world temperance missionary, reassured her Glasgow audience that Scots the world over were in the van of temperance progress.[293] Dr Anna Potts of the Women's Medical College Philadelphia made two trips to lecture on the laws of health to the Glasgow masses.[294] The most renowned visitor came in 1893, Francis Willard. The driving force behind the WCTU, she gave a series of addresses at rallies in Glasgow and Edinburgh in association with her friend, Lady Henry Somerset. Such continuous activity, big name visits and growing influence in the town council gave Glasgow prohibitionists every encouragement. Even in the schools, temperance textbooks on physiology were making headway. Sir William Collins had commissioned Dr William Snodgrass, Muirhead Demonstrator in Physiology in Glasgow University, to write a textbook for schools. Snodgrass, an American-born graduate of the university, extolled the virtues of American schools' physiology teaching as worthy of imitation.[295] The next generation seemed safe for temperance.

The growing success of prohibitionists in America in the early twentieth century encouraged their Glasgow brethren. By 1914 nine American states had gone dry and half of total population lived in no-licence areas. Encouraged by these successes, the Anti-Saloon League had secured legislation preventing the introduction of alcoholic beverages into dry areas and inaugurated a national prohibition campaign.[296] It seemed the only effective solution. Even in Glasgow enforcement of existing law was often inadequate. The police were less professional than might have been expected. In 1899, 131 policemen had been found drunk—or ten per cent of the force.[297] Total prohibition would eliminate such abuses, so it was believed.

In 1900 a World Temperance Congress was held in Edinburgh. A host of Americans descended upon Scotland to meet and exchange views on progress.[298] Revd George Gladstone of Glasgow attended the Edinburgh meetings and brought several delegates back to address the meeting in the city. Mrs Catherine Lant Stevenson of the Massachusetts WCTU and Mrs Boole, President of the New York WCTU, addressed a great rally in Glasgow City Halls. Shortly afterwards Joshua L Baily, the Philadelphia Quaker who had known Maine for forty years, and had recently toured prohibitionist states came and addressed the Scottish Permissive Bill and Temperance Association in Glasgow.[299] Other less well-known American temperance advocates were horrified by the sight of Glasgow drunkenness, like Revd George Reith's American guest.[300] At the same time a certain antipathy if not outright prejudice against immigrants began to appear both in America and in Glasgow temperance circles. The Anti-Saloon League began to fear that their successes were being offset by the growing alien drinking population through mass immigration. Two million converts a year to prohibition, it was claimed, would be needed to offset their influence. That sentiment appears in Scottish visitors' reflections on America. In 1900 the American movement was far ahead of its Scottish counterpart in securing cheap and efficient orderly government. Unfortunately the reactionary European immigrants brought their destructive attitudes with them. New England policemen for example were invariably Irish and corrupt. After three months in Maine, it was clear that 90 per cent of the sellers of alcoholic drinks were foreign born and 70 per cent of the drunks were foreign. The 'true' American was a prohibitionist.[301]

Other visitors found happiness was essentially dry.[302] The Anti-Saloon League view and the propaganda of the New Voice of New York were increasingly accepted and circulated in the Glasgow movement.[303] The prohibitionist states were idealised.[304] The passage of the Scottish Temperance Act (1913) gave great confidence to the prohibitionsts. The whole world seemed to be moving dry. The new American President Woodrow Wilson, of Scottish descent, and William Jennings Bryan were making very public gestures of their dry sympathies.[304] More American states seemed to be going dry; Virginia in 1914, South Carolina 1915; Oregon 1914; Oklahoma 1917; and many areas also went dry under local option.[305] Scottish observers were on the spot to send back glowing accounts of astonishing social transformations. Dr W L Reid, of Glasgow, saw the change in Charlottesville, Virginia, in 1914. In one area, following state prohibition, where there were formerly 16 saloons and only 3 butchers' shops, there no saloons and 16 butchers. Revd John Lamond toured

America and closely observed the Ohio State Prohibition Convention in Columbus in November 1913. Renowned as the Scottish John B Gough, Lamond had been born in Troon, graduated from Edinburh University, held a charge at Skelmorlie before going to Edinburgh Greenside in 1899, a charge he held until he left to become a spiritualist. He died in London in 1932.[306] After attending the World Temperance Congress in Oregon he returned very impressed by the strength of temperance convictions. The success of the anti-tobacco campaign, particularly in Nebraska and South Dakota, together with prohibitionist controls, made for health and order. To a large extent that was attributable to the influence of temperance teaching in schools. Scotland likewise had to educate her children for the future. Only backward European immigrants posed any serious threat to the triumph of purity.[307] To the Scottish Temperance League preacher, Sylvester Horne MP, Glasgow graduate, Congregationalist minister and Member of Parliament, America invariably promised the highest fulfilment for man: in prohibition 'the common people of the nation showed the world that Christianity was not dead nor dying, that it could purify a land of its iniquity'.[308]

To some extent then wartime produced an even more intense Protestant search for political realism. On the eve of the First World War, Glasgow town council held a referendum on the question of licences. The electorate of 203,014 in 37 wards showed only mild interest, with only 55 per cent (111,315) voting. Over 76,000 did not vote and 6500 spoiled their papers. Though over 96,000 opposed any new licences only a majority of 7557 voted unequivocally for a reduction in licences.[309] The figures were ominous for the 1920 vote in the city. The prohibitionists were clearly going to be dependent on America for more than inspiration. And so it proved.

The war enabled much restrictive legislation to be passed as necessary to the successful prosecution of the war. Restriction of the production of beer, hours of opening and the liquor business generally was considerable. Labour leaders and labour-minded churchmen like Revd James Barr supported restrictions even to prohibition.[310]

The general failure to influence the Catholic press in favour of prohibition, to secure Catholic clergy for the prohibitionist platform, and after 1916 the rising tensions engendered by the Irish question were indicative. The virtual absence of concern with prohibition from the pages of the Catholic Glasgow Observer, the reply of only one priest to a prohibition circular, and a growing class consciousness were important developments in the war at home. Many Catholics might not have the vote in local elections but sufficient did to be apprehensive about the resurgent Protestantism, as in Ulster from 1914. Other groups were more concerned with the Bolshevik Revolution in 1917 which focused attention on the structures rather than the sinfulness of society. In addition the liquor interests were well prepared and organised for the campaign in which they could cleverly represent the prohibitionist drive as essentially American and alien. To workers, America appeared increasingly reactionary and unattractive. Even moderate British working class opinion would cast a protest vote against 'American' intrusion.[311]

The prohibitionist interests were gathering their forces. As W J Allison, secretary of the Scottish Permissive Bill and Temperance Association, wrote in the Anti-Saloon Yearbook 1919, the various organisations were seeking to establish a tight organisation for the whole of Scotland 'without overlapping or duplication of effort'.[312] This National Citizens Council was a development of the National Temperance Council of Scotland which comprised all the national and denominational bodies: the Scottish Temperance League, the Scottish Permissive Bill and Temperance Association, the Good Templars, and the British Women's Temperance Union of Scotland. In close co-operation with the Anti-Saloon League of America, this body secured speakers to campaign the length and breadth of Scotland but particularly in the Glasgow area. Everyone knew that whichever way Glasgow went the rest of the country would follow. It would also be a beacon to the world.

The American connection had been in abeyance for much of the war. With American entry into the war in 1917, large numbers of American clergymen and social workers were coming over to work among their troops in France. En route many seem to have stopped off to campaign in Glasgow. Canadian prohibitionists co-operated in several series of meetings. From early in 1918 Americans and Canadians were moving through Scotland. In May 1918 three visitors had given some 110 addresses before they left for home: Dr Daniel A Poling, of Massachusetts Anti-Saloon League, who was also associate president of the United Society of Christian Endeavour and author of numerous articles in the *National Enquirer,* had been visiting American troops in France. Professor John A Nicholls, General Secretary, and Revd John Steele, Assistant Secretary of the American Presbyterian Board.[313] Together with Newton Tyle of Canada, these gentlemen had formed the vanguard of a prohibitionist 'invasion'.[314] The colourful W E 'Pussyfoot' Johnson arrived in October. Already familar with Glasgow from his visit for the *New Voice* in 1900, Johnson was now a publicist, associate editor of the American Anti-Saloon League press bureau and editor of its *American Issue.* For several weeks he went campaigning through Ayrshire, Lanarkshire and the North East of Scotland, went to London where he lost an eye in a fracas with London University students and returned again to Glasgow. In April 1920 he returned to America and after a whirlwind tour through virtually every major American city he returned to Glasgow once more.[315] Drink was the experiment which had failed for Americans after three hundred years. Prohibition was the wisdom of experience.[316]

While R A Munro of the Scottish Permissive Bill and Temperance Association attended the World Prohibition Congress in Columbus, Ohio, and was overcome by emotion amid the moral fervour and addresses of William Jennings Bryan, the great Democratic orator, Glasgow was experiencing more American fervour. Lesser known figures poured in, Revd W F Dickens of New York, Revd Cyrus P Keen of the American YMCA, and others.[317] A considerable number of Canadians came to give testimony to the benefits of prohibition in their state and localities: there were two agents to the Dominion Alliance of Canada, Revd. John Bailey and Cecil J Bell; George Bell MP from British Columbia; the former mayor of Renfrew, Ontario, W E Smallfield, Revd Hugh Macrae and Revd J Craig of Vancouver, formerly of Glasgow; J McComb and Dr Grenfell of Labrador.[318] They were assisted by reinforcements from New Zealand, Mrs Harrison Lee, British Wesleyans and Revd Samuel Chadwick of Cliff College Sheffield who boasted of thirty years' American experience of prohibition.[319] Guy Hayler of the United Kingdom Temperance Federation arrived as did one Catholic priest, Revd Fr Hays of Beeston, Nottingham. No Scottish Catholic priest appears to have been involved.[320] These were but additions to the American presence.

The American Anti-Saloon League was involved at every level. Revd George Safford, the state superintendent of the Minnesota Anti-Saloon League, sent materials, including posters, which had been used in successful campaigns in North America.[321] The Anti-Saloon League also seconded several leading figures to campaign in Scotland. They usually spent four to six weeks on the stump around the whole of Scotland but inevitably heavily concentrating on Glasgow as the key election. Charles M Sheldon, the author of the best seller, *In His Steps,* was again in Britain in 1918 and lent his support to the campaign.[322] W E 'Pussyfoot' Johnson wrote numerous articles for the temperance press.[323] The message was essentially that the true patriot is always an abstainer. State superintendents of the Anti-Saloon League also came to speak on a long-term loan basis. The California state superintendent, Revd Dr D M Gandier, came on a second three-month tour early in 1919.[324] At the annual general meeting of the Scottish Temperance League, the keynote address was given by Revd Professor Charles Scanlon of Pittsburgh, Pennsylvania. The thirteenth son on an Irish immigrant, he had served the prohibitionist cause in over twenty tours around the United States.[325] He was in effect a one-man prohibition movement. He was a member of the American Presbyterian Church Temperance Board, the permanent chairman of the National Prohibition Convention which organised the Prohibition Party presidential campaigns, the secretary of the National Dry Federation with some thirty-seven organisations affiliated to it; secretary of the Federal Council of Churches commission on temperance representing some 20 million Christians; treasurer of the International Prohibition Confederation; and he had even stood for governor with a campaign charabanc, brass band and quartet in support. Other less well-known figures also lent support at the same time; Revd Cyrus Keen of the American YMCA and Revd Dr Andrew Melrose Brodie of Wichita Kansas.[326]

The formidable Bishop James Cannon Jr, chairman of the National Executive of the Anti-Saloon League, lent his aid to the Glasgow campaign. Known as 'the Dry Messiah' he had graduated from the Princeton seminary and university. He then became principal of a failing academy for girls which he placed on a sound footing before he became a Southern Methodist Bishop in 1918. As president of the Virginia Anti-Saloon League he had helped the state go dry in 1914. An influential figure in southern Democratic party politics, he was to play an important role in the later defeat of Al Smith, the first Catholic to run for President in 1928.[327] At the time of his visit to Glasgow he was the chairman of the national executive committee of the Anti-Saloon League. Addressing Glasgow businessmen, he stressed the social efficiency gained through prohibition—increased productivity, control of rapacious blacks, safeguarding of womenhood and the future stock of the nation together with lower crime and taxes. Prohibition, he claimed, was essentially a labour protection law. He was clearly appealing to his audience but the entrepreneurial spirit of American 'normalcy' was more apparent than social reconstruction. That was something the 'wet' interests could exploit.[328]

Cannon was but the tip of the dry iceberg. Towards the close of 1919 the Scottish prohibitionists received several more American lecturers on loan from the Anti-Saloon League. Professor Nicholls was still touring the country on behalf of the drys when reinforcements arrived.[329] Revd Dr Henry Beache Carre, vice chairman of the Anti-Saloon League, deputising for Cannon, addressed a meeting of Glasgow ministers on the popular democratic will behind American prohibition.[330] As a teacher at Vanderbilt University Nashville and President of the Tennessee Anti-Saloon League, he was from a state legally dry since 1909[331] A personal witness on the local veto issue, Revd George A Henry, a Canadian born minister, was one of six originally secured for the campaign in 1919; the number later dropped to four.[332] Others did come, however, for the transatlantic prohibitionists realised the critical nature of the contest: 'It will determine the attitude of parliament for years to come.'[333]

Revd Dr W C Poole and Miss Ida Green of the California Anti-Saloon League gave their services under the auspices of the American Anti-Saloon League.[334] With assorted support from local leaders, visitors like Mrs Lloyd George and other Americans like Revd Steele of Pittsburgh and a Mr and Mrs Coulee, they travelled extensively throughout the country, addressing meetings large and small, in villages and major cities, with only an occasional disruption as at Dumfries.[335] In addition Mrs Howland of the Boston branch of the WCTU worked in the west and north east of Scotland.[336]

Other support came from returning visitors to America; Ex-Bailie Gardiner twice returned trumpeting the massive increases in productivity, quality, reliability and general standard of living of dry America.[337] Ex-Bailie John King on a visit to the American Chamber of Commerce Convention in Atlanta was particularly impressed by the quality of working class housing in America as a result, he believed, of prohibition.[338]

Sir Samuel Chisholm and the Citizens Council organized a celebration on first saloonless day in America, 16 January 1920.[339] Mrs Howland, Miss Green and Revd Dr Henry listened to an address by Revd W C Poole of California in which he proclaimed; 'Having made the world safe for democracy America addressed herself seriously to the task of making her democracy safe for the world.'[340] The other Americans stressed the benefits of child care improvements and of education, and as Miss Green said 'the bringing of God's kingdom on earth'.[341] To Sir Samuel Chisholm 'the event was worthy of a hallelujah chorus'.[342] At the same time the prohibitionists were slowly being forced on to the defensive by the Anti-Prohibitionist

League propaganda. For the trade had very well organised forces and an excellent publicity machine which portrayed the whole prohibitionist effort as undue American interference in Scotland's domestic affairs.[343] It would seem that xenophobia and class consciousness were beginning to undermine the traditional dry constituency. As businessmen emphasised, the better regulation of work and labour would seem to have become very suspicious. Whatever the leadership might have said, the rank and file were restive. Bigger profits seemed more in view than bigger pay packets.

The propaganda war ground on relentlessly. Mrs Knox Livingstone returned to her Glasgow home again from Massachusetts WCTU to address the annual general meeting of the Scottish Temperance League. Prohibition, she claimed, was a considered established policy which had developed naturally over the years. The war had exercised little influence: in 1914 some 28 states had already been dry. Mrs Livingstone then joined the roster of Citizens Council speakers with the various Canadian visitors above.[344] Mass meetings, demonstrations all over the country, but especially in the west, continued. A new phenomenon was the drawing-room meeting. These meetings usually took place in select west-end residences with an address by a visiting American. In that their message was to be converted the impact could only be inspirational rather than politically persuasive. Few voters were persuaded.[345] There might be flying visits from Bishop Cannon and a Mr Weatherill but with the return of W E 'Pussyfoot' Johnson to America from mid April to September the campaign seems to have peaked.[346] Revd Dr Henry stayed on far beyond his allocated six-week stint and Mrs Armour of Georgia WCTU returned again after a lapse of ten years.[347] The liquor interests had in turn secured American speakers against prohibition: a former minister Hon C A Windle and Mrs Minona Jones.[348] Immediately on his return in September Pussyfoot Johnson became embroiled in controversy with the liquor speakers. A close result seemed in prospect. Revd Dr Henry extended his stay once more as speakers from Canada and England were brought in to bolster the attack.

Johnson stressed the essential Scottish nature of the reform. He defensively argued that Glasgow had taught America everything valuable in the last generation. America seemed but Scotland across the sea: 'We owe so much good to Scotland. Men and women of Scottish blood have been in the forefront of everything good in America.' For over ten years he had received the reports of all the Glasgow Corporation departments which he used 'all over America with telling effect. The result was that in nearly every city in America thanks to Glasgow's example these enterprises were now operated by the municipalities for the benefit of the people. We owe this in large part to your experience. We followed your example and through all these years we have been reaping the benefits of your example.'[349]

The *Glasgow Herald* strongly supported the prohibitionists. It was the only major British paper to do so.[350] It also printed articles and letters from America supporting prohibition.[351] The wet forces printed and distributed eight million cards on the streets. 2.5 million anti-prohibition shopping bags; 260,000 posters; 60,000 coloured posters; and 20,000 sixteen-sheet coloured posters. The wets advertised at football grounds, at licensed grocers, public houses and virtually any available site. That campaign lasted seven months and in the event proved successful, with abundant quotations against prohibition from Samuel Gompers, the President of the American Federation of Labour. The drys were unable to counter this wealth of publicity nor effectively rebut the charge of American intervention in Scottish affairs: 'The result to put it bluntly was a complete fizzle. Not a single bad area went dry.'[352]

The failure at the polls was a severe blow to the drys. American prohibitionists still came to exhort, rally and inspire their Scottish brethren. The structure of the poll might have prevented dry success. They had to secure a 55 per cent majority of no-licence resolution. That majority also had to represent 35 per cent of the total electorate. A bare majority for the limitation of licences was sufficient to succeed if that represented 35 per cent of the total electorate. Four areas, all in the suburbs, went no-licence, as the table shows: Nine other suburban areas opted for limitation whilst twenty-four areas including the worst slum districts wanted no change. Only 99 licences were suppressed from 1604. From 253 areas in the whole of Scotland 206 had voted no change, 24 for limitation and 23 for no licence.

The following year Dr Howard H Russell, the founder of the Anti-Saloon League visited Scotland. After addressing gatherings in Glasgow and Edinburgh he gave a speech to the general meeting of the Scottish Temperance League.[353] The emphasis seemed to be upon the benefits to business, the maintenance of constitutional law and the protection of children. It seemed an essentially utilitarian approach. He was supported by Revd Dr W C Poole, formerly of the California Anti-Saloon League, now in London, and by an American lady preacher, Mrs Varney, also stationed there.[354] While they seem to have made only brief lecture tours, Russell spent a month touring mainly the west of Scotland, from Ayr to Glasgow and Coatbridge.[355] These continuing dreams were further sustained by Revd Norman J Bennett of Jonesburg, USA, the son-in-law of a former Scottish Temperance League worker. He had emigrated to study for the Methodist Episcopal Church eight years earlier and now returned to hold a series of meetings throughout the west and south west of Scotland in February 1921.[356] Returning visitors from America still portrayed prohibition as an unqualified success. An Australian businessman told his Glasgow friends after travelling three months in America about the considerable economic benefits. The only opponents seemed to be alien elements in New York city.[357]

The Church of Scotland delegates to the Pan Presbyterian Alliance gave similar testimony. The chairman of the temperance committee of the church felt that Boston, though 'owned by Jews and run by Irishmen,' still prospered under prohibition. At the second anniversary celebration of American prohibition Revd Dr R J Fleming, the historian and then secretary general of the Presbyterian Alliance, told of his five months in America. Well acquainted with the country from his three previous visits, he believed that the Scots would follow American example if the churches were to work together and the women were to be organised for the struggle. Scots flourished in a dry land: why not at home?[358] At a rally there were numerous glowing accounts of the American experience, an ideal sullied only by ignorant alien Catholics.[359] Encouraged by yet another tour by J G Woolley, the old Prohibition Party candidate, and the deliverance of the temperance committee of the General Assembly of the Church of Scotland, the prohibitionists remained confident.[360] A further delegation confirmed these impressions the following year. Amid the general affluence only the disgruntled alien Catholic groups wished for the return of the saloon.[361] The parallels and similarities to American public attitudes were remarkable. The normalcy of America and the antipathy to immigrants was reflected in Scottish attitudes as in the General Assembly deliverances upon the Irish in Scotland at the same time. In both countries an old dominant group was celebrating the triumph of its principles at the very moment the respective societies were irrevocably changing. The old monolithic cohesive order was passing on both sides of the Atlantic. Prohibition and the attempt to introduce it into Scotland was the last fling of an old regime. The shopkeepers' millenium was misplaced in the corporate society—or a socialist municipality.

The motives and attitudes may have been high-minded and geared to social improvement. Unfortunately, they were too closely identified with a particular social, religious and ethnic group. That is not to exclude other elements but to recognise the dominant features of the movement. America could appeal to the radicals in the early nineteenth century as a free democratic land of manhood suffrage free from industrial—and soon hopefully chattel—slavery, and the slavery of drink. By the 1920s that dream seemed to many groups in Glasgow a nightmare. It seemed that a small unrepresentative group allied to business interests had forced the worker to a new form of slavery: prohibition was a symbol of that capitalist dominance. At the same time the radical left in Glasgow and the west went dry. Cambuslang, Kilsyth and a ward in Clydebank allegedly saw the triumph of prohibition and bolshevism as closely linked.[362] Whatever the reasons, 1920 showed that Glasgow and America were drifting apart in certain areas. Jealousy in the face of American economic success as Glasgow declined slowly. The new nature of Scottish democratic politics followed the 1918 enfranchisement of the masses, with the emergence of Labour, the Russian revolution, the image of American business, and perhaps the Glasgow Irish antipathy to a nation which had failed their nation at the treaty of Versailles, all coalesced to produce an anti-prohibitionist party in Glasgow. An auld alliance was in decline—though the memory lingered. As an American observer wrote in 1922:

> If Scotland had gone dry, America would stay dry without question. If America goes back to wetness, or even to dampness, there is scarcely any power on earth that can make Scotland dry.[363]

Perhaps in one sense the new Democratic party of Franklin D Roosevelt had its origins in the streets of Glasgow in 1920. The Irish, the blue collar workers and the ethnic urban groups were not to be driven along the old road of the Protestant ethic epitomised in prohibition. What Glasgow does today the world. . . .

Chapter Five

The Civic Ideal

Efficiency and Morality in Local Government

The story of Glasgow has especial interest for Americans because of its rapid growth and because it contains a large proportion of the same element which has been for sixty years and more the chief element of drink and corruption in New York and because, in spite of the fear that liquor is as plentiful and as cheap as in New York, Glagow has been able to keep this element in some order, and, above all, to prevent it from seizing the offices and plundering the finances of the city. The contrasts which suggest themselves are as startling as they are painful.[1]

So, in 1895, wrote the reviewer of Albert Shaw's book on municipal government in *Christian Work*. Shaw's work highlighted the problems of urban government in Glasgow and demonstrated how an efficient business-like honest administration curbed the alien and Catholic, supported temperance and provided a vast array of public services at very low cost.[2] In short, Glasgow had preserved her cultural traditions, expanded and grown rich, and retained a strong sense of public probity and duty; she was Protestant, prosperous and progressive.

The links between Glasgow and the United States had been and continued to be wide ranging, diverse and profitable in many ways. An essentially nineteenth-century city, Glasgow's development, as Weber suggested, had much to teach Americans.[3] Glasgow was at once an example, inspiraton and clearing house for ideas among American progressive reformers. Glasgow's motto, Let Glasgow Flourish, and its traditional continuation 'by the preaching of the Word' epitomised the attractions of the city to reformers: confidence, business acumen and enterprise for the future and a positive commitment to the public Christian ethic. As Washington Gladden and F C Howe observed, Glasgow businessmen served with pride and professional efficiency as Lord Provosts and city councillors.[4] It was a view expressed in the *Municipal Review*, that 'city shall cease to be the haunt of the time server and become the shrine of democracy to which all the people shall make stated pilgrimage'.[5] Glasgow was the Holy Grail, the New Jerusalem for the chivalric reformers of America. Glasgow, the Second City of the British Empire, had grown wealthy, particularly through coal, engineering and shipping. Though that wealth might not be equitably distributed, the most successful businessmen, like Sir William Burrell, did not shirk their civic responsibilities: they served with pride. The Lord Provost, American reformers noted, was 'almost as busy as the President Roosevelt and yet he has not as much power as the Mayor of Evanston or Waukegan'.[6] Natural pride in public service stood in marked contrast to the vulgar corruption and self-seeking of major American cities. Glaswegians, far from abandoning civic responsibility to corrupt political machines, were active in promoting civic moral uplift and in practical improvements in their great city. That was to the taste of Washington Gladden. A seemingly disinterested high-mindedness permeated the respectable classes of Glasgow: there was, as F C Howe observed, 'something akin to religious enthusiasm for Glasgow'.[7]

As a provincial metropolis, Glasgow was especially attractive to American provincials. Few American progressive reformers came from the eastern seaboard, but multitudes came from the mid-west: Jane Addams, F C Howe, Albert Shaw, Henry Demarest Lloyd and others. J R Commons found himself more at home in Glasgow than in London.[8] Robert A Woods, the Boston settlement worker, found his religious faith received a cold bath in the east end of London, but was revitalised in Glasgow. Dr Alice Hamilton of Hull House was, perhaps, near the truth when she observed: 'Our English visitors sometimes surprised us by combining social radicalism with a total lack of democratic feeling.'[9] Even the working-class champions, Edward Aveling and Eleanor Marx, found the average American 'indescribably unpleasant'.[10] Glasgow was not only homogeneous, but homely and without English snobbery. As Joseph Lee, the vice president of the Massachusetts Civic League, said, the Scotch race were 'the most respected of any on this planet'.[11] Glasgow embodied the highest ideals of the race.

In one sense the American interest was an outcome of the improved relations between Britain and America. Still more, it was the result of W T Stead's activities in seeking to promote better understanding between the English speaking communities, particularly through his Civic Church and his Association of Helpers. Glasgow in 1893 was one of the first cities to establish such a body: 'a spiritual counterpart of the town council.'[12] Through this 'moral caucus' the government of cities in the Atlantic world would uphold the highest standards of human dignity and integrity. When Stead's programme is considered, Glasgow was already well on the way to having a fully working model in operation: hospitals, cheap guaranteed milk, playgrounds, educational opportunity and access to university, temperance, better housing and cheap, rapid transportation within the city.[13] Significantly the American edition of the *Review of Reviews* was to be edited by Albert Shaw, *the* Glasgow publicist.

The city of Glasgow itself was the community church idealised by American reformers like Stanton Coit and Charles Zueblin: 'What the Civic Church can do is to generalise for the benefit of all the advantages which have hitherto been confined to the few.'[14] It was, as Frederic Harrison saw, 'the Positivist ideal of the republic in which these—the main ends of social like—are attained by moral means, by religious training, by education, by an intensely active social opinion'.[15] To such men, Glasgow was a dynamic expression—and proof—of the social democratic faith.

The city provided a guide to the future. Intellectually, James McCosh had come from Scotland to America. A former Glasgow and Edinburgh student who had studied under Thomas Chalmers, he was president of Princeton University from 1868 until 1894. Armed with Scottish Common-Sense philosophy, he introduced an awareness of evolutionary religion into America.[16] The old static dogmatic forms were having to adapt to the challenges of popular Darwinism. That optimistic idealism was continued by others with Scottish connections. John Fiske, who came to Scotland on a lecture tour, promoted idealism and evolution in his *Cosmic Philosophy* and *The Destiny of Man*.[17] The Aberdeenshire born John A Gordon from his Boston Pulpit gave warm support to the 'forward' movement of liberal Christianity.[18] By the close of the century Professor Henry Drummond of Glasgow, the author of the *Ascent of Man* and popular speaker, had reinforced that religious optimism.[19] At a more sophisticated level the Idealism of Edward Caird, Professor of Glasgow, spread through many American colleges and universities.[20] From Michigan to California, from Professor Sylvester Morris to Professor G H Howison, his Idealism spread through intellectual strength and personal contact.[19]

That challenge had a racial aspect in America and to a degree in Glasgow. The flood of immigrants was altering the old order in America dramatically. The cities grew rapidly with little control over developments, industrial locations or the provision of public services. Without an urban tradition to draw upon, the new urban population was left to its own devices: nine out of ten were totally new to the city in America. As James Bryce pointed out in his *American Commonwealth,* the city was the failure of American democracy.[21] The need to infuse a sense of identity, of local and national patriotism upon the polyglot masses, was a glaring necessity.

Sensitive, educated, usually élite Protestant groups cast around for a solution. Their doctrinal positions were eroding, their real centres of power and strength were increasingly in the suburbs and countryside. The new Americans were largely not of their religious persuasion, of their ethnic group or their democratic tradition. So the Protestant churches had to abandon their fixed positions in doctrine, in social concerns and intellectual approaches to the contemporary world. A more flexible, fluid response was required. Increasingly mobile Americans needed a portable, efficient set of values. Free from the burdens of the past and the barrage of doctrinal intricacies, and accessible to all, the various denominations were drawn together into social involvement.[22]

In the late nineteenth century, the outlook had become general among leading groups of Christians and professionals. As Washington Gladden claimed, St John's vision was 'none other than your city as it might be and as you might help to make it'.[23] 'Religion must be a free plastic, progressive, versatile life, ever embodying itself in new forms as the ages unfold. The moment it stiffens into organisation and settles into final statements, the ages begin to struggle with it, to shake it off and to leave it behind.'[24]

Bascom was originally president of Wisconsin University and taught the leading Progressive Robert Lafollete. It was time to lay 'the foundations of the kingdom of heaven, as a present social structure, broadly, wisely, conspicuously'.[25] The church was identified with the democratising forces in contemporary life. It made God the democratising tide and the national purpose. Civic duty and social reform, the church and nation, individual and international peace were interchangeable ideas. Each contributed to a cohesive social order.[26]

Glasgow seemed to have produced religious apologists like McCosh and civic critics like James Bryce who could see through the prevailing urban morass. Glasgow as a city seemed a working model of their ideas. It was worthy of attention. It was part of the modernisation of liberalism.[27] That process enabled those who were concerned with improved social efficiency and those apprehensive about the limited nature of future resources to ally for social reforms.[28] For local and national needs social cohesion was a necessity. The warfare and welfare states were both concerned with social amelioration.[29] In the absence of alternatives, religion was a predictable means to that end. In the absence of social engineers and bureaucrats, it was the only means. Evolutionary practicable religion would bring results: 'The nation herself is the living church of her citizens. National idealism in the hearts of the citizens is in the nature of worship, of religious praise and of the sense of spiritual communion and dependence which inform prayer.'[30] More than that, 'Christianity as soon as it has become transfused with the spirit and transformed by the method of modern science will bring about the Millenium.'[31]

The two most renowned Glasgow figures were Sir Samuel Chisholm, a wholesale provision merchant, and Sir Daniel Macaulay Stevenson, a considerable coal exporter.[32] Both served as Lord Provost in the heyday of Glasgow's success. Both were Liberals and both failed at parliamentary contests. They therefore remained local men of substance and influence: unlike Joe Chamberlain, they did not leave a faltering civic base to pursue more national career interests. Chisholm, a staunch temperance advocate, emphasised the *legal* enforcement of the 'good life' as when he made all municipally-owned properties dry. But Stevenson, a far wealthier, more intellectual character, stressed the innate potential goodness of man which could be liberated through art, music and literature. Emphasising moral suasion, Stevenson was a phenomenal benefactor of Glasgow, Liverpool and London Universities, the Glasgow School of Art and the Academy of Music. The brother of a noted artist of the day, Stevenson, whom Bryce described as 'one of the most distinguished private citizens of Britain', was a persistent peace advocate: during the First World War, he was a member of the Union of Democratic Control.[33] In this Stevenson was more in tune with the views of Brand Whitlock and the 'soft' wing of progressive reform than with the 'hard' views of Chisholm and Roosevelt.[34]

Chisholm and Stevenson with their enlightened—or perhaps self-interested—businessmen in the Glasgow city council, were responsible for the creation of a model municipality. While Chisholm could mobilise public opinion around temperance, Stevenson improved the efficiency of the city council, introduced the idea of all councillors sharing in some committee work and cut borrowing expenses. In addition, he was a leading advocate of free public libraries and the Sunday opening of galleries, and largely responsible for the foundation of the Glasgow Civic Society.[35] The gas, water, electricity and other public services were a tribute to their imaginative enterprise though these initiatives were unable to eliminate the root problem of poverty within the city. Humanitarianism, or welfare capitalism operating at municipal level, sought to enable the deserving to help themselves: the undeserving would be taken in hand and given suitable treatment and assistance. Liberalism with a large injection of Christian duty forced the consideration of urban problems. It was perhaps a feeling of guilt, a realisation that, but for the grace of God and the luck of the trade cycle, they too might be among the unfortunate. A social demand that they be seen to be actively involved in some form of charitable activity further stimulated this concern. To conservative American critics, like Robert P Porter, municipal socialism was but a poor substitute for private enterprise.[36] To critics on the left, municipal reform was merely a cosmetic operation, but the fact is that businessmen did make the effort and did have some considerable success in some areas.

To that extent Glasgow stood far superior to the American experience: 'The majority of our municipal charters as they stand today entirely fail to represent the experienced judgement of the most capable men in the community as to what is the best and most practical organisation of the administrative agencies of local government.'[37] American businessmen were reassured that reform was good for business rather than a prelude to socialism: 'In its present stage of development municipal ownership is inspired by no ideal of a changed social order, and the movement is likely to continue to be one for improved service, for business thrift, for the relief of taxpayers from the burden of taxation, and for increased revenue for the community.'[38] The Glasgow 'revolution' was staffed by businessmen, 'earning their living by the sweat of their brow', a reassuring American way.[39] Glasgow's Lord Provosts were neither 'gentlemen' nor corrupt political bosses, but men of keen practical business sense drawn from the local successful professional groups: even the Labour councillors included a doctor and a wholesaler. Drawn from a common social-cultural background, they could unite in a non-partisan manner for the common good: divisive issues were removed from politics. That tone of politics was further sustained by what American observers considered a restrictive municipal franchise: 'The whole body of men who are ignorant, vicious and irresponsible are practically outside the pale of politics.'[40] Albert Shaw and J R Commons saw that limited suffrage had much to commend it: immigrants and blacks would have to earn the vote and so exercise the franchise in a responsible manner.[41] But the thrust of American progressive argument was the businessmen should involve themselves in local affairs. Efficient businessmen made an efficient local community and an efficient nation: 'A community of purpose,' wrote Hugo Munsterburg, 'is more effective than tradition because it pervades the whole of man'.[42] That was the vital point for, as Henry James emphasised, America lacked 'a visible church, a visible state, a society, a visible past'.[43]

Glasgow offered a practical working model of efficient municipal government. Theory and practice combined to produce a humanitarian caring council within a cohesive community: social concern paid in personal, communal and financial terms. Glasgow seemed to have achieved a revolution in government through education, an active public opinion and a responsive social democracy in the city council. In that, Glasgow may not have differed significantly from any other British or German city. But Glasgow seemed to have gone further in her municipal enterprise in scale, convenience and, even more startlingly, in profitability: Glasgow seemed to have a superabundance of what Lord Bryce called 'intelligence, self-control and conscience'.[44] The vibrant, vital provincial centre offered a solution to the 'outsiders in American society'. Above all her tramway system, an integrated service which physically bound the city together in a community, was a mode of technical improvements: a boon to the public in its services, and still more, in the application of its profits, through the Common Good Fund, to better public facilities and in the opening up of new areas of economic opportunity and recreation. The tramway symbolised the public control of the most advanced technology in the interests of the whole community.

Americans showed great interest in Glasgow's profitable humanitarianism. At the turn of the century, Americans were increasingly conscious of their background, ancestry and traditions.[45] With the influx of millions of variegated immigrants, largely from southern and eastern European peasant stock, Americans were apprehensive for their future. Millions of Catholics and Jews, and in California, hundreds of thousands of Asians, posed a racial, religious, cultural threat to American homogeneity. The newcomers seemed to be characterised by poverty, illiteracy and unacceptable customs, like drinking and anti-sabbatarianism. As quantity threatened American quality, so the older stock sought refuge in various expedients: they campaigned to exclude various classes or races of immigrants, as in the New England Immigration Restriction League: they urged some restriction on American voting privileges, a sentiment which found its most extreme expression in the South: or they compensated for their present impotence by emphasising their superior culture, as in Henry Adams, or more pertinently, in their Anglo-Saxon ancestry; Brand Whitlock, E A Ross, J R Commons, R T Ely among others.[46] Many came from a strong, frequently Presbyterian, religious background. This cultural tradition made for a dynamic mixture as epitomised in that eminent Scots-Irishman, Woodrow Wilson. That sense of duty, service and the obligation to educate one's fellowman, seemingly frustrated in some social and political areas of American life in recent times, had demonstrated their vitality in Glasgow, the vibrant centre of their cultural homeland.

Among the Glasgow exports of the time was the Boys' Brigade. By 1893-4, there were more than 300 companies in America: The Boston Brigade had some 800 members.[47] When the founder, Colonel Smith, visited President Roosevelt in 1907, he found four officers, former members of the original Glasgow 1st Brigade, running units in Baltimore and Pittsburgh. Glasgow notions of service, discipline and order could flourish in an American context: 'The object of the Brigade shall be the advancement of Christ's Kingdom among Boys, and the promotion of habits of Reverence, Discipline, Self-Respect, all that tends towards a true Christian Manliness.'[48]

Associated with Revd Dr John B Paton, an Ayrshire-born Congregationalist minister, Smith rejoiced that the future generation would maintain patriotism within a sense of universal brotherhood.[49] Like Paton and many Americans, Smith wanted to give order and structure to the lives of the untutored children of the masses. Assisted by Professor Henry Drummond, the inspirational writer, he inculcated a sense of individual discipline and social service.

In an era of growing affluence, rising expectations and a new intelligentsia, many men and women graduates of the new educational institutions were able to combine scholarship, pleasure and a pilgrimage to the old land. Not surprisingly, many like Jane Addams came to Glasgow initially in pursuit of Scott and Burns, but found themselves even more impressed by the city's municipal achievements. The various summer schools, at Edinburgh University, or on Chatauqua type tours, or at the great missionary gathering in 1911 in Edinburgh, widened the knowledge of Glasgow's achievements.[50] Glasgow became a part of a social democratic grand tour: pleasure had to have a strong dose of duty.

Glasgow represented the theory and practice of effective, efficient municipal government. The reputation and accomplishments of the various municipal enterprises under *professional* control responsible to the elected council seemed the solution to the American ills. The record of John Young and his successor, James Dalrymple, in establishing and developing a thriving municipal tramway system, proved that responsible collective control could provide cheap and profitable community services. The Medical Officers of Health, Chalmers and Russell, showed the value of community health under municipal control.[51] Housing, thanks to Chisholm, was a model for housing the poorer classes in society. Homes for widows, for tramps and for the unemployed at Glasgow and Midlocharwoods, under the Scottish Labour Colony, and for alcoholics at Girgenti, were further evidence of reforming efficiency.[52]

Like many other British cities, Glasgow had extended its control of public services: gas, water, electricity, housing and even telephones. To contemporaries, the scale and extent of public regulation in building, health and education were impressive. Public laundries, markets, slaughterhouses, concert halls, and even an inebriates' home had been established. Although there were shortcomings, the cheap and efficient operation of the public services produced considerable benefits: 'The city is being inspired by a new morality,' it was said in 1907.[53] Yet in all these activities, the tramway was the peak of municipal enterprises.

In 1894, Glasgow had municipalised her tramway system; and, as the first major city in the world to undertake this public service, found herself under close scrutiny. Under the management of John Young and his successor, James Dalrymple, the enterprise proved extremely successful.[54] In the initial phase, houses, cars and depots had to be acquired with great speed. In 1898, after Young had toured American systems, electrification began, and was completed by 1901. Between 1896 and 1903 the Glasgow track mileage was doubled to 130 miles, the number of passengers annually carried more than doubled to reach 177.1 million; and, although fares were reduced, receipts were almost doubled from £328,000 to £653,000. By 1914 indeed, 336.6 million passengers were carried, ninety per cent of them usually at fares of a penny or less. Every year the system showed a substantial surplus, from £83,000 in 1896 to £68,000 in the troubled year of 1911; and in 1910 the reserve funds more than covered the whole capital of nearly £4 million. To meet an increasing demand on the service, the number of cars rose from 220 to over 600 in 1904, when ninety per cent of them were built in the municipal workshops. Better wages, shorter hours and various benefit schemes improved the morale of the workforce. The original 92 employees had risen thirty years later to almost 9000. The public enjoyed a comfortable, frequent and cheap service. The junction of Jamaica Street and Renfield Street was allegedly the busiest in the world—466 cars an hour passed on weekdays; 516 on Saturdays.[55] With service for twenty of the twenty-four hours in constantly improved cars, Glasgow was justifiably proud of her municipal enterprise, efficiency and profit; and the surplus, which was applied to the Common Good Fund, benefited the whole city. The achievement appears all the greater when we remember the competition not only of the surburban railways but also from the newly constructed underground railways.

Between 1894 and 1914, therefore, Glasgow's trams were at the centre of an American debate about the quality of social, economic and political life. Between 1894, when Pullman, the modern town of paternalistic capitalism, was effectively destroyed by a major strike, and the First World War, when welfare capitalism, the garden suburb and the automobile were establishing the good consumer society in America, Glasgow provided a middle way between the capitalist and the socialist: it was the honest broker.[56] That appeal diminished only as the image of Glasgow changed and American private enterprise recovered its self-confidence.

The tramcar was thus not merely an asset but a symbol. In the selective view of the Progressives, it symbolised the industrial order under public regulation. There the most sophisticated machinery was put at the disposal of the public and not of private profit. Labour, in the drivers and conductors, was also placed in public service rather than sectional interest. The tram, in a sense, transcended the politics and social dissensions which confronted the uneasy American middle class; for 'conscience', morality, businesslike methods and public service were almost interchangeable words expressing the values of those who sought a middle way between the extremes of concentrated wealth and socialism.[57] The tram expressed a generalised faith, or moral law, which every man could grasp and co-operate towards achieving, in a mutual search and agreement on both means and ends, towards the good life and the common good. The Progressive, sensitive to economic pressures, believed his social position enabled him to define 'the good society' in acceptable, disinterested terms; in order to reconcile class interest, open and honest discussion was necessary; men of goodwill, rising above party and class interest, could unite to promote the common good. The tram typified that dynamic democratic society, opening up new areas of opportunity and improvement but united in a common purpose.[58]

The public interest was to be second to none. In Glasgow the best example of public interest was, as John Young claimed, the total absence of advertising from public transport. Aestheticism preceded profit.[59] Even the trolley posts and wires were, as at Kelvinbridge, carefully designed and selected: and in the Glasgow of Charles Rennie Mackintosh and of notable art collectors, this was understandable. Again by their cleanliness and good appearance, their prompt service, and their neatly uniformed crews, the trams were mobile advertisements for hygiene, efficiency and a disciplined order. An apprehensive middle class sought improvement through example: their duty as custodians of democracy required the integration, or 'domestication' of the newcomer to industrial society: 'There are some classes in every modern society composed of those who are virtually children'[60] Although the number of Glasgow's immigrants was by American standards miniscule, there were opportunities for moral stewardship. The tram fulfilled the demand. It symbolised certain basic rights and so acted as 'an engine of democracy'. Glasgow trams flourished just as Labour was beginning to organise in the Scottish Co-operative Wholesale Society and, through Glasier and Keir Hardie, in the Independent Labour Party.[61] By placing the different classes physically side by side, perhaps the tram fostered egalitarian notions, or encouraged aspirations to middle class tastes. By spreading the population—though by no means to American satisfaction—the Glasgow trams potentially opened up better housing, better recreation and better health for all. Business benefited from cheap fares and the increased mobility of labour.[62]

American Progressives saw the tram as a means of diminishing the appeal of Labour, The American socialist vote had risen dramatically between 1896 and 1904, but as reformism grew so too the socialist vote dropped between fifty and eighty per cent in the elections of 1904–5.[63] The public, naturally an honest and just employer, would pay a fair wage and so reduce the appeal of radicalism. Violence would also disappear. By providing cheap access to the country and thus offering alternatives to the saloon, the trams seemed to act as a showpiece of 'second economy and perfect solvency'.[64] Municipal ownership meant morality and business could unite for the common good. Glasgow was a 'concrete reality'.[65] That was particularly important to several academic reformers. Several of these had been dismissed for their 'socialist' views or their attacks on monopoly. E W Bemis had been dismissed from the University of Chicago, 1895, for his anti-monopoly views, and then again with Frank Parsons from Manhattan College in Kansas, 1899, and Syracuse, 1899.[66] Even the redoubtable R T Ely had to justify himself before a university court of regents. These economic heretics had to ground their theories in practicality, in Glasgow, for self-defence. Far from being dreamers, they were realists—efficiency experts, combining humanity with profitability.

This transatlantic connection found its strength in the traditional cultural links, the present municipal successes of Glasgow and the confidence in a future consensus. Education, an enthusiastic public opinion and an effective social democracy within an expanding religious culture were as ever the key elements. Again, a traditional sense of guilt and a reproach to

American nationalist pride from 'decadent' Europe, was hurtful. But a reproach from Glasgow, the most 'American' European city made such warnings and example a little more acceptable: 'The Nation, thus ordained by God, and entrusted by him with a portion of the earth's surface as its domain and treasure house, exists in the earth for the fulfilment of divine purpose, for the establishment here of righteousness and peace, for the maintenance of freedom and order, for the building up of the kingdom of heaven. The end which it must seek is not the welfare of certain favoured classes, but the welfare of all—the physical, intellectual and moral welfare of the whole people.'[67] Americans could rely on Glasgow sympathy and understanding.

At that time America was in desperate straits. Rapid urbanisation, massive immigration, the consolidation of gigantic monopolies and the increasing militancy of organised labour presented considerable problems. If public life was bleak, private life was too.[68] The family was in a crisis: a declining birth rate, a fourfold increase in divorce since the Civil War and women, educated or not, seeking careers outside the home. The fluid situation was exaggerated by the mobile population: few stayed long in any one location and many became part of the vast army of casual labour.[69] Ever on the move, with no commitments and no real stake in the existing order, these rootless people would naturally fall prey to the saloon, vice, or wild socialist theories. Only religion seemed to be a stable element. Between 1880 and 1910 the proportion of the population formally affiliated to a religious body doubled to 40 per cent. By 1914, 52 million were attached to some church or sect (and this as a time when voter turnout at national elections was declining).[70] Everything then devolved on religion. It provided solace and reassurance but, above all, stability and a means of conservation. Neither blindly conservative nor wildly innovative, religion meant initiative *and* containment within an evolutionary process. In the final analysis much of this romantic sentiment was doomed to failure: As Reinhold Neibuhr said, American progressives wanted 'a God without wrath who brought men without sin into a kingdom without judgement, through the ministration of a Christ without a Cross'.[71] Theirs was a gentle, well-mannered, antiseptic world, inoculated with optimism against grim reality.

America was therefore in the midst of a cultural crisis. To many needs Glasgow was at least a palliative. To those like Edward T Devine, it offered social cohesion: 'Embryonic philosophy was so formulated as not to exclude any who were willing to face facts and to co-operate in the eradication of demonstrable evils.'[72] To those like Vida Dutton Scudder, Glasgow offered a practical answer: 'Middle class radicalism desperately needed to be purged of its Utopian ideology.'[73] To Fabian social democrats like Henry Demarest Lloyd, it was an ideal haven:' To an American accustomed to the fierce passions which rage in our industrial world, going to a co-operative land is like reaching harbour after a tempestuous journey.'[74] To religiously inspired reformers like Robert A Woods, Glasgow was racially and religious attractive. 'There is sometimes a strong relation between classes where they have the same blood and same traditions as in Scotland'[75] Glasgow met these demands.

Not all Americans were admirers. Henry James, predictably, found Glasgow 'blackened beyond redemption from any such light of the picturesque as can hope to irradiate fog or grime'.[76] For Glasgow, said Bret Harte, one time American consul there, had 'no gaiety, no brilliancy, no sense of enjoyment visible but a stern stupid respect for the art of business, as if they were intoxicated from a sense of duty'.[77] Whatever its external failings, Glasgow more than compensated by a resilient interior, that psychic human solidarity beloved of progressives. Glasgow had that quality, which F C Howe described: 'Duty was always first, happiness was to be analysed'.[78] Indeed the new economists, like Ely and Commons who admired the city, hailed from rural backgrounds and had a preacherly cast of mind. Glasgow, with its missionary tradition would naturally endorse Dewey's belief that 'the teacher always is the prophet of the true God and the usherer in of the true Kingdom of God'.[79] It was zeal epitomised in the work of an unreserved admirer of Glasgow, Edward W Bemis.[80] An organiser of libraries, branches of the American Economic Association and University extension classes, Bemis at one point regularly commuted between St Louis and Nashville each week to give extra-mural lectures.

The radical ingredient is perhaps best represented by Henry Demarest Lloyd.[81] When he came to Scotland, Lloyd already had succumbed to Shaw's roseate description. He also met and was impressed by Lord Kelvin and John Young. Though he had met Keir Hardie and other Fabian socialists, he found Scotland a co-operative haven in a restless oppressive world of rapacious capitalists. Perhaps he felt more at home amid the many Scottish emergent radicals. He was tapping a growing tradition. After all Henry George had found many supporters for his land tax schemes in Glasgow. Indeed at least one Glasgow Labour pioneer, had joined the Knights of Labour. There were several branches in the West of Scotland. Bellamy found supporters there too: a volume in the British Bellamy library dealt with Scottish Home Rule. Indeed, Bellamy's closest supporter, Sylvester Baxter, returned from a European Tour in 1894–5 to laud Glasgow to the skies.[82] Lloyd had already been in correspondence with Scottish shale oil producers and had, in Robert Donald's *Daily Chronicle,* exposed the dangerous trusts.[83] With the Scottish Wholesale Society he found himself sharing in an ideal model community. Armed with slides from Scottish Co-operative Wholesale Society, he returned to spread the message through the United States:

The fanatical avarice which is destroying municipal ownership in gas works and city transit is a University extension course in economic democracy. We want to know how much inferior city owned transit in Glasgow is, to that of New York and Chicago, but the dullest of us is clever enough to see that the real comparison is not between Glasgow and New York, but between Glasgow municipalised, and Glasgow un-municipalised. We want the statistics and the political economy of municipal ownership of course, but we want them all. Nothing misleads like figures, if you do not put in all the figures. What is the political economy of the slow wearing away of the lives of tired men, women and children, who must walk because they cannot afford to ride, and the political economy of the death-rate, the misery, and the deterioration of the tenement districts congested because fares, and the rates of speed, and the number of cars run, are determined by the demand of stockholders for dividends, and a short-sighted demand at that of making less for itself than it might make?[84]

The provinces were the vital centres. J B Glasier wrote to Henry Demarest Lloyd on 20 October, 1897: 'Don't judge British Socialism by what you see of socialism and socialists in London. Come to the provinces. It is the provinces that have initiated every great reform in our country. Come to Glasgow.'[85] Even the good men in London were 'colleged in Scotland'. Though Glasgow socialists might send Keir Hardie to America to spread their ideal, Americans were also influential in developing Glasgow socialist sentiment. In the circles around David Kirkwood, the influence of Henry George and Edward Bellamy was considerable. Indeed there were even McGlynn clubs in Glasgow, as well as pamphlets of the unfortunate priest of the IWW, Fr Thomas Hagerty.[86] Henry George had enjoyed tremendous influence in Glasgow. The Scottish Land League had been encouraged by his ideas. On his tour of 1884–5, George was appalled by the proverty of Glasgow: 'Right on these streets of yours the very stranger can see sights that he could not see in any tribe of savages in anything like normal conditions.'[87] It was a view echoed by the Medical Officer of Health who believed a man would be safer beneath a tree in an African jungle than beneath a lamp-post in the Bridgegate.[88]

The strength of these views found expression in the journal *Single Tax* which flourished in Glasgow until 1902, when it changed its title to *Land Values* and moved to London. Indeed, it is alleged that 48 of the 75 councillors elected in 1896 were favourably disposed to land tax ideas. Glasgow was in some difficulty by the turn of the century. With a massive commitment to municipal enterprise and a constricted tax base, the city saw private enterprise reaping unearned increments through civic improvements. Landlords were able to demand high prices for land required by the city for municipal purposes. By withholding land, owners were able to prevent social improvements, increase the cost to ratepayers and prevent the city increasing its own revenues. The pressure therefore from the city was considerable for the taxation of land values. Glasgow was prominent in urging parliament to introduce such legislation throughout the period 1900–10. With the people truly represented in parliament for the first time in history in 1906, according to that great supporter of municipalisation, Robert Donald, the pressure mounted and the new Liberal government was deluged with demands.[89]

The influence of American single taxers was considerable: Glasgow was fighting their battle. Joseph Fels, the millionaire soap manufacturer and single taxer, came.[90] Having moved to London, he was persuaded by D M Stevenson and Professor Smart to come to Glasgow. Shortly afterwards Tom Johnson came, though he was clearly a very sick man following his defeat in Cleveland. Louis Post, a confidant of Mayor Dunne of Chicago, was another single taxer who warmly supported Glasgow's efforts.[91] As editor to *The Public*, a single tax journal, Post emphasised the importance of the Scottish League for the Taxation of Land Values in setting the tone for all other local British organisations. In 1910, Post himself came to Glasgow and worked for the election of the radical liberal, Dundas White. He rejoiced in his success and that of Francis Neilson, the President of the English League for the Taxation of Land Values. Neilson was well known in the United States: he had lived there from 1885 to 1887, had toured the country in 1910 and 1912 in support of progressive campaigns in Oregon, Kansas City, St Louis, Chicago and New York. Among his audience of 200 at the Chicago City Club was ex-baillie Burt of Glasgow.[92] Neilson, a great friend of Brand Whitlock, Mayor of Toledo, accompanied him on his visit to Glasgow in November, 1912. Together they attended a dinner in their honour at the Scottish League for the Taxation of Land Values. Whitlock was also guest of honour at a dinner given by D M Stevenson.[93] There was a strong transatlantic conviction that the community should profit from the fruits of its labour. As one social settlement worker, Marcus T Reynolds, wrote, 'Glasgow may serve as an excellent example of expropriation.'[94]

Terence V Powderly was a member of the Land League and some of his identifiable union members in Glasgow were prominent in the Scottish Land League. However, when Powderly came later in connection with his federal government work on immigration, his main interest seems to have been taking photographs of Glasgow trams.[95]

Perhaps more significant was the American involvement in Glasgow's traditional socio-religious crusade. Glasgow did provide a receptive audience to new enthusiasms however utopian. One of Thomas Lake Harris's associates was Mr Pearce, who subsequently played host to Charlotte Perkins Gilman. The renowned feminist preached on two occasions in Glasgow in 1896: 'Well received and appreciated by a few—a week of foregoing failure, hard work and heavy sledding in general. Pay $16.25.'[96] And though suitable hotel accomodation seemed hard to come by, she left greatly impressed by Keir Hardie, Bruce Glasier and the model municipal tenements.

American Fabians were usually very impressed by Glasgow's achievements. Their dreams had substance. The short lived *American Fabian* lavished praise on the municipal tram as a sign of a caring social democracy.[97] Frank Parsons, a life-long admirer of the city, was especially active in promoting Glasgow's image in America. Not only did he extol Glasgow as a model municipality in public lectures and debates in the eastern and mid-western United States, but also in his book *The City for the People*.[98] He claimed that the city, cheaply and efficiently run, emphasised the social gains from superior safety records, the absence of strikes and violence. Monopoly existed for public rather than private benefit.

Those comments might be reassuring to some American reformers like Edward T Devlin, who though admiring Glasgow felt that European cities 'notwithstanding their progress in socialism are crowded with a class who look upon anarchy and the reign of destruction which it advocates, as the only remedy for existing municipalities. We believe the application of strictly business principles will be more effective moral preaching.'[99] Glasgow clearly met both requirements.

But nothing impressed 'Big Bill' Haywood when he came to the city in 1911. He was—predictably—unimpressed by the much vaunted image of Glasgow: drunken women seemed to be everywhere. After touring the surrounding mining districts and making several speeches in Glasgow and Cambuslang, he went south to join Hyndman. But he was part of that tradition which included James Connolly and Daniel De Leon, both of whom were instrumental in founding the Socialist Party of Great Britain in the east end of Glasgow.[100] For the thoroughgoing socialist, progressive reform was merely reform in the interests of the rich, a device to forestall the advent of socialism, or, as Marcuse would argue, 'an ideological defence of middle class society'.[101] With the seasonal migration of labour, these socialist links must have been more substantial, if unrecorded. Unable to tackle basic problems, capitalism was as always, in crisis. But for the majority of American visitors, Glasgow seemed to have discovered the right formula. To the respectable American observer the city, the locality, the province, had engendered a staunch civic pride within a happy harmonious community. Class antagonism was buried in mutual endeavour and co-operation.[102] That was attributable to the religious impulse. It was wideranging religious sentiment born of conviction, conditioned reflexes, a well established tradition, an imaginative conservatism. For all shades of opinion were agreed on containment: no one desired revolution. That was a tactical device to scare sluggish elements into action. Religion became democratised and secularised in the process of establishing a community, an identity for the individual in a restless society. Democracy was evolving its own internal regulating mechanisms. Glasgow had built the first working model. Glasgow was a place of pilgrimage.

To American visitors, Glasgow was invariably a reassuring experience. Some progressives like C E Russell, may have found English snobbish condescension only marginally worse than perpetually hymn singing Scots—and he, after all, was a socialist.[103] But the majority felt very much at home in the city. Jane Addams was amazed at the American standards of St Enoch's Hotel: it was like the Palmer House with lifts, a gas fire in every room and even a rocking chair. As she said, 'There is no help to the imagination like locality'.[104] Glasgow seemed to have everything. Other lady visitors might bemoan the quality of hotel accommodation but they were clearly impressed by the spirit of the place. To Brand Whitlock, Glasgow was 'immensely modern' like Chicago: but unlike Chicago, it had cleansed itself, even its slaughterhouses which bore absolutely no relation to Upton Sinclair's *Jungle*.[105] Though even here Glasgow's John McLean would disagree. But the environment seemed American. Even the bitterest critic of Glasgow's municipal enterprises, Robert P Porter, was prepared to make that concession.[106] One American visitor extolled Glasgow's virtue as a holiday resort with numerous attractions, galleries, parks and beautiful countryside at hand, with the added attraction of not being so foreign: a walk down Sauchiehall Street, so like Manhattan, would immediately cure any homesickness. Glasgow was still *the* American city of Europe.[107]

Equally in the United States, Scots integrated well. Scottish immigrants, Chisholm said, don't stand apart but become 'a living part of yourselves'.[108]

Scots were renowned as engineers, as managers and foremen. Glasgow similarly showed great pride in her wares, industrial and intellectual, at the great exhibitions of the time; at her own international exhibition in 1901, at St Louis in 1904, and at the New York tenement house exhibition in 1901. 'I belong to Glasgow' was a proud boast of no mean city.[109]

The Glasgow gospel was therefore known. It had to be propagated by education, which in turn would stimulate public opinion and produce a responsive city council. Far from being a tentative working hypothesis, Glasgow existed and worked. As Carlyle had written years before, all true work was religion, a notion which would readily be transformed into the canonisation of Main Street in the 'twenties in America. But the traditional Calvinist ideal had to be restated in a modernised form with a dose of scientific humanitarianism. Democratic aspiration had to be united with realistic assessment. Henry Drummond's 'love story' of science and religion had to be brought to fruition.[110] In America that was to be seen in the University of Michigan, and Johns Hopkins University. Michigan—according to Dilke, the most democratic university in the world—was perhaps the most advanced state university and one of the first to develop a graduate school.[111] Education, self-realisation was to be available to everyone in a truly democratic moral society. Johns Hopkins, on the other hand, the Germanic university, represented the new scientific spirit. Research and practical application rather than classical aloofness characterised this new institution. Both universities were outside the traditional university centres. They were part of the provincial and urban renaissance. With each of them Glasgow had important connections: Glasgow had not a little to do with the emergence of the intellectual as a social type.[112]

To this new intelligentsia, invariably the first of their family to graduate, the appeal of public service was considerable. The missionary impulse was secularised, and the individualistic impulse was socialised. In that respect these graduates followed the Glasgow tradition of John Buchan, the Revd David Watson and John Reith.[113] For the Scottish tradition of democratic intellect was far stronger than anywhere else in Britain. Americans could naturally respond to that ideal. Indeed, several leading American educational innovators and administrators show a marked similarity to Scottish reformers. Both Andrew Sloan Draper and William H Maxwell were of Scots-Irish ancestry; William T Harris was strongly influenced by neo-Hegelian thought; and John Dewey stressed the importance of environment in communicating the desirable, traditional culture.[114] In the absence of a cultivated hereditary class, the necessity of trained leaders able to assert their cultural dominance over a fragmented society was clear: a modernised religious philosophy, education and racial background provided the basis for conflict leadership in the evolving community. But the influences were far more tangible than that.

If, as Josiah Strong said, 'The Kingdom of God is Utopia made rational and destined to be made actual', then Glasgow, largely through the influence of Michigan and Johns Hopkins, acquired that quality for many American reformers.[115] A third university, Toronto, also seems to have played a part in beaming the Glasgow gospel into the United States.[116]

Professor R M Wenley of the University of Michigan is perhaps the best example of that traffic.[117] With J H Muirhead he had been a pupil of Edward Caird. Though forced by illness to withdraw from the university for a spell, he returned to graduate with distinction. Like his mentor, Caird, he was particularly interested in promoting university education for women. As examiner in philosophy and secretary of the university extension board, he won the high regard of Professor A C Bradley. For Wenley was prominent in promoting university extension work on both sides of the Atlantic. No other lecturer in the whole of Scotland gave so many university extension lectures or travelled so widely. A prolific if superficial writer, Wenley contributed to the *Contemporary Review,* the *Scottish Review, Modern Church* and wrote several books. All were marked by a strong Christian idealism. As Caird said, he hoped that Wenley's teaching had 'stimulated life which will take care of itself'.[118] Certainly Wenley was confident in the superior ability of the Anglo-Saxon races to act as moral stewards for mankind.

Unsuccessful in his application for the chair of logic at the University of Edinburgh, Wenley secured a chair in the University of Michigan in January, 1896. Though Caird reasssured him, 'You have found a place of action in Dewey's chair', Wenley still retained a strong interest in Scotland.[119] Partly from misgivings about his position in Michigan, Wenley returned to share in Patrick Geddes's summer school in Edinburgh. He was also active in the Sociological Society with Lord Bryce.[120] When his friend, James Mavor, secured a chair in Toronto, Wenley tried unsuccessfully to join him. Closely associated with G Stanley Hall, Wenley was caught up in the progressive tide, which for him was a distinctly Scottish tide:

> Were a constant stream of the select minds of America to be directed towards Scotland, the results could not fail to be of the most fortunate augury. I say deliberately Scotland. For here more than in England, the American finds himself at home. Partly by temper, by force of circumstances, the Scot is a citizen of the world. This is the main reason why he is so popular with Americans. Perhaps too they regard him as a member of a nationality that has been downtrodden by the English. But I would remind them that Scotland has only been subdued twice. John Knox conquered her head and Robert Burns won her heart. Otherwise she stands where Wallace and Burns put her, and this is yet another reason why the free people of the great republic find it easier to come to terms with her sons. More cautious and for a little, seemingly less approachable, the Scot has none of the Englishman's *morgue*: poor and less the prey of social conventions, he is, if not a more pleasant then a more suggestive companion. There is more "to him" as the expressive phrase has it. These characteristics have passed from him into the university system. Nowhere has so much been accomplished on so little: the income of the four universities is but a bare half of that enjoyed by Oxford. And this has been done by individual effort. This must always be an attractive feature to the quick and independent American. Scotland for him is the best gateway to an understanding of the inwardness of the Scottish people.[121]

Wenley's experience at Michigan confirmed his beliefs in the city's excellence. For not only was the Professor of Naval Architecture, Charles

Sadler, a fellow Glaswegian, but so also was John A Fairlie, Professor of Political Science, from 1900–9, a member of the National Municipal League, and editor of the *Political Science Quarterly*.[122] In addition to being involved in the Bureau of Corporations, Fairlie also wrote several books on municipal government. But rather than eulogise systems, he preferred to urge higher standards of public morality. As he said in his book on municipal administration: 'So much has been published in the United States about the municipal enterprises of Glasgow that it may seem useless to offer anything more.'[123] Even so he lavishly praised the extraordinarily successful tramways of Glasgow and strongly rebutted any criticism: 'There is no substantial foundation for recent attempts to minimise the extent of that success.'[124]

R T Ely of Johns Hopkins, the leading 'new' economist, was inspired by religious idealism to a marked degree. That conviction drove him to found the American Economic Association, promote the American social Christian Union and to lecture at Chatauqua. He was anxious to spread his idealism. For him stability meant the safeguarding of the family within a decentralised, diverse and balanced society. Local control of local business and public services was crucial: 'Great wealth also tends to concentrate in one or two immense cities while men of moderate fortunes are more likely to be found in every part of the country. . . . Men of moderate wealth are also better able than the excessively rich to use their wealth to alleviate distress because they come in closer contact with their fellow men.'[125] An efficient society required varied creative centres: monopoly therefore bred inefficiency. That was especially true in local public services in private hands: municipalisation meant the better utilisation of productive forces. Glasgow naturally would appear a model to men of such views. Now, Johns Hopkins had strong links with Glasgow. Lord Kelvin and James Bryce lectured at this increasingly prestigious institution in 1883. It saw itself like Kelvin's dynamo as generating light throughout the Union. Bryce in particular was associated with the new history school under Herbert Baxter Adams.[126] Dedicated to institutional history, above all municipal history, Adams was an important figure in spreading the Glasgow gospel. His students' name read like a roll call of progressive reformers: Woodrow Wilson, Walter Hines Page, Abraham Flexner, F C Howe, Albert Shaw, E R L Gould, E W Bemis and Amos Warner to name but a few.[127] Many received their first experience in urban problems and reform in Baltimore, an enterprise in which the example of Glasgow was readily invoked.

Albert Shaw was one of the distinguished group of graduates from this new 'Germanic University'. Like his fellow graduates, E R L Gould, Edward Bemis, Woodrow Wilson and a little later, F C Howe. Shaw emerged with a strong sense of public service and duty derived from the new economics of Professor Ely and the 'democratic' history of Herbert Baxter Adams. Together those ingredients inspired many reformers. The intellectual as a social type had emerged. To graduates reform had an obvious appeal as a career in itself or a means of establishing a new profession, either in social welfare or in a purified civil service: 'I want an outlet for my men in government work and am going to have it one way or another.'[128] In that he was merely reiterating to Shaw the views of Bryce: 'It is from the action of such men as yourself and some of your fellow students there, scattered over the continent as professors and journalists that one expects the most powerful influence for good on politics, literature and social life.'[129] Certainly the intention was scholarly but it was unmistakably didactic in inculcating desirable social objectives. The old Calvinism was being modernised, the old ethic more secularised. The crises of faith, identity, career and sexuality were commonplace: the old purpose had to be restated in an urban industrial world. The individual graduate would find purpose in service to the community.

Albert Shaw appropriately enough wrote his doctoral thesis on ideal communities.[130] Not surprisingly he turned his attention subsequently to contemporary cities. He found the ideal in contemporary Glasgow. As he said in a newspaper interview on his return to America: 'I have seen nothing like Glasgow in the whole of the United States.'[131] In particular he was impressed by 'the extraordinary care that was taken by the authorities to look after the interests of the poorer classes. It was quite wonderful and without any precedent in my American experience. I think the experience of Glasgow is full of lessons for our new communities that are springing up all over the United States.'[132] As Professor Smart of Glasgow saw, Scotland had one clear unequivocal message for corrupt American cities—reform.[133]

Shaw was the best publicist the city of Glasgow has ever had. After visiting the city, he returned to America, published several articles, gave interviews and then published his book *Municipal Government in Great Britain*, which gave a very favourable view of municipal enterprises.[134] The book was timely and was rapturously welcomed by concerned citizens in the major metropolitan areas. Glasgow made a career for Shaw and generated a growing reform movement. The press was fulsome and lavish in its praises. American newspapers gave the work warm enthusiastic reviews.[135] The Chicago Civic Union wanted Shaw's assistance in discussing the municipalisation of public services. Students like Charles Zueblin, Leo S Rowe and others sought his aid in teaching and research; Delos F Wilcox wanted help with his book on municipal government. E W Bemis and Frank Parsons hoped to further their ideas for municipal ownership through Shaw.[136] Students sought information for debates on municipalisation. Shaw also acted as an examiner for Milo R Maltbie's doctoral thesis on municipal enterprises. Glasgow had had an impact in no uncertain manner.

The work proved a rallying cry for reformers. Hazen Pingree and Jacob Riis wrote admiringly.[137] The cry was taken up by numerous newspapers and periodicals throughout the United States. Henry Demarest Lloyd, the social democrat, immediately after reading the chapter on Glasgow, the longest in the book, wrote enthusiastically, 'Your book it really seems to me may prove to be a turning point in the remaking of America.'[138] So it proved. British friends were also impressed. Lord Bryce who had encouraged Shaw was particularly interested in his views on Glasgow while Professor Ashley asked whether Shaw had made the acquaintance of his friend D M Stevenson, 'The combination of business ability and social enthusiasm marks him as a most interesting man.'[139] Shaw had a close friendship with Robert Donald, the editor of the *Municipal Journal, London,* and the *Daily Chronicle.* They had first met during 1888–9 and their correspondence continued until late in the First World War. Donald sent Shaw pamphlets and leaflets and articles on Glasgow to keep his friend informed. But Shaw. who had become well acquainted with Glasgow officials, was himself already on the city council's official mailing lists and received the annual returns and report on municipal undertakings. He subsequently visited Glasgow in 1918 on official war business with Professor Kemp Smith of Princeton, a former member of the Glasgow University staff. Even in 1939 Shaw was again in Glasgow leaving the city as war broke out.[140]

If the foundation had been laid, Edward W Bemis consolidated it. A fellow graduate of Johns Hopkins, Bemis had served as a university extension organiser and lecturer in the University of Chicago and elsewhere. For a time he seems to have flirted briefly with Fabian ideas before working closely with W T Stead during his visit to Chicago. As a result he was largely responsible for the establishment of the Chicago Civic Federation. Unfortunately his social views proved too advanced for Chicago University and Manhattan College, Kansas and in both instances he was dismissed. In 1899 he edited a collection of essays on *Municipal Monopolies* which contributed to the debate on Glasgow in America.[141] Subsequently he served as head of the Cleveland Water Works under Mayor Tom Johnson.

The same year, 1899, Milo R Maltbie examined Glasgow's city administration at first hand.[142] During that summer he spent his time studying the various municipal enterprises and their cost effectiveness. Duly impressed he published some articles praising the gas and transport services. Charles Zueblin, the Chicago sociologist, later editor of the *Twentieth Century Magazine* also knew Glasgow fairly well through his visit to the Edinburgh Summer School under his friend Patrick Geddes.[143] His interest in cohesive societies and his book *American Municipal Progress* suggest that he was well acquainted with the much publicised Glasgow parks, swimming pools, playgrounds and the late opening of schools for recreational purposes, during his visit.[144] Following a visit to Glasgow, another of this group, John A Fairlie, wrote his *Essays in Municipal Administration.* He was well aware that his was a well worn theme for in his earlier book *Municipal Administration* (1901), Fairlie had already given great attention to his native city. He was a leading figure in the New York Charity Organisation Society and a great admirer of E R L Gould's City and Suburban Homes Company.[145] He strongly believed that progressive social action depended on religion. Any other philosophy or form of social engineering was inadequate to the task.

F C Howe following in that tradition. His work invariably focused on Glasgow's successful municipal enterprises. On his three visits Howe always greatly appreciated the city. His reports to the Commissioner of Labour, his books on *Municipal Government in Great Britain, European Cities at Work,* or *The City, the Hope of Democracy,* all paid glowing tribute to Glasgow.[146] Indeed one book spent almost half its length on Glasgow, particularly Chisholm. As an academic administrator and a close confidant of Tom Johnson, Howe was well placed to urge imitation of Glasgow.

Cleveland eventually secured cheap trams on Glasgow lines, employed professional administrators like Howe and Bemis and even introduced labour and alcoholic colonies as in Glasgow.

Edward Ralston Lowell Gould embodied the twin thrusts of social awakening and the techniques of mobilising that spirit into effective, creative channels.[147] A graduate of Toronto and Johns Hopkins, Gould, like Bemis and Shaw, had studied under Ely and Herbert Baxter Adams and he received his doctorate with Woodrow Wilson. After teaching in Washington DC with hopes of a university post, Gould entered government service in the newly developing administration. He then undertook studies of working class houses in Europe and temperance regulation, both interests which naturally took him to Glasgow. There he became acquainted with D M Stevenson and the Glasgow Workman's Dwelling Company.[148] Gould also studied the Gothenburg system of drink regulation and seems to have become acquainted through D M Stevenson with the Public House Trust. This scheme (whereby model public houses would apply profits to social improvement) though originating in England, was first given practical application in Glasgow through Stevenson and his friends like Sir John Mann.[149] Indeed, Sir John Mann, Jr, the son of a major Glasgow accountant, carried on a considerable correspondence with Gould for many years. As the secretary of the Glasgow Workman's Dwelling Company, the Public House Trust and several other progressive enterprises, Mann played a leading role in publicising many of Glasgow's achievements through private enterprise. He was responsible for organising the Glasgow Workman's Dwelling Company's exhibition and pamphlets for the New York tenement house exhibition in 1901. Significantly, he was a former pupil of Edward Caird, and Caird supported the Glasgow Workman's Dwelling Company, both intellectually and financially. From his activity in Baltimore, Gould would also seem to have taken a close look to the Glasgow Labour Colony and its activities. For under Gould's leadership, the tramp problem was largely solved in Baltimore.[150] No longer were unemployed given shelter in police stations but they were given food and accommodation in return for labour under Charity Organisation direction.

As an economic expert Gould was called to give important evidence to the British Royal Commission on Labour.[151] He was also in great demand as a lecturer on municipal government and social problems: for those in Ohio and Chicago he naturally drew on the Glasgow model. Acquainted with Bryce and Stead, Gould gave an impressive series of lectures at Johns Hopkins on European social problems, but decided his future lay elsewhere: 'I will lead more of a public life and escape much of the drudgery and grinding incident to a purely practical life.'[152] Shortly after, Gould was largely responsible for the foundation of the City and Suburban Homes Company in New York. That enterprise tapped American traditions in New York City but it also bore striking resemblances to the Glasgow Workman's Dwelling Company in its activities, policy and profitability. Its directors were almost duplicates in social standing and concerns as their Glasgow counterparts.[153] From then until his untimely death, Gould was to play a leading role in that philanthropic enterprise. Through his friend, Albert

Shaw, his firm received great attention in the *Review of Reviews*.[154] The company expanded into Brooklyn and other areas, providing good quality accommodation at reasonable rates, and later ownership on advantageous terms within healthy accessible localities to the city on cheap lines of transportation. A leading figure in the Citizens Union and other reform organisations through which he seems to have become well acquainted with Patrick Geddes, Gould later became Controllor of city finance under the reforming Seth Low Administration in New York.[155] Certainly he enjoyed a considerable reputation for probity and imaginative administration during his short term. In many ways he was not unlike his friend D M Stevenson.

The University of Toronto also beamed the Glasgow gospel into the United States in several ways. E R L Gould after all was a graduate of Toronto. But more pertinent was W J Ashley, the 'new' economic historian, who had succeeded a Glasgow graduate at Toronto and knew Glasgow well through D M Stevenson.[156] He was, after Harvard, to become Chancellor of Birmingham University, that civic institution which was consciously modelled by Chamberlain on Glasgow University.[157] He was succeeded by James Mavor of Glasgow. Already associated with reforming elements in Glasgow, he came strongly recommended by R T Ely. He was to retain his close links with progressive sentiment in Glasgow by frequent trips to lecture in summer schools. In addition to being involved in Toronto reform, he became closely acquainted with American municipalities in 1903 during a tour.[158] He came to know John Graham Brooks, Jane Addams, Henry Demarest Lloyd, E W Bemis and Lilian Wald. Through him, Ely became acquainted with Patrick Geddes.

Ely also helped to secure William Smart his chair at Glasgow.[159] For his friend, one of the earliest members of the American Economic Association, Ely wrote a very strong recommendation: Smart was appointed the first professor of political economy in the University of Glasgow. Though Smart visited America at least three times, 'but only on the unpleasant business to save my American investments', he did offer constant support in his writing to American civic reformers.[160] Though he might set limits to municipal enterprise, Smart was anxious to uplift and provide people with the opportunities to help themselves. As a former businessman, deeply involved in progressive reforms in Glasgow, he was very attractive to American idealists.

The University of Pennsylvania with which Glasgow also had long established connections, contributed, too, to the progressive impulse. Professor Simon N Patten of the Wharton School of Economics believed that 'public control should be extended to everything that lowers the vitality of the working population. . . . Bad streets, incongruous buildings and glaring advertisements depress men, reduce their productive power and check the growth of social feelings.'[161] Students with this ideal before them would obviously consider Glasgow of some consequence. Significantly, the first lectureship in municipal government was established at Pennsylvania in 1894: the first appointee, was Leo S Rowe, an unrepentant admirer of Glasgow.[162] Another graduate of this university was Clinton Rogers Woodruff, whose admiration for Glasgow and involvement in municipal reform was considerable.[163] Their role was essentially educational.

Religion was an important educational link. The religious connections between Glasgow and America were greatly increased as we have seen in the last quarter of the nineteenth century. American evangelists paid several successful visits to Glasgow. In the opposite direction, Glasgow sent Henry Drummond and many students to Northfield and the early Chatauqua. The writings of Professors F W Robertson, A B Bruce and John Orr went out from Glasgow whilst Union Theological College, New York, retained a strong Scottish flavour.[164] The international gatherings of the Alliance of Reformed Churches, largely a Presbyterian organisation were examples of this trend. The gatherings were held alternately in Scotland and the United States. In 1896 the assembly was in Glasgow and in Washington DC in 1904: Samuel Chisholm was present with Woodrow Wilson and Hoke Smith at the latter.[165] Chisholm had been in America in 1901 and returned again in 1906 during the course of a world tour. Another transatlantic figure, the Revd John Hunter of Trinity Church, Glasgow, numbered the Cairds, Professors Jones, Smart, Bradley as well as D M Stevenson among the members of his congregation.[166] A great friend of Professor A B Bruce, Hunter ran a very progressive church. For example, a lecture series devised by him included among his speakers, Cobden-Sanderson, Keir Hardie, Edward Carpenter and Professor Smart.[167] In 1901, he was the preacher at the International Peace Congress held in Glasgow. On at least two occasions he visited the United States. In 1907, he went to Michigan and to Chicago where he met Jane Addams, Dr Hillis and R G Moulton. Three years later, he was visiting Columbus, Ohio, home of a fellow Congregationalist, Washington Gladden.[168]

A friend of Hunter's Revd J B Paton, another Congregationalist, was well known in the Atlantic world for his philanthropic enterprises. Born in Ayrshire where he frequently spent his summers, Paton was a correspondent of Professor Herbert Baxter Adams, and an associate of Revd Josiah Strong in the Institute for Social Service, which flourished on both sides of the Atlantic.[169] Strong was a visitor to Glasgow in 1904. Both he and Paton were staunch advocates of Anglo-Saxon leadership and unity throughout the world. That was perhaps symptomatic of the great rapprochement between Britain and America. But Paton was extremely important in encouraging common initiatives. He was particularly important in stimulating the foundation of institutions which subsequently became the British provincial universities, in promoting university extension and Chatauqua type enterprises, the greater utilisation of school facilities for the community after hours and in vacations.[170] Another Glasgow social reformer, the Revd David Watson, was influenced by meeting Paton.[171] A graduate of Glasgow University Watson was also deeply influenced by the writing of the American Social Gospellers, Rauschenbusch, Gladden and others. A firm supporter of the Glasgow Workman's Dwelling Company, Watson was to play a decisive role in turning the Church of Scotland towards social reform.

Education, the Progressives believed, would provide immediate and long term social gains. It would broaden horizons now and prepare the rising generation for the new urban industrial world. All shades of opinion would agree upon the value of education but, in addition, the enforcement of school attendance, school health inspection and school leaving certificates effectively regulated industry.[172] Education was a means of legislating for government interference in areas where direct legislative enactment would have been totally unacceptable: a *laissez-faire* society could never have passed such wide-ranging social legislation. In a sense, conservative claims that socialism was creeping into acceptance were not altogether inaccurate. At any rate, education was building a new community and, hopefully, a new society. The Chatauqua and University extension movement merged into one general movement for amelioration. Culture, education and a sense of belonging had to be brought to the masses through evening classes, summer schools, popularly available classical literature and music. Indeed reading some of the lecture courses, programmes and recommended books, it is hard not to feel that the masses were being gently introduced into the political process on the side of reform: education was a gentle means of politicisation. However admirable and socially desirable the end, the means was essentially through guided democracy. in both Glasgow and the United States, clergy and reformers encouraged popular participation in sport as a means of encouraging abstinence from excesses in tobacco, drink, sex, or delinquency.[173] In slum areas where children were inevitably forced into adult life at an early age, the opening of school facilities after hours and the availability of playgrounds provided a counter-balance to undesirable parental influences or stultifying environments. It also admitted the child, even unconsciously, into the dominant culture. Liberation could be a liberty to conform. In the best circumstances, 'the outsider' could bring the best aspects of culture to the community and enrich both: it was a delicate operation.[174]

The settlement house movement was in most instances a more secularised version of the old fashioned Christian involvement.[175] On occasion the settlement workers in finding their own identity might adopt patronising roles towards the local people, but equally the settlement house was in the best sense a people's university, a university of popular experience and sharing, and if properly conducted—or guided—might be a formative democratic experience. The difficulty was to establish an acceptable democratic norm or to inject your value system subtly into the enterprise in order to make a majority of the participants believe that they themselves had evolved their own values which just happened to be yours. It was liberal, liberating and paradoxically social engineering in the kindest sense at the same time. In that interim stage of society, it was all of them and none.[176] But Glasgow was a step ahead of the new urban provincial universities in that it already existed and had an existing tradition. It could lead the way. Bryce emphasised *The Menace of Great Cities* in 1913 as cutting citizens off from nature, segregating people into classes in unhealthy environments which proved particularly harmful to the natural develop-ment of children and encouraged revolutionary consciousness. Mary Richmond saw clearly that migration within the city should be encouraged as a means of elevating the masses.[177] University extension classes together with various other American patriotic education classes together with enforcement of school attendance would have salutary effects. Florence Kelley went further and saw the best means would be to prevent the employment of children.[178] That would immediately yield an improvement. Public education and cheap public transport together with informed attempts to regulate the work of women and children, Glasgow and its leading citizens softened—at least somewhat—the worst abuses of man by man. That did not pass unnoticed. Charles Zueblin was no stranger to Glasgow. Well acquainted with Professor Smart and his writings, Zueblin seems to have visited Glasgow during his close association with Patrick Geddes of Edinburgh: 'A comprehensive improvement can be expected only when idealism becomes infectious'.[179] That means having a high sense of civic pride, as in Glasgow, fostered by respectable participation in politics, didactic architecture and healthy environments promoting social harmony and peace. Municipal enterprise brought that happy end.

The Church had then gone into social life, social life must then come to the church and give rise to a civic church, a focus of unity, informed and caring consideration of the pressing social issues of the day. That was W T Stead's ideal. It was to energise all the institutions that make for righteousness'.[180] This 'Moral Caucus' would create a new community ethos. It would enable the 'good' people in the Anglo-Saxon world to rule effectively as a laboratory for social initiatives and mutual support. 'As the Civic Church is in advance of the State so the individual reformer is ever in advance of the Civic Church. The heretic always leads the van. What the Civic Church can do is to generalise for the benefit of all the advantages which have hitherto been confined to the few.'[181] Glasgow seemed especially receptive to this reawakening of public interests and concern, in every aspect of social life: child rearing, nurture and health, drink, education and labour, housing and cheap transport.

Other leading American writers and social critics who visited Glasgow during this period included Israel Zangwill, 1895; William James; Thorsten Veblen; G W Cable; and Charles M Sheldon, author of *In His Steps*.[182] That last work together with W T Stead's *If Christ Came to Chicago*, contributed to the common Christian attack on social injustice. Glasgow was the first and most successful Civic Church advocated by Stead.

It was in Glasgow that these ideas were carried to their greatest fulfilment. Thanks to the enormous generosity of D M Stevenson, inspired by Patrick Geddes, an annual lecturership in citizenship was established and subsequently a chair of social study.[183] That initiative was the result of the activities of the Glasgow Civic Society stimulating influential public interest. University professors and businessmen combined to educate popular opinion: Henry Jones and D M Stevenson were typical. In effect Glasgow had achieved what Cobden-Sanderson had long desired: 'Assuredly there should be at the university a chair of the "Ideal Community", a chair which should set out, in the main line, Society as it is, with all its many occupations and aims, based upon the past and such a society as it should be as a norm.'[184] The University was the new church.

If the Church, university and new democracy were interchangeable, identical forms of aspiration, then the social settlement was the perfect vehicle for the realisation. Glasgow also provided a model settlement movement. Robert A Woods, the Boston social settlement founder from Andover College, who became preeminent in the social movement as president of the NCCC also gained some insights from Glasgow.[185] He was a regular contributor to the Glasgow paper, *Modern Church*. As he told Revd Walter Wragge, he had articles accepted, and he urged Wragge to send his paper on Toynbee House for publication. Well acquainted with Professor A B Bruce, Woods continued to send in contributions on the American social gospel and political developments during 1891–2. The paper showed considerable interest in America with frequent Letters from America by Revd James M Whiton. During Whiton's summer vacations, Revd G B Safford, a widely travelled American minister who was the manager of Brooklyn charities, sent wide-ranging informative reports. In particular they reported the exposure by Jacob Riis and Revd Louis A Banks of conditions among the poor: they also reported the reforming activities of Revd Dr Parkhurst. In addition the journal carried news about presbyterian and congregational developments throughout the North Atlantic world, discussions of major American writers, and articles from Edward Caird, R M Wenley and J H Muirhead. In all, Woods contributed at least six signed and possibly more unsigned articles on Andover and related theological matters. He knew Mr Shelley, the editor, presumably from his Glasgow visit and found the journal 'has a good deal of spring in it and has a wide range. It aims to include all the Scotch Churches but it is run in the Broad Church interest'.[186]

Clearly the British visit had awakened Woods to the social dimension of Christianity: 'As to the theological questions I seem to care less and less about them.'[187] Social Christianity was a personal and a social necessity. For Woods saw that the Protestant Churches of Boston had virtually no influence among the working classes. Church involvement in effective local government as in Glasgow was a necessity for training the masses in democracy and morality: 'The state has its being in the village sense of the people who pass their days in spontaneous neighbourhood relationships which they have learned to direct to effective ends.'[188]

Woods was a protestant modernist, a humanitarian whose Calvinist heritage died hard. His *City Wilderness*, which he published in consultation with professor W J Ashley, had a imperialist, almost racist turn of mind.[189] Social reform was moral rather than structural reform.

For as Woods said, following his experience in Glasgow: 'The tendency of Christian people in Scotland seems to be to meet the social problems without the use of Church machinery. This is quite possible in Scotland where sectarian boundaries are easily passed over, and where the poor people, having had early religious training, are quite open to the simpler and more distinctive influence of religion.'[190] A strong religious community, with a strongly religious-preferably Protestant—tradition, could easily be mobilised in support of social reforms. Its latent sense of duty merely needed to be tapped. Americans had to establish an accessible tradition. C S Loch perhaps best expressed something of that tension within progressive thinking about amelioration: 'For justice lies not in the distribution or non-distribution of means with a view to equality but in the development and enforcement of function with a view to the fulfilment of duty.'[191] Woods was still under the influence of his older tradition to a greater extent that he realised: 'There are times when the greater love must even leave the starving to starve.'[192] Woods' old moralistic assumptions often clouded his scientific judgement, as his writings indicate.

Woods' friend, Jane Addams, also followed Glasgow development with interest. In the public mind Hull House and the Glasgow University settlements were linked.[193] Jane Addams had visited Glasgow in 1883 before she had found her purpose in life. Suitably impressed with the city, she hoped to return on her European visit in 1896. Meanwhile, George D Hooker, a reforming minister and lawyer from Chicago, had visited the city during his European tour in 1894–5. Well known for his investigations in municipal government, he gave Jane Addams letters of introduction to Mr Maclehose to visit the new municipal thriving enterprises; the cleansing department, the family home, the municipal lodging houses, the civic improvement trust houses, the settlements and the Peoples Palace. She was also given introductions through Mrs Ker of Edinburgh to various people including Patrick Geddes. Unfortunately the visit fell through when after visiting London and meeting Robert Donald she went off to see Tolstoy instead. Woods had been unsuccessful shortly before in persuading Professor Smart to visit America though other Glasgow figures might attend a proposed conference.[194] Professor Drummond would be 'a drawing card' for Addams was still influenced by religious motives to a far greater degree than she later confessed. As John Trevor wrote to her 'in many directions where the old religious forms of faith have been set aside as inadequate, God appears to be breaking through in the new life of the spirit and gaining the confidence of those who seek him in the services of their fellow men'.[195] Activity, ceaseless experience rather than any *a priori* assumptions, guided her. She was determined to judge situations through her own experience. Glasgow—at least in a secondhand way—was part of that experience.

Julia Lathrop, Jane Addam's friend also came to Scotland. In 1898, she came to see the institutions for the care of the insane and, like Charles Loring Brace, returned with vivid impressions of the advanced methods and intensive care in Lanarkshire.[196] The humane treatment and the boarding out of patients greatly impressed her. Others were equally moved by Scottish medical care. Abraham Flexner, another graduate of Johns Hopkins, on a tour of European medical centres was particularly impressed by the high standard of Glasgow hospitals and training. Dr Ann Howard Shaw came as part of her European tour in aid of women suffrage, though war prevented Dr Alice Hamilton of Hull House making her planned visit.[197] But many others came. Glasgow and the West of Scotland was a land of enchantment and fable, literary and political. Even the dynamite factory at Ardeer attracted attention for its welfare and safety record, allegedly far better then the average American foundry or factory.[198] Glasgow was clearly second to none.

Inspired by these ideals and perhaps under pressure from their electors, practising politicians came to inspect the municipal wonders of Glasgow. Sam Jones came in 1897, Edward Dunne and William Jennings Bryan came later. Each put his impressions into political effect, Dunne in Chicago politics to win the 1905 election and Bryan to make municipal ownership part of the democratic platform in 1904.[199] Sam 'Golden Rule' Jones returned to spread the Glasgow gospel throughout America and to give it immediate practical effect in Toledo, Ohio. As early as 1894, his predecessor as mayor had demanded information from Albert Shaw on Glasgow.[200] At the opening of the first children's playground in Toledo, he recalled the first publicly 'designated' playgrounds he ever saw were in Glasgow two years earlier:

> When I turned a corner I saw a spot of ground alive and merry with children's play and a beautiful legend on the fence, saying 'Citizens, protect your property'. Now I say to the children of Toledo, 'this is your property' and we know that you will take care of it, won't you? So I congratulate the children of Toledo and the citizens of Toledo upon this great step forward. I congratulate you because it marks the dawn of a better day when the world is ruled by love instead of by hate. . . . I want to save the children from the grave and from the jail, and I know of no better way then to manifest our love by doing something for them. I want to give them a place where they may play safe from the electric cars and from the temptations of the street, where they may get together and learn to love each other. That is what is to save this nation and will make it the greatest of all the nations of the earth.[201]

Exactly one week later, Jones addressed the League of American Municipalities in Detroit in a stirring address enthusiastically lauding municipal ownership as 'a love story':

> Glasgow leads the cities of Great Britain and the world in ministering to the social needs of her people through the medium of collective ownership. Glasgow owns not only the water works, lighting plant, street railways and parks, but in addition public baths, wash houses, lodging houses, model homes for widowers, model homes for widows: tumbled down rookeries and filthy disease ridden haunts for vice and crime were purchased by the municipality, torn down, and in their places, beautiful buildings were erected to minister to the needs of the people in the many ways indicated: the great municipality of Glasgow bringing light, air and sunshine to the downmost men and women, who before on account of their poverty, were compelled to live in foul tenements that disgraced the city. Public wash houses for the poor are a benefaction. The poor woman living with her children in a rented room with perhaps no conveniences for washing or drying her clothes, goes to a public wash house and for a penny is furnished with tub, mangle, wringer and steam drier, and in an hour's time is back home with her washing nicely done, and for less expense than the cost of the fuel that would have been necessary in her own crowded quarters. Working men unable to find respectable quarters for lodging can now go to the lodging house provided by their mother, the municipality—a beautiful, stone building four stories high, where they have bath, laundry, lavatories, library and game rooms, and all these at minimum cost with

no thought of making profit to enrich some individual, but with the thought uppermost in the mind of the municipality making men to enrich all and thus enrich the municipality.[202]

Just over three weeks later, Jones was writing to Frank Parsons that Bemis had been to Toledo and 'went down well'.[203] Evidently, the evangels of Glasgow were gaining converts.

Ohio, indeed, played a prominent role in spreading the Glasgow gospel. Not only did Washington Gladden frequently cite the Glasgow model but Tom Johnson of Cleveland came and shared in the single tax movement in Glasgow—though by then he was a tired, broken, ailing man.[204] Shortly afterwards, in 1912, Brand Whitlock came as part of his campaign to secure Home Rule for the cities of Ohio. He sent some thirteen articles on Glasgow and a handful on other European cities to the Toledo press, in order to demonstrate what could be done by local people in public interest—power to and from the people. D M Stevenson in particular was praised.[205] As a host, progressive, and superb Lord Provost, Stevenson greatly impressed Whitlock. Once again the old stories of Glasgow's triumphs echoed around America. Correspondents from as far afield as San Francisco congratulated Whitlock. Ben Lindsey, the Denver progressive judge, urged him to work the Glasgow articles into a book as important contributions to the work of American progressives.[206]

In the event Whitlock did not. But he did seek to improve his local fire service through the Glasgow example. He sent the Methodist Episcopal minister, Revd Dr Guild, armed with introductions to Glasgow. He sent two young businessmen, G E Swartzburgh and John S Gager, to D M Stevenson.[207] On their return, Gager was to play a leading role in establishing the magnificent Toledo Museum of Art. The impact was there.

But perhaps Whitlock's visit indicates some of the strains and tensions which were creeping into the loose liberal alliance. In Glasgow, Whitlock was accompanied by the Mayor of Dublin and he had spoken forcefully in support of Home Rule for Ireland. In that respect he was like Lilian Wald: 'To a believer in democracy, Irish Home Rule is as inevitable as votes for women. Both are expressions of the same movement.'[208] On both sides of the Atlantic few were so consistent or logical. There were limits to progressivism. There was a finality to municipal enterprise and reform. These developments were foreshadowed in the early years of the century. The trans-Atlantic debate about municipalisation largely centred on Glasgow in the years 1900–11. The two main protagonists were Robert Donald and Robert P Porter.[209] Donald, a liberal party national executive member born in Banffshire, had been a journalist throughout his life. He had worked on the *Pall Mall Gazette* and then established the *Municipal Journal* and *Yearbook* as well as editing the *Daily Chronicle*. Porter had been a census official and a member of the American tariff commission investigating team. He had been brought to London by private enterprise. Their debates were intensified by growing American criticism of private unfettered enterprises in public service industries. Charles Yerkes, the Chicago traction magnate now in London, was the epitome of that abuse. The elections of reforming mayors (Hazen Pingree, in Detroit; Tom Johnson, in Cleveland, 1901-9; Sam Jones and Brand Whitlock in Toledo) with strong views on municipalisation heightened feelings.[210] The Parliamentary Commission on Municipal Trading, the Massachussetts State Commission and the National Civic Federation Commission tried to establish firm conclusions.[211] The rise of the muckraking press which gave prominence to urban reform provided widely circulated propaganda. In addition there were numerous academic studies which kept the issue before the public.

Donald had been publishing favourable reports on Glasgow in his journal, *London*.[212] With the introduction of electric traction into Great Britain his articles were seen as a challenge by the new electrical power interests. Porter therefore was recruited to rebut municipal schemes. In response, Donald enjoyed the public support of B O Flower, F C Howe, Henry Demarest Lloyd and Frank Parsons.[213] These debates continued throughout the years 1900 to 1906. In that year two studies appeared; by Meyer of Chicago and Darwin of Harvard.[214] But the issue had been largely resolved elsewhere: on the streets of Chicago and in the National Civic Federation Commission's Report. The first event was Dalrymple's visit to Chicago in 1905.

The long battle over the proposed municipalisation of the street railways of Chicago seemed to have ended with the election in 1905 of Edward F Dunne, on a platform of immediate municipalisation: 'It is the greatest victory for municipal ownership ever won in this country.'[215] It was seemingly a victory for the disinterested voice of public opinion; Dunne, a Democrat, had won in a city where Roosevelt, the Republican presidential candidate, had a 20,000 majority only the year before. In his zeal to make Chicago 'the Glasgow of America', Dunne immediately requested the loan of James Dalrymple, Glasgow's transport manager.[216] He claimed that like Yerkes, the notorious traction magnate, he had gone to borrow Glasgow's best brains—a reference to Young, the original tramway manager, who had gone to work for Yerkes in London. Chicago, notorious for its slums, vice, and stockyards, had a tramway system which was described as 'a picturesque lot of junk' with 'ancient ill-smelling, vermin-infested cars which have gone uncleaned for months.[217] Clearly, the advice of Dalrymple was sorely needed.

Chicago naturally awaited Dalrymple with eager anticipation. Chicago would be a test case for the Glasgow plan in America. The *Chicago Tribune* sent a special reporter to give exhaustive reports on Glasgow, which were with a few reservations generally favourable.[218] Unfortunately, Dalrymple arrived amid the Russo-Japanese War and a three-month-long teamster strike which was marked by considerable racial violence. Front-page coverage was far less than expected by the reformers. Besieged by pressmen and attacked by a hostile press, Dalrymple, as one commentator observed, suffered every indignity, except having his picture in the 'yellow press'.[219] On arrival in New York, Dalrymple was given a tremendous reception at what was, in effect, a national rally of Progressives.[220] But his natural caution and reluctance to proselytise on behalf of municipal ownership proved very disappointing to his hosts. When he was whisked from Chicago to a major Democratic Party rally in Cleveland, Ohio, Dalrymple gave a speech in which he expressed his inability to understand the purpose of the meeting, and warned that Americans were not prepared for municipal ownership, a very demanding and exacting enterprise.[221] With that address, he effectively killed the municipal ownership movement in the United States. His cautionary views became part of the conservative counter-attack. His report to Mayor Dunne subsequently destroyed the movement in Chicago.

Though American reformers might import Mr Bellamy, the general manager of Liverpool municipal tramways and a former Glasgow employee, to address the New York City Club, and though Dunne might earnestly confer with Tom Johnson of Cleveland, the municipal movement was already in decline.[222] W L Fisher of the Chicago Civic Federation stressed the moves in Glasgow to disfranchise the growing army of municipal employees: the flow was dimming. As for Dunne, 'he is deader than a mackerel that has been in a pickle for six months. He could not be elected constable for his own ward. His downfall has really been pitiful.'[223] His brief visit to Glasgow and Dalrymple's visit to Chicago had been disastrous.

The second event was the visit of the National Civic Federation Commission to Great Britain in 1906.[224] Their object was to investigate municipal and private ownership in Great Britain and Ireland. Naturally much of their interest focused on Glasgow. Although the Commission included those who were favourably disposed to municipalisation like F J Goodnow, Milo R Maltbie, E W Bemis and Frank Parsons, they were balanced by substantial conservative interests. Dunne, supported by John Graham Brooks and J R Commons, had backed the nomination of Frank Parsons to the Commission in the face of surprising opposition from E W Bemis. The former carried the day: 'He is absolutely honest and the common jibe that he is a crank is not truth enough to warrant a reply.'[225] Parsons indeed did not let his prejudices rule him. Already a sick man, he spent some two months with Dalrymple at his summer home and in his office, long after the Commission had concluded its rapid visit to Glasgow.

If American ardour for municipally owned tramways was waning, the visit of the National Civic Federation to Glasgow pushed it further into decline. Although the Glasgow Corporation were admitted to have the best paid employees, the cheapest fares, the most passengers and the highest profits, the conservative members of the commission were unimpressed— though one did concede, 'This is the finest street railway system I ever saw.'[226] They felt that municipalisation was 'already three fourths dead' and 'on the junk pile of impossibilities'.[227] It was but thinly disguised socialism. The 'red scare' helped to halt the movement as private enterprise recovered its self confidence.

Robert Donald continued his admiration of Glasgow in spite of the attacks of Robert Porter, Lord Avebury and Professor Meyer of Chicago, but the situation had changed. With the failure of the above visits, and the rise of radicalism in Britain and America, Glasgow's image was changing. The increasing militancy of labour, culminating in the 1911 tramway strike, destroyed the myth of good industrial relations.[228] That myth finally collapsed in the aftermath of the 1926 strike. After a riot in the city council, Dalrymple was forced to resign.[229] Other forms of city administration were attracting American attention—the commission and the city manager.[230] In 1908, the appointment of a city manager was mooted in Glasgow. It was an indication that the city was a little less confident, with immigration less homogeneous and socially less harmonious.

American interest was shifting from the city to the state government, a point best exemplified in F C Howe's work.[231] It also emphasised the very different constitutional and political arrangements in America. The secretary of the Chicago Civic Federation scorned Glasgow's appalling costly trams as part of the drift 'nearer governmental and industrial chaos'.[232] Old advocates like L S Rowe defended Glasgow but they were a diminishing band. As Frank Parsons died and others drifted into socialism, journals began to lose interest: the *Annals* and others dropped their columns on municipal government. When they did show interest, they were concerned purely with American solutions to American conditions.[233] Muckraking had passed its climax and journals were turning to broader social issues like health and unemployment insurance.[234] Welfare capitalism was coming into its own. Progressivism began to wane and disintegrate: the process had marked similarities with the fate of the British Liberal-Imperialists. The Progressives were facing the real test. The reformer had been doing things for or to the unfortunate, but the unfortunate now wanted to do things for himself in his own way. It was a shock: they were less democratic than they realised. By 1920, as a result of the shift to conservatism, 'normalcy' in the United States becomes understandable. The trams had reached the terminus: the motor car took over.

Glasgow still retained great charm for Howe, Brand Whitlock and others. Even as late as 1919, the Federal Electric Railway Commission believed Glasgow was 'the premier British city with respect to tramway policy'.[235] But the dreamlike quality had gone. America must have an American solution for an American problem; that was embodied in the motor car even by 1914. The frenzied patriotism of the First World War, the antipathy to immigrants and the return to 'normalcy' in the twenties, meant that Glasgow and her trams had no relevance to America. The image of Red Clydeside had even less.

But whatever the difficulties of municipal government, Glasgow remained attractive and attentive to three other groups; women reformers, temperance crusaders and peace advocates.

The peace movement followed a similar pattern. Glasgow's influence gradually receded. The Glasgow tradition was again considerable from the days of Elihu Burritt, the Quaker cobbler, through Robert Monteith, the Catholic apologist. In 1901, Glasgow was host to the International Peace movement. Benjamin Trueblood, Edward Mead and R T Paine came to spread their ideals.[236] Revd Robert Hunter preached to the gathering. D M Stevenson, a member of his congregation, developed a more sophisticated and realistic approach to peace. A coal exporter with interests in France and Germany, as well as a sister married to the Mayor of Hamburg, Stevenson was philosophically opposed to war. As he said in 1912, he would prefer the Clyde to resound to the building of merchant ships rather than to the construction of warships.[237] In 1907 and 1912, Stevenson was largely responsible for bringing influential groups of Germans to Glasgow as a means of fostering friendships and understanding in order to diminish the dangers of war. Ironically, although his brother was a manager of an armaments firm in Pennsylvania, Stevenson was instrumental in bringing two major peace propagandists to Glasgow: Norman Angell and the American David Starr Jordan.[238]

Glasgow was the first city in Britain to establish an International Polity Club.[239] That followed the publication of Norman Angell's *The Great Illusion*.[240] Largely under the aegis of Stevenson, that body was effectively organised and began a full programme of lectures from John Hilton, Randal Cremer, and Norman Angell himself.[241] Supported by wealthy and influential businessmen, the organisation inspired other groups in Britain. Stevenson himself promised financial support to the government's journal, *War and Peace,* whilst his secretary attended the Le Touquet conference.[242] In Stevenson, Angell had secured a life long friend and supporter.

David Starr Jordan came in the autumn of 1913.[243] A leading zoologist and president of Stanford University, Jordan had written extensively against war. In modern warfare the primitive barbarism of man destroyed the sophisticated progressive impulses in society, which was impoverished, degenerated and fell easy prey to monopolistic enterprises. The finest species was destroyed and the incompetent survived to exacerbate the ills of society. Bearing this message, Jordan came to Glasgow at the start of his Scottish tour. Greatly impressed by the spirit of Glasgow, Jordan lectured to the University, to the students and to the Catholic social affairs club.[244] At each gathering, Stevenson was in close attendance and support. Interestingly enough, at the last meeting, the father of Sir Denis Brogan, who had recently returned with his family from California, was on the platform. From Glasgow Jordan went to Edinburgh, Dundee and Aberdeen on a triumphal tour.[245] In the process he made a firm friend in Glasgow, a Miss Milne, who was to correspond with him throughout the First World War and support his pacifism in a tireless way. Supporters in other parts of Scotland wavered in their commitment and endorsed the war, but Miss Milne did not.[246]

Likewise Sir Daniel Macaulay Stevenson remained a committed peace advocate, not on intuitive but on rational grounds. Following his work on behalf of the Belgian refugees in Glasgow, Stevenson was drawn into the Union for Democratic Control. In spite of unpopularity, Stevenson remained firm in his support. Under pressure he even delivered an address for Bertrand Russell who had been banned by the government.[247] His alleged sympathy for Germany, his rumoured business dealings with the enemy though disproved in court stuck, and contributed to his post war defeat in a parliamentary election.[248] Though he might enthusiastically support the League of Nations and endow the chair for the study of International Relations in London University, Stevenson failed to adequately appreciate the changed nature of politics. He could not understand why the electorate had deserted their traditional leaders, the Liberals, and gone over to Labour. The war had proved extremely costly. The old confident liberalism was shattered; in Britain, the masses were now fully enfranchised for the first time from 1918; and Glasgow no longer so prosperous and thriving. Socialism had arrived on Clydeside. Or perhaps, as Jordan had prophesised, degeneracy had taken over. But again the point was made. Glasgow had become a ward of American humanitarianism; its image was not that of a model; and socialism had nothing to offer to the abrasive postwar American business community.

Intellectual and emotional strains were apparent as the First World War progressed. Intellectually, the correspondence of the Glasgow University constitutional historian, W S McKechnie with Professor C B Adams of Yale University is illustrative.[249] Both were great constitutional historians and McKechnie was largely responsible for organising the seven hundredth anniversary celebrations of Magna Carta during the war. Both men were convinced of the righteous allied cause. At the same time McKechnie revealed an unease about the future prospects for democracy. In the crisis over the House of Lords veto over legislation in 1910–11, he saw new interests taking over high principle in politics.[250] Special interest groups like trade unions could enforce irresistible demands now. The Parliament Act of 1911 and the War meant that self restraint had vanished: 'Absolute equality, irrespective of moral worth, of services to the community or of fitness for civic life, is the fundamental principle of democratic theory.[251] As a result the House of Commons 'represents pensioners and would-be pensioners on the national bounties'. The party which pandered to such hopes would invariably succeed: 'The bill of costs includes the rapid increase of the submerged class, the multiplication of individuals unwilling or unable to help themselves clinging like a millstone round the necks of the more deserving.'[252] The only hope lay in some kind second chamber of experts or in a devolved federal system against 'the prolific riff-raff'. The limits of Progressive reform were clear.

That comment on the prolific poor found echoes later in the 1923 report to the General Assembly on the Menace of the Irish Race to Our Scottish Nationality.[253] Many Scots, like many Americans, felt they and their traditional culture were threatened by aliens in their midst. It was symptomatic of profound social and economic changes: the immigrant was the convenient scapegoat for different expectations, lowered status and a more diverse culture. In Scotland old resentments resurfaced. The activities of transatlantic agitators like 'Angel Gabriel' Orr and Alessandro Gavazzi, who had produced considerable rioting on both sides of the Atlantic in the mid-nineteenth century had largely subsided.[254] The ritual of disturbances on the Orange and Green days had emphasised the essential stability of the community. An Ulster Protestant, John Ferguson, had led the Irish nationalists in demands for Home Rule until his death in a Glasgow Corporation tramway accident in 1906.[255] Condemned by the Church and shunned by the local Irish population, the American Fenian movement received little support: the last person publically hanged in Britain was a Glasgow Fenian in 1868. Nonetheless, former Glaswegian Thomas

Gallagher, was sent over to aid in a terrorist campaign. Tradeston Corporation Gas Works were blown up but Gallagher and his associates were soon captured.[256] In more ways than one, the nationalist movement foundered on municipal enterprises. Public ownership of public utilities naturally bred the desire among Glasgow socialists for greater extension of public utilities. After 1918, they were in a position to seek those demands at national level. The working class and Catholic vote was recruited for the new Labour Party.[257]

By 1920 Glasgow had lost its cohesion. It was divided by class, religion and political party in a markedly polarised fashion. There were some similarities to contemporary America but Glasgow was presiding over a declining local economy. In a declining economy the competition for the available jobs and resources had a sharper edge. Social, religious and political distance were intensified. Only after 1945 would they greatly diminish.

Glasgow had been a model for American Progressives; a community facing its massive social problems in a humane, professional and efficient manner. Distress was alleviated in a painless way. A middle course between capital and labour was maintained. Arrogating to himself the voice of the community, the Progressive was convinced that, like himself, the municipality should be a dispassionate focus of social unity. But mesmerised by the techniques of social engineering in Glasgow he became somewhat repetitive and inflexible. Novelty was essential, particularly as the Garden City movement was under way.[258] Perhaps the tradition to the suburb confirmed him in the belief that a society of equal opportunity already existed, for the trams, like Carnegie, gave aid to those willing to help themselves. The trams like the Progressives, provided opportunity amid poverty, but they did not materially alter the structure of society. They provided, literally, a running commentary on American reform between 1894 and 1914.

Chapter Six

Conclusion

Glasgow and the United States had enjoyed a century of continuous close friendly relations between 1820 and 1920. Theirs was essentially a relationship of peoples rather than governmental institutions. As Scotland was not an independent state it could hardly be otherwise. At the same time, such a relationship did vindicate the democratic, voluntarist, self-help tradition in the Atlantic world. The various groups of interested Scots and Americans were able to unite and cooperate in pursuit of common goals. Through their activities they created and sustained a climate of opinion favourable to progress in both countries. Their attitudes, their pressure, their propaganda campaigns and mutual support ensured that their ethos prevailed. In short they guaranteed or underwrote the democratic experiment on both sides of the Atlantic. We tend to forget that there was nothing inevitable in the continuance of stable democratic institutions. At that time there was precious little evidence to suggest that communities in other parts of the world could readily agree to differ, to transfer power from one political party to another with little disturbance—apart from occasional unruly political demonstrations—and generally respect the religious and political views of all. Even since that time the tenuous nature of democracy in many areas highlights the strength and stability of the Scottish-American ideal.

Scotland through her philosophers had contributed massively to the Declaration of Independence. Through her educational institutions she had produced leaders who in turn would reproduce other leaders of calibre in the United States. Glasgow University and other Scottish universities played a major role in this work. Even more impressive was the achievement of popular education through the agency of many Scottish educationalists in the nineteenth century. Their importance lies in that they democratically educated an educated democracy. They morally informed a moral majority, not in the pejorative sense, though that did happen on occasion, but in the safeguarding and securing of democratic ideas and institutions in the hearts and minds of the people at large. Scots in a very real sense exported their sense of identity. That identity's main characteristic was a useful flexible frame of mind which they could readily adapt to American needs and conditions. It was not something they kept to themselves alone. Like most of their contributions to American development it was utilitarian.

Glasgow contributed to a sense of American identity in many ways and at many levels. In particular they gave a self confidence, based on literacy, moral purpose, social responsibility and a cohesive community. Like all such ideals, on occasion it failed—in the case of nativism and the bitterness against Irish immigrants in the mid-nineteenth century. But in the main, the Glasgow mentality, I would suggest, provided a means of disciplining and ordering a fluid fluctuating and somewhat frantic society. Devoid of a traditional aristocracy, law or deferential spirit, the United States needed some acceptable guidelines in her developing years. Like all children she was likely to abandon the precepts of her childhood, but they were useful in the meantime. By emphasising religious values of self restraint, the work ethic and education, the Scottish contribution was to provide the instruments for American success.

If Glasgow provided the intellectual tools, her people frequently provided the skills for social and economic development. Social engineering was in a double sense a Glasgow achievement; the formulating and articulating the desired social values and in providing the practical technicians to bring that happy economic state to pass—in the early stages, skills like weaving and machine building, later with coal mining, then in managerial capacities in mining, engineering, department stores and the like. With these abilities went an attitude of mind that wanted usefulness, efficiency and a good self conceit in a job well done. It was a form of nationalism. It did not belong to a territorial area. It was a state of mind. Scotland went with them wherever they went. Unlike the Irish they did not think in terms of an independent country except in the few notable cases. What is significant is that an increasing awareness of Scottish nationalism grew as opportunities seemed to be drying up in America: David Macrae in his writings and the Bannockburn commemoration in the early twentieth century were indicative of deeper subtle changes. As the traditional strength of the Glasgow region began to decline somewhat in the years preceding the First World War, attitudes slowly altered.

What many American observers had repeatedly highlighted in Glasgow, the existence of two groups, the haves and the have-nots, the West End and the Saltmarket, developed an ideological view. The growth of the labour movement, the heightening class consciousness, the rising expectations in the wake of municipal socialism and the incipient welfare state of the Liberal government gave added impetus to the growing Labour party. The increasing militancy of organised labour, as in the 1911 tramway strike and during the first World War, would be effective schooling for the newly enfranchised in the post-war era. Another group with a new world view, the socialists, were aggressively asserting their version of the future. The success of the Russian Revolution encouraged the wildest dreams. Newly enfranchised workers might be mobilised by effective propaganda. The Red Clydeside of 1919 seemed, at least to some at the time and since, to be the only thoroughgoing way forward. It promised more immediate and tangible results rather than the indirect benefits of municipal enterprise. The changes would be real rather than cosmetic. The benefits would be for all rather than merely the middle classes and the municipal employees who gained disproportionate advantages from civic amenities in utilities, transport and, in the latter case, housing.

America as an inspiration had waned. No longer was the United States seen as the land of the future community development. The image of monopoly capital, anti-labour, anti-intellectual and fundamentalist America did not appeal either to the intelligentsia or to the working class. As a model it was not acceptable. At the same time the opportunities for individual self improvement in the new consumer industries of the twenties proved irresistible—if we analysé the immigration figures.[1] Hollywood proved extraordinarily popular in Glasgow at the popular and the sophisticated level. Most Glaswegians preferred American to English movies and John Grierson said 'it was from America that we in Glasgow, Scotland, got our first sight of most things new in the arts'.[2] To such men America was still a lively vibrant imaginative society— but then he was meeting the finest America could offer on a Rockefeller scholarship: 'He was a revolutionary, but his bombs were verbal and visual.' By temperament a Calvinist preacher 'he enraged his congregation by simply holding a mirror up so that they could see themselves'.[3] That was the difference. The city and its inhabitants had to radically re-examine themselves. It had to find a new inspiration and use it to improve itself.

Hitherto a city run by an élite group ostensibly for the good of its city, now it was allegedly a working class city run by the working class for the working class. The problems which had been evaded, ignored or inadequately treated now pressed. A declining economic base in the post-war period was hardly one on which to build the New Jerusalem. Poverty and unemployment bedevilled efforts at improvement in housing and health. Religious antagonism, class conflict and political polarisation changed the city's image.

In America the consumer revolution, the new leisured individuality epitomised in the proliferation of the motor car rather than the civic tram car, distanced them from Glasgow. The dominant mood of conservatism had little in common with Glasgow. In one interpretation, the twenties in America might seem to be the vindication of the older Glasgow tradition; the triumph of white Anglo-Saxon Protestantism. The end of mass immigration from Southern and Eastern Europe, the enactment of Prohibition, the reinvigorated Protestantism as in the Fundamentalist controversy suggest a *legal* triumph. In fact affluence and the diversity it brought were eroding those successes: Middletown had changed. That old moral earnestness, the community consciousness and cohesion were irrevocably changed. In similar manner the relationship between Glasgow and America was altered.

The goodwill and personal contacts would persist, encouraged by the Second World War, the entertainment and leisure industries. A certain resentment, jealousy and fear of American power since 1945 tempered that association. The children had grown up and the parents had to recognise the differing life styles. Too many Glaswegians looked to the socialist model of the future—and it worked—where Americans looked to the future—and it played.

In one hundred years Glasgow had provided and gained much in her relationship with the United States. It is time to recognise that fact. America similarly gained and gave much in the informal alliance. Americans can begin to realise their debt to Glasgow and the West of Scotland. Both sides can only gain through this mutual appreciation.

Notes

INTRODUCTION

1   Andrew Hook, Scotland and America, 1750–1835 (Glasgow 1975); T M Devine, The Tobacco Lords (Edinburgh 1975); W R Brock, Scotus Americanus (Edinburgh 1982)

2   See Alastair M Dunnett, The Donaldson Line: A Century of Shipping 1854–1954 (Glasgow 1960) and below

3   Horace Greeley, Glances at Europe in a Series of Letters (New York 1851) p 305

4   This paragraph is based on Lewis Perry, Radical Abolitionism: Anarchy and the Government of God in Anti-Slavery Thought (Ithaca 1973). Also see his Childhood, Marriage and Reform: Henry Clarke Wright, 1797–1870 (Chicago 1980)

5   See Arthur H Williamson, Scottish National Consciousness in the Age of James VI: The Apocalypse, the Union and the Shaping of Scotland's Public Culture (Edinburgh 1978) and Katharine R Firth, The Apocalyptic Tradition in Reformation Britain 1530–1645, (Oxford 1979) vol III p 149. Also Ernest Lee Tuveson, Redeemer Nation: The Idea of America's Millenial Role (Chicago 1974 edn)

6   See C Gordon Strachan, The Pentecostal Theology of Edward Irving, (London 1977) and later chapters of this book. Also David Brown, Christ's Second Coming: Will It Be Pre-Millenial (Edinburgh 1849 edn)

7   See W M Mathew, The Origin and Occupations of Glasgow Students 1740–1839 Past and Present no. 33 (1966) 74–94; J B Morrell's articles, The University of Edinburgh in the late Eighteenth Century: Its Scientific Eminence and Academic Structure, Isis 62 (1971) 158–71; Professors Robison and Playfair and Theophobia-Gallia: Natural Philosophy, Religion and Politics in Edinburgh 1789–1815, Notes Records of the Royal Society of London 26 (1971) 43–64; Practical Chemistry in the University of Edinburgh 1799–1843, Ambix 16 (1969) 66–80; The Chemist Breeders: The Research School of Lilby and Thomas Thomson, Ambix 19 (1972) 1–46. An identical case could be made for Glasgow University

8   This paragraph is based mainly on Lawrence J Friedman, Gregarious Saints: Self and Community in American Abolitionism, 1830–1870 (Cambridge 1982); T Scott Miyakawa, Protestants and Pioneers; Individualism and Conformity on the American Frontier (Chicago 1964); John G Cawelti, Apostles of the Self Made Man (Chicago 1965) pp 24–25; Charles E Cunningham, Timothy Dwight, 1752–1817 (New York 1942) pp 293–334

9   D Bogue, On Universal Peace, Being Extracts from a Discourse Delivered in October 1813 (London 1835 edn). Also Richard Lovett, History of the London Missionary Society 1795–1895 2 vols (London 1899) vol I passim: Also D Brown, Christ's Second Coming esp pp 409–28: William Garden Blaikie, David Brown (London 1898) pp 32–9. Brown was associated with James Nisbet, the Scottish evangelical bookseller in London. On that aspect of trans-atlantic propaganda see Anne Scott MacLeod, A Moral Tale: Children's Fiction and American Culture 1820–1860 (Hamden Conn 1975) and J S Bratton, The Impact of Victorian Children's Fiction (London 1981)

10   On the religious background see A C Cheyne, The Transforming of the Kirk: Victorian Scotland's Religious Revolution (Edinburgh 1983), and Andrew L Drummond and James Bulloch, The Church in Victorian Scotland 1843–1874 (Edinburgh 1975). On the American side see W G McLoughlin Pietism and American Character, American Quarterly 17 (1965) 163–86, his introduction to William G Finney, Lectures on Revivals of Religion, (Cambridge Mass 1960 edn) and his Revivals, Awakenings and Reform: Religion and Social Change in America 1607–1977 (Chicago 1978)

11   Cf Lewis Perry, p 34 and L J Friedman, p 109

12   Cf L Perry, p 37; L J Friedman, p 97 and Tuveson, passim

13   See John Fraser, America and the Patterns of Chivalry (Cambridge 1982) and on Britain, Mark Girouard, The Return to Camelot: Chivalry and the English Gentleman (New Haven 1981)

14   See A C Cheyne, pp 110–56; J Fraser, pp 111–48, 191; and Peter J Frederick, Knights of

the Golden Rule: The Intellectual as Christian Social Reformer in the 1890s (Lexington Ky 1976)
15   James Hedderwick, Backward glances (Edinburgh 1891) p 9

CHAPTER 1

1   W Brownlee, The Whigs of Scotland: or the Last of the Stewarts, 2 vols (New York 1833) vol I p ii. He was born in Torfoot, Lanark in 1787, educated at Glasgow University, emigrated to America following his ordination to the ministry where he held charges in Philadelphia, New Jersey and New York, 1813–26, as well as being Professor of Languages, Rutgers University from 1825. Given a DD by Glasgow in 1824, he wrote a tract, Popery an Enemy of Civil and Religious Liberty, 1834, edited the Protestant Vindicator and died in 1860. (Dictionary of American Biography and Glasgow University Matriculation Album)
2   Letter describing J Jamieson of Ayr to R Mackay, editor of the Social Reformer, published in the July 1880 issue
3   Remarks to the New York Council Presbyterian meeting Pan Presbyterian Congress reported in Temperance Leader (Glasgow) 7 Aug 1909.
4   D Macrae, American Presidents and Men I have Met (Glasgow 1908) p 121
5   Quoted Macrae, Presidents p 123
6   D Macrae, Amongst the Darkies and Other Papers (Glasgow 1876) p 35
7   David Riesman with R Denny and N Glazer, The Lonely Crowd (New Haven 1950) p 9. Also see Marshall McLuhan, The Gutenberg Galaxy: The Making of Typographic Man (Toronto 1965 edn) p 28
8   See my The Scottish Religious Identity in the Atlantic World 1800–1914 in S Mews (ed), Religion and National Identity: Studies in Church History, vol 18 (Oxford 1982) pp 505–18
9   See Richard D Brown, Modernisation: The Transformation of American Life 1600–1865 (New York 1976)
10   J D Rockefeller quoted in Edward C Kirkland, Dream and Thought in the Business Community, 1860–1900 (Ithaca New York 1956) pp 20–1. Also see I G Wyllie, The Self-Made Man in America: The Myth of Rags to Riches (Rutgers 1954)
11   cf Rex Burns, Success in America: The Yeoman Dream and the Industrial Revolution (Amherst 1976) pp 2, 66; James B Gilbert, Work Without Salvation: American Intellectuals and Industrial Alienation 1880–1910 (Baltimore 1977); John G Cawelti, Apostles of the Self-Made Man (Chicago 1975); D T Rodgers, The Work Ethic in Industrial America, 1850–1920. (Chicago 1978)
12   A Carnegie, The Gospel of Wealth and Other Timely Essays, ed E C Kirkland (Cambridge Mass 1965) p 49
13   Quoted in R G McCloskey, American Conservatism in the Age of Enterprise, 1865–1910 (Cambridge Mass 1951) p 144. Also see Robert G Gutman, Protestantism and the American Labour Movement; The Christian Spirit in the Gilded Age, pp 79–117 in his Work Culture and Society in Industrialising America; Essays in American Working Class and Social History (Oxford 1977)
14   James D Young, Changing Images of American Democracy and the Labour Movement, International Review of Social Studies 13 (1973) 69–89
15   See J Gunnison and J Gilfillan, Third Statistical Account (Glasgow 1958) p 619
16   See Table 1
17   Redelia Brisbane, Albert Brisbane (New York 1969 edn) p 159
18   cf my article, The Scottish Religious Identity in the Atlantic World 1880–1914, Religion and National Identity: Studies in Church History 18, ed Stuart Mews (Oxford 1982) 505–18
19   Louis B Wright, Culture on the Moving Frontier (Bloomington Indiana 1955) p 40
20   The Literary Diary of Ezra Stiles DD LL D, President of Yale College, ed Franklin Bowditch Dexter (New York 1901) p 184
21   George S Pryde, The Scottish Universities and the Colleges of Colonial America (Glasgow 1957) p 3
22   Quoted Richard Eburne, A Plain Pathway to Plantation (1624 edn); Louis B Wright (Ithaca 1962) p xxv; John Mason, A Brief Discourse of the Newfoundland, with the Situation, Temperature and Commodities Thereof, Inciting Our Nation to go Forward in That Hopeful Plantation Begun (Edinburgh 1620); Robert Gordon, Encouragement for Such as Shall Have

Intention to Be Undertakers in the New Plantation of Cape Breton, Now New Galloway in America (Edinburgh 1625) cited Eburne pp xvii–xix, xxv

23 E Keble Chatterton, English Seamen and the Colonisation of America, (London 1930) p 288

24 T D Devine, The Tobacco Lords (Edinburgh 1975). For fuller bibliography see Bumsted and Brock cited below

25 William Thom, A Candid Enquiry into the causes of the late and the Intended Migrations from Scotland in a letter to J R Esq of Lanarkshire (Glasgow 1771) p 19. Thom was minister of Govan 1748–90, graduated MA from Glasgow University 1732. Fasti, vol 3 pp 412–13

26 Thom, p 33

27 Thom, pp 28–9, 40–1, 50–3

28 Thom, p 39

29 Thom, p 37

30 M Thom, The Defects of a University Education and Its Unsuitableness to a Commercial People With the Expenditure and Necessity of Erecting at Glasgow and Academy for the Instruction of Youth (London 1762)

31 John Fergus̀on, From Glasgow to Missouri, (Glasgow 1878) was just one of many works

32 See Michael Kraus, The Atlantic Civilisation; Eighteenth Century Origins (Ithaca 1949) p 39

33 Dugald Stewart quoted in Richard Olsen, Scottish Philosophy and Mathematics, 1750–1830, Journal of the History of Ideas 32 (1971) 29–44, 42

34 See Malcolm Gray, Scottish Emigration: The Social Impact of Agrarian Change in the Rural Lowlands, 1775–1875, Perspectives in American History, 7 (1973) 95–174, and J M Bumsted, The People's Clearance: Highland Emigration to British North America (Edinburgh 1982); W I Adam, Highland Emigrations of 1770 Scottish Historical Review 16 (1919) 280–93, and The Causes of the Highland Emigrations 1783–1803, S H R 17 (1920) 73–89; Ian C C Graham, Colonists from Scotland, Emigration to North America, 1707–1803 (Ithaca 1956); Duane Meyer, The Highland Scots of North Carolina, 1732–1776 (Chapel Hill 1961); R J Dickson, Ulster Emigration to Colonial America 1718–1775 (London 1966) has much on Scotland

35 John M Duncan, Travels through Parts of the United States and Canada in 1818 and 1819 (Glasgow 1823)

36 Edwin Hodder, Sir George Burns Bart, His Times and Friends (London 1890) pp 189–203 and F E Hyde, Cunard and the North Atlantic, 1840–1873 (London 1975) pp 2–19

37 N P Bonsor, North Atlantic Seaway (Prescot 1955) p 54

38 R S McLellan, Anchor Line 1856–1956 (Glasgow 1956); Alastair M Dunnett, The Donaldson Line; A Century of Shipping 1854–1954 (Glasgow 1960); N P Bonsor, North Atlantic Seaway 5 vols (Newton Abbot/Jersey, 1975–9), vol I pp 422–50, 998–1007; R Perren, The Meat Trade in Britain 1840–1914 (London 1978) pp 106–32, 157–75

39 R S McLellan, Anchor Line pp 38–40. The Christian Instructor reported that not a single oath was ever heard on the trip

40 Frances Wright, Views of Society and Manners in America (Cambridge Mass 1963 edn); John M Duncan, Andrew Bannatyne, eldest son of Andrew Bannatyne, educated Glasgow University, emigrated to New Jersey, died in New York 1894 (MSS List of the Members of the Faculty of Procurators, Glasgow); his book entitled The Government of the United States appeared in 1887

41 Emma Willard, Journals and letters from France and Great Britain (Troy New York 1833) p 365

42 E K Washington, Echoes of Europe or World Pictures of Travel (Philadelphia 1860) p 219

43 Letter, Jane Addams Papers, Chicago Campus, University of Illinois; 30 Sept 1983. Francis C Sessions, On the Way Through Europe (Columbus Ohio 1880) p 44; Wilbur Fisk Travels in Europe (New York 1838) p 656; I McLellan Jr, Journal of a Residence in Scotland (Boston 1834) p 182; Eleanor Childs Meehan, Memoir of a Red Letter Summer (Cincinnati 1903) p 181

44 E C Benedict, A Run Through Europe (New York 1860) p 527; The Papers of Woodrow Wilson, ed A Link vol 9 (Princeton 1970) p 523, 21 June 1896; also T W Silloway and Lee L Powers, The Cathedral Towns and Interesting Places of England, Ireland, Scotland (Boston 1853) p 220

45   Revd Charles Weston Winchester, The Gospel of Foreign Travel (Rochester 1891) p 294
46   Morton Byan Wharton, European Notes and What I saw in the Old World, (Atlanta 1884) p 343
47   Daniel Webster in England: Journal of Harriette Story Paige, ed Edward Gray (Boston 1917) pp 242–63 gives several illustrations
48   E C Benedict p 524; W Harlan Cora, A Knight Templar Abroad (St Louis 1885) p 451; Grace Greenwood, Haps and Mishaps of a Tour in Europe (Boston 1854) p 128
49   Grace Greenwood pp 117–18; E C Benedict p 528; Loretta J Post, Scenes in Europe: Or Observations by an Amateur Artist (Cincinnati 1874) p 115
50   E K Washington, p 224
51   Mrs W Parker, Wandering Thoughts and Wandering Ships (Philadelphia 1880) pp 293–4
52   Quoted in Julia Ward Howe, Margaret Fuller (Wesport Conn, 1970 edn) p 177
53   Margaret Fuller, At Home and Abroad (New York 1971 edn) p 159
54   Caroline White Diary 23 May 1835, Manuscript Collection, American Antiquarian Society, Worcester, Mass. On her next visit thirty years later she found the city smoky, dirty and busy, Diary 5–8 Aug 1885
55   R R Gurley, Mission to England on behalf of the American Colonisation Society (Washington DC 1841) p 45; also see Amelia M Murray, Letters p 221. G A Shepperson, Harriet Beecher Stowe and Scotland, SHR 32 (1952) 40–9
56   cf. Louis Simond, An American in Regency Britain: The Journal of a Tour 1810–1811 (London 1968) pp 77–8; James Mott, Three Months in Great Britain (Philadelphia 1841) p 71 among many others
57   Z Allen D. Am. Biography; and his The Practical Tourist 2 vols (Providence Rhode Island 1832); Louis C Hunter, A History of Industrial Power in the United States 1780–1930 vol. I (Charlottesville Va 1979) pp 162–3
58   Louise A Wallace, An American Child in Europe (np 1914) p 29; James M Hoyt, Glances on the Way at Foreign Lands (Cleveland 1872) p 169; Randal W McGavock, A Tennessean Abroad (New York 1854) p 96; Nathaniel H Carter, Letters from Europe, Comprising the Journal of a Tour Through Ireland, England Scotland, France, Italy and Switzerland in the years 1825, 1826 and 1829, 2 vols (New York 1829) vol 1 pp 280, 317; Loretta J Post, Scenes in Europe, pp 110, 124, 130; Zachariah Allan,.The Practical Tourist or Sketches of the State of Useful Arts and of Society and Scenery, etc in Great Britain, France and Holland, 2 vols (Providence Rhode Island) vol II pp 337–8; E K Washington, p 208: Benjamin Moran, The Footpath and Highway or Wanderings of an American (Philadelphia 1853) p 169; Eleanor Childs Meehan pp 100, 138
59   Quoting Notebook Sept 1846 in T W Higginson, Margaret Fuller Ossoli (New York 1968 edn) p 226; also see Nathaniel M Carter, vol I p 244
60   See James M Hoyt p 169; E K Washington p 219; Henry Day, A Lawyer Abroad (New York 1874) p 26
61   Papers from Over the Water (New York 1869) p 190
62   Orrin Z Hubbell, A University Tramp (Elkhart Indiana 1889) pp 10–11, and Samuel Watson, A Memphian's Trip to Europe with Cook's Educational Party (Nashville 1874) p 343. Also see Fernando Henriques, Modern Sexuality (London 1968) pp 92–153
63   Emma Goldman, Living My Life, 2 vols (New York 1931) vol 1 pp 225–6, 262; Margaret Sanger, An Autobiography (London 1939) pp 12–33 and 1913, Glasgow, draft manuscript in Margaret Sanger Papers, Library of Congress
64   The Letters of Bret Harte, ed Geoffrey Bret Harte, (Boston 1926) p 193 19 Jan 1881
65   Letters p 214 letter 11 Oct 1882
66   Letters p 215, also see pp 232–3, 253, 271
67   Wilbur Fisk, Travels in Europe (New York 1838) p 649
68   For a full discussion see Andrew Hook, Scotland and America: A Study in Cultural Relations, 1750–1835 (Glasgow 1975) esp pp 116–73
69   E C Benedict, pp 527–8
70   Dunn Browne, Experiences in Foreign Parts (Boston 1857) p 279
71   Emma Willard, Journals p 366
72   Glances, vol I p 254
73   Journal of a Visit to Europe and the Levant (Princeton N J 1955) p 57
74   J M Bailey, England, From a Back Window with Views of Scotland and Ireland (Boston

1879) p 268, describing Edinburgh, p 269 describes the sight of thirty women with black eyes hours after the pubs had closed. On Glasgow Margaret Fuller, At Home and Abroad (New York 1971 edn) (1856) p 160

75   Orrin Z Hubbell, A University Tramp; E J Rockwell, Scenes p 320 C W Winchester, The Gospel of Foreign Travel (Rochester New York 1891) pp 293–5

76   See George Buckham, Journal of a Tourist 2 vols (New York 1890)

77   cf Dunn Browne, Experiences p 279

78   cf Benjamin Moran, The Footpath and Highway or Wanderings of an American (Philadelphia 1853) pp 165–6

79   Letter, 1886, Jane Addams Papers (Chicago) and Evelyn R Stetson, Rapid Transit Abroad (New York 1879) p 29; W Harlan Cord, A Knight Templar Abroad (St Louis 1885) p 540; Clement A Pearson, A Journal of Travels in Europe During the Summer of 1881 (Washington 1885) p 16; William Stevenson, Sights and Scenes In Europe or Pencillings by the Way, (Flint Michigan 1882) p 25

80   Rodney Glison, Two Years in Europe (New York 1887); p 99

81   P Neilson, Six Years in America (Glasgow 1830); Letter of Neal Dow on Maine in Scottish Reformer, July 1880

82   cf Fergus Ferguson, From Glasgow to Missouri (Glasgow 1878) which is a catalogue of such meetings

83   Thomas Hamilton, Men and Manners in America (Edinburgh 1833 edn) introduction; also his novel Cyril Thronton London 1846; John Dunmore Lang, Religion and Education in America (London 1840 p 256

84   Hamilton, p xviii

85   Impressions of America and American Churches (Edinburgh 1845) p 35

86   Three Years Among the Working Classes in United States London 1865) pp 168–247

87   See Bernard Wall, Andrew Carnegie (New York 1970) and Sigmund A Lavine, Allan Pinkerton (London 1965) pp 1–7

88   Hamilton, p 130

89   See Allen, The Practical Tourist vol II pp 349–50

90   H Murray, Historical Account of Discoveries and Travels in North America with Observations on Emigration 2 vols (London 1829) vol II p 531

91   The New World Journal of Alexander Graham (Dunlop 1845) eds David Sinclair and Germaine Warkentein (Edinburgh 1976) pp 32–40, 73

92   Revd E J Rockwell, Scenes and Impressions Abroad (New York 1860) p 320

93   W C Bryant, Letters of a Traveller or Notes of Things Seen in Europe and America (London 1850) p 192

94   P L Groome, Rambles of a Southerner (Greensboro NC 1891) p 332. Orrin Z Hubbell, A University Tramp p 9; Revd C W Winchester, The Gospel of Foreign Travel (Rochester NY 1891) p 293

95   Robert P Porter, Breadwinners Abroad (New York 1885, p 29

96   Mrs E A Forbes, A Woman's First Impressions of Europe, Being Wayside Sketches Made During a Short Tour During the year 1863 (New York 1865) p 49

97   Mrs E A Forbes, pp 48–9; M B Wharton, European Notes of What I Saw in The Old World (Atlanta Ga 1884) p 345; Zechariah Allen, The Practical Tourist or Sketches of the State of the Useful Arts and of Society and Scenery and co. in Great Britain, France and Holland, 2 vols (Providence Rhode Island 1832) vol 2 p 350

98   R P Porter, p 16

99   Z Allen, The Practical Tourist p 350

100   E K Washington, Echoes of Europe or World Pictures of Travel, (Philadelphia 1860) pp 216–18; E C Benedict, A Run Through Europe, (New York 1860) p 528; Loretta J Post, Scenes in Europe, Or Observations by an Amateur Artist Cincinnati 1874) p 116

101   R Van Wert/E D Clarke, Rip Van Winkle's Travels in Foreign Lands, (New York 1881) p 34; also see Randal W McGavock, A Tennessean Abroad, (New York 1854) p 95

102   Grace Greenwood, Haps and Mishaps of a Tour of Europe (Boston 1854) p 122

103   John B Latrobe, Hints on Six Monthes in Europe (Philadelphia 1869) p 353; Emma Willard, Journals and Letters from France and Great Britain (Troy New York 1833) p 355; J H Latrobe, 1803–1891, pursued a varied career as lawyer, inventor and public servant, D Am B. Miss Willard as we shall see played a leading role in educational innovation

104   Wilbur Fisk, Travels in Europe (New York 1838) p 648; H Melville, Journal of a Visit to Europe and the Levant (Princeton NJ 1955 edn) p 57; O Z Hubbell, A University Tramp, p 13

105   G Buckham, Journal of a Tourist, 2 vols (New York, 1890) vol II p 512; a more favourable example is Mrs W Parker, Wandering Thoughts and Wandering Steps (Philadelphia 1880) p 238

106   Henry P Tappan, Steps from The New World to The Old, 2 vols (New York 1852) p 237

107   cf Richard Hofstadter and C Dewitt Hardy, The Development and Scope of Higher Education in the United States (New York 1952) pp 28, 46, 62. Scholarships for study in Scotland were recommended as vital to American development, I McLellan Jr, Journal of a Residence in Scotland (Boston 1834) p 353

108   Passages from the English Notebooks, 2 vols (Boston 1870) vol II pp 242 and 246/1857

109   Nathaniel Hawthorne, Passages from the English Notebooks, vol II p 242 and Benjamin Moran, The Footpath and Highway or Wanderings of An American (Philadelphia 1853) p 165

110   B Moran, p 165

111   Rodney Glison, Two Years in Europe (New York 1887) p 98

112   B Moran, p 165

113   Morton Bryan Wheaton, p 343

114   N Hawthorne, vol II p 244

115   Nathaniel Wheaton, A Journal of A Residence of Several Months in London, including Excursions through the Various Parts of England and A short Tour in France and Scotland in the Years 1823 and 1824 (Hartford Conn 1830) pp 484−5

116   Dunn Browne, Experiences of Foreign Parts (Boston 1857) p 279. He was the editor of the Springfield, Mass, Republican paper

117   Mrs Lydia Sigourney, Pleasant Memories of Pleasant Lands (Boston 1856 edn) p 99; N. Wheaton, p 485; B Moran, p 168; Mrs Sigourney felt inspired to write a poem about The Necropolis at Glasgow, pp 101−4, Loch Lomond, pp 104−8

118   B Moran, p 166

119   N Hawthorne, vol II p 24, Also see Harriet Beecher Stowe, Sunny Memories of Foreign Lands (London, 1854) p 26 on the beauty of all Glasgow children

120   Godfrey T. Vigne, Six Months in America, 2 vols (London 1832) vol 1 p 245. He has an account of Scottish farming success in the west vol II p 35

121   John Regan, The Emigrant's Guide to the Western States of America (London 1853) pp 234, 242

122   Alexander MacKay, The Western World and Travels in the United States in 1846−1847, 3 vols (London 1849) vol 3 pp 80−3

123   Mackay, vol 3 p 169 and A M Maxwell, A Run Through the United States During the Autumn of 1840, 2 vols (1841) vol I pp 250−5

124   Hugo Reid, Sketches in America (London 1861) pp 42−3, 261

125   See the chapter on temperance

126   J D Borthwick, p 66

127   Craib, Congregational Miscellany (Dec 1876) p 148

128   Craib, Jan 1877 pp 4−5

129   Borthwick, p 68

130   P Shirreff, A Tour 1835, p 55

131   Edward Potts Cheyney, History of the University of Pennsylvania (Philadelphia, 1940

132   D MacFarlan, The Revivals of the Eighteenth Century particularly at Cambuslang (London 1845); Arthur Fawcett, The Cambuslang Revival: The Scottish Evangelical Revival of the Eighteenth Century (London 1971); W J Couper, 'The Glasgow Periodical Press in the Eighteenth Century, Records of the Glasgow Bibliographical Society 8 (1930) 99−135, 106−7

133   See Perry Miller, Nature's Nation (Cambridge Mass 1967), esp pp 92−108; Charles Roy Keller, The Second Great Awakening in Connecticut (New Haven 1942); Wesley M Hewehr, The Great Awakening in Virginia, 1740−90 Durham NC 1930) ch II pp 251−62; T Scott Miyakawa, Protestants and Pioneers: Individualism and Conformity on the American Frontier (Chicago 1964)

134   John Campbell, Memoirs of David Naismith (London 1844); W L Alexander, Memoirs of Ralph Wardlaw (Edinburgh 1856) pp 273−4; R Carwardine, Transatlantic Revivalism: Popular Evangelicalism in Britain and America 1790−1865, Westport, Conn 1978) p 95 also see the chapter on temperance

135   See W G McLoughlin, Revivals, Awakenings and Before: American Religion and Social Change in America 1607–1977 (Chicago 1978) and his edition of W G Finney, On Revivals of Religion (Cambridge Mass) p 19; William Adamson, The Life of Fergus Ferguson (London 1900) pp 36, 48; Tim Jeal, Livingstone (London 1974) p 13

136   W J Couper, Scottish Revivals (Dundee 1918), pp 135–6; J G Lorimer, The Recent Great Awakening in America (Glasgow 1859); R Ferguson and A M Brown, Life and Labours of John Campbell (London 1868); Recollections of Reginald Radcliffe by his wife (London nd) pp 91–3, 177; Richard Carwardine, Transatlantic Revivalism: Popular Evangelicalism in Britain and America 1790–1865 (Westport Conn 1978)

137   Andrew Reed and James Matheson, A Narrative of the Visit . . . vol II p 4

138   Quoted J F C Harrison, Robert Owen and the Owenites in Britain and America (London 1969) p 120. Also see W Anderson Smith, 'Shepherd' Smith the Universalist, The Story of a Mind Being a Life of the Revd James E Smith MA (London 1892); Andrew L. Drummond, Henry Irving and His Circle (London 1938); Margaret O W Oliphant, Life of Edward Irving 2 vols (London 1862; C Gordon Strachan, The Pentecostal Theology of Edward Irving (London 1973); W H Oliver, Prophets and Millenialists: The Uses of Biblical Prophecy in England From the 1790s to the 1840s (Auckland New Zealand 1978) pp 197–203; Timothy L Smith, Revivalism and Social Reform in Mid-Nineteenth Century America (Nashville 1957)

139   John Vicker, Thomas Coke (London 1960) p 237. Coke 1747–1814 D N B b Brecon son of doctor, JP, educated Oxford, president of the Irish Conference 1782, one of the instigators of missionary endeavours in America 1784, served in Baltimore and travelled extensively in America. One of his American Methodist friends, a Mr Pilmoor served in Scotland for a time before giving up the ministry and returning to America

140   cf Peter Cartwright, Illinois Methodist quoted in T Scott Miyakawa, Protestants . . . p 201

141   John Campbell, David Naismaith (London 1844)

142   See C Howard Hopkins, History of the YMCA in North America, (New York 1951), and his John R Mott 1865–1955 (Geneva 1979) pp 287, 322, 330, 442; Clyde Binfield, George Williams and the YMCA: A Study in Victorian Social Attitudes (London 1973) p 137; J R Mott, Addresses and Papers 6 vols (New York 1946–7) vol 1 p 288 and vol 2 pp 337, 360

143   E J Goodspeed, A Full History of the Wonderful Career of Moody and Sankey in Great Britain (New York 1876) pp 73–120; James F Findlay Jr, Dwight L Moody: The Evangelist 1837–1899 (Chicago 1969) pp 154, 356

144   F and H L Wayland, A Memoir of the Life and Labours of Francis Wayland, DD LL D, 2 vols (New York 1867) vol I p 99

145   Lydia M Sigourney, Sunny Memories of Pleasant Lands (Boston 1856 edn) pp 95–6

146   N H Carter, Letters from Europe, pp 335–6. Also see Revd John Mitchell, Notes from Overseas Consisting of Observations made in Europe in the Years 1843 and 1844, 2 vols (New York 1845) vol I p 181 for Chalmers' preaching 'A New England sermon'

147   W Burns, The New Era of Christianity (London 1828); W H Channing, W E Channing, 3 vols (London 1848) vol II pp 401, 422, 426. W E Channing, Lectures on the Elevation of the Labouring Portion of the Community (Boston 1840)

148   James Hedderwick, Backward Glances (Edinburgh 1891) pp 3–9; On James Hedderwick see The Bailie (21 Dec 1887). He had revisited USA in 1885. Robert Hedderwick, The Bailie (8 July 1894)

149   J Hedderwick to W E Channing, 1 Dec 1835, 30 July 1839, 18 Apr 1840, 27 Sept, 2 Oct 1838, 12 Sept 1837. W E Channing Papers, The Boston visitors were Thomas Gannett and Mr Thatcher

150   See R Griffin to W E Channing, 27 Mar, 31 Oct 1840 and copies of W E Channing to J Hedderwick, 1 Feb 1841, Channing Papers. Printed copies of the two parties legal statements are also in the papers.

151   J Hedderwick to W E Channing, 12 Sept, 29 Oct, 1837. Also see letters of 3 June 1837, 18 April 1839, 30 July 1841

152   L Baker Short, T F Palmer 1747–1804—From Eton to Botany Bay, Transactions of the Unitarian Historical Society 13(1963–6) 37–68; and his William Christie and the First Unitarian Church in Scotland, ibid 14 (1967–70) 10–27, 78–92; on Priestley see appendix

153   Earl Morse Wilbur, Unitarianism in Transylvania, England and America (Cambridge Mass 1952) pp 319–22. On Yates 1789–1871, studied at Glasgow, York, Edinburgh before

graduating from Glasgow in 1811, founded the Scottish Unitarian Association in 1813 see DNB
154   William E Gannett, Ezra Stiles Gannet (Boston 1875) pp 169–72 and J Hedderwick to
W E Channing, 24 Oct 1838 and 18 Apr 1939
155   On Brooks, 1795–1872 see D Am B
156   On Thatcher, D Am B 1809–40; J Hedderwick to W E Channing, 12 Sept 1837
157   See G Thompson, Voice to the United States: Report of the Discussion American Slavery
in Dr Wardlaw's chapel between Mr George Thompson and the Revd R J Breckenridge,
Glasgow 1836; C Duncan Rice, The Scots Abolitionists 1833–1861 (Baton Rouge 1981)
pp 59–79; and below
158   See Daniel T McColgan, Joseph Tuckerman: Pioneer in American Social Work,
(Washington, DC 1940) pp 93–116; P Colquhoun, Treatise on Indigence (London 1806)
159   J Tuckerman, On the Education of the Poor, (nd, np) pp 39, 57
160   Margaret S Carhart, Life and Work of Joanna Baillie (New Haven 1923)
161   31 Jan; 1, 19 Feb 1834, Tuckerman Journal, Houghton Library, Harvard University
162   Journal 19–26 Apr 1834
163   Tuckerman Journal, 19 Apr 1834; Lucretia Mott Journal 1841, Swarthmore Papers,
Swarthmore College, Pennsylvania
164   See Richard T Hughes, 'From Primitive Church to Civil Religion: The Millenial Odyssey
of Alexander Campbell, Journal of the American Academy of Religion 44 (1976) 87–103. Also
Robert Frederick West, Alexander Campbell and Natural Religion (New Haven 1948)
165   James Brown, The Religious Denominations of Glasgow (Glasgow 1860) pp 107, 116; Dr
Russell E Miller, unpublished paper on the Universalists' Scottish mission for which I am
deeply grateful; Geoffrey Rowell, The Origins of Universalist Societies in Britain 1750–1850,
Journal of Ecclesiastical History 22 (1971) 35–56
166   See Russell E Miller, The Larger Hope: The First Century of the Universalists Church in
America 1770–1870 (Boston 1979) for numerous references to Sawyer and Smith
167   See John C Gibson, Life and Letters of Peter Hateley Waddell (London 1925). He
received a DD from an American University. He was also in correspondence with American
ministers. See Alexander Craib, America and the Americans (Paisley 1892) p 131
168   Dr Russell E Miller, unpublished manuscript on the Scottish mission
169   Alan Seaburg, Missionary to Scotland Caroline Soule, Transactions of the Unitarian
Historical Society 14 (1967) 28–41; Sullivan Holmes McCollester, After Thoughts of Foreign
Travel (Boston 1883) pp 3–9
170   The Reverend Samuel Davies Abroad: The Diary of a Journey to England and Scotland
1753–1755, ed. Samuel J Baird (Urbana 1867) p 103
171   William L Sachse, The Colonial American in Britain (Westport Conn 1978 edn) p 114,
and C T Foreman, Indians Abroad (Norman Okla 1943) pp 82–92
172   C T Foreman, pp 150–67
173   See Mae Reed Porter and Odessa Davenport, Scotsman in Buckskin: Sir William
Drummond Stewart and the Rocky Mountain Fur Trade (New York 1963); The West of Alfred
Jacob Miller, ed Marvin C Ross (Norman Okla 1968); Braves and Buffalo: Plains Life in 1837
(Toronto 1973)
174   See Altowan or Incidents of Life and Adventures in the Rocky Mountains by an amateur
traveller, 2 vols (New York 1846) and Edward Warren (London 1854)
175   George Catlin, Notes of Eight Years Travels and Residence in Europe, 2 vols (London
1848 vol 2, pp 173–7); and C T Foreman, pp 189, 206
176   Letters of James Gillespie Birney 1831–1851, ed Dwight L Drumond, 2 vols (New York
1938) vol II pp 585–7
177   C Duncan Rice, passim; I McLellan Jr, p 157
178   See John P Green, Fact Stranger Than Fiction, Cleveland 1920; and see chapter on
temperance
179   W E B DuBois, Autobiography (New York 1968) pp 14,373 and Dusk of Dawn (New
York 1968 edn) p 233
180   J F Potts, Letters from America (London 1880) p 245
181   H L Schneider and George Lawton, A Prophet and a Pilgrim (New York 1942) and J W
Slade, Historical Sketch of Thomas Lake Harris, Laurence Oliphant and the Brotherhood of
the New Life (nd, np) microfilm edition, Thomas Lake Harris Papers, Columbia University
and Wagner College, Staten Island New York.

182   Philip Henderson, The Life of Laurençe Oliphant (London 1956)
183   See W H G Armytage, Heavens Below: Utopian Experiments in England, 1560–1960 (London 1961) pp 126–81; Anne Taylor, Laurence Oliphant (Oxford 1982) pp 240–59
184   T L Harris, The New Republic (London 1891) p 15
185   A A Cuthbert, Life: The Fundamental Principle of All Phenomena. A Lecture (Glasgow 1887); The life and Work of Thomas Lake Harris from Direct Personal Knowledge (Glasgow 1908)
186   Dec/Jan 1887
187   2 vols (Edinburgh 1891)
188   Evening Citizen 29 Dec 1891 also rebutting a letter in the previous day regarding sexual scandals in the California colony
189   The Medium and Daybreak (2 Oct 1891, 27 Oct 1892); R. McCully, The Brotherhood of the New Life and Thomas Lake Harris (Glasgow 1893)
190   See Glasgow Directories 1895–1927. The business appears afterwards without a California connection until 1955–6 at 85 Queen Steet. The Pearces were hosts to Charlotte Perkins Gilman, the American Fabian and Journalist. See below.
191   E W Berridge, Brotherhood of the New Life: An Epitome of the Work and Teaching of Thomas Lake Harris, 16 vols (Glasgow 1896–1917)
192   Mrs Harris to Kanaye, Fountaingrove, 9 July 1903, Microfilm Harris Papers. On Kanaye see Paul Kagan, New World Utopias (London 1975) pp 19–35
193   Letters Mrs Harris, 16, 20, 23 June; 3, 9 July 1903; Dairy July-Oct 1903, Harris Papers
194   Bella Pearce to F Markham, 18 Jan, 6 May 1911, 8 May, 1 June 1923; T Watson Duncan to Bella Pearce, 24 Aug 1910; Anna H Pearce to G Lawton 23, 31 July, 23 Sept 1930. The new house was 25 Tinto Road Hillpark Newlands Glasgow. The Pearce family disappear from the Glasgow Directory after 1933–4
195   Theosophy in Scotland (May, Nov 1910; July 1911; Mar, Apr, June 1912, Mar 1913)
196   Missionaries of the Church of Jesus Christ of the Latter Day Saints, 1839–48 in the Church archives, Salt Lake City Utah
197   ibid 1839, and Manuscript History of the British Mission in the Church archives, Salt Lake City
198   Manuscript History, 14 Jan 1840
199   ibid, 15 June 1840
200   British Mission—Scotland Manuscript History, Church archives, Salt Lake City Utah, 2 Sept 1840
201   Glasgow Conference LDS, Records, Church History archives
202   9 May 1847
203   Frederick Stewart Buchanan, The Emigration of Scottish Mormons to Utah, 1849–1900, unpublished MSc. (Utah 1961) and his essay Imperial Zion: The British Occupation of Utah, in The Peoples of Utah, ed Helen Z Papanikolas, (Salt Lake City 1974) pp 61–114
204   J F C Harrison, Robert Owen and the Owenites in Britain and America, London 1969; R W Leopold, Robert Dale Owen (Cambridge Mass 1940); for fuller information on Maclure and Frances Wright see the chapter on education
205   Letter of a native American quoted in Merle Curti, The Making of an American Community (Stanford California 1959) p 92
206   C K Yearley, Britons in American Labour pp 220–1. See William Maxwell, History of Co-operation in Scotland (Glasgow 1910)
207   See G J Holyoake, Travels in Search of America and Canada: A Settler's Guidebook (London 1844) pp 12, 69, 135, 145; Edward Royle, Victorian Infidels: The Origins of the British Secularist Movement 1791–1866 (Manchester 1974)
208   Ray Boston, British Chartists in America (Manchester 1971) p 88; Forres Gazette (23 Oct 1872); Scottish Temperance League Journal (3 May 1873); letters of Margaret Crawford Kerr 1 July 1889 and 31 Jan 1892, Manuscript Collection, Minnesota Historical Society, St Paul Minnesota; W S Shepperson, Emigraton and Disenchantment (Norman Okla 1965)
209   J M Bumsted, The People's Clearance: Highland Emigration to British North America, 1770–1815 (Edinburgh 1981) pp 59–80
210   J F Gordon, Scotichronicon, 6 vols (Glasgow 1867) Appendix III p 453
211   See Bernard J Canning Irish Born Secular Priests in Scotland 1829–1979 (Greenock 1979) pp 18, 66, 47, 70, 90

212   See R Monteith-O A Brownson correspondence 1853–5, Brownson Papers, University of Notre Dame, Indiana, USA, also Revd J Cumming, Glasgow to O A Brownson, Brownson Papers
213   See my article on Brownson and Monteith in the Innes Review 23 1982 pp 75–6
214   See Michael J Haynes, History of the Diocese of Cleveland (Cleveland 1953) pp 113–93 and George F Houk, A History of Catholicity in Northern Ohio and in the Diocese of Cleveland, 2 vols (Cleveland 1903) vol II pp 101–61
215   Houk p 121 and Hynes pp 123–5
216   B J Canning, pp 134–5
217   See Henry J Browne, The Catholic Church and the Knights of Labour (Washington DC 1949) for a discussion of Gilmour's views esp pp 283–4
218   Church of St Mary's Irvine Century 1875–1975 (Irvine 1975); Glasgow Observer (21 Sept 1889)
219   William Stamer, The Gentleman Emigrant (London 1874); Maurice Farrar, Five Years in Minnesota (London 1880); A Mord, The English Colony at Fairmont in the Seventies, Minnesota History 8 (1927) 140–9. The colony included 24 Scots: Glasgow Observer (29 Aug 1885) reporting the visit to the Scottish Land Restoration League of Revd Duncan McGregor, Chicago; (22 Sept 1888) Revd James Nichol, Denver, Mr J Donnelly, Memphis Tennessee, M J Condon, Knoxville, author of The Irish Race in America to a nationalist meeting; also see 23 Jan, 22 May, 12 June, 10, 24 July 1886 and 5 Mar, 30 July 1887 for excellent examples
220   Edward K. Bennet, Father Nugent of Liverpool (Liverpool 1949) and J P Shannon, Catholic Colonisation on the Western Frontier, New Haven, 1957; Glasgow Observer (8 Oct 1887)
221   eg Buffalo Bill in Glasgow Observer (21 Nov 1891)
222   J S Tait, Who is the Man: A Novel of the Scottish Borders (London 1890); The Cattle-fields of the Far West (Edinburgh 1884): W Turrentine Jackson, The Enterprising Scot: Investors in the American West after 1873, (Edinburgh 1968) pp 42–3
223   A A Robinson, The Resources and National Advantages of Florida, (Tallahassee Fla 1882); Florida Land Agency, Florida. Its Soil, Climate Health, Productions, Resources and Advantages with a Sketch of Its History (Jacksonville Fla 1875); Reports of the Commissioner of Lands and Immigration 1873–88; G E Pozzetta, Foreigners in Florida: A Study of Immigration Promotion, 1865–1910, Florida Historical Quarterly 53 (1974–5) 164–80
224   See London Times (12–23 Apr 1883) and Edinburgh Courant (1 May 1885); Florida Mortgage and Investment Co 1412/3 (16108) Companies Register, Edinburgh
225   Catholic Observer (29 Aug, 12 Sept 1885); Dr P Letters 1849–1910 b Stirling, graduate of Aberdeen University, MB, CM 1870, MD 1887, wrote early article on blood transfusion in the Lancet (1878) pp 116–17 contributed numerous articles to medical and health journals, left Dundee c 1887, for Ireland, settled at Valentia Island 1893 and died there in 1910. Medical Register 1912; Fr James Browne was ordained in 1882 according to the Scottish Catholic directories of 1883 and 1885 and attached Our Lady of Victories, Dundee. He officiated at Arbroath marriages and baptisms between April and August 1885. Information from Revd Peter Foylan. I have been unable to trace where he was ordained or where he went later in Britain, Ireland and the USA
226   A A Robinson, pp 67–8. Bishop John Moore 1835–1901. B Westmeath, Ireland, emigrated to Charleston SC 1848, educated Charleston, France, Rome, ordained 1860, Charleston 1860–77, St Augustine 1877–death. Sylvester Malone, Edward McGlynn, New York 1978 edn
227   See George E Pozzetta, Foreign Colonies in South Florida 1865–1910, Tequesta, Journal of the Historical Association of South Florida 34 (1974) 45–56
228   John Tebbel, A History of Book Publishing in the United States 2 vols (New York 1972–5) vol II pp 377–9
229   See appendix
230   Mrs Eliza Fletcher, Autobiography (Boston 1876) p 71; W C Lehmann, John Millar of Glasgow, 1735–1801; His Life, Thought and Contribution to Sociological Analysis (Cambridge 1960); G P Fisher, Life of Benjamin Silliman, 2 vols (New York 1860) vol 1 pp 109–10; John Maclean, Memoir of John Maclean (Princeton 1885)
231   Grant Thorburn, Fifty Years Reminiscences of New York or Flowers from the Garden of Lawrie Todd (New York, 1845) and his Men and Manners in Britain or A Bone to Knaw for the

Trollopes, Fidlers, etc. Being Notes From a Journey on Land and Sea, 1833–1834 (Glasgow 1835)

232   British Chartists in America pp 88–97

233   Bernard Wall, Andrew Carnegie (London 1970): S A Lavine, Pinkerton (London 1965)

234   See James D Young's excellent Changing Images of American Democracy and the Labour Movement, International Review of Social History 13 (1973) 69–89

235   See Henry Pelling, The Knights of Labour in Britain, Economic History Review 9(1956–7) 313–31, and the correspondence in the Powderly Papers, Catholic University of America, Washington DC

236   See his photographs taken in Glasgow. He does not seem to have recorded much of the city in print

237   Charlotte Erickson, Invisible Immigrants: The Adaptation of English and Scottish Immigrants in Nineteenth Century America (London 1972) p 247 for example

238   Quoted Charles L Sanford The Quest for Paradise: Europe and the American Moral Imagination (Urbana Illinois 1961) p 164 (1961) p 164. Also see pp 159–62

239   David J Jeremy, British Textile Technology Transmission to the United States: The Philadelphia Region Experience 1770–1820, Business History Review, 47 (1973) 24–52, especially pp 30 and 51. Also see Cynthia Shelton, Labour and Capital in the Early Period of Manufacturing: The Failure of John Nicholson's Manufacturing Company, 1793–97, Pennsylvania Magazine of History and Biography, 106 (1982) 341–63. Frances W. Gregory, Nathan Appleton, Merchant and Entrepreneur, 1779–1861 (Charlottesville 1975) pp 143–5

240   Caroline F Ware, The Early New England Cotton Manufacture: A Study in Industrial Beginnings (Boston 1931) p 203

241   See Daniel J Walkowitz, Worker City, Company Town: Iron and Cotton Workers Protests in Troy and Cohoes, New York, 1855–1884 (Urbana Illinois, 1978) p 61. Also see tables 1.4, 2.4, 2.7; Tamara K Hareven, Family Time and Industrial Time: The Relationship Between the Family and Work in the New England Industrial Community (Cambridge Mass 1982) pp 16, 20, 45, 123

242   See Ray Ginger, Labour in a Massachusetts Cotton Mill 1853–1860, Business History Review 28 (1953) 67–91

243   Ginger, p 78

244   Ginger, p 80

245   Constance McLaughlin Green, Holyoke, Massachusetts; A Case History of the Industrial Revolution in America (New Haven 1939) pp 48–9, 76

246   Daniel Creamer, Recruiting Contract Labourers for the Amoskeag Mills, Journal of Economic History 1(1941) 42–56

247   Charlotte Erickson, American Industry and the European Immigrant 1860–1888. (Cambridge Mass 1957) pp 36–8

248   Rowland T Berthoff, British Immigrants in Industrial America, 1790–1850 (Cambridge Mass 1953) p 44; Frances W Gregory, The American Industrial Elite in the 1870s: Their Social Origins, in William Miller ed. Men In Business: Essays on the Historical Role of the Entrepreneur (New York 1962 edn) p 197

249   Hugh Murray, Historical Account of Discoveries and Travels in North America with observations on emigration 2 vols (London 1829) vol II p 517, quoting Westminster Review

250   Murray, vol II p 528

251   Murray, vol II p 531, also see Henry Bradshaw Fearon, Sketches of America, A Narrative of a Journey of five Thousand Miles through the Eastern and Western States of America (London 1819) p 437

252   cf Hugh Murray, The United States of America, Their History from the earliest period, their commerce, etc, 3 vols (Edinburgh 1844) vol 3 p 344; J. Dawson Burn, Three Years Among the Working Classes in the United States during the War (London 1865) p 301, advice to unskilled; J. Keir Hardie in Forward, 1912–13

253   Maurice Corina, Fine Silks and Oak Counters: Debenhams 1778–1978 (London 1978) p 42

254   See H A Gibbons, John Wanamaker, 2 vols (New York 1926); Alfred D Chandler Jr, The Visible Hand: The Managerial Revolution in American Business (Cambridge Mass 1977) pp 209–26

255   cf S Thernstrom, Poverty and Progress: Social Mobility in the American City (Cambridge Mass 1963) and his The Other Bostonians (Cambridge Mass 1973)
256   See above
257   Arthur Wilson, William Wilson (Glasgow 1920)
258   See H A Gibbons, John Wanamaker, vol I pp 117, 123, 248
259   John Thomas Scharf, History of St Louis City and County, 2 vols (Philadelphia 1883) vol II pp 12, 41—2
260   James Cox, Old and New St Louis (St Louis 1894) pp 216—18, St Louis Hornet (8 Apr 1882); J Thomas Scharf, History of St Louis City and County St Louis, 2 vols (1913), vol II p 1302. I am most grateful to the Missouri Historical Society for their help in locating this material
261   See W Turrentine Jackson, The Enterprising Scot: Scottish Investment in the American West after 1873 (Edinburgh 1968); W M Pearce, The Matador Land Company, (Norman, Oklahoma, 1964); W. G. Ker, Scottish Capital on the American Credit Frontier (Austin Texas 1976); W Turrentine Jackson, British interests in the Range Cattle Industry, in M Frink, W T Jackson and A W Sping, When Cattle Was King (Boulder Colorado 1956); James MacDonald, Food from the Far West (Edinburgh 1878); John Clay, My Life on the Range (Chicago 1924); Lewis Atherton, The Cattle Kings (Bloomington Ind 1961); Louis Pelzer, The Cattleman's Frontier: A Record of the Trans Mississippi Cattle Industry From Oxen Trains to Pooling Companies 1850—1890 (Glendale Cal 1936)
262   Atherton, p 190
263   W Turrentine Jackson, The Enterprising Scot: Investment in the West after 1873 pp 161, 187, 192, 204
264   W G Ker, Scottish Capital on the American Credit Frontier (Austin Texas 1976) pp 269—72. There are a fair number of other Glasgow enterpreneurs scattered through the book.
265   Cedric Watts and Laurence Davies, Cunninghame Graham (Cambridge 1979) p 45
266   Quoted in Memoir and Correspondence of Mrs Grant of Laggan (ed J P Grant, 3 vols (London 1844) vol 3 p 232 in 1832. Also see vol 3 pp 112, 137, 148 and Andrew Hook, Scotland and America, pp 181—99
267 Hiram Martin Chittenden, The American Fur Trade in the Far West, 2 vols (Stanford 1954) vol I p 159 and 381—82
268   Quoted Lewis O Saum, The Fur Trader and the Indian (Seattle 1963); Chittenden, vol I pp 52—3, 384—6
269   Altowan, 2 vols (New York 1846); Edward Warren (London 1854); also see the correspondence of Sir William Drummond Stewart in the Sublette Papers, Missouri Historical Society, St Louis, and in the Webb Papers, Beinedecke Library, Yale University; and in the Grandtully Papers, the Scottish Record Office, Edinburgh; The West of Alfred Jacob Miller, ed Marvin C Ross (Norman Okla 1968); Braves and Buffalo: Plains Indians Life in 1837, ed Michael Bell (Toronto 1973); Mae Reed Porter and Odessa Davenport, Scotsman in Buckskin: Sir William Drummond Stewart and the Rocky Mountain Fur Trade (New York 1963); Thomas Hancock, Personal Narrative of the Origin and Progress of the Caoutchouc or India-Rubber Manufacture in England (London 1857) p 82; J Cecil Alter, Jim Bridger, (Norman Okla 1973); James L Crouthamel, James Watson Webb: A Biography (Middletown Conn 1969)
270   cf Edward Warren, p 66. Also see Roderick Marsh, Wilderness and the American Mind (New Haven 1971 edn); Lewis O Saum, 'The Fur Trader and the Noble Savage, American Quarterly 15 (1963) 554—71
271   W J Anderson, Sir William Drummond Stewart and the Chapel of St Anthony the Eremite, Murthly, Innes Review 15 (1964) 151—170
272   Alexander Wilson and C L Bonaparte, American Ornithology or the Natural History of the Birds of the United States, 3 vols (London 1837 edn) vol I pp ix—cvii; Sir William Jardine, Memoir of Alexander Wilson, in the Naturalists Library, 27 (Edinburgh 1843) 17—50; Elisa Guerdrum Allen, The American Career of Alexander Wilson, Atlantic Naturalist 8 (1952) 61—76; Ernest Earnest, John and William Bartram: Botanists and Explorers, 1699—1777 and 1739—1823 (Philadelphia, 1940) pp 166—73. William Maclure, the Ayrshire merchant educator and supporter of New Harmony was also a renowned geologist and collector of natural history. See the chapter on education. Alexander Wilson taught Edwin Forrest the renowned American actor elocution: Forrest was to visit Glasgow on his first British tour in 1836—7. W R

Alger, Life of Edwin Forrest, 2 vols (New York 1972 edn) vol I pp 57–8, 194, 409 and Richard Moody Edwin Forrest (New York 1960) p 16

273   See the Ord Papers, American Philosophical Society, Philadelphia for their large correspondence; C Waterton, Wanderings in South America, (Everyman edition); Philip Gosse, The Squire of Walton Hall: The Life of Charles Waterton (London 1940)

274   Journal Kept by David Douglas During his Travels in North America, 1823–1827 (London 1914)

275   See Susan Bryant Dakin, A Scotch Paisano in Old Los Angeles: Hugo Reid's Life in California 1832–1852, derived from his correspondence (Berkeley, 1978 edn); H H Jackson, Ramona (Boston 1907 edn) and her Century of Dishonour (New York 1881)

276   Dakin, p 203 lists eleven Scots who are known to have resided in California between 1824 and 1831. See Martha Vogt's article in SHR 52 (1973) 137–48

277   Roger W Lotchin, San Francisco 1846–1856; From Hamlet to City, (New York 1974), and R A. Burchell, The San Francisco Irish 1848–80 (Manchester 1979) pp 9–10, 22, 27; Peter Donahue appears in the National Cyclopaedia; and California Biography. There is a manuscript life in the Bancroft Library, University of California, Berkeley.

278   Anonymous typescript life in Bancroft Library; Ira B Cross, Financing an Empire: History of Banking in California, 4 vols (Chicago 1927) vol I pp 233, 374–5; Anon, Sketch of the Life of Peter Donahoe of San Francisco, 1822–1885 (San Francisco 1888). Ruth Reiser, Charleston: An Industrial Milestone, California Historical Quarterly, 25 (1946) 39–53, 41–3; Robert Ryal Miller, The Camanche First Monitor of The Pacific, California Historical Quarterly 45 (1966) 113–24; John H White Jr, The Railroad Reaches California: Men, Machines and Cultural Migration, California Historical Quarterly, 52 (1973) 131–44

279   St Mary's Centenary Brochure 1840–1940 (Glasgow 1940); information provided by Sister archivist, San Francisco archdiocesan archives

280   See his obituary notices in the Davenport Democrat 3, 6 Oct 1884

281   See California Biography, The background will be found in Robert Seager. Some Denominational Reactions to Chinese Immigration to California, 1856–1892, Pacific Historical Review 28 (1959) 49–66

282   Men Who Made San Francisco p 139, copy in San Francisco Public Library

283   A R Kimball, The Blue Ribbon (New York 1894) pp 22–222; John Leng, America in 1876 (Dundee 1877) p 85

284   William S McKinstry, Alexander Winton: An Unsung Genius (Cleveland, nd); William Garrison Rose, Cleveland: The Making of a City (Cleveland 1950) pp 533, 585, 601, 680, 712–13; Leslie J Flink, America Adopts the Automobile 1895–1910 (Cambridge Mass 1973) pp 25, 37–8; G R Doyle, The World's Automobiles 1880–1955 (London 1931) pp 161–3; Anthony Bird, The Motor Car 1765–1914 (London 1960) pp 172–3, 200, 209–10, 230–1

285   See the classic account in Robert and Helen Lynd, Middletown (New York 1929)

286   J L Carvel, One Hundred Years in Timber (Glasgow 1950) pp 15–22; F H Young, A Century of Carpet Making (Glasgow 1944–5); Michael S Moss and John R Hume, The Making of Scotch Whisky: A History of the Scotch Whisky Distilling Industry (Edinburgh 1981) pp 91–2, 145–72

287   28 Aug 1885 quoted in S B Saul, Technological Change in the United States and Britain in the Nineteenth Century (London 1970) p 161. Also see W H Marwick, Economic Development in Victorian Scotland (London 1936) p 80 and Robert B Davies, Peacefully Working to Conquer the World: The Singer Manufacturing Company in Foreign Markets 1854–89, Business History Review 44 (1969) 299–325

288   See Leila Sellers, Charleston Business on the Eve of the American Revolution (Chapel Hill 1934) p 119; Paul G E Clemens, The Atlantic Economy and Colonial Maryland's Eastern Shore: From Tobacco to Grain (Ithaca 1980) p 157; T M Devine, The Tobacco Lords (Edinburgh 1975); Jacob M Price, France and the Chesapeake, 2 vols (Ann Arbour 1973) vol 1; and his Buchanan and Simson 1759–83: A Different Kind of Glasgow Firm Factoring on the Chesapeake, William and Mary Quarterly 40 (1983) 3–41. Robert C Nash suggests Glasgow merchants may have prospered through inefficient customs far removed from London, in The English and Scottish Tobacco Traders in the Seventeenth and Eighteenth Century: Legal and Illegal Trade, Economic History Review 35(1982) 354–72

289   Dorothy R Adler, British Investment in American Railways (Charlottesville Va 1970)

p 125 and Peter Temin, Iron and Steel in Nineteenth Century America: An Economic Inquiry (Cambridge Mass) pp 58–9
290   J Nichol, American Literature (Edinburgh 1882) p 13
291   Samuel J May, Some Recollections of Our Anti-Slavery Conflict (New York 1968 edn) pp 385–6; The Letters of William Morris, ed Philip Henderson (London 1950) p 218; Anna M Stoddart, Elizabeth Pease Nichol (London 1899); W Knight, Memoir of John Nichol (Glasgow 1896) and his Some Nineteenth Century Scotsmen, Edinburgh 1903, pp 221–45
292   J P and E Nichol to W L Garrison, 9 May 1854; among a large number in the Garrison Papers, Boston Public Library; E P Nichol to Lucretia Mott, 20 Dec 1800, Mott Papers; Elizabeth Cady Stanton to E Pease, 12 Feb 1842, Angelina Grimke Weld to E Pease, 14 Aug 1839; Frederick Douglass to E Pease, 8 Nov 1849; Boston Public Library Collection; J P Nichol to Edward Everett 18 Jan 1848, Everett Papers, Massachusetts Historical Society, Boston: J P Nichol to M Bouvier, 17 Nov 1856; J P Nichol to Alexander Dallas Bache, 17 July 1851, 2 Aug 1859, Huntington Library Manuscript Collections, San Marino California; Historical Sketch of the Salem Lyceum, Salem Mass 1879 p 49. Also see John Harvie, The Lights of Liberalism: University Liberals and the Challenge of Democracy 1860–1886 (London 1976): John Nichol to Hiram Barney, 22 Aug 1867, 21 June 1870, 20 Aug 1872, 20 Jan 1873. Barney A New York lawyer, confidant of Abraham Lincoln and Collector of the Port of New York, 1861–4. J. Nichol to Alice Fields, 24 Aug 1872, a minor poet friend of Longfellow, introducing the feminist Emily Faithfull of the Victoria Press, London, Huntington Library Manuscript Collections: J. Nichol to Miss C. Weston, 22 Dec 1865 with copies of poems he wrote, Boston Public Library Collections: E Faithfull, Three Visits to America (Edinburgh 1884)
293   Ruskin quoted E T Cook, The Life of John Ruskin, 2 vols (London) vol II p 390, and W M Rossetti, Some Reminiscences, 2 vols (London 1906) vol II pp 485–6
294   The Life and Letters of Thomas Campbell, ed William Beattie, 3 vols (London 1849); A Hook, Scotland and America p 142
295   See visitors Book, Lord Provost of Glasgow, Glasgow City archives
296   The Scottish Association Football Annual 1891–2 pp 75–8
297   SAF Annual 1892–3 p 76
298   SAF Annual 1892–3 p 75
299   See appendix
300   See list in appendix
301   Capt J E Alexander, Transatlantic Sketches Comprising Visits to the Most Interesting Scenes in North and South America and the West Indies, 2 vols (London 1833) vol II pp 302–3

CHAPTER 2

1   H Barnard Papers on Preventive, Correctional and Reformatory Institutions and Agencies in Different Countries (Hartford Conn 1857) p 343. See Anna Lou Blair, Henry Barnard, School Administrator, Minneapolis 1938
2   (Glasgow 1975) He concentrates on higher education
3   See W R Brock, Scotus Americans (Edinburgh 1982) pp 87–113 and Gary Wills, Inventing America: Jefferson's Declaration of Independence (New York 1979 edn) for the pervasive Scottish influence
4   J F C Harrison, Robert Owen and the Owenites in Britain and America: The Quest for a New Moral World (London 1969) p 170: Theodore Stanton and Harriet S Blatch (eds), Elizabeth Cady Stanton, 2 vols (New York 1922) vol 1 pp 18–23. Revd Simon Hosack who had studied at Glasgow University; on Cunningham see below.
5   Margaret S Carhart, The Life and Work of Joanna Baillie (New Haven 1923) and Memoir and Correspondence of Mrs Grant of Laggan (ed) James P Grant) 3 vols (London 1845)
6   H F May, The Enlightenment in America (New York 1976) p 342
7   Ibid p 346. On Scottish philosophy see Gladys Bryson, Man and Society: The Scottish Inquiry of the Eighteenth Century (Princeton 1945); S A Grave, The Scottish Philosophy of Common Sense (London 1960); Douglas Sloan, The Scottish Enlightenment and the American College (New York 1971); Howard Miller, The Revolutionary College: American Presbyterian Higher Education 1707–1837 (New York 1976); Garry Wills, Inventing America (Garden City New York 1978); D H Meyer, The Instructed Conscience: The Shaping of the American

National Ethic (Philadelphia 1972). Also see Nathan D Hatch, The Sacred Cause of Liberty: Republican Thought and the Millenium in Revolutionary New England (New Haven 1977) esp pp 139–65 and E L Tuveson, Millenium and Utopia: A Study in the background of the Idea of Progress (Gloucester Mass 1972) pp 191–201 and his Redeemer Nation: The Idea of America's Millenial Role (Chicago 1968) for Scottish Ideas

8 Quoted in Carl Siracusa A Mechanical People: Perceptions of the Industrial Order in Massachusetts 1815–1880 (Middletown Conn 1979) p 100

9 Quoted in D H Meyer, p 40

10 A Tyrell, Political Economy, Whiggism and the Education of the Working Class in Scotland 1817–40, Scottish Historical Review 48 (1969) 151–65, 153 and R Olson, Scottish Philosophy and Mathematics 1780–1830, Journal of the History of Ideas, 32 (1971) 29–44.

11 cf W E Channing, The Obligation of A City to Watch Over the Moral Health of Its Members (Glasgow 1841) is almost identical to Chalmers' Christian Civics.

12 Robert Baird, Religion in the United States of America (Glasgow 1844) p 237

13 For example David Nasau, Schooled at Order: A Social History of Public Schooling in the United States (New York 1979) esp pp 38–49. It also influenced the Deep South: Anne C. Loveland, Southern Evangelicals and the Social Order 1800–1860 (Baton Rouge 1980) and E Brooks Hollifield, The Gentleman Theologians: American Theology in Southern Culture 1759–1860 (Durham NC 1978) pp 110–26

14 Merle Curti, Human Nature in American Thought: A History (Madison Wis 1980) for example has much material which would sustain that point

15 Kathryn Kish Sklar, Catherine Beecher: A Study in American Domesticity (New Haven 1973) pp 78–84; Raymond A Mohl, Humanitarianism in the Pre-Industrial City: The New York Society for the Prevention of Poverty 1817–23, Journal of American History 57 (1970–1) 576–9; Merle Curti, The Social and Political Ideas of American Educators (Totowa NJ 1971 edn); Selwyn K Troen, The Public and the Schools: Shaping the St Louis System 1838–1920 (Columbia Mo 1975) pp 2–53; M J Heale, From City Fathers to Social Critics: Humanitarianism and Government in New York, 1790–1860, Journal of American History 63 (1976) 21–41

16 George Davie, The Democratic Intellect: Scotland and Her Universities in the Nineteenth Century (Edinburgh 1961) and Lawrence James Saunders, Scottish Democracy 1815–1840 (Edinburgh 1950) are the classic statements. T J Wertenbaker, Early Scottish Contributions to the United States (Glasgow 1945) is an early pioneering example.

17 J M D Meiklejohn, An Old Educational Reformer Dr Andrew Bell (Edinburgh 1881); P Colquhoun, New and Appropriate System of Education for the Labouring People (London 1806); Iatros, A Biographical Sketch of the Life and Writings of Patrick Colquhoun, (London 1818)

18 John Abercrombie, Inquiries Concerning the Intellectual Powers and the Investigation on Truth (Edinburgh 1830) and his The Philosophy of Moral Feelings (London 1833); Henry Brougham, Practical Observations on the Education of the People (London 1825); George Combe, The Constitution of Man (Edinburgh 1828); Thomas Dick, On the Improvement of Society by the Diffusion of Knowledge (Edinburgh 1843); George Jardine, Outlines of Philosophical Education (Glasgow 1825 edn). I am grateful to Dr J V Smith, Dundee University for his unpublished paper, Manners, Morals and Mentalities: Reflection on the Popular Enlightenment of Early Nineteenth Century Scotland. Also E Halevy, Thomas Hodgskin (London 1956) pp 86–7

19 Robert Burns, Memoir of the Revd Stevenson Macgill DD (Edinburgh 1842). Macgill in his reformism and local pride was developing defences against revolutionary upset pp 25–33; Thomas McCrie, Life of John Knox, 2 vols (Edinburgh 1813) and his life of Andrew Melville, 2 vols (Edinburgh 1819)

20 William Maclure (1763–1818). See Samuel George Morton A Memoir of William Maclure (Philadelphia 1841). On Fanny Wright see below. Frances Wright D'Arusmont, Life Letters and Lectures (New York 1972 edn) p 152.

21 Wright, Life, Letters and Lectures p 103

22 An Outline of the System of Education at New Lanark (Glasgow 1824). See also R W Leopold, Robert Dale Owen: A Biography (Cambridge Mass 1940).

23 Most recent writing on early American education betrays a strong bias of varying intensity towards interpretations emphasising social control: Barbara Finkelstein, Pedagogy as

Intrusion: Teaching values in Popular Primary School in Nineteenth Century America, pp 239–70 in Donald R. Warrend (ed), History, Education and Public Policy (Berkeley 1978): Samuel Brooks and Herbert Gintis, Schooling in Capitalist America: Education Reform and the Contradictions of Economic Life (London 1976) ch 6, Origins of Mass Public Education pp 151–79; Stanley K. Schultz, The Culture Factory: Boston Public Schools 1789–1860 (New York 1973); David Nasau, Schooled to Order: A Social History of Public Schooling in the United States (New York 1979); Michael B. Katz, The Irony of Early School Reform: Educational Innovation in Mid Ninteenth Century Massachusetts (Cambridge Mass 1968); these ideas have been strongly challenged by Louis Banner, Religious Benevolence as Social Control: A critique of An Interpretation, Journal of American History 60 (1973–4) 23–41. See her Religion and Reform in the Early Republic: The Role of Youth, American Quarterly 23 (1971) 677–95; John L. Thomas, Romantic Reform in America 1815–1865, American Quarterly 17 (1965) 656–81; Timothy L. Smith, Protestant Schooling and American Nationality 1800–1860, Journal of American History 53 (1966–7) 679–95; David Tyack, The Kingdom of God and the Common Schools: Protestant Ministers and the Educational Awakening in the West, Harvard Educational Review 36 (1966) 447–69; D G Mathews The Second Awakening as an Organising Process 1780–1830: An Hypothesis, American Quarterly 21 (1969) 23–40

24   The difficulties of readjustment are readily summarised in Thomas Bender, Toward an Urban Vision: Ideas and Institutions in Nineteenth Century America (Lexington Kentucky 1975)

25   See for example D. H. Mayer, The Instructed Conscience: The Shaping of the American National Ethic (Philadelphia 1972) for an important discussion of these points. Ch 4, The Legacy of the Scottish Enlightenment, pp 35–42 is central.

26   See Orville Dewey, Works (London 1844) p 617 and the Philadelphia Committee Report in J R Commons et al, History of Labour in the United States, 2 vols (New York 1918) vol 1 p 226

27   Quoted in G D Lillibridge, Beacon of Freedom: The Impact of American Democracy Upon Great Britain 1830–1870 (Philadelphia 1954) p 99

28   ibid pp 18, 36–9, 94 and David Stow in conversation 22 Dec 1836. Alexander Dallas Bache, Journal, Bache Papers, Library of Congress

29   Anne L Kuhn, The Mother's Role in Childhood Education: New England Concepts, 1830–1860 (New Haven 1947). The earlier background is in Linda K Kerber, Women of the Republic: Intellect and Ideology In Revolutionary America (Chapel Hill 1980) esp pp 136, 189, 235

30   cf David J Rothman, The Discovery of the Asylum; Social Order and Disorder in The New Republic (Boston 1971). The Glasgow graduate and minister John Dunmore Lang, Religion and Education in America (London 1840) p 3, saw the crusade as inseparable from an anti-Papal campaign. He was to be a major figure in Australian educational, religious and political developments. See biographical list.

31   See for example R J Breckenridge, Discourse on the Formation and Development of the American Mind before the Literary Society of Lafayette College, Easton, Pennsylvania on 20 Sept 1836 (Baltimore 1837) and C S Rosenberg, Religion and the Rise of the American City: The New York City Mission Movement 1812–1870 (Ithaca 1971)

32   See John A Andrew, Rebuilding the Christian Commonwealth; New England Congrega-tionalists and Foreign Missions (Lexington Kentucky 1976) pp 33–69

33   eg Bertram Wyatt-Brown, Lewis Tappan and the Evangelical War Against Slavery (Cleveland 1969) esp pp 46–69; Timothy L Smith, Revivalism and Social Reform (Nashville 1957); John L Thomas, Romantic Reform in America 1815–1865, American Quarterly 17 (1965) 656–81

34   Robert Cunningham, Thoughts on the Question Whether Seminaries Ought to be Distinct Establishments or Ingrafted on Colleges? Being an Inaugural Address on his Inauguration as Professor of Ancient Languages in Lafayette College, Easton, Pennsylvania, 1 Jan 1838 (Philadelphia 1838) p 5

35   Annual Report of the Board of Missioners of the Presbyterian Church 1849, quoted in John R Bodo, The Protestant Clergy and Public Issues 1812–1848 (Princeton 1954) p 190

36   eg William Russell, Suggestions on Teachers' Institutes (Boston 1848) pp 10–11

37   See Biographical list: J M Duncan, Travels Through Part of the U.S., vol 2 p 324:

Raymond A Mohl, Humanitarianism in the Pre-Industrial City: The New York Society for the Prevention of Pauperism 1817–1823, Journal of American History 57 (1970–1) 576–99 and M J Heale, From City Fathers to Social Critics: Humanitarianism and Government in New York 1790–1860, Journal of American History 63 (1976) 21–41. William Charvat, Francis Jeffrey in America, New England Quarterly 14 (1941) 309–34

38   R D Owen, An Outline of the System; John Griscom, A Year in Europe, 2 vols (New York 1823) vol II pp 373–93. His later Memoir With Some Account of the New York High School: The Society for the Prevention of Pauperism; the House of Refuge and Other Institutions (New York 1859) pays more attention to Pestalozzi and Edinburgh High School. Boston High School was allegedly also modelled on Edinburgh. Nelson R. Burr, Education in New Jersey 1630–1871 (Princeton 1942) p 284. See below.

39   eg J F C Harrison, Robert Owen pp 139–63 and J Griscom, A Year, p 373

40   Kate Silber, Pestalozzi: The Man and His Work (London 1960) pp 304–5

41   Elizabeth Hamilton, Hints addressed to the Patrons and Directors of Schools Principally Intended to Show that the Benefit Derived from the New Modes of Teaching may be increased by the partial adoption of the plan of Pestalozzi (London 1815); p 89 for Bell and Lancaster; Letters on the Elementary Principles of Education, 2 vols (Edinburgh 1810) the Mitchell Library copy presented by Lord Kelvin; Series of Popular Essays Illustrative of Principles Essentially Connected with the Improvement of the Understanding, the Imagination and the Heart, 2 vols (Edinburgh 1813). In additon she wrote several religious works, on philosophy and a novel. Elizabeth Ogilvie Benger, Memoirs of the late Mrs Elizabeth Hamilton 2 vols (Edinburgh 1818). J Abercrombie, The Philosophy of Moral Feelings p 46

42   Quoted in Kate Silber, Pestalozzi, p 149

43   Revd C and Miss Mayo, Practical Remarks on Infant Education (London 1837) p 42. Also see their Lessons on Shells at the Pestalozzian School at Cheam Surrey (London 1838 edn)

44   Thomas Chalmers, The Christian and Civic Economy of Large Towns, Glasgow 1821; Stewart J Brown, Thomas Chalmers and the Godly Commonwealth in Scotland (Oxford 1983); cf W E Channing, Self-Education (Edinburgh 1839) pp 6–8; K S Inglis, The Churches and the Working Class in Victorian Scotland (London 1963) pp 5–18; On Badham and his sons see Venn, Cambridge Graduates, and W H G Armytage, Heavens Below, pp 174–5; John Henry Newman brought up in an evangelical household later talked of conscience as 'the aboriginal vicar of Christ' which is suggestive see John Griscom A Year, vol 2 pp 395–9; W E Channing, The Obligation of A City to Watch Over the Moral Health of Its Members with remarks on the life and character of the Revd Dr Tuckerman, founder of the ministry at Large (Glasgow 1841): D T McColgan, Joseph Tuckerman; Pioneer in Social Work (Washington DC 1940) pp 93–116

45   S G Morton, William Maclure; James D Hardy John Jensen and Martin Wolfe (eds), The Maclure Collection of French Revolutionary Material (Philadelphia 1966) has an excellent account of Maclure, pp xvii–xxi. William Maclure, Opinions on Various Subjects dedicated to the Industrious Producers (New Harmony 1831) 2 vols remains the best collection of his political and social views. Also see W H G Armytage, Heavens Below: Utopian Experiments in England 1560–1960 (London 1961) pp 113, 129 and J F C Harrison, Robert Owen and the Owenites in Britain and America: esp pp 36–42

46   (Philadelphia 1839). Phrenological Journal 14 (1841) 62–3 reported 600 at the exhibition in the evening. Also see William Stanton, The Leopard's Spots: Scientific Attitudes Towards Race in America 1815–1859 (Chicago 1959) pp 24–53

47   W Maclure to B Silliman, 19 Oct 1822 quoted in W H G Armytage, Heavens Below, p 118. On Silliman see biographical list and G P Fisher, Life of Benjamin Silliman, 2 vols (New York 1866); Gerald Lee Gulick, Joseph Neef: The Americanisation of Pestalozzianism (Alabama 1978)

48   J R Commons et al, History of Labour, vol 1 pp 181, 223–6; Maclure, Opinions, vol 1 pp 33, 34, 44, 47, 57 and 59 and many more throughout the work

49   W Maclure, Opinions, vol 1 p 34

50   ibid vol 1 p 59

51   ibid vol 1 p 21

52   ibid vol 1 p 57

53   George B Holloway, The New Harmony Experiment (New York 1905) ch 20 pp 209–93

54   W H G Armytage, Heavens Below, quoting New Harmony Disseminator (16 Jan 1828)

55   On Fanny Wright, see her Views of Society; W R Waterman, Frances Wright (New York 1924); A J G Perkins and Theresa Wolfson, Frances Wright, Free Enquirer (New York 1939); Margaret Lane, Frances Wright and the Great Experiment (Manchester 1972); Cecilia H Payne Gapaschkin, The Nashoba Plans for Removing the Evil of Slavery: Letters of Frances and Camilla Wright 1820–1829, Harvard Library Bulletin 23 (1975) 221–61
56   Frances Wright, Views, p 217
57   Frances Wright, Address to the Industrious Classes: A Sketch of a System of National Education (New York 1830) p 4
58   Outline (Glasgow 1824) and R W Leopold, Robert Dale Owen (Cambridge Mass 1940) pp 11–28. Also see Frances Wright D'Arusmont, Life Letters and Lectures (New York 1972) p 103
59   Houghton MSS Collection, Harvard University. On the background see Louis H Arky, The Mechanics Union of Trade Associations and the Formation of the Philadelphia Working-men's Movement, Pennyslvania Magazine of History and Biography 75 (1952) 142–76; Merle Curti, Robert Rantoul, The Reformer in Politics, New England Quarterly 5(1932) 264–80; Walter Hugins, Jacksonian Democracy and the Working Class: A Study of the New York Workingmen's Movement 1829–37 (Stanford 1960); Sidney L Jackson, Labour, Education and Politics in the 1830s, Pennsylvania Magazine of Biography and History 66 (1942) 279–93
60   Robert Baird, Religion in the United States p 327. The figures appear on pp 328 and 337. On the background of disorders see Ray A Billington, The Protestant Crusade, 1800–1860 (Chicago 1964 edn) and Leonard L Richards, Gentlemen of Property and Standing: Anti-Abolitionist Mobs in Jacksonian America (New York 1970)
61   William Fraser, Memoir of the Life of David Stow (London 1868) and Stewart Mechie, The Church and Scottish Social Development, 1780–1970 (London 1960): Marjorie Cruickshank, History of the Training of Teachers in Scotland (London 1970) pp 13–50; Thomas A. Markus, The School as Machine: Working Class Scottish Education and the Glasgow Normal Seminary in his collection of essays, Order in Space and Society: Architectural Form and Its Context in the Scottish Enlightenment (Edinburgh 1982) pp 201–61. Scotland was far ahead even in Sunday School education. G Dyer, The Complaints of the Poor People of England (London 1793) p 29 and Guy Kendall, Robert Raikes: A Critical Study of the Founder of the Sunday School (London 1939) p 94. The Glasgow method was suited to developing countries. See M A Laird, Missionaries and Education in Bengal 1793–1837 (Oxford 1972) pp 180–222
62   See R D Owen, An Outline: Amariah Brigham, Remarks on the Influence of Mental Cultivation and Mental Excitement Upon Health, with notes by R MacNich (London 1844 edn). On Mann the standard account is Jonathan Messerli, Horace Mann (New York 1971). John Dunmore Lang wanted a dozen teachers to take to Australia for his schemes
63   DNB and Edwin Hodder, Sir George Burns Bart, His Times and Friends (London 1890); James C Mohr, Abortion in America (New York 1978) p 8. The dates are for Glasgow publication
64   DNB:R Burns, Stevenson Macgill pp 291, 310–11
65   Life, Letters and Journal of George Ticknor (ed Anna Ticknor) 2 vols (London 1876) vol 1 pp 278, 282. qv supra and Alma Lutz Emma Willard Daughter of Democrary (Boston 1929) p 168. She was also associated with the American Colonisation Society pp 243–55
66   Like James Simpson for example who wished to leave the religious instruction to the individual religious groups
67   See James Murphy, The Religious Problem in English Education (Liverpool 1959)
68   cf Barbara Finkelstein, Pedagogy as Intrusion. See Note 23 above
69   James Simpson, Necessity of Popular Education as a National Object (Edinburgh 1843) p 43
70   ibid p 250
71   Glasgow Herald (24 Oct 1834). See James Murphy, The Religious Problem in English Education: The Crucial Experiment (Liverpool 1959) pp 37, 41, 144–6. J C Colquhoun, MP for Kilmarnock was the main opponent of these schemes. James Simpson wrote a rebuttal Anti-National Education or the Spirit of Sectarianism Morally Tested by means of certain speeches and letters of the member for Kilmarnock (Edinburgh 1837). On Thomas Wyse, Lady Noel Byron wrote Revd J Tuckerman 12 Sept 183? that he was 'the most judicious and capacious minded of all the philanthropists with whom I have had any intercourse. No one has

been more diligent in bringing forward evidence to prove that religious instruction may be given to all denominations of Christians without distinction in our parochial school.' Tuckerman Papers, Harvard-Amherst Collection. J J Auchmuty, Thomas Wyse (London 1939) is the only biography. It was a question which also posed difficulties for American national cohesion.

72   R Knox, The Races of Man (London 1850 edn) p 259

73   DAmB: J G Cogswell, On the Means of Education and the State of Learning in the USA, Blackwood's 4 (1818–19) 546–53 and On the State of Learning in the USA, pp 641–9. The quotes are on pp 547 and 647.

74   J G Cogswell, pp 644–6, 646 quote. Basil Hall, Travels in America, 3 vols (London 1829 edn). Mrs F Trollope, Domestic manners of the American, 2 vols (London 1832) vol 1 p 126 and vol 2 p 176; Isaac Fidler, Observations on Professions; Literature and Manners and Emigration in the United States and Canada made there during a residence there in 1832 (London 1833) pp 77–8, 81–2, were sceptical about the prospects for American education

75   See George Davie, The Democratic Intellect: Scotland and Her Universities in the Nineteenth Century (Edinburgh 1961) pp 3–25: Outlines of Philosophical Education (Glasgow 1825 edn) esp pp 404, 524; Theodore Dwight Bozeman, Inductive and Deductive Politics: Science and Society in Ante-Bellum Presbyterian Thought, Journal of American History 64 (1977–8) 704–22; Richard Olson, Scottish Philosophy and Mathematics, 1750–1830, Journal of the History of Ideas 32 (1971) 29–44. Also useful on this point, Christine Chapman Robbins, David Hossack: Citizen of New York (Philadelphia 1964) and Ernst Earnest, John and William Bartram (Philadelphia 1940) pp 166–79. Several Scots appear in the last book.

76   John Wood, Account of the Edinburgh Sessional School, (Edinburgh 1828) p 81

77   1778–1864, DNB; Principles of Elementary Teaching (Edinburgh 1828) and Contributions to the Cause of Education (London 1836) p 185

78   John Abercrombie, The Philosophy of Moral Feelings and his Inquiries concerning the Intellectual Powers and the Investigation of Truth (Edinburgh 1830); Thomas Dick, 1774–1857, DNB, and his On the Improvement of Society by the Diffusion of Knowledge (Edinburgh 1843). I am grateful to Dr J V Smith of Dundee University for his help

79   New York Review quoted in F L Mott, A History of American Magazines 1741–1850 (Cambridge Mass 1939) pp 487–88, also p 148. The Pickets, father and son went west to Cincinnati to establish the Western Literary Institute, an enterprise in which they associated with the Scottish author and teacher, Alexander Kinmont. His views were circulated in Glasgow by D G Goyder in the Phrenological Almanac (Glasgow 1846), Address before the College of Professional Teachers Cincinnati, pp 41–60. Also see R C Buley, The Old North West, 2 vols (Bloomington Indiana 1951) vol 2 pp 379–82. Report of the Commissioner of Education 1898–9 (Washington DC 1900) vol 2 pp 2263–470 carries a detailed survey of the beginning of normal schools.

80   Russell has usually been neglected by American historians of education. Paul H Mattingly, The Classless Profession: American Schoolmen in the Nineteenth Century (New York 1975) is an important exception, though the older William S. Monroe, History of the Pestalozzian Movement in the United States (New York 1969 edn) has several mentions. Judge McPherson Berrien was the patron of the first library in Savannah, a staunch states rights politician who eventually gravitated to the Nativist party. See E M Coulter, A Short History of Georgia (Chapel Hill 1933) and J H Broussard, The Southern Federalists 1800–1816 (Baton Rouge 1978)

81   Suggestions on Education relating particularly to the Method of Instructing Commonly Adopted in Geography, History, Logic and the Classics (New Haven 1823). See Henry Barnard, Normal Schools and Other Institutes, Agencies and Means Designed for the Professional Education of Teachers (Hartford Conn 1851) 2 vols in one. And Richard Emmons Thrusfield, Henry Barnard's American Journal of Education (Baltimore 1945) pp 31, 45, 87, 99, 123, 130, 188

82   See American Journal of Education (1826); Odell Shepard, Pedlar's Progress: The Life of Bronson Alcott (London 1938) p 122. The Phrenological Journal 7 (1831–2) 165–75 gives a full report on the Germantown school. For their correspondence see the Letters of Bronson Alcott, ed R L Herrnstadt (Ames Iowa 1969)

83   Quoted in F B Sanborn and F T Harris, A Bronson Alcott: His Life and Philosophy, 2 vols (London 1893) vol 1 p 159

84   See Address on Infant Schools delivered at the Request of the Managers of the Infant School Society (Boston 1829). It has all the Pestalozzian hallmarks with the practices of Stow. W S Monroe, History of Pestalozzianism, p 130; Jonathan Messerli, Horace Mann (New York 1972) pp 244–51 show Mann influenced by Brougham, James Simpson and the American Journal of Education. William Russell to F Parkman 6 Jan 1868, Parkman Papers, Massachusetts Historical Society Boston. Among those who attended the American Institute of Instruction and closely followed Scottish development was Henry Clarke Wright 1797–1870. He was to spend considerable time in Glasgow lecturing on abolitionism, peace and other millenarian pursuits. Lewis Perry, Childhood, Marriage and Refom; Henry Clarke Wright, 1797–1870 (Chicago 1980)

85   Quoted by H R Warfel, Noah Webster (New York 1936) p 182

86   W Russell, Address on Infant School, p 9. Also see Stow's remarks to Alexander D Bache in several meetings in Glasgow, Bache's Journal 1836–7

87   W Russell, Harper's New York Class Book (New York 1844) p iv. Also see Ruth Miller Elson, American Schoolbooks and 'Culture' in the Nineteenth Century, Mississippi Valley Historical Review 46 (1959–60) 411–34

88   See F and M L Wayland, A Memoir of the Life and Labours of Francis Wayland, DD, LLD, 2 vols (New York 1867) vol 1 pp 205–11 and vol 2 pp 334–6; Francis Wayland, Thoughts on the Present Collegiate System in the United States (Boston 1842); The President of the University of Michigan, Henry Philip Tappan also visited Scotland. Charles M Perry, Henry Philip Tappan: Philosopher and University President (Ann Arbor 1933) pp 142–50. Also see D H Meyer, The Instructed Conscience, pp 13–14

89   John Maclean, A Memoir of John Maclean the First Professor of Chemistry in the College of New Jersey (Princeton 1885); A Lecture on a School System for New Jersey (Princeton 1829); his son John Maclean wrote History of the College of New Jersey from its Origin in 1746 to the commencement of 1854, 2 vols (Philadelphia 1877). The copy in Glasgow University Library is his presentation copy. Also see Nelson R Burr, Education in New Jersey, pp 120, 220–70. Anna Lou Blair, Henry Barnard p 40. W McGavin, The Protestant (Glasgow 1818–19) was widely reprinted in the USA. Wilbur Fisk, Travels in Europe (New York 1838) pp 645–6. Fisk was the President of Wesleyan University, McGavin's Sunday School talks will be found in the Library of Congress Catalogue. R Baird, Religion in the United States had an introduction welcoming the work from Professor David Welsh, W. Cunningham and R Buchanan

90   See P H Mattingly, The Classless Profession, pp 84–112; W E Channing, Treatise on Self-Culture (Edinburgh 1839) p 78; S L Jackson, America's Struggle for Free Schools: Social Tension and Education in New England and New York 1827–1942 (Washington DC 1941) p 23

91   W Russell, On Associations of Teachers: An Address delivered at a meeting held in Dorchester on Wednesday 8 Sept for the Purpose of Forming an Association of Teachers for Norfolk County, Boston 1830 and his Address at the Dedication and Opening of the New England Normal Institute at Lancaster, Mass, Wednesday 11 May 1853, Boston 1853. These ideas reflected D Stow, Moral Training (Glasgow 1834) pp 10–43 and The Training System (London 1853 edn) pp 123–34. Also John Gordon, Report on the Deficiencies of Elementary Education in Scotland (Edinburgh 1845) pp 372–3 and W E Channing, Lectures on the Education of the Labouring Portion of the Community (Boston 1840) pp 69, 71. Anne L Kuhn, The Mother's Role in Childhood Education: New England Concepts 1830–1860 (New Haven 1947) p 59 and Kathryn Kish Sklar, Catherine Beecher, p 81

92   W Russell, Address on Infant Schools, pp 14–15

93   Quoted in Ruth Miller Elson, 'American Schoolbooks and Culture', pp 418–19. The Library of Congress Catalogue shows numerous editions of Russell's textbooks

94   Common School Journal 5 (1843) 15 Dec 1843

95   Common School Journal (1 Oct 1841) quoting 5th Report of the Glasgow Education Society Normal Seminary. The Connecticut School Journal (1 July 1840) pp 253–6 discusses Glasgow High School and Glasgow Educational Society.

96   S L Jackson, America's Struggle for Free Schools p 23

97   See for example R Doherty Society and Power: Five New England Towns 1800–60 (Amherst 1977) p 81. The classic works in this now considerable literature are by Stephan Thernstrom Poverty and Progress: Social Mobility in a Nineteenth Century City (Cambridge

Mass 1963) and The Other Bostonians: Poverty and Progress in the American Metropolis 1880–1970 (Cambridge Mass 1973). Such ideas were even more pronounced in the late nineteenth and early twentieth century America.

98   Anna Lou Blair, Henry Barnard, pp 38–40, 50, 93 for the influence of Brougham's rectorial address and other Scottish influences

99   See the considerable correspondence of W Russell with Barnard in Barnard Papers, New York University, New York. W Russell, Suggestions On Teachers' Institutes (Boston 1848); H. Barnard, Object Teaching and Oral Lessons on Social Science and Common Things, 2nd series (New York 1860) reprinted from the American Journal of Education, 21–48, 57, 91, 294–320. The first series includes W Russell, Intellectual Education, pp 11–156 P H Mattingly The Classless Profession has numerous references to Barnard

100   cf H Barnard, Normal Schools and Other Institutions, 2 vols in one

101   See the W Russell, H Barnard correspondence 1841–56, and P H Mattingly, The Classless Profession, passim

102   American Journal of Education (March 1826) pp 134–44, 'Mechanics Institutes'; Grammar School of Glasgow (Sept 1826) pp 571–2; Parish Schools of Scotland (Dec 1827) pp 712–20. Russell as already noted had published Alcott's translation of Pestalozzi in 1827. On Vaux see DAmB and Phyllis Dain, the New York Public Library: A History of Its Founding and Early Years (New York 1972) pp 10–11

103   Quoted S E Ahlstrom, A Religious History of the American People (New Haven 1972) p 416: See Charles Roy Keller. The Second Great Awakening in Connecticut (New Haven 1942) is a standard account. Other aspects are covered in numerous studies including Niels Henry Sonne, Liberal Kentucky 1780 (New York 1939) and R A Billington, The Protestant Crusade 1800–1860 (New York 1964 edn)

104   See DNB, DAmB and biographical list: Sheila Marriner, Rathbones of Liverpool (Liverpool 1961) pp 3–12; W H Channing, Life of Channing; Stephen Nissenbaum, Sex, Diet and Debility in Jacksonian America; Sylvester Graham and Health Reform (Westport Conn 1980) p 8. Significantly the health crusade was in keeping with William Maclure's ideas. Asahel Nettleton who toured Scotland in 1831–2 appears in W B Sprague, Annals of the American Pulpit, 8 vols (New York 1857–65) vol 2, pp 542–54. Interestingly Sprague had a Glasgow graduate mininstering in the Albany presbytery; J D Lang, Religion and Education in America p 8. Lang also met Alexander D Bache and other figures in his travels

105   DNB. Also see David Murray, Members of the Old College of Glasgow (Glasgow 1927) p 247; Dugald J Bannatyne, Andrew Bannatyne and his wife Ann Stirling (Glasgow (1896); Hedderwick had intended to settle near Albany New York but returned to Glasgow to enter into printing and newspapers. See James and Robert Hedderwick in The Bailie (21 Dec 1887, 8 July 1894): James Hedderwick, Backward Glances (Edinburgh 1891). He was associated with Kossuth, Louis Blanc and Gavazzi.

106   Life, Letters and Journals of George Ticknor, 2 vols (London 1876) vol I pp 274–82, 325, 393 and vol 2 pp 153–65

107   P H Mattingly, The Classless Profession p 125

108   Letters and Extracts from the Manuscript Writings of James Pierrepoint Greaves (ed Alexander Campbell) 2 vols in one (Ham Common Surrey 1843) vol 1 p 89. Greaves recommended Alexander Kinmont's The Natural History of Man (Cincinnati 1839) qv supra. Charles Badham 1789–1845 became Regius Professor of Surgery at Glasgow in 1827. His son Charles, 1813–84, after eduction with Pestalozzi and at Eton eventually became Professor of Classics in the University of Sydney 1867–84. His brother David, 1806–57, became a doctor then entered the Church and wrote for Blackwood's and Fraser's. W Anderson Smith, Shepherd Smith, The Universalist (London 1892); Alexander Cullen, Adventures in Socialism (Glasgow 1910) on Alex Campbell.

109   Quoted in W H G Armytage, Heavens Below p 178; see also F B Sanborn, Bronson Alcott at Alcott House and Fruitlands New England 1842–4 (Cedar Rapids 1908) and W H G Armytage 'Alcott House: An Anglo-American Educational Experiment, Educational Theory 8 (1958) 129–42

110   John D Davies, Phrenology, Fad and Science: A Nineteenth Century American Crusade (New York 1971 edn); Madeleine B. Stern, Heads and Headlines: The Phrenological Fowlers (Norman Oklahoma 1971); T M Parssinien, Popular Science and Society: The Phrenology Movement in Early Victorian Britain, Victorian Studies 8 (1974–5) 1–20; R E Riegel, 'The

Introduction of Phrenology to the United States, American Historical Review 39 (1928–9) 73–8
111   On Dr Caldwell, DAmB, on MacNish 1802–37 see D M Moir, The Modern Pythagorean: A series of Tales, Essays and Sketches by the late Robert MacNish LL D 2 vols (Edinburgh 1838). Also see below
112   Phrenological Journal 5 (1829) 161–2. 250 attended the public lectures and some 60 doctors the professional specialist addresses: 6(1830) 418–20: 12(1839) 295 for report of 13 Nov 1838
113   A Brigham, 1798–1849 became superintendent of the Connecticut Asylum, Hartford then the New York Asylum 1842–7 and established the American Journal of Insanity in 1844. R MacNish, An Introduction to Phrenology in the Form of Questions and Answers (Boston 1836). With James Simpson, MacNish edited Brigham's book and sold over 1000 copies in six weeks in 1836 in Glasgow. D M Moir, vol 1 pp 127, 354
114   M B Stern, pp 28–9; John D Davies, Phrenology pp 74, 83, and Phrenological Journal 14 (1841) 51–3
115   DNB: Combe lectured in Glasgow in 1825 Phrenological Journal 2 (1825) 158–9. James Simpson, Hints on the Formation and Conduct of a General Model Normal School (Edinburgh nd); The Philosophy of Education (Edinburgh (Edinburgh 1836) p 205, Dumfries, p 264 Manchester and Liverpool, 13 lectures in each on alternate days
116   ibid p 196
117   ibid pp 134, 201, It began after the American Annals of Education
118   ibid p 208, also pp 206, 235–6 and his Hints, p 8
119   R Cunningham 1799–1883 b Stranraer, educated at Edinburgh University, licensed Haddington 1825 but never held charge, attached to George Watson's 1827–32, when he founded his Edinburgh Institution; married Elizabeth Jeffrey; at Easton Pa 1837–9; Glasgow Normal School to 1843 then Blair Lodge Polmont for a decade (now the site of a Borstal Institution), minister in charge of Polmont 1843–6 holding services in the classroom; seat in presbytery to 1851; lived in Edinburgh until 1859 then returned to Stranraer to his death in 1883. Corresponded with Barnard 4 July 1839; nd and 29 Oct 1852, 24, 30 Mar, 14 Nov 1853, 2 June, 20 Aug 1855. (Barnard Papers) Obituary in Free Church Magazine (1883)
120   Cunningham, Report on the Studies Pursued in the Edinburgh Institute for Languages, Mathematics and c. submitted to the parents of pupils 30 July 1835 (Edinburgh 1835) p 4. John Griscom, A Year in Europe, vol 2 pp 402–4: Mirror with some account of the New York High School; Society for the Prevention of Pauperism, p 284. 'R C' was described as a pupil (teacher?) of Dr Pillans
121   Connecticut School Journal (Aug 1839); The Educator (Apr 1838–Aug 1839). I am indebted to the Librarian of Easton College for his help
122   Educator (30 July, 17, 31 Dec 1838): R Cunningham, Thoughts on The Question Whether Normal Seminaries Ought to be Distinct Establishments or Ingrafted on Colleges, Being the Inaugural Address on his Inauguration as Professor of Ancient Languages in Lafayette College, Pa. January 11 1838 (Philadelphia 1838) p 5; David Bishop Stillman, The Biography of a College Being the History of the First Centenary of the Life of Lafayette College, 2 vols (Easton Pa 1932) vol 1 pp 50–1, 118–19
123   Thoughts on the Question pp 6–27. Cunningham urged state grants for intending teachers with accommodation well paid for qualified teachers
124   R Cunningham, Education in the USA, Free Church Education Journal no 3 (1848) 35–7. Also see his other articles some of which are signed 'R. C.' no 1 3–6 no 5 69–72 and 136–9
125   George Combe, Notes on the United States of America during a Phrenological Visit 1838–40, 3 vols (Edinburgh 1841) vol 3 pp 443, 450; R Cunningham to H Barnard, 4 July 1839, nd, 1852, 29 Oct 1852, 30 Mar 1853, Barnard Papers. He sent Barnard copies of the Educator and reviewed Barnard's work in the Witness.
126   15 Jan 1842. The editor was H Barnard F L Mott, A History pp 694–5
127   MS Journal of Horace Mann 22 June 1843, Mann Papers, Massachusetts Historical Society, Boston. The Mann Papers were unavailable when I was writing so I am grateful to Mrs Nina D Wyatt Donald of Antioch College Ohio for a copy. Lydia H Sigourney, Pleasant Memories (New York 1856 edn) pp 96–8 visited the Normal School and was suitably impressed by Cunningham. She contributed to The Glasgow Infant School Repository. There

were also Glasgow Infant School Magazine and Glasgow Infant School Instructor. They combined sample lessons with poems songs and uplifting thoughts. Also see Harold Schwartz, Samuel Gridley Howe, Social Reformers 1801–1876 (Cambridge Mass 1956) p 146. Howe had previously taken an Edinburgh man to help him in his institution for the blind.
128   Horace Mann, Second Annual Report (Boston 1868 edn) p 281. That may be related to his views on Bible training and those practised in Scotland. Raymond B Culver, Horace Mann and Religion in the Massachusetts Public Schools (New Haven 1929) and Michael B Katz, The Irony of Early School Reform (Cambridge Mass 1968)
129   A J D Dorsey to George Combe, Combe Papers, National Library of Scotland correspondence: Dorsey's father's name appears in the Glasgow Directory in the 1820s as a coal agent. Significantly Haunchwood House adjoined a coalmine and brickworks by Nuneaton. I am grateful to Mr M W Farr, the Warwick Record Office for information on Haunchwood House. Later the father seems to have run a coffee house. See also Glasgow University Matriculation Album 1830
130   Glasgow Herald (11 Oct 1833; 20, 24 Oct, 17 Nov 1834, 25 Dec 1835). From July to Dec the paper carried many adverts for Dorsey's classes. Dorsey went from 6 Croy Place 1830–1, Glasgow Directory to 1832–3, West Nile Street 1833–4, 32 Dunlop Street 1835–6, 96 Regent Terrace: Dalbeth House 1846–7; 1850–1 9 Claremount Terrace; 1851–2 2 New Terrace; 1852–3 2 Kew Terrace
131   Phrenological Journal 12 (1839) 191; 14 (1841) 51–3 Dorsey addressed the third annual Phrenological Association Meeting in Glasgow in September 1840
132   Phrenological Journal 12 (1839) 191
133   ibid
134   Glasgow Herald (27 July 1835) and A D Bache, Journal (Dec 1835). Jan 1836, Dorsey played the harp for his guest
135   Phrenological Journal 10 (1836–7) 385 lecturing in Forfar; 9 (1834–5) 570; 10 (1836–7) 384; 12 (1839) 191; 13 (1840) 186–7; 14 (1841) 51; Glasgow Herald 29 May, 6, 16 Nov, 18 Dec 1935); 1 July 1836 Cowgate Edinburgh; 7, 14 Nov 1836. His resignation is in 12 June 1835; Post Office Directory 1835–6 notes Dorsey as lecturer at Anderston, Bridgeton, Mile End and Calton Mechanics Institutes. He later return in 1840–1 to give 12 lectures with others at Calton. Also see J Smith, Our Scottish Clergy, 2nd series (Edinburgh 1849) pp 359–68 for a description of Dorsey's preaching
136   Bache, Journal; M L Walker, St John's Episcopal Church Cranstonhill 1850–1950 Centenary Brochure (Glasgow 1950). A J D Dorsey, Education in Madeira Prospectus (nd, np) in Mitchell Library; S George West, Alexander J D Dorsey 1812–94, Biblos 51 (1975) 173–82. I am indebted to Dr Harry Ashmall for this last item
137   Lucretia Mott Journal 1840, Lucretia Mott Papers, Swarthmore College, Pennsylvania. She and her husband went with an introduction from George Combe. Alexander D Bache, Journal, Dec 1836–Jan 1837
138   Prenological Journal 12 (1839) 295 and 19 (1846) 81: D G Goyder, A Treatise on the Management of Infant Schools (London 1826) and a Biographical Sketch of the Life of Revd Thomas Goyder, Minister of the New Church Ipswich (London 1850); he also edited The Magazine of Popular Information on Capital and Secondary Punishments (Glasgow 1846) I have been unable to trace any copies. I am grateful to Mrs C P Dawson of the Swedenborgian Society, London for full biographical information
139   Phrenological Journal 14 (1841) 51–3; 16 (1843) 19, 27 and 15 (1842) 383–4
140   ibid and C Mayo, Memoir of Pestalozzi (London 1828) p 27
141   1 Nov, 25 May 1837 Alexander D Bache, Journal. He also met Revd Mr Yates, the former Glasgow Unitarian minister, 1789–1871, Mr Smith of Jordanhill and many other local figures
142   Bache, Journal, 30 Dec 1835
143   ibid 19 Dec 1836
144   ibid 30 Dec 1836
145   ibid 12 Jan 1837
146   ibid 29 Dec 1836
147   ibid
148   ibid 10 Jan, Simpson; 3 Feb, Pillans; 16 Jan, Wood; 13 Jan, Combes; 18 Jan, Chambers. He also met Lord Cockburn and Mrs Grant of Laggan

149   Carl Bode, The American Lyceum: Town Meeting of the Mind, (Carbondale Ill 1968 edn) pp 118–19
150   Henry Brougham, Inaugural Discourse on Being Installed Lord Rector of the University of Glasgow (Glasgow 1825) p 46
151   ibid pp 49, 50. Brougham also claimed that Glasgow had been responsible for encouraging the formation of mechanics libraries and institutes in Boston, Philadelphia, Albany and New Orleans. The Franklin Institute of Philadelphia had sent visitors to Glasgow's Institute
152   Thomas Kelly, George Birkbeck: Pioneer of Adult Education, (Liverpool 1957) pp 20, 36, and 56–75 Also see the appendix on the Glasgow graduate Granville Sharp Pattison, pp 282–3. He later taught in the USA
153   H Brougham, Practical Considerations Upon Education of the People (London 1825), pp 2–18. The institution was controlled by its members. As one British Observer said, 'The education of a free people, like their property, will always be directed more beneficially for them when it is in their own hands. When government interferes it directs its efforts more to make people obedient and docile than wise and happy. Man had better be without education so called for nature herself teaches us many valuable truths than be educated by their rulers.' T Hodgskin quoted in E Halevy Thomas Hodgskin (London 1956) p 86
154   American Journal of Education (1826) pp 134–44; Carl Bode, The American Lyceum, pp 5–18; W Beattie, and Letters of Thomas Campbell, 3 vols (London 1849) vol I, pp 23–7. He had nearly emigrated to join his relatives in Virginia, one was married to a daughter of Patrick Henry. On Holbrook see biographical list
155   Carl Bode, The American Lyceum, pp 22–6 and P H M Mattingly, The Classless Profession, pp 8–43
156   N R Burr, Education in New Jersey, p 263; James Lauder, The Glasgow Athenaeum: A Sketch of Fifty Years Work (Glasgow 1897) p 77; 1848–9 Programme in Essex Historical Society Salem Massachusetts
157   A D Bache, Journal, 19 Dec 1836; F Wayland, Thoughts on the Present Collegiate System in the United States (Boston 1842) p 129
158   F and M L Wayland, A Memoir, vol II p 44
159   J M Duncan, Travels Through Part of the United States and Canada in 1818 and 1819 (Glasgow 1823) pp 125–80, 154
160   David J Rothman, The Discovery of the Asylum: Social Order and Disorder in the New Republic (Boston 1971). On Glasgow see Thomas Ferguson, The Dawn of Scottish Welfare (London 1948). Also for example Wilbur Fisk, op cit p 647
161   P Colquhoun, Treatise on Indigence (London 1806) pp 110–38. Also see Frank Dekker Watson, The Charity Organisation Movement in the United States (New York 1922) pp 27–38
162   Orlando F Lewis, The Development of American Prisons and Reformation (New York 1896) pp 16–154; R Burns, Stevenson Macgill 46; Max Grunhut, Penal Reform a Comparative Study (Oxford 1948) p 71; but see H Barnard, Papers on Preventive, Correctional and Reformatory Institutions and Agencies in Different Countries (Hartford Conn 1857) pp 343–7
163   F H Wines, Punishment, p 154. Also see Blake McKelvey, American Prisons: A Study in American Social History Prior to 1915 (Chicago 1936) pp 6–11. Horace Mann and S G Howe visited European but not Scottish prisons. S G Howe, An Essay on Separate and Congregate Systems of Prison Discipline being a Report to the Boston Prison Discipline Society (Boston 1846)
164   Phrenological Journal 4 (1827) 560. 559–66 on the Glasgow Bridewell. W. Brebner, A letter to the Lord Provost on the Expediency of a House of Refuge for Juvenile Offenders (Glasgow 1829); J Griscom, A Year in Europe, vol 2 p 410; Samuel L Knapp, The Life of Thomas Eddy (New York 1834). Eddy corresponded with P Colquhoun and W Roscoe of Liverpool
165   Nathaniel C Carter, Letters from Europe Comprising the Journal of a Tour Through Ireland, England, France, Italy and Switzerland in the Years 1825, 1826 and 1827, 2 vols (New York 1829) vol 1 p 255. See A D Bache, Journal, 29 Dec 1836 for scathing comments on Baillie Alston: 'This is a peculiar man full of happiness and self esteem; overflowing with the milk of human kindness; fond of approbation and especially that of Baillie Alston'
166   Randal W MacGavock, A Tennessean Abroad (New York 1854) p 95
167   J M Duncan, Travels vol 2 p 324 and Isabella Graham. See biographical list

168   Quoted in Dorothy Clarke Wilson, Stranger and Traveller: The Story of Dorothea Dix (Boston 1975) p 221: 'No country ever exceeded Scotland in the grossness of its superstition and the unhappy consequence which flowed from it'
169   Sir William Jardine, Life of Alexander Wilson, pp 17–50; Wilson taught elocution to the renowned American actor, Edwin Forrest; Richard Moody, Edwin Forrest (New York 1960) p 16; W R Alger, Life of Edwin Forrest, 2 vols (New York 1877) vol 1 pp 57–8, 294, 409; C L Bonaparte, American Ornithology, 3 vols (London 1837) vol 1 pp ix–cvii; W Maclure, Observations on the Geology of the United States (Philadelphia 1817); G P Fisher, Life of Benjamin Silliman, passim; C Bode, American Lyceum p 8; W Wilks (ed), Journal Kept by David Douglas During His Travels in North America 1823–1827 (London 1914)
170   Thomas Hamilton, Men and Manners in America (Edinburgh 1843 edn) p 50; Orville Dewey, Works (London 1844) p 617; J D Burn, Three Years Among the Working Class in the United States During the War (London 1865) p 168
171   A Bronson Alcott to W Russell, in Letters (ed R L Herrnstadt) pp 426–7. The Journal of Speculative Philosophy has numerous articles by W T Harris and Thomas Davidson
172   J David Hoeveler Jr, James McCosh and the Scottish Intellectual Tradition (Princeton 1981) pp 31–2. J H Vincent, the architect of the popular Chatauqua education movement, spent some time in Glasgow and greatly admired Professor Henry Drummond. Leon H Vincent, John Heyl Vincent (New York 1925) pp 58, 153
173   Patricia Hollis, The Pauper Press; A Study in Working Class Radicalism of the 1830 (London 1970) p 6. Compare with Thomas Wyse, Education Reform, London 1836, 386 where he claims the Glasgow unemployed have shown much can be endured and how well. What other community ever exhibited such temper and patience and under such conditions more striking than in those very towns where education is most advanced'
174   Patricia Hollis, The Pauper Press, p 9

CHAPTER THREE

1   qv supra
2   See above and also Joanna Baillie to B Tuckerman 28 Mar 1838, Tuckerman Papers. J P Grant (ed), Memoir and Correspondence of Mrs Grant of Laggan 3 vols (London 1844); Miss Berryer, Memoirs of Elizabeth Hamilton 2 vols (London 1818)
3   New York 1832 edn
4   T Currie Gregory, On Street Railways, Proceedings Philosophical Society of Glasgow 5 (1860–4) 41–50
5   See Peggy Chambers, A Doctor Alone; A Biography of Elizabeth Blackwell, The First Woman Doctor 1821–1910 (np, nd); Ishbel Ross Child of Destiny: The Life Story of the First Woman Doctor (London 1950): Rachel Baker, The First Doctor: The Story of Elizabeth Blackwell M D (London 1946). Her autobiography in the Everyman Library edition remains indispensable
6   The Religion of Health published Edinburgh 1878
7   ibid pp 10–11
8   Essays on Medical Sociology, 2 vols (London 1902) vol 2 p 181
9   See the Blackwell Papers, Schlesinger Library, Radcliffe College USA, Cambridge Mass
10   See E J Dingwall's introduction to Emma Hardinge Modern American Spiritualism, (New York 1970 edn (1870))
11   See Medium and Day Break (27 Oct 1892, 3 Aug, 7 Sept, 1894, 22 Mar 1895)
12   Theosophy in Scotland (Nov 1910, Nov 1913). Anna Howard Shaw, Memoirs of a Pioneer (New York 1911), claimed Scottish descent and had visited Glasgow
13   On this point see Logie Barrow, Socialism in Eternity: The Ideology of Plebian Spiritualists 1853–1913, History Workshop Journal 9(1980) 37–69
14   See her Sunny Memories of Sunny Lands (London 1854); Charles Edward Stowe, Life of Harriet Beecher Stowe (London 1889) pp 210, 213; F J Klingberg, Harriet Beecher Stowe and Social Reform in England, American Historical Review 43 (1937–8) 542–52; George Shepperson, Harriet Beecher Stowe and Scotland, SHR 32 (1953) 40–6. His other articles provide important background, The Free Church and American Slavery, SHR 30 (1951)

126–43 and Thomas Chalmers, The Free Church of Scotland and the South, Journal of Southern History 17 (1951) 517–37
15 Sunny Memories, pp 144–150 and SHR 32 (1953) 43
16 See C Duncan Rice, The Scots Abolitionists 1833–1861 (Baton Rogue 1981) 80–115
17 See Memoranda of Visit 1840, Lucretia Mott, Mott Papers, Swarthmore College, Pennsylvania; also printed version F B Tolles (ed), Slavery and the 'Woman Question': Lucretia Mott's Diary of her Visit to Great Britain to attend the World's Anti-Slavery Convention of 1840, Journal of the Friends Historical Society (1952); J Mott, Three Months in Great Britain (Philadelphia 1841)
18 Lucretia Mott Memoranda
19 Lucretia Mott Memoranda
20 See Aileen Kraditor, Means and Ends in American Abolitionism: Garrison and his Critics of Strategy and Tactics 1834–1850 (New York 1969) and L. Perry, Radical Abolitionism; Anarchy and the Government of God in Anti-Slavery Thought (Ithaca New York 1973)
21 See Duncan Rice, Scottish Abolitionists, pp 105–8
22 E P Nichol to Lucretia Mott, 20 Dec 1880 and L Mott to E P Nichol, Mott Papers
23 Angelina Grimké to E Pease, 14 Aug 1839; E C Stanton to E Pease 12 Feb 1842, Pease Collection. Also see Clare Taylor, British and American Abolitionists: An Episode in British and American Understanding (Edinburgh 1974) esp pp 11–12, 54–63; Christine Bolt, The Anti-Slavery Movement and Reconstruction: A Study in Anglo-American Co-operation 1833–1877 (London 1969)
24 1804–59
25 Pease Collection, Boston Public Library
26 qv infra; J Nichol, History of American Literature (London 1882)
27 Historical Sketch of Salem Lyceum (Salem 1879) p 49
28 W L Garrison to E P Nichol 22 Feb 1859, Pease Collection; J P Nichol to E Everett 4, 18 Jan 1848, Everett Papers, Massachusetts Historical Society, Boston
29 J P and Elizabeth P Nichol to Garrison, 9 May 1854 sending the University of Glasgow Album with their son's poems. 51, 327, Garrison Paper; J Nichol to W L Garrison,—Aug 1872, ibid; F Douglass to E Pease 11 Mar, Mar 1847, 8 Nov 1849, Pease Collection
30 J Nichol to Garrison, Aug 1872, Garrison Papers
31 W L Garrison to E P Nichol, 9 Oct 1865, Pease Collection, and W Knight, Memoir of John Nichol (Glasgow 1896) pp 271, 275
32 1815–1902
33 Theodore Stanton and Harriet S Blatch, Elizabeth Cady Stanton, 2 vols (New York 1922) vol 1 pp 18–23
34 ibid p 98
35 Elizabeth C Stanton to Susan B Anthony, 1 Mar 1853 quoted in Stanton and Blatch vol 2 p 29. On the background see Eleanor Flexner, Century of Struggle (Cambridge Mass 1966); Alan P Grimes, The Puritan Ethic and Woman Suffrage (New York 1967); Andrew Sinclair, The Better Half (London 1967); Aileen S Kraditor, The Ideas of the Woman Suffrage Movement 1890–1920 (New York 1967); Ross Evans Paulson, Woman's Suffrage and Prohibition: A Comparative Study of Equality and Social Control (Glencoe Illinois 1973); William L O'Neill, Everyone was Brave; The Rise and Fall of Feminism (Chicago 1969) p 224; Constance Rover, Love, Morals and the Feminists (London 1970); C Smith-Rosenberg and Charles Rosenberg, The Female Animal: Medical and Biological Views of Woman and Her Role in Nineteenth Century America, Journal of American History 60 (1973) 332–56, in the large and growing literature.
36 Stanton and Blatch, vol 11 p 70
37 ibid and later Charlotte Perkins Gilman, see note 77 below
38 Jane Addams, A New Conscience and An Ancient Evil (New York 1911) and Mark Thomas Connelly, The Response to Prostitution in the Progressive Era (Chapel Hill 1980)
39 ibid pp 95–6
40 cf William Logan, The Great Social Evil (London 1871 edn) Fernando Henriques Modern Sexuality (London 1968), vol 3 of Prostitution and Society: pp 144–9; part of Oscar Slater's problems stemmed from his association with the demi-monde of Glasgow
41 See my own Social Catholicism and Health: Dr and Mrs Thomas Low Nichols, pp 249–70 in Studies in Church History 19 (Oxford 1982); James C Whorton, Tempest in a Flesh Pot; The

Formulation of a Physiological Rationale for Vegetarianism pp 315–330 in Sickness and Health in America: Readings in the History of Medicine and public Health (eds Judith Walzer Leavitt and Ronald L Numbers) (Madison Wisconsin 1978)

42 qv supra and Madeleine B Stern, Heads and Headliners: The Phrenological Fowlers (Norman Oklahoma 1971), pp 45, 193

43 Commonwealth, 26 July 1865. See also J Metcalfe, Memoir of William Metcalfe (Philadelphia 1866)

44 cf Gwendolyn Wright, Moralism and the Model Home (Chicago, 1980) esp ch 5, Model Housewives and Model Homes, pp 150–71; Dolores Hayden, The Grand Domestic Revolution: A History of Feminist Designs for American Houses, Neighbourhoods and Cities (Cambridge Mass 1981) esp ch 9, Charlotte Perkins Gilman pp 183–205; W L O'Neill, Divorce in the Progressive Era (New York 1973 edn, originally New Haven 1967); John Spargo, The Bitter Cry of the Children, (Chicago 1968 edn (1906)); Lawrence J Pivar, Purity Crusade: Sexual Morality and Social Control 1868–1900 (Westport Conn 1973)

45 cf Anti-Saloon Yearbook (1910) p 238. Gladden was a vice president of the League. Also F C Howe Confessions of a Reformer (Chicago 1969 edn)

46 G Stanley Hall, Adolescence, 2 vols (London 1894) vol 2 p 579

47 Daniel Scott Smith, Family Limitation, Sexual Control and Domestic Feminism in Victorian America, Feminist Studies 1 (1973) 40–57

48 See for example J R Commons, Races and Immigrants in America (New York 1907). Arnold White, The Destitute Alien in Great Britain (London 1892), showed a similar concern in Britain

49 'Mother' Eliza Daniel Stewart, The Crusader in Great Britain, (Springfield Ohio 1893) passim

50 C E Dilke, Greater Britain (London 1879 edn)

51 Mrs E C Stanton to Harriet Stanton Blatch, Saturday morning nd, Elizabeth Cady Stanton Papers, Library of Congress, Washington DC, Glasgow Herald (4 Nov 1882) gives scant attention to the speech

52 1846–1911. Her tour was marked by frequent disturbances

53 See Glasgow Herald (Dec 1908–Jan 1909) and Herbert Asbury, Carry Nation (New York 1929)

54 Ida Husted Harper, The History of Woman Suffrage, vol 6 pp 238–43, 405, 689

55 Theodore Stanton (ed), The Woman Question in Europe: A Series of Original Essays (London 1884) p ix acknowledges the aid of Mrs Lorna Maclaren of Edinburgh

56 Elizabeth Cady Stanton, Susan B Anthony and Matilda Joslyn Gage, History of Women Suffrage, vol 4 pp 84, 124

57 ibid vol 6 pp 805–62

58 Helen Marshall, Dorothea Dix (Chapel Hill 1937) pp 161–4

59 David J Rothman, The Discovery of the Asylum: Social Order and Disorder in the New Republic (Boston 1971) 240–52

60 E C Wines, The Insane Hospitals of Europe, National Conference on Charities and Correction 6 (1879) 59–73, and F B Sanborn, Public Charities in Europe, 18(1891) 167–86

61 Julia C Lathrop, Village Care for the Insane, National Conference 29 (1902) 185–99. The essay was republished as a book (Boston 1902)

62 Mrs Henrietta O W Barnett, Life of Samuel Barnett, 2 vols (London 1918)

63 1860–1935. See Alan F Davis, American Heroine: The Life and Times of Jane Addams (New York 1973) and David Levine, Jane Addams and the Liberal Tradition (Madison Wis 1971)

64 Jane Addams, letter 30 Sept 1883, Jane Addams Papers, University of Illinois Chicago Circle Campus

65 ibid The Palmer House was *the* Chicago hotel

66 ibid

67 C Lasch (ed), The Social Thought of Jane Addams (Indianapolis 1969) p 24

68 cf her Twenty Years at Hull House (New York 1910). On Chicago and Jane Addams see T L Philpott, The Slum and the Ghetto: Neighbourhood Deterioration and Middle Class Reform, Chicago 1880–1930 (New York 1978) pp 7–100; John C Farrell, Beloved Lady: A History of Jane Addams' Ideas on Reform and Peace (Baltimore 1967)

69 Jane Addams et al, Philanthropy and Social Progress (New York 1893) p 86

70   R A Woods to Jane Addams, 5 May 1893, Jane Addams Papers, Swarthmore College, Pennsylvania

71   F H Stead to Jane Addams, 24 Apr 16, 20 May 1896, Jane Addams Papers, Swarthmore College

72   George Hooker, Chicago to Mr Maclehose, Glasgow, letter of introduction, Jane Addams Papers

73   G E Hooker to Mrs Kerr, Edinburgh, 27 Apr 1896; G E Hooker to Alderman W White, Birmingham, 27 Apr 1896, Jane Addams Papers

74   Ellen Gates Starr to C Rowley, 22 Apr 1896, Jane Addams Papers

75   Philanthropy and Social Progress, p 96

76   See the papers presented at the Twenty-Third Meeting of the National Conference on Correction and Charities 1902, Katherine Bennet Davis, Civic Efforts of Social Settlements, pp 131–7; Dr W Caldwell, English and Scotch Settlements 110–7; J S Reynolds, The Settlement and Municipal Reform, pp 138–42; Graham Taylor, The Social Settlements and the Labour Movement, pp 143–9; R Hunter, The Relation Between Social Settlements and Charity Organisation, pp 302–14. Werner Picht, Toynbee Hall and the English Settlement Movement (London 1914)

77   See Charlotte Perkins Gilman, The Man Made World: Our Androcentric Culture (New York 1911), her The Living of Charlotte Perkins Gilman: An Autobiography (New York 1935), and Mary A Hill, Charlotte Perkins Gilman: The Making of a Radical Feminist, 1860–1896 (Philadelphia 1980). Florence Kelley may have been in Glasgow at a Co-operative conference on the eve of the First World War but I was unable to establish the point in the Florence Kelley Papers, Columbia University (New York)

78   See Jane Addams, The Spirit of Youth and the City Streets (New York 1912) pp 102, 119; David J Rothman, Conscience and Convenience; The Asylum and its Alternatives in Progressive America (Boston 1980) p 53

79   Edward E Hale, Home Rule in the Cities, Cosmopolitan 10 (1893–4) 735–8, 736

80   cf Mary Klein and Harvey A Kantor, Prisoners of Progress: American Industrial Cities, 1800-1920 (New York 1979), p 257; Paul Boyer, Urban Masses and Moral Order in America 1820–1920 (Cambridge Mass 1978) 22; Joseph Lee Constructive and Preventive Philanthropy (New York 1913 edn) pp 4, 157, 187–8

81   cf Helen Buckler, Mary Fiedler, Martha Allen, Wo-He-Lo: The Story of the Camp Fire Girls (New York 1961)

82   cf Clarence Lee Rainwater, The Play Movement in the United States (Chicago 1922)

83   Alice Henry, Women and the Labour Movement (New York 1971 edn (1923); Alice Hamilton, Mary MacArthur (London 1925)

84   Quoted Gladys Denny Schultz and Daisy Gordon Lawrence, Lady From Savannah: the Life of Juliette Gordon Low (Philadelphia 1958) p 161

85   Juliette Gordon Low Papers, University of North Carolina (Chapel Hill) and also at the Georgia Historical Society, Savannah. There are numerous trips to Inverness, North Berwick, Glen Lyon and Glasgow in the correspondence

86   Juliette Gordon Low to Mother, 12 July 1884, Low Papers, Savannah. The cellar description was also used by Bret Harte

87   Letter Juliette Gordon Low, Aug 1911, Georgia Historical Collection

88   See Letters 21, 29 June, 15 July, 4, 6, 7, 11 Aug 1911

89   Baden Powell to Juliette Gordon Low, 21 Aug 1911, Low Papers, Chapel Hill

90   Gladys D Schultz and Daisy G Lawrence, Lady from Savannah, pp 300, 379; also see Anne Hyde Choate and Helen Ferris, Juliette Gordon Low and the Girl Scouts: The Story of an American Woman Garden City (New York 1928). E E Reynolds, Baden Powell (Oxford 1942) does not mention her

91   Letter 23 Apr 1914 Low Papers, Chapel Hill records her meeting with Jane Addams and others at Hull House

92   1854–1914 See note 68

93   Smith was to found a Girls Life Brigade in 1902, visit his many former Glasgow leaders in America and meet President Theodore Roosevelt

94   1860–1935 See F P Gibson, W A Smith (London 1953 edn)

95   The Living of C P Gilman (New York 1935) and Mary A Hill, Charlotte Perkins Gilman: The Making of Radical Feminist 1860–1896 (Philadelphia 1980)

96   Originally published in Boston 1898
97   Labour Leader (5, 12, 19, 26 Sept 1896) and Charlotte Perkins MSS, Diary 1896, Library of Congress Washington DC
98   ibid and Labour Leader (19 Sept 1896)
99   Gilman Diary
100 The Living p 213 and Labour Leader (14 Nov 1896)
101 See Emma Goldman, Living My Life, 2 vols (New York 1931) and Richard Drinnon Rebel in Paradise: a biography of Emma Goldman (Boston 1970 edn)
102 See Living My Life, vol 1 pp 225–7 and the classic Henry David, The History of the Haymarket Affair (New York 1968 edn)
103 Emma Goldman to Mrs J D Campbell, Redcott, Alton Road, Paisley, 30 Jan 1925, Emma Goldman Papers, New York Public Library
104 Emma Goldman, Living My Life, vol 1 p 225–2, vol 2 p 262
105 W Paul, The State Its Function and Origin (Glasgow 1917) cited in Elizabeth Wilson, Women and the Welfare State (London 1977) pp 31–32
106 Forward (11 Mar 1911). Also see 1 Apr 1911 and the article by Sylvia Pankhurst in 30 July 1912
107 Margaret Sanger, An Autobiography (London 1939) pp 12–33
108 ibid p 94
109 1913 Glasgow draft MSS, Margaret Sanger Papers, Library of Congress
110 Autobiography p 96
111 ibid p 95
112 ibid p 97
113 ibid p 110
114 Forward (22, 29 May, 26 June, 3, 10, 17 July 1920) and Autobiography pp 267–9
115 ibid p 267
116 ibid p 268
117 Also see Guy Aldred, No Traitor's Gait (Glasgow 1957) p 431
118 Spur (Aug, Sept 1914, Mar, Apr 1915). The Mitchell Library, Glasgow copy is apparently that of Aldred and Witcop themselves
119 Feb, June, Aug 1915, Mar 1916
120 ibid and Forward (21, 28 Feb 1920)
121 Herald of Revolt (Aug, Sept, Nov 1913); Paul Avrich, An American Anarchist: The Life of Voltairine de Cleyre (Princeton 1978) pp 18–69 and Margaret S Marsh, Anarchist Women 1870–1920 (Philadelphia 1981) pp 123–50
122 P Avrich, pp 110–14
123 Scotch reservation as de Cleyre observed
124 Voltairine de Cleyre to Will and Maggie Duff, 28 May 1898 and 6 Aug 1001, Ishill Collection, Houghton Library, Harvard University. Also quoted in P Avrich, 117
125 W Duff to J Ishill, nd, Ishill Collection; P Avrich, p 118; John Quail, The Slow Burning Fuse: The Lost History of the British Anarchists (London 1978) 214–17
126 W Duff to J Ishill, nd, 3 Aug 1931 and one of the series written about 1937–9; P Avrich, p 118
127 W Duff to J Ishill, 3 Aug 1935, Ishill Collection
128 John Paton, Proletarian Pilgrimage: An Autobiography (London 1935) pp 120, 156, 218–19; J Quail, The Slow Burning Fuse 274–7
129 J Quail, p 292
130 See Blanche Wiesen Cook (ed), Crystal Eastman: Woman and Revolution (New York 1978) and William L O'Neill, Max Eastman (New York 1978) pp 3–29
131 W L O'Neill ibid p 15 quoting John Spargo
132 Blanche W Cook, pp 6–29
133 Workers of the Clyde, Liberator (1919), reprinted in Blanche Cook, pp 336–49
134 ibid p 343
135 ibid
136 ibid p 340
137 Forward (6 Sept 1919) reporting her speech at McKeesport

CHAPTER FOUR

1   Revd J J Mackay, quoted in Temperance League Journal (2 Apr 1982)
2   Temperance League Journal (27 Feb 1892)
3   Councillor Battersby, League Journal (2 Apr 1892)
4   League Journal (30 Jan 1886; 29 Dec 1888)
5   Forward (1 June 1918)
6   Forward (3 Apr 1920)
7   B Harrison Drink and the Victorians: The Temperance Question in England 1815–1872 (London 1971)
8   The Universal Tendency to Association in Mankind (London 1840) p 29
9   Select Committee on Drunkenness, Report Minutes of Evidence, etc. Parliamentary Papers 1834 (559) p vii. I am grateful to Dr J F McCaffrey for this reference
10 eg J Dunlop, The Universal Tendency pp 68, 220
11 cf A E Dingle, The Campaign For Prohibition in Victorian England: The United Kingdom Alliance, 1872–1895 (London 1980)
12 Jane Hume Clapperton, Scientific Meliorism and the Evolution of Happiness (London 1885) p 427
13 Ira V Brown, Lyman Abbott: Christian Evolutionist: A Study in Religious Liberalism (Westport Conn, 1970 edn) p 203
14 Timothy L Smith, Revivalism and Social Reform in Mid-Nineteenth Century America (Nashville 1957)
15 See J A Krout, The Origins of Prohibition (New York 1925)
16 J S Buckingham, National Evils and Practical Remedies with the plan of a Model Town London 1849 vol II: F W Farrer and B W Richardson, How Workingmen May Help Themsleves (London nd) 12, pp 15–16: B W Richardson, Hygeia: City of Health (London 1876)
17 Scottish Reformer (26 March 1898; 21 Oct 1899)
18 ibid and A R Sennett, Garden Cities in Theory and Practice 2 vols (London 1905) vol II p 671
19 J Dawson Burn, Temperance History 2 vols (London 1889–90) vol 1 pp 34–5
20 Edward Morris, The History of Temperance and Teetotal Societies in Glasgow from their origin to the present time (Glasgow 1855)
21 Temperance Society Record (Apr, May, Dec 1831; Mar, Apr, May, June 1833; Sept 1835); First Annual Report Glasgow and West of Scotland Temperance Society 1830 esp pp 35–8
22 Temperance Society Record (Dec 1831, Apr 1833) Revd Baxter Dickinson of New Jersey (Sept 1832)
23 Temperance Society Record (Jan 1833)
24 Glasgow and West of Scotland Temperance Society 2nd Annual Report (1831)
25 E Morris, op cit pp 22, 46
26 William Reid, Temperance Memorials of the late Robert Kettle, Esq (Glasgow 1853) pp xxx–xxxviii
27 Scottish Temperance Society Record 1st Annual Report (1830) p 9
28 December 1831; also J A Krout, The Origins of Prohibition pp 132–60
29 Oct 1833, A Scot from the Clyde Valley promoted similar ideas later, see Archibald Prentice, A Tour in the United States with Two Lectures on Emigration (London 1849) pp 186–212. He was a leading newspaper editor and temperance advocate in Manchester with the Anti-Corn Law League
30 Scottish Temperance Journal (15 Jan 1839)
31 H Humphrey, Great Britain, France and Belgium: A Short Tour in 1835 2 vols (New York 1838) vol 2 p 7
32 J Dawson Burn, Temperance vol 1 pp 100–21
33 Revd Dr Asahel Nettleton to Revd Lyman Beecher 1829, quoted in League Journal (30 June 1860)
34 STJ (9 Apr, 18 June, Aug 1839)
35 STJ (Jan, Mar 1846)
36 Scottish Temperance Record (Oct 1846)
37 STR (Mar, Apr, May 1850)

38   STR (Apr 1851), with the Crafts, a couple who had escaped from slavery
39   S Graham, Lectures on the Science of Human Life (London 1854) p 425
40   ibid p 487
41   S Graham, The Philosophy of Sacred History Considered in Relation to Human Ailment and the Wines of Scripture (New York 1855 edn) p 40
42   ibid p 58
43   On the background see S Nissenbaum, Sex Diet Debility on Jacksonian America: Sylvester Graham and the Health Reform (Westport Conn 1980) and W H G Armytage, Heavens Below: Utopian Experiments in England 1560–1960 (London 1961) pp 178–83
44   These ideas may be traced to Thomas Tyron 1634–1703 in his writings, Wisdom's Dictates or Aphorisms and Rules, Physical, Moral and Divine (London 1691); The Way to Make All People Rich or Wisdom's Call to Temperance and Frugality (London 1685); The Way to Health, Long Life and Happiness, (London 1883); and A Treatise of Dreams and Visions (London nd) Tyron demands simple food, clothes and abstinence 'to extinguish exorbitant desires', Wisdom's Dictates p 7. Advocating temperance, vegetarianism and sexual abstinence Tyron's ideas were taken up and developed by nineteenth-century writers like Joseph Ritson, An Essay on Abstinence from Animal Food as a Moral Duty (London 1802), Lewis Gompertz and as we shall see Thomas Low Nichols. They were to exercise some influence in Scotland
45   League Journal (28 Aug, 5, 12, 26 Oct, 30 Nov, 1861); Madeleine B Stern, Heads and Headliners: The Phrenological Fowlers (Norman Oklahoma 1971) pp 178–88; P T Winskill, The Temperance Movement and its Workers 4 vols (London 1893) vol 3 p 258
46   M B Stern, p 244
47   Thomas Low Nichols, Forty Years of American Life (New York 1937 edn); and my Social Catholicism and Health: Dr and Mrs Thomas Low Nichols in Britain, Studies in Church History vol 19 (Oxford 1982) pp 240–70
48   The British Library possesses the only copy which seems to have survived
49   Reformer (7, 24 Oct 1885, 19 Nov 1892); Scottish Reformer (Nov 1883); Dietetic Reformer and Vegetarian Messenger 1879–80
50   Reformer (Dec 1880); League Journal (23 Oct 1897, 14 May 1898; 10 June 1899); Scottish Reformer (Feb 1901); Forward (3 Nov 1917)
51   See my article above and Forward (29 Nov 1913, 19 June 1920)
52   R Metcalfe; The Rise and Progress of Hydropathy in England and Scotland (London 1906) pp 31–40. R Simpson 1807–87 b Saltcoats, draper in the Trongate, Glasgow at 19 until 1885. Studied at Glasgow University, Congregational Theological studies, joined Evangelical Union, active with close friend Fergus Ferguson in the formation of churches. League Journal (9 Apr 1887)
53   Hygeian Journal (1832–3); The Aberdeen Water Cure Journal esp Oct 1860; R T Trall, The Water Cure for the Million: The Processes of the Water Cure Explained (New York 1860); League Journal (10 June 1876)
54   R Metcalfe, op cit pp 157–62; Christian News (3 Jan 1873, 17 Feb 1877); A Munro, The Family Hydropathic Guide: A Practical Water Cure Manual (Glasgow 1870); League Journal (12 Aug 1871) for the opening of the Waverley Hydro.
55   On the background see R Metcalfe, The Water Cure: A Plea for Hydropathic Dispensaries (London 1878) and his Sanitas Sanitatum et Omnia Sanitas (London 1877)
56   League Journal (11 Aug 1888; 17 Jan 1891; 12 Nov 1892) letter from Mrs R H Morton of USA. Her daughter was taught by Paderewski. Also see Weekly Journal (19 Oct 1861; 9 Aug 1862); Obituary, League Journal (26 Apr 1902), A Philp b Dumfermline, opened hotel in Kirkcaldy initially and then built up chain which included interests in the Swan, Harrogate and Conishead Priory. Also see the adverts in the Scottish Temperance League Register annual volumes
57   Evelyn R Stetson, Rapid Transit Abroad (New York 1879) p 29; W Harlan Card, A Knight Templar Abroad (St Louis 1885) p 540; Clement Pearson, A Journal of Travels in Europe during the Summer of 1881 (Washington 1885) p 16. The lady whom I have been unable to identify came from Louisiana
58   League Journal, (3 May 59 9 Aug 1862; 13 June-25 July 1863)
59   League Journal (3 Sept 12 Nov 1864); Temperance Congress Volume (London 1862) p 56–60 for a full account

60   eg League Journal (17, 24 Dec 1864)

61   League Journal (19 July 1879 for agm; 31 July 1880)

62   Dietetic Reformer (1861) pp 10–16

63   Social Reformer (June, July Nov 1879)

64   Social Reformer (Dec 1880) and Reformer (25 Dec 1886)

65   eg A Munro in League Journal (28 July 1866; 15 Aug, 4, 18 Sept 1875); Coates in Social Reformer (Nov 1883)

66   John Davie 1800–91 b nr Stirling, drapery business in Dunfermline, became total abstainer in 1830, health food reformer, hydropathic supporter, member International Arbitration Society, Standard Encyclopaedia of the Alcohol Problem: P T Winskill, The Temperance Movement, 4 vols (London 1893) vol 3 p 28; W Reid Temperance Memorials; Herald of Health (1 June 1889); League Journal (14 Mar 1891)

67   Dietetic Reformer and Vegetarian Messenger (May 1879); Social Reformer (April 1879)

68   League Journal (19 July 1879, 31 July 1988), Dietetic Reformer (Jan 1880)

69   Dietetic Reformer and Vegetarian Messenger (May, June, Nov 1879, Jan 1880); letters from Coates, Social Reformer (Nov 1883) and Reformer (19 Nov 1892)

70   Dietetic Reformer (1 Nov 1879, 1 Dec 1880), League Journal (23 Oct 1897, 14 May 1898); Reformer (Aug 1893); Social Reformer (Feb 1901), Forward (29 Sept, 3 Nov 1917)

71   League Journal (9 Oct 1872, 4 Oct 1873); R B Walker, Medical Aspects of Tobacco Smoking and the Anti-Tobacco Movement in Britain in the Nineteenth Century, Medical History 24 (1980) 391–402

72   Animals Guardian (June, July 1891)

73   Scottish Reformer 3 (10 June 1899), for example. On the ethnic social and political conflict see Paul Kleppner, The Cross of Culture: A Social Analysis of Mid-Western Politics (New York 1970); Richard Jensen, the Winning of the Mid-West: Social and Political Conflict 1888–1896 (Chicago 1971); J M Kousser, The Shaping of Southern Politics: Suffrage Restriction and the Establishment of the One Party South, 1880–1910 (New Haven 1975)

74   Thomas Service obituary, League Journal (9 Oct 1880); Robert Smith profile, Temperance Leader Journal (29 Apr 1905); James Allan obituary, League Journal (28 Aug 1880); Bryce Allan obituary, Temperance Journal (9 Apr 1892); William Reid, The Temperance Autobiography (Glasgow 1895) pp 73, 183–6

75   R Simpson, League Journal (9 Apr 1887) obituary and Winskill vol 3 p 208

76   Sir William Collins profile, Temperance Leader (13 May 1905). Also see the biographies of father and son in the Standard Encyclopaedia on the Alcohol Problem

77   George Gallie obituary, League Journal (29 Jan 1876) and The Advance and Congregational Miscellany (Mar 1876), also son obituary (5 Nov 1898)

78   William Reid, Temperance Memorials of the Late Robert Kettle Esq (Glasgow 1853); Edward Morris, The History of the Temperance and Teetotal Societies in Glasgow from their Origin to the Present Time (Glasgow 1855)

79   Bailie Torrens obituary, Social Reformer (Nov 1884) and Winskill, vol 3 p 97; Scottish Temperance Review (Apr 1850)

80   Patricia Hollis and Brian Harrison, Robert Lowery (London 1979). Also see League Journal (23 Nov 1861, 4 Oct 1862, 12 Sept 1863 (obituary)

81   Revd Thomas Adam, League Journal (3 Mar 1877)

82   Thomas Smith, League Journal (20 June 1868)

83   James McNair obituary, in Temperance League Register (1885) p 60: James Browning White, Winskill vol 4 p 106

84   Robert Reid obituary, League Journal (8 Feb 1908); William Reid obituary, Temperance Leader (18 Mar 1905); John McGavin obituary, Temperance Leader (15 Apr 1905); Dr Joseph Brown obituary, League Journal (17 Apr 1897) and Winskill vol 3 pp 17–18; Dr W M Taylor obituary, League Journal (16 Feb 1896); Revd Dr Storrs, DAmB, Revd J Newman Hall, DAmB; John Guthrie obituary, League Journal (14 Aug 1875); John Brown, Brown and Polson obituary, Temperance Leader (25 Mar 1905)

85   Temperance League Journal (27 Apr 1872)

86   ibid (23 Aug 1873)

87   ibid (27 Feb 1864)

88   League Journal (12 Sept 1868)

89   Temperance leader (7 Aug 1909)

90   Forres Gazette (23 Oct 1872)
91   League Journal (3 May 1873)
92   cf James P Shannon, Catholic Colonisation on the Western Frontier pp 10–11 for details of George Sheppard the Northern Pacific land agent with whom Kerr was associated and later evidence of Catholic temperance colonisation efforts. Kerr was to die at Tomah, Wisconsin 29 June 1890—information from Miss Moira Innes
93   Temperance Leader (8 Feb 1908)
94   Temperance Leader (11 Jan, 22, 29 Feb 1908)
95   League Journal (13 Mar 1869)
96   ibid (4 Sept 1886)
97   ibid (16 June 1888)
98   See list from Scottish Temperance Register membership lists for America in appendix
99   See below
100 Weekly Journal of the Scottish Temperance League (16 June 1860)
101 P T Winskill, The Temperance Movement vol 2 pp 268–70
102 A E Dingle, The Campaign for Prohibition in Victorian England: especially pp 13–30
103 UP Magazine new series 16 (1872) 540
104 William G McLoughlin, The Meaning of Henry Ward Beecher: An Essay on the Shifting Values of Mid Victorian America, 1840–1870, (New York 1970) pp 116–17, 172–3, 186–7. The title of the book itself is revealing
105 See for example George Fredrickson, The Inner Civil War, (New York 1965) pp 161–5 and the later chapter here on reform
106 Scottish Temperance Journal (June 1840, Jan, Mar 1846); League Journal (27 July 1867)
107 Social Reformer (Aug 1880) article, Early Prohibitionists
108 Scottish Reformer (6, 13 Jan 1900)
109 Dawson Burns, Temperance History vol 1 pp 360–1
110 Frank L Byrne, Prophet of Prohibition: Neal Dow and his Crusade, (Madison Wis 1961) pp 55–6
111 W J Couper, Scottish Revivals (Dundee 1918) pp 135–6
112 Scottish Temperance Review (Nov 1850) and Theodore Davenport Bacon, Leonard Bacon: A Statesman in The Church (New Haven 1931) p 321
113 Scottish Temperance Review (Oct 1852). He claimed descent from a Convenanter at Bothwell Brig. His funeral notice appears in League Journal (16 Jan 1858)
114 Scottish Temperance Review (Apr, May 1852) and J B Gough, Autobiography (London 1870 edn) pp 279–80
115 League Journal (16 June 1860)
116 Frank L Byrne, Neal Dow and His Crusade (Madison Wis 1961) pp 11, 35, 56; Neal Dow Reminiscence (Portland Me 1898)
117 Reminiscences p 570
118 Weekly Journal (16 May 1857)
119 J B Gough, Autobiography (London 1870 edn) pp 19, 158
120 Autobiography p 281
121 John Marsh, Temperance Recollections: Labours, Defeats, Triumphs, (New York 1866) p 121. Also see his horrific account of Glasgow drunkenness p 154
122 Autobiography p 347 quoting Christian News
123 Weekly Journal (19 Sept 1857). A Revd Mr Gould of America was with him
124 eg ibid 26 Sept, 10, 17, 24, 31 Oct, 7, 14, 21, 28 Nov, 5, 12, 19, 26 Dec 1857
125 See appendix
126 W W Brown, Three Years in Europe or Places I have Seen And People I have Met (London 1852) pp 163–82. His Sketches of Places and People Abroad, (Boston 1855), though largely the same omits his Glasgow meeting
127 League Journal (30 June, 7 July 1877). Gladstone obituary, Temperance Leader (21 May 1910). Winskill, vol 3 pp 199–208
128 League Journal (22 June 1878; 26 July 1879). The delegates in Liverpool included Revd Bishop Campbell, a black from Georgia; Revd W H Hillery of the AME Church; J C Dancy, a black from N Carolina; Revd E M Pinckney, S Carolina; Mrs H N K Goff of New York; and delegates from Florida, Pennsylvania, Virginia and West Virginia

129   Scottish Temperance Review (Mar, May 1850, Apr 1851); League Journal (29 Sept, 20 Oct 1877)

130   League Journal (9, 16, 23, 30 Aug 1862; 7, 14 Mar 1863; 14 Oct 1865; 25 Feb 1860). A Revd George Blyth brought some New York black ladies' handiwork for sale at the temperance bazaar in 1852. Glasgow United Total Abstainers Association Second Annual Report (1853) p 19

131   Scottish Temperance Journal (Dec 1839 Mar 1840); Edward Morris, pp 92–9; J F Maguire, Father Mathew (London 1863)

132   eg Revd J J Messrs, Monks and Monasteries as they were: with remarks on genuine Christianity, Puseyism, Teetotalism, etc., League Journal (4 Jan 1868). Also 8 May 1858 Gavazzi. The UP Magazine has a similar predictable bias running through its pages though it had very favourable views of Cardinal Manning's temperance work though he was 'untypical'

133   cf H F Kearney, Fr Mathew: Apostle of Modernisation, pp 164–75 in Studies in Irish History Presented to R Dudley Edwards, eds Art Cosgrave and Donal McCartney (Dublin 1979)

134   League Journal (1 June, 10 Aug 1872, 4 Jan 1873)

135   League Journal (19 Apr 1873)

136   19 Apr 1873, 27 Apr 1872, 10 Nov 1870

137   10 Nov 1870

138   League Journal (10 Aug 1872, 23 Nov 1872)

139   Glasgow Post Office Directory (1877–8) at 280 George Street

140   ibid (1866–7). The Baptist chapel became a Church of Christ the following year

141   See Robert Frederick West, Alexander Campbell and National Religion (New Haven 1948) esp pp 197–206

142   Glasgow Post Office Directory (1913–14)

143   League Journal (7 Jan 1899)

144   Scottish Reformer (May, June 1921)

145   ibid (Mar 1922)

146   League Journal (23 Aug 1873), Christian News (26 Dec 1874, 7 July 1877) reports his health broken; J Dawson Burn, Temperance History vol 2 p 123; Norman Longmate, The Waterdrinkers; A History of Temperance, (London 1968) pp 214–15

147   League Journal (23 Aug 1872)

148   The delegates to the Independent Order of Good Templars international gathering in Glasgow 1873 included the following: Mrs Cleland Brown, Ohio; Sarah E Wills, New York; Mrs S B Chase, Pennsylvania; Mrs Jane Dow, Wisconsin; Mrs Anne Weichman, Pennsylvania; Mrs M L Johnson, Pa; Miss E C Rice, Conn; Miss E D Stacey, Minnesota; Revd John Russell, Michigan; Revd O M Consen, Maine, J B Yard, New Jersey; Thomas Polson, Maryland; Hon J Black, S B Chase and Col MacFarlane, Pa; Hon S D Hastings, Wisconsin; T Needham, Kentucky; Revd J M Yearnshaw, Nebraska; Revd G K Morris, New Brunswick, New Jersey; Revd D C Ridgeway, Milford, Delaware; Ely Marsh, Frankfort, New York; J S Carrigus, Kokomo, Indiana; J T Dow, Sisters Dow, Wells and Chirton, New York, Sister Strong, Minnesota, W M B Sorrell, Colorado; E P P Ellis, Missouri. League Journal (19 July 1873). Theodore M Ramsey, N Carolina; J R Van Doorn, Illinois were noted at later meetings, League Journal (23 Aug 1873). Fannie Du Bois Chase 1828–1902 b Hallstead Pa, married Simeon Brewster Chase lectured in USA and Europe throughout her life on temperance. Presbyterian vice president of Pennsylvania WCTU 1874, president 1879–81, and her husband Simeon Brewster Chase 1828–1909, teacher, lawyer, newspaper editor, Republican politician associated with various temperance organisations became chairman of the first Prohibition Party national convention 1872, ran for governor twice, church elder. Standard Encyclopaedia of the Alcohol Problem

149   League Journal (16 May 1857)

150   ibid

151   ibid

152   ibid (28 Jan, 2 June, 20 Oct, 2, 9, Mar 1861) for example

153   ibid (20, 27 Oct 1866)

154   ibid (19 Sept 1868)

155   ibid (7 Nov 1874)

156   17 Feb 1866

157 4 July 1866
158 eg 24 Mar 1866
159 4 Apr 1866
160 17 Feb 1866
161 13 Feb, 27 Feb 1864
162 21 May 1864
163 6 Aug 1864
164 ibid (17 Feb 1866)
165 League Journal (30 June 1900), Social Reformer (23, 30 June 1900)
166 William Jennings Demorest 1822–95, b New York, dry goods merchant and later publisher began the New York Illustrated News 1850, the Demorest's Family Magazine 1864, abolitionist and temperance advocate, joined the Prohibition Party 1884, candidate for mayor of New York 1888, later for lieutenant governor. He instituted the Demorest Medal contests in 1886 for prohibitionist recitations by youngsters, later taken over by WCTU. He visited Glasgow in 1892. Standard Encyclopaedia of the Alcohol Problem; League Journal (6 Aug 1892)
167 Obituary in League Journal (18 May 1895)
168 Scottish Temperance League Register (1894) p 75
169 Social Reformer (7 July 1900). He was also president of the American National Temperance Society
170 eg T L Cuyler, Moral Duty of Total Abstinence, League Journal (24 Feb 1872); Neal Dow to R Mackay, Social Reformer (July 1883). Numerous other examples could be cited
171 The Scottish Reformer also reported Ian McLaren, Agnes Slack of the BWTU on prohibition America (24 Mar, 12 May 1900); Bailey (11 Aug 1900); Hayler (4 Jan 1902, 2 Apr 1917); League Journal, W S Caine (29 Oct 1898, 2 Dec 1899; 2 Jan 1886)
172 Temperance Leader (11 Jan 1908)
173 League Journal (22 Mar 1879) reports the establishment the previous November of Glenboig Total Abstinence Society. Four priests were present and 75 per cent Catholics were allegedly members of the organisation: trip to Catholic orphanage at Lanark (26 July 1877); figures (8 Aug 1891, 4 Dec 1897); obituary James Dunnachie (5 July 1890) also notes an American professor visiting the Glenboig Fire Clay Factory as the finest in the world
174 League Journal (11 Aug 1894). Any gathering of the League of the Cross under Cardinal Manning invariably received lavish coverage
175 See for example Forward (19 Aug 1911) in the aftermath of the unsuccessful municipal tramway strike. Also 16 Jan 1915, 15 Mar 1919
176 See Albert Barnes, The Throne of Iniquity (London 1852) and his Life at Three Score (London 1858). Barnes seems to have visited Glasgow
177 H A Gibbons, John Wanamaker 2 vols (New York 1926) vol 1 p 123 and esp vol 1 pp 181–94 and vol 2 pp 328–44 and Marion L Bell, Crusade in the City: Revivalism in Nineteenth Century Philadelphia (Lewisburg USA 1977) ch 10, Businessmen's Revivals pp 169–99
178 Obituary League Journal (28 Oct 1893) Breze was born in Chile; League Journal obituary D D Robertson (4 Mar 1899)
179 R Hood, League Journal (13 Jan 1894)
180 League Journal (5 Apr 1905)
181 League Journal (3 Oct 1903); Temperance Leader (16 June 1906)
182 Temperance Leader (4 Sept 1909). Revd William Ross, Rothesay and later Cowcaddens as a leading Good Templar visited America several times, Temperance Leader (30 Apr 1904) obituary
183 Scottish Temperance Register (1867) report
184 League Journal (16 June 1888) obituary, also see 17 Jan 1874
185 League Journal (7 May 1898) obituary
186 League Journal (18 Aug 1900) obituary, also see 1 Jan 1886
187 League Journal (19, 26 Mar 1898). Also see the obituary of Mrs Thomas Arnot, New Brighton Pennsylvania, League Journal (1 Aug 1891)
188 Social Reformer (Jan, Apr, Sept 1879)
189 Scottish Temperance League Register 1888–92 under USA and Ayr
190 This is based entirely upon Fergus Ferguson, From Glasgow to Missouri (Glasgow 1878)

191   Jan 1876, Dec 1877. A version with additional articles appeared later, Alexander Craib, America and the Americans (Paisley 1892)
192   Sept and Oct 1877
193   Sept 1877 p 101
194   Scottish Reformer (9 June 1894)
195   17 Feb 1894
196   Letters from America (London 1880) p 260
197   Dr Edmond wrote a full account in several issues of the *UP Magazine* new series 16 (1872)
198   18 June 1870
199   UP Magazine 1872 p 103
200   p 443
201   p 493
202   p 494
203   p 494–5
204   p 538
205   p 539
206   eg League Journal (25 Oct, 6 Dec 1873)
207   eg at Ardrossan (27 Jan 1866)
208   21 Sept 1867
209   30 Nov 1867, 8, 15, 22 Aug, 5 Sept 1868
210   23, 30 May 1867
211   19 Sept 1868, 20 Jan 1869
212   19 Sept 1868
213   26 Sept 1868
214   3, 10, 17, 31 Oct 1868
215   14, 21, 28 Nov 1868
216   26 Dec 1868
217   30 Jan 1869
218   6 Feb 1869
219   20, 27 Feb 1869
220   6 March 1869
221   STL Register 1861, 28 Aug 1869
222   20 Nov 1869
223   4 Sept 1869
224   3 Sept 1870
225   UP Magazine (1872) pp 532–37
226   ibid p 540
227   League Journal (1, 8 June, 10 Aug 1872)
228   16 Nov 1872 and 3 May 1873
229   19 July 1873
230   28 March 1874
231   Christian News (18 Apr 1874)
232   18 Apr 1874
233   18 Apr, 12 Dec 1874, 13 Mar 1875
234   31 Oct 1874, also 17 Jan 1874
235   3 Apr 1875
236   3, 10 Apr 1875; UP Magazine pp 525–6
237   League Journal (9 Oct 1875)
238   18 Dec 1975, 30 Dec 1876. Details of his career are in N Longmate, The Waterdrinkers, pp 76–88 and passim
239   League Journal (8 Jan 1876), see Winskill vol 3 p 111
240   League Journal (25 Mar 1876)
241   12 Feb 1876
242   18 Sept 16 Oct 6 Nov 1876
243   28 Dec 1875, 12 Feb, 8 Apr 1876
244   8, 15, 22 Apr, 10 June 1876
245   1 July 1876
246   23 Dec 1876

247 5 May, 16 June 1877
248 25 June 1877 no name; 11 Aug, 18, 25, 1, 29 Sept 1877, Mr Sawyer
249 19 Oct 1878, 16 Apr 1879, 26, 20 Sept 1879
250 31 May 1879
251 J B T Marsh, The Story of the Jubilee Singers (London 1885)
252 Winskill vol 3 pp 199–200
253 League Journal (26 July 1877)
254 30 June, 7 July 1877
255 29 Sept 1877
256 14 Sept 1878
257 League Journal (2 Jan 1886, 27 Aug 1887)
258 N Longmate pp 214, 234–6
259 League Journal (22 June 1889)
260 20, 29 June, 6, 13, July 1889
261 27 July 1889
262 3, 24 Aug 1889
263 10, 17 Aug 1889
264 24 Aug 1889 at Rothesay
265 24 Aug 1889
266 Temperance Leader (15 Aug 1908)
267 Temperance Leader (9 Nov 1895)
268 Scottish Reformer (10 Sept 1898)
269 eg 23 July 1904
270 9 Sept 1905, 27 Aug 1904, 7 Oct 1905
271 7 Aug 1909
272 Death of Revd W Reid (18 Mar 1905); William Johnston (22 July 1905); T L Cuyler
(8 Feb 1908, 20 Mar 1909); Ex Provost Clark of Paisley (12 Mar 1910). In addition through
February-May 1905 a series of historical articles appeared
273 4th AGM Vigilance Association (20 Oct 1906); R M Hunter (29 May 1909; 24 July 1909)
274 11 Jan 1908
275 4 Sept 1909
276 16 June 1906
277 23 Aug 1909 for example
278 18 Sept 1908
279 In Celebration of the Ministerial Jubilee of the Revd Joseph Brown DD Kent Road UP
Church Glasgow 1884, p 48
280 Temperance Journal (17 Apr 1897, 1 Apr 1916)
281 League Journal (25 Mar 1901)
282 Temperance Leader (16 Jan, 4 June, 27 Aug 1904; 7 Oct 1905); League Journal (26 July
1902; 28 Nov 1901), also see J Rowntree and A Sherwell, British Gothenburg Experiments and
Public House Trusts (London 1901)
283 See E R L Gould, The Gothenburg System and our Liquor Traffic, Forum 17 (1893)
103–13; The Gothenburg System in America, Atlantic 72 (1893) 538–45
284 Raymond Calkins, The Committee of Fifty Substitutes for the Saloon (Boston 1901)
p 184 quoting the Glasgow Herald (24 Jan 1898)
285 E R L Gould, Popular Control of the Liquor Traffic (London 1894) p 60
286 Reformer (26 Dec 1885)
287 1856–1933. He gave lavish gifts of land to the city. See chapter 5
288 K L Roberts, Why Europe Leaves Home (London 1922) p 309
289 J B Gough Papers; League Journal (19 Oct 1878, 19 Apr, 20 Sept 1879)
290 Councillor Pinkerton promoted the meeting of the Glasgow women in support of their
sisters in the Ohio Whisky War, 18 Apr 1874. Social Reformer (Dec 1881, Jan to Dec 1882);
N Longmate, The Waterdrinkers p 216
291 League Journal (24 Aug 1889)
292 Mr Aitken of USA at Crosshall League Journal (12 Dec 1891; 1 Sept 1887); T H
Campbell and Mrs and Mr Aitken at Crosshall (25 Aug 1888)
293 League Journal (7 Aug 1889); Mary Earhart, Frances Willard (Chicago 1944) pp 340–1,
353, 362

294 Scottish Reformer (9 Feb 1895)
295 Information from Mrs Simpson, Glasgow University Archives
296 Anti-Saloon Year Book (1914) pp 3–8
297 Scottish Reformer (4 Nov 1899)
298 League Journal (20 Jan, 16, 30 June 1900) W E Johnson was over
299 Scottish Reformer (28 Oct 1899, 7 July 1900). Among the delegates listed at the World Temperance Congress in Edinburgh 1900 were: Miss Stevens Maine; Mrs Stevenson, Mass; Mrs Burt, Mrs Boole, Madame Demorest, Dr Funk from New York; C M Sheldon the writer from Kansas; Dr Mary Wood Allen, Miss Brehm, Mrs. F J Barnes, Miss Marianne Framingham, Miss Greenwood, Dr Myra Gillette, Gordon Gulick and Anna Gordon, Miss Willard's former secretary. Mrs Lovell, Pennsylvania; Mrs Thatcher, New Jersey; Mrs Barney, Providence Rhode Island. The Fisk Jubilee Singers were also present. Scottish Reformer (16, 30 June 1900)
300 League Journal (12 Dec 1901)
301 Scottish Reformer (17 Mar 1900)
302 League Journal (27 June 1901), Guy Hayler, North of England Temperance League
303 Temperance Leader (25 June 1904, 4 Mar 1905)
304 Temperance Leader (18 Sept 1909 and 5 Apr, 3 May 1913)
305 Anti-Saloon Year Book 1919; Temperance Leader (15 Aug 1914, 9 Oct 1915)
306 21, 28 June, 26 July, 1 Nov 1918, 28 Feb 1914; Fasti
307 Temperance Leader (28 Feb 1914)
308 League Journal (30 Jan 1892), Temperance Leader (9 May 1914) also W B Selbie, The Life of C S Horne (London 1920)
309 See Appendix
310 eg Barr in Forward (1 June 1918) Scottish Society and Alcohol Prohibition; 19 Jan 1918 Guy Hayler
311 cf Forward (15 Feb 1919) on the Chicago Socialist trial. Also see Kenneth L Roberts, Why Europe Leaves Home (London 1922) p 340
312 Anti-Saloon Yearbook (1919) p 259 and Scottish Temperance Register (1920) p 17
313 Scottish Reformer (May 1918)
314 The Anti-Saloon Yearbook (1919) p 406 and Scottish Temperance Register (1920) p 35. Professor Charles Scanlon 1869–1942 educated Minnesota and Valparaiso University, Indiana, teacher, then lecturer for the Prohibition Party in 1903 Board of Temperance Presbyterian Union USA. Prohibition candidate for governorship of Minnesota 1902, later chairman Prohibition Convention, President National Temperance Society, editor Pittsburgh Moral Welfare, New York National Advocate. Who Was Who in America 1897–1942
315 Scottish Reformer (Sept, Oct 1918, Dumfries, Kilmarnock, Motherwell; Nov 1918, Aberdeen; Jan 1919 Buckie, Inverness, Beauly, Pulteney, Kingussie)
316 ibid (Feb 1919)
317 Jan, Mar 1919
318 ibid (Apr 1919; June, Aug, Sept, Oct, Nov, Dec 1920); League Journal (15 Mar 1920)
319 Scottish Reformer (Aug, Nov 1920). Revd Samuel Chadwick B Burnley, Lancs 1850 ed Didsbury Training College, ordained 1888, served Edinburgh 1886 and Clydebank 1887–90 then Leeds until appointed principal of Cliff College, Sheffield 1907. One time editor Joyful News. 1918 President, Wesleyan Methodist Conference and in 1921 president of the National Council of Free Churches. Vice President Leeds Temperance Council. Standard Encyclopaedia of the Alcohol Problem
320 ibid (Dec 1920)
321 Temperance Leader (1 Jan 1920)
322 ibid (1, 15 Feb 1918)
323 eg Temperance Leader (2 Sept 1918); Scottish Reformer (Feb, June, July 1918)
324 Temperance Reformer (Mar 1919)
325 Temperance Leader (1 Mar, 1 Apr 1919); Anti-Saloon Yearbook (1919) p 429
326 Scottish Reformer (Mar 1919). Mr Chandler also appears to have offered his support
327 Temperance Leader (1 Apr, 15 June 1918); Scottish Reformer (Apr 1919); Virginius Dabney, Dry Messiah: The Life of Bishop Cannon (New York 1951) merely notes his British visit
328 See poster. The capitalist dry looks remarkably like Sir Samuel Chisholm

329   Temperance Leader (1, 15 Nov 1919); Scottish Reformer (Oct, Nov, Dec 1919)
330   Temperance Leader (1 May 1919); Scottish Reformer (May 1919)
331   See Paul E Isaac, Prohibition and Politics: Turbulent Decades in Tennessee 1885–1920 (Nashville 1965). Revd Henry Beach Carrel 1871–1928 b New Orleans, educated Tulane, Vanderbilt, Chicago and Germany; ordained Methodist Episcopal Church minister 1893; Professor Biblical theology and exegesis Vanderbilt 1903–19; president Tennessee Anti-Saloon League; on executive of the Anti-Saloon League of America, World League against Alcoholism, worked in France of the YMCA in World War I. Standard Encyclopaedia of the Alcohol Problem
332   Scottish Reformer (May, Aug 1919)
333   ibid (Aug 1919)
334   Scottish Reformer (Dec 1919, Apr 1920)
335   Scottish Reformer (Oct–Dec 1919, Jan, Feb 1920), Temperance Leader (1, 15 Nov, 1 Dec 1919). Poole made play with his Scottish ancestry
336   Feb 1920
337   Temperance Leader (15 Dec 1919), Scottish Reformer (Mar 1922)
338   Temperance Leader (16 Feb 1920)
339   Scottish Reformer (Feb 1920), Temperance Leader (2 Feb 1920)
340   ibid
341   ibid
342   ibid
343   See cartoon
344   Scottish Reformer (Mar, Apr, May 1920); Temperance Leader (15 Mar, 1 Apr 1920)
345   eg Dr Henry was the guest at Mr and Mrs Service, 10 Belmont Street, Mrs A A Dick 24 Eglinton Drive and Miss Green at Huntingfield, Albert Drive, Scottish Reformer (June 1920)
346   ibid (May, June 1920)
347   ibid (Oct 1920)
348   ibid (Oct 1920); Temperance Leader (16 Aug, 15 Oct 1920): Kenneth L Roberts, Why Europe Leaves Home pp 341–5
349   Scottish Reformer (Oct 1920)
350   K L Roberts, Why Europe Leaves Home p 352
351   Temperance Leader (15 May 1920)
352   K L Roberts, Why Europe Leaves Home p 353, also pp 348–52, see appendix for figures
353   Scottish Reformer (May, June, Oct, Nov, Dec 1921)
354   ibid (Nov 1921)
255   ibid (Dec 1921)
256   Scottish Reformer (Apr 1921)
357   ibid (Nov 1921)
358   ibid (Feb 1922)
359   ibid (Mar 1922). Speakers included Dr Norman Maclean, Revd W S Mathieson, Galashiels, Ex-bailie Gardiner, Revd Dr MacGilchrist, Revd Mr Russell
360   ibid (May, June, Aug 1922); Report of the Proceedings of the General Assembly of the Church of Scotland (1922)
361   Report of the Commission of Scottish Churchmen: Prohibition in the United States and Canada (Edinburgh 1923). The committee included Revd Malcolm, Revd J Johnston, Robert Gibson and Roderick Mason. See Fasti 1 145: 8 314; 9 378
362   K L Roberts, Why Europe Leaves Home p 354
363   K L Roberts, Why Europe Leaves Home p 356

CHAPTER FIVE

1   Clipping in Albert Shaw Papers, New York Public Library, New York. The standard life of Lloyd J Graybar, Albert Shaw, (Lexington Kentucky 1975). Also Century Magazine 50 (1895) 314–15. The advanced nature of Glasgow's municipal socialism can be gauged by comparison with London. See Ken Young, Local Politics and the Rise of Party: The London Municipal Society and the Conservative Intervention in Local Elections, 1894–1963 (Leicester 1975) pp 34–112, and H V Emy, Liberals, Radicals and Social Politics, 1892–1914 (Cambridge 1973)

2   An examination of the backgrounds and occupations of the Glasgow town councillors between 1880–1914 shows an increasing representation of businessmen, temperance activists and social reformers, latterly more partisan, entering public life (Glasgow City Archives)

3   Adna F Weber, The Growth of Cities in the Nineteenth Century: a study in statistics (Ithaca 1963 edn) pp 57–64

4   Washington Gladden, Civic Religion (Philadelphia 1904), and the Christian Pastor and the Working Church (Edinburgh 1898) p 329

5   Charles Zueblin to Patrick Geddes, 30 Dec 1915, Geddes Papers (National Library of Scotland, Edinburgh)

6   Chicago Tribune (7 May 1905) one of the series of special reports on Glasgow. On Burrell the remarkable art collector and entrepreneur see biographical list

7   F C Howe European Cities at Work (London 1913) p 273. Also Washington Gladden, The Christian Pastor, pp 439 and 466; his Social Salvation (London 1902) p 192; the Social Facts and Forces (New York 1897) p 189. The tradition was of long standing. See Robert Chambers, Picture of Scotland, 2 vols (Edinburgh 1834) 2 vols; (Edinburgh 1834) 2 vols, vol 1 p 366: 'Among the manufacturers of Glasgow are to be found men of prodigious wealth and at the same time elevated and enlightened minds who form a sort of nobility. These men in general raised from a very humble rank in life display a munificence of disposition and proud feeling of honour in their dealings which might add lustre to coronets and garters. It is perhaps their noblest characteristic that whatever may be their superiority over the rest of the citizens in point of capacity they show no disposition to withdraw themselves from or to lord over their less eminent brethern. . . . Altogether their public spirit and their talent, their well won and well used wealth, their greatness and their humility, entitle them to the admiration of even those who may be least disposed to applaud greatness in the first generation.' Others were less sure of such high minded motives in civic reformers. See E P Thompson, William Morris: Romantic to Revolution (London 1955) p 666, quoting Morris and E A Ross, the Social Trend, (New York 1922) pp 180–1

8   J R Commons, Races and Immigrants in America (New York 1907) p 38. Robert A Woods, the Boston Settlement also felt the same way. R A Woods

9   Alice Hamilton, Exploring the Dangerous Trades (Boston 1943) p 85

10 Edward Aveling and Eleanor Marx, The Working Class Movement in America (London 1891) p 12

11 Joseph Lee, Constructive and Preventive Philanthropy (New York 1902) 1913 edn p 205

12 Review of Reviews (September 1893) p 314. A full statement appears on pp 316–19. He was about to publish his If Christ Came to Chicago (London 1894. On his return from USA he gave his first address in Glasgow. Also see the writings of his brother, F H Stead, a former Glasgow University student, Federation of the English Speaking Peoples, in International Congregational Council (London 1891) authorised record of the proceedings with an introduction by R W Dale, London vol 1 (1891) pp 229–33 and his The Story of Social Christianity 2 vols (London 1924) pp 203–4

13 Review of Reviews (Sept 1893) p 314. See similar views in Canon H O Barnett, The Ideal City (Bristol nd) pp 10, 14; Stanton Coit, National Idealism and A State Church (London 1907) pp 372–3; Charles Zueblin, American Municipal Progress (New York 1902) p 20; Brand Whitlock On the Enforcement of Law in Cities (New York 1910) p 8, and many others

14 Review of Reviews

15 Frederick Harrison, George Washington and Other Addresses (London 1901) p 186

16 See Hoeveler; James McCosh, The Method of Divine Government, Physical and Moral (Edinburgh 1859 edn) and his The Religious Aspect of Evolution (London 1898 edn); W R Hutchison, The Modernist Impulse in American Protestantism (Cambridge Mass 1976); Herbert Schneider, The Influence of Darwin and Spencer on American Philosophical Theology, Journal of the History of Ideas 6 (1945) 3–18; Bert J Loewenberg, Darwinsim Comes to America 1859–1900, MVHR 28 (1941) 339–68

17 2 vols (New York 1874) and (New York 1884)

18 George A Gordon, My Education and Religion and W R Hutchinson, The Modernist, passim

19 The Ascent of Man (London 1894); George Adam Smith, Henry Drummond (London 1899)

20 See Edward Caird's correspondence with Professor R M Wenley, Wenley Papers,

University of Michigan collections; Professor George Howison, Howison Papers, Bancroft Library, University of California, Berkeley; Professor Adam Shortt, a former student at Queen's University, Kingston, Canada, 8 March 1886 Shortt Papers; Professor John Mavor, Mavor Papers, Toronto University; G Spiller, The Ethical Movement in Great Britain (London 1934); A J M Milnes, The Social Philosophy of English Idealism (London 1962); Sir Henry Jones and J H Muirhead, The life and Philosophy of Edward Caird (Glasgow 1921); and his own The Moral Aspect of the Economical Problem. Jane Addams was a great admirer, Twenty Years at Hull House (New York 1910): R M Wenley, The Life and Work of George Sylvester Morris (New York 1917) pp 166–70 recounting the visit of the Michigan Professor to Glasgow in 1885

21   James Bryce, The American Commonwealth 2 vols (London 1910 edn). See Robert Howie, The Churches and the Churchless in Scotland (Glasgow 1891): Aaron I Abell, The Urban Impact on American Protestantism (Cambridge Mass 1942); Henry F May, The Protestant Churches and Industrial America (New York 1949); Charles H Hopkins, the Rise of the Social Gospel in American Protestantism (New Haven 1940). For a contemporary statement see James McCosh ed., Problems of American Civilisation: Their Practical Solution the Pressing Christian Duty of Today (New York 1888) pp 105–18 and 155–68

22   Robert A Woods et al, The Poor in Great Cities (London 1896) esp pp 6 and 76

23   Washington Gladden, Civic Religion p 9; Also R T Ely, The Social Aspects of Christianity (London 1896) pp 74, 79

24   John Bascom, Sociology (New York 1887) p 178. On Bascom saw biographical list

25   J Bascom, Sociology p 241. Also Walter Rauschenbusch, Christianity and the Social Crisis (New York 1907)

26   See Henry Warren, Church History in the Age of Science; Historiographical Patterns in the United States 1876–1918, (Chapel Hill 1971); A L Tracy, New Immigration and American Culture: An Analysis of the Attitudes of Charles Ellwood, Shailer Mathews and Graham Taylor towards the The New Immigration, unpublished PhD dissertation American University 1975

27   Michael Freeden, The New Liberalism: An Ideology of Social Reform (Oxford 1978). Much of the evidence comes from Glasgow figures

28   H G C Mathew, The Liberal Imperialists; The Ideas and Politics of a Post Gladstonian Elite (London 1973) and Bernard Simmel, Imperialism and Social Reform (London 1960)

29   The contrast can be seen in Homer Lea, The Valour of Ignorance, (New York, 1909) and David Starr Jordan, The Human Harvest (1972) 1907 edn

30   Stanton Coit, The Soul of America (New York 1914) p 89

31   S Coit, The Soul p 247. Also his National Idealism and a State Chruch, (London 1907), and Samuel Lane Loomis, Modern Cities and their Religious Problems (New York 1970) 1887 edn; H Stuart Hughes, Consciousness and Society: The Reconstruction of European Social Thought, 1890–1930 (London 1959)

32   See biographical list

33   W J Ashley to Albert Shaw, 1894, Albert Shaw Papers, New York Public Library

34   The former sought to persuade, the latter to coerce by legislation

35   Chisholm was largely responsible for the remodelling of the Saltmarket area of Glasgow in the 1890s

36   Porter was a persistent critic. Traction and Transmission 2 (1901) 20–5, 81–9, 140–51, 228–33; 3 (1901) 220–6; 6 (1903) 252–9 are but a few examples

37   p 612 in W R Grace, The Government of Cities in the State of New York, Harper's 67 (1883) 609–16

38   F C Howe, Municipal Ownership, in Great Britain, Bulletin of the Bureau of Labour (Washington DC 1906) p 2. Also see his article in the Publications of the American Economic Association 3rd series 7 (1906) 113–32

39   Sylvester Baxter in Cosmopolitan 18 (1894–5) 55

40   Albert Shaw, Municipal Government in Great Britain (London 1904) pp 42, 50–5

41   J R Commons, Races and Immigrants p 43. Also A Shaw, Relations of Municipal Administration, in Congress of Arts and Science: Universal Exposition (St Louis 1904); American Journal of Sociology 10 (1904–5) 794; Street Railway Journal (1902) pp 156–7. James Bryce and a former Lord Provost of Glasgow Sir John Ure Primrose endorsed that view though the American Leo S Rowe strongly opposed, Chicago Tribune (8 May 1905), L S Rowe. Problems of City Government (London 1909) p 89

42 H Munsterberg, The Americans (London 1905) p 5

43 Henry James, The American Scene (London 1968 edn) p 135

44 Lord Bryce, Hindrances to Good Citizenship (New Haven 1909) p 7; also see my article, Glasgow Trams and American Politics 1894–1914, SHR 56 (1977) pp 64–84

45 John Higham, Strangers in the Land: Patterns in American Nativism 1860–1925 (New Brunswick NJ 1955), and Barbara M Solomon, Ancestors and Immigrants: a changing New England Tradition (Boston 1956)

46 J M Kousser, The Shaping of Southern Politics: Suffrage Restriction and the Establishment of the One Party South 1880–1910 (New Haven 1974); Brand Whitlock, Forty Years of It, (New York 1925); J R Commons, Myself (New York 1934); E A Ross, Seventy Years of It; E A Ross, Seventy Years of It; R T Ely, Ground Under Our Feet (New York 1938) pp 1–5; Ray Stannard Baker, Native American: The Book of My Youth (New York 1941). A Link, Woodrow Wilson and His Presbyterian Inheritance, in Essays in Scotch-Irish History, ed. E R R Green (London 1969) pp 1–17

47 F P Gibbon, William A Smith of the Boys' Brigade (London 1953 edn) pp 104–8 and 145–5 on Smith's two trips to USA

48 ibid p 60

49 ibid pp 104, 135–6. John Lewis Paton, John B Paton (London 1914) pp 271, 311–12, 317, 415, 436–8

50 See Christopher Lasch, The New Radicalism in America 1889–1963: The Intellectual as a Social Type (New York 1969 edn). Also the visits of Jane Addams and the temperance activists in earlier chapters. Charles Zueblin attended Edinburgh University Summer School met Patrick Geddes and investigated Glasgow. C Zueblin maintained a correspondence with Geddes from 1898 to 1920. Zueblin introduced Professor J H Raymond of Chicago, 26 Feb 1901, Geddes Papers. Geddes was in contact with Sir Daniel M Stevenson (Glasgow), E R L Gould, James Mavor. He was also largely responsible for promoting halls of residence in the University of Glasgow. See Henry Jones to P Geddes, 12, 15 Feb 12 Dec 1895 Geddes Papers.

Geddes lectured to several Glasgow groups, town planners and others. P Geddes to J M Biggar, 1 May, 1 Oct 1911. See P Geddes, City Development (Edinburgh 1904) in which he emphasises the important role of teachers and clergy p 266. Philip Boardman, Patrick Geddes, Maker of the Future (Chapel Hill 1944) and Paddy Kitchen, A most Unsettling Person; An Introduction to the Ideas and Life of Patrick Geddes (London 1977)

51 See Dr J B Russell's evidence to The Royal Commission on the Housing of the Working Classes vol 5 (1885) C4409; J F J Sykes, Public Health Problems (London 1892) among others. A K Chalmers paper on the city's health in Annals American Academy of Political and Social Science 25 (1905) 273–89, and Robert Crawford former city councillor, The Struggle Against Preventable Diseases: Typhoid and Tuberculosis, Annals, 29 (1907) 184–203. Full discussion will be found in J B Russell, Public Health Administration in Glasgow (Glasgow 1905) and A K Chalmers, The Health of Glasgow 1818–1925 (Glasgow 1930)

52 See for example Report on the Homes of the People and Sketches of Some Dwellings in Glasgow (Glasgow 1882); Corporation of Glasgow, Report of the Proceedings at the Conference as to Cheap Dwellings 24, 25 Sept 1901 (Glasgow 1901); The Glasgow Presbytery Commission on Housing (Glasgow 1904); and (E R L Gould) Eighth Special Report of the Commissioner of Labour: The Housing of the Working People (Washington DC 1895): Transactions of the Fourth International Home Relief Congress held in Edinburgh, June 7–10 1904 (Edinburgh 1905) where Glasgow's municipal work was well publicised. James Grahame, the founder of the Glasgow Society for the Prevention of Cruelty to Children was supposed to have got the idea from the visit to America p 35. Scottish, Labour Colony Association Ltd, 3rd Annual Report (Glasgow 1900) gives a full history: D M Stevenson, Labour Colonies Abroad, New Review 7 1892 492–504; The Times, 30 Sept 1902 gives a staggering catalogue of municipal enterprises.

53 F C Howe, The British City: The Beginnings of Democracy (London 1907). See similar ideas in Frank Parsons, The City For the People (Philadelphia 1900); J R Commons, Social Reform and the Church (1894) (New York 1967 edn)

54 See annual Reports of the Glasgow Corporation Tramways from 1895–6 to 1923–4: Glasgow Corporaton Tramways: Report by the General Manager and Engineer on Tramway Traction and Operation in American Cities (Glasgow 1896); J Dalrymple, Chicago's Tramways (Glasgow 1906); J Dalrymple, Notes by the General Manager on a Visit by the

Master of Works and himself to the United States and Canada (Glasgow 1914). He was to go over afterwards in 1923. Glasgow Herald (31 Oct 1923/16 Jan 1924)

55   Report of the National Civic Federation: Municipal and Private Ownership and Operation (New York 1907) pt 1 p 288

56   Stanley Buder, Pullman (New York 1967). See S P Hays, The Politics of Reform and Municipal Government in the Progressive Era, Pacific Northwest Review 45 (1964) 151–9; Blake McKelvey, The Urbanisation of America, 1860–1915 (New Brunswick 1963); Stuart D Brandes, American Welfare Capitalism, 1880–1940 (Chicago 1976)

57   For example, J Gilbert, Designing the Industrial State (Chicago 1972); J Weinstein, The Corporate Ideal in the Liberal State 1900–1918 (Boston 1968); H V Emy, Liberals, Radicals and Social Politics, 1892–1914 (Cambridge 1973) pp 4–14

58   R Donald in Politics have bearing on Municipal ownership, Street Railway Journal 21 (1903) 76; and Frank Parsons, The Municipal Movement: Tramways Report of the National Civic Federation, vol I pt i pp 260–301; Leo S Rowe, in Annals of the American Academy of Political and Social Science 10 (1898) 269

59   See ibid 27 (1906) 14; Outlook 34 (1905) 463; F C Howe, The Modern City and Its Problems (New York 1915) 1969 edn p 180; The Advertisement Menace, New Review 9 (1893) 466–81

60   R T Ely in Century 55 (1897–8) 781. Also D C Gilman, University Problems in the United States (New York 1898) p 90, various writers 'show us what man is without a history'. Discipline was ruthlessly enforced. National Civic Federation found stern discipline. A five-year reference was required, regulation uniform worn, very tight supervision. 1085 of 2433 employees were of less than three years' standing. Outlook 27 May 1905 reported that men were dismissed for wearing uniform in public house. It is also worth noting the art-reform connection. James Mavor had been the founding editor of the Scottish Art Review and a contributor; D M Stevenson had an artist brother; Walter Crane, Ideals in Art (London 1905) pp 121, 191 also contributed his influence. Also Thomas Howarth, Charles Rennie Mackintosh and the Modern Movement, (London 1977 edn)
     On immigrants see W H Allen, Poor Man's England, Chatauquan 4 (1905) 264–70 which deals with Glasgow Jews; Royal Commission on Alien Immigration (1903) 16605, 20860–998; Glasgow Herald (14, 21, 28 Oct, 4 Nov 1911) for a series of articles on Jews, Germans, Scandinavians and Germans in Glasgow. The Destitute Alien in Great Britain, ed. Arnold White, (London 1892) attacks Jews and Italians, as does J D Whelpley, The Problem of the Immigrant (London 1905)

61   E P Thompson, William Morris: Romantic to Revolutionary (London 1956); Laurence Thompson, The Enthusiasts: A Biography of Katherine and Bruce Glasier (London 1971); Bruce Glasier, William Morris and the Early Days of the Socialist Movement (London 1921); Emrys Hughes, Keir Hardie (London 1956); David Kirkwood, My Life of Revolt, show the strength of Glasgow sentiment, a feature generally overlooked in K O Morgan, Keir Hardie (London 1975)

62   See R Crawford, Glasgow's Experience with Municipal Ownership and Operation, Annals . . . 27 (1906) 1–19

63   Ira Kipnis, the American Socialist Movement 1897–1912 (New York 1972) pp 167–9

64   A Shaw, Glasgow A Municipal Study, Century 39 (1890) 721–36, 736 and T C Devlin, Municipal Reform in the United States (New York 1906) p 174

65   F C Howe, The British City p 161

66   R Hofstadter and W P Metzger, A History of Academic Freedom In the United States (New York 1955) pp 420–59

67   Washington Gladden, Tools and the Man (Boston 1893) p 74

68   From the massive literature on American Progressivism the most relevant from our purpose are: Martin J Schiesel, The Politics of Efficiency: Municipal Administration and Reform in America 100–1920 (Berkeley 1977); B J Bledstein, The Culture of Professionalism: The Middle Class and the Development of Education in America (New York 1976); Paul Boyer, Urban Masses and Moral Order in America 1820–1920 (Cambridge Mass 1978); R Sennett, Families against the City: Middle Class Houses of Industrial Chicago 1972–1940 (Cambridge Mass 1970); Robert M Crunden, Ministers of Reform: The Progressive Achievement in American Civilisation, 1889–1920 (New York 1982); David Rothman, Conscience and Convenience; The Asylum and Its Alternatives in Progressive America (New York 1980); M

Klein and Harvey A Kantor, Prisoners of Progress: American Industrial Cities, 1880–1920 (New York 1976)
69   G Stanley Hall, Adolescence, 2 vols (New York 1904) vol 2 pp 579–637; William L O'Neill, Divorce in the Progressive Era (New York 1973 edn); Paul T Ringenbach, Tramps and Reformers, 1873–1916; The Discovery of Unemployment in New York (Westport Conn 1973); see the numerous urban studies like Stephan Thernstrom, The Other Bostonians: Poverty and Progress in the American Metropolis 1880–1970 (Cambridge Mass 1973); Howard P Chudacoff, Mobile Americans Residential and Social in Omaha, 1880–1920 (New York 1972)
70   US Historical Statistics Introduction by Ben J Wattenberg (Washington DC 1976) form· the basis of these figures
71   Reinhold Niebuhr, the Kingdom of God in America (New York 1950)
72   E T Devine, Progressive Social Action (New York 1833) p 120
73   Vida Dutton Scudder, On Journey (New York 1937) p 171 and her Socialism and Character (New York 1912 pp 67, 111, 154, 177
74   Quoted in Caro Lloyd, Henry Demarest Lloyd, 2 vols (New York 1912) vol 2 pp 74–5. Also see C E Russell, Barehands and Stonewalls: Some Recollections of A Side-Line Reformer (New York 1933) p 181
75   Robert A Woods, Modern Church (9 Apr, 21 May, 16 July, 10 Sept, 9 Nov 1891, 3 Mar 1892); Americans in Process: A Settlement Study, ed. R A Woods (Boston 1903) pp 50, 147, 354–5; The City Wilderness; A Settlement Study, ed. R A Woods (Cambridge Mass 1898) pp 227–30
76   Henry James, The American Scene (London 1968 edn) p 76
77   Quoted in G R Stewart, Bret Harte: Argonaut and Exile (Boston 1931) p 285
78   F C Howe, The Confessions of a Reformer (Chicago 1967 edn) p 34
79   John Dewey, Democracy in Education (New York 1963 edn) pp 41–53 and John Macunn, The Making of Character (Cambridge 1900) pp 91–117
80   E W Bemis, ed. Municipal Monopolies (New York 1899). He spent some considerable time in Glasgow about 1898–9
81   See his Labour Cọ-partnership (London 1898) pp 299–325; Letters to H D Lloyd from J G Gray, 26 Oct, J N Forsyth, 22 Oct and James Deans, 22 Oct, 10 Dec 1897; Same Jones to H B Lloyd, 6 Dec 1897, Henry Demarest Lloyd Papers (Wisconsin Historical Society Madison Wisconsin). All the letters to the SCWS were destroyed when the society moved its premises
82   S Baxter, Public Control of Urban Transit, Cosmopolitan 18 (1894–5) 54–60, and A E Morgan, Edward Bellamy (Philadelphia 1974 edn) pp 94, 261
83   H D Lloyd to D R Stewart, Broxburn Oil Co Broxburn, 14 Nov 1896, 16 Feb 1897; D R Stewart to H D Lloyd, 27 Oct 1895, 15 Mar 1897, with public letter published in Daily Chronicle. R Donald was the editor. C McA Destler, Henry Demarest Lloyd and the Empire of Reform (Philadelphia 1963). Lloyd's wife was a Scot
84   H D Lloyd, typescript of address delivered to Nineteenth Century Club (New York 10 Feb 1898), Lloyd Papers. Also see Similar views in Samuel Jones, address to the League of American Municipalities, 3 Aug 1898, typescript in Jones Papers
85   J B Glasier to H D Lloyd, 20 Oct 1897, Lloyd Papers
86   See Sheridan Gilley, Catholics and Socialists in Glasgow 1906–12, in Hosts, Immigrants and Minorities, Historical Responses to Newcomers in British Society, 1870–1914, ed. Kenneth Lunn, pp 160–200. John Wheatley reprinted the pamphlet, Economic Discontent. Robert E Doherty, Thomas J Hagerty The Church and Socialism, Labour History 3 (1962) 39–56 Daniel De Leon, the American Socialist Labour Party leader visited Glasgow in August 1904 and was largely responsible for the formation of the Scottish Socialist Labour organisation, continuing other contacts through James Connolly, and promoting the idea of Industrial Unionism, Socialist (Edinburgh) Nov 1904 and Aug 1914 De Leon contributed articles to the paper through that period. Neil Maclean was his main Glasgow supporter. See also Raymond Challinor, The Origins of British Bolshevism (London 1977) pp 24–42 on Connolly and De Leon in Scotland
87   Henry George quoted Anna George de Mille, Henry George p 129
88   J B Russell, the Glasgow medical officer of health, in Sanitation and Social Economics: An Object Lesson, Proceedings of the Glasgow Philosophical Society 21 (1889–90) 8. Also in A K Chalmers (ed), Public Health Administration in Glasgow: A Memorial Volume of the work of J B Russell (Glasgow 1905) p 266

89   See above; R Donald, British Democracy in Power, Outlook 83 (1906) 204–10 and his The British Government and Social Legislation, Outlook 83 (1906) 326–9

90   D M Stevenson to J Fels, 13 Oct 1906 and to P Geddes, 13 Oct 1906; J Fels of P Geddes, 6 June 1907; P Geddes to J Fels, 12 June 107. Also Arthur Power Dudden, Joseph Fels and The Single Tax Movement (Philadelphia 1971) pp 141, 217, 247

91   The Public 25 Sept 1908, 9 Oct 1908, 1 Oct 1909, 21 July 1911, 15 Aug 1913. The Louis F Post Papers in the Library of Congress contain a manuscript autobiography describing in detail his two trips to Glasgow. On the first he met Keir Hardie, Joseph Fels, John Paul and Baillie Burt. On the second he was accompanied by Henry George Jr. They spoke for Dundas White in Dumbarton and in other areas around Glasgow

92   Francis Neilson, My Life in Two Worlds 2 vols (Appleton Wis 1952) vol 1 pp 245, 296 vol 2 p 10; Brand Whitlock, Letters and Journals, ed. Allan Nevis 2 vols (New York 1936) vol 2 pp 156, 169; The Public (4 Oct 1912). Post wrote his own impressions in The Public II, 18 (25 Feb 1910). Colonel Greig, the brother-in-law of Judge Edward O Brown of Chicago had won the affection of Glasgow land values supporters and election to parliament. See biographical list

93   Brand Whitlock, Letters and Journals, ed. Allan Nevins vol 2 pp 156, 169; Robert M Crunden, A Hero in Spite of Himself; Brand Whitlock, in Art Politics and War (New York 1969) p 226

94   Marcus T Reynolds, The Housing of the Poor in American Cities (Baltimore 1893)

95   The Powderly Papers Catholic University Washington DC proved disappointing for Scottish interests. There is a good organisational history in the catalogue of the microfilm edition of his papers. Henry Pelling, The Knights of Labour in Britain. See the photograph taken at Jamacia Street bridge in Glasgow from Powderly's collection; also Economic History Review 2nd Series 8 (1955–6) 1–17

96   Charlotte Perkins Gilman diary, C P Gilman papers

97   Frank Parsons, The Wisdom of Glasgow, American Fabian (Dec 1896); also see Feb 1897, Jan 1898

98   The City For the People (Philadelphia nd); Eugene Debs, the socialist wrote extolling its value 4 Apr 1900 and Washington Gladden distributed it among Columbus city councillors 8 Apr 1900 Albertson Papers; his The Public Ownership of Monopolies (Boston 1894) pp 6, 13 quoting Glasgow's example and his Legal Doctrine and Social Progress (New York 1911 edn); Thomas P Jenkin, The American Fabian Movement, Western Political Quarterly 1 (1948) 113–23

99   E T Devlin, Quarterly 1 (1948) 113–23

100   W D Haywood, Bill Haywood's Book, pp 234–5: H M Hyndman, Further Reminiscences (London 1913). S Levenson, James Connolly (London 1973); B Pribicevic, The Shop Stewards Movement and Workers Control 1910–1922 (Oxford 1959), pp 12, 111; L Glen Seretan, Daniel De Leon: The Odyssey of An American Marxist (Cambridge Mass 1979); Ian Wood, Irish Immigrants and Scottish Radicalism 1880–1906, in Essays in Scottish Labour History; A tribute to W H Marwick, ed. Ian MacDougall (Edinburgh 1978) pp 65–89

101   H Marcuse, Reason and Revolution (London 1968 edn) p 342

102   eg F C Howe, The British City, p 45 and E S Rowe, Annals . . . 10 (1897) 269

103   C E Russell Diary, Russell Papers 1905 on his Pacific tour. He mellowed a little in his 1914–15 diary, retaining his admiration for Scotland but his utter contempt for Winston Churchill

104   30 Sept 1883 letter of her trip Addams Papers (Chicago)

105   Brand Whitlock, Letters and Journals vol 2 pp 156, 169; J Tager, The Intellectual as Urban Reformer: Brand Whitlock and the Progressive Movement (Cleveland 1968). John Maclean, The Greenock Jungle (Glasgow 1908)

106   R P Porter, The Breadwinners Abroad, p 30

107   See Charles Phelps Cushing, Glasgow The Chicago of Scotland, Travel (July 1915). 'When I was growing a little homesick for Manhattan, a walk down Sauchiehall Street lifted the gloom. I found myself on Broadway again, but by some odd transformation such as dreams produce all the people were chattering away with an unmistakeable accent of Scotch.'

108   Address in New York at the Alliance of the Reformed Churches holding the Presbyterian System, 9th General Council (New York 1909) pp 34–5

109   Harry Lauder popularised the song about this period

110   Henry Drummond, The Ascent of Man (London 1894), eg pp 297, 443
111   C W Dilke, Greater Britain: A Record of Travel in English Speaking Countries Diary 1866–1867 (London 1868) esp p 85, 'With that earnestness which is seen in the Scotch universities at home.'
112   C Lash, The Emergence of the Intellectual; Daniel C Gilman, The Johns Hopkins University 1876–1889 (New York 1890) p 33; Allan Nevins, The State Universities and Democracy (Urbana 1962) pp 23, 98–9
113   Janet Adam Smith, John Buchan (London 1965) pp 13–45; John Reith, Wearing Spurs (London 1966); The Reith Diaries, ed. Charles Stuart (London 1975) pp 17–46: David Watson, Chords of Memory (Edinburgh 1936). Watson was to become a leading social gospel character in the Church of Scotland. See his American-influenced works: Social Problems and the Church's Duty (London 1908); Social Advance: its meaning, method and goal (London 1912); The Church at Work (Edinburgh 1926); and his report with W P Paterson, Social Evils and Problems, edited for the Church of Scotland Commission in the War (Edinburgh 1918). Also see The Scottish Social Christian Union and How It Can Be Found (Glasgow 1901); Child Life in Cities (Glasgow 1901); Social Problems and the Church's Duty (Glasgow 1908)
114   See biographical list
115   Josiah Strong, The Next Great Awakening (London 1901) p 115
116   For example Mavor was on the staff in contact with numerous American Progressive reformers. My Window on the World vol 2 pp 152–96
117   See biographical list. Sir Henry Jones and J H Muirhead, The Life and Philosophy of Edward Caird (Glasgow 1921); See the Caird correspondence in the Wenley Papers, University of Michigan. Also the testimonials from A C Bradley and others. W M Wenley, The University Extension Movement in Scotland (Glasgow 1895); W H Marwick, Early Adult Education in the West of Scotland, Journal of Adult Education 4(1930) 191–202 and earlier efforts in his Adult Education in Glasgow Eight Years Ago, Proceedings Philosophical Society of Glasgow 59 (1930–1) 86–97. On the broader implication see John M Knapp, The Universities and the Social Problem (London 1895); Amos Warner, American Charities (New York 1908 edn) p viii; H B Adams, University Extension in the United States, Review of Reviews II (1891) 510–22 and Public Libraries and Popular Education, Home Education Bulletin (31 May 1900); C Hanford Henderson, University Extension, Popular Science Monthly 40 (1891) pp 1–15; James E Russell, Extension of University Teaching in England and America, Publications of the University Extension Board 10 (1895); S Skidmore, University Extension, Lippincott's Magazine 46(1890) 549–58; Joseph E Gould, The Chataquan Movement (Albany New York 1972); Malcolm S Knowles, The Adult Education Movement in the United States (New York 1962); W H Draper, University Extension 1873–1923; Margaret T Hodgen, Workers Education in England and the United States (London 1925) pp 134–5
    J B Paton to H B Adams, 2 Jan 1900, H B Adams Papers, Johns Hopkins University, tells of the holiday Reading Centre at Ardconnell on the Clyde
118   E Caird to W M Wenley, 21 Apr 1894, Wenley Papers, University of Michigan
119   E Caird to W M Wenley, 28 Jan 1896, Wenley Papers
120   See Sociology as an Academic Subject, Sociological Papers (London 1907) introduction James Bryce vol 3 pp 281–92
121   Anglo Saxon and the Scandinavian produce the best citizens, p 286: R M Wenley to P Geddes, 5 Feb 1896, Geddes Papers, National Library of Scotland. Article by Wenley in The Educational Review (1897) quoted in Review of Reviews (May 1897) p 349. See G S Hall in biographical list
122   See biographical list
123   Essays in Municipal Administration (New York 1908) p 287
124   Essays in Municipal Administration, p 290. Also see his The Street Railway Question in Chicago, Quarterly Journal of Economics 21 (1906–7) 371–404
125   R T Ely, Socialism (London 1895) pp 312–13. See his autobiography, Ground Under our Feet (New York 1938) and Sidney Fine, R T Ely, Forerunner of Progressivism 1880–1901, MVHR 37 (1950–1) 599–624; B G Rader, The Academic Mind: The Influence of R T Ely; American Life (Lexington K Y 1966)
126   W Stull Holt (ed) Historical Scholarship in the United States 1876–1901; as revealed in the Correspondence of Herbert Baxter Adams (Baltimore 1938); see William Thomson (Lord Kelvin) to D C Gilman, President Johns Hopkins University, 2 Sept 1882, 10 May 1877, 2 Oct

1883, 5 Feb 1884, 7 Nov 1885, 23 June 1896, Gilman Papers, Johns Hopkins University Baltimore; D C Gilman to daughter, 17, 24, 31 July, 7 Aug 1892 on his visit to Lord Kelvin in Glasgow and Largs, Gilman Papers
127   See Biographical list
128   H B Adams to A Shaw, 5 May 1887, Shaw Papers also 24 Dec 1889 and 30 June 1894
129   James Bryce to A Shaw, 27 Nov 1884. Also see the Bryce-Shaw correspondence Shaw Papers
130   Icaria (New York 1884). It was a study of the ideas of the French communitarian Etienne Cabet and his experience in America
131   Municipal Government in England (Baltimore 1889) p 3
132   ibid p 8
133   William Smart, Glasgow and Its Municipal Industries, Quarterly Journal of Economics 9 (1894–5) 188–94
134   New York
135   See Lyman Abbott in Outlook (2 Feb 1895): Christian Work (31 Jan 1895); St Paul Dispatch (26 Apr 1895); New York Mail and Express (1895); San Francisco Chronicle (27 Jan 1895); Scrapbook in Shaw Papers
136   eg F Parsons to A Shaw, 20 Dec 1897; Edmond Kelly to A Shaw, 20 Mar 1894; S Rowe to A Shaw, nd; C Zueblin to A Shaw, 30 Aug 1897; Delos F Wilcox, 12 Feb 1896; R T Paine to A Shaw, 13 Nov 1897; E W Bemis To A Shaw, 19 Oct 1889, A Shaw Papers
137   Hazen Pingree to A Shaw, 12 Apr 1895 to J Riis to A Shaw, 10 July 1896, Shaw Papers
138   Henry Demarest Lloyd to A Shaw, 9 Feb 1895, Shaw Papers. 'I stop at the close of your chapter "A Study of Glasgow" to let off some of my enthusiasm. Your book it really seems to me may prove to be a turning point in the remaking of America.'
139   James Bryce to A Shaw, 27 Nov 1884 and W J Ashley to A Shaw 11 Jan 1895, Shaw Papers
140   R Donald to A Shaw, 28 June 1895; 20 June, 12 Oct 1896; 12 May 1897; Peter Fyfe to A Shaw, 28 Apr 1894. Thomas Dunlop to A Shaw, 31 Aug 1894, 4 Feb 1897 sent various Glasgow municipal reports. Dairy 19–21 Sept 1918; A Shaw to R S Baker, 25 Sept 1939, Shaw Papers
141   New York 1899; there is a considerable correspondence with Shaw 1883–1912
142   Milo R Maltbie, English Local Government Today: A Study of the relations between central and local government (New York 1897); his Municipal Functions: A study of the development and scope and tendency of municipal socialism, Municipal Affairs 2 (1898) 579–799; Glasgow's Municipal Tramways, Municipal Affairs 4 (1900) 40–59; and Conditions of Municipal Success, Municipal Affairs 6 (1902–3) 800–2. He later served on the National Civic Federation Commission which visited Glasgow in 1906
143   C Zueblin to P Geddes, 26 Feb 1901, 1 July 1911 3 June 1912, 17 Apr 1920
144   American Municipal Progress, New York. Geddes Papers, National Library of Scotland Edinburgh. H E Meller, Patrick Geddes. An Analysis of His Theory of Civics 1880–1904, Victorian Studies 16 (1972–3) 291–317. See Philip Boardman, Patrick Geddes, Maker of the Future, (Chapel Hill 1944), and Paddy Kitchen, A Most Unsettling Person: An Introduction to the Ideas of Patrick Geddes (London 1977)
145   Dictionary American Biography
146   Published in New York
147   On Gould see biographical list. Information provided by the office of records and administration, Johns Hopkins University. See E R L Gould–A Shaw correspondence, Shaw Papers; E R L Gould: A Memorial (New York 1915)
148   Gould wrote the Eighth Report of the Commissioner of Labour on European housing conditions which included a considerable study of Glasgow municipal and the Glasgow Workman's Dwelling Company Housing schemes. He also wrote numerous articles on drink and slum problems see below: Minute Book Glasgow Workman's Dwelling Company, Glasgow
149   A N Cumming, Public House Reform (London 1901) pp 89–90, 124–35; John Mann, Better Houses for the Poor—Will They Pay?, Proceedings Glasgow Philosophical Society 30 (1898–9) 83–124; his Housing the Very Poor, Municipal Affairs 6(1902–3) 431–7; Reformed Public Houses, Proc. Glasgow Philosophical Soc. 24 (1892–3) 9–28 for example were identical to E R L Gould, The Gothenburg System and Our Liquor Traffic, Forum 17(1893)

103–13; The Gothenburg System in America, Atlantic 72(1893) 538–45; The Popular Control of the Liquor Traffic (London 1894); (Raymond Calkins), The Committee of Fifty: Substitutes for the Saloon (Boston 1901). Gould served on the committee. He wrote The Temperance Problem: Past and Future, Forum 18 (1894–5) 339–51 to support the committee's ideas; E R L Gould, The Economics of Improved Housing (Boston 1896); The Social Condition of Labour (Baltimore 1893); copy of Manuscript of Life of Sir John Mann, Glasgow
150 E R L Gould, How Baltimore Banished the Tramps and Helped the Idle, Forum 17 (1893) 477–504; Amos Warner, American Charities (New York 1908 edn); J B Crooks, Politics and Progess: The Rise of Urban Progressivism in Baltimore 1895–1911 (Baton Rouge 1968) esp p 168; E R L Gould to A Shaw, 23 Jan, 14 May 1894, Shaw Papers. Charles Hirschfield, Baltimore 1870–1900, Studies in Social History (Baltimore 1941) esp p 159
151 Royal Commission on Labour: Fifth and Final Report part I (1894) p 89 and part II questions 6428–827: E R L Gould to A Shaw, 31 Jan 1893, Shaw Papers. Cf D M Stevenson, The Poor of Glasgow and How to Help Them with suggestions for forming A Glasgow Social Union, privately printed (Glasgow 1889)
152 E R L Gould to A Shaw, 1 Mar 1892, Shaw Papers
153 E R L Gould to A Shaw, 11 Jan 1897, Shaw Papers. Shaw published an article Homewood boosting Gould's housing schemes in Review of Reviews (July 1897) pp 43–51; I am most grateful to the City and Suburban Housing Company for allowing me to utilise their records for the Years to 1920 in their headquarters in New York City. The Company's annual reports proved invaluable.
     Glasgow and the United States had a longstanding connection housing reform. In 1843, James Lumsden, the Lord Provost of Glasgow had visited the USA to return and establish model dwellings. It seems likely that he may have been influenced by the building programmes of the New York Association for Improving the Conditions of the Poor, though such ideas were current in Edinburgh and the model Scottish factory villages. A similar organisation flourished in Glasgow. Roy Lubove, The New York Association for Improving the Condition of the Poor: The Formative Years, New York Historical Society Quarterly 43(1959) 307–28; James Lumsden, American Memoranda (Glasgow 1844); Frank Worsdall, The Tenement: A Way of Life: A Social Historical and Architectural Study of Housing in Glasgow (Edinburgh 1979) pp 84–6 attributed the building to Lumsden's son. On later developments see Enid Gauldie, Cruel Habitations: A History of Working Class Housing 1780–1918 (London 1971); Alfred T White, Thirty-Five Years Experience as an Owner (New York 1912); The Tenement House Building Company, The Tenement Houses of New York (New York 1891); Federal Housing Administration, Four Decades of Housing with a Limited Dividend Corporation (Washington DC 1939); Tenement House Building Company Papers 1887–1904, New York Public Library: Richard Welling, As The Twig is Bent (New York 1942) shows the similarities and interests in Glasgow and America see Marvin E Gettelman, Charity and Social Classes in the United States, 1874–1900, American Journal of Economics and Sociology 22 (1963) 313–29 and 417–26. Not all were impressed: City of Liverpool: Report of the Deputation of the Housing Committee to Glasgow etc (Liverpool 1901); Builder Feb 1848
154 Review of Reviews (July 1897); E R L Gould to A Shaw 11, 14 June, 2 July 1897, Shaw Papers
155 E R L Gould, Annual Report of the Chamberlain of the City of New York 1902 (New York 1903). Harold Coffin Syrett, The City of Brooklyn 1865–1898 (New York 1944) pp 106–34. Gerald Kurland, Seth Low: the Reformer in an Urban and Industrial Age (New York 1971); obituary New York Times (19 Aug 1915). League For Political Education, E R L Gould 1860–1915; A Manual (New York 1916). The limits of Gould's and Progressive trust in popular democracy can be seen in his invitation to Tom Watson of Georgia, a militant segregationist, to lecture to the New York Nineteenth Century Club on suffrage restriction. E R L Gould to A Shaw, 5 Oct 1900. J M Kousser, The Shaping of Southern Politics: Suffrage Restriction and the Establishment of the One Party South (New Haven 1971). The Social Gospel advocates in some cases endorsed that view: Nathaniel S Shaler, European Peasants as Immigrants, Atlantic 71 (1893) 646–55. The 'new' was 'in essentially the same state as the Southern negro', p 649. The same writer described the Scots as 'qualified by a body of impulses which exactly fit the machinery of our civilisation and enable him to command all its great engines', p 516 in The Scotch Element in the American People, Atlantic 77 (1896) 508–16

156 W J Ashley to A Shaw, 11 Jan 1895, Shaw Papers
157 Anne Ashley, William James Ashley (London 1932) p 97
158 See the correspondence Jane Addams to J Mavor, 17 Aug 1903, 29 Nov 1910 in the Mavor Papers, the University of Toronto, Canada and James Mavor, My Windows on the Street of the World vol 2 pp 152–96: J Mavor to R T Ely, 11 Feb, 8 Jun, 7 Nov 1892, Ely Papers, Wisconsin Historical Society, Madison Wisconsin
159 W Smart to R T Ely, 24 Apr, 30 May 1895, Ely Papers
160 W Smart to R T Ely, 30 May 1895, Ely Papers
161 Simon N Patten, The Theory of Prosperity (New York 1902) p 226
162 See for example his 'Taxation in Glasgow' City and State, 30 Dec 1897 pp 210–11. He also contributed a regular admiring report on Glasgow to the Annals 6 (1895) 179; 8 (1896) 267–9, 578–84; 9 (1897) 132–33; 11 (1898) 430–4, 301–23; and his Problems of City Government (London 1909)
163 C R Woodruff The Municipal Problem, Chatauquan 36 (1902–3) 177–82. Also see biographical list
164 Robertson greatly influenced G D Herron, the Christian socialist; Bruce visited the United States on a number of occasions to lecture and Orr did likewise as well as being a contributor to the Fundamentals (1910). Alan Preston Neely, James Orr: A Study in Conservative Christian Apologetics, unpublished PhD dissertation, South Western Baptist Theological College Fort-Worth (Texas 1960), copy in Glasgow University Library
165 Alliance of the Presbyterian Churches Holding the Presbyterian System Sixth General Council, Glasgow 1896, London 1896, Eighth 1904, London 1906, Ninth New York 1909, Ninth New York 1909, London 1909. The list of American delegates and their Scottish brethren is invariably large
166 Leslie Hunter, John Hunter (London 1922) p 87
167 John Hunter, pp 122–6. He supported Women Suffrage
168 John Hunter, pp 226–9, 233–9
169 John Lewis Paton, John B Paton (London 1910) pp 217–18. Also his editorship of Christ and Civilisation (London 1910). Strong was promoting his Institute of Social Service in Britain. It had been publicised at the 1901 Glasgow Exhibition
170 See above and W H G Armytage, Civic Universities (London 1956)
171 Chords of Memory (Glasgow 1938)
172 eg Sophonisba P Breckinridge (ed), The Child in the City (London 1912) and Report of an Inquiry conducted for the Scottish Council for Womens' Trades: The Employment of Children (Glasgow 1901). Josephine Goldmark, Fatigue and Efficiency; a study in Industry (New York 1912)
173 Lawrence J Pivar, Purity Crusade: Sexual Morality and Social Control 1868–1900 (Westport Conn 1973). Frederic Whyte, The Life of W T Stead 2 vols (New York nd) pp 159–86. Mark Thomas Connelly, The Response to Prostitution in the Progressive Era (Chapel Hill 1980)
174 For example, Stanton Coit, Neighbourhood Guilds: An Instrument of Social Reform (London 1892); E R L Gould, Park Areas and Open Spaces in Cities American Statistical Association, new series 2–3 (June–Sept 1888) 49–61: Clarence Lee Rainwater, The Play Movement in the United States: A Study of Community Recreation (Chicago 1921)
175 James Addams, Democracy and Social Ethics (Cambridge Mass 1964) pp xii, 7, 274; The Social Thought of Jane Addams, ed C Lasch (Indianapolis 1964) p 24; Graham Taylor, Religion in Social Action (New York 1913) p 224; Louise C Wade, Graham Taylor; Pioneer For Social Justice, 1851–1938 (Chicago 1964); Ray Lubove, The Professional Altruist: The Emergence of Social Work as a career, 1880–1930 (Cambridge Mass 1965)
176 Jane Addams, Twenty Years at Hull House, shows all these qualities
177 The Menace of Great Cities 1913–1912. Also see his The Hindrances to Good Citizenship (New Haven 1909) and The Government of British Cities: Address Before the City Club of New York 8 March 1911 (New York 1911)
178 Quoted in Mary E Richmond, Friendly Visiting Among the Poor, (Montclair N J 1969 (1899) p 82 and see Florence Kelley, Some Ethical Gains Through Legislation (New York 1905)
179 Charles Zueblin, American Municipal Progress New York 1902–20. The Glasgow reformers had contributed to the Scottish Art Review 1 (1888–9) edited by James Mavor, a series of articles in this vein: Edward Caird, Patrick Geddes and others

180   Review of Reviews (Sept 1893) p 314
181   Review of Reviews (Sept 1893) p 315
182   Glasgow Evening News (6 June 1905); Arlin Turner, George Washington Cable: a biography (Durham NC 1956) pp 311–12; Visitors Book Glasgow's Provost; DAmB
183   D M Stevenson to Mrs L Cunningham, 10 Sept 1936, Geddes Papers
184   The Journals of T J Cobden-Sanderson 1879–1922 2 vols (London 1926) vol 1 23 Dec 1888. Also Samuel Barnett, The Ideal City, (np nd). On the University–Church idea see Herbert Baxter Adams, The Church and Popular Education (Baltimore 1900) p 16; R G Moulton, University Extension and the University of the Future (New York 1891) pp 5, 10, 11; Daniel C Gilman, University Problems in the United States (New York 1898) pp 52, 198; J R Commons, Social Reform and the Church. On the background to this transatlantic attitude see J O Baylen, A Victorian's Crusade in Chicago 1893–94, Journal of American History 51 (1964–5) 418–34 and his The New Jerusalem in Victorian Britain, Australian Journal of Political History 18 (1972) 367–85; Hugh McLeod, Class and Religion in the Late Victorian City (London 1974); Stephen Koss, Nonconformity in Modern British Politics (London 1975); John F Glaser, English nonconformity and the decline of Liberalism, American Historical Review 68 (1957–8) 352–63; J H S Kent, The Role of Religion in the Cultural Structure of the Late Victorian City, Transactions of the Royal Historical Society, 5th series, 23 (1973) 153–74; Ferenc M Szasz, Protestantism and the Search for Stability 1875–1925, pp 88–102, in Building the Organisational Society, ed Jerry Israel (New York 1972)
185   R A Woods to Revd Mr Wragge, 22 June 1891, Robert A Woods Papers, Houghton Library, Harvard University, Wood's articles appeared in The Modern Church 9 Apr, 2 May, 16 July, 10 Sept, 19 Nov 1891 and 3 Mar 1892. Other contributions included George Eyre Todd, Leaves From the Life of a Scottish Man of Letters (Glasgow 1934) pp 97–9: Shelley seems to have become a Roman Catholic later. He wrote pamphlets for the Irish Catholic Truth Society, Dublin but unfortunately their successors, Veritas were unable to trace any records. Wenley, Edward Caird and J H Muirhead contributed as well as the American biblical writer, Revd J Whitton
186   R A Woods to Revd Walter Wragge, Conway, New Hampshire, 22 June 1891 Woods Papers Houghton Library Collection, Harvard University
187   R A Woods to Revd W Wragge, 22 June 1891, Woods Papers
188   Stanton Coit, Neighbourhood Guilds (London 1891); his The Soul of America, p 89; Simon N Patten, The Development of English Thought: A Study in the Economic Interpretation of History (New York 1899) p 338; his Theory of Prosperity (New York 1902) p 207; Mary P Follett, The New State: Group Organisation and the Politics of Popular Government (London 1934 edn (1918)) pp 51, 103, 161; Gustave Le Bon, The Crowd (London 1912 edn (1896)) pp 68, 71; Margaret Timms, Jane Addams (London 1961) p 61
189   ibid
190   Quoted R A Woods, English Social Movements (London 1895), p 166. Also see his edited work, Americans in Process: A Settlement Study (Boston 1903) pp 50–1, 195, 354–5; and his The City Wilderness: A Settlement Study (Cambridge Mass 1898) pp 227–30, 307
191   C S Loch, Charity and Social Life (London 1910)
192   R A Woods to Jane Addams, 4 Sept 1895, Addams Papers (Swarthmore)
193   Sir John Gorst, Settlements in England and America pp 3–29 in John M Knapp, The Universities and the Social Problem (London 1895). It was his inaugural address as Lord Rector of Glasgow University in 1894
194   George Hooker to Mr Maclehose, 27 Apr 1896, R A Woods to Jane Addams, 5 May 1893 Jane Addams Papers, 5 May 1893 (Swarthmore College, Pennsylvania); G Hooker to Mrs Kerr, 27 Apr 1896
195   John Trevor to Jane Addams, 3 June 1896, Addams Papers
196   Julia Lathrop, Village Care for the Insane, National Conference on Social Welfare Report of Proceedings (1902) pp 185–99
197   Abraham Flexner, Medical Education in Europe (New York 1912) p 122. Ann Howard Shaw, Story of a Pioneer (New York 1915) and Alice Hamilton, Exploring the Dangerous Trades (Boston 1943) pp 161–2
198   H J W Dain, The Great Dynamite Factory at Ardeer, McClures 9 (1897–8) 823–36. Leisure interest encouraged many holiday articles: T L James, A Summer Tour of the Scottish Highlands, Cosmopolitan 21 (1896) 571–81; J M Gleeson, Drummond Castle, Century 66

(1903) 833–5; A C Gordon's Climbing The Scottish Alps, Cosmopolitan 33 (1902) 635–40: W W Smith, The Characteristics of the Scottish People, Chatauquan 27 (1898) 642–52

199   See below and Paola E Coletta, William Jennings Bryan, 4 vols (Lincoln Nebraska 1964–9) vol 1 pp 316–18

200   G G Mayor to A Shaw, 14 Dec 1894, Shaw Papers

201   Typescript of address 26 July 1899 in Samuel 'Golden Rule' Jones, Papers, Toledo, Ohio, Public Library. Also see Samuel M Jones, The New Right: A Plea for Fair Play through a More Just Social Order (New York 1899) pp 75, 282, 301, 334, 349–50

202   Typescript of address 3 Aug 1889 to the League of American Municipalities, Jones Papers. It was similar to Henry Demarest Lloyd's 'Municipal Ownership' address to the New York Nineteenth Club 10 Feb 1898, M D Lloyd Papers typescript

203   Sam Jones to F Parsons, 28 Aug 1898 Albertson Papers

204   Washington Gladden, Papers State Historical Society contain a fair number of sermons on Glasgow Themes of municipal ownership and the ideas of Henry Drummond. His writings also show a close familiarity with the city; Social Facts and Forces (New York 1897) pp 158–61, 172–4, and Social Salvation (London 1902) invariably refer to Glasgow: At the International Congregational Council 1891 he appeared with George Gladstone of Glasgow at one session. J H Dorn, Washington Gladden Prophet of the Social Gospel (Columbus Ohio 1967) shows him in England in 1888, 1891, 1894, 1898 but his papers do not prove conclusively that he visited Glasgow although his sermons show many Glasgow interests. Also see Robert H Bremner's series of articles under the general heading The Civic Revival in Ohio, American Journal of Economics and Sociology, 8(1948) 62–8; The Single Tax Philosophy in Cleveland and Toledo, 9 (1949–50) 369–76; Municipal Ownership and Economic Privilege, 9 (1949–50) 478–82; Self-Government, (1950–1) 185–206; Tax Equalisation in Cleveland, 10 (1950–1) 301–12; Gas and Ice Monopolies in Toledo, 10 (1950–1) 417–29; Hoyt L Warner, Progressivism in Ohio, 1897–1917 (Columbus Ohio 1964)

205   Brand Whitlock, Letters and Diaries, ed Allan Nevins (New York 1936) p 156. His articles appeared in the Toledo Bee 22 Nov to 14 Dec 1912 with lavish illustration. They were invariably spread across the front page. On 25 Nov 1912 there was a large photo of the Kelvin Galleries. Brand Whitlock to John D Barry, San Francisco Bulletin (26 Feb 1913), 'I had the opportunity of studying the most wonderfully governed city that is from the standpoint of democracy in the English speaking world', Brand Whitlock Papers Library of Congress

206   Ben Lindsey to Brand Whitlock, 5 Feb 1913; Brand Whitlock to Ben Lindsey, 24 Jan 1913, Brand Whitlock Papers; Charles Larsen, The Life and Times of Ben Lindsey (Chicago 1972); M Sabinsky of Cleveland Dept of Public Safety, 23 Dec 1912 regarding Glasgow Fire Dept, B Whitlock to M Sabinsky, 30 Jan 1913; Mr J Langlands, Glasgow Street Lighting Dept to B Whitlock, 6, 9 Dec 1912; O Hamilton to B Whitlock, 12 Dec 1912; The City of Ashtabula to B Whitlock, 2 Dec 1912: Booster Club of East Liverpool to B Whitlock, 28 Dec 1912; Cleveland Women's Club to B Whitlock, 11 Dec 1912; W Morgan to B Whitlock 1 Feb 1913; Cincinnati City Club to B Whitlock, 11 Dec 1912: Mayor S Schilling, Canton Ohio to B Whitlock, 11 Dec 1912, Whitlock Papers. The reports were reprinted in the Cleveland Press, Toledo Blade, New York Rochester Times, Scrapbook, Brand Whitlock Papers

207   B Whitlock to James Busby, Scottish League for the Taxation of Land Values 17 Feb 1913; to Revd R S Horne MP, 17 Feb 1913; to R McGhee MP and F Neilson MP, 11, 26 Feb 1913. B Whitlock had spoken for Horne and the Progressive candidates at St Pancras, Westminster Gazette (30 Oct 1912); General letter of introduction for Revd John Bayne Ascham. Whitlock had found time to play golf. He wrote the local Scottish golf professional, Alexander Auchterlonie, Springfield Ohio 18 Feb, 3 Nov 1913 who had a sports shop in St Andrews to tell of his caddy there with three sons professionals in Florida: 'I can imagine nothing finer than a holiday at Turnberry.' He had also taken some 300 photos which were turned into a movie presumably for political purposes. Secretary to E E Maryin, Cleveland Press. He had come home to confer with Newton Baker Mayor of Cleveland to press for home rule in the state legislature, a point carried in 1913

208   Lilian Wald to Sylvia Pankhurst, 17 May 1912 replying to S Pankhurst to L Wald, 30 Apr 1912, Wald Papers, New York Public Library and Whitlock reported in Toledo 12 Dec 1912. He also attended and spoke at a meeting of the United Irish League, Townhead Branch, Glasgow. Belfast Irish Weekly and Ulster Examiner (26 Oct 1912) clipping in Brand Whitlock Papers

209   Amid the numerous articles and countercharges about the quality of Glasgow municipal services see Henry Demarest Lloyd, Labour Copartnership (London 1898), pp 168, 279: R Donald, The case for Municipal Trading, Contemporary Review 83 (1903) 485−500 and 622−39; his The Commercial Audit of Municipal Accounts, Contemporary Review 84 (1903) 724−7; his Municipal Trading, Traction and Transmission 1 (1903) 244−52, 3 38−46, 7 84−89; Practical Engineer (29 Sept 1899) 306; Outlook 83 (1906) 204−10, 326−9; R P Porter, Traction and Transmission, i (1901) 20−5, 81−9, 140−51, 228−33; 2 (1901) 220−6; 6 (1903) 252−9, and Municipal Affairs 6 (1902) 3 539−78. Others on the benefits of Glasgow include F C Howe, Municipal Ownership in Great Britain, Bulletin of the Bureau of Labour (Washington DC 1906); Frank Parsons, The Public Ownership of Monopolies (Boston 1894); and his article Glasgow's Great Record, Arena 32 (1904) 461−71; John Creelman, Municipal Non-Partisanship in Glasgow, Century 80 (1910) 667−74—he spent six months in Glasgow. A much neglected aspect of Progressive reform, pure milk, received attention in Glasgow, see John Spargo, The Commonsense of the Milk Question (New York 1908); John Sinclair, The Milk Supply and Public Health (Dundee 1901); A K Fallows, A City's Campaign for Pure Milk, Century 66 (1903) 555−65. Councillor Robert Crawford contributed Glasgow's Experience with Municipal Ownership and Operation, Annals 27 (1906) 1−19 and to The Struggle Against Preventable Diseases: Typhoid and Tuberculosis: A Symposium, Annals 29 (1907) 184−203
210   Melvin G Holli, Reform in Detroit: Hazen Pingree and Urban Politics, (New York 1969); Tom L Johnson, My Story (London 1913); H L Warner, Progressivism in Ohio, p 295 et seq
211   Every conceivable aspect of Glasgow municipal life and organisation was examined by American commissions: House Report on the Massachusetts Special Committee Appointed to investigate the Relations Betweeen Cities and Towns and Street Railway Companies, February 1898. Charles Francis Adams examined Glasgow and added an appendix by R P Porter pp 205−61: The Mayor's Committee of New York City: Report on Public Baths and Comfort Stations (New York 1897); Report of the Industrial Commission on Transportation (Washington DC 1900) p 4; The New York Tenement House Commission Report 1894 (Albany 1895); Eight Special Report of the Commissioner of Labour; The Housing of the Working People (Washington DC 1895); Report of the Industrial Commission on Transportation (Washington DC 1900); Report on Municipal Ownership of the American Street and Interurban Association, Street Railway Journal 29 (11 May 1907) 839−45; The National Civic Federation Commission; Municipal and Private Operation of Public Utilities; Report to the National Civic Federation Commission; Municipal and Private Operation of Public Utilities; Report to the National Civic Federation; Commission on Public Ownership and Operation (New York 1907): National Civic Federation commission on Foreign Inquiry; The Labour Situation in Great Britain and France 1919 (New York 1919). Proceedings of the Federal Electric Railways Commission, July−October 1919 (Washington DC 1920). In addition there were the British government reports which were widely publicised in America in The Report Municipal Operations 1900, Housing Royal Commission 1885 vol 5, and labour. There were also the Presbytery of Glasgow Investigations Report of the Commission on the housing of the poor in relation to their Social Condition (Glasgow 1891); Corporation of Glasgow: Report on Proceedings at conference as to Cheap Dwellings held 24−5 September 1901 (Glasgow 1901); Glasgow Municipal Commission: The Housing of the Poor Report (Glasgow 1904); Sir Samuel Chisholm, Municipal Enterprises (Glasgow 1901). The work of the Civic Improvement Trust was well publicised as was the work of the Medical Officers of Health, Drs Russell and Chalmers. Given such material and the host of American visitors to the city, Glasgow received coverage such as no other city in Britain or Europe remotely approached. The articles cascaded out in every conceivable journal invariably praising the city to the heights. I have found only one article on Birmingham, one on Nottingham and four on Berlin. See for example J Edward Mussey Hartwell, Public Baths in Europe, Bulletin of the Department of Labour no 11 (1897), 434−85: John Martin, Municipal Ownership, World's Work 2 (1901) 833−6; Charles Mulford Robinson, The Improvement of Towns and Cities (New York 1901); William H Tolman, Municipal Reform Movements in United States (New York 1895); R W De Forest and L Veiller (eds), The Tenement House Problem 2 vols (New York 1903) has much on Glasgow as did their articles in Annals 20 (1902) 83−95 and 25 (1905) 248−72; Lettice Fisher, Municipal Housing in British Cities, Municipal Affairs 6 (1902−3) 357−74; E R L Gould, The Housing Problem, Municipal Affairs 3 (1899) 108−31: A R Bennett, Municipal Telephony in Great Britain, Municipal Affairs 6 (1902−3) 683−700; C E

Russell, Soldiers of the Common Good, Everybody's 14 (1906) 42–55; H N Shepard, Municipal Housekeeping in Glasgow, American City 6 (1912) 709–13; W H Maxwell, The Removal and Disposal of Town Refuse (London 1908) and his British Progress in Municipal Engineering (London 1904) pp 108–23. Numerous other articles appeared in the Street Railway Journal eg 11 July 1908 traction and transmission, Railway World, American Gas Light Journal and many other journals.

212   London 28 June 1894

213   For example as early as 14 Oct 1894 the New York Times had examined Glasgow's street railways in a special article: R Donald Municipal Ownership of Street Railways in Glasgow, Outlook 80 (1905) 431–5; B O Flower's Arena magazine consistently supported municipal ownership eg 34 (1905) 88–9, 36 (1906) 424–6, S S Mclure the leading muckraking journal's owner, specialising in revelations of graft and corruption in public life had spent his childhood in Glasgow. P Lyon, Success Story: The Life and Times of S S Mclure (Delaware Fla 1967) pp 4–5; B O Flower, Progressive Men and Movements of the last Twenty-Five Years (Boston 1914) pp 139–40; F C Howe, The British City and his European Cities at Work (London 1913), The London Morning Leader described Porter as 'a man hallowing at a cyclone'

214   H R Meyer, Municipal Ownership in Great Britain (New York 1906); W G Fowler socialism in local Government (London 1908); Leonard Darwin, Municipal Trade (London 1903) and Municipal Ownership (London 1907); Lord Avebury, On Municipal Trading (London 1906); T D A Cockerell, Municipal activity in Britain, American Journal of Sociolology II (1905–6), 817–29. He was the brother of the renowned British bookbinder and on the staff of the University of Colorado; Benjamin Taylor, Municipal Glasgow, North American Review 184 (1907) 590–603 were conservative statements. The left was even more cynical: William English Walling, Socialism as It is (New York 1915) pp 50–1, 92–3, 163, 238–393; W E Walling and Harry W Laidler (eds) State Socialism: Pro and Con (New York 1917) pp 546–80; Gaylord Wilshire, Wilshire Editorials (New York 1906), pp 122–33 and 171–9; the Chicago traction magnate, Charles Yerkes, who later moved to London was invariably the villain, C E Russell, The Uprising of the Many, London (1907) pp 39–52, and Lawless Wealth (London 1908). A leading American socialist and muckraking writer, Russell was a typical in both instances. See David Chalmers, The Social and Political Ideas of the Muckrakers (New York 1964) and Harold S Wilson, McClure's magazine and the Muckrakers (Princeton 1971). The American lag in municipal activity and control can be readily seen throughout the nation in Pollution and Reform in American Cities 1870–1930, ed Martin V Melosi (Austin Texas 1980) esp pp 105–34 and Socialism and the Cities, ed Bruce M Stave

215   New York Times (5 Apr 1905). Street railways were at the centre of reform battles: Tom L Johnson, My Story; Clay MacShane, Technology and Reform; Street Railways and the Growth of Milwaukee, 1887–1900 (Madison Wis 1974). On the European aspect see John P McKay, Tramways and Trolleys: The Rise of Urban Mass Transport in Europe (Princeton 1976) and T C Baker and Michael Robbins, A History of London Transport 2 vols (London 1963–74) vol 2 pp 61–84

216   New York Times (8 Apr 1905); Public Opinion 38 (1905) 481–2, 574–5

217   C E Russell in Everybody's 17 (1907) 355

218   Chicago Tribune (5–12 May 1905)

219   Quoted Glasgow Herald (30 June 1905). D M Stevenson, the Lord Provost, made complaints about misrepresentation when he visited America in 1913. Mavor, 10 Aug, 19 Sept, Mavor Papers

220   New York Times (28 May 1905); Chicago Tribune (28, 30, 31 May 1905) C O'Malley, Mayor Dunne A Practical Idealist, Public Opinion (15 Apr 1905) pp 574–5

221   Cleveland Plain Dealer and Chicago Tribune (3, 4 June 1905); Street Railway Journal (13 May, 10 June 1905); Glasgow Herald (13 July 1905, 22 Feb, 13 Mar, 31 May, 1906). J Dalrymple Chicago's Tramways (Glasgow 1906)

222   W L Fisher to Tom L Johnson, 1 Dec 1905, Fisher Papers, Library of Congress: Also amid Tom L Johnson's municipalisation campaign, the Cleveland Leader ran a series of articles on Glasgow tramways in 1908. Street Railway Journal 31 (7 Mar 1908); F C Howe, The Case for Municipal Ownership, Publications of the American Economic Association 3rd series 7 (1906) 113–32; Winthrop D Daniels, Municipal Ownership, ibid pp 133–43; James Marwick (of Glasgow) Municipal Ownership of Street Railways: with an analysis of the accounts of the City of Glasgow Tramways, reprinted from the Wall Street Journal 3 June 1905 (np nd); Leo S

Rowe, Municipal Ownership and Operation: the Value of Foreign experience, American Journal of Sociology 12 (1906–7) 241–53: Hayes Robbins, Public Ownership versus Public Control, ibid 10 (1904–5) 787–813; F C Howe Municipal Ownership in Great Britain, Bulletin of the US Bureau of Labour Statistics No 62 (Jan 1906) 1–123. The issue continues in the National Civic Federation Review (Sept 1905—Dec 1906, Feb 1908). It moved increasingly to the right: R F Phillips, Insidious Methods of the Socialist Press Propaganda (July 1909) is a scaremongering outburst

223   John E Eastman to Brand Whitlock, 22 Nov 1905, Whitlock Papers: W L Fisher to A W Cooley Civil Service Commission (Washington DC 25 May 1905), Walter L Fisher Papers, Library of Congress. Fisher was in Europe May–Aug 1905

224   National Civic Federation 3 vols (New York 1901); pt 1 is mainly concerned with Glasgow

225   John Graham Brooks to R M Easley, 23 Sept 1905, National Civic Federation Papers. Also see the considerable correspondence between E W Bemis and R M Easley (1905) especially 29 Sept 1905; E W Bemis to F Parsons, 18 July 1905. Parsons' enthusiasm can be seen in his various publications already cited and in the notes for lectures in his papers (Portland Me 18 Jan 1906) the Economic Club of Boston (9 Feb 1906) as well as undated typescripts, proofs and leaflets for debates. In all Glasgow figures prominently as a model municipality, Albertson Papers. Parsons remained in Glasgow to write a special report. J R Commons to Charles Niell, Commissioner of Labour 17 Sept 1907, Albertson Papers, (Yale University Library). Commons was less impressed by the Commission's methods and remained in Glasgow after the official visit to work with Dalrymple. Myself pp 116–17. See Arthur Mann, Frank Parsons: The Professor as Reformer, MVHR 37 (1950–1) 471–90

226   In National Civic Federation vol i p 288

227   In National Civic Federation vol i p 421

228   The strike was widely reported and discussed in the American Press eg Electric Railway Journal 38 (1911) p 378. The full story appears in Daily Record and Mail (12, 14 Aug), Glasgow Herald (12, 14 Aug 1911), Evening News (14, 15, 16 Aug 1911), Evening Citizen (14 Aug 1911), Forward (12, 19 Aug 2, 16 Sept 1911), Glasgow Catholic Observer (12, 19 Aug 1911). Also see below

229   See the Corporation Minutes 1911–26, Strathclyde Regional Archives, City Chambers Glasgow; The Tramway Committee Minutes 5 June 1911–7 Aug 1912; the minutes between 1913–15 show increasing tension between Dalrymple and the trade union interests

230   See J Weinstein, Organised Business and the City Commission and Manager Movements, Journal of Southern History 38 (1962) 167–81; Bradley Robert Rice, Progressive Cities: The Commission Government in America 1901–1920 (Austin Texas 1977). R G Miller, Fort Worth and the Progressive Era: The Movement for Charter Reform 1899–1907, pp 89–125 in Essays in Urban America, ed R F Oates et al (Austin, Texas, 1975)

231   F C Howe Wisconsin, An Experiment in Democracy (New York 1912) p vii: 'The State is Probably our Most conspicuous Political Failure.'

232   W W Brown in American Journal of Sociology 12 (1906–7) 340

233   C E Russell and Lincoln Steffens became socialists. Annals dropped the word 'municipal' from its index in 1909

234   Federal Government Reports, Workmen's Compensation in the USA and Foreign Countries (Washington DC 1910) and Annals

235   Proceedings of the Federal Electric Railways Commissions, July-October 1919 (Washington DC 1920), also pp 1202–77; National Municipal Review 4 (1915) 272–6

236   See proceedings of the Tenth Universal Peace Congress Glasgow 10–13 September 1901 (London 1902). American Peace Society Annual Report (1902) pp 6, 8: Trueblood had already visited Scotland in 1886. See his articles in The Osculoosa, Iowa, Saturday Globe clippings in the American Peace Society Papers. Elihu Burritt, A Walk From London to John O'Groats (London 1864); and Peter Tolis, Elihu Burritt, Crusader for Brotherhood (Hamden Conn 1968). Burritt sent a minor Scottish poet, J B Syme to America but he abandoned the peace movement for the Free Soil Party p 63n; Merle Curti, The American Peace Crusade 1815–1860, (New York 1965 edn) pp 143, 206–8; W Evans Darby, International Tribunals (London 1904 edn); my article The Scottish Dimension; Robert Monteith and the Origins of Modern British Catholic Social Thought, Downside Review 97 (1978) 46–68. Burritt was associated with a former Glasgow student and Chartist, Arthur O'Neill who was a minister in

Birmingham, Herald of Peace (Jan 1896, 1 Sept 1896). On the American background and the relation to social reform see Sondra R Herman, Eleven Against War (Stanford 1969) and C R Marchand, The American Peace Movement and Social Reform 1898–1968 (Princeton 1972). The standard accounts of the movement are Peter Brock, Pacifism in the United States: From the Colonial Era to the First World War (Princeton 1968) and his Pacifism in Europe to 1914 (Princeton 1972)

237   Glasgow Herald (26 Dec 1912): War and Peace (Aug 1914) claims Stevenson founded the Glasgow body in May 1912. On the background see Howard Weinroth, Norman Angell and The Great Illusion: An Episode in Pre-1914 Pacifism, Historical Journal 17 (1974) 551–74 and his Left Wing Opposition to Naval Armaments in Britain before 1914, Journal of Contemporary History 6 (1971) 93–129; P J A Morris, The English Radicals Campaign For Disarmament and the Hague Conference of 1907, Journal of Modern History 43 (1971) 367–93

238   See Glasgow Herald (2, 8, 14 Nov 1912), and the Peacemaker 1 May (1912) 68–9; 1 Dec 1912. The Peace Yearbook (1911) and (1912)

239   Glasgow Herald (14 Nov 1912). See Norman Angell, The Foundations of International Polity (London 1914) esp ch 6

240   The Great Illusion (London 1912 edn) p 190

241   See above, War and Peace (Oct Nov Dec 1913) and Howard Evans, Sir Randal Cremer (London 1909), p 120; Norman Angell, After All: The Autobiography (London 1951) p 170; Edna Hilton, Life of John Hilton (London 1946) pp 52–5

242   Confidential Report; Circular, Letters Aug 1913, 1 Sept 1913. Listing of attenders at Le Touquet Conference 19–22 September, Angell Papers 1913; War and Peace (Aug 1914)

243   David Starr Jordan, The Days of Man 2 vols (New York 1922) vol 2 pp 539–47. Daniel Macaulay Stevenson and Professor J Graham Kerr, Zoology, Glasgow University were his Glasgow hosts. See also his The Human Harvest (New York 1972 edn) (1903) p 57: 'Almost every Anglo-American has, if he knew it, noble and royal blood in his veins'; his War and Waste (New York 1972 edn (1914)) esp pp 26–7, 156, 164; his War and the Breed (Boston 1915) p 182: 'I never knew that there were such Scotchmen alive as I saw in the slums of Dundee'

244   D S Jordan to his wife 1 Dec 1913 after addressing 600 Dreadnought workers and about to address the students union: 'Scotch folks are much more democratic than the English and much more our kind.' Glasgow is less aristocratic and conservative than Edinburgh; 2 Dec 1913 reports the students as cruder than our folks. Whatever they like they cheer 'vociferously' with their feet and when they disapprove they move their feet sideways across the floor. On the whole they approved but they were dazed by some things: 'The people here are democratic often radical, but most of the stuff I have given them they have never heard before.' 5 Dec 1913 he felt more at home in Scotland than in England and 7 Dec 1913 wrote, 'Scottish students seem more manly and better bred than the undergraduates of Oxford and Cambridge', David Starr Jordan Papers, Hoover Institution, Stanford University California. Glasgow Observer and Catholic Herald (29 Nov, 6 Dec 1913)

245   D S Jordan to his wife, 2, 3, 4, 5, 7 Dec 1913, Jordan Papers and his The Days of Man vol 2 pp 544–8

246   Miss A Milne to D S Jordan, 19 Jan 1914, 1 Feb, 26 July 1915; 30 Mar, 28 Sept, 20 Dec 1916; 25 May 1917; 7 Feb and 28 Dec 1918 and copies D S Jordan to Miss A Milne 21 Oct 1914, 2 Mar 1915. I have been unable to establish her identity. She was associated with the Glasgow mining experts John and Charles Stewart McArthur, an organiser of a peace study circle, a supporter of the Union for Democratic Control, a homeopathic and anti-vivesectionist enthusiast. The changed mood appears in J Graham Kerr to D S Jordan 23 Sept 1915 and Mrs Maud A Ferguson to D S Jordan, 24 Jan, 23 June, 9 Sept 1915; 2 Aug, 12 Oct 1916. D S Jordon to Mrs M A Ferguson, 17 Dec 1915, D S Jordan Papers. Her son, James, a former Stanford student who had studied in Scotland before taking a medical degree at Johns Hopkins, returned home, joined the Black Watch and died in France

247   D M Stevenson to Norman Angell, 5 Mar 1914, Angell Papers, Ball State University, Muncie Indiana; War and Peace (Aug 1914). Addresses were given by Norman Angell, Viscount Esher, John Hilton and others. It was hoped to expand the meetings to surrounding towns. On the Bertrand Russell incident see Ronald W Clark, The Life of Bertrand Russell (London 1975) pp 302–3. Also the Glasgow Herald (2, 8, 14 Nov 1912). His correspondence

with Norman Angell continued through 1934, Angell Papers. The collection also contains a fair correspondence between Angell and the Glasgow Union of Democratic Control 1928–9 with which Stevenson was closely associated as a former president. He had been active in promoting municipal peace links with Germany. Peacemaker (May 1912, Mar 1914). His brother John was involved in the heavy industry and armaments manufacturing in Sharon Pa J G White, A Twentieth Century History of Mercer County (np Pennsylvania 1909) 2 vols, vol 2 pp 573–4. I am indebted to Vivian A Johnson, Buhl-Henderson Community Library, Sharon Pa, for this reference. See biographical list

248   Glasgow Herald (13 Oct, 3, 24 Nov, 23 Dec 1920)

249   W S McKechnie to C B Adams, 2 May, 26, 31 Oct 1905, 20 Mar 1909, 29 Aug 1915, C B Adams Papers, Yale University Collections. McKechnie was largely responsible for establishing the Honours School of History in Glasgow University and the Historical Association, R S Rait to Mrs McKechnie 5 July 1930; D J Merk to Mrs McKechnie 5 July 1930; Andrew Browning to Mrs McKechnie, 3 June 1930, Glasgow University Archives and West of Scotland Branch of the Historical Association Minute Books. The two men seem to have been drawn together following the favourable review of McKechnie's book, Magna Carta: A Commentary on the Great Charter (Glasgow 1905) by Professor P Vinogradoff in Law Quarterly Review 21 (1905) 250–7

250   See his The Reform of the House of Lords (Glasgow 1909) and his The State of the Individual: An introduction to Political Science with special reference to socialistic and individualistic theories (Glasgow 1896)

251   The New Democracy and the Constitution (London 1912) p 8

252   ibid p 143. The term riff-raff appears on the same page. Even social gospel ministers endorsed that view. David Watson, Social Advance: Its Meaning, Method and Goal (London 1912) pp 196–7 for an attack on 'offscourings of Europe' entering Scotland. They were the Poles

253   The Menace of the Irish Race to Our Scottish Nationality, report to the General Assembly of the Church of Scotland (1923). The same sentiments can be seen in the horrors associated with Italian ice cream shops in the temperance newspapers and in police reports. They provide interesting background to the Oscar Slater case. Slater a foreigner had assocations with the underworld of gambling and vice, eg J R Motion, Memorandum on a Social Evil in Glasgow (Glasgow 1911) pp 32, 35; Glasgow Herald (27 May 1911) Chief Constable and Town Clerk Depute; Social Evil in Glasgow Report (1911) Appendix no 2 p 22 claims similar worries surfaced in contemporary America, Jane Addams, A New Conscience and an Ancient Evil (New York 1912); Lawrence J Pivar, Purity Crusade

254   Robert Sylvain, Alexandre Gavazzi 1809–84 2 vols (Quebec 1962) vol 1 pp 268–70; vol 2 p 444; Ray Allen Billington. The Protestant Crusade 1800–1860 (Chicago 1964 edn) pp 301, 306, 319. Orr had a Scots father and West Indian mother and was born in Demerara. Orr had precipitated riots in Greenock in 1851, Tablet (26 July 1951). Gavazzi gave several addresses in Glasgow. The Mitchell Library has the penny pamphlets summarising each talk: also see Problems of American Civilisation: Their Practical Solution the Pressing Christian Duty of Today, ed James McCosh (New York 1888) for this continuing undercurrent

255   Obituary Glasgow Herald (24 Apr 1906)

256   K R M Short, The Dynamite War: Irish-American Bombers in Victorian Britain (Dublin 1979) pp 102–53. On the background William D'Arcy, The Fenian Movement in the United States (Washington DC 1947). On Gallagher see biographical lists

257   On this complex development see John F McCaffrey, Politics and the Catholic Community Since 1878 in Modern Scottish Catholicism 1878–1978, ed David McRoberts pp 140–55. The general increase in labour militancy can be seen in The Socialist in the wake of Daniel De Leon's visit in 1904, the formation of the IWW and the trial of Bill Haywood in the United States (Aug, Oct 1904; July, Oct, Dec 1905; Jan, Apr 1906). Henry Pelling, America and the British Left (London 1956) is a useful survey. R H Tawney was a young lecturer in Glasgow University, involved in social work in the city's east end. Ross Terrill, R H Tawney and His Times: Socialism as Fellowship (Cambridge Mass 1973), esp pp 174–9

258   See A R Sennett, Garden Cities, in Theory and Practice 2 vols (London 1905)

CHAPTER SIX

1   See Table 1, p 246
2   Forsyth Hardy, John Grierson: A Documentary Biography (London 1979) p 32 quoting an interview given in 1962
3   ibid p 262. The film connection is another interesting aspect. The son of the Glasgow Metropole Theatre manager, Stan Laurel attended Rutherglen school and Queens Park Academy before leaving to make his name in America in 1910. He and Oliver Hardy visited Glasgow in the thirties and enjoyed a massive popular reception: thirty were hospitalised. In 1935 they made their movie, Bonnie Scotland. John McCabe, Mr Laurel and Mr Hardy (London 1976) pp 14–23, 189, 194. Edward G Robinson came during the Second World War. In addressing the Clydeside workers he found immediate rapport by mimicking his role in Little Caesar to their great satisfaction. Edward G Robinson, All My Yesterdays (London 1974) p 229. Also see T Louden, The Cinemas of Cinema City (Glasgow 1983) on Glasgow movie-going

Tables

TABLE 1

Scottish-born population in the United States: 1850–1950

		Total Scottish population (millions)
1850	70,550	2.8
1860	108,518	5.05
1870	140,835	3.3
1880	170,136	3.7
1890	242,231	4.0
1900	233,524	4.3
1910	261,076	4.7
1920	254,570	4.8
1930	354,323	4.82
1940	279,321	5.0 1939 estimated
1950	244,200	5.09
1960	213,219	5.17
1970	170,134	5.22

R T Berthoff, British Immigrants in Industrial America (Cambridge Mass 1953) p 7 based on Sixteenth Census of the US; Seventeenth Census; and Statistical History of the United States From Colonial Times to the Present, ed B J Wattenberg (Washington DC 1976); B R Mitchell, Abstract of British Historical Statistics, Cambridge, 1962; Scotland Census Population Tables 1971 (Edinburgh 1974).

TABLE 2

Scottish immigration to the United States 1820–1970

1820–30	3,180
1831–40	2,667
1841–50	3,712
1851–60	38,331
1861–70	38,769
1871–80	87,564
1881–90	149,869
1891–1900	44,188
1901–10	120,469
1911–20	78,357
1921–30	159,781
1931–40	6,887
1941–50	16,131
TOTAL	749,905

From R T Bertoff, British Immigrants, p 5 from Statistical Abstract of the United States 1951, p 94.

TABLE 3

Job tenure of sixty-six women weavers imported from Glasgow to Holyoke by the Lyman Mills, May 1853

	1	2 (per cent)	3	4	5	6
1853	July 2	0	66	100.0	0	176
	July 30	1	66	100.0	0	152
	Aug 27	2	58	87.18	0	142
	Sept 24	3	57	86.3	0	149
1854	July 1	12	46	69.6	0	167
	Oct 28	15	35	53.0	0	153
1855	Jan 27	18	24	36.3	0	159
	July 28	24	25	37.8	5	180
1856	July 26	36	15	22.7	1	171
1857	July 25	48	10	15.1	1	162
1858	July 31	60	11	16.6	3	168
1859	July 2	72	3	4.5	0	161
1860	July 28	84	4	6.0	3	180
1861	July 27	96	3	4.5	2	154
1862	June 28	108	2	3.0	0	144
1863	July 25	120	3	4.5	2	100

Key: column 1, date of payroll; 2 time elapsed in months since payroll of 2 July 1853 when the names of the 66 women first listed; 3, the number of the original 66 still on the payroll; 4, percentage of original 66 women still on the payroll; 5, number of original 66 women on the payroll at this check-date but not on the payroll at the immediately preceding check date; 6, total number of weavers on the payroll at Mill no. 2
Source: R Ginger, Labour in a Massachusetts Cotton Mill 1853–60, Business History Review 28 1954 p 84

TABLE 4

Company Town (Cohoes): factory (textile) workers aged ten and over and ethnicity, 1860

		Male	Female	Total	Percent of population (ten and over)	Factory workers (%)
Cotton workers	N	610	940	1,550		
manufacturing census	%	39.4	60.2	23.3		
Textile workers	N	778	1,103	1,881		
ten and over)	%	41.4	58.6	28.3		
Native-born						
American	N	197	293	490		
	%	40.2	59.8		22.8	26.0
Irish	N	377	617	994		
	%	37.9	62.1		31.6	52.8
English	N	101	74	175		
	%	57.7	42.3		30.0	9.3
French Canadian	N	50	74	124		
	%	40.3	59.7		26.2	6.5
Scottish	N	39	35	74		
	%	52.7	47.3		30.9	3.9
Other	N	14	10	24		
	%	58.3	41.7		—	1.5

Source: Daniel J Walkowitz, Worker City, Company Town: Iron and Cotton Worker Protest in Troy and Cohoes, New York, 1855–84 (Urbana Ill. 1978) p 61

TABLE 5

Percentage and relative concentration of selected Cohoes workers by ethnicity, 1860

Percentage

	Unskilled						Skilled						
	Managerial[a]	Clerical[a]	Labourer[a]	Service[b]	Factory (textile) Worker Male	Factory (textile) Worker Female	Weaver Male	Weaver Female	Spinner[a]	Dresser[a] Carder	Seamstress Milliner Dressmaker[b]	Carpenter[a]	Machinist[a]
USA	70.4	54.5	8.8	17.5	25.3	26.5	2.4	32.6	16.6	46.1	53.3	52.7	38.1
Ireland	13.1	24.6	80.3	77.7	48.4	55.9	36.6	32.6	25.0	7.6	21.6	23.1	27.0
England	8.1	7.7	1.0	0	12.9	6.7	46.3	32.6	50.0	30.7	5.0	8.3	17.5
French Canada	0	0	9.1	1.8	6.4	6.7	12.2	0	0	7.6	3.3	11.1	0
Scotland	6.5	6.4	0.2	1.8	5.0	3.1	0	2.1	8.3	7.6	1.6	2.8	11.1

Relative concentration
(Proportion among gainful workers in all occupations = 100)

	Managerial[a]	Clerical[a]	Labourer[a]	Service[b]	Factory (textile) Worker Male	Factory (textile) Worker Female	Weaver Male	Weaver Female	Spinner[a]	Dresser[a] Carder	Seamstress Milliner Dressmaker[b]	Carpenter[a]	Machinist[a]
USA	222	172	28	55	80	84	8	103	52	145	168	166	120
Ireland	29	55	178	159	107	114	81	67	55	17	44	51	60
England	82	78	10	0	130	86	468	418	505	310	64	84	177
French Canada	0	0	123	26	86	97	318	64	0	103	48	150	0
Scotland	61	77	5	55	132	94	41	46	218	200	48	74	292
N	77	372	372	108	778	1,103	41	46	12	13	60	108	63

[a] all males [b] all females

Source: Daniel J Walkowitz, Worker City, Company Town: Iron and Cotton-worker Protest in Troy and Cohoes New York, 1855–1884 (Urbana Ill 1978) p 64

TABLE 6

Selected ironworkers and ethnicity, 1880 (raw totals, and percentage of the total in the trade)

Father's birthplace		Population (1)[a]	Managerial (2)	Labourer (3)	Molder (4)	Puddler (5)	Heater roller rougher (6)	Stove-mounter (7)	Pattern-maker (8)	Machinist (9)	Total columns 3–9 (10)
Ironworkers' birthplace: USA		39,809	87	730	497	12	82	148	86	182	1837
USA	N		54	169	153	5	13	58	58	108	564
	%	31.8	48.6	11.2	18.5	2.3	5.8	29.0	42.3	38.1	16.7
Ireland	N		19	936	511	166	171	94	26	65	1969
	%	46.4	15.7	62.4	61.9	79.0	73.3	47.0	18.9	22.9	58.2
England	N		22	161	63	22	28	11	18	51	354
	%	6.1	18.1	10.7	7.6	10.4	12.5	5.5	13.1	18.0	10.5
Canada	N		5	88	27	11	4	23	12	12	177
	%	6.2	4.1	5.8	3.2	5.2	1.9	11.5	8.7	4.2	5.3
Scotland	N		7	75	29	2	2	0	3	26	137
	%	1.5	5.7	5.0	3.5	0.9	0.9	0	2.1	9.1	4.0
Germany	N		3	55	34	1	3	11	19	19	142
	%	1.6	0.8	1.5	0.9	1.4	2.3	1.5	0.7	0.7	1.3
Total	N	56,747	111	1,507	825	210	224	200	137	283	3,386

[a] The ethnic breakdown is based upon a 4 per cent sample of every twenty-fifth person listed in the 1880 manuscript census tract.
Source: Daniel J Walkowitz, Worker City, Company Town: Iron and Cotton-worker Protest in Troy and Cohoes, New York, 1855–1884 (Urbana Ill 1978) p 36

TABLE 7

Characteristics of old and new immigrant groups at time of arrival, 1910

Origin	Percentage illiterate	Percentage with less than $50
Old		
Dutch and Flemish	2.7	65
English	0.5	49
French	10.8	52
German	5.7	66
Irish	1.4	81
Scandinavian	0.1	86
Scottish	0.4	56
Welsh	0.6	47
New		
Bohemian and Moravian	1.1	82
Croation and Slovenian	33.5	96
Dalmation, Bosnian, and Herzegovinian	39.3	93
Greek	24.0	93
Hebrew	28.8	87
Italian (north)	7.2	84
Italian (south)	51.8	92
Lithuanian	50.0	95
Magyar	11.8	90
Polish	35.0	97
Roumanian	36.5	94
Russian	38.1	93
Slovak	21.3	94

Source: S Lieberson, 1963, Ethnic Patterns in American Cities (Glencoe Ill. 1963) Table 16 p 72 and also in his A Piece of the Pie: Black and White Immigrants since 1880 (Berkeley 1980) p 28

TABLE 8

Western American mining enterprises registered in Scotland

		regis- tration date	nominal capital (£)	Scottish head- quarters	winding up	active	location
1	Utah Cotton Wood Mining and Smelting Company Ltd	1872	6,000	Glasgow	1872	no	Big Cottonwood Canyon, Utah
2	Kirkland Gold and Silver Mining Company Ltd	1875	4,000	Glasgow	1884	yes	Placer County, California
3	Atchison Mining Company Ltd	1875	6,000	Dundee	1880	yes	Boulder County, Colorado
4	Scottish Pacific Coast Mining Company Ltd	1881	100,000	Edinburgh	1899	yes	Sierra County, California
5	Arizona Copper Company Ltd	1882	875,000	Edinburgh	1921	yes	Graham County, Arizona
6	Scottish Colorada Mining and Smelting Company Ltd	1884	250,000	Glasgow	1894	yes	Boulder County, Colorado
7	Richardson Gold and Silver Mining Company Ltd	1884	50,000	Glasgow	1885	yes	Gilpin County, Colorado
8	Colorado Silver Mines Ltd	1884	200,000	Glasgow		no	San Juan County, Colorado
9	Feather-Fork Gold Gravel Company Ltd	1886	300,000	Glasgow	1902	yes	Plumas and Sierra Counties, California
10	Creston Gold Mining Company Ltd	1889	160,000	Edinburgh	1891	yes	Saguache County, Colorado
11	Grass Valley, California, Gold Extracting Company (Pollok Patents) Ltd	1890	30,000	Edinburgh	1894	yes	Nevada County, California
12	Poorman Silver Mines (of Colorado) Ltd	1891	130,000	Glasgow	1899	yes	Boulder County, Colorado
13	Mining Development Syndicate (of Colorada) Ltd	1892	20,000	Glasgow	1900	no	Colorado
14	Gold and Silver Extraction Company of America	1893	110,00	Glasgow	1904	yes	Colorado
15	Bear Creek Alluvial Gold Mining Company Ltd	1894	65,000	Glasgow	1898	yes	Rocky Bar, Idaho
16	California Gold Production Syndicate Ltd	1894	55,000	Glasgow	1899	yes	Sierra County, California
17	Prescott Development Syndicate Ltd	1895	100,000	Glasgow	1902	no	Arizona
18	Alaska (Glasgow) Gold Mine Ltd	1895	44,000	Glasgow	1901	yes	Nevada County, California
19	Redhill Ltd	1895	75,000	Glasgow	1899	yes	Nevada County, California
20	Diamond Hill Gold Mines Ltd	1896	455,000	Glasgow	1908	yes	Broadwater County, Montana
21	Gold Basin Mining Company Ltd	1896	150,000	Glasgow	1896	no	Mohave County, Arizona
22	Glasgow and Western Exploration Company Ltd	1896	30,000	Glasgow	1921	yes	Utah, Nevada and Colorado
23	Jumper Gold Syndicate, California, Ltd	1896	45,000	Glasgow	1914	yes	Tuolumne County, California
24	California Consols Ltd	1896	60,000	Glasgow	1912	yes	Tuolumne and Shasta Counties, California
25	Atlas Mines Syndicate Ltd	1896		Glasgow	1902	yes	Tuolumne County, California
26	Highland Chief Mining Company Ltd	1897	30,000	Glasgow	1897	no	Deadwood, South Dakota
27	Bull Creek Mineral Estates Ltd	1897	42,000	Glasgow	1897	no	Christian County, Missouri
28	Longfellow Gold Syndicate Ltd	1898		Glasgow	1902	yes	Tuolumne County, California
	Nonpareil Gold Syndicate Ltd	1906	6,000– 10,000	Glasgow	1910		Tuolumne County, California
29	Scottish California Mining Syndicate	1898		Glasgow		no	Tuolumne County, California
30	Crystalline Gold Mines Ltd	1898	65,000	Glasgow	1902	yes	Tuolumne County, California
	Crystalline Mining Company Ltd	1902		Glasgow			
31	Arizona Copper Syndicate Ltd	1899	100,000		1900	no	Graham County, Arizona
32	Mineral Hill Copper Syndicate Ltd	1900	5,000		1905	no	Yavapal County, Arizona
33	St Patrick Gold Mine Ltd	1900	80,000	Glasgow	1908	yes	Cripple Creek, Colorado
34	Herman Mining Company Ltd	1903	30,000	Glasgow	1907	yes	Placer County, California
35	California Copper Syndicate Ltd	1901	30,000	Glasgow	1902	yes	Fresno County, California
	Fresno Copper Company Ltd	1902	175,000– 400,000	Glasgow	1907	yes	
	Fresno Copper Company Ltd	1907	100,000	Glasgow	1914	yes	
36	Scottish Tonopah Gold Mining Company Ltd	1904	3,000	Glasgow	1908	yes	Esmeralda County, Nevada
37	British Arizona Copper Company Ltd	1913	25,000	Dundee	1924	yes	Arizona

Source: W Turrentine Jackson, The Enterprising Scot: Investors after 1873 (Edinburgh 1968) pp 188–189

Appendix 1

Lydia Huntley Sigourney (1791–1865)

Lydia H Sigourney, the Connecticut poetaster visited Glasgow in 1839. A popular writer of American religious revivalism, she wrote numerous novels, children's tales and inspirational works in which death was a major preoccupation. Known as 'the sweet singer of Hartford' and 'the American Mrs Hemans', she enjoyed enormous popular success with more than sixty books. An early advocate of higher education for women, she established a female seminary. She was also an early supporter of the American Colonisation Society which resettled freed slaves in Africa. In addition she edited various religious and juvenile periodicals and publications. With her religious and educational interests she came to Glasgow to the British Assocation for the Advancement of Science meeting. Although appalled by the poverty and wealth of Glasgow she found much to admire including Dr Robert Cunningham's work at the Normal Seminary, Glasgow hospitality and various distinguished clergymen: Dr Thomas Dick, the Christian philosopher also impressed her. Like numerous other tourists she attended Dr Thomas Chalmers' service: 'Dr Chalmers repeatedly spoke with his characteristic forcefulness and power. He has none of the gracefulness of the practised orator and his countenance is heavy until irradiated by his subject. Then mind triumphs over matter and makes the broad Scotch a pliant vehicle with eloquent thought.'* On her visit to the city she was moved to write two poems printed below. They illustrate her preoccupation with death, the attraction of the Necropolis, with the Knox statue to American tourists generally and the feeling of being at home in Glasgow.

* Lydia H Sigourney, *Pleasant Memories of Pleasant Lands* (3rd edn. Boston), pp 95–6. The poems are printed on pages 101–9. She wrote her autobiography, *Letters of A Life,* in 1866. Her biographer Gordon S Haight wrote *Mrs Sigourney* (New Haven 1930). She had contributed the *Glasgow Infant School Annual* but I have been unable to identify the poems in the volumes available in the Glasgow collection, Mitchell Library Glasgow.

THE NECROPOLIS AT GLASGOW

Come o'er the Bridge of Sighs, some twilight hour,
When dimly gleams the fair Cathedral-tower,
And lingering daybeams faintly serve to show
The tombstones mouldering round its base below;
—Come o'er that bridge with me, and musing think
What untold pangs have marked this streamlet's brink,
What bitter tears distilled from hearts of woe,
Since first its arches spanned the flood below.
Here hath the mother from her bleeding breast
Laid the young darling of her soul to rest;
Here the lorn child resigned the parent stay,
To walk, despairing, on its orphan way;
Here the riven heart that fond companion brought
By years cemented with its inmost thought;
Here the sad throng in long procesion crept,
To bear the sage, for whom a nation wept,
Or deep in dust the reverend pastor lay,
Whose pure example taught to Heaven the way.

253

Approach through winding paths yon terrace high,
Whose statued column strikes the traveller's eye,
Or rove from cell to cell, whose marble door
The inhospitable tenants ope no more,
Or on their tablets read the labored trace,
That asks remembrance from a dying race,
Or mark the flowers, whose lips with fragrance flow,—
The sweetest tribute to the loved below.
Poor child of Judah, exiled and oppressed,
How wrapped in shades thy lowly spot of rest!
Type of thy fate, for whom no sunbeam falls
In peace and power, on Zion's sacred walls;
But by strange streams thy silent harp is hung,
and captive numbers tremble on thy tongue.
Dark is yon gate, through which thy mourners pass
To hide their idols 'neath the matted grass,
And sad the dirge, no Saviour's name that knows
To gild with glorious hope their last repose.
Oh! turn thine eye from Sinai's summit red,
Our Elder Sister, fly its thunders dread;
List to the lay that flowed o'er Bethlehem's plain,
Whe star and angel warned the shepherd train;
Thou lov'est our Father's Book,—its seers believe,
To thy torn breast the Holy Cross receive
Bind to the frowning Law the Gospel sweet,
And cast thy burdens at Messiah's feet.

But whether this secluded haunt we tread,
Where Caledonia shrouds her cherished dead,
Or where the Turk funereal cypress rears,
Or the poor Cambrian plants his vale of tears,
Or search Mount Auburn's consecrated glades,
Mid lakes and groves and labyrinthine shades,
Or Laurel Hill, where silver Schuylkill flows,
Quiescent guarding while its guests repose,
Or near the Lehigh's rippling margin roam,
Where the Moravian finds his dead a home,
In lowly grave, by clustering plants o'ergrown,
That half conceals its horizontal stone,
One voice, one language, speaks each sacret scene,
Sepulchral vault, or simpler mound of green,
One voice, one language, breathes with changeless
        power,
Graved on the stone, or trembling in the flower.

That voice is love for the pale clay, that shrined
And fondly lodged the never-dying mind,
Toiled for its welfare, with its burdens bent,
Wept o'er its woes, and at its bidding went,
Thrilled at its joys, with zeal obeyed its will,
And 'neath the stifling clod remembers still.
Though on the winds its severed atoms fly,
It hoards the promise of the Archangel's cry,
Though slain, trusts on, though buried, hopes to rise,
In ashes fans a fire that never dies,
And with the resurrection's dawning light
Shall burst its bonds, revivify, unite,
Rush to its long lost friend, with stainless grace,
And dwell forever in its pure embrace.

LOCH LOMOND

While down the lake's translucent tide
With gently curving course we glide,
Its silver ripples, faint and few,
Alternate blend with belts of blue,
As fleecy clouds, on pinions white,
Careering fleck the welkin bright.

But lo! Ben Lomond's awful crown
Through shrouding mists looks dimly down;
For though, perchance, his piercing eye
Doth read the secrets of the sky,
His haughty bosom scorns to show
Those secrets to the world below.
Close-woven shades, with varying grace,
And crag and cavern mark his base,
And trees, whose naked roots protrude
From bed of rock and lichens rude;
And where, 'mid dizzier cliffs are seen
Entangled thickets sparsely green,
Methinks I trace, in outline drear,
Old Fingal with his shadowy spear,
His gray locks streaming to the gale,
And followed by his squandrons pale.
Yes, slender aid from Fancy's glass
It needs, as round these shores we pass,
Mid glen and thicket dark, to scan
The wild MacGregor's stormy clan,
Emerging, at their chieftain's call,
To foray or to festival;
While nodding plumes and tartans bright
Gleams wildly o'er each glancing height.

But as the spectral vapours rolled
Away in vestments dropped with gold,
The healthier face of summer sky,
With the shrill bagpipe's melody,
Recal, o'er distant ocean's foam,
The fondly treasured scenes of home;
And thoughts, on angel-pinions driven,
Drop in the heart the seeds of heaven,
Those winged seeds, whose fruit sublime
Decays not with decaying time.
The loving child, the favorite theme
Of morning hour or midnight dream,
The tender friend so lowly laid
Mid our own church-yard's mournful shade,
The smitten babe, who never more
Must sport around its father's door,
Return they not, as phantoms glide,
And silent seat them at our side?
Like Highland maiden, sweetly fair,
The snood and rosebud in her hair,
Yon emerald isles, how calm they sleep
On the pure bosom of the deep:
How bright they throw, with waking eye,
Their lone charms on the passer-by;

The willow with its drooping stem,
The thistle's hyacinthine gem,
The feathery fern, the graceful deer,
Quick starting as the strand we near,
While, with closed wing and scream subdued,
The Osprays nurse their kingly brood.

High words of praise, the pulse that stir,
Burst from each joyous voyager;
And Scotia's Streams and mountains hoar,
The wildness of her sterile shore,
Her broken caverns, that prolong
The echoes of her minstrel song,
Methinks might catch the enthusiast-tone,
That breathes amid these waters lone.
Even I, from fair Columbia's shore,
Whose lakes a mightier tribute pour,
And bind with everlasting chain
The unshorn forest to the main;
Superior's surge, like ocean proud,
That leaps to lave the vexing cloud;
Huron, that rolls with gathering frown
A world of waters darkly down;
And Erie, shuddering on his throne
At strong Niagara's earthquake tone;
And bold Ontario, charged to keep
The barrier 'tween them and the deep,
Who oft in sounds of wrath and fear,
And dark with cloud-wreathed diadem,
Interpreteth to Ocean's ear
Their language, and his will to them;
I reared amid that western vale,
Where nature works on broader scale,
Still with admiring thought and free,
Loch Lomond, love to gaze on thee,
Reluctant from thy beauties part,
And bless thee with a stranger's heart.

Appendix 2

The itinerary of John B Gough in Scotland
(See Chapter Four)

Aberchirder   22 Oct 1858

Aberdeen   15/16 Feb 1855, 24/25 Dec 1857, 2/3 Nov, 15/16 Sept 1858, 14/15 and 21 Nov 1859, 9 Apr, 10 Sept 1879

Airdrie   11 Oct 1854, 18 Nov 1857

Alexandria   27 Oct 24 Nov 1859

Alloa   28 Feb 1855, 16 Nov 1857

Arbroath   12 Feb 1855, 6 Jan 1858

Auchterarder   7 Jan 1859

Ayr   27 Oct 1854, 12 Apr 1855, 24 Nov 1857, 8 Dec 1858

Aytoun   25 Nov 1858

Banchory   6 Oct 1858

Banff   6 Oct 1851

Barrhead   26, 30 Aug 1853, 14 Feb 1854, 6 Dec 1858, 25 Oct 1859

Bathgate   20 Nov. 1854

Beith   9 Apr 1855

Bervie   4 Nov 1854

Berwick   7 Dec 1854

Biggar   16 May 1855, 3 Dec. 1858

Blairgowrie   21 Dec 1857

Brechin   7 Jan 1858

Broughty Ferry   21 Feb 1855, 4 Jan 1858

Burntisland   17 Nov 1858

Campbelltown   15/16 Oct 1857

Carluke   19 Nov 1857

Carnwath   19 Nov 1858

Cartsdyke   13 Oct 1857

Castle Douglas   1 Dec 1859

Coatbridge   2 Feb 1855, 9 Nov 1857

Coldstream   26 Nov 1858

Coltness   1 Nov 1859

Crieff   26 Feb 1855

Cumbernauld   5 Feb 1855

Cupar, Fife   22 Feb, 24 Apr 1855, 5 Jan 1855

Cumnock   17 Oct 1854, 10 Apr 1855, 26 Nov 1857

Dalkeith   23 Jan 1854, 8 Jan 1855, 30 Nov 1858

Dornoch   28 Sept 1857

Doune   6 Jan, 22 Nov 1859

Dumbarton 2 Oct 1854, 10 Nov 1857

Dumfries   6/7 Feb, 19 Oct 1854, 21 Apr 1879

Dunbar   22 Nov 1858, 31 Oct 1859

Dunblane   27 Feb 1855

Dundee   16/17 Feb 1854, 19/20, 23 Feb, 27 Apr 1855, 11/12 Jan 1858, 13/14 Jan, 7/8 Nov 1859, 8 Apr, 9 Sept 1879

Dunfermline   18 Jan 1854, 8 May 1855, 15 Nov 1858

Dunkeld   8 Feb 1855

Duns   21 Nov, 6 Dec 1854, 23/24 Nov 1858

Edinburgh   1/2 Sept, 31 Dec 1853, 2, 4, 6, 9, 11, 16, 18, 19, 20, 26 Jan 1854, 16 May, 8, 13, 15, 18, 27, Nov 1854, 1, 3, 4, 9, 11, 13, 19 Jan, 6, 21 Apr, 7, 23, 24 May 1855, 2, 4 Nov 1857, 1 Jan, 9 Sept 8-10 Nov 1858, 20/29 Jan 1859, 16/17 Oct 1878, 5, 7, Apr 1879

Elgin   13 Oct 1858

Ewart Park   24 Nov 1854, 1 Feb 1855, 28 Dec 1857

Falkirk   9 Feb 1854, 1 Feb 1855, 28 Dec 1857

Forfar   23 Dec 1857

Forres   1, 2 Oct 1857, 14/15 Oct 1858, 14/15 Oct 1859

Fraserburgh   27 Oct 1858, 17 Nov 1859

Galashiels   24 Aug 1853, 10 Nov 1854, 1 May 1855

Garlieston 23 Oct 1857

Gatehouse 27 Oct 1857

Girvan   25 Nov 1859

Glasgow   25, 31 Aug 1853, 1, 3, 11, 21, 23, 27, 28 Feb 17/18 May, 26/27 Sept 7, 10, 14, 21, 30 Oct, 3 Nov 1854, 2 Jan, 6 Feb, 16 Apr, 11, 18, 21, 22, May 1855, 14 Sept, 11, 13, 23 Nov, 14, 29, Dec, 1857, 7 Sept, 9 Nov 1858, 11, 21, Jan, 26 Oct, 2 Nov 1859, 21/22 Feb 1860, 14/15 Oct 1878, 14 Apr, 16 Sept 1879

Gourock   24 Feb 1854

Grangemouth   15 Dec 1857

Greenloan   22 Nov 1854

Greenock   20 Feb, 1 March, 4 Oct 1854, 14 May 1855, 10 Jan 1859, 17 Apr 1879

Haddington   16 Nov 1854, 5 Jan 1859

Hamilton   29 Sept 1854

Hawick   29 Nov, 1 Dec 1854, 6 Nov 1857

257

Helensburgh   15 Sept 1857
Huntly   11 Oct 1858

Inverary   18 Nov 1859
Inverness   29/30 Sept 1857, 18/19 Oct 1858
Irvine   30 Jan 1855

Jedburgh   28 Nov 1854, 5 Nov 1857
Johnstone   31 Jan, 13 Apr 1855

Keith   5 Oct 1857
Kelso   12 Jan, 23 Nov 1854
Kilwinning   24 Oct 1854
Kilmarnock   2 Mar, 26 Oct 1854
Kilsyth   17 Apr 1855
Kinross   12 Jan, 20 Sept 31 Dec 1859
Kirkintilloch   2 Nov 1854
Kirkcaldy   4/5 Dec 1854, 9 May 1855, 10 Nov 1858
Kirkpatrick   28 Oct 1857
Kirkwall   21/22 Sept 1857, 22/23/24 Sept, 1858
Kirriemuir   9 Feb 1855, 22 Dec 1857, 19 Jan 1859

Lanark   17 May 1855, 2 Dec 1858
Langholm   30 Nov 1854
Lasswade   14 Nov 1854
Lauder   30 Apr 1855
Laurencekirk   17 Jan 1859
Leith 10 Jan, 7 Nov 1854, 17 Jan 1855, 3 Nov 1857
Leslie   23 Apr 1855
Lesmahagow   1 Dec 1858
Leven   13 Jan 1858
Linlithgow   24 Jan 1854
Lochwinnoch   1 Nov 1854 (illness prevented 23 Oct meeting)
Lockerbie   29/30 Oct 1857

Melrose   9 Nov 1854
Methven   (?) 1 Nov 1858
Montrose 13/14 Feb 1855, 8 Jan 1858, 18 Jan 1859, 10 Apr 1879

Musselburgh   16 Jan 1855

Nairn   20/21 Oct 1858
Newmilns   25 Nov 1857
Newton Stewart   21/22 Oct 1857

Old Meldrum   7 Oct 1858

Paisley   29 Aug 1853, 2, 13, Feb, 28 Sept, 5 Oct 1854, 15 May 1855, 7 Dec 1858, 11 Sept 1879
Peebles   18 Jan 1855, 3 Nov 1859
Penicuik   5 jan 1854, 10 Jan 1855
Perth   15 Feb 1854, 7 Feb 1855, 18 Dec 1857, 10/11 Nov 1859, 15 Apr 1879
Peterhead   8 Oct 1857, 28/29 Oct 1858
Pollokshaws   16/17 Sept 1857
Port Glasgow   13 Oct 1854, 12 Oct 1857

Rothes   12 Oct 1858
Rothesay   31 Oct 1854, 12 Nov 1857, 15 Sept 1879

Saltcoats   24 Jan 1859
Stewarton   25 Oct 1854
Stirling   25 Jan, 10 Feb 1854, 18 Apr 1855, 13/14 Sept 1858, 8 Sept 1879
Strain   1 Mar 1855
Stranraer   19/20 Oct 1857, 28/29 Nov 1859
Strichen   26 Oct 1858
Stuartfield   16 Nov 1859
St Ninian's   19 Apr 1855

Thornhill   18 Oct 1854
Turriff   7 Oct 1857, 25 Oct 1858

Waterbeck   (?) 2 Dec 1859
West Linton   4 Nov 1859
Whithorn   26 Oct 1857
Wick   24/25 Sept 1857
Wigton   30 Nov 1859
Wishaw   12 Oct 1854, 20 Nov 1857
Woodside   (?) 9 Oct 1857

Source: J B Gough Papers, American Antiquarian Society, Worcester, Mass

Appendix 3

Ned Duncan's Dream;

Or, The Great International

Scotland *v.* America, 1901

(*By Glenavon*)

While on holidays, enjoying myself at a quiet and beautiful sea-side village on the shores of the Firth of Clyde, I received a note from a friend reminding me that an old football chum was still on the sick list, and making little or no progress towards recovery. In fact, his life, which had recently been enfeebled by an incurable malady, was slowly but surely drawing to a close. Last time I saw him he referred to the fact that he had some manuscript, which he wished me to read over, and when this came into my mind I resolved to repair to Glasgow at once, ere it might be too late.

It was just as well that I did, for poor Ned Duncan was fast sinking when I got permission from his widowed mother to visit the bedside. Ned, I may mention, was one of the most enthusiastic players of his day that ever kicked a ball, but was obliged to give up practice in consequence of the unfortunate circumstances I have just mentioned, and of late had only been a spectator at the leading games. He received me that evening with a kind smile of recognition, and his pale face beckoned me to come near. I was certainly much touched with my old friend's appearance, and tried as much as possible to cheer him, but it was of no use.

He said he knew he was going to the silent land. The doctor, in fact, had told him he had only a few days to live, and he was glad I had come to bid him farewell, and take over some straggling notes he had compiled last summer about the football of the future. 'Going home one evening,' he continued, 'after an International match, I fell into a deep sleep, and had a remarkable dream. I thought I saw a great match between Scotland and America. Real genuine players glided past, scrimmaging with each other for the ball; thousands of spectators, new and beautiful youthful faces, graced the area allotted to spectators; the hum of thousands of excited voices greeted my ears, and'—Here poor Ned's voice failed.

After a few minutes repose, the old player gasped, 'But what need I tell you more. Here is the manuscript, and make what use of it you like.'

My dear old friend is now under the turf he loved so well to play on when in the zenith of his fame. Keeping in mind that the *Scottish Association Football Annual* was nearly due, and that Mr John McDowall, the editor, would most likely think poor 'Ned Duncan's Dream' in a certain sense public property, or at least the property of all genuine Association football players, I considered it my duty to give the *Annual* the first chance.

Having eventually opened the packet, the first sentence which met my eyes was 'Ned Duncan's Dream; or, The Great International of 1901'.

I will, therefore, leave poor Ned to tell his own tale, and what he saw in his vision, which at any rate has the merit of originality about it. As more extraordinary dreams have come to pass, there is no saying what the beginning of the twentieth century may bring forth, for International football matches with Australia, America, and Canada have been talked of during the past year or two, and may become accomplished facts.

I must, however, return to the manuscript, which reads after the following style:

It was in April, 1901, on a Saturday afternoon, that the Yankees came to Scotland to play a match with our crack Eleven. The Universal Postal Service, which scattered letters all over the world at the rate of one half-penny per ounce, conveyed a formal challenge from the

Americans to Scotland that the Yankees would be delighted to meet an eleven of that country in an even game of football. The New World men of course meant business, and our secretary, who was a capital fellow, much liked by the Scottish Football Association for his kind and obliging disposition, was instructed to accept the challenge and welcome the strangers to Glasgow.

Previous to the time I speak of, the Americans had beaten the Australians and Canadians, and were considered by their own friends invincible even to the extent of a couple of goals. The Canadians, by the aid of the Electric Express Line's fast steamers, had been able to leave Montreal in the morning and return in the evening from New York, defeated but not disgraced. The Australians were a little longer on the way, as the improved appliances for driving ships had not yet attained the perfection there which had been shown in most of the ports and rivers of the British Isles. They were experimenting, however, and some good in that direction was looked for daily, and a new Express Company floated. The Americans had also beaten the Englishmen the previous year at New York, and, as their own newspapers had it, 'came over to crow in the Land o' Cakes'. The great shipping trade of the Clyde ere this was, so to speak, causing a new order of things to arise all over the world. Large and beautifully-built steel and bronze vessels left the Clyde every day for all parts of the earth.

They had annihilated space and bridged the Atlantic in earnest, and the 'electrics' (once called steamers) could go from Glasgow to New York in little over twenty-four hours. Yes. 'Daily to New York, Montreal, California, and New Mexico. Splendid accommodation for first-class passengers; 110 knots per hour, and no vibration.' So read the advertisement in the leading Glasgow newspapers. Why! what did it all mean? One hundered knots per hour—2400 in twenty-four hours! To New York in little over a day! I had certainly heard of the swallow taking an early breakfast at the uttermost part of England and picking up a late dinner on the shores of Africa all in one day; but 100 knots an hour with a vessel, it was just enough for flesh and blood to comprehend at once.

'Well,' said a friend of mine with some experience in the marine engineering line. 'I have long thought on electricity as the great motive power of the future, provided it could be properly stored, and now you see what it has come to.'

In fact, our coal supply—one of the sources of Britain's greatness—was getting exhausted, and electrical appliances had become an absolute necessity. The Strain could no longer be borne of one huge vessel consuming 500 tons of coal in twenty-four hours, and those blessed electrics were not introduced a moment too soon.

The learned men of France, who had long been working earnestly to solve the problem of electric economy, were beaten in the race, and a perfect system of stored electricity introduced and successfully applied to the propulsion of ships, patented by Professor Scotland Thomson, nephew of the late Sir William Thomson of blessed memory.

Lots of other remarkable events had been occurring in our history, but none so marked as the introduction of the 'electrics'. The people of Scotland had very nearly lost their individuality. Old Caledonia was to have been simply a name. Englishmen invaded Glasgow, Edinburgh, Dundee, and even Ultima Thule, and overran the country with their ideas of social life. They made slow progress at first, but came in hordes, and the invasion was irresistible. They, of course, introduced all their new-fangled ideas about games, and pastimes, and compelled us to submit.

Parliament had got so mixed up and thoroughly disgusted with the question of Irish Home Rule, which cropped up every session, that in an evil mood it had threatened puir auld Scotland with assimilation of the Law of Jurisprudence, but failed. King Albert the First, however, had out of respect to the great city of Glasgow—the Second City in the Empire—created his third son Duke of Glasgow, you must know the House of Peers was still extant, but greatly reformed and limited in power. It could only veto a law passed by the Commons once, and there was no more about the matter.

The match, you may be sure, was the general topic of conversation all over Scotland several weeks before it came off, and on the Friday evening when the Americans arrived and put up at the Express Hotel, Glasgow, the excitement was great. The preparations and arrangements for the struggle were on a grand scale, and good weather alone was wanting to make it a success. That evening several of the Scotch team strolled into the billiard-room of the Express Hotel to welcome the young Americans, and had a chat with them about football in general and the spread of the Association rules all over the world.

The eventful day at last dawned, and a finer April morning could not have been desired. Play was announced to begin at 2.30 p.m. and long before that time Bruce Park, Cathcart Road, was half filled with spectators, and presented a fine sight.

The crowd around the field was certainly the most remarkable that had ever gathered together in Glasgow. As the game was no ordinary one, they flocked from all quarters. Most of the towns in Scotland supplied their quota to swell the multitude, and as railway travelling was cheap and convenient now compared to the original football days of the Queen's Park, Clydesdale, Vale of Leven, Rangers, Dumbarton, Granville, 3rd Lanark Volunteers, Partick, Eastern, Parkgrove, and a host of other clubs, a two-hundred mile journey, which was easily accomplished in an hour-and-a-half, was considered next to nothing. They were there—young men and maidens from London, Manchester, Liverpool, Edinburgh, Blackburn, Darwen, and Sheffield—all bent on making a day of it. The road to Bruce Park, indeed was a sight to see, despite the fact that the Cathcart railway carried its thousands that afternoon to the South-Side. There were not a few buxom country girls in the crowd, enticed thither by no great love of the game—which, of course, they did not understand—but by their sweethearts, just to let the young persons of the place see that they had lads as well as their neighbours. There was one winsome lassie among them, however, who would have done credit to Burns' incomparable 'Queen o' the Glen'.

Emma was the only sister of a young farmer in the district. It is a mistaken notion to suppose that farmers in Scotland are by far too plodding a class to indulge themselves in anything savouring of English games and pastimes, particularly football, but this is a mistake. I know several farmers in the country who love the dribbling game dearly, and do their best to promote its interests in the way of supplying ground to not a few young clubs dotted over the country. In fact, Emma was the beauty of the whole parish, and all the young men for miles around were well aware of it. No one could deny it, and even the most unreasonable of fellows, Charley McGowan, the schoolmaster, and Alfred Walker, the lawyer's clerk, were forced to acknowledge it.

'Talk about Sidney's heavenly Geraldine,' said young McGowan to me one afternoon on the road to practice, 'she beats her hollow.' McGowan, however, was a bit of a cynic, and Emma soon cast him off for Walker. He was a fine singer, and in after years, when he became a confirmed bachelor, delighted to sing songs about the inconstancy of the fair sex. He used to hum out Goethe's 'Vanatos', and more particularly that verse with reference to the fickle fair ones, which ran—

> I set my heart upon woman next—
>   Hurrah!
> For her sweet sake was oft perplexed;
>   but ah!
> The false one looked for a daintier loot—
> The constant one wearied me out and out—
>   The best was not easily got.

The Yankees, however, had a high opinion of our feminine beauty, and the impressions made on the gallent youths that Saturday afternoon were of the most favourable order. The Romans, in fact, were not more captivated with the beauty of the Sabine maidens than were the young Americans with the lovely Scottish girls who gave them such a hearty reception at Bruce Park in April, 1901.

Walts Vanderbilt, their captain, was a fine-looking young fellow, about twenty-five years of age. Ere this, the young Americans had completely discarded whiskers, and Walt formed no exception to the rule with his closely-shaven cheeks and well-formed moustache. Good work in the field in the way of practice had made Walt's form show complete development, and I am inclined to think that a finer specimen of a football player never toed a ball. The goal-keeper of the team, too, young Lincoln, was rather a nice-looking fellow, nearly six feet high, and well proportioned, with eyes sparkling with humour, but he lacked the fine open countenance of his captain.

The other members of the team were much of the ordinary type of humanity, just like our average football club men, with any amount of nerve and energy. If they felt excited at the magnitude of the work they had taken in hand they concealed it well, and looked as if they were merely entering the field to do a little practice. They wore the sign of the American eagle, dotted over with the emblematical stars and stripes. Our fellows had also an imposing appearance, with the lion-rampant on their jerseys, and although looking rather douce and uncertain about the game, determination was depicted on every face.

The names of the gentlemen who entered the field were as under:

SCOTLAND: F Wallace (South Side Swifts), goalkeeper; T Glen (Queen's Park), D Smollet (Vale of Leven), backs; W McMillan (Dumbarton), F McNeil (Rangers), half-backs; K McGeake (Pollokshields Athletic), P Livingston (Kilmarnock), K Watt (Edinburgh Rovers), T Stewart (Volunteer AC) T D Coats (Paisley Combination), and G F Turnbull (Renfrewshire Nomads, forwards).

AMERICA: W R C Lincoln (New York Caledonian), goalkeeper; V H Grant (Texas Rovers), W C Vanderbilt (Hamilton State Swifts), backs; J H Armstrong (Chicago Association, D Steel (Nebraska Electric), half-backs; D C Bramey (Victoria Boys), R S Chandler (Utah Gentiles), P Whitehouse (Newhaven), J S Bryan (Alaska Pilgrims), W D Bangle (San Francisco Racers), and T Lawrence (Washington House), forwards.

UMPIRES: J W Marindin (South Australia) and D Y Jones (Canadian Association). Referee—W H Littleton (English Association).

Before the game began, the Yankees offered to bet level money, and some of their red-hot plungers even went to the length of two to one on the chances; but they were promptly told that the days of betting and wagering at football matches, cricket, horse-racing, and all genuine sport, were now numbered with the past in the United Kingdom.

Gentlemen, in fact, who loved and enjoyed sport for its own sake, and for that part of it, ladies too, had voted betting 'low and unmanly', and even degrading, and as Parliament had been repeatedly petitioned on the subject, a bill was almost unanimously passed in the dying year of the nineteenth century, abolishing betting.

The loyal Irish Party (late Home Rulers), and the Rado-Toro Democratic Party (led by Lord Randy Chapel-Mountain), whose hair was beginning to get silvery-grey, and his long moustache to match, did not even oppose the bill, and it passed. Never did a legislative enactment work such improvement among the masses as this Bill. It completely banished all needy souls and black-legs from the arena of honest sport, and left the field to those who came of an afternoon and evening to enjoy themselves in an honest way.

The coarse language, too, of which our forefathers justly complained twenty years ago, had almost disappeared, whether through the effects of the School Board, I would not like to say, but one could now take sweetheart or wife to enjoy themselves, provided always, of course, the weather was at all suitable.

As for professional football players, no such thing had been heard of for years. They certainly died hard, but eventually no club would have anything to do with them.

'What is that?' 'Oh, it's the bell to begin.'

Well, the game did begin in earnest, immediately after a fair lady had thrown out the leather ball from the Grand Stand at the right-hand side of the field. There was no tossing for choice of ends, for a new rule had been just added to the revised code enacting in a most chivalrous way that strangers or visitors be allowed to select the side of the ground they preferred to play on for the first half-hour—for you must know, my readers, the term now allowed for the game was one hour, and that when the ball was kicked into touch, there was no throwing back into play with the hands, but it was kicked from the touch-line straight out before play was again resumed.

For some time the forwards kept the leather close to themsleves, and the Yankees on the left wing, by a fine piece of manoeuvring, were successful in getting it away, amid tremendous cheering. Chandler, who was one of the fastest sprinters in the world, and had beaten the record in San Francisco in the fall of last year, got through his men in brilliant form, and came down on the goalkeeper like 'winkum'. Just as he was poising himself, however, for a final shot, McNeil deliberately crossed the field from the opposite side, and after dodging about the young American, rushed in and took the leather away, and keeping it between his feet for a couple of seconds, kicked it clear to the Scotch goal. A good deal of heading afterwards occurred near the home goal—the ball getting close on the lines several times, and even passing them. Many considered before the game began that the Americans would never have a 'look in' at all, and great was their dismay when they actuallly held their champions hotly pressed on their own ground, and looked like losing the day. With a brilliant charge the Yankee forwards crowded round the Scotch sticks like a hive of bees on a June morning, and a straight shot from the foot of D Steel, who rushed in from his place at half-back, caused the ball to glide past the Scotch goalkeeper like a rocket.

This was the signal for tremendous excitement. Crowds of partisans and friends who had come over with the strangers, and many enthusiastic lovers of the game and fair play, raised a loud cheer, again and again renewed, at this piece of grand play on the part of the Yankees. The intensely interested Scotchmen, however, while they certainly admired the pluck and fine play of the visitors, and cheering in the mild kind of a way, even though an enemy wrung it from them, kept very quiet, and not a few white faces might have been seen about the wire fence which kept spectators and players apart on Bruce Park on that memorable day. They, however, kept their own council, and quaintly said to the Yankees who chaffed them on the point, that howling was a very good thing in a way, but it should not be indulged in till people were out òf the wood.

The teams then faced each other in midfield, and the ball had no sooner left the Scotch captain's foot than it was taken away, and dribbled down the centre of Bryan, Whitehouse, and Lawrence, and when half-time was called the latter was just finishing a good shy, which sent the ball over the bar. According to the new rules a quarter of an hour was allowed as an interval, and during that time speculation ran high as to what was destined to be the final issue.

To indulge for a moment at the idea of the Americans beating the Scottish on their own ground in the great International was a sore point for the bulk of the spectators with Scotch faces, but they said very little. They had a secret hope that their champions would eventually pull off the game, even though they had a goal to make up, and only half-an-hour to do it. They had, it was remembered with pride and satisfaction, pulled through many a doubtful match before, and Scotchmen, it was well known, were not easily beaten.

The young lady again threw up the ball, and Tam Glen, getting a good hold of it at his left foot, made one of the finest fly-kicks ever seen in a match, and the forwards on the Scotch side following well up, completely puzzled the Yankees backs and half-backs by their brilliant passing. Before you could say Jack Robinson, McGeake shied for the American goal, and the ball knocked of the cap of the goalkeeper, and hitting the bar, bounded back into the field of play. A hard and exciting scrimmage followed, and amid breathless excitement, the Yankees cleared their goal. Five minutes of very even play followed, and then the Scotchmen set their teeth and made a desperate effort for victory.

Only ten minutes of the game now remained to the good, and there was, you may be sure, no time to lose. One goal behind, and at the great International, too! It would never do to allow America to whip creation even at football! One final effort; no, two final efforts, and it was done.

The Scotch captain was seen to whisper something to his team, and in a few minutes the grandest run which was probably ever witnessed since football became a scientific sport in the world, was started, and before the American backs, half-backs, and goalkeeper could realise their position, the Scotchmen bore down on the visitors' goal, and literally dribbled the ball clean through. This way, you may be sure, the signal for an outburst of cheering, which must have been heard over the half of the big city of Glasgow, which now contained over a million of inhabitants.

The game, however, was not yet won—it was only a tie—and when the representatives of Brother Jonathan again started the ball only four minutes remained, but it proved a bad four minutes for the representatives of the stars and stripes. Another run, backed up by a shooter from the left foot of Turnbull, settled the great International for that year at any rate. Those who had hitherto viewed the game in moody silence began to come out of their shells (talking piscatorically) and join in the universal huzzah.

The Yankees were now fairly cowed, and when another grand piece of play by Stewart, backed up at the proper moment by Watt, put a third goal to the credit of the Scotchmen, the visitors, in the most gentlemanly way, heartily joined in the cheering for the victors. When the referee's whistle was sounded, 'the Scotchmen were declared the winners of a hard-fought field by 3 goals to 1'. The crowd completely besieged the pavilion at Bruce Park at the close and cheered lustily as the Scotch champions made their way up the steps. Nor were the vanquished strangers forgotten. They came in for a round of hearty cheers for their pluck.

There was a dinner given the distinguished strangers, in the evening, and the annual complimentary toasts proposed, and duly acknowledged, but as I was not present, I am unable to say who spoke best, gave the most enjoyable song, or drunk the heaviest quantity of sparkling champagne or zoedone.

At any rate, a happy evening was passed, and, after spending a day in Glasgow, the Yankees sailed on the following Monday morning for New York, where they duly arrived without any mishap, after the fastest passage on record—having covered the distance from Greenock to Sandy Hook in twenty-three hours fifty-nine and three-quarter minutes!

Such is 'NED DUNCAN'S DREAM, OR THE GREAT INTERNATIONAL'.

Source: Scottish Association Football Annual 1884–1885, pp 115–21

THE SCOTS-AMERICAN CONNECTION

*a comprehensive bibliography
and biographical list
extracted from*

PORTABLE UTOPIA

Glasgow and the United States

Bernard Aspinwall

Bibliography

Manuscript Sources
Those marked with an asterisk were particularly useful for this study

AMERICA

CALIFORNIA

Stanford University, Hoover Institution, Palo Alto:
* David Starr Jordon Papers
San Marino, Huntington Library:
* A D Bache Papers
  Ida Harper Papers
  Harriet Beecher Stowe Papers
  W C Bryant Papers, and several autograph and other smaller collections which contained Scottish material
San Francisco, Public Library, Special Collections:
* Local History, pamphlets, cuttings and various rare items of local importance
California Historical Society:
* Local history and Scottish material, especially relating to the Donoghue brothers from Glasgow
Berkeley, University of California, Bancroft Library:
  Bancroft Papers, including his manuscript histories of San Francisco, etc.
  Fremont Older Papers
* James D Phelan Papers
* W George Mooney Papers
  George Davidson Papers
Los Angeles, University of Southern California, Philosophy Library MSS Collections:
* George Howison Papers
  W T Harris Papers
  Gomperz Papers and several small collections
Stockton, California, University of the Pacific:
* John Muir Papers

CONNECTICUT

New Haven, Yale University Library:
  Benjamin Silliman Papers
* Thomas Davidson Papers
  Timothy Dwight Papers
  Henry Ward Beecher Papers
  D L Moody Papers
  D C Gilman Papers
  A J MacDonald Collection
  The Wright Family Papers
  G B Adams Papers
  J W Webb Papers

FLORIDA

Gainesville, Florida, University of Florida:
  Gov Broward Papers
  W H Gleeson Papers
  Swan Papers and numerous pamphlets, land company reports and promotional literature for intending immigrants as well as the Florida Immigration reports, 1870–90

GEORGIA

Savannah, Georgia, Georgia Historical Society:
* Juliette Gordon Low Papers and several minor collections of some Scottish interest.
Athens, Georgia, University of Georgia:
Hoke Smith Papers

ILLINOIS

Chicago, Historical Society:
* Several volumes of clippings relating to the rise and defeat of Mayor Dunne 1904–8
Newberry Library:
Graham Taylor Papers and some small collections
Moody Bible Training Institute:
Moody Papers and Moodiana
Chicago, University of Illinois Chicago Circle Campus
* Jane Addams Papers

INDIANA

Ball State University, Muncie, Indiana:
* Norman Angell Papers

MICHIGAN

Michigan Historical Collections, University of Michigan, Ann Arbor, Michigan:
* R M Wenley Papers

MASSACHUSETTS

Boston, Public Library:
* W L Garrison Papers
* Bronson Alcott Papers (copies)
* Pease Collection
* S J May Papers
Cambridge, Harvard University, Houghton Library:
Charles Sumner Papers
Henry Ward Beecher Papers
Frances Wright Papers
Phillips Brooks Papers
John Freeman Clarke Papers
Josiah Royce Papers
Joel Barlow Papers
G W Cable Papers
* Dorothea Dix Papers
* Margaret Fuller Papers
T W Higginson Papers
S G Howe Papers
W L Garrison Papers
Louis Agassiz Papers
O G Villard Papers
Julia Ward Howe Papers
Francis Parkman Papers
Edward Everett Papers
* Ishill Collection
Massachusetts Historical Society:
George Bancroft Papers
* Horace Mann Papers—unavailable—in microfilming stage
Amasa Walker Papers
Amos Lawrence Papers
Henry W Bellows Papers
Ezra Stiles Gannett Papers
Theodore Parker Papers
John Pierce Papers

Joseph Tuckerman Papers
Noah Worcester—Peace Papers
S G Howe Papers
New England Freedman's Aid Society Papers
R T Paine Papers
Edward Atkinson Papers
Harvard Divinity School:
* Unitarian Collections, especially Joseph Tuckerman Papers
Radcliffe College, Women's Collections:
Julia Ward Howe Papers
Anna Shaw Papers
Harriet Beecher Stowe Papers were in microfilming stage—not available
Worcester, Mass—American Antiquarian Society:
E Abbott Papers
Scioto Land Company Papers
* J B Gough Papers
* R A Hallam Diaries
Joseph Lancaster Papers
* Andrew Bigelow Diaries
Caroline White Papers
Salem, Mass—Essex Historical Institute:
George Peabody Papers
J G Whittier Papers and several small miscellaneous collections of travels in Europe

MARYLAND

Baltimore, Johns Hopkins University Library:
* Herbert Baxter Adams Papers
* C P Gilman Papers
F G Goodnow Papers

MISSOURI

St Louis, Missouri, Missouri Historical Society:
* Sublette Papers
* W T Harris Papers

NEW JERSEY

Princeton N J, Princeton University Library
* Mormon Diaries copies from Brigham Young University of British Missions
Mudd Library:
McCosh Papers

NEW YORK

New York City:
* City and Suburban Housing Company Papers at Company Head office
Columbia University:
* Elizabeth Blackwell Papers
Homer Folks Papers
G F Holls Papers
Mary Richmond Papers
* Edwin Markham Papers and Thomas Lake Harris Papers. Special collections—Van
    Ariage, G Watson and Felix Arnholm
New York University:
* Henry Barnard Papers
Taniment Library:
* Socialist Party Papers, materials on Debs, London, Hillquit and municipal government
New York Public Library:
* Albert Shaw Papers
* Henry George Papers
* John Griscom materials

Benjamin Tucker Papers
* Elizabeth Blackwell Papers
W G Simms Papers
E A Poe Papers
* Alfred S Roe Diary
* Tenement House Building Company
National Civic Federation Papers
Staten Island, Wagner College:
* Edwin Markham Papers
* Thomas Lake Harris Papers (with those sections in Columbia University)
The archives of the Community Service Society which included the papers of The New York Association for Improving the Condition of the Poor, the New York Charity Organisation Society, and others had been transferred to Columbia University for sorting and copying and were unavailable. Union Theological College Collections were closed on the two occasions I went up there.

NORTH CAROLINA

University of North Carolina, Chapel Hill NC:
* Juliette Gordon Low Papers and several diaries and letters of Scottish immigrants in the early and mid-nineteenth century

OHIO

Cleveland, University of Western Reserve:
* The Green Papers, now available on microfilm
Toledo-Lucas County Public Library:
* Samuel Jones Papers
Columbus Ohio, Ohio State Historical Collections
* Temperance Collections
Washington Gladden Papers

PENNSYLVANIA

Easton, Pennsylvania, Lafayette College:
* Materials and rare pamphlets, etc., relating to Professor Cunningham of Glasgow and Edinburgh
Philadelphia, American Philosophical Society:
Benjamin Vaughan Papers
Joseph Priestley Papers
A D Bache Papers
John Vaughan Papers
Richard Price Papers
* George Ord Papers
Academy of Natural Sciences:
Benjamin Silliman Papers
* McClure materials in various collections
Historical Society:
Frederick Douglass Papers
US Sanitary Commission, Phil. section, Papers
* Joel Poinsett Papers
Joseph Fels Papers
Several small collections including autograph items
Presbyterian Historical Society:
A thorough search of their nineteenth- and twentieth-century material proved disappointing for this study.
Swarthmore, Friends and Peace Collections:
* Lucretia Mott Papers
William Ladd Papers

RHODE ISLAND

Providence, Historical Society:
* Channing Papers

UTAH
  Salt Lake City, Mormon Archives:
  * Here I found some 50 autobiographies, memoirs, letters and correspondence relating to
    Scottish immigrants and their experiences. Also the manuscript histories of the
    British, Scottish and Glasgow missions

VERMONT
  Bennington College:
    John Spargo Papers

WASHINGTON DC
  Catholic University of America
  * Terence V Powderley Papers
  Library of Congress:
  * Bache Papers
    Ezra Stiles Papers
    Lester Ward Papers
    Ida H Harper Papers
  * John A Kingsbury Papers
    Jacob Riis Papers
  * Margaret Sanger Papers
    Tappan Papers
    Elizur Wright Papers
  * Frances Wright Papers
    Andrew Carnegie Papers
    G F Peabody Papers
    The Breckenridge Family Papers
    American Colonisation Society Papers
  * American Peace Society Papers
    National Women's Trade Union League Papers
    Neil Jamieson Papers
  * Elizabeth Cady Stanton Papers
  * Frederick Douglass Papers
    Carrie Chapman Catt Papers
    Daniel Webster Papers
    W C Langdon Papers
  * W L Fisher Papers
    Alexander J McKelway Papers
    Clarence Darrow Papers
    T De Witt Talmage Papers
    John Fiske Papers
  * Charles Edward Russell Papers
  * Brand Whitlock Papers
    William Jennings Bryan Papers
    William Allen White Papers
    National Consumers League Papers
    Booker T Washington Papers

WISCONSIN
  Madison Wisconsin, Wisconsin State Historical Society:
  * J R Ely Papers
  * Henry Demarest Lloyd Papers
    Daniel De Leon Collection

CANADA

TORONTO
  Queens University, Toronto:
  * James Mavor Papers

SCOTLAND

EDINBURGH

Edinburgh National Library of Scotland:
* George Combe Papers
* Patrick Geddes Papers

GLASGOW

Mitchell Library:
* Glasgow Emancipation Society, Smeal Collection
Strathclyde Regional Archives:
* Minutes of the Town Council and Tramways Committee
* Councillors' Biographical Clippings and Obituary Book—The Doomsday Book

Books

The works listed here proved particularly useful in writing this book. Fuller listings will be found in the various chapters.

Alexander, John K	Render Them Submissive: The Response to Poverty in Philadelphia 1760–1800 (Amherst 1980)
Allen, H C and Thompson, Roger	Contrast and Connection: Bicentennial Essays in Anglo-American History (London 1976)
Armytage, W H G	Heavens Below: Utopian Experiments in England 1560–1960 (London 1961)
Bebbington, D W	The Nonconformist Conscience: Chapel and Politics 1870–1914 (London 1982)
Berger, Max	The British Traveller in America, 1836–1860 (New York 1943)
Berthoff, Rowland, Tappan	British Immigrants in Industrial America, 1790–1850 (Cambridge Mass (1953)
Bestor, Arthur	Backwoods Utopias: The Sectarian and Owenite Phases of Communitarian Socialism in America 1663–1829 (Philadelphia 1950)
Black, George Fraser	Scotland's Mark on America (New York 1921)
Bolt, Christine	Victorian Attitudes to Race (London 1971)
Boston, Ray	British Chartists in America 1839–1900 (Manchester 1971)
Brock, William R	Scotus Americanus: A Survey of the Sources for the Links between Scotland and America in the Eighteenth Century (Edinburgh 1982)
Bryson, Gladys	Man and Society: The Inquiry of the Eighteenth Century (Princeton 1940)
Bumsted, J M	The People's Clearance: Highland Emigration to British North America (Edinburgh 1982)
Campbell, John	Memoirs of David Nasmith: His Labours and Travels (London 1844)
Carwardine, Richard	Transatlantic Revivalism: Popular Evangelicalism in England and America 1790–1865 (Westport Conn 1978)
Checkland, Olive	Philanthropy in Victorian Scotland: Social Welfare and the Voluntary Principle (Edinburgh 1980)
Cremin, Lawrence	The Transformation of the School (New York 1961)
Crook, David Paul	American Democracy in English Politics 1815–1840 (Oxford 1965)
Davie, George	The Democratic Intellect: Scotland and her Universities in the Nineteenth Century (Edinburgh 1961)

Dickson R J — Ulster Emigration to Colonial America, 1718–1775 (London 1966)

Dudden, Arthur Power — Joseph Fels and the Single Tax Movement (Philadelphia 1971)

Erickson, Charlotte — American Industry and the European Immigrant 1860–1885, (Cambridge Mass 1957)

— Invisible Immigrants: The Adaptation of English and Scottish Immigrants in Nineteenth Century America (London 1972)

Ferguson, Thomas — The Dawn of Scottish Social Welfare (London 1948)
Scottish Social Welfare, 1864–1914 (Edinburgh 1958)

Findlay, John L — Canada in the North Atlantic Triangle: Two Centuries of Social Change (Toronto 1975)

Fladeland, Betty — Men and Brothers: Anglo-American Anti-Slavery Co-operation (Urbana Ill 1972)

Ford, Henry James — The Scotch Irish in America (Princeton 1915)

Graham, Ian Charles Cargill — Colonists from Scotland: Emigration to North America, 1707–1783 (Ithaca 1956)

Grave, S A — The Scottish Philosophy of Common Sense (Oxford 1960)

Hanna, Charles A — The Scotch-Irish or the Scot in North Britain, North Ireland and North America, 2 vols (New York 1902)

Hareven, Tamara K and Langenbach, Randolph — Amoskeag: Life and Work in an American Factory City in New England (London 1979) (contains interviews with Scottish immigrants)

Harrison, J F C — Robert Owen and the Owenites in Britain and America: The Quest for the New Moral World (London 1969)

Holloway, Mark — Heavens on Earth: Utopian Communities in America 1680–1880 (New York 1966)

Hook, Andrew — Scotland and America 1750–1835 (Glasgow 1975)

Hoeveler, J David Jr — James McCosh and the Scottish Intellectual Tradition, (Princeton 1981)

Horowitz, Helen, Leflowitz — Culture and the City: Cultural Philanthropy in Chicago from the 1880s to 1917 (Lexington Ky 1976)

Jackson, W Turrentine — The Enterprising Scot: Investors in the American West after 1873 (Edinburgh 1973)

Jeremy, David J — Transatlantic Industrial Revolution. The Diffusion of Textile Technologies between Britain and America 1790–1830s (Oxford 1981)

Johnston, H J M — British Emigration Policy 1815–1850 (Oxford 1972)

Johnston, S C — Emigration from the United Kingdom to North America, 1763–1912 (London 1966 edn)

Kelley, Robert — The Transatlantic Persuasion: The Liberal Democratic Mind in the Age of Gladstone (New York 1969)

Kelly, Thomas — A History of Adult Education in Great Britain (Liverpool 1970)

Kenin, Richard — Return to Albion: Americans in England 1760–1940 (New York 1979)

Kerr, W G — Scottish Capital on the American Credit Frontier (Austin Texas 1976)

Klingberg, F J and and Abel, A H — A Sidelight on Anglo-American Relations, 1839–1858 (Lancaster Pa 1927)

Kraus, Michael — The Atlantic Civilisation: Eighteenth Century Origins (Ithaca 1966 edn)

Landon, Fred — Western Ontario and the American Frontier (New York 1970 edn)

Lane, Margaret — Frances Wright and the 'Great Experiment' (Manchester 1972)

Lawrence, Elwood P — Henry George in the British Isles (East Lansing Michigan 1957)

Leopold, R W — Robert Dale Owen (Cambridge Mass 1940)

Lillibridge, G D — Beacon of Freedom: The Impact of American Democracy Upon Great Britain, 1830–1870 (Philadelphia 1954)

McCalla, Douglas — The Upper Canada Trade 1834–1872: A Study of the Buchanan's Business (Toronto 1979)

MacDonald, Norman — Canada, Immigration and Colonisation, 1841–1903 (Aberdeen 1968 edn)

MacDougall, D — Scots and Scots Descendants in America (New York 1917)

MacLean, J P — An Historical Account of the Settlements of Scotch Highlanders in America Prior to 1783 (Baltimore 1978 edn)

Mattingly, Paul H — The Classless Profession: American Schoolmen in the Nineteenth Century (New York 1975)

Mesick, Jane Louise — The English Traveller in America 1785–1835 (New York 1922)

Metcalfe, R — The Rise and Progress of Hydropathy in England and Scotland (London 1906)

Meyer, D H — The Instructed Conscience: The Shaping of the American National Ethic (Philadelphia 1972)

Moore, R Laurence — European Socialists and the American Promised Land (New York 1970)

Mulvey, Christopher — Anglo-American Landscapes: A Study of Nineteenth Century Anglo-American Travel Literature (New York 1983) [appeared as this book was going to print]

Niebuhr, Reinhold and Heimert, Alan — A Nation so Conceived: Reflections on the History of America from its Early Vision to Its Present Power (London 1964)

Nolan, James Bennett — Benjamin Franklin in Scotland and Ireland, 1759 and 1771 (Philadelphia 1938)

Nord, David Paul — Newspapers and New Politics: Mid-western Municipal Reform 1890–1900 (Ann Arbor 1979)

Pelling, Henry — America and the British Left: From Bright to Bevan (London 1956)

Perry, Lewis — Radical Abolitionism: Anarchy and Government of God in Antislavery Thought (Ithaca 1973)

Rattray, W J — The Scot in British North America, 4 vols (Toronto 1888)

Raish, Marjorie Gamet — Victoria: The Story of a Western Kansas Town (Topeka Kansas 1947) a settlement with considerable Scottish interest

Reid, W Stanford (ed) — The Scottish Tradition in Canada (Toronto 1976)

Rice, C Dunean — The Scots Abolitionists 1833–1861 (Baton Rouge 1981)

Rothman, David J — The Discovery of the Asylum: Social Order and Disorder in the New Republic (Boston 1971)

Sandeen, Earnest R — The Roots of Fundamentalism, British and American (Chicago 1970)

Saunders, L C — Scottish Democracy 1815–1840 (London 1950)

Schiesel, Martin J — The Politics of Efficiency: Municipal Administration and Reform in America 1800–1920 (Berkeley 1977)

Sloan, Douglas — The Scottish Enlightenment and the American College Ideal (New York 1971)

Smith, Timothy L — Revivalism and Social Reform: American Protestantism on the Eve of The Civil War (New York 1965 edn)

Taylor, Clare — British and American Abolitionists: An Episode in Transatlantic Understanding (Edinburgh 1974)

Temperley, Howard — British Anti-slavery 1833–1870 (London 1972)

Thistlethwaite, Frank — The Anglo-American Connection in the Early Nineteenth Century (Philadelphia 1959)

Watson, Frank Dekker — The Charity Organisation Movement in the United States (New York 1971 edn)

Wilson, Gordon M — Alexander McDonald: Leader of the Miners (Aberdeen 1982)

| Woodroofe, Kathleen | From Charity to Social Work in England and the United States (London 1974 edn) |
| Yearley, Clifton K Jr | Britons in American Labour: The Influence of the United Kingdom Immigrants on American Labour 1820–1914 (Baltimore 1957) |

Articles

Adam, Margaret I	The Causes of Highland Emigration of 1783–1803, Scottish Historical Review 17 1920 73–89
Ahlstrom, Sydney E	The Scottish Philosophy and American Theology Church History 24 1955 257–72
Aspinwall, Bernard	Scottish Religious Identity in the Atlantic World, 1880–1914, Studies in Church History: Religion and National Identity 18 1982 505–18
—	Social Catholicism and Health: Dr and Mrs Thomas Low Nichols in Britain, Studies in Church History: The Church and Healing 19 1982 240–70.
—	Glasgow Trams and American Politics, 1894–1914, Scottish Historical Review 56 1977 64–84
Bailyn, Bernard and Clive, John	England's Cultural Provinces: Scotland and America, William and Mary Quarterly 3rd series II 1954 200–13
Charvet, William	Frances Jeffrey in America, New England Quarterly 14 1941 309–34
Clarke, P F	The Progressive Movement in England, Transactions of the Royal Historical Society 5th series, 24 1974 159–81
Cooter, Roger	Phrenology and British Alienists, 1780–1835 58–104, in Madhouses, Mad Doctors and Madmen: The Social History of Psychiatry in the Victorian Era (London 1981, ed Andrew Scull)
Creamer, Daniel	Recruiting Contract Labourers for the Amsokeag Mills, Journal of Economic History I 1941 42–56
Eklund, Emmet	The Scottish Free Church and its Relation to Nineteenth Century Swedish and Swedish-America Lutheranism, Church History 51 1982 405–18
Elson, Ruth Miller	American School-books and 'Culture' in the Nineteenth Century, Mississippi Valley Historical Review 46 1959–60 411–34
Fingerhut, Eugene	From Scots to Americans: Ryegate's Immigrants in the 1770s, Vermont History 35 1967 186–207
Ginger, Ray	Labour in a Massachusetts Cotton Mill, 1853–1860, Business History Review 28 1953 67–91
Gray, Malcolm	Scottish Emigration: The Social Impact of Agrarian Change in the Rural Lowlands 1775–1875, Perspectives in American History 7 1973 95–174
Griffin, Clyde	The 'Old' Immigration and Industry: A Case Study 176–204, in Immigrants in Industrial America 1850–1920, (Charlottesville, Va 1977, ed Richard L Ehrlich)
Harrison, Lowell H	Thomas Simpson Carson, New Mexico Rancher; New Mexico Historical Review 42 1967 127–43
Hays, Samuel P	The Politics of Reform in Municipal Government in the Progressive Era, Pacific Northwest Quarterly 55 1964 157–69
Horne, Robert M	James Fergus in the Colorado Goldfields, Colorado Magazine 50 (1973) 41–56

Hughes, J T — From Primitive Church to Civil Religion: The Millenial Odyssey of Alexander Campbell, Journal of American Academy of Religion 44 1976 87–103

Hunter, James — The Gaelic Connection: The Highlands, Ireland and Nationalism 1873–1922, Scottish Historical Review 54 1975 178–204

Landsman, Ned — Revivalism and Nativism in the Middle Colonies: The Great Awakening and the Scots Community in East New Jersey, American Quarterly 34 1982 149–64

Lubove, Roy — The New York Association for Improving the Condition of the Poor: The Formative Years, New York Historical Society Quarterly 43 1959 307–327

Mann, Arthur — British Social Reform Thought and American Reformers of the Progressive Era, Mississippi Valley Historical Review 42 1956 672–92

Mathew, W M — The Origin and Occupations of Glasgow Students 1740–1839, Past and Present 33 1966 74–94

Miller, Helen — Cities and Evolution: Patrick Geddes as an international prophet of Town Planning before 1914 199–224, in Anthony Sutcliffe, The Rise of Modern Urban Planning, 1800–1914 (London 1980)

Murray, Janette Stevenson — Lairds of North Tama, Iowa Journal of History and Politics 40 (1942) 227–260

— Women of North Tama, Iowa Journal of History and Politics 41 (1943) 287–318

Nash, Robert C — The English and Scottish Tobacco Traders in the Seventeenth and Eighteenth Century: Legal and Illegal Trade, Economic History Review 35 1982 354–72

Olson, Richard — Scottish Philosophy and Mathematics 1750–1830, Journal of the History of Ideas 32 1971 29–44

Pelling, Henry — The Knights of Labour in Britain 1880–1901, Economic History Review 2nd series 9 1956–7 313–37

— The American Economy and the Formation of the British Labour Party, Economic History Review 2nd series 8 1955–6 1–17

Quarles, Benjamin — Ministers Without Portfolio, Journal of Negro History 39 154 27–42

Roth, Randolph A — The First Radical Abolitionists: The Reverend James Milligan and the Reformed Presbyterians of Vermont, New England Quarterly 44 1982 540–63

Shepperson, George A — Thomas Chalmers, The Free Church of Scotland and the South, Journal of Southern History 17 1951 517–37

— The Free Church of Scotland and American Slavery, Scottish Historical Review 30 1951 126–43

— Frederick Douglass and Scotland, Journal of Negro History 38 1953 307–21

— Writings in Scottish-American History: A Brief Survey, William and Mary Quarterly 3rd series II 1954 163–78

— Harriet Beecher Stowe and Scotland, Scottish Historical Review 32 1953 40–6

Tyson, R E — Scottish Investment in American Railways: The Case of the City of Glasgow Bank 1856–81, in Studies in Scottish Business History (London 1967, ed P L Payne)

Vogt, Martha — Scots in Hispanic California, Scottish Historical Review 52 1973 137–48

Wilson, William H — The Ideology, aesthetics and politics of the City Beautiful Movement 166–89, in Anthony Sutcliffe, The Rise of Modern Urban Planning 1800–1914 (London 1980)

Wright, Esmond	Education in the American Colonies: The Impact of Scotland 18–45, in Essays in Scotch-Irish History (London 1969, ed E R R Green
Young, James D	Changing Images of American Democracy and the Labour Movement, International Review of Social History 13 1973 69–89

Novels by Scottish Immigrants to America with a Scottish Theme

Barr, Amelia Edith Huddleston	Scottish Sketches (New York 1883); A Daughter of Fife (New York 1886); A Border Shepherdess (New York 1887); The Mate of the Easer Bell and Other stories (New York 1893); The Flower of Gala Water (New York 1895); Prisoners of Conscience: A Story of Scotland (New York 1897); Christine, A Fife Fishgirl (New York 1917) Cluny McPherson (New York 1883)
	She wrote many other novels with Scottish themes, but claimed to have forgotten how many novels she had written. Various authorities attribute between 75 and 80 to her. See her autobiography Amelia Edith Huddleston Barr, All the Days of My Life (New York 1980 edn) Her sister-in-law was married to David Colville the great iron and steel magnate of the West of Scotland.
Brownlee, William C	The Whigs of Scotland; or The Last of the Stewarts, 2 vols (New York 1833)
Tait, J S	Who Is the Man: A Tale of the Scottish Borders (London 1890)

Scottish Poets and Writers on American Themes

Blake, George	The Constant Star (London 1945) and The Innocence Within (London 1955)
Galt, John	Lawrie Todd or the Settlers in the Woods 3 vols (London 1830); Grant Thorburn
Hamilton, Thomas	Cyril Thorton (Edinburgh 1846)
Murray, Charles Augustus	The Prairie Bird (London 1846)
Stevenson, Robert Louis	The Amateur Emigrant; Across The Plains; The Silverado Squatters; The Old and New Pacific Capitals From the Collected Works 35 vols (Edinburgh 1891–2)
Stewart, Sir William Drummond	Altowan, 2 vols (London 1846); Edward Warren (London 1854)
Thomson, James	Religion in the Rocky Mountains, in William David Schaefer, The Speedy Extinction of Evil and Misery; Selected Prose of James Thomson (Berkeley 1967) pp 66–79. It was the only work Thomson is known to have written while in America

Scottish Impressions of America

EMIGRANT GUIDES

Abbott, Joseph	The Emigrant to North America, from Memoranda of a Settlement in Canada (Edinburgh 1844)
Burton, John Hill	The Emigrants' Manual (Edinburgh 1851)
Fraser, William	The Emigrants' Guide or Sketches of Canada with some of the Northern and Western States of America (Glasgow 1857)

Alexander J E	Transatlantic Sketches 2 vols (London 1833)
Anon	Ayrshire Schoolmaster's Pedestrian Tour of a Scottish Immigrant in the Middle States of America, Tait's Edinburgh Magazine vol 6 1839 pp 381–92, 444–52, 724–34
Allardice, R B (Capt Barclay)	Agricultural Tour in the United States and Canada (Edinburgh 1842)
Baxter, W E	America and the Americans, London 1855
—	The Social Condition of the Southern States of America: a Lecture delivered in the Corn Exchange Hall, Dundee on 5 November 1852 (London 1852)
Berry, C B	The Other Side: How It Struck Us (London 1880)
Bishop, Isabella L(Bird)	An Englishwoman in America (London 1856) (Although born in Yorkshire, Mrs Bird settled in Edinburgh and amid her many travels she sought to eliminate the Edinburgh slums)
—	Aspects of Religion in the United States of America (London 1859)
—	A Lady's Life in the Rocky Mountains (London 1879)
Borthwick, J D	Three Years in California (Edinburgh 1857)
Brechin, Hugh	Letters from America, a series in the Glasgow Herald 1881.
Bryce, James	The American Commonwealth 3 vols (London 1888)
Burn, J Dawson	Three Years Residence Among the Working Classes of America During the Recent Civil War (London 1865)
Caird, Sir James	Prairie Farming in America (London, 1859)
Campbell, Sir George	White and Black: The Outcome of a Visit to the United States (London 1879)
Campbell, John Douglas Sutherland, Marquis of Lorne, later Duke of Argyll	A Trip To the Tropics and Home through America (London 1867)
Campbell, J Kerr of Stirling	Through the United States and Canada, being a Record of Holiday Experience (London 1886)
Carson, Thomas Simpson	Ranching, Sport and Travel (London 1911)
—	The World as Seen by Me (London 1923)
Chambers, William	American Slavery and Colour (Edinburgh 1862)
—	Things As They are in America (London 1854)
Clay, John	New World Notes (Kelso 1875)
—	My Life of the Range (Chicago 1924)
Combe, George	Notes on the USA During a Phrenological Visit 1838, 1839, 1840 3 vols (Edinburgh 1841)
Craib, Alexander	America and the Americans (Paisley 1892)
Davis, Stephen	Notes of a Tour in America in 1832 and 1833 (Edinburgh 1833)
Dudgeon, Thomas	A Nine Years' Residence and a Nine Months' Tour on Foot in the States of New York and Pennsylvania for the Use of Labourers, Farmers and Emigrants (Edinburgh 1841)

Duff, Alex	An Address (Washington DC 1854)
Duncan, John M	Trends Through Part of the United States and Canada in 1818 and 1819 (Glasgow 1823)
Dunlop, Alexander Graham	The New World Journal (1845) eds David Sinclair and Germaine Warkentin (Edinburgh 1976)
Edmond, Revd Dr	America and Americans, United Presbyterian Magazine vol 16 ns 1872 12 articles
Fagan, James O	The Autobiography of an Individualist (London 1913)
Ferguson, Fergus	From Glasgow to Missouri and Back (Glasgow 1878)
Ferguson, William	America by River and Rail; or Notes By The Way (London 1856). He also claimed to have written The Illinois Central and Co, but I have been unable to trace this work.
Fergusson, Adam	Practical Notes During the Tour in Canada and a portion of the United States (Edinburgh 1833)
Forbes, Alexander	California: A History of Upper and Lower California (London 1839) reputedly the first book in English on the area
Forbes, Archibald	Souvenirs of Some Continents (London 1885)
Hall, Basil	Fragments of Voyages and Travels 3 vols (London 1829)
Hamilton, Thomas	Men and Manners in America (Edinburgh 1843 edn)
Hogben, John	First Impressions of America (Leith 1904)
Howison, John who *may* have been a Scot wrote	Sketches of Upper Canada, Domestic Local and Characteristic to which are added practical details for the information of emigrants of every class (Edinburgh 1821) (with a section on the USA) and Foreign Scenes or Travelling Recreations 2 vols (Edinburgh 1825) with some fleeting references to America
Johnstone, James F W	Notes on North America: Agricultural Economic and Social 2 vols (Edinburgh 1851)
Kelland, Philip	Transatlantic Sketches (Edinburgh 1858)
Lang, John Dunmore	Religion and Education in America (London 1840)
Lang, J Marshall	The United States and their People, Catholic Presbyterian 5 (1881) 90–9
Leng, John	America in 1876 (Dundee 1877)
—	Letter from the United States and Canada (Dundee 1905)
Leng, William C	The American War (Dundee 1863)
Lewis, George	Impressions of America and the American Churches (Edinburgh 1845)
Logan, James	Notes of a Journey Through Canada, the United States and the West Indies (Edinbrugh 1838)
Lorimer, John G	The Past and Present Conclusion of Religion and Morality in the United States: An Argument Not for Voluntary But For Established Churches (Glasgow 1833)
Lumsden, James	American Memoranda (Glasgow 1844)
MacGregor, John	Our Brothers and Cousins: A Summer Tour in Canada and the United States (London 1859)
Mackay, Alexander	The Western World and Travels in the United States in 1846–1847 3 vols (London 1849)
Mackay, Charles	Life and Liberty in America 2 vols (London 1859)
McLean, John	Notes of a Twenty-Five Years' Service in the Hudson Bay Territory 2 vols (London 1849)
Macrae, David	The Americans at Home (Glasgow 1885 edn)
—	Home and Abroad: Sketches and Gleanings (Glasgow 1871)
—	Among the Darkies and Other Papers (Glasgow 1876)
—	America Revisited and Men I have Met (Glasgow 1908)
Marjoribanks, Alexander	Travels in North and South (London 1853)
Mathieson, R	How We Saw The United States (Dunfermline 1883)
Maxwell, A M	A Run Through the United States in the Autumn of 1840 2 vols (London 1841)

Montgomery, James	A Practical Detail of the Cotton Manufacture of the United States of America and the State of Cotton Manufacture of that country contrasted and compared to that of Great Britain (Glasgow 1840)
Muirhead, James F	America, The Land of Contrasts: A Briton's View of his American Kin (London 1898)
Murray, Charles Augustus	Travels in North America 1834–1836 2 vols (New York 1839)
Murray, Henry A	Lands of the Slave and the Free 2 vols (London 1855)
Neilson, Peter	Recollections of a Six Years' Residence in the United States (Glasgow 1830)
Oliphant, Laurence	Minnesota and the Far West (Edinburgh 1855)
—	Patriots and Filibusters (London 1860)
—	On The Present State of Political Parties in America (Edinburgh 1866)
Oliver, William	Eight Months in Illinois (Newcastle-on-Tyne 1843)
Playfair, Robert	Recollections of a Visit to the United States and the British Provinces of North America (Edinburgh 1856)
—	Tour in the United States and British North America with Useful Hints to Tourists and Emigrants (Edinburgh 1849 edn)
Potts, John Faulkner	Letters from America (London 1880)
Prentice, Archibald	A Tour in the United States with Two Lectures on Emigration (London 1849)
Regan, John	The Emigrants' Guide to the Western States of America (Edinburgh 1853 edn)
Reid, Hugo	The American Question in a Nutshell; or Why We should Recognise the Confederate State (London 1862)
—	Sketches in North America (London 1851)
Rosebery, Lord	North American Journal—1873 ed A R C Grant with Caroline Combe (London 1967)
Ross, Alex	The Fur Hunters of the Far West (1855) (Norman Oklahoma 1956 edn)
Shirreff, Patrick	A Tour Through North America (Edinburgh 1835)
Simpson, Sir George	Narrative of a Tour Round the World During the Years 1841 and 1842 2 vols (London 1847)
Stirling, James	Letters from the Slave States (London 1858)
—	Letters from the Slave States (London 1857)
Stuart, James	Three Years in North America 2 vols (Edinburgh 1833)
Tait, J S	Emigration by Colony For the Middle Classes (Edinburgh 1885)
—	The Cattlefields of the Far West (Edinburgh 1884)
Thomson, William	A Tradesman's Travels in the United States and Canada (Edinburgh 1842)
Thorburn, Grant	Fifty Years Reminiscences of New York, or Flowers From The Garden of Lawrie Todd (New York 1845) also his Forty Years Residence in America (London 1834)
Turnbull, Jane M E and Marion	American Photographs 2 vols (London 1859) The authors seem to be the daughters of Dr Alexander Turnbull, MD 1794/5–1881, an Edinburgh University graduate.
Weston, John	A Visit to the United States and Canada in 1833, with a view to settling in America (Glasgow 1836)
Wilkie, David	Sketches of a Summer Trip to New York and Canada (Edinburgh 1837)
Wright, Frances	Views of Society and Manners in America—in a series of Letters from that Country to A Friend in England During the Years 1818, 1819, and 1820 (London 1821)

Also see:
Memoir of a Life Chiefly Passed in Pennsylvania Within the Last Sixty Years, ed John Galt
(Edinburgh 1822)

Baird, Robert	Religion in the United States of America (Glasgow 1844 edn) was an influential work by an American Presbyterian missionary to European Catholics. Its endorsement of voluntaryism had obvious Scottish implications

American Impressions of Scotland

Allen, Zachariah	The Practical Tourist and Sketches of the State of the Useful Arts and of Society and Scenery and co. in Great Britain, France and Holland 2 vols (Providence RI 1832)
Bache, Alexander Dallas	Report on Education in Europe (Philadelphia 1839)
Bailey, J M	England From the Back Window With Views of Scotland and Ireland (Boston 1879)
Benedict, E C	A Run Through Europe (New York 1860)
Bigelow, Andrew	Leaves From the Jounal or Sketches and Rambles in Some Parts of Western Britain and Ireland chiefly in the year 1817 (Boston 1821)
Breckinridge, R J	Memoranda of Foreign Travel: Containing Notices of a Pilgrimage Through Some of the Principal States of Western Europe 2 vols (Baltimore 1845)
Brown, William Wells	The American Fugitive in Europe (New York 1969 edn) (1855)
Browne, Dunn	Experiences in Foreign Ports (Boston 1857)
Bryan, William Jennings	The Old World and Its Ways (St Louis 1907)
Bryant, William Cullen	Letters of A Traveller or Notes of Things Seen in Europe and America (London 1850)
Buckham, George	Journal of a Tourist 2 vols (New York 1890)
Bushnell, Horace	Life and Letters ed Mary Bushnell Cheny (New York 1880)
Carter, Nathaniel Hazeltine	Letters from Europe Comprising the Journal of a Tour Through Ireland, England, Scotland, France, Italy and Switzerland in the Years 1825, 1826 and 1827 2 vols (New York 1829)
Codman, John	Narrative of a Visit to England (Boston 1836)
Coffin, Levi	Reminiscences (New York 1976 edn) (1898)
Coghill, James Henry	Abroad: Journal of a tour through Great Britain and the Continent (New York 1868)
Colton, Calvin	The Americans in London (London 1833)
—	Four Years in Great Britain 1831–1835 2 vols (New York 1835)
Cooke, Arthur B	With The Tourist Tide (New York 1907)
Cord, W Harlan	A Knight Templar Abroad (St Louis 1885)
Day, Henry	A Lawyer Abroad (New York 1874)
Dewey, Orville	The Old World and the New; or, a Journal of Reflections and Observations Made on a Tour in Europe 2 vols (New York 1836)
Durbin, John Price	Observations in Europe Principally in France and Great Britain 2 vols (New York 1844)
Eastman, Crystal	On Women and Revolution, ed Blanche Wiesen Cook (New York 1978)
Finney, Norton	Letters From Across The Sea (Philadelphia 1909)
Finney, William Grandison	Autobiography (London 1892 edn)
Fisk, Wilbur	Travels in Europe (New York 1838)

Flexner, Abraham	Medical Education in Europe: A Report to the Carnegie Foundation for the Advancement of Learning (New York 1912)
Flynt, (Willard), Josiah	Tramping With Tramps (New York 1899)
Forbes, Elizabeth A Mrs	A Woman's First Impressions of Europe Being Wayside Sketches Made During a Short Trip in the Year 1863 (New York 1865)
Fuller (Ossoli), Margaret	At Home and Abroad (New York 1971 edn) (1856)
Gibson, William	Rambles in Europe (Philadelphia 1839)
Gilson, Rodney, MD	Two Years in Europe (New York 1887)
Gough, John B	Autobiography and Personal Reminiscences (London 1870 edn)
Greeley, Horace	Glances at Europe (New York 1851)
Green, John P	Fact Stranger than Fiction: Seventy-Five Years of a Busy Life (Cleveland 1920)
Greenwood, Grace (Sara Jane Lippincott)	Haps and Mishaps of a Tour in Europe (Boston 1854)
Griscom, John	A Year in Europe, Comprising a Journal of Observations in England, Scotland, Ireland, France, Switzerland, the North of Italy and Holland in 1818 and 1819 2 vols (New York 1823)
Groome, P L	Rambles of a Southerner in Three Continents (Greensboro NC 1891)
Gurley, R R	Mission To England on Behalf of the American Colonisation Society (Washington DC 1841)
Hawthorne, Nathaniel	Passages From The English Notebooks 2 vols (Boston 1870)
Howe, F C	The British City: The Beginnings of Democracy (London 1907)
Hoyt, James M	Glances on the Wing at Foreign Lands (Cleveland 1872)
Hubbell, Orrin Z	A University Tramp (Elkhart Indiana 1889)
Humphrey, Herman	Great Britain, France and Belgium: A Short Tour in 1835 (New York 1838)
Hunter, Robert	Socialists at Work (New York 1908)
Irving, Washington	Tour in Scotland 1817, and other Manuscript Notes, ed Stanley T Williams (New Haven 1927)
King, Horatio	Sketches of Travel or Twelve Months in Europe (Washington DC 1878)
Knox, Thomas Wallace	The Boy Travellers in Great Britain and Ireland (New York 1891)
Latrobe, John M B	Hints on Six Months in Europe (Philadelphia 1869)
Linskill, Charles F	Travels in Lands Beyond The Sea (Wilkes-Barre Pa 1888)
McCollester, Sullivan Holmes	After Thoughts of Foreign Travel (Boston 1883)
McCulloch, Oscar Carleton	The Pastor Abroad, pp 53–177 in Plymouth Congregational Church, Indianapolis Yearbook 1887 (Indianapolis 1888)
McGavock, Roderick W	A Tennessean Abroad (New York 1854)
McLellan, I, Jr	Journal of A Residence in Scotland (Boston 1834)
Meehan, Eleanor Childs	Memories of a Red Letter Summer (Cincinnati 1903)
Mellish, John	Travels in the United States in the Years 1806 and 1807 and 1809, 1810, and 1811: including an Account of Passages Betwixt America and Britain and Travels Through Various Parts of Great Britain, Ireland and Upper Canada 2 vols (Philadelphia 1812).
Melville, Herman	Journal of a Visit to Europe and the Levant (Princeton N J 1955)
Mitchell, John	Notes From Over the Sea; consisting of Observations Made in Europe in 1843 and 1844 2 vols (New York 1845)
Morgan, Benjamin	The Footpath and Highway or Wanderings of an American (Philadelphia 1853)

Morphy, John*	Recollections of a Visit to Great Britain and Ireland in the Summer of 1862, Quebec 1863. Also his Ned Fenton's Portfolio (Quebec 1863)
Morrison, Leonard Allison	Among the Scotch-Irish and a Tour in Seven Countries (Boston 1891)
Parker, Mrs W	Wandering Thoughts and Wandering Steps (Philadelphia 1880)
Parkman, Francis	The Journals, ed Mason Wade 2 vols (London 1946) European Journal 1834–44 in vol 1
Pearson, Clement, MD	A Journal of Travels in Europe During the Summer of 1881 (Washington 1885)
Porter, Robert P	Bread Winners Abroad (New York 1885)
Post, Loretta	Scenes in Europe or Observations by an Amateur Artist (Cincinnati 1874)
Prentis, Noble L	A Kansan Abroad (Topeka 1878)
Rockwell, E J	Scenes and Impressions Abroad (New York 1860)
Sessions, Frances C	On The Way Through Europe (Columbus Ohio 1880)
Severance, Frank H	The Journeys and Journals of an Early Buffalo Merchant (John Lay 1822–24) Buffalo Historical Society Publications 4 (1896) 125–45
Shaw, Albert	Municipal Government in Great Britain (New York 1895)
—	Municipal Government in England (Baltimore 1899)
Sigourney, Lydia M	Sunny Memories of Pleasant Lands (Boston 1856 edn)
Silliman, Benjamin	A Journal of Travels in England, Holland and Scotland and of Two Passages Over the Atlantic in the Years 1805 and 1806 2 vols (New York 1810)
Silloway, T W and Powers, Lee L	The Cathedral Towns and Interesting Places of England, Ireland, Scotland (Boston 1883)
Simond, Louis	An American in Regency Britain: The Journal of a Tour 1810–1811 (London 1968)
Stuart, James	Three Years in North America 2 vols (New York 1833).
Stewart, Charles S	Sketches of Society in Great Britain and Ireland 2 vols (Philadelphia 1834)
Stewart, Eliza P 'Mother'	The Crusader in Great Britain (Springfield Ohio 1893)
Stetson, Evelyn	Rapid Transit Abroad (New York 1879)
Stevenson, William	Sights and Scenes in Europe or Pencillings By The Way, (Flint Michigan 1882)
Stowe, Harriet Beecher	Sunny Memories of Foreigh Lands (London 1854)
Symons, Jelinger C	Arts and Artisans at Home and Abroad (Edinburgh 1839)
Tappan, Henry P	Steps From the New World to the Old 2 vols (New York 1852)
Thorburn, Grant	Men and Manners in Britain or a Bone to Knaw for the Trollopes, Fidlers &c. Being Notes From a Journey on Sea and Land 1833–1834 (Glasgow 1835)
Thwing, Edward P	Outdoor Life in Europe (New York 1888)
Topcliffe, Samuel	Letters From Abroad in the Years 1828 and 1829 (Boston 1906)
Wall, James W	Foreign Eldings or Outline Sketches of the Old World's Pleasant Places (Burlington N J 1856)
Wallace, Louise A	An American Child in Europe (np 1914)
Wayland, Francis	Thoughts on The Present Collegiate System in the United States (Boston 1842)
—	A Memoir of the Life and Labour by F Wayland and M L Wayland 2 vols (New York 1867) vol 2 especially
Washington, E K	Echoes of Europe or World Pictures of Travel (Philadelphia 1860)

* Canadian

Watson, Samuel	A Memphian's Trip to Europe With Cook's Educational Party (Nashville Tenn 1874)
Webster, Daniel	In England: Journal of Hariette Story Paige, ed Edward Gray (Cambridge Mass 1917)
—	The Private Correspondence ed Fletcher Webster 2 vols (Boston 1857)
van Wert, Rupert (Clarke, E D)	Rip Van Winkle's Travels in Foreign Lands (New York 1881)
Wharton, Morton Bryan	European Notes or What I Saw in the Old World (Atlanta Ga 1884)
Wheaton, Nathaniel S	A Journal of Residence during Several Months in London, Including Excursions Through Various Parts of England; and a Short Tour in France and Scotland; in the Years 1823 and 1824 (Hartford Conn 1830)
Willard, Emma	Journals and Letters from France and Great Britain (Troy New York 1833)
Willis, Nathaniel Parker	Famous Persons and Places (New York 1854)
Winchester, Charles Wesley, Revd	The Gospel of Foreign Travel (Rochester New York 1891)
Young, Edward*	Labour in Europe and America: A special Report (Montreal 1879)

* Canadian

Theses Consulted

Bingham, Robert LeBaron	The Glasgow Emancipation Society 1833–1876 (M Litt Glasgow University 1973)
Buchanan, Fred Stewart	The Emigration of Scottish Mormons to Utah 1849–1900 (MSc University of Utah 1961)
Stuart, Jace Meyer	William English Walling: A Study in Politics and Ideas, (Columbia University 1968)

Autobiographies by Glaswegians and other Scots with views on America

Barr, James	Auld Lang Syne (Glasgow 1949) Labour, prohibitionist minister in USA 1912
Bell, Robert	Reminiscences of an Old Physician (London 1924) Glasgow graduate prominent gynaecologist in USA 1891
Dickson, Sir Alexander	Journal in America 1814–15, ed J H Leslie in Journal Society of Army Historical Research 8 1929 pp 79–113 and 133–78. The Battle of New Orleans
Dutton, Joseph E	An Evangelist's Travels (Kilmarnock 1927) Liverpool born son of Allan Line captain; he ministered five years in New Orleans
Fagan, James O	The Autobiography of an Individualist (London 1913) East Indian Company soldier's son from Inverness. After wide travels in Africa and S America, settled in Massachusetts as railwayman
Forbes, Archibald	Souvenirs of Some Continents (London 1885) Banffshire graduate of Aberdeen, war correspondent, lectured in USA 1880

Gordon-Cumming, Constance F	Memoirs (Edinburgh 1904) Aristocratic Morayshire lady who wrote Fire Fountains: The Kingdom of Hawaii, 2 vols (Edinburgh 1883) and The Granite Crags of California (Edinburgh 1884). She also wrote extensively in many major Victorian quarterlies
Hunter, George McPherson	When I was a Boy (Boston 1920) A Glasgow childhood and emigration to America
Kerr, J Lennox	Back Door Guest (Indianapolis 1930) and The Eager Years (London 1940) Paisley man who visited America
Lauder, Sir Harry	Roamin' in the Gloamin' (London 1928) His first US tour in 1907
Lipton, Sir Thomas	Leaves From Among the Lipton Logs (London 1931) The Rutherglen entrepreneur made good
McAlpine, James	Genuine Narratives and Concise Memoirs (Greenock 1780 reprinted 1883) a loyalist minister caught in the midst of the War of Independence
MacKenzie, Kenneth	Been Places and Seen Things (London 1935) and Living Rough (London 1936). Son of Gallowgate Salvation Army family, in US forces, gangsters, IWW, boxing and Hollywood. On Bonus March and later deported
Oliphant, Laurence	Memoirs of a Rolling Stone (Edinbrugh 1881)
Stoddart, J H	Recollections of a Player (New York 1902). Actor for many years in Glasgow who emigrated to better things in America. See DAmB
Wigham, John	Memoirs of a Life (London 1842) Aberdeen Quaker in America

American Autobiographies with Scottish interest

Burr, Aaron	The Private Journals, 2 vols (Rochester New York 1903) ed W H Samson. Notorious American who visited Scotland
Irving, Peter	Travel Diaries (1807) Bulletin of the New York Public Library 44 1940 888−914

Biographical List and Index of Names

This list is intended to serve several purposes. It gives some basic outline of most characters who appear in the book: chapter references are given after their names. It also provides information about many people who do not appear in the book. The numbers of all those clergy, educators, entrepreneurs, technicians, artists and others from Scotland go to reinforce the view that no other country contributed so many formative influences to American development. That contribution was not merely intellect or expertise imported from Scotland: it was a host of people accomplished in many skills which were desperately needed in the developing United States. Some migrated backwards and forwards across the Atlantic, maintaining associations with friends or relations, and pursuing common humanitarian or business interests. Others merely secured honorary degrees from American colleges or universities. It might be difficult to justify a place for some of them individually in the list, but in the sum total of connections between Scotland and the United States they reinforce the contention about the strength of that link. That new cultural world was made, manufactured, sustained and serviced by Scots at virtually every level. In particular the west of Scotland loomed large in that common culture. Glasgow was unique not merely in Scotland but in Britain and probably in the world in its 'American consciousness'. No other country, region or city could compare in that respect.

Many more characters could easily be added to this collection. Some individuals were described as having gone to America. In some instances they may have gone to Canada but the reference works are not always clear on that point. For simplicity I have cited the basic reference works for individuals. In very many instances I could have referred to standard biographies and so forth but that would merely have complicated the list.

Over a hundred more Scots and a hundred more Americans might also be added from the delegates to the joint gatherings of the Presbyterian Alliance. See the lists of delegates in the published proceedings of each meeting: Report of the Proceedings of the First General Presbyterian Council (Edinburgh 1877): Second (Philadelphia 1880): Third (Belfast 1884): Fourth (London 1888) (London 1889): Fifth (Toronto 1892) (London 1892): Sixth (Glasgow 1896) (London 1896): Seventh (Washington DC 1899) (London 1899): Eighth (Liverpool 1904): Ninth (New York 1909) (London 1909): Tenth (Aberdeen 1913) (Edinburgh 1913). Many other lesser lights appear in Peter Ross, The Scot in America (New York 1896). Even more will be found in the numerous state county histories which appeared in great numbers around the First World War. Those of Iowa, Minnesota, Ohio and North Dakota proved particularly useful. Gordon Donaldson, The Scots Overseas (London 1966) is a very useful compilation while Donald Whyte, Dictionary of Scottish Emigrants to the USA (Baltimore 1972) covers the period to 1854.

Abbreviations used in Biographical List

Addison	W Innes Addison (ed), The Matriculation Album of the University of Glasgow, From 1728 to 1858 (Glasgow 1913)
Berthoff	Rowland Tappan Berthoff, British Immigrants in Industrial America 1790–1850, (Cambridge, Mass 1953)
Black	George F Black, Scotland's Mark on America (New York 1921)
Boase	Frederic Boase, Modern English Biography
Boston	Ray Boston, British Chartists in America 1839–1900 (Manchester 1971)

Canning	Bernard J Canning, Irish Born Secular Priests in Scotland 1829–1979 (Greenock 1979)
Carwardine	Richard Carwardine, Transatlantic Revivalism: Popular Evangelicalism in Britain and America 1790–1865 (Westport, Conn 1978)
Congress	Biographical Directory of the American Congress 1774–1961 (Washington DC 1961)
CUYB	Congregational Yearbook
DAmB	Dictionary of American Biography
DNB	Dictionary of National Biography
Ewan	Joseph Ewan, Biographical Dictionary of Rocky Mountain Naturalists, 1682–1932 (Utrecht 1981)
Ewing	William Ewing, Annals of the Free Church of Scotland 1843–1900, 2 vols (Edinburgh 1914)
Fasti	Fasti Ecclesiae Scoticanae, ed Hew Scott, 8 vols (Edinburgh 1915–50)
Glasgow 1909	George Eyre-Todd, Who's Who in Glasgow 1909 (Glasgow 1909)
LPOG	The Lord Provosts of Glasgow, 1833 to 1902 (Glasgow 1902)
Lamb	John A Lamb, Fasti of the United Free Church of Scotland 1900–1927 (Edinburgh 1956)
Macrae	Jean M Macrae, Scots Wha Ha'e: The Scottish Legacy to the United States and to the Duluth Area (Duluth, Minn 1976)
MacDougall	D MacDougall, Scots and Scots Descendants in America (New York 1917)
MacKelvie	William MacKelvie, Annals and Statistics of the UP Church of Scotland (Edinburgh 1873)
Miller	Russell E Miller, The Longer Hope: The First Century of the Universalist Church in America, 1870–1970 (Boston 1979)
NAW	Notable American Women, 4 vols (Cambridge Mass 1971–80) Vols 1–3 eds Edward T James and Janet Wilson James, with Paul S Boyer. Vol 4 eds Barbara Sicherman and Carol Hurd Green with Ilene Cantov and Hariette Walker
POG	James R Anderson, The Provosts of Glasgow 1609 to 1832, ed James Gourlay (Glasgow 1942)
Procurator Mss	Procurators Library Glasgow Manuscript Biographical Dictionary of Members
Ross	M C Ross ed, The West of Alfred Jacob Miller (Norman, Oklahoma 1968)
Seaburg	Alan Seaburg, Missionary to Scotland: Caroline Augusta Soule. Transactions of the Unitarian Historical Society 14 (1976) 28–41
Small	Robert Small, History of the Congregations of the United Presbyterian Church from 1733 to 1900, 2 vols (Edinburgh 1904)
Smith	Alice E Smith, George Smith's Money: A Scottish Investor in America (Madison, Wisconsin 1966)
Sprague	William B Sprague, Annals of the American Pulpit, 9 vols (New York 1857–69)
St Andrew	An Historical Catalogue of the St Andrews Society of Philadelphia 1749–1907 (Philadelphia 1907)
Stenton	Who's Who of British Members of Parliament, 1832–1886 vol 1 (Hossacks Sussex 1976) ed Michael Stenton
Stenton and Lees	Who's Who of British Members of Parliament, 1886–1945 vols 2 and 3 (Hossacks Sussex 1978–79)

Whorton	J C Whorton, Crusaders for Fitness: The History of American Health Reformers (Princeton 1982)
Wilson	Gordon M Wilson, Alexander MacDonald: Leader of the Miners (Aberdeen 1982)
Winther	O O Winther, Old Oregon Country (Stanford 1950)
Wright	L C Wright, Scottish Chartism (Edinburgh 1954)
Yearley	Clifton K Yearley Jr, Britons in American Labour: A History of the Inflence of the United Kingdom Immigrants on American Labour 1820–1914 (Baltimore 1957)

Biographical List

ABERNETHY, George 1807–77
Son of Aberdeen Shoemaker: b in New York, went to Pacific Northwest; great business interests in lumber and fish.   DAmB

ADAM, Thomas
(Johnstone) Associate Burgher Class 1823, gave up for medicine—Barrhead; emigrated to USA.   MacKelvie

ADAM, William 1800–83
Relief minister: b Glasgow, matriculated at Glasgow University. Relief minister in Dumfries 1837–8. At Chambersburg Pa 1840 and later a bookseller in Washington DC.   Addison

ADAMS, Charles Francis
Railroad expert, civic leader, historian: b Boston, ed Harvard. Served in Civil War. In Europe 1865–6. Became authority on railroad management and development. Served on the Massachusetts Commission to investigate municipal ownership (1898). Visited Britain twice in 1913 during which he delivered his lectures on Trans Atlantic Historical Solidarity.   DAmB

ADAMS, Herbert Baxter, 1850–1901   Ch 5
Professor and promoter of historical studies: b Massachusetts, ed Amherst and Heidelberg. At Johns Hopkins University developed 'new' Scientific History. His students became leaders in academic and reforming political life.   DAmB

ADAMSON, W
(Glasgow) DD Waynesbury.   CUYB 1908–9

ADDAMS, Jane, 1860–1935   Chs 1, 3, 5
Social reformer: b Illinois, ed Rockford College. Spent 1883–5 in Europe, visiting Glasgow. In Britain 1887. Inspired by Toynbee House. Started Hull House settlement in Chicago. Inspired social reform. Staunch peace campaigner.   DAmB

AFFLECK, Thomas, 1812–68
Agricultural writer: b Dumfries. Emigrated to America 1832. Moved to west became junior editor Western Farmer and Gardener 1840 (Cincinnati). Toured South and after his marriage settled in Mississippi. 1857 migrated to Texas to lumber and livestock business. After the Civil War sought to promote Scottish emigration. Promoted beef packing for Europe.   DAmB

AIKMAN, John Logan 1820–85
b Lanark, ed Glasgow. UP Moderator, 1885, DD New York 1869, Glasgow 1885, minister Anderston, Glasgow 1856–85.   Addison

AINSLIE, Hew 1792–1878
b Ayrshire, ed Ballantrae and Ayr; studied law in Glasgow; emigrated to USA 1822; on farm 3 years before going to New Harmony for a year. Wrote Pilgrimage to the Land of Burns 1822; settled in Louisville. In Scotland in 1855 and 1862.   DAmB

AITKEN, Robert 1734-1802
Printer, publisher: b Dalkeith. In Philadelphia 1769 as a bookseller. Produced one of the first tradesmen's annuals and the first complete English Bible printed in America.   DAmB

AITKEN, Thomas c1800-1884
Minister: from Falkirk, ed Glasgow University. At St Andrews Secession church 1829-38. Emigrated and ministered to Genessee and Sparta, New York. Died in Sparta.   Addison

AITKEN, William
London—Pell Street 1839-41. To America 1843. Became minister Smiths Fall, Canada East.
                                                                                         MacKelvie

ALCOTT, Amos Bronson 1799-1888   Chs 2, 3
Educator and transcendentalist. Teacher for many years in association with William Russell in Pennsylvania and Boston. Married sister of Samuel J May. In contact with James Pierrepoint Greaves and Ham Common group; visited Britain; formed model community Fruitlands, USA. Thomas Davidson of Aberdeen later associated with him in the Concord School of Philosophy.   DAmB

ALCOTT, Louisa May 1832-88
Second daughter of A B Alcott. Author: famous for Little Women, 1868. Woman suffrage and temperance supporter.   DAmB

ALCOTT, William Andrus 1798-1859   Chs 2, 4
Educator and physical education pioneer. Qualified as a medical practitioner. Drawn into American Pestalozzian education group. Health reformer.   Whorton: DAmB

ALEXANDER, J E 1803-85
b Clackmannan; ed Glasgow University; joined army; served in Burma, Crimea, etc, travelled widely. Wrote Transatlantic Sketches, 2 vols (London 1833).   DAmB

ALEXANDER, James 1691-1756
Lawyer, politician and patriot: b Scotland, Jacobite supporter; fled to America. Member of New York and New Jersey Council.   DAmB

ALEXANDER, John 1808-72   Ch 1
b Mauchline, Ayrshire: joiner; moved to London 1830s; Chartist, close personal friend of Bronterre O'Brien; left for Texas colony to found Cabot community 1848; wrote letters for O'Brien's paper The Reformer (May). Returned disenchanted 1849.   Boston p 88

ALEXANDER, John 1803-63
b Renfrew: at Glasgow University 1825; minister of Church of Scotland 1836-43. Joined Free Church. DD Rutgers NJ 1855.   Addison

ALISON, Francis 1705-59   Ch 1
b Donegal; ed Glasgow University; to America 1735, established college in Pennsylvania. Great reputation as classical scholar.   DAmB

ALISON, Mathew
Kilbarchan 1818-41 Moderator Relief Synod 1837. Emigrated to Mifflington, Jamieta, Pennsylvania 1841.   MacKelvie

ALLAN, John 1746/7-1805
Revolutionary Soldier: b Edinburgh Castle. Emigrated to Nova Scotia; fought for the colonists in the Revolutionary Wars with success.   DAmB

ALLEN, Zachariah 1795-1882   Ch 1
Scientist, inventor, reformer: b Providence RI, ed Brown University; developed water works, hydraulic waterpower, other innovations in textiles and solar energy. Defender of Indian rights. Visited Glasgow. Wrote Philosophy of the Mechanics of Nature (New York 1852). God ordained power origin.   DAmB

ANDERSON, Alexander 1802-87
Advocate, banker and entrepreneur: b Strichen, Aberdeen; partner in Adam and Anderson law practice, Aberdeen; launched North of Scotland Bank Co and North of Scotland Fire and Life

Insurance Co. Later promoted heavy investment through George Smith (qv) in Illinois and the western states; promoted Aberdeen Market Co, Gas Company and Great North of Scotland Railway; Lord Provost of Aberdeen; knighted 1863.   Smith

ANDERSON, Andrew
Dundee-School. UP Class 1799; did not complete; became teacher; emigrated to USA.
MacKelvie

ANDERSON, David
Perth (Moyness) Emigrated 1839 to Carlisle, Pennsylvania. DD 1841 Philadelphia   MacKelvie

ANDERSON, Ebenezer
Minister: b Cadder, ed Glasgow University. Old Secession minister at Cupar, Fife 1819–35. Emigrated to America.   Addison

ANDERSON, John
1771 Class. Missionary to Pittsburgh 1788.   MacKelvie

ANDERSON, Joseph
Minister: b Glasgow, ed Glasgow University. Became Irish Presbyterian minister 1826–34. Resigned and emigrated to America.   Addison

ANDERSON, K C
Congregational minister in Dundee Scotland. DD Union, USA; trained at Yale.
CUYB 1902–3

ANNAN, James Craig
b 1864 Hamilton, ed Anderson's College. Photographer; exhibited widely in Europe and USA. On International Committee for Photography at St Louis Exhibition.   Glasgow 1909

ANNAN, Robert
(Ceres) 1757 Class, 1761 missionary—became minister in Philadelphia.   MacKelvie

APPLETON, Nathan, 1779–1861   Ch 1
Banker, politician and textile mill owner. Visited Scotland to examine model villages 1810–11; returned again later; served in Congress. Extremely heterodox religious and political views.
DAmB

ARCHER, Frederic 1838–1901
Organist: ed Oxford, London, Leipzig; after work in London, conductor Glasgow Select Union Choir 1878–80, composed and edited part songs for them. 1881 emigrated to USA; organist in HW Beecher's church, Brooklyn; then in New York, Chicago RC Church. Pioneer of organ revival.   DAmB

ARCHER, Thomas
London-Oxendon Street 1832–64. DD from Princeton 1844.   MacKelvie

ARTHUR, Peter M 1831–1903
b Paisley; emigrated to America 1842; began to work on railways at 18 and rose to be head of Loco Engineers Union 1863–1903. Transformed it into successful aggressive organisation. Reluctant to strike but never failed in any. Successful real estate speculator in Cleveland.
DAmB

ASHLEY, Sir William James 1860–1927   Ch 5
Economic Historian: ed Oxford. Professor of Political Economy and Constitutional History, Toronto University 1888–92, Harvard 1892. Professor at Birmingham 1901–25.   DNB

AUCHMUTY, Robert
Colonial jurist: died 1750. Qualified and called to the English bar 1711. Emigrated to Boston and won a considerable reputation for wit and shrewdness.   DAmB

AUDSLEY, George Ashdown 1838–1925
Architect, organ designer and author: b Elgin. Won reputation in neo-gothic architecture in Britain. Emigrated to New York 1892. Designed Milwaukee Art Gallery and many notable buildings.   DAmB

BACON, Leonard 1802–81   Ch 4
Congregationalist clergyman: ed Yale and Andover. Held same charge 41 years. Professor of
Divinity Yale 1866–7. Visited Glasgow temperance movement.
                                         T D Bacon, Leonard Bacon, (Chicago 1931) p 321:DAmB

BAILLIE, Joanna 1762–1851   Chs 1, 3
Author: b Hamilton. Professor of Theology, Glasgow University. Went to London. Became
minor poet, playwright, staunch Unitarian and entertained numerous American visitors.
                                                                                              DAmB

BAIN, George Luke Scobie 1836–91
Merchant miller: b Stirling, ran away to sea at 15; to Montreal; then via Portland, Chicago to
St Louis 1865 where he became biggest shipper of flour and made city milling centre of USA.
Involved in various philanthropic and fraternal activities.   DAmB

BAIRD, Archibald
Paisley-James Street, 1825–57, from Greyfriars Glasgow. DD from Washington College Pd
1844.   Small

BALCH, Emily G 1867–1961
Pacifist and American Social Reformer. Mainly concerned with immigrants. Visited Glasgow
in 1886. Wrote Our Slavic Fellow Citizens (New York 1910).   DAmB

BANKS, John
Kilmeny. Emigrated to USA 1796, Philadelphia, then Professor to Associate Synod USA. Died
1826.   Fasti

BANKS, Revd John c1763–1826
Minister and educator: b Stirling. Emigrated 1796 to New York, then to Philadelphia where he
opened in 1816 a school for Latin and Greek, also Hebrew for private pupils: associated with
the University of Pennsylvania. Professor at Easton Theological seminary 1820.   St Andrew

BANNATYNE, Andrew 1798–1871   Ch 1, 2
Eldest son of Dugald J; Glasgow University 1813; apprenticed to Alex McGrigor 1831; m 1828
Margaret d of James Millar of Millheugh, Professor of Mathematics Glasgow University.
Dean of Faculty 1860–5. LL D Glasgow 1868. In partnership with brother Dugald J.
                                                                        Glasgow Procurators MSS

BANNATYNE, Dugald Jr c1836–1894   Chs 1, 2
Eldest son of Dugald; Glasgow University 1852; emigrated to New Jersey; published
Handbook of Republican Institutions in the USA (1887). Died New York.
                                                                        Glasgow Procurators MSS

BARCLAY, Mathew 1789–1865
DD New Jersey.   Ewing

BARLAS, William
Buchan-Whitehill 1779–97; deposed. Emigrated to New York; teacher and bookseller. A
correspondent of Revd John Newton. Died 1817.   Small

BARR, Amelia Edith Huddleston 1831–1919
Novelist: b Ulverston. Daughter of a Methodist Minister. She trained at the Glasgow Normal
School but left before completing the course to marry Robert Barr, son of a Minister, owner of
a Glasgow woollen business. Bankrupt, the family emigrated to America 1853. After working
in Chicago, Memphis and Austin, Mr Barr died 1866. Galveston Scots aided her. Henry Ward
Beecher whom she had met in Glasgow encouraged her to write for the Christian Union. She
and her daughters wrote 1000 articles in ten years. She also began writing popular novels and
was able to spend summers in Scotland.   NAW

BARR, Charles 1864–1911
Captain of racing yachts: b Gourock; grocery assistant; 1884 delivered cutter to USA;
remained, worked for wealthy yacht owners, including August Belmont, the Vanderbilts and
others. Figured in Americas Cup successes.   DAmB

BARR, Revd James, 1862–1949   Ch 4
b Ayrshire, ed Kilmarnock Academy and Glasgow University, Glasgow Free Church College.
MP for Motherwell 1924–31 and Coatbridge 1935–45. Served on government committees on
housing and capital punishment.   Stenton and Lees

BASCOM, John 1827–1911   Ch 5
Philosopher and university president: b New York state, ed Williams, Auburn and Andover.
Became President of the University of Wisconsin 1874. Strong prohibitionist. Resigned to
become a lecturer in sociology at Williams 1891. Populariser of reform ideas.   DAmB

BAXTER, Sylvester 1850–1927   Ch 5
Publicist: b Massachusetts; studied in Leipzig and Berlin 1875–7; promoter of Boston public
parks. Wrote on German municipal government and served on civic improvement bodies.
Visited Glasgow.   DAmB

BAXTER, William Edward 1825–90
b Forfarshire, ed Edinburgh University. Liberal MP for Montrose 1855–85. Toured America
1845, 1853–4; wrote America and the Americans (1855).   Stenton

BEATTIE, Alexander O
Glasgow-St Vincent Street. MD Glasgow University 1831. DD Oxford, Ohio 1844.   MacKelvie

BEECHER, Catherine 1800–78   Chs 2, 4
Reformer and educator. Eldest daughter of Lyman Beecher, the evangelical preacher, sister of
Harriet Beecher Stowe. Promoted female education but she was opposed to woman suffrage.
                                                                       DAmB

BEECHER, Henry Ward 1813–87   Ch 4
Clergyman: b Litchfield Conn, ed Amherst. Entered Lane Theological Seminary of which his
father, Lyman, was head. Popular preaching and popular writing, brought him to Brooklyn
Plymouth Church 1847. Opposed to slavery like his sister Harriet Beecher Stowe. 1863 visited
Scotland and in 1886. Scandal of impropriety later overshadowed his career 1870–76.   DAmB

BEGG, James 1808–83
Moderator of the Free Church 1865: b New Monklands, ed Glasgow University. After holding
charges at Maxwellton, Edinburgh, Paisley and Liberton went over to the Free Church at the
Disruption. Minister at Newington. DD Lafayette College 1847.   Addison

BELL, Alexander Graham 1847–1922
Inventor of the telephone: b Edinburgh; taught in various schools before emigrating to work
with deaf children. Numerous inventions and interests in science. Established Science journal
1883.   DAmB

BELL, Alexander Melville 1819–1905
Educator, father of Alexander Graham Bell. Taught elocution for 22 years in Edinburgh. 1868
toured America lecturing. Settled in Canada before joining son in Washington DC 1881.
                                                              DAmB

BELL, Robert, 1732–84
Publisher, bookseller and book auctioneer; b Glasgow; emigrated about 1766 to join several
friends in Philadelphia. Widely promoted sale of books, maintained a circulating library,
published first edition of Paine's Common Sense.   DAmB

BELL, William
(Airdrie) UP Class 1810; emigrated to USA; Minister in Perth.   MacKelvie

BEMIS, Edward Webster 1860–1930   Ch 5
Economist; ed Johns Hopkins; served as professor at Vanderbilt University, Nashville,
1889–92; University of Chicago 1892–5. Manhattan College, Kansas 1897–9. Supt of
Cleveland Water Department 1901–9 under Tom L Johnson. Became municipal expert and
consultant.   Who Was Who in America

BENNETT, James Gordon 1795–1872
Editor; b Keith, Banffshire; trained at Catholic Seminary Aberdeen; visited Glasgow;

emigrated 1819 to Nova Scotia. Settled in Boston, then New York. Made a reputation as a newspaper correspondent. Returned to Scotland for five months 1838. Again in Boston 1843. His New York Herald flourished. Retired 1867.   DAmB

BERMAN, Nathan S S   Ch 4
Pastor first Presbyterian Church, Troy. Moderator of the First Assembly New School Presbyterians. Visited Glasgow on temperance business 1830s.   L G Vander Velde
                    The Presbyterian Churches and the Federal Union (Cambridge, Mass 1932) p 480

BERRIEN, John MacPherson 1781-1856   Ch 2
US Senator and judge; b New Jersey; settled in Savannah. Became judge 1810-21. State Senator 1822-3, US Senate 1824-31 and 1841-52. Supreme Court of Georgia Justice. Employed William Russell in his early days.   Congress

BETHUNE, Joanna Graham 1770-1860   Ch 1
Social worker and activist in schooling for children: b Fort Niagara Canada. Brought up in Scotland, ed in Paisley and at Mrs Graham's School for Ladies, Edinburgh. Lady Glenorchy sent her to train as a teacher in Holland. 1798 the family emigrated to America. She taught in Mrs Graham's School. (qv) Married D Bethune, Scottish Merchant in 1795. Devoted to orphanages, Sunday Schools and general amelioration. Described as the 'mother of American Sabbath Schools'. With John Griscom founded New York Infant School Society.   NAW

BEVERIDGE, Thomas
(Alloa) Class of 1775; sent to America as missionary, Cambridge, New York; died of fever 1798.   MacKelvie

BILES, John Harvard
b 1854; Naval Architect. Clydebank Shipyard: b Portsmouth. LL D Yale. Widely travelled in USA.   Glasgow 1909

BISHOP, Robert
(Longridge) Associate Presbytery Class of 1798; emigrated; became Professor of Theology, Miami, Oxford, Ohio.   MacKelvie

BLACK, David
Dunfermline—Charles Street 1789-1824. DD 1817 from an American College.   MacKelvie

BLACK, Hugh 1868-1953
b Rothesay; ed Glasgow University 1888; appointed to Chair of Practical Theology Union, Theological College NY 1906-38. DD Yale 1907. DD Princeton 1911; Litt D Pittsburgh 1913.
                                                                                           Lamb

BLACK, James
Minister: b Glasgow 1834, ed Glasgow University. Served in Canada from 1860. Then returned to England. Became a Unitarian minister, on their Missionary Board, a missionary and private teacher in Topeka, Kansas.   Addison

BLACKIE, John Alexander
b 1850; Chairman of Blackie Publishers; ed at Blair Lodge School, Polmont (qv infra William Cunningham). Germany and Glasgow University. Widely travelled in America.   Glasgow 1909

BLACKWELL, Elizabeth 1821-1910   Ch 3
First Woman doctor. Emigrated from England 1832. Started a school in Cincinnati 1838. Studied medicine in America and Europe. Opened a hospital 1857 and became the first Professor of hygiene. Settled in London 1871. Professor of gynaecology 1875. Vigorous sanitary reformer. Buried at Kilmun.   DNB: DAmB

BLAIR, James 1655-1743
Founder and first president of William and Mary College: b Scotland, ed Edinburgh University. Anglican clergyman. Emigrated 1685; began the College in 1691.   DAmB

BLAIR, Robert
Minister UP church. At Glasgow University 1827. Minister at Galashiels 1838-80, when he died, DD from Philadelphia 1844.   Addison

BOAG, John Toshack
b 1895 Dunfermline; ed St Andrews University, Union Theological NY. Ultimately appointed
to Glasgow Govan Memorial.   Lamb

BONNAR, James 1810–80
Episcopalian president: b Edinburgh. Became a teacher of languages in England. Persuaded to
go to Kenyon College Ohio. In Pennsylvania 1840; in Ohio 1858–72 and Maryland 1872–80.
                                                                                      St Andrew

BORLAND, William
Bailie: b Ayrshire; founder City Iron Foundry; 1903 Glasgow Town Councillor. Visited 22
states of America c1889.   Glasgow 1909

BORTHWICK, Peter
(Penicuik) UP Class 1824. Became Episcopalian; ed Oxford. Served West Indies. Opposed the
abolitionist George Thompson. Twice elected MP Evesham. Connected with Morning Post;
died 1852.   MacKelvie

BOWEN, Francis 1811–1910
Philosopher; b Massachusetts, ed Harvard. 1839 in Europe. 1843 Editor of North American
Review, 1853 Professor of Natural Religion, Moral Philosophy and Civil Polity, Harvard.
Particularly anxious to reconcile philosophy and Christianity.   DAmB

BOYD, John
(West Kilbride 1849–66) DD from Monmouth College, Illinois. Died 1881.   Small

BOYD, William 1832–1905
b Kilmun, matriculated Glasgow University 1847. Served on the Govan and Glasgow
schoolboard 1888–1903. LL D Greenville College, USA.   Addison

BOYD, William
(Milnathort-A-Brugher 1860–82) From Paisley, ordained 1860. LL D from Greenville College
USA.   Small

BRACE, Charles Loring 1826–90   Ch 5
Philanthropist: ed Yale; teacher. Went on walking tour of Britain 1850. Visited again in 1854.
Founded Christian Aid Society 1853. Pioneer social reformer.   DAmB

BRACKENRIDGE, John
Class of 1750; emigrated to Pennsylvania.   MacKelvie

BRACKENRIDGE, William 1810–93
Botanist: b Ayr. A gardener he studied extensively in the continent. To USA 1837. Appointed
to US expedition to the Pacific as chief botanist 1838–42. Retired to Maryland estate 1855.
                                                                                  DAmB: Ewan

BRADLEY, AC 1851–1935   Ch 5
Literary critic: ed Cheltenham and Bristol, Oxford. Professor of English, University of
Glasgow 1890–1900. Great Shakespearean authority.   DNB

BRADLEY, John 1768–1823
Naturalist; b Scotland. Collected specimens in USA for Liverpool Botanic Garden 1808–11.
Went up the Missouri with Pacific Fur Co, 1811; with Thomas Nuttall, the famous nativalist
on his travels in Missouri. Mentioned in Washington Irving, Astora.   Ewan

BRAILSFORD, Henry Noel 1873–1958
Author and journalist: ed Glasgow University. Worked on the Nation 1907–22. Joined ILP
1907. Editor New Leader, formerly Labour Leader 1922–26. London correspondent of the
New Republic from 1915. Wrote War of Steel and Gold 1914, America Our Ally 1940. Several
visits to USA.   DNB

BRASH, John
East Campbell Street Glasgow (Wamphray) 1851–4. Called to Cameronian Church, NY 1854
then S Boston and Amboy, NJ.   Small

BRECHIN, Hugh 1846–1915
Businessman and councillor: b Cumbernauld. Successful butchering business. In the Glasgow
Town council 1886–1911. Bailie 1891–4. Master of Works 1901–2. Church of Scotland elder.
Widely travelled in Europe and USA. Director John Swan and Sons, Edinburgh (cattle
company) and of Glenburn and Dunblane hydropathic establishments.
                                    Glasgow 1909: Glasgow City Archives: Glasgow Herald 27 July 1915

BRIGHAM, Amariah 1798–1849
Physician: b Mass. Studied as a doctor and spent several months in Europe. Became Professor
of Anatomy and Surgery in New York College of Physicians. Became superintendent of
Hartford Asylum for the Insane 1840–42 then took over the New York asylum. Pioneer in
treatment. Wrote Remarks on the Influence of Metal Cultivation on Health 1832. Scottish
editions were published by R MacNish in Glasgow and John Simpson in Edinburgh.   DAmB

BROOKS, Charles 1795–1872   Ch 1
Unitarian clergyman. Educator. Examined Prussian and Glasgow Schools 1833–4. Promoted
teacher training schools in USA. 1839–1843 in Europe. Wrote Remembrances of Europe 1846.
                                                                                      DAmB

BROOKS, John Graham 1846–1938   Ch 5
Sociologist and reformer: ed Harvard. Entered Unitarian Ministry. Studied in Europe 1882–5.
Radical critic though not a socialist. Active in Progressive reform movement. Supporter of
Mayor Dunne of Chicago.   DAmB

BROWN, AK, RSA, RSW, c1850
Artist: b Edinburgh. Widely exhibited in major American cities.   Glasgow 1909

BROWN, Hugh
UP minister: b Glasgow, ed Glasgow University. Left for USA 1861. Ministered in Greensboro
Alabama 1863–7, then in Decorah Iowa and Caledonia, Wisconsin 1867–76. Died 1876.
                                                                                      Small

BROWN, John
(Broughton Place 1829–58) DD Jefferson College; died 1858.   MacKelvie

BROWN, John
(Glasgow—Kent Road 1863–1897) DD Amherst 1850. After 29 years in Dalkeith, to Glasgow
1863. Moderator UP 1873.   Small

BROWN, William 1752–92
Physician: b Haddingtonshire, ed Edinburgh University. Emigrated to Alexandria, Virginia.
Acquainted with Washington, Jefferson, Madison. Served with Revolutionary Army.   DAmB

BROWN, William S 1812–75
Glasgow printer; preacher moral force; secretary of the Glasgow Charter Association; left for
Boston Mass 1850; returned 1875.   Boston

BROWN, William Wells c1816–84
Negro reformer, historian: b Lexington, Kentucky, son of slave; escaped to Ohio 1834.
Employed as anti-slavery lecturer 1843–9. Visited Britain 1849. Visited Glasgow. Established a
reputation as the black historian of his day.   DAmB

BROWNLEE, James
(Falkirk-South) UP Class 1822, son of minister there; emigrated; minister of Slater Island NY.
                                                                                   MacKelvie

BROWNLEE, WC 1783–1860   Ch 1
Writer, editor; b Lanarkshire; ed Glasgow University. Emigrated to USA. In Philadelphia,
New Jersey and New York. DD from Glasgow. Professor at Rutgers. Wrote the Whys of
Scotland. Editor Protestant Vindicator. Became minister Dutch Reformed Church
                                                                          MacKelvie: DAmB

BROWNSON, Orestes A   Ch 1
American Catholic controversialist. Became by turns a minister of Universalist and Unitarian

faiths. Friend of Frances Wright and Robert Dale Owen. Catholic 1844. Corresponded with Robert Monteith of Carstairs. Ran Brownson's Quarterly Review almost single-handed for over twenty years.   DAmB

BRUCE, Alexander Balmain 1831−98   Ch 5
Theologian: b Abernethy, Perthshire, ed Edinburgh University. Entered Free Church Ministry. Served among other places Lochwinnoch and Cardross. 1875 became Professor of Apologetics and New Testament with Free Church College, Glasgow to death. Several visits to USA. Daughter married to New Yorker.   DNB

BRUCE, George 1781−1866
Typefounder: b Edinburgh; emigrated to Philadelphia. Established printing and publishing business in New York; brought over the secret of stereotyping from England. Produced popular editions of the Bible. President of New York Mechanics Institute for many years.
                                                                                     DAmB

BRUCE, Robert 1778−1846
Presbyterian educator and clergyman: b Scone, Perthshire. Became a minister in Associate Church, Class of 1802. Emigrated to America. Moderator 1810. Became principal of New Western University of Pennsylvania. His faculty included John Black of Glasgow:
                                                                          DAmB: MacKelvie

BRYAN, William Jennings 1860−1925   Chs 4, 5
Politician: b Salem, Illinois; entered law and politics. Renowned for his 'Cross of Gold' speech at 1896 Democratic Convention. Thrice unsuccessful Democrat presidential candidate. Lecturer on Chatauqua circuit. Secretary of State under Woodrow Wilson; resigned on pacifist principle. Involved in the Darwinian controversy in 1920s.   DAmB

BRYANT, William Cullen 1794−1878   Ch 1
Poet, editor; leading Democratic journalist, radical on labour and slavery in New York Evening Post. Went on four trips to Europe. Visited Glasgow. Remained a radical through the Civil War.   DAmB

BRYCE, James 1838−1922   Chs 1, 5
b Belfast, ed Glasgow; Oxford Regius Professor of Civil Law 1870−1893. Liberal MP 1880−1906. Chancellor of the Duchy of Lancaster 1892−4; President of the Board of Trade 1894−5; Chief Secretary for Ireland 1905−6; Ambassador to the USA 1907−13. Viscount 1914. Renowned for his American Commonwealth 1884. Made 8 visits to and resided in USA six years.   DNB

BUCHANAN, Hugh 1823−90
b Ayrshire, emigrated to Vermont; lawyer Georgia 1845; State Senator 1855−7; delegate to Democratic National Conventions 1856 and 1868; presidential elector of the Democratic ticket of Breckinridge and Lane 1860; Confederate Army 1861−5; representative in Congress 1881−5.   Congress

BUCHANAN, James
Merchant partner in Virginia firm of Buchanan Hastie & Co. Provost 1768−9, 1774−5.   POG

BUCHANAN, James 1804−70
Minister: b Paisley, ed Glasgow University. Held charges at Roslin, Leith and the High Church 1827−43 when he joined the Free Church. Professor at New College 1845−65. DD Princeton 1844.   Addison

BUCHANAN, Thomas 1744−1815
Merchant. b Glasgow; ed Glasgow University. Family involved in transatlantic shipping. Neutral in the American Revolution; he continued trading with Scotland for over 30 years though his business greatly maimed by various wars.   DAmB

BUFFOM, Arnold 1782−1859   Ch 4
Quaker anti-slavery lecturer. 1825−31 several business trips to Europe led to British abolitionists fundships. Fall River Schools established on return. President New England Anti-Slavery Society. Lectured in Midwest against slavery. Visited Glasgow.   DAmB

BULLIONS, Alexander
(Logiealmond) Class of 1802, went to New York, became Professor of Theology there.
MacKelvie

BULLIONS, Peter c1790–1863
(Logiealmond) 1813 Class. Went to Argyle, Washington County then Troy, New York.
MacKelvie

BURDEN, Henry 1791–1871
Ironmaster, inventor: b Dunblane, Stirlingshire, ed Edinburgh University. Emigrated 1819; settled eventually in Troy, New York and established one of the largest iron factories in the country. Patented numerous industrial products. 1846 established with Glasgow capitalists Atlantic Steam Ferry Co.   DAmB

BURGESS, Alex
(Banff) Parochial School master. Deserted charge for America 1795. Died there.   MacKelvie

BURN, James Dawson 1806–89   Chs 1, 2, 4
Glasgow weaver and physical force Chartist; moved to London in 1850s; active temperance; wrote Autobiography of a Beggar Boy 1855; in New York and New Jersey 1862; in munitions factory; wrote Three Years Among the Working Classes of the United States During the War 1865; returned to Britain; wrote The Beggar Boy 1882.   Boston and Boase

BURNET, John James 1857–1938
Architect: ed Paris. Numerous city of London commissions; toured USA 1896.
DNB: Glasgow 1909

BURNS, Sir George 1795–1889   Ch 1
A founder of the Cunard Shipping Company: b Glasgow; entered business in New Lanark Spinning Co; influenced by Thomas Chalmers; active in various benevolent works; invested in shipping and subsequently played a part in the founding of Cunard. Philanthropist.
Edwin Hodder, Life (London 1890)

BURNS, John 1774–1850
Professor Glasgow University; brother of James. Specialist in obstetrics. Wrote The Principles of Midwifery (10 editions 1814–37), Observations on Abortion (1806) as well as The Principles of Christian Philosophy (1828).   DNB

BURNS, John
(Fenwick) UP Class 1792; emigrated as Minister to Niagara NY. Died 1822.   MacKelvie

BURNS, Lucy 1879–1966
Suffragist: b of Irish Catholic parents in Brooklyn, ed at Vasser, Yale and German Universities. In Britain she became closely associated with English women militants and campaigned in Scotland, where she later served as an organiser in Edinburgh 1910–12. She joined forces with another American militant, Alice Paul to form the American Congressional Union 1913, and later the National Woman's Party. Edited The Suffragist 1915–16. By 1919 she had spent more time in jail than any other suffragist. Died still a devout Roman Catholic.
NAW

BURNS, Robert 1809–83
b Glasgow, ed Glasgow University. Emigrated with father to USA 1830. Wanted to enter Episcopalian clergy but studied pharmacy.   St Andrew

BURNS, Robert 1826–96
Minister: b Paisley, ed Glasgow University. Served in Canada 1847–67, 1870–5 and at the Chicago Scottish Church 1867–70. DD Hamilton College, USA 1866.   Addison

BURNS, William of Saltcoats   Ch 1
Regular correspondent of W E Channing the Boston Unitarian. Wrote the New Era of Christianity (1831). Beyond that I have been unable to establish his identity.
See Life of Channing

BURRELL, Sir William 1861–1958   Ch 5
Art collector. Entered family shipping business, served on the Glasgow council 1899–1906.
Very interested in housing reform. Inveterate collector. Loaned 160 works of art to the
Glasgow Exhibition in 1901. Sold out his shipping interest 1917 and settled at Hutton Castle.
Gave his massive collection to Glasgow 1944. Now to be housed in the new Pollock gallery.
                                                                                  DNB

CABLE, George Washington 1844–1925   Chs 1, 5
Author: b New Orleans. Served in Southern Army in the Civil War and was severely wounded.
Started in journalism after the War. His outspoken views on Southern life encouraged his
move to the north. Strong reforming views. Visited Glasgow.   DAmB

CADELL, Henry
Naturalist: b Linlithgow, Scotland, ed Edinburgh University. Wrote on Yellowstone and other
western features.   Ewan

CAIRD, Edward 1835–1908)   Chs 3, 5
Professor of Moral Philosophy, Glasgow University; Master of Baliol; ed Glasgow and St
Andrews Universities 1857–60. Baliol 1860–63. Influenced by T H Green. Idealist
philosopher, radical in politics.   DNB

CAIRD, John 1820–98
Principal of Glasgow University; b Greenock, ed Glasgow University. Entered Church of
Scotland ministry. Became Professor of Theology 1862, Principal 1873 to his death.   DNB

CALDERHEAD, Alexander
(Horndean 1787–1802) Accompanied Dr Mason of New York back to USA. Minister in Ohio.
Died there.   MacKelvie

CALLENDER, James Thomson 1758–1803
Political writer: b Scotland. Writer in Edinburgh. Political radical stance forced him to flee to
America 1793. Patronised by Jefferson, produced tracts and papers. Disappointed in politics;
deteriorated and died from drowning while drunk.   DAmB

CALVIN, Samuel 1840–1911
Geologist: b Wigtownshire. Associated with Thomas Wilson (qv) at school. Family emigrated
to Iowa 1851. A teacher he became Professor of Natural History at Iowa State University 1874.
One of the founders of the American Geologist 1888 and editor in chief to 1894.   DAmB

CAMERON, Andrew
b Berwickshire; 17 years printing; editor; leading figure in Illinois Grand Eight Hour League;
State Labour Assembly and Chicago Trades Assembly; leading figure in National Labour
Union; involved in numerous reform movements; editor of Workingmen's Advocate.   DAmB

CAMERON, Archibald c1771–1836
Presbyterian Minister: b Lochaber. Emigrated with family 1773–4, eventually settled in
Kentucky. Trained for the ministry at Transylvania College, Lexington. A travelling preacher
he built numerous orthodox churches.   DAmB: Sprague

CAMERON, Robert
(East Kilbride 1817–41) Emigrated to America.   MacKelvie

CAMPBELL, Duncan
(Comrie) Entered medicine as probationer; went to USA.   MacKelvie

CAMPBELL, Donald   Ch 3
Teacher: ed Glasgow University. Held several teaching posts in the West of Scotland before
becoming head of John Neilson Institution 1912 for 19 years. Went to Canada with Guild of
Europe 1927. His wife, the organiser of Guild. She also invited Emma Goldman to Paisley.
Died 1931.   Addison:
                            Paisley and Renfrewshire Gazette 12 September 1931

CAMPBELL, Sir George 1824–92
Indian administrator and author: b nr Cupar, Fife, ed St Andrews. Pursued distinguished career in India, wrote on Indian culture. Stood then withdrew as a liberal candidate for Dunbartonshire. Wrote on the Irish land question. Presided over 1874 Social Science Congress, Glasgow. MP Kirkcaldy 1874–92. Wrote Black and White: The Outcome of a Visit to the United States 1879.   DNB

CAMPBELL, John 1653–c1728
Journalist; b Scotland. Established first newspaper in America.   DAmB

CAMPBELL, John Coats 1721–1804
Virginia merchant; Provost 1784–5.   POG

CAMPBELL, Thomas
Class of 1792; emigrated to USA 1796.   MacKelvie

CAMPBELL, Thomas 1777–1844   Ch 1
Poet: b Glasgow, ed Glasgow University. Tutor, travelled extensively in Europe. Settled near London 1804 to death. Supported founding of London University; Lord Rector Glasgow University 1826–29.   DNB

CANT, James
(Linlithgow-East) UP Class 1819; emigrated to USA.   MacKelvie

CARDOZO, Francis L
Coloured American, described as from Hutchesontown; ed 1861 class UP Church Hall, teacher New York, Charleston, member S Carolina Convention, Sec State S Carolina for black schools Charleston.   D Macrae, The Americans at Home, p 210: MacKelvie

CARNACHAN, James
Minister: b Glasgow, ed Glasgow University 1849–53. Died aged 74 at Meadville Pennsylvania 1903.   Addison

CARNEGIE, Andrew 1838–1919
Son of Chartist; left 1848 for Pittsburgh; author of Triumphant Democracy 1886; endowed libraries; philanthropist, industrialist.   DAmB

CARNEGIE, William 1801–1972
(Dunfermline) Handloom weaver; close friend of John Fraser; wrote for Cobbett's Political Register and also letters in The True Scotsman July 1838; left from Glasgow 1848 for Pittsburgh.   Boston

CARPENTER, Edward 1844–1929
Writer on social issues: ed Cambridge University; ordained 1869, resigned orders 1874. Visited USA; friend of Walt Whitman. Settled in model community near Sheffield 1883–1922. Best known for Towards Democarcy 1883.   DNB

CARRUTHERS, William 1830–1922
Botanist and palaeontologist: ed Edinburgh University in British Museum Botany 1871–95, Agricultural Society 1871–1909. At British Association for the Advancement of Science, Montreal 1884, travelled in Utah collecting specimens.   Ewan

CARTER, James Gordon 1795–1849
Educational reformer: ed Harvard University. Prominent in the common school movement, writing pamphlets and articles. Helped found the American Institute of Instruction and the education of factory children. Elected State representative and Senator.   DAmB

CASTILLO, Joachim 1801–78
Mexican diplomat. Matriculated at Glasgow University 1816. Served his country in both England and the United States.   Addison

CHALMERS, P MacGregor
Architect: b 1859 Glasgow. Designed numerous Scottish Churches; travelled extensively including America.   Glasgow 1909

CHAPMAN, David
Church of Scotland minister: b Kirkintilloch, ed Glasgow University. Minister at Girvan 1860–72. Resigned. Died in Virginia 1893.   Fasti

CHARLES Richard 1800–63
Physician: b Co Tyrone, ed Glasgow University. Practised at Angelica, New York and was apparently an innovator.   Addison

CHASSELS, Angus McNab
b 1817. Matriculated Glasgow University 1844. Teacher in Glasgow. Later farmer at Cadzow Hill, Sparta Randolph County, Illinois.   Addison

CHINIQUY, Pastor   Ch 4
b 1810. A former Canadian Catholic priest. renowned for his temperance activity. In 1851 served in Illinois. Then chapel given to Irish led to conflict and ultimately his excommunication from the church. Became a popular lecturer in America. Visited Scotland 1860. Wrote a famous autobiography.   UP Magazine 4 (1860) 479–80

CHISHOLM, Hector
(Logiealmond 1753–55) Emigrated to America without notice.   MacKelvie

CHISHOLM, Sir Samuel 1836–1923   Chs 1, 4, 5
Wholesale grocer: Dalkeith. Settled in Glasgow 1870. Elder Kent Road UF Church. Successively chairman and president of the Glasgow Foundry Boys Religious Society over 37 years. Town Councillor 1888; strong prohibitionist. 1891 Convener City Improvement Trust; defeated 1895 Camlachie parliamentary candidate. 1899–1904 Lord Provost, during which he bestowed freedom of the city on Andrew Carnegie. Pan-Presbyterian Alliance delegate. His second wife, the widow of Thomas Henderson founder of the Anchor Line.
                                                    Who Was Who: Glasgow 1909: LPOG

CHRISTIE, Alexander Mackenzie
b Lochee Scotland. Emigrated to Mobile, Alabama 1887–9. Returned—inducted to Methven-Perth 1892. Died 1910.   Small: Lamb

CHRISTIE, Robert Merchant
Provost 1756–57. Married to coloured lady. One of his sons, Robert, attended Glasgow University and successfully engaged in business in Maryland. Died 1780 Maryland.   POG

CLARK, Thomas
b 1744, Class 1754; Missionary to America; settled Salem, New York.   MacKelvie

CLARK, William
b Glasgow, matriculated Glasgow University. Died Youngstown Ohio 1874.   Addison

CLARK, William
b 1843 in Glasgow. Cotton Manufacturer and insurance business. Widely travelled in USA.
                                                                                        Glasgow 1909

CLARKE, Robert 1829–99
Publisher: b Annan; emigrated to Cincinnati 1840. Opened bookshop and soon importing and publishing considerable quantities of books of antiquarian and archeological interest.   DAmB

CLARKSON, James
1768 Class. Went as missionary to America 1772.   MacKelvie

CLOW, William McCallum 1853–1930
b Glasgow, ed New Zealand, California and Glasgow University 1878. Chair of Christian Ethics Glasgow College 1911. Principal 1921–8.   Lamb

CLUER John C 1806–86
Glasgow weaver; forceful local Chartist leader; left Scotland 1839 for New York City and Lowell Mass. Member of the National Reform Movement and a leading figure in the New York Ten Hours Movement. One of the first to link the British and American short hours movement as a common struggle. Promoted peace motion at Lynn Ten Hour convention in 1846.   Yearley pp 31–2: Boston 90

COATES, James   Ch 4
Resident in Glasgow late nineteenth and early twentieth century. American spiritualist; health food advocate. Settled in Crosshill, Glasgow, with his American wife. Went south to London. Associated with W T Stead, the radical journalist.   Temperance Register

COBDEN-SANDERSON, Thomas James 1840–1922   Ch 5
Bookbinder and printer. Called to the bar 1871. Closely associated with William Morris and Burne Jones. Influential in the arts and crafts movement.   DNB

COCHRANE, Revd William 1831–98
Clergyman: b Paisley, ed Glasgow University and Hanover College, Indiana; ordained 1859. Served in Brantford, Ontario, Canada for many years. Acted as President of Brantford Ladies College.   Commission on Education 1898 p 99

COGHILL, William Calder, JP
b Wick 1835. Printing business. Prominent in YMCA and founding of Scottish Prohibition Society 1856. Went to USA 1907–8.   Scottish Temperance

COKE, Thomas 1747–1814   Ch 1
Methodist leader: b Wales. Spent much time in USA, Scotland and England as a missionary.
                                                                                                                            DNB

COLBY, Clara Dorothy Bewick 1846–1916
Suffragist: b Gloucester, England. Emigrated with her parents 1849; ed University of Wisconsin. On marriage moved to Nebraska, where her husband served two terms in the State Senate. Adopted two children including one found in dead mother's arms at Wounded Knee. Active in state suffrage movement and then in the national organisation. Edited Woman's Tribune which became suspect for its support of The Woman's Bible (1895–8). Divorced, she moved to Oregon. Frequently in Britain lecturing and at congresses. She spent six months studying Glasgow. A Congregationalist she had great interest in the New Thought movement.
                                                                                                                            NAW

COLLINS, Sir William   Ch 4
b 1817. Publisher, Lord Provost 1877–80. Closely associated with American temperance movement.   LPOG

COLQUHOUN, Patrick 1745–1820
Spent time as merchant in Virginia, returned Provost 1782–3; went to London 1789. Wrote major works on social questions.   DNB: POG

CONNOLLY, James 1868–1916   Ch 5
Socialist: b Edinburgh. Served in British Army. Became socialist activist in Scotland, Ireland and USA, which he toured in 1902. Emigrated 1903–10. Helped IWW in early days. Executed after 1916 Irish rising.   Boylan, A Dictionary of Irish Biography

CORBETT, A Cameron, MP 1856–1933   Ch 4
Educated privately; married Alice Polson 1887; MP 1885–1911 for Tradeston, Glasgow, on various party labels, Liberal, Liberal Unionist, Independent Liberal Free Trader. Created Baron Rowallan 1911.   Stenton & Lees

COUTTS, David
(Logiealmond) Associate Burgher Hall class of 1827. Went to America then Canada West.
                                                                                                                       MacKelvie

COVENTRY, R M G, ARSA RSW
Artist; b Bridgeton. Studied in Paris. Exhibited in Europe and USA   Glasgow 1909

COWIE, George Gray 1843–1916
Chief clerk Minnesota Board of Charities and Corrections; studied law in Edinburgh 1869–72; emigrated to Canada 1880; to Minnesota 1884 with the Northern Pacific Railroad; became chief clerk for 13 years.   Minnesota Historical Soc Mss

CRAIB, Alexander   Ch 4
Scottish UP minister. Toured extensively in USA Wrote America and the Americans 1892.
                                                                  A Craib, America and the Americans (1892)

CRAIG, Hector 1775-1842
b Paisley; emigrated to New York 1790; founded town of Craigsville with paper, grist and sawmills; served on Congress as representative, Jackson Democrat, 1823-5 and 1829-30; surveyor of the Port of New York 1830; US Commissioner of Insolvency; New York Surveyor of Customs 1833-9.   Congress

CRAIK, James 1730-1814
Chief physician and surgeon of the Continental Army: b Arbigland, Dumfries; ed Edinburgh University. Emigrated via W Indies to America. Close friend of Washington to his death.
                                                                                                                      DAmB

CRAWFORD, Archibald
Minister: b Grangemouth, ed Glasgow University. In Newark NJ 1869.   Addison

CRAWFORD, David
UP Minister: b Glasgow, ed Glasgow University. Minister at Earlston 1815-34 and Portobello 1834-43. Resided in Edinburgh. Acted as sub-treasurer for the church. DD University of New York 1863.   Addison

CRAWFORD, Dugald   Ch 1
b 1830 (Argyllshire). Apprenticed to Arthur of Glasgow dry goods. Emigrated via Canada to St Louis 1864. Soon had a thriving department store business.   St Louis Records

CRAWFORD, Robert 1845-1915   Ch 5
Reformer: b Milngavie. Member Cathcart School Board. Member Glasgow Town Council 1883-96, Bailie 1885-86, Master of Works 1892-93. Lectured on Municipal Socialism around the Glasgow district; attracted American attention to the city. Promoted health building regulations act. Interested in cleansing the Clyde, pure milk, tramways, the art galleries etc. LL D Glasgow University 1902. In business with Burn Crawford and Co.
                                                                                                       Glasgow City Archives

CRAWFORD, William (1760-1823)
b Paisley; studied medicine at Edinburgh University; graduated 1781; emigrated to Emmitsburgh Pa; 1785 farm on Marsh Creek, practised medicine there; Judge 1801-8; House of Representatives as Democrat 1809-17; resumed medical practice to death.   Congress

CREE, John
(Perth—N). Associate Presbytery Class of 1781. Went as missionary to New York Congregation 1790.   MacKelvie

CROCKETT, Samuel R 1860-1914
Novelist: ed Edinburgh University, entered Free Church Ministry. Wrote several popular novels, The Stickit Minister 1893, The Raiders and The Lilac Sunbonnet 1894. Resigned ministry 1895.   DNB

CROSS, John
(Paisley) 1832 UP Class. Emigrated to USA as probationer.   MacKelvie

CROSS, John
b Paisley: ed Glasgow University 1828. Emigrated to Middletown Pa. Died at Mechanicsburg Pa 1851. Widow returned to Scotland. Possibly the same as UP probationer.   Addison

CROSS, William 1809-62
ed Glasgow University. Partner in Dennistoun, Cross and Co, Glasgow with agents in New York and New Orleans.   Addison

CROSSER, Robert 1874-1957
b Holytown, Lanark. Emigrated to Cleveland, Ohio 1881; then Salineville, Ohio; ed Kenyon College, Columbia University and Cincinnati Law School; practised law Cleveland; State Representative 1911 and 1912: House of Representatives 1913-19, 1923-55. Failed to win renomination in 1954.   Congress

CUMMING, Kate c1828-1909
Confederate hospital administrator and diarist: b Edinburgh. Emigrated via Montreal to

Alabama. Inspired by Florence Nightingale's example, nursed in the Civil War, later taught school.   NAW

CUNNINGHAM, John George 1835–1907
Son of Robert Cunningham, Polmont FC: ed Glasgow University; DD Lafayette College 1895; served Edinburgh–Queen Street and continental stations.   Lamb

CUNNINGHAM, Robert 1799–1883   Ch 2
Educator: b Stranraer; ed Edinburgh University. Emigrated to Easton College, Pennsylvania. Returned to head Glasgow teacher training seminary. Left at the Disruption. Ran school in Polmont. Retired to Edinburgh. Returned to Stranraer 1859.   Ewing: Free Church
                                                                                                            Record (1883)

CURR, William Allan
(London-Bow 1869–71). Emigrated to America.   Fasti

CURRIE, Charles George
b Edinburgh, matriculated Glasgow University 1847. Minister in Wheeling West Virginia 1868.
                                                                                                          Addison

CUYLER, Revd Dr Theodore L   Ch 4
Reforming minister, prominent temperance advocate with very strong links with Glasgow.
                                                                                                           DAmB

DALRYMPLE, James   Ch 5
Manager of Corporation Tramways. Succeeded John Young 1904. Visited USA 1905, 1912, 1922. Presided over expansion of the system with strong authoritarian hand.   Glasgow 1909

DALRYMPLE, James R.
(Thornliebank 1837–45). Resigned; emigrated to America, minister of Hamilton, West Canada. 1852 returned to Britain; emigrated to Victoria, Australia; died 1858.   MacKelvie

DAVIDSON, David
Associate Presbtery, Class 1811. Went to America as probationer.   MacKelvie

DAVIDSON, Thomas 1840–1900   Ch 2
Philosopher, scholar, educator: b Old Deer Aberdeen, ed King's College Aberdeen. Rector Aberdeen Grammar School before going to teach in England. Emigrated to Canada 1866. Then moved to Boston and St Louis where he taught under W T Harris and was associated with the Neo-Hegelians. In Boston 1875. Spent most of the period 1878–84 with the Rosminians in Italy. Began Fellowship of the New Life which laid the foundation for the Fabians 1883. Returned to America where he established a Breadwinner's College for the working class; worked with Bronson Alcott and promoted summer schools. Brother of J Morison Davidson, the Scottish radical who had spent some time in Colorado. Also he was closely associated with William James and wrote numerous works on education.   DAmB

DAVIS, Jefferson 1808–99
President of Confederate States of America. Visited Glasgow after the Civil War.   DAmB

DAWSON, W J 1854–c1925   Ch 4
Former Glasgow Wesleyan Minister; emigrated to USA. Temperance activist.
                        Who Was Who in America: Temperance League Journal 11 January 1908

DEAS, William
(Auchterarder) UP Class 1825. Emigrated to America then to Canada.   MacKelvie

DE CLEYRE, Voltairine 1866–1912   Ch 3
Anarchist feminist: b Michigan, ed at a convent in Ontario. Became an active public speaker and writer on behalf of anarchism. Visited Glasgow in 1897 and 1903. Associated with the Scottish anarchists Thomas Bell and Will Duff.   P Avrich, An American Anarchist:
                                                            The Life of Voltairine de Cleyre (Princeton 1978)

DELANY, Martin 1812–85
Early black nationalist and Pan-Africanist: b Virginia. Settled in Canada and then Cleveland Ohio. Attended the National Association for the Promotion of Social Science meeting in Glasgow 1860. Persuaded some Glasgow merchants to support his scheme for raising 'free' cotton in West Africa. Tried unsuccessfully to enter southern politics during Reconstruction. Died Wilberforce Ohio.   Cyril E Griffith, The Africian Dream:
Martin R Delany and the Emergence of Pan African Thought,
(University Park Pa 1975)

DELAVAN, Edward Cornelius 1793–1871   Ch 1, 4
Reformer, publisher: b New York. Spent 1814–16 in Europe. Real Estate speculator. Organised New York State Temperance Society. 1836 chairman American Temperance Union; gave $10,000 to its funds. Published Enquirer, a temperance journal. Visited Glasgow.
DAmB

De LEON, Daniel 1852–1914
Socialist: b Curaçao, Dutch West Indies of Jewish ancestry. Studied in Germany. Emigrated to America 1874: ed Columbia University. Became a lawyer. Supporter of Henry George, and other radical causes. Joined Socialist Labour Party 1890. A doctrinaire divisive figure. At the founding of the Industrial Workers of the World 1905. Visited Scotland. Greatly admired by Lenin.   DAmB

DEMOREST, Ellen Louise Curtis 1824–98   Ch 4
Businesswoman and fashion arbiter: b New York State. Married William J Demorest, a dry goods merchant, 1858. She promoted the idea of paper pattern making. Began Demorests Illustrated Monthly Magazine. One of the founders of the New York Woman's Club, Sorosis, which took up welfare work. A Prohibitionist. Visited Glasgow.   NAW

DENNEY, James 1856–1917
b Paisley, ed Glasgow University. Chair of Systematic Theology F C College 1897. Principal 1915. DD Chicago, Princeton and Aberdeen. Visited USA several times.   Lamb: DNB

DEVINE, Edward Thomas 1867–1948   Ch 5
Social worker: b Iowa; ed University of Pennsylvania and Germany. Involved in University extension work; drawn into New York Charity Organisation Society. Active in housing and health reforms.   DAmB

DEY, Alexander
Inspector of Schools: b Banffshire, ed Aberdeen and Cambridge University. Fellow of St Peters College. LL D Cambridge 1889. He and his brother John, established Dey Time Register factory, Syracuse, New York. Married to a Californian.   Glasgow 1909

DICK, John
(Glasgow Greyfriars 1801–33) DD Princeton 1815.   MacKelvie

DICK, Mungo
(Newbiggin) Associate Presbytery Class of 1798. Emigrated to Mount Home, Pennsylvania.
MacKelvie

DICK, Thomas 1774–1857   Ch 2
(Dundee). Renowned writer, astronomer, educator. LL D Union College, Schenectady. Renowned for his Christian Philosopher.   DNB

DICKIE, George William 1844–1918
Engineer: b Arbroath. Parochial school and associated with many leading scientists of the day. Emigrated to San Francisco 1869. Became General Manager, Hymon Ironworks 1883–1905. Prominent in organising American Society of Naval Architects.   DAmB

DICKSON, Robert 1765–1823
Fur Trader: b Dumfries; emigrated via Canada to America. Married Sioux chief's sister. Considerable interest in the upper Mississippi.   DAmB

DINWIDDIE, Lawrence 1696–1764   Ch 1
Provost 1742–3. Merchant. Brother Robert Governor of Virginia 1751–7.   POG

DOBIE, John
(Shamrock Street). Received DD from a Western American University 1871.   MacKelvie

DONAHOE, James c1820–63   Ch 1
Emigrated to USA 1835? Foundry apprentice. Worked in South for health. Joined two
brothers in California. Dogged by ill health retired.
Journal Glasgow Chamber of Commerce (1981)

DONAHOE, Michael 1817–84   Ch 1
b Glasgow. Emigrated to New York 1831. Foundry apprentice. Went to Cincinnati 1844.
Served in Mexican-American War. Successful with brother Peter. Returned east to Davenport,
Iowa. Again economic success and mayor of city.
Journal Glasgow Chamber of Commerce (1981)

DONAHOE, Peter 1822–85   Ch 1
b Glasgow. Emigrated to USA 1833. Foundry apprenticeship. Sailed to deliver steamship to
Peruvian Navy. Found way to San Francisco and with brother built flourishing diverse
enterprise in land, railways and shipbuilding.   Journal Glasgow Chamber of Commerce (1981)

DONALD, Robert 1724–1803
Virginia merchant; Provost 1776–77.   POG

DONALD, Sir Robert 1860–1933   Ch 5
b Banffshire. Journalist; Editor Daily Chronicle. Established Municipal Journal 1893,
Municipal Yearbook 1897, urged ministry of information on Lloyd George. Served on
committee on local government. Chairman Publicity Committee British Empire Exhibition
1924, and Empire Press Union 1915–26. Strong admirer of Glasgow's municipal schemes.
DNB

DONALDSON, David
1811 Class; emigrated.   MacKelvie

DONALDSON, John
(Cupar-Burnside). To America as probationer. 1808 Class.   MacKelvie

DONALDSON, Lawrence
Businessman; b Milnathort, Kinross; apprenticed to Glasgow dry goods merchant; emigrated
1878 to Scottish dry goods house in Providence, Rhode Island. Joined with his brother in
partnership in 1884 (qv).   Minnesota Historical Society

DONALDSON, William 1849–97
Businessman; b Milnathort, Kinross; apprenticed to Glasgow dry goods merchant emigrated to
work with Scottish dry goods firm in Providence, Rhode Island in 1877; settled in St Paul 1881;
began his own business 1882 with massive success; built huge 5 storey business with some 900
employees with buyers all over USA and in Paris; chairman Businessmens Union of
Minneapolis; leading civic figure and Presbyterian. Still a prosperous business.
Minnesota Historical Society

DORSEY, Alexander James Donald, 1812–94   Ch 4
Educator and Anglican priest: b Nuneaton, England, ed Glasgow University. Active in
promoting workmen's education, influenced by phrenology. Master at Glasgow High Scool.
Ordained 1847. Incumbent St John's Anderston 1846–50. In Madeira 1850–9, chaplain and
lecturer at Cambridge 1860–4, then at King's College, London 1864–84. Deep interest in
public health reforms.   Boase

DOUGALL, John 1808–86   Ch 4
Journalist: b Paisley. Emigrated to Canada at 18 as commercial traveller. Became editor of the
Canada Temperance Advocate. Founded, extremely successful, Montreal Witness 1846.
Founded similar paper in New York, Daily Witness 1871–78, though continued by Weekly
Witness. Died in Long Island NY.   Macmillan Dictionary of Canadian Biography

DOUGLASS, David 1798–1834   Ch 1, 2
Botanist: b Scone. Gardener to Earl of Mansfield, then at Culross. Became assistant to

Professor William Hooker in Glasgow. Went to USA 1823, 1824–7, 1829–34. He died in Hawaii after an accident. David Douglass, Journal ed W Wilks (London 1914): Ewan

DOUGLASS, Frederick 1817–95 Ch 1, 3, 4
Abolitionist, orator, journalist. Escaped from slavery 1838. Became agent for Massachusetts Anti-Slavery Society. Travelled to Glasgow 1846. In Scotland again after the failure of the John Brown Raid. After the Civil War he was ambassador to Haiti. Supported woman suffrage. DAmB

DOUGLASS, William 1691–1752
Physician of Boston: b Gifford, Haddington, ed Edinburgh, Leyden, Paris. Emigrated to Boston 1718. DAmB

DOW, John
b 1885 Angus, ed St Andrews University; appointed to Chair at Knox College, Toronto 1925–52, St Andrews 1952–3. Lecturer in Canadian and American Summer Schools. Lamb

DOW, Neal, 1804–97 Chs 1, 4
Temperance reformer; successful entrepreneur from Portland Maine. Mayor of Portland 1851 and 1855. Lectured in Europe and Scotland on prohibition 1857, 1866–7, 1873–5. DAmB

DOWIE, John Alexander 1847–1907
Founder of the Christian Apostolic Church in Zion: b Edinburgh; emigrated to Australia; ed Edinburgh University. Returned to Australia. Went to San Francisco 1888, then Chicago 1890–6. Increasingly claimed divine inspiration. Established Zion City for 5000 of his followers. Eventually collapsed amid scandals. DAmB

DRAPER, Andrew Sloan 1848–1913 Ch 5
Politician, educator of Scots-Irish Descent. Teacher, lawyer. 1886 State superintendent of Instruction, New York. President University of Illinois 1894. Commission of New York State Education 1904. DAmB

DRUMMOND, Henry 1851–97 Chs 3, 5
Theological writer: b Stirling, ed Edinburgh University. Entered Free Church divinity course. Promoted Moody and Sankey 1874–5 and worked with them in London. Invited to Philadelphia by Moody; refused. 1879 went to USA on archaeological expedition with Sir Archibald Geikie. Visited Moody in Cleveland. Worked among Glasgow workers. Aided Moody in 1882. Published Natural Law in the Spiritual World (1883); visited Africa, 1883; America, 1887; gave 1893 Lowell Lectures, Boston, published as The Ascent of Man 1894. Supported Boys Brigade from 1885. DNB: Ewan

DRUMMOND, Revd Robert, MA DD
Minister of Belhaven Church, Glasgow: b 1828, ed Glasgow and Edinburgh. Travelled widely in USA. Glasgow 1909

DRUMMOND, Thomas (1780–1835)
Naturalist: b Scotland. Curator Belfast Botanical Garden. Assistant naturalist to Sir John Franklin's second land Arctic expedition 1825–27. In the American Southwest 1831–35. Ewan

DRYER, Oliver
(Presbytery of Dalkeith) b 1881 Sanquhar; ed Glasgow University. Lectured on International Affairs in European and American Universities. Lamb

DRYSDALE, Anderson
(Houghton-le-Spring) 1843–53. Emigrated to America. Returned. Ran a Boarding School. Suspended 1866. MacKelvie

DUBOIS, WEB 1868–1963 Ch 1
Historian, sociologist, crusader: black leader, b Mass; ed Fisk, Harvard, Berlin. University teacher and NAACP activist. Moved to Marxism. Visited Scotland, USSR. Became Pan-Africanist and Communist. Settled in Ghana 1961. DAmB

DUFF, Alexander 1806–76
Toured extensively in N America as moderator of the Free Church of Scotland. Ewing

DUFF, John
Emigrated to America. Minister in Albion and Vaughan Canada West.   Fasti: Lamb

DUNBAR, Robert 1812–90
Engineer, inventor: b Carnbee, Fife. Emigrated to Dunbarton, Canada, founded by grand-father. Moved to Buffalo, New York; established ironworks. Specialist in grain, elevator design.   DAmB

DUNBAR, William 1749–1810
Planter, scientist: b near Elgin; ed Glasgow and London. Emigrated 1771. Built up plantations in the south. Surveyor and explorer, correspondent of Jefferson. Later a Chief Justice and a member of Mississippi territorial legislature.   DAmB

DUNCAN, James 1857–1928
Labour leader: b Kincardine. Emigrated to USA at 23 as a granite cutter. Played a prominent part in the founding of the AFL with his friend Samuel Gompers. A vice-president of AFL from 1894. Frequently delegate to international conferences.   DAmB and Supplement

DUNCAN, Abram
b Glasgow 1798. Woodturner and trade union spokesman; Chartist pastor in Arbroath; returned home after music hall tour of Eastern US cities with daughter.   Boston

DUNCAN, James
(Kincardineshire). Leader and secretary of stone cutters and granite workers. Vice-president American Federation of Labour.   Yearley: Berthoff

DUNKIN, Christopher 1811–80.
b London, ed Glasgow University. Greek lecturer at Harvard 1834–5. Went to Canada. Editor Montreal Morning Chronicle. Called to the Bar 1846, QC 1867, MP Canadian Parliament. Provincial Treasurer of Canada 1867–9, Minister of Agriculture and Statistics 1869–71, Puisne judge Supreme Court, Quebec 1871.   Addison

DUNLOP, John Aitken 1808–67.
b Beith; ed Glasgow University, studied theology 1828–30 but entered tobacco business as merchant in Louisville and Owensboro, Kentucky. Died in Glasgow.   Addison

DUNLOP, Alexander 1684–1747
Professor of Greek, Glasgow University: b Carolina; appointed to chair in 1706. Son of former Principal William Dunlop.   DNB

DUNLOP, Colin 1706–77
Merchant in Colonial tobacco trade. Provost 1770–71. Raised 100 men to fight against American rebels.   POG

DUNLOP, Henry 1799–1867
Cotton spinner/manufacturer. Lord Provost 1837–40. Associated with Glasgow Bible Society and similar bodies. Spent some time visiting son in America.   LPOG

DUNLOP, William c1649–1700
Principal Glasgow University. Emigrated to Carolinas. Returned after 1688. Soldier, merchant and chaplain. Appointed Principal 1690. Director of the Darien Company. Historiographer Royal 1693.   DNB

DUNMORE, John Burray, Earl of 1732–1809
Colonial Governor: b Scotland. One of the representative Scottish peers 1761–70. Appointed Governor of New York 1770, Virginia 1772, left 1775.   DAmB

DUNNE, Edward F 1853–1937   Chs 1, 5
Governor of Illinois, Mayor of Chicago: b Connecticut, ed Trinity College, Dublin. Became lawyer 1877, Judge Cook County, Illinois 1892–1905, Mayor of Chicago 1905–07, Governor 1913–17; President League of American Municipalities 1906–7. Wrote a history of Illinois. Roman Catholic.   Who Was Who in America 1897–1942

DWIGHT, Timothy 1752–1817   Chs 2, 4
College president: b Mass, grandson of Jonathan Edwards; ed Yale. Principal of Hopkins Grammar School 1771. Tutor at Yale 1772. President from 1795. An immense evangelical influence.   DAmB

EASTON, George 1808−1884   Ch 4
b Portobello. Temperance agent for 30 years. STL Visited USA.   Social Reformer
February 1884

EASTON, John Arnot
Surgeon: b Dumfriesshire, ed Glasgow University. Died New York 1875.   Addison

EASTON, Robert,
(Morpeth 1798−1802). Emigrated to America, minister to Montreal Congregation.   MacKelvie

EATON, Alexander
(Kirkintilloch) Miles Land-London 1799−1802. Emigrated to America 1804.   MacKelvie

ECKFORD, Henry 1775−1832
Marine architect and shipbuilder: b Irvine, Scotland. Emigrated to New York via Quebec.
Established shipyards on Long Island. Renowned for speed and strength. Praised by
Fennimore Cooper in his History of the American Navy. Staunch Democrat in 1820s. Died in
Turkey.   DAmB

EDGAR, John 1798−1866   Ch 4
Minister and temperance advocate: b near Ballynahinch, Ireland, ed Glasgow University.
Minister in Belfast 1820−48. Professor of Divinity for the Secession Church 1826−48 and the
General Assembly of the Irish Presbyterian Church 1848−66. Moderator of the General
Assembly 1842. DD Hamilton College 1836. Associated with Glasgow temperance reformers.
Died in Dublin.   Addison

EDWARDS, John
(Greenhead). DD from University of Philadelphia.   MacKelvie

EMERSON, Ralph W 1803−82   Chs 1, 2
Transcendentalist, literary giant: ed Harvard. Established his reputation as writer, critic and
speaker. Visited Glasgow.   DAmB

ENGLISH, William Watson
b 1832. Anglican priest: ed Glasgow and Oxford Universities. Served as curate and vicar in
several English parishes. DCL University of the South 1885.   Addison

ERSKINE, Robert 1735−80
Geographer: b Dunfermline, ed Edinburgh University. Emigrated to supervise American Iron
Company Mines New Jersey, 1771. Firm supporter of American revolution.   DAmB

EVERETT, Edward 1794−1865   Chs 2, 3
Unitarian clergyman, teacher and statesman: b Massachusetts, ed Harvard. 1815 began four
years in Europe. Became editor of North American Review. Served five terms in Congress.
1835 Governor of Mass. Particularly interested in common schools. 1841−45 Ambassador to
Britain, 1852−53 Secretary of State. Ran as Vice-president on Constitutional Union Ticket
1860.   DAmB

FAGAN, James O
b 1859 Inverness. Railwayman and YMCA activist; travelled extensively in South America and
Africa before settling in Boston 1881 where he worked as a signalman.
Autobiography (1913)

FAIRLIE, John Archibald 1872−1947   Ch 5
Political scientist, educator; public official: b Glasgow. Father a Chartist who emigrated to
New York in 1879 following failure of soft drinks venture. Went to Jacksonville Florida 1881.
Though both parents died of yellow fever in 1888, he went to Harvard. Studied under F J
Goodrow at Columbia University. Wrote Municipal Administration 1901. Became professor at
Michigan, then Illinois. Founded American Political Science Association 1905. Active in
promoting municipal reform.   DAmB

FARQUHAR, John McCreath (1832–1918)
b near Ayr, ed Ayr Academy. Emigrated to Buffalo, New York as boy; printer editor and publisher for 33 years; president International Typographical Union 1860–62; served in Civil War 1862–65; gained Congressional Medal of Honour; House of Representatives as Republican 1885–91; member of US Industrial Commission 1898–1902. Retired.
Yearley: Congress

FEINER, William 1787–1835
(Paisley-Oakshaw Street). DD from Princeton 1822.   Fasti

FERGUS, David 1805–22
(Campbelltown). Emigrated to USA in 1822. Died Cincinnati.   MacKelvie

FERGUSON, Fergus 1824–97   Chs 1, 4
EU Minister, Montrose Street Glasgow 1845–97: b Glasgow; ed Glasgow University. Vigorous temperance advocate. Travelled widely in USA: published From Glasgow to Missouri and Back. DD University of Lebanon, Tennessee.   Addison

FERGUSON, John 1787–1856
Founder of the Ferguson Bequest: b Irvine. Spent four years with uncles in America. Retired 1810. Inherited large sums through uncles. Left £400,000 in trust to promote education and religion in Scotland.   DNB

FERGUSON, John 1836/7–1906   Ch 5
Irish nationalist; businessman: b Ulster. Protestant. Partner in Glasgow Wholesale Stationers, London and Glasgow. Elected to Town Council 1893. Advanced social reformer; land taxer; leading Home Ruler; associated with Davitt and Parnell. Invariably principal speaker at Irish rallies in West of Scotland and sometimes in Dublin. Widely read, courteous debater and frequent contributor to the press. Died in a tramway accident. Glasgow Herald 24 April 1906:
Evening News 24 April 1906

FERGUSON, Peter
(Bridge of Teith). Ass Burgher Presbytery. Class of 1824. To America-Canada West.
MacKelvie

FERGUSON, David
(Thornhill). Ass Presbytery Class 1815. Went to America as probationer.   MacKelvie

FERRIE, William 1815–97
Free Church minister: b St Andrews; son of Professor of Church History, St Andrews. Educated there. Emigrated 1861, New York 1863, Canada 1869. New York State for 28 years as minister.   Ewing

FERRIER, Andrew
(Airdrie-South Street 1833–41). Emigrated to USA, then to Canada. Believed to have DD from a US College.   MacKelvie

FERRIER, Thomas
(Perth-North). Ass Presbytery Class 1810; west to America.   MacKelvie

FINDLAY, Hugh 1731–1801
Merchant: b Scotland. Emigrated via Canada 1760 where he opened post offices. Surveyed potential postal routes through the colonies 1772–4. Remained in Canada after American Independence.   DAmB

FINLAY, James
(Tollcross 1827–37). Emigrated to become a minister in New York State.   Lamb

FINLAY, Kirkman 1727–90   Ch 2
Merchant. Raised troops against American Colonists. Father of the free trade advocate Kirkman Finlay 1773–1842.   POG: DNB

FINNEY, William Grandison 1792–1875   Ch 1
Revivalist preacher of immense influence. Stimulated reformist enterprise in temperance, abolitionism and urban problems. Visited Scotland 1859.   DAmB

FISK, Wilbur 1792–1832
Methodist clergyman and President of Wesleyan University, USA: Visited Glasgow. Wrote Travels in Europe 1838. b Vermont, ed Brown University. Promoted education of his persuasion and became first president of Wesleyan University. Temperance advocate and supporter of African Colonisation Society for freed slaves. DAmB

FISKE, John 1842–1901 Ch 5
Historian, popular lecturer: b Hartford Conn; ed Harvard. Toured Scotland lecturing in late nineteenth century. Friend of Herbert Spencer. Visited Britain three times. DAmB:
J S Clark, Life and Letters of John Fiske:
H Burnell Pannill, The Religious Faith of John Fiske, Durham NC 1957

FLEMING, John H 1764–1800
Printer and loyalist: b Scotland. Arrived in Boston 1764. Began regular, weekly paper. Died in France. DAmB

FLEMING, Wilhelmina Paton Stevens 1857–1911
Astronomer: b Dundee. Teacher. Emigrated 1878. Took a post in the Harvard College Observatory and soon had charge of the Photographic section. DAmB

FLEMING, William 1729–95
Soldier statesman: b Jedburgh, ed Edinburgh University and emigrated to Virginia 1755. Served on various commissions on western lands. DAmB

FLETCHER, Alexander
(London-Albion Church Moorfields) DD from Delaware College 1845. MacKelvie

FLEXNER, Abraham 1866–1959 Ch 5
Jewish-American; educational reformer: ed Johns Hopkins University. Became educational researcher and writer. Examined European Medical Education 1912 and numerous other studies. DAmB

FLINT, Robert 1834–1910
Minister, academic and author: b Dumfriesshire, ed Glasgow University. LL D and DD from Edinburgh and Glasgow Universities. Professor Moral Philosophy at St Andrews 1864–76. Professor of Divinity at Edinburgh University 1876–1903. Stone Lecturer at Princeton 1880.
Addison

FORBES, Archibald 1838–1900
Newspaperman: b Banffshire, ed Aberdeen University; army service; editor of the London Scotsman 1867–71; widely travelled war correspondent: Lecture tour of USA 1880. Boase

FORBES, John 1769–1823
Merchant: b probably Aberdeenshire. Emigrated. Became partner in trading company and head in 1804. Declining fortunes. He emigrated to Cuba 1817. DAmB

FORGAN, James Berwick 1852–1924
Banker: b St Andrews. Emigrated via Canada to Minnesota 1885. Became Vice-President First National Bank Chicago. DAmB

FORREST, Revd A F Ch 4
(Caledonian Road Glasgow). Minister, Renfield Street UF Church Glasgow 1885–1921. Several visits to USA in the summer. Ordained 1876. Died 1922. Small: Lamb

FORREST, James
Unitarian minister and real estate entrepreneur: b Renfrewshire. Graduated Glasgow University 1833. Minister at Greenock 1835–40, Devonport 1840–1. Emigrated to New York. Acquired suburban lands as real estate man. Died Fairmount NY 1858. Addison

FORREST, Robert
(Saltcoats-Countess Street) 1798–1802). Accompanied Dr Mason back to USA. Minister in New York, then Stanford, Delaware. Died 1846. MacKelvie

FORSYTH, Robert 1846–1916 Ch 1
b Lanarkshire. Trained with Randolph Elder, Glasgow. Served with Pacific Navigation Co,

Pacific Mail Steamship Co, Risdon Iron Works, Engineer in Chief Union Iron Works, San Francisco. Later President.   Men Who Made San Francisco

FRASER, Alexander Gordon
b 1814 New York. Studied at New York and Edinburgh University. Ordained 1845. Eventually joined Church of England.   Ewing

FRASER, Donald 1773−1841
Ordained 1794. (Kennoway), DD Jefferson College, 1833.   Small

FRASER, John 1794−1879   Ch 4
b Johnstone, near Glasgow. Schoolmaster, journalist. Founder Edinburgh Radical Association 1836; Member Edinburgh Technical Association, advocate of Hygeism; reported trial Glasgow Cotton Spinners for Northern Star 1838; editor of the True Scotsman, Chartist paper. Left for Boston USA 1848. Believed returned home 1870.
                                                Boston, p 91: Social Reformer 1879

FRASER, Thomas
b Kilbarchan (King's Park-Edinburgh) 1819−26. Emigrated to Canada. Also served in the Dutch Reformed Church, Niagara USA. Died 1884.   Roll of Graduates

FRENCH, William 1733−1802
Virginia merchant. Provost 1778−79.   POG

FRIAR, John
(Galashiels) Associate Burgher Hall. Class of 1829. Emigrated to America, took up farming.
                                                                                    MacKelvie

FRYER, George Robert
b 1869 Chicago, ed in USA and England. Mission work in China 1891−7. Various charges in Britain until Paisley, Mossvale 1923.   Lamb

FULLER, Sarah Margaret (Marchioness d'Ossoli) 1810−1850   Chs 1, 3
Social reformer: b Massachusetts. Precocious intellect. She was acquainted with the leading Transcendentalists. Wrote Woman in the Nineteenth Century (1845) a feminist apology. 1846 in Europe; visited Glasgow. In 1847 married Angelo d' Ossoli. Involved in Roman Revolution 1848. Drowned on voyage home.   DAmB

FULTON, Andrew
(Glasgow Duke Street). Associate Presbytery. Class of 1789. Settled in Kentucky 1797.
                                                                                    MacKelvie

FULTON, David, RSW
Artist. Apprenticed as engraver. Began exhibiting 1872. Elected Royal Scottish Society Watercolour Artist 1890. Had exhibited in USA including St Louis.   Glasgow 1909

FYFE, Maxwell 1856−1934
Land agent: b Angus, son of gamekeeper, worked on estates at Glamis and Landertis; sent to America as manager for the Glasgow American Land and Colonisation Co about 1883; rancher and later superintendent of Indiana and Ohio universities farm schools.
                                                Minnesota Historical Society MSS

FYFE, Peter
b 1854. Chief Inspector Glasgow Sanitary Dept Engineering apprentice 1870−6. To USA for a time 1879; entered Corporation service 1885 Chief Inspector. Author of numerous pamphlets on public health.   Who's Who in Glasgow 1909

GALLAGHER, Thomas 1851−1925
Medical doctor, terrorist: b Glasgow; worked as a child in local foundry; emigrated to America about 1875−6; became a doctor in Brooklyn; active in Fenian movement; came to Britain in 1883 on bombing campaign. Arrested and imprisoned until 1896. Emerged insane and died in New York sanatorium.   K R M Short, The Dynamite War (London 1979)

GALLIE, George c1793–1876   Chs 3, 4
Bookseller; congregationalist. Member of Greville Ewing's church in Glasgow. An elder for 41
years. Travelled widely to support revivals. American religious visitors greatly impressed him.
Active in the Glasgow Emancipation Society, tract distributor and Sunday School teacher.
                                        Advance and Congregational Miscellany March 1876

GALT, John 1779–1839
Author: b Irvine Ayrshire. Began his writing career early, moved to London 1803. Employed
in various business schemes by Kirkman Finlay of Glasgow. Wrote Life of Benjamin West, the
American artist 1816–20; the Ayrshire Legatees 1820; Annals of the Parish 1821; Lawrie Todd
1830 and many others. Secretary to the Canada Company. Edited Grant Thorburn's Forty
Years Residence in America 1836.   DNB

GANNET, Ezra Stiles 1801–71
Unitarian clergyman: ed Harvard. Married daughter of President Ezra Stiles of Yale: assistant
to WE Channing; driving force in founding American Unitarian Association 1835; assistant
editor Christian Register; spent 1836–38 in Europe. Moderate opponent of slavery but averse
to abolitionists.   DAmB

GARDEN, Alexander c1730–91
Naturalist: b Aberdeenshire, ed Edinburgh and Aberdeen Universities. Settled in South
Carolina. Associated with the botanist Cadwaller Colden and John Bartram, naturalist. As a
loyalist left the colonies for London during the American Revolution.   DAmB

GARDEN, Alexander 1757–1829
Revolutionary soldier. Son of the above; b in S Carolina, ed Glasgow University. Served in S
Carolina assembly; visited Britain 1792. Published history of the colonial revolt.   DAmB

GARDINER, John 1861–1900
Naturalist: b Annan, Dumfries, son of Presbyterian minister; ed London University. First
Professor of Biology, University of Colorado. Emigrated around 1887. Appointed to
University 1889. On sabbatical 1894; fell ill; never recovered; retired 1898.   Ewan

GARDNER, Henry
Merchant's Son: b Georgia, matriculated Glasgow University 1809.   Addison

GARNET, Henry Highland 1815–82
Educator, clergyman and black militant: b into slavery in Maryland, escaped at an early age;
ed Oneida Institute. A Presbyterian minister, lectured for the American Anti-Slavery Society.
In 1843 clashed with Frederick Douglass by urging slave rising. Served in Troy, New York
pastorate 1843–48. Spent three years in Europe. A missionary for the Scottish UP Church to
Jamaica. Returned to New York. In Washington DC 1864. Minister to Liberia 1881.   DAmB

GARRISON, William Lloyd 1805–79   Chs 1, 3, 4
Abolitionist: b Newburyport Mass. Served as printer's apprentice. Became deeply involved in
anti-slavery activity through his paper, The Liberator. Became corresponding secretary of the
New England Anti-Slavery Society and an agent 1831–32. In Britain 1833, 1840, 1846, 1867,
1877. In Scotland closely associated with Glasgow and Edinburgh abolitionist societies. A
vigorous uncompromising character.   DAmB

GARTH, William
b Glasgow, ed Glasgow University. Died Paducah Kentucky at his brother's home 1869.
                                                                                        Addison

GARVIE, Thomas
UP Class 1792. Changed to medicine. Emigrated to USA 1803 as surgeon.   MacKelvie

GAVAZZI, Alessandro 1809–1889   Chs 4, 6
Italian nationalist and former priest. Toured Scotland and the USA lecturing on the dangers of
Popery. In the wake of his American rallies, disturbances usually followed. Largely
responsible for the riotous reception which greeted the papal legate, Archbishop Bedini in
America. Bedini was allegedly responsible for the brutal repression of the Bologna rising in
1848.   R Silvain, Life 2v (Quebec 1962): Glasgow Herald October 1854

GEDDES, James 1763–1838
b Scotland. Chief Engineer on the Erie Canal.   Black

GEDDES, Sir Patrick 1854–1932   Ch 5
Biologist, sociologist, educationalist and town planner: ed Perth Academy, Paris and under
T H Huxley. Professor of Botany, Dundee, 1899–1914. Worked in India and France. A
seminal influence.   DNB

GEIKIE, Archibald 1835–1924
b Edinburgh, ed Edinburgh University. Professor. Went to Rocky Mountains with Henry
Drummond. Lectured at Johns Hopkins 1897.   DNB: Ewan

GELLATLY, Alexander
1748 Class. 1753 Missionary. Settled Octara, Pennsylvania; died 1761.   MacKelvie

GEMMELL, Thomas c1834–1909
Mining engineer: b Glasgow, ed Glasgow University. Settled in Baltimore. Died in London.
                                                                                          Addison

GEORGE, Henry 1839–97   Chs 1, 3, 5
Economic reformer: b Philadelphia. His grandfather was from Glasgow. Brought up in intense
evangelical religious household. Went to sea. Visited Australia. Settled in California. Worked
as a newspaperman and developed his land theories. Published Progress and Poverty 1880.
Went to New York. Toured Great Britain. Ran unsuccessfully for mayor of New York city.
                                                                                            DAmB

GEORGE, Henry Jr 1862–1916   Ch 5
Son of above. Land taxer, journalist and congressman: b Sacramento, Cal. Reported on his
father's tour of Great Britain for the Brooklyn Eagle 1883–4. Visited Tolstoy. In Glasgow
also. Member of Congress 1911–15.   DAmB

GEORGE, James 1800–70
b Muckhart Perthshire, ed Glasgow University. Emigrated to USA. Served as minister in New
York state of Philadelphia before 1833. Went to Canada as Professor, Queen's College
1833–53; 1846–53 Professor of Systematic Theology; 1853–62 Professor of Moral
Philosophy; Vice Principal 1854–7.   Addison

GEUBLE, John
(Ireland) Class of 1800. Minister in Ireland then emigrated to America.   MacKelvie

GIBSON, Hugo
Minister: b Irvine. Minister Biggar Relief church 1820–36. At New York Broadway
Tabernacle, then Otis Mass, 1840–50. Also served in Pennsylvania. Resided in Vineland NJ
1856–71 where he died.   Addison

GIBSON, James
East Campbell Street Glasgow (Brechin-High Street) 1848–56. Emigrated to Canada. Died
New York 1860.   Small: MacKelvie

GIBSON, Walter 1643–1723
Lord Provost 1688–9. Merchant. Allegedly greatest merchant of his day in Glasgow. In
American colonial trade. He offered cheap passages to America and 70 acres for any settler at
a penny an acre per year. His brother James transported Covenanter prisoners to Carolina.
                                                                                             POG

GILCHRIST, Alexander 1858–1930
b Cromarty, ed USA; ordained Chicago 1890 to Springburn-Johnstone Memorial 1905–1930.
                                                                                       Small: Lamb

GILLESPIE, Mother Angela 1824–87
b Argyllshire; joined religious order; became superior Sisters of Holy Cross St Mary's;
associated with Fr Sorin of Notre Dame.   DAmB

GILLIE, George W
b 1880 Berwickshire; emigrated 1882; Kankakee, Illinois 1882, Fort Wayne 1884; successful
veterinary surgeon, sheriff. House of Representatives Republican 1939–49.   Congress

GILLIES, Revd John   Ch 1
Minister of Cambuslang. Deeply involved in the religious revivals in Scotland and New
England. Corresponded with leading figures. Wrote Life of Whitefield and edited his works, 6
vols 1770–72.   Arthur Fawcett, The Cambuslang Revival (1971)

GILMAN, Charlotte Perkins Stetson 1860–1935   Chs 3, 5
Feminist, social reformer: b Hertford Conn. Unhappy childhood and marriage. Divorced
1894. Married her cousin G H Gilman 1900. Interested in Bellamy's Nationalist movement and
Fabian Socialism. Lectured in America and Scotland. Her Woman and Economics 1898 is a
classic study. Ran the Forerunner, 1909–16, social reform journal.   DAmB

GILMOUR, Richard 1824–91   Ch 1
Roman Catholic Bishop of Cleveland: b Glasgow. Emigrated as a child. Converted to
Catholicism, he entered the priesthood. Wrote numerous textbooks for schools and as bishop
crushed ethnic divisions in his diocese. Moderate supporter of working men. Visited Scotland
several times.   DAmB

GLADDEN, Washington 1836–1918   Chs 3, 4, 5
Congregational clergyman: b Pottsgrove Pa, ed Williams College. Entered ministry with
strong social bent. Became minister in Columbus, Ohio 1882–1918. Moderator of the National
Council of Congregational Churches. Well known in Britain which he visited 1891, 1898.
Social Gospel advocate, reformer and author of numerous books.   DAmB

GLASIER, John Bruce 1859–1920   Chs 3, 5
Socialist: b Glasgow. Chairman ILP 1900–03. Editor of Labour Leader 1904–9. Associated
with Henry Demarest Lloyd (qv) and contributed to Revd WDP Bliss's Encyclopaedia of
Social Reform.   DNB

GODKIN, E L
Editor of the Nation. Emigrated from Belfast to USA 1856. Returned many times to Europe;
several visits to Scotland. Generally considered 'Mugwump', old style elitist reformer.
                              DAmB: The Gilded Age Letters of E L Godkin, ed
                                    William M Armstrong (Albany New York 1974)

GOLDMAN, Emma 1869–1940   Chs 1, 3
Anarchist lecturer and birth control advocate: b Kovno, Lithuania Russia, ed in St Petersburg.
Emigrated to USA 1885. Associated with J Most and his radical friends. Became Editor of
Mother Earth 1906–17 and wrote numerous pamphlets. Deported from USA 1919. Visited
Glasgow 1895 and later in 1930s   NAW

GOODNOW, Frank Johnson 1859–1939   Ch 5
Political scientist and university president: b Brooklyn, New York, ed Amherst and Columbia.
Became university teacher, Columbia 1883–1914. Spent 1884 in Europe. Investigated British
municipal government 1906; President Johns Hopkins University 1914. Helped redraft New
York City Charter 1900. Served on the National Civic Federation in Britain 1906. Served as
adviser to Sun-Yat-Sen in China 1913. Wanted greater home rule for cities. Republican and
Congregationalist.   DAmB

GOODWILLIE, David (Leslie)
Class of 1772; to USA as missionary 1788 then a Professor of Theology in Vermont.
                                                                                MacKelvie

GOOLD, William A 1830–1912
Alabama coal miner prospector: b Near Glasgow. Emigrated to Pennsylvania 1852. Brought
wife and child over two years later. Went to Alabama and produced the first coke in the state.
Did much prospecting for coal and opened several mines.   DAmB

GORDON, Alexander
(Montrose). 1812 Class; emigrated as probationer.   MacKelvie

GORDON, Alexander 1813–73
Naturalist. Travelled in America for Covent Garden Seedsman. Wrote on travels and hints for emigrants in Gardener's Magazine 1837. On Sir William Drummond Stewart's 1843 expedition. Sent specimens to Sir William Hooker.   Ewan

GORDON, Peter
(East Campbell Street). UP Class 1825; emigrated as minister to USA.   MacKelvie

GORDON, Peter
(Peebles-Brechin). Emigrated 1807 to Prince Edward Island. Died 1809.   Lamb

GORDON, Robert
Banker 1829–96: b Dumfries, matriculated Glasgow University 1845. Banker in New York and London. Home, Betchworth Surrey.   Addison

GORRIE, Peter Douglas 1813–84
b Glasgow. Clergyman and historian of the American Methodist Church.   Black

GORST, Sir John Elden 1835–1916
Mayor and political MP 1875; member of the 'Fourth Party' 1880–4. Rector Glasgow University 1895. Settlements in England and America. Glasgow Rectorial Address.   DNB

GOULD, Elgin Ralston Lovell 1860–1915   Chs 4, 5
b Oshawa, Ontario, ed Johns Hopkins 1881–6. Research in Europe for Gothenburg System of Liquor Traffic 5th Special Report. US Commissioner of Labour 1893. The Housing of the Working People 8th Special Report of the US Commission of Labour 1895. Taught at Johns Hopkins and Chicago 1896; organised City and Suburban Homes Company New York. President of the 34th Street Bank. Civic reformer.   DAmB

GOWANS, William 1802–70
Bibliophile and publisher: b Lanarkshire near Falls of Clyde. Emigrated 1821, went to west; returned to New York, opened shop; boarded with E A Poe family. Had some 250,000 volumes at death.   DAmB

GOYDER, David G 1796–1878
Educator: b Westminster. A noted schoolmaster in Bristol Infant School. A Swedenborgian, he spent some years in Glasgow with reforming phrenological friends. Lecturer on phrenology.
                                                                                                Boase

GRAHAM, Revd Ambrose   Ch 1
(St Mary's Irvine). Emigrated to Cleveland Ohio 1888   Private Information

GRAHAM, Isabella Marshall 1742–1814   Ch 2
Philanthropist and promoter of New York Charitable organisation: b Lanarkshire. Grew up in Elderslie; sat under Witherspoon. In 1765 she married Dr. John Graham of Paisley who served in N America with British Army 1722. She returned to settle in Cartside Paisley before beginning a boarding school in Edinburgh. In 1789 on the advice of Witherspoon, returned to New York and established a school for young ladies. Introduced the Penny Society to New York. In 1797 involved in the foundation of the New York Society for the relief of poor widows and children, the earliest such body in America. Presided at the Organisation of the New York Orphan Asylum Society 1806. Presided over the New York Magdalen Society 1811. Her funeral sermon preached by Revd John Mason.   DAmB

GRAHAM, John
b Bute; ed Glasgow University. Minister at Wishawton 1832–45, Ayr 1845–58 and Liverpool 1858–76. DD Geneva College Pa 1856.   Addison

GRAHAM, Peter 1773–1849
Merchant: b Ecclefechan; ed Glasgow University. Emigrated to Philadelphia. His brother, John established the firm of John Graham in New York as an extension of William Graham of Glasgow.   St Andrew: DAmB

GRAHAM, Sylvester 1794–1851   Chs 2, 4
Health reformer: b West Suffield, Conn. Grandson of John Graham, clergyman and physician (Glasgow University 1714); ed Amherst. Became preacher then agent for Pennsylvania

Temperance Society 1830. Toured lecturing on health and diet. Enjoyed enormous success to 1840 but thereafter waned.   Whorton: DAmB

GRAHAME, Robert 1759–1851   Ch 1
Merchant, Lord Provost 1833–4. Staunch defender of American and French Revolutions. Defended Thomas Muir in 1794 Treason Trial. President of Glasgow Emancipation Society from foundation to death. Lord Rector of Glasgow University 1785.   LPOG

GRANT, Revd George Munro, 1835–1902
Naturalist: b Albion Mines, Nova Scotia; ed Glasgow University. Accompanied Sandford Fleming of Kirkcaldy 1827–1915. Wrote Ocean to Ocean 1877. Chief Engineer, Canadian Pacific Railway on trip to Rocky Mountains. Wrote England and Canada; A Summer Tour 1884.   Ewan

GRANT, (MacVicar) Anne, 1755–1838
b Glasgow. Father served in Army in American Colonies. Settled in New York with lands in Vermont. Returned to Scotland 1768. Became a popular literary celebrity. Hostess to numerous Americans.   DNB

GRANT, William Morton
b Drumoak 1895, ed University of Aberdeen. NY Union Theological 1923 (Falkirk West).
                                                                                   Lamb

GRAY, James
(Ireland) Ass Burgher Hall. Class 1817. Emigrated to America.   MacKelvie

GRAY, James
Minister: ed Glasgow University. In Washington, New York and Philadelphia. Later ran a school in Baltimore.   Addison

GRAY, John 1817–72.
Roman Catholic bishop: b Buckie, Banff; ed Blairs and Rome. Served in Glasgow and Airdrie. In USA 1848–9 with Bishop Alexander Smith. Consecreted bishop 1862. Succeeded to Glasgow. Confronted with the difficult Free Press issue. Resigned and retired to Rothesay 1868.   Peter F Anson, The Catholic Church in Modern Scotland 1560–1937 (London 1937)

GRAY, Michael
Son of manufacturer from Grafton NH; matriculated 1808 at Glasgow University.   Addison

GREAVES, James Pierrepoint 1777–1842
Educator. Widely travelled advocate of Pestalossian methods, experimental schools and community at Main Common, Surrey. Associated with Robert Owen, 'Shepherd' Smith and A Bronson Alcott. Vegetarian, water drinker and hydropathic advocate.   DNB

GREEN, John P
Black leader, Republican from Cleveland. Visited Europe several times. Had close links with William Smeal of Glasgow.   Autobiography (1920)

GREENWOOD, Grace 1823–1904
One of 11 children. Began writing 1844. Spent 15 months in Europe 1852–3. Married October 1853. Edited juvenile papers. First woman correspondent to an American newspaper.   DAmB

GREGG, John Hunter
Minister: b Donegal, matriculated Glasgow University 1845. Assistant minister at Letterkenny, Donegal. Then emigrated to USA. Died in Chicago 1896.   Addison

GREIG, John
1760 Class. Missionary in Pennsylvania   MacKelvie

GREIG, John 1779–1858   Ch 1
b Moffat, Dumfries; attended Edinburgh High School; to USA 1797; lawyer, practised in Canadaigua, New York; president Ontario Bank 1820–56; regent of the State University of New York 1825, vice-chancellor 1845 to death; a founder of Ontario Female Seminary; president of Ontario Agricultural Society; House of Representatives Whig 1841.
                        Congress: A M Maxwell, A Run Through The United States
                        During the Autumn of 1840, 2 vols (London 1841) I 250–5

GRENFELL, Sir Wilfred Thomason 1865–1940   Ch 4
Medical missionary: b Chester, England; ed Oxford University. Settled in Labrador 1892.
Established hospitals, orphanages and nursing stations. In Glasgow during the temperance
referendum.   The MacMillan Dictionary of Canadian Biography

GRIEVE, Miller 1801–c1878
Journalist, diplomat: b Edinburgh. Emigrated to Savannah 1817. Dominated Southern
Recorder newspaper 1833–53, the unofficial Whig paper of Georgia. Served as minister to
Denmark 1852. Promotor of railways, education and Presbyterian Church.   DAmB

GRISCOM, John 1774–1852   Ch 2
Philanthropist, teacher: ed Columbia and Rutgers. A Quaker. Organised New York School,
principal Friends School, Rhode Island 1831. Involved in New York Society for the Prevention
of Poverty, the reform of juvenile delinquents, penal and food reform.   DAmB

GUNION, Andrew Jeffrey
(Greenock) 1868 LL D from Tusculum College, Tennessee. Died 1873.   Small

HADFIELD, Robert c1816–65
b Lancashire, ed Glasgow University. Trained for the law. Interest in literature. Died Buffalo.
His son MP, solicitor and one of the founders of the Lancashire Independent College.
                                                                                      Addison

HALL, Basil 1788–1844
Naval Officer, author: b Haddingtonshire; ed Edinburgh High School. Entered navy 1802.
Served in America and East Indies. Wrote Travels in North America 1829 a critical view of
American democratic culture.   DNB

HALL, David 1714–72
Printer and bookseller: b Edinburgh. Settled in London. Emigrated to join Benjamin Franklin
in Philadelphia partnership.   DAmB

HALL, John 1829–98   Ch 4
Minister and temperance speaker: b Armagh, ed Dublin. Emigrated to the USA 1867. Twice
anniversary preacher for the Scottish Temperance League and author of several STL pictorial
tracts.   League Journal 24 September 1898

HALL, G Stanley 1844–1924   Ch 5
Psychologist, philosopher and educator: b Mass, ed Williams College, Union Theological,
Germany and Harvard. Lectured at Antioch College, associated with W T Harris and the Neo-
Hegelians. Founding president of Clark University. Wrote extensively on child study and
education. Best known for his Adolescence (1904). Literally brought Sigmund Freud to
America.   DAmB

HALLEY, Ebenezer
(Leith-Kirkgate 1828–38). DD Emigrated to USA. Salem, then to Troy, New York: Albany
1855–75. Retired. Died 1881.   Small

HALLEY, James 1854–1920
b Stirling. Emigrated to USA 1857. Teller First National Bank Deadwood Dakota 1879.
Founder 1884 and President First National Bank Rapid City, Mayor of Rapid City.
                                                             Who Was Who 1897–1942

HALLEY, William M
(Dunbarton-High Street 1847–1881). DD Union, New York 1879.   Small

HAMILL, James Macafee 1867–1912
b Antrim. Missionary in Nebraska; Edinburgh-Lauriston Place, resigned. Died in Philadelphia
                                                                                       Lamb

HAMILTON, Alexander 1712–56
Physician and Social Historian. Studied in Edinburgh. Emigrated to Maryland 1738–39.
Wrote an account of travels through the colonies.   DAmB

HAMILTON, Alice 1869–1970   Ch 5
Physician, social reformer: b New York, ed University of Michigan and in Germany. Joined
Hull House, Chicago and became active in reform circles. In 1911 she became special
investigator for the US Dept of Labour. She specialised in dangerous industrial processes.
Active in the 1915 Women's peace effort. She later became the first woman professor at
Harvard. Critical of Communism and Nazism. Opponent of the Vietnam War.   NAW

HAMILTON, Elizabeth 1758–1816   Chs 2, 3
Educationist, novelist: b Belfast. Brought up in Stirlingshire. Became involved in Female
House of Industry, Edinburgh and wrote two works advocating Pestalozzian methods of
Education.   DNB

HAMILTON, Thomas 1789–1842   Chs 1, 2
Author. Younger brother of Sir William Hamilton; ed Glasgow University. Served in army in
Spain and Canada. Became writer for Blackwood's 1818. After death of his wife went to USA.
Wrote Men and Manner in the USA 1834 and Cyril Thomlan 1837 an autobiographical novel.
                                                                               DNB

HAMILTON, Sir William 1788–1856
Philosopher: b Glasgow in the college, ed Glasgow University. Toured Germany. Became
Professor of Moral Philosophy Edinburgh University 1836. Very influential commonsense
approach. His library bought by Glasgow   DNB

HANNAN, Revd Joseph   Ch 1
Priest of the Eastern District of Scotland. His brother founded Hibernian FC. Friend and
correspondent of Bishop Gilmour of Cleveland.   Canning

HARDIE, James Keir 1856–1915   Chs 1, 3, 6
Labour leader. Lanarkshire miner. Leading figure in miners' union. Became chairman Scottish
Labour party 1888, founded Labour Leader 1889. MP 1892–95, 1900–15. Chairman
Independent Labour Party 1893–1900, 1913–15. First leader of the Labour Party in parlia-
ment. Frequently visited America.   DNB

HARDIE, Thomas
(Ceres) 1815 Class. Emigrated to USA as a teacher.   MacKelvie

HARDINGE, Emma 1823–99   Ch 3
Spiritualist: b London. An actress, she went to New York in 1855. Became a Spiritualist 1857.
Travelled extensively in USA, Australia, New Zealand and Britain. Vigorous supporter of the
Union in the Civil War; Campaigned for Lincoln's re-election 1864. Frequently commuted
across the Atlantic. Visited Glasgow 1867. Settled latterly in Manchester editing spiritualist
journals.   D J Dingwall introduction to her Modern American Spiritualism
                                                                    (New York 1970 edn)

HARKNESS, or HARKINS, James
(Ecclefechan 1832–39). Emigrated to America, New York. Died 1878.   Small

HARKNESS, William 1837–1903
Astronomer: b Ecclefechan. Son of clergyman who emigrated to New York 1839. Newspaper
reporter, homeopathic doctor.   DAmB

HARPER, James
(Presbytery of Ireland). First minister ordained in Knockcloughgorm, opened by Glasgow
Burgher Presbytery 1771. Emigrated 1798 to USA. His son James also a minister, followed in
1801.   Fasti

HARPER, James
b 1819 (North Leith). DD Jefferson College Pennsylvania 1843.   Small

HARPER, James
(Glasgow Duke Street). Ass Burgher Hull Class 1824. Went to America.   MacKelvie

HARRIS. Thomas Lake   Ch 1
Mystic. Former Swedenborgian minister, founded model communities at Brocton, New York

and Santa Rosa, California. Associated with Laurence Oliphant. Spent several months in Glasgow.   DAmB

HARRIS, William Torrey 1835–1909   Chs 2, 5
Philosopher, educator, superintendent St Louis Schools 1868. Edited Journal of Speculative Philosophy 1867–93 in which many leading American philosophers first appeared. After associating with Concord School of Philosophy and the Scot, Thomas Davidson, he became US Commissioner of Education 1889–1906.   DAmB

HART, James MacDougal 1828–1901
Painter: b Kilmarnock. Emigrated with parents 1831. Studied in Germany. Opened studio in Albany then New York.   DAmB

HARVEY, Alexander
b Glasgow, ed Glasgow University; entered Relief Hall 1842, joined Free Church 1843. Emigrated to New York. Died there 1852.   Addison

HAUGHEY, Thomas 1826–69
b Glasgow; emigrated with father to New York City; moved to Alabama 1841; studied medicine New Orleans; served as surgeon in 3rd Regiment, Tennessee Volunteer Infantry in Union Army 1862–65; resumed practice Decatur, Alabama; House of Representatives Republican 1868–69. Assassinated in renomination campaign.   Library of Congress

HAWTHORNE, Nathaniel 1804–64   Chs 1, 2
Novelist: b Salem, Mass, ed Bowdoin College. Began writing, became editor of the American Magazine of Useful and Entertaining Knowledge. Joined transcendentalist Brook Farm. Wrote several successful novels: Scarlet Letter 1850, The House of Seven Gables 1851, The Blithedale Romance, 1852. US Consul in Liverpool 1853–60. Visited Scotland.   DAmB

HAY, James
(Kinross West). DD from Miami University, Oxford Ohio 1838. Died 1849.   Fasti: Small

HAYWOOD, William Dudley 1869–1928   Chs 3, 5
Labour activist: b Salt Lake City: lost an eye aged 6; in the mines aged 9. Became leading figure in Western Federation of Miners. In 1900 Secretary-treasurer. Involved in the bitter Colorado labour struggles. Founder member of the Industrial Workers of the World 1905. Stood trial for the assassination of ex-governor Steunenberg of Idaho 1906–7. Joined Socialist Party of America. Visited Scotland. Addressed miners. National secretary IWW 1917. Fled to Russia after his arrest in USA. Died in Russia.   DAmB

HAZLITT, William
Unitarian minister: ed Glasgow University. Served in several localities including Philadelphia 1783–86. Father of the essayist William Hazlitt.   Addison

HEDDERWICK, James David   Chs 1, 2, 3
Stockbroker, Publisher: b Glasgow 1845, ed Glasgow University. Widely travelled in USA.
                                                                            Bailie

HENDERSON, Daniel McIntyre 1851–1906
Bookseller, poet: b Glasgow. Book-keeper to Scottish Permissive Bill and Temperance Association. Emigrated 1873 to Baltimore. Proprietor of the University Bookstore, Johns Hopkins University. Wrote poems admired by leading American critics.   DAmB

HENDERSON, David Bremner 1840–1906
b Old Deer, Aberdeen. Emigrated to Illinois 1846; to Iowa 1849; served.in Civil War 1861–5 with loss of leg; lawyer 1865; House of Representatives Republican 1883–1903. Speaker in 56th and 57th Congresses.   Congress

HENDERSON, Mathew
1753 Class. Missionary. Minister at Charteris Pennsylvania. Died 1795.   MacKelvie

HENDERSON, Peter 1822–90
Horticultural writer; b Pathhead; gardner at Dalkeith 1837–43; worked for George Thorburn 1843–4; partner in seed store, later owner in New York of garden and seed supply house. Contributed widely to garden and agricultural journals.   Who Was Who in America

HENRY, Alice 1857−1943
Journalist and trade union leader: b Melbourne, Australia of Glasgow parents. Became journalist in Melbourne papers, publicising health reforms and needs. In Britain in 1905 and USA in 1906. At Hull House, Chicago. Met reform minded women and began editing labour union paper for American Women's Trade Union League. Adopted genteel Marxist views.
NAW

HERRON, George Davis 1862−1925
Clergyman, lecturer and writer: b Indiana of Scottish parents, ed Ripon College, Westonson. Entered ministry. Appointed Professor of Applied Christianity, Grinnell College, Iowa 1892−99. Joined the Socialist Party. Divorced, remarried and moved to Italy. Continued to write numerous works in social reform vein.   DAmB

HEUGH, Hugh c1782−1846   Ch 4
(Glasgow-Regent Place). DD Pittsburgh College 1881. Entertained several American visitors on trips to Glasgow.   MacKelvie

HEWAT, Alexander c1745−c1829
Presbyterian clergyman, Loyalist, historian: b Scotland, ed Edinburgh University. Emigrated to S Carolina 1763. Wrote first history of S Carolina on return to England.   DAmB

HEWITT, Revd Dr Nathaniel 1788−1867   Ch 4
ed Yale and Andover. Temperance activist sent to Britain by the evangelical Tappans.
Library of Congress

HILLIS, Newell Dwight 1858−1929
Clergyman, author: b Iowa, ed Lake Forest College, Illinois and McCormick Theological College, Chicago. Renowned as Sunday School organiser and preacher. Called to Henry Ward Beecher's Plymouth Church, Brooklyn in 1899. Wrote some 25 theological works.   DAmB

HINTON, Colonel Richard
Correspondent of Boston Weekly Voice. Writer on labour questions. Visited Glasgow to investigate co-operation, 1867−68.   Yearley

HOLBROOK, Josiah 1788−1854   Ch 2
Educator. Actively promoted the Lyceum movement, published his Association of Adults for the Purpose of Mutual Education; established Lyceums in Massachusetts; in 1837 established Lyceum villages in Ohio and western New York state but they collapsed with heavy financial losses. Introduced children to botany, geology and science at an early age. Inspired by British example. Drowned 1854.   American Journal of Education 8(1860) 229−45

HOLMS, John 1830−91
Spinner. Liberal MP; b Paisley. Became partner in W Holms Bros, Glasgow. Lord of the Treasury 1880−82; Secretary to the Board of Trade. JP Lanark, Middlesex and Westminster. Deputy Lieutenant Tower Hamlets. MP Hackney 1868−85. Travelled in USA.   Stenton

HOLYOAKE, George Jacob   Ch 1
Co-operator and secularist. Formerly in Glasgow and retained contacts with co-operators there and America.   DNB

HOME, William
(Carnwath 1823−33). Emigrated to be minister to Scots settled at Caledonia. Later to Switzerland and India. Died 1848.   Fasti

HOME, William
Associate Presbytery Class 1796. Emigrated to USA. Settled in Nashville or Kentucky.
MacKelvie

HOOKER, Sir William Jackson 1785−1865   Chs 1, 2
Professor of Botany, Glasgow University 1820−41; Director of Kew Gardens 1841−65. Host of many American visitors to Scotland.   DNB

HOOKER, Joseph Dalton 1817−1911
Son of the above: travelled extensively in America 1877 to collect 1000 specimens.   DNB

HOPEKIRK, Helen 1856–1945
Concert artist and composer: b near Edinburgh. Appeared in her first concert in Edinburgh 1874. Studied in Germany and taught at New England Conservatory, Boston. Produced Seventy Scottish Songs (1905). Returned to Edinburgh 1919–20 but settled in Boston.   NAW

HORNE, Charles Silvester 1865–1914   Ch 5
MP Ipswich 1910–14: ed Glasgow University and Oxford. Congregational minister. Frequent visitor to USA.   DNB

HOSACK, David 1769–1835
b Elgin, Scotland, son of British artillery officer; ed Princeton University; visited Scotland 1792. Year at Edinburgh University; in 1794 returned to USA. Established Medical Philosophical Register 1810–14. His son Alexander Eddy Hosack 1805–71 eminent surgeon.
                                                                                          DAmB

HOUSTON, Andrew
Ass Burgher Hull. Class of 1780. Emigrated as probationer to America.   MacKelvie

HOWAT, Hugh Taylor
(Dundee-Broughty Ferry 1860–88). DD New York 1882.   Small

HOWE, F C 1867–1940   Chs 3, 4, 5
Reformer, lawyer, public servant. Worked with Tom L Johnson and Cleveland reformers. Expert on municipal government. Woodrow Wilson friend from Johns Hopkins. Commission of Immigration 1914. Worked later with the New Deal.   DAmB

HOWE, Julia Ward 1819–1910   Ch 2
Unitarian author, reformer, married Samuel Ward Howe. Came to Glasgow on wedding trip 1843. Abolitionist famed for The Battle Hymn of the Republic. Engaged in Woman's movement.   DAmB

HOWISON, George 1834–1916   Ch 5
Philosopher: b Maryland; ed Marietta and Lane Theological Colleges. Taught at St Louis, MIT Michigan. Chair at University of California. In Europe 1881–2, 1900. In touch with Edward Caird and Thomas Davidson.   Howison Papers U of California: DAmB

HUME, William
(Auchtermuchty North) Class of 1796. Went to USA as missionary 1800. Settled in Nashville, possibly in Kentucky.   MacKelvie

HUMPHREY, Revd Herman 1779–1861   Ch 4
b Connecticut, ed Yale. Congregational minister, President of Amherst College 1823. Organised Anti-Wine Society 1830. Visited Glasgow.   DAmB

HUMPHREYS, Alexander Crombie, 1851–1927
Mechanical engineer, educator: b Edinburgh. Built up international gas plant construction company. President of the Stevens Institute of Technology.   DAmB

HUNTER, Revd John   Ch 5
Congregational minister: b Aberdeen. Appointed to Glasgow 1886. Went to London. Returned to Glasgow.   L S Hunter, Life (1921)

HUNTER, Robert
Royal Governor New York and New Jersey: b Hunterston, Ayrshire. Served in Spanish Succession War. Emigrated 1707. Brought 3000 refugees from Germany with him. Died 1734.
                                                                                          DAmB

HUNTER, Robert 1874–1942
Social reformer: b Terre Haute, Indiana, son of a wealthy Scottish businessman; ed Indiana University. Worked with the Chicago Charity Organisation Society 1896–1906. At Hull House. Wrote on tenement conditions. In London 1899. Visited Keir Hardie in Ayrshire. Published his influential Poverty (1904). Joined Socialist Party of America but abandoned the party in the First World War and became a bitter critic of the New Deal later.   DAmB

INMAN, Henry 1801-46
American artist: b Utica New York. Travelled widely painting portraits. Given commission by James Lenox and others to paint Wordsworth, Chalmers etc in Britain. Visited Sir William Drummond Stewart with J W Webb, the New York newspaper proprietor.   DAmB

IRONS, Martin
Scot, emigrated at 14 after five years in industry. Famous as Knights of Labour strike leader 1884-86   Yearley

IRVIN, Richard c1799-1888
b Glasgow, son of merchant; ed Glasgow University. Entered business in New York with considerable success. Died Oyster Bay Long Island.   Addison

IRVINE, James Fergus
Minister and educator: b Derry, ed Glasgow University. Irish Presbyterian church 1817. Attended University of Pennsylvania 1832. MD 1834. Served as minister and doctor in Limavady, Ireland 1834-6. Returned to America. President of several colleges and academies in Pennsylvania and Ohio. Began New Brighton Academy Pa 1851. Retired after the Civil War to Newark Ohio. Died 1872.   Addison

JACK, Alexander c1794-1868
(Dunbar). DD Monmouth College, Illinois 1862.   MacKelvie

JACK, William James
b 1864 Carlisle, ed Edinburgh University. Served various charges until Shiskine-Kintyre 1926. STD from Evangelical Association of America, North-Western College, Napierville, Illinois.
                                                                                              Lamb

JAMES, George
(Auchterarder). Ass Burgher Hull. Class 1825. Went to America, Canada West; Professor and Vice-President Queen's College, Kingston.   MacKelvie

JAMES, Henry 1843-1916   Ch 5
Novelist: b New York City. Spent much time in Europe in 1850s and eventually settled in England 1875. Visited Glasgow.   DAmB

JAMES, John
Canadian (Wolverhampton). Ordained 1857 in Canada, returned to Scotland 1862. Returned to Canada 1864-5, Wolverhampton 1869 to Slate Street Church, Albany USA 1871 MacKelvie

JAMES, John
b 1839 Nitshill; in pits at 10; moved to Johnstone; joined Miners' Association of Great Britain; influenced by Alexander McDonald; blacklisted; emigrated 1865; organiser Illinois miners; contributed to the Workingmans Advocate.   Yearley

JAMES, William 1842-1910
Philosopher and psychologist: b New York City. Spent much of formative years in Europe; ed by Scot, Robert Thompson 1855, among many others; at Harvard 1861; qualified as a doctor 1868; appointed to faculty 1872; taught physiology, then from 1877 philosophy; assisted at the formation of the American Society for Psychical Research 1884; gave the Gifford Lectures at University of Edinburgh 1897 and 1902, later published as The Varieties of Religious Experience (1902); numerous other influential studies. Closely associated with Thomas Davidson (qv).   DAmB

JAMIESON, Arthur Foote Campbell 1836-54
b Brodick, Arran, ed Glasgow University. Died Oregon City, USA.   Addison

JAMIESON, David 1660-1739
Colonial Lawyer: b Scotland. Transported 1685 for his religious views. Defended Revd Francis Makemie in court. Chief Justice of New Jersey 1711. Anglican.   DAmB

JAMIESON, James   Ch 4
Textile manufacturer Ayr. Spent several years in Kansas before returning to Ayr c1892.
                                        Social Reformer, September 1879: Temperance Register

JAMIESON, John
(Forfar 1780−91). DD Princeton.   Fasti

JAMIESON, John c1749−1819
(Bathgate-Livery Street). Emigrated 1983 to America.   MacKelvie

JAMIESON, John
(Scone 1777−1853). Served in same church 61 years. DD Jefferson College, 1841.
                                                                            Lamb: MacKelvie

JEFFREY, George
(Glasgow-London Road) DD from New York 1861. Refused call to Ass Reformed Church
New York 1853.   MacKelvie

JEFFRY, John 1826−54
Naturalist: b Perth. Sent by Edinburgh horticulturalists to Oregon to complete David Douglas'
work.   Ewan

JOHNSON, Tom L 1854−1911
Inventor, street railway operator, steel producer, member of Congress, reforming Mayor of
Cleveland: b Blue Spring, Kentucky. Chequered youth. Invented first fare box for coins.
Associated with street railways in Louisville, Indianapolis, Cleveland. He had interest in
establishing two steel works, inventing 'trilby' rail and the machine to make it. Converted to
the ideas of Henry George. Elected Mayor of Cleveland 1901−10. He made Cleveland 'the best
governed city' in America. Visited Glasgow.   DAmB

JOHNSON, William Eugene 'Pussyfoot' 1862−1945   Ch 4
Prohibition lecturer: b Coventry, NY, ed University of Nebraska. Journalist; editor,
prohibitionist New York New Voice 1895−99 and associate editor Chicago New Voice
1899−1905. Federal Enforcement Officer in Indian Territory 1906−11 securing 4,400
convictions. Editor, New Republic 1913−16. Wrote numerous books, tracts and gave over
4,000 lectures on prohibition.   Who Was Who in America 1941−50

JOHNSTON, David 1803−90
b Haddington, East Lothian; weaver then apprentice baker in Edinburgh and London; moral
force Chartist; shop wrecked by Chartist rowdies 1848; to Chicago 1848 where he lived and
worked until 1890. Wrote Autobiographical Reminiscences of an Octogenarian 1885.
                                                                            Boston p 92

JOHNSTON, Gabriel 1699−1752
Royal Governor of North Carolina: b Scotland, ed St Andrews University. Appointed
Governor 1734. Promoted free schools.   DAmB

JOHNSTON, George
(Edinburgh-Nicholson Street). DD Rutgers 1854. Died 1871.   Fasti

JOHNSTON, James Brown
(Glasgow-Duke Street 1854−68). DD Hamilton College, New York.   MacKelvie

JOHNSTON, John 1791−1880
Agriculturist: b New Galloway. Emigrated 1821. Utilised Scottish drainage techniques and
improving methods.   DAmB

JOHNSTON, John c1784−1864
(St Vincent Street 1825−41). Emigrated to Jersey City. Returned to Scotland 1854. Died
Moffat.   MacKelvie

JOHNSTON, John 1836−1904
Banker; b Aberdeen, graduate Aberdeen University; emigrated to Milwaukee 1856; accountant
with Wisconsin Marine and Fire Insurance Co and later a bank vice-president; numerous
directorships and educational positions including President Board of Regents, University of
Wisconsin. Gave land for Milwaukee city hospital subsequently named after him.
                                                    University of Wisconsin (Milwaukee) MSS

JOHNSTON, John Brown 1882–1960
b Glasgow; emigrated to Brooklyn 1886: New York Law School. House of Representatives Democrat 1919–21: continued successful legal career. In 1953 appointed official referee to Supreme Court. Congress

JOHNSTON, Samuel 1733–1816
b Dundee; emigrated to North Carolina 1736, lawyer 1760, member state assembly. Moderator of Revolutionary Convention 1775, State Senator 1779. Continental Congress 1780–82, Senator US Senate 1789–93, Judge of Superior Court NC 1800–03. Congress

JOHNSTONE, James F W 1796–1855
Chemist: b Paisley, ed Glasgow University. At Durham University 1833–55 although he resided in Scotland out of term time. His Catechism of Agricultural Chemistry (1844) widely used in America which he visited 1849–50 FRS DNB

JONES, Sir Henry 1852–1922 Ch 5
Philosopher: ed Glasgow University, 1878 MA; influenced by Edward Caird (qv); Professor of Philosophy and Political Economy, Bangor UCNW 1884; Professor of Logic, St Andrews 1891; Professor of Moral Philosophy Glasgow University 1894–1922; Knighted 1912. DNB

JONES, John Paul 1747–1792
Naval officer: b Kirkcudbrightshire. Became sailor. Served with distinction in the Revolutionary Wars. Spent his last years in Paris. Father of the American Navy. DAmB

JONES, Samuel 'Golden Rule' 1846–1904 Ch 5
Manufacturer and Mayor of Toledo: b Caernarvonshire, N Wales. Emigrated 1849. Worked in oil industry and began his own company with very benevolent relations with employees. His models were Tolstoy, Edward Bellamy and Walt Whitman. Mayor 1897–1904. DAmB

JONES, Thomas P
b Glamorgan S Wales; in Monklands with John Edwards, future leader of the Sons of Vulcan; worked in Govan Bar Iron Works, Glasgow; emigrated 1862; organised labour unions in Chicago mills; founded National Association of Iron and Steel Heaters; first president; leading figure in merger of Sons of Vulcan and Iron Rollers into Amalgamated Iron and Steel Workers in 1875. Yearley

JORDAN, David Starr, 1851–1931 Ch 5
Naturalist, teacher, university president and peace advocate: b New York State; ed Cornell University. After holding several teaching positions he went to California, becoming president of Stanford University 1898. Wrote extensively on peace and the future of the race. Visited Glasgow 1913. DAmB

KAY, Archibald, RSW
Artist: b Glasgow 1860. Exhibited at St Louis Exhibition. Glasgow 1909

KAY, James, RSW
Artist: b Lamlash 1858. Exhibited in USA Glasgow 1909

KAY, John
b Muthill, Perthshire. Church of Scotland minister; ed Glasgow University. Served at Howwood 1868–72, left for Port Austin Michigan, and after three charges in Canada, returned to Port Austin. Returned to Scotland about 1907. Fasti

KEEP, Revd John
Oberlin College. Came seeking funds in 1839 with Dawes for support of new abolitionist institution. Carwardine

KEIR, John
(Glasgow-Duke Street).
Class of 1803. Emigrated to Nova Scotia. DD from an American College. MacKelvie

KEITH, George c1638–1716
Founder of Christian Quakers, schoolmaster and Anglican missionary: ed Aberdeen

University. Emigrated to New Jersey 1685, later entered the Anglican Church as priest.
Returned as missionary 1702–04.   DAmB

KEITH, Sir William 1680–1749
Governor of Pennsylvania and Delaware: b Inverugie. Surveyor General for the Southern
Colonies 1714.   DAmB

KEITH, William 1839–1911
Painter, engraver: b Old Meldrum, Aberdeenshire. Taken to America as child. Worked for
Harpers; in California 1859; studied in Germany. Associated with John Muir.   DAmB

KELLAND, Professor Philip 1808–79
Mathematician: ed Cambridge University. Professor of Mathematics 1838–79 Edinburgh
University. First Englishman totally educated in England to hold an Edinburgh Chair. Wrote
on Scottish education. President Edinburgh Royal Society 1878–9.   DNB

KELLEY, Florence 1859–1932   Chs 3, 5
Social reformer: b Philadelphia, daughter of industrialist WD 'Pig-Iron' Kelley; ed Cornell.
Married and divorced from Russian emigre socialist. She made the first English translation of
Engels 1887. Joined American Socialist Labour Party. Joined Hull House settlement. Became
first woman factory inspector in Illinois. Active in anti-child labour campaigns. Secretary
National Consumer League.   DAmB

KELMAN, John 1864–1929
b Dundonald, ed Edinburgh University. After several charges went to New York 1919.
Returned to London 1924. Retired 1925. DD Yale 1917. D Litt Lafayette 1921.   Lamb

KEMP, James 1764–1827
Second Bishop of the Protestant Episcopal Diocese of Maryland. b Aberdeenshire: ed
Aberdeen. Emigrated 1787. Became Anglican priest and later bishop.   DAmB

KENNEDY, Alexander
(Cumnock) 1830 UP Class. Missionary to Trinidad, USA then Canada.   MacKelvie

KENNEDY, Archibald 1685–1763
Colonial Official: b Scotland. Emigrated in youth to New York. Land speculator. His son
succeeded as 11th Earl of Cassillis 1792.   DAmB

KENNEDY, John Fitzgerald, 1917–1963
President of the United States: b Brookline Mass; ed Harvard. Visited Glasgow in 1939 on
behalf of his father, then the American ambassador to Britain. He visited the survivors of the
'Athenia' and was entertained to lunch by Lord Provost Dollan. After his war service Kennedy
entered politics as a representative 1946–52, Senator 1952–60 and became the first Catholic
elected President in 1960. Assassinated 1963.   Information supplied by Dr Gerard Rice

KENNEDY, John Stewart 1830–1900
Capitalist and philanthropist: b Blantyre, ed in Glasgow public schools. Travelled in USA for
an iron and coal firm 1850–52. Returned to USA 1857 and as a banker developed considerable
interest in Western Railroads. Director of several lines. On boards of numerous educational
and philanthropic institutions. Member of New York Committee of Fifteen on Prostitution
1901–02. Great friend of J J Hill of the N Pacific Railroad.   DAmB

KENNEDY, Patrick Beveridge 1874–1930
Naturalist: b Mount Vernon, Scotland; ed University of Toronto. Worked for the US
Department of Agriculture Washington DC 1896–1900. Professor University of Nevada
1900–13 then at Berkeley.   Ewan

KENNEDY, Thomas
b 1824 Blantyre, UP minister: ed Glasgow University, DD Princeton.   Addison

KENNEDY, William, 1799–1871
Author: b Dublin; ed Glasgow University. Secretary to Lord Durham as Governor General of
Canada 1838. British consul in Galveston, Texas 1841–7. In Glasgow 1847–9. Retired to live
near London and in Paris. Minor poet and miscellaneous writer.   Addison

KENNEDY, William
Artist: b Paisley 1860. Exhibited in Europe and America several times.   Glasgow 1909

KERR, Andrew
(Dennyloanhead) Class of 1791. Missionary but then followed secular calling, emigrated to America.   MacKelvie

KERR, Daniel 1836–1916
b Near Dalry, Ayrshire; emigrated to Illinois 1841, lawyer; served in Union Army 1862–65; Illinois House of Representatives 1868; moved to Iowa, Mayor of Grundy Center 1873; representative State Assembly 1883; House of Representatives Republican 1887–91. Delegate to Republican Natural Conventions 1888, 1896. Defeated as Democratic candidate 1902. Moved to Pasadena, California.   Congress

KERR, John   Chs 1, 4
Congregational minister of Forres: b Kilmarnock. Author and promoter of unsuccessful temperance colony in Minnesota.

KERR, Dr Norman 1834–99   Ch 4
Temperance medical activist in Glasgow. After working on the Allen Line, settled in London.
          Scottish Reformer 10 June 1899

KETCHEN, Thomas
1810 Class. Emigrated to S Carolina congregation.   MacKelvie

KIDD, William c1645–1701
Private: b Greenock. Allegedly son of a minister. Pursued a colourful career until executed.
          DAmB

KINKELL, James
Class of 1815. Ordained early to emigrate to New York   MacKelvie

KINLOCH, Samuel
(Paisley-Abbey Close). Emigrated to America. Returned 1769. Resigned 1800, died 1808
          Fasti

KINMONT, Alexander 1799–1838   Ch 2
Educator: b Aberdeenshire. Emigrated to USA. Began teaching. Moved to Cincinnati where he was involved in Western Education Society, the promotion of new ideas and techniques of teaching. Wrote The Natural History of Man 1839.
          See preface to The Natural History of Man

KIRKWOOD, Robert 1793–1866
Minister: b Paisley, ed Glasgow University. Emigrated to Courtandville Dutch Reformed Church New York, then at Auburn and Sandbach New York. Home missionary in Illinois 1839–46. Bible and Tract Society agent 1846–57. Joined Presbyterian Church 1857. Latterly in Yonkers, New York.   Addison

KNOX, Robert 1791–1862   Ch 2
Anatomist: b Edinburgh, ed Edinburgh University. MD 1814. Became army surgeon. On continent 1821. Associated with Burke and Hare. Lectured at Portland Street Medical School, Glasgow 1844. Went to London 1856. His racial ideas very influential in USA.   DNB

LAIDLAW, James
British consul in Oregon. Son of the minister of Wanlockhead: ed Glasgow University, matriculated 1913.   Addison

LAIDLAW, John
(Dunning 1805–14). Missionary to Nova Scotia. Died Pittsburgh 1824.   MacKelvie

LAIDLAW, William Grant 1846–1908
b Near Jedburgh, Roxburgh. Emigrated 1852 to Franklinville, NY. Lawyer. House of Representatives Republican 1887–91.   Congress

LAING, Robert
(Dunse East 1785–93). Deposed. Emigrated to be a minister in Buffalo, New York. MacKelvie

LAIRD, William
b Balornock. At Glasgow University 1827. Died Mobile Alabama 1849.   Addison

LANG, John Dunmore 1799–1878   Ch 1
Presbyterian clergyman, educator, promoter and organiser of emigration to Australia: b
Greenock: ed Glasgow University under Stevenson Macgill and deeply influenced by Thomas
Chalmers. Emigrated to Australia 1822. Constantly travelling between there and Britain in
pursuit of his schemes. In the USA 1840 in eleven states. Later sought to promote cotton
cultivation in Australia to undermine slave produce in America.
                                                Dictionary Australian Biography

LATHROP, Julia 1858–1932   Chs 3, 5
Social reformer: b Rockford, Illinois, ed Rockford and Vassar. Joined Hull House settlement
with her friend Jane Addams (qv). First woman on Illinois Charities Board. Visited Glasgow
1898. First head of the Federal Children's Bureau 1912.   DAmB

LAWRENCE, George
(N Leith) 1829 UP Class. Emigrated as missionary.   MacKelvie

LAWRIE, James
(Edinburgh-Bristo Street) UP Class 1793. Emigrated to Washington DC.   MacKelvie

LAWSON, James 1799–1880
Author, editor, insurance expert: b Glasgow; ed Glasgow University. Emigrated to New York.
Literary and business interests. Great friend of the actor, Edwin Forrest and Edgar Allan Poe.
Became newspaper editor and then insurer.   DAmB

LAWSON, Peter 1772–1846
Engraver: b Lanark. Emigrated to USA. Engraved plates for Wilson's Ornithology.   DAmB

LECKIE, John
(Peebles) UP Class 1817. Completed study but did not licence. Emigrated to become classics
teacher University High School NY. Died 1841   MacKelvie

LEIPER, Thomas 1745–1825
Merchant: b Strathaven, Lanark. Emigrated 1763. Became successful tobacco merchant.
Active in the Revolutionary Cause. Mechanical innovator in various fields. A Director of the
Bank of the United States; a founder of the Franklin Institute, Philadelphia.
                                                                St Andrew: DAmB

LESLIE, Andrew
Virginia merchant's son; matriculated Glasgow University 1819.
                                                Matriculation Album: Addison

LETTERS, Dr Patrick 1849–1910   Ch 1
Surgeon: b Stirling, ed Aberdeen University. Wrote numerous articles in medical journals. In
Dundee tried unsuccessfully to promote Catholic emigration to Florida.
                                                                Medical Register 1912

LEVISON, Nahum
b 1888 Palestine, Son of Rabbi; ed in various schools in Britain, Syria and Chicago; BD 1916.
Served in Wyoming and Arizona. Enlisted in British forces in Chicago 1916. Served in War
Office. Went to Blantyre Anderson 1929.   Lamb

LEWIS, George 1803–1879   Chs 1, 2
Educator, presbyterian minister: ed Glasgow, Edinburgh and St Andrews Universities.
Secretary to the Glasgow Educational Society. Served in Dundee and Perth before joining the
Free Church. One of the delegation on slavery to visit America. Wrote Impressions of America
and the American Churches 1845.   Boase: Fasti

LEWIS, James c1806–72
Free Church minister, ed Glasgow University. Leith FC 1843–72, and in Rome Italy 1864–72.
DD Princeton 1871.   Addison

LIEBER, Francis 1800-72
Political scientist, educator: b Berlin Germany, ed Jena. Enlisted in the Greek revolutionary cause. Emigrated to Boston via England. Prepared the constitution of Girard College, Philadelphia 1834. Professor of Political Economy, South Carolina 1835. Columbia, New York 1856. Promoted codification of international law. DAmB

LILLIE, James
(Montrose-John Street 1839-43). Emigrated to New Jersey. Later Professor of Theology in Maclay College, Toronto. Died Kansas. Fasti: Lamb

LILLIE, John AM
DD (Kelso) 1830 Class UP. Emigrated to USA, became Surgeon. MacKelvie

LINCOLN, Mary Todd 1818-82
Widow of President Lincoln: b Lexington Kentucky, married Abraham Lincoln 1842. His assassination and family deaths contributed to her later instability. Visited Scotland in 1869. Overwhelmed by beauty of Clyde and Trossachs as well as Edinburgh; a last joy before her tragic end. Illinois Historical Society Journal 49 (1956) 7-34: DAmB

LIND, William
(W Calder) 1828 Ass Burgher Hull. Emigrated to Jefferson County Congregation in USA. MacKelvie

LINDSAY, Robert Burns
b 1824 Dumfriesshire: ed St Andrews. Became 19th Governor of Alabama 1870-1872. Black

LINDSEY, Ben 1869-1943 Ch 5
Judge and social reformer: b Tennessee, ed University of Notre Dame, Indiana. Family moved to Denver. Entered law. Won reputation for innovation of children's court. Associated with leading Progressive reformers. Caused sensation with his Revolt of Modern Youth (1925) and Compassionate Marriage (1927) for their liberated sexual views. DAmB

LIPTON, Thomas Ch 1
Lived in Crown Street, Glasgow. Cabin boy on Belfast Steamers. To USA 1865. Travelled widely, returned after three years. Specialised in commodities. 20 stores by 1880. Direct meat imports from USA. Buried in Glasgow Southern Necropolis.
Alex Waugh, The Lipton Story NY 1950

LITTLE, William
b 1832. Presbyterian minister: b Millport, ed Glasgow University. Served at Longtown, Carlisle and Michigan USA. Addison

LIVINGSTON, Robert 1654-1728
Lord of the Livingston Manor. b Ancrum, Roxburghshire. Emigrated 1674. Became considerable landowner in New York. DAmB

LIVINGSTONE, Deborah Knox Ch 4
President Rhode Island Womens Temperance Union: b Glasgow. Already in Band of Hope before she emigrated at 10 to USA. State President 1904. Temperance 28 May 1910

LIVINGSTONE, Martin W
(Kilsyth-Musselburgh-Mill Hill 1853). Emigrated to America. Settled in Ontario with Church of Scotland connection. Died 1887. Small

LLOYD, Henry Demarest 1847-1903 Chs 4, 5
Journalist: b New York city; ed Columbia University. Lawyer. Moved to Chicago and took up reform. Worked for the Chicago Tribune. In Britain 1885. Later in Glasgow. Began critical evaluation of US society with his A Strike of the Millionaires Against the Miners 1890; Wealth Against Commonwealth 1894; Labour Copartnership 1898; Man The Social Creator 1906. Also organised the Milwaukee streetcar workers 1893 and very active in Chicago municipal reform. An American Fabian. DAmB

LOCH, Sir Charles Stewart 1849–1923   Ch 5
Social worker: b Bengal, ed Oxford. Influenced by T H Green and A Toynbee. Became
secretary of Charity Organisation Society. On various government commissions 1893–1909
and influence on the poor law report. Professor of Economic Science and Statistics 1904–08.
Knighted 1915.   DNB

LOCHEAD, William
b Glasgow, ed Glasgow University; studied at the Relief Hall and eventually settled as a
minister in Albany New York. Matriculated 1816.   Addison

LOCHRIE, John
b 1861 Bishopbriggs. Miner. Emigrated at 18. Worked in Pennsylvania, Colorado and W
Virginia. Began own business in 1903. Soon president of several coal companies. Frequently in
Scotland.   MacDougall

LOCKHART, Charles 1818–1905
Pioneer oil producer, refiner and early promoter of the Standard Oil Trust: b Wigtownshire.
Emigrated 1836. In provision business then oil 1852. President 1874 Standard Oil of
Pittsburgh. Considerable manufacturer also of iron and steel products.   DAmB

LOFTUS, Cissie 1876–1943
Actress and impersonator: b Glasgow, ed in Blackpool Convent. Made her stage debut in 1892
in Scotland. Eloped with Justin MacCarthy, ex-MP 1894, divorced 1899. Her career declined
after 1905 but then recovered with the 'talkies' in America.   NAW

LOGAN, William
1770 Class. Missionary to America 1770.   MacKelvie

LORIMER, John G 1804–68   Ch 1
Church of Scotland Minister: b Haddington, ed Edinburgh and St Andrews Universities.
Joined Free Church 1843. Served Glasgow St Davids 1843–68. Wrote two books on American
developments.   Fasti

LOUDON, John Campbell, 4th Earl of May 1705–82
b Ayrshire: British Commander-in-Chief N America, 1756–57. Agricultural improver. DAmB

LOW, Juliette Gordon 1860–1927   Ch 3
Founder of the American Girl Scouts. After somewhat unhappy marriage, developed interest
in British Scout movement and on one of her many visits to Scotland began her movement.
                                                                                        DAmB

LOWERY, Robert 1805–63   Ch 4
b Newcastle-on-Tyne; tailor; moral force Chartist; associated with Robert Monteith of
Carstairs; temperance leader; to USA 1862 to join daughter and Chartist husband; worked in
New York and Boston; died in Canada.   Boston p 92

LOWRIE, Walter 1784–1868
b Edinburgh, emigrated 1791 to Pennsylvania; schoolteacher, surveyor, State Representative
1811, 1812. State Senator 1813–19. US Senator Democrat 1818–26. Secretary US Senate
1825–36. Secretary Presbyterian Board of Foreign Mission 1836–68.   Congress

LUBBOCK, Sir John, 4th Baronet and 1st Lord Avebury   Ch 5
Banker, scientist, author: ed Eton. MP Maidstone 1870–80, London University 1880–1900.
Secured Bank Holidays Act 1871; Act for the Preservation of Ancient Monuments 1882; Early
Closing Act 1904. Author of numerous scientific and ethical works. Opposed to municipal
ownership.   DNB

LUMSDEN, James 1778–1856
Printer specialising in popular illustrations and portraits. Built model lodging houses,
promoted Clydesdale Bank, Gas Company, etc. Visited Canada and USA 1843. Wrote up his
trip in the Glasgow Argus.   LPG

LUMSDEN, William 1812–42 Physician. Studied at Glasgow University, then took medicine
1830–2 then studied in Philadelphia, MD Glasgow 1836, LRCS Edinburgh 1835. Died in
Glasgow.   Addison

LUNDIE, John 1857–1931
Engineer inventor: b Arbroath, ed Edinburgh University. Emigrated to USA to work on railroad projects. Largely responsible for the suburban electrification of the Illinois Central. Adviser on numerous major international projects.   DAmB

LYALL, David 1817–95
Naturalist: b Auchinblae, Aberdeen. Graduated in medicine University of Aberdeen. Served in the Royal Navy. Travelled to New Zealand. Worked in the Rocky Mountains.   Ewan

LYALL, James 1836–1901
Inventor, manufacturer: b Auchterarder, Perth. Emigrated 1839. Designed and manufactured cotton looms and other machinery. Established several cotton and jute mills. Invented tubular wheeled tyre 1897.   DAmB

MacADAM, John
b Glasgow, son of merchant; matriculted Glasgow University 1810. Died Sullivan's Island, near Charleston, S Carolina 1823.   Addison

MacALESTER, Charles 1765–1832
Merchant, entrepreneur: b Campbeltown, Argyll. Emigrated to Philadelphia 1786. Remarkably successful trader with E Indies and Europe. Bank director, president insurance company and founder of a Presbyterian Church in Philadelphia. His son, Charles 1798–1873. Banker, real estate speculator. Land for Macalester College, Minneapolis a gift from him in 1873.   DAmB

McALESTER, James 1840–1913
Educator: b Glasgow. Emigrated to Wisconsin 1850. Lawyer. Superintendent of Milwaukee Schools 1873. Reorganised Philadelphia Schools 1883. Presided over establishment of Drexel Institute Art, Science and Industry. Frequently in Europe. Member Committee of Fifty to study the Liquor Problem. Trustee University of Pennsylvania 1885–97.   DAmB

McALLISTER, John 1753–1830
Noted craftsman in wood: b Glasgow; emigrated to New York around 1775 and settled in Philadelphia 1781.   St Andrew

McALPIN, James 1761–1847
b Glasgow. In Virginia during American Revolution. A noted Episcopalian.   St Andrew

McARTHUR, Arthur 1817–96
b Glasgow. Emigrated with widowed mother to Massachusetts: ed Amherst and Wesleyan University. Lawyer, settled Milwaukee, 1849. Became lieutenant-governor Wisconsin 1855 and very briefly Governor. Judge; became Associate. Justice of the US Supreme Court to 1888. Popular lecturer. Grandfather of General Douglas McArthur.
                                    Wisconsin Dictionary of Biography

McARTHUR, John 1823–90
Architect: b Bladenock, Wigton. Emigrated as child with uncle to USA. Carpenter in Philadelphia. Began designing noticeable buildings eg Lafayette College, Easton Pa and in 1869 Philadelphia town hall, one of the largest public buildings in USA.   DAmB

McARTHUR, John 1826–96
Manufacturer and soldier: b Erskine. Emigrated 1849. Joined brother-in-law, Carlile Mason in boilermaking partnership in Chicago 1854. Served in Civil War with some distinction. 1866–72 commissioner of public works, Chicago, 1873–7 postmaster Chicago. Lost heavily in bank and store manufacturing crash.   DAmB

MacARTHUR, Mary 1880–1921   Ch 3
Trade Unionist: b Glasgow. Visited USA several times, in 1919 for three months. Associated with Women's Trade Union League of America. Suffragist. First woman adopted as a parliamentary candidate. Married to Will Anderson, MP (Sheffield, A Hercliffe). Favourite poem—F Markham, The Man With a Hoe.
                                    Mary A Hamilton, Mary MacArthur (London 1925)

MacBETH, James
b Ayrshire. Minister in Church of Scotland at Arbroath and Lauriston, before joining the Free
Church 1843−50. Deposed. Emigrated to America.   Addison

McBETH, Susan Law 1830−93
Presbyterian missionary: b Doune, Scotland. Emigrated 1832. Served in the Far East.   NAW

McBRYDE, Archibald 1766−1816
b Wigtownshire. Emigrated as child to N Carolina. Lawyer. Representative Democrat
1809−13. State Senator 1813−14.   Congress

McCLEAN, John Robinson 1813−73
b Belfast; ed Glasgow University. Civil engineer Brown, Harker and Co, railways, and
numerous other projects including Singapore harbour. Chairman Anglo-American Telegraph
Co. FRS 1869.   Addison

McCLELLAND, James 1799−1879
Accountant. First President of the Institute of Accountants 1853. Friend of George Combe.
Phrenologist. Associated with Glasgow Sunday Educational Association 1849, later Glasgow
Secular School Society. Went to USA a second time 1872. Returned to London.
              Portraits of One Hundred Glasgow Men 2 vols (Glasgow 1886) v 2

McCLURE, Samuel Sidney 1857−1949
Journalist: b Antrim Northern Ireland. In Glasgow 1865 when father killed in shipyard
accident. Emigrated to join relatives in Indiana: ed Knox College, Galesburg Ill. Began cycling
magazine The Wheelman before embarking on syndicated feature article scheme. In Scotland
1887. Began McClure's Magazine which soon set the pattern for muckraking with its
investigative journalism and exposés, continued to 1914, later revived.   DAmB

McCOLL, Alexander c1804−72
Minister: b Glasgow, ed Glasgow University. In Canada 1847−9. Served at Niagara Falls and
Seneca Falls. Died in Philadelphia.   Addison

MacCOLL, John Robertson
b 1856 Glasgow. Engaged in drapery business. Emigrated 1881. Became President New
England Cotton Manufacturers Association 1905. President Rhode Island Anti-Tuberculosis
Association 1907−13.   MacDougall

McCOLLESTER, Sullivan Holmes   Ch 1
Universalist Minister who visited Glasgow and wrote a travel book on his experiences in 1883.
                                                                                     Miller

McCORRY, Peter
Editor Glasgow Free Press, a former school teacher who wrote under the name Shandy
McSherry. Began Irish Catholic Banner 1868. Failed. Emigrated to USA. Became editor of
Irish People, then the Catholic Herald in Boston and New York.
              P Quinlivan and P Rose, The Fenians in England 1865−1872 (London 1982)

McCOSH, James 1811−94
President of Princeton University; clergyman: b Ayrshire, ed Glasgow and Edinburgh
Universities (under Thomas Chalmers). Held charges in Arbroath and Brechin before Belfast
1852−68, President of Princeton 1868−88, retired.   DAmB

McCOSH, Andrew James 1858−1908
Naturalist: b Scotland, son of James McCosh; ed Princeton. Medicine at Columbia and
practised in New York. Spent summers in Europe.   DAmB: Ewan

MacCRATE, John
b 1885 Dumbarton. Emigrated with mother to Brooklyn 1893 to join father. Lawyer.
Representative Republican 1919−20, Justice of New York Supreme Court 1920, Official
Referee NY State Supreme Court 1956−58.   Congress

McCUE, James
(Old Meldrum). DD Princeton 1861.   MacKelvie

McCULLOCH, Oscar Carleton 1843–91
Congregational divine and advocate of the social gospel: b Ohio. After working as a salesman, entered the ministry; ed Chicago Theological College. Minister in Wisconsin then at Plymouth Church, Indianapolis 1877 to death. Prominent in the National Conference of Charities and Correction. Initiated savings banks, baths, children's aid and other welfare agencies in Indianapolis. Visited Scotland.   DAmB

McDONALD, Alexander 1821–81
Miner's leader and MP: b New Monklands. Miner at 8. Teacher 1851–5. Secretary Miners' Association, later president of the union 1863–81. MP Stafford, 1874–81. Travelled widely in USA. Founded McDonald Bursaries for miners at Glasgow University.   Addison: Wilson

McDONALD, Henry Rainy
b Glasgow; matriculated Glasgow University 1844. Died St Louis 1887.   Addison

MacDONALD, John Lewis 1838–1903
b Glasgow. Emigrated to Nova Scotia, then to Pittsburgh 1847. Minnesota 1855; Lawyer 1859; State House of Representatives 1869–70; State Senate 1871, 1873–6; Mayor of Shakopee 1876; judge 1876; Representative Democrat 1887–89. To Kansas City Mo 1898.   Congress

McDONNELL, Aeneas
One of the first Catholic doctors in Glasgow with his brother, Dr R W McDonnell. He spent seven years working in America before returning to Glasgow.
                                        Tablet 21 August 1852 and 30 April 1853

McDOUGALL, Alexander 1731–1786
b Islay. Emigrated to New York 1740. Ardent patriot in Revolutionary conflict, wrote pamphlets. Member of Continental Congress. State Senator 1783–6. Reputed as 'The Wilkes of America'.   Congress

McDOUGALL, Alexander 1845–1923
Businessman: b Islay. Emigrated to Canada 1854. In Chicago at 16. Engaged in shipbuilding on Great Lakes. 1892 built first steamship in Pacific North West and founded Everett Washington Hydro-electrics.   DAmB

MacDOUGALL, Clinton Dougald 1839–1914
b near Glasgow. Emigrated 1842 via Canada to Auburn NY. Banker 1856–9. Served with distinction in Union Army 1861–5. Representative Republican 1873–7; US Marshal in NY State 1877–85 and 1901–10.   Congress

MacDOUGALL, Revd Donald
Scot. Editor of Caledonian in USA. Believed Glasgow would awake American civic pride.
                                                        Chicago Tribune 28 August 1905

MacDOUGALL, William E
Free Church Minister: b 1841. Studied in USA, ordained Plato Indiana 1871. To Scotland 1878. Coatbridge 1883. Left charge 1900.   Ewing

McDOWALL, James
Merchant. Provost 1780–91, 1796–7. In 1782 married as second wife Margaret Jamieson of New York, daughter of Neil Jamieson, merchant, a former Glasgow student.   POG

McEWAN, Alexander R
b Glasgow, matriculated Glasgow University 1844. Died Brooklyn, New York 1860.   Addison

McFARLAN, Duncan
Minister: b Renton, ed Glasgow University. Minister Anderston 1827–30, Renfrew 1830–43. In Free Church 1843–53. DD Union College, Schenectady New York.   Addison

MacFARLANE, Andrew
(Falkirk-Erskine) DD Union College, New York, 1854.   MacKelvie

McFARLANE, Frederick
(Montrose-Mill Street). Involved in considerable controversy in his charge. Went to America and settled in Long Island, New York.   Small: MacKelvie

MacFARLANE, Robert 1801-55
Glasgow dyer knew Pinkerton; to New York 1842, worked in Buffalo and Albany; Founded
Mechanics Mutual Protection Society in Albany 1845; died in Brooklyn.   Yearley

McFEE, Daniel 1811-99
Minister: b Renfrew, ed Glasgow University. Minister in Scotland 1848-69. Pittsburgh
1872-7, Seattle 1877-8 Freeport 1878-9, Port Townsend 1879-81, Cambria CA 1881-6. In
Craiglockhart poor house under the name David Simpson 1893-9.
                                                                Matriculation Album: Addison

McGAVIN, James
(Irvine-East). DD Princeton 1858, wrote Sailors Prayer book suitable for passengers and
emigrants.   Small

McGAVIN, John
(Dundee-Tay Square). DD Princeton 1858.   Small

McGAW, Alexander 1831-1905
b Stranraer. Bridge builder who erected the pedestal for the Statue of Liberty.   Black

MacGILL, Patrick
Writer: b Glenties, Donegal. Worked as a navvy in the west of Scotland, took up writing;
joined Socialist party in Glasgow; joined Dawn as a writer in about 1909; served in First World
War, then emigrated to USA 1930. Lived and worked in California and Florida. Buried in Fall
River, Mass. Best known for his autobiographical Children of the Dead End (1914). His other
renowned works include The Rat Pit (1913) and Moleskin Joe among over twenty other works.
                        Bro James Handley, unpublished life in possession of B Aspinwall

McGILL, Stevenson 1765-1840   Chs 1, 2
Professor of Theology Glasgow University: b Port Glasgow, ed Glasgow University; preceded
Thomas Chalmers in the Tron Church; wrote Discourse on Education 1811. Prominent in
promoting the Knox memorial in the Glasgow Necropolis.   DNB

McGILVRAY, Walter
Free Church minister; ed Glasgow University; DD Lafayette College 1847. Died 1880.
                                                                                     Addison

MacGREGOR, George
(Hogarth Carnaby 1892). b Aberdeen, ed Cambridge University, New College, Edinburgh;
D Lit Glasgow 1929. Professor of New Testament Hartford Theological Seminary, Conn USA
1929 (Glasgow St John's and Renfield and Hyndland).   Lamb

McGUFFEY, W H 1800-73
Educator of Scots-Irish ancestry. His grandfather emigrated from Scotland to Pennsylvania in
1774. Became Professor at Miami, Ohio, 1829; licensed as Presbyterian minister but never held
a charge. 1839 President, Ohio, University. 1845 President University of Virginia. Began
producing his influential children's Readers in 1836. Enthusiast for common schools.   DAmB

McINDOE, Walter Duncan 1819-72
b Dunbartonshire. Emigrated to US 1834; in business New York, Charleston, St Louis before
settling in Wisconsin in timber business. Representative Republican 1863-7.   Congress

McINNES, Thomas c1791-1824
Minister: b Logie, Stirling, ed Glasgow University. In Halifax NS 1815-20 then 9th
Presbyterian Church, Philadelphia 1820-4.   Addison

McINTOSH, Lachlan 1725-1806
b Badenoch, Scotland. Emigrated to Georgia 1736. Surveyor. Delegate to the Continental
Congress 1784.   Congress

McINTOSH, James
(Shiels-Belhelvie 1828-50). Went to America 1855.   Small

MacINTYRE, Hugh
(Ireland-Loanends Templehill). DD from University of Pennsylvania 1849.   Fasti

MacIVER, Robert Morrison 1882-1970
Political scientist: b Stornoway, ed Edinburgh University. After lecturing at Aberdeen University 1907-15, became Professor of Political Science, Toronto 1915-27, Columbia 1927-50. President of the New School of Social Research 1963-5, Vice-Chancellor 1965-6. Author of numerous works on Politics. Who Was Who in America 1969-73

MACKAY, Alexander 1808-52 Ch 1
b Scotland, ed Toronto. In USA 1846. Called to Emissary for Glasgow Chamber of Commerce in India 1851. Wrote The Western World or Travels in the United States in 1846 or 1847. 3 vols (London 1949) DNB

MACKAY, Charles 1814-89
Poet, journalist: b Perth, ed London. Sat under Edward Irving's preaching for three years. At the Eglinton Tournament. Edited Glasgow Argus; Illustrated London News. Visited USA 1857-8 and acted as the Times correspondent in America 1862-5. DNB

MACKAY, James 1759-1822
b Kildonan. Emigrated 1776. Involved in early development of Missouri. DAmB

MACKAY, Robert 1827-1900 Ch 4
b Aberdeen. Edited Social Reformer, Reformer, Previously Chartist sympathies. Attended 1893 International Temperance Congress, New York. Scottish Reformer, 13 Jan 1900

McKECHNIE, W S 1863-1930
Professor of Conveyancing and constitutional historian: ed Glasgow University. Became lecturer in constitutional law, wrote on Magna Carta, the House of Lords and the 'new' democracy. Professor of conveyancing Glasgow University 1916-27. Friend and correspondent of Professor G B Adams, the American constitutional historian. Glasgow University

McKELLAR, Peter
Artisan; emigrated from Anderston, Glasgow to Vermont 1848; his son had already 'tramped' America as a craftsman in 1841-2; by 1851 settled in Iowa on farm; many other relatives followed to America. Died c1867. Minnesota Historical Society MSS

McKELVIE, William (Balgeddie) 1829-66
DD from Hamilton College, New York, 1846. Small

MACKENNAL, Alexander 1835-1904
b Cornwall, ed Glasgow University and DD 1887. Several tours of USA. Congregational Minister. Dugald MacFadyean, Alexander MacKennal (London 1905)

MacKENZIE, Alexander 1775-1820 Ch 1
Entrepreneur, naturalist: b Scotland. Employed by the North West Fur Company. Went to America 1779. Became the first European to cross the Rocky Mountains via Peace River, Pass and Fraser River 1793; returned to Britain 1801. Ewan

MACKENZIE, Donald 1882-1941
b Stornoway, ed Aberdeen University. On University staff 1906-9. Appointed to chair of systematic Theology, Pittsburg Theological Seminary USA 1928 then to Princeton later. Lamb

McKENZIE, George Ross Ch 1
A Scot largely responsible for locating Singers in the West of Scotland. Later president of the Company. Marwick

MacKENZIE Kenneth 1797-1861
Merchant fur trade: b Ross/Cromarty, Canada, NW Company. 1822 to St Louis, Columbia Fur Co. 1827 amalgamated with American Fur Company. In Europe, returned 1835. Brought in foreign workers. DAmB

MACKENZIE, Murdo 1850-1939
Cattleman: b near Tain Ross, Scotland; 1876 Manager Prairie Cattle Company. 1891 Matador Land and Cattle Company. President American National Livestock Corporation 1904-11. President Theodore Roosevelt appointed him to the National Conservation Commission. To Brazil 1912. Prohibited drinking and gambling among employees. DAmB

McKERROW, John 1793–1867
(Bridge of Teith 1813–6). Author and promoter of missions. DD Washington College, 1841: from Mauchline, Ayrshire.   Small

McLACHLAN, James 1852–1940
b Argyllshire. Emigrated to New York State 1855, teacher then lawyer. Moved to California 1888. District Attorney Los Angeles 1890–92. Representative Republican 1895–7 1901–11.
                                                                    Congress

McLANE, John, 1852–1911. Governor of New Hampshire 1905–7: b Lennoxtown; emigrated as child. Manufacturer of post office equipment. State Senator 1891–3.   Black

McLARDY, David
Glasgow town councillor 1894–6. Draper in Buchanan St and later in Nelson St Glasgow. Active Values supporter. Toured USA 1902–3. Died 1922.
                                                                    Glasgow Directories and City Archives

MacLAREN, Ian (John WATSON) 1850–1907
Free Church minister and author: b Essex, ed Edinburgh University. Held charges at Logiealmond and Glasgow before serving in Liverpool for 25 years. Established his popular reputation with Beside The Bonnie Brier Bush (1894). Toured USA 1896, 1899 and 1907. DD Yale 1896. Died in Mount Pleasant Iowa.   DNB

McLAREN, John 1846–1943
b Bannockburn; largely responsible for the Golden Gate Park, San Francisco.
                                                                    Gordon Donaldson, The Scots Overseas (London 1966) p 121

McLAUGHLIN, Daniel
Lanarkshire miner emigrated in 1868 to Braidwood Illinois; friend of James Siney, Alexander McDonald; ceaselessly promoting miners union; leader Illinois State Miners' Union; on executive of Miners National Association; driving force in and later president National Federation of Miners; Vice-President of American Federation of Labour. Active in Greenback movement and Knights of Labour; Mayor of Braidwood, Illinois 2 years; in state legislature helped pass state's first Mine Law 1872.   Yearley

McLEAN, Andrew
b 1848 Renton, Dumbarton. Editor: Emigrated 1863. Served in US navy in the Civil War. Worked on the Brooklyn Daily Eagle and founded Brooklyn Daily Citizen 1886. A Democrat. An annual visitor to Scotland.   MacDougall

McLEAN, James Henry 1829–86
b Ayrshire, brought up in Nova Scotia. Emigrated to Philadelphia 1842; to St Louis 1849; briefly in New Orleans. Doctor 1863. Representative Republican 1882–3.   Congress

McLEAN, John 1771–1814   Chs 1, 2
Son of British Army Surgeon, orphaned—Guardian Charles Mackintosh of raincoat fame; studied at Glasgow University also at Edinburgh, London and Paris. Emigrated 1795 to New Jersey. Professor of Chemistry Princeton 1797–1812. At William and Mary College 1813.
                                                                    DAmB

MACLEAN, John Jr 1800–86   Ch 2
Son of above: ed Princeton. Ordained minister 1828; Professor of Mathematics 1823; Languages 1829, Greek 1827 and then the Principal at Princeton to 1868. Succeeded by James McCosh (qv).   DAmB

MacLEAN, Magnus
Professor of Electrical Engineering, Glasgow and West of Scotland Technical College; member of the Moseley Education Mission to the United States Oct-Dec 1903.
                                                                    Mission Report London 1904 pp 235–45

MacLEAN, Neil MP 1875–1953   Ch 4
b Mull; active socialist from 1893; MP for Govan 1918–50 associated with Danial De Leon.
                                                                    Lees and Stenton

McLELLAN, John
(Braehead 1833–45). Emigrated to Detroit—Canada West.   Fasti

McLELLAN, William
(North America) 1766 Class returned home later.   MacKelvie

McLEOD, Alexander 1774–1833   Ch 4
Reformed Presbyterian minister from Mull, emigrated 1792. After teaching Greek in
Schenectady NY helped organise American Colonisation Society.   Sprague 9 (1869)

McLEOD, John 1788–1849
Botanist: b Scotland. Fur Trader and Botanical Collector. Served the North West and
Hudson's Bay Co. Met Sir William Drummond Stewart 1837.   Ewan

MacMILLAN, Alexander 1818–96
Publisher: b Irvine, ed there. Worked at Nitshill family farm near Glasgow before he and his
brother Daniel went to London 1839. Established house and opened New York House in 1869.
                                                                        DNB

McMILLAN, Margaret 1860–1931
Social reformer: b New York; ed Inverness. Founder member ILP 1893. First Elementary
School Medical inspector. Pioneered open air nursery school 1917, CBE 1917, Ch 1930.
                                                                        DNB

McNAUGHT, James T 1833–94
b near Kilmarnock, ed Glasgow University. Minister in Glasgow Market Street 1862–76 and
Abbotsford church 1876–94. DD Central University, Kentucky 1885.   Addison

MACRAE, David   Ch 1
Minister and writer. Studied at Glasgow and Edinburgh. 1867 toured USA. 1871 in Gourock.
1879 expelled from UP Church. Called to Dundee, returned. Already pressing Scottish Claims.
Founder President of Scottish National Association. Visited USA again. Died Pollokshields
1907.   Glasgow 1909

MacVICAR, Malcolm 1829–1904
Educator and author: b Dunglass, Argyle. Emigrated to Canada aged 6. Became Baptist
Minister 1856, then turned to education in American normal schools. Appointed to McMaster
University 1881.   DAmB

MAIR, Hugh 1797–1854
b Newmilns, ed Glasgow University. Emigrated to USA. Pastor in New York state 1828,
Johnston 1830–43, then Waterloo county Canada, 1847–54. DD University of New York
1842.   Addison

MAIRS, James
(Ireland) Associate Burgher Hull, Class 1788, ordained went to USA.   MacKelvie

MALLOCH, John Russell 1875–1963
Naturalist, b Stirlingshire, ed Glasgow University. Emigrated to America 1909. Served on
Unions Natural History Survey 1913–21 US Bureau. Biological Survey 1921–34.   Ewan

MALTBIE, Milo R
Municipal expert: b Hinckley, Illinois 1871, ed Iowa, North Western and Columbia Uni-
versities. Secretary of Reform Club on Municipal Administration. Editor of Municipal
Affairs.   Who Was Who in America v 5

MANN, David c1829–1911
UP minister (Wamphrey-Braehead): ed Glasgow University. Minister at Wamphrey until 1871.
Held two charges in USA. Retired 1899.   Lamb: Addison

MANN, Horace, 1796–1859   Ch 2
Educator: b Massachusetts; ed Brown University. A lawyer, he served in the state legislature
1827–37. Prominent in education issues. Became Secretary of the Board of Education and

produced twelve influential reports. Editor of the Common School Journal 1838–48. In Glasgow 1843. Became president of Antioch College, Ohio. Influenced by George Combe.

DAmB

MANN, John   Ch 5
b 1827. Accountant, social reformer. One of the first followers of Pitman in Glasgow, prominent in intellectual and social societies like the Glasgow Philosophical Society.

Bailie 23 July 1900

MANN, John Jr   Chs 4, 5
b 1863. Accountant, social reformer. Glasgow graduate active in Civic Society, Glasgow Workmen's Dwelling Company. Public House Trust and Cremation Society.

Bailie 22 April 1903: Glasgow 1909

MANN, Ludovic McClellan
Archaeologist. Saved Glasgow Tolbooth from demolition, knew USA. Manager Western Assurance Co. Chief of Mann, Ballantyne Co, Insurance Brokers.   Bailie 19 March 1923

MANTELL, Robert Bruce 1854–1929
Actor: b Irvine. Became an actor and made first appearance USA 1874 and continued on American stage for 40 years.   DAmB

MARKHAM, Edwin 1852–1940   Ch 1
Poet: b Oregon. Brought up by Campbellite mother. Fell under the influence of Thomas Lake Harris (qv supra). Ethical social reformer with a vision of the Christian Kingdom of Comrades. His poem The Man with the Hoe made him the Progressive reformers' poet. Corresponded with Tolstoy and involved in the American Social Gospel movement. In touch with T L Harris's Glasgow funds.   P J Frederick, Knights of the Golden Rule:
The Intellectual as Christian Social Reformer in the 1890s
(Lexington Ky 1976) pp 187–209

MARSHALL, Andrew
(Kirkintilloch) DD 1841 Jefferson College, LL D 1842 Washington College.   MacKelvie

MARSHALL, William
1761 Class. In Philadelphia 1765.   MacKelvie

MARSHALL, William
(Coupar-Angus) DD Hamilton College 1872 and City University of New York 1865.   Small

MARSHALL, William
Minister: b Glasgow, ed Glasgow University. Relief Church Minister 1823–9 in Scotland. Minister at Pickshill New York, 1832–43 then went into education work. Died 1864.   Addison

MARTIN, James
(Bangor-Ireland) 1749 Class. Emigrated to America 1777.   MacKelvie

MASON, John   Chs 1, 2
(Craigmailen 1755). Class 1760. Missionary to America. New York visited. Joined Reformed Synod.   MacKelvie

MATTHEWS, George Duncan
Presbyterian clergyman: b Kilkenny 1828, ed Dublin and Glasgow Universities. DD Western University, Pennsylvania; LL D Westminster College, New Castle Pa. Stranraer UP 1854–68, Jane Street, New York 1868. American secretary of the Presbyterian Alliance 1873–88. General Secretary of the Alliance from 1888.   Addison

MATTHEWS, William 1822–96
Bookbinder and writer. b Aberdeen Emigrated 1843, establishing his own binding business.

DAmB

MAVOR, James   Ch 5
University Professor: b Glasgow. Involved in social reform movements. Emigrated to Canada to take post in Toronto. In contact with leading American Progressives.

J Mavor, My Windows on the World. 2 vols (London 1923)

MAXTON, James, MP 1885−1946   Ch 4
b Glasgow; ed Glasgow University. Chairman ILP 1933−39. Represented Glasgow, Bridgeton
1922−46.   Stenton and Lees

MAXWELL, Dr William 1760−1834
Doctor. Studied Edinburgh and Paris. Deeply committed to the French Revolution.
Occasioned Edmund Baker's famous 'dagger' speech by his support for the French. At the
execution of Louis XVI, returned to Scotland. Invited to go to America by Thomas Cooper,
Manchester as medical and later college president; refused. Remained in Dumfries. Returned
to Edinburgh.   Bernard Aspinwall in Recusant History v 15, 1980, 194−200

MAXWELL, William Henry 1852−1920   Ch 5
Educator: b Tyrone, Ireland. Claimed descent from John Knox. Emigrated to USA 1874.
After working in the press became a teacher. Became superintendent of Brooklyn, then New
York Schools, 1898. Sponsored teacher training. Allegedly one of the greatest American
educators with W T Harris and A S Draper since Horace Mann.   DAmB

MAY, Samuel Joseph 1797−1871   Ch 2
Unitarian clergyman reformer: ed Harvard, assistant to W E Channing; supported
temperance, woman's rights and the abolition of slavery. Close friend to W L Garrison.
Associated with William Russell in education.   DAmB

MEEK, William
b Linlithgow; at Glasgow University 1824. Died near San Francisco 1861.   Addison

MEEKISON, David 1849−1915
b Dundee. Emigrated to Napoleon Ohio 1855, printer. US army 1866−9. 1873 Banker;
established Meekison Bank, Napoleon 1886. Mayor of Napoleon 1890−7. Representative
Democrat 1897−1901.   Congress

MEIKLE, James
(Beith 1812−70). DD Princeton 1856.   Small

MEIKLE, William
Ayre (Anstruther) 1848−53). Emigrated to Mobile, Alabama.   MacKelvie

MEIKLEHAM, David Scott 1804−49
ed Glasgow University. Snell Exhibitioner, Oxford, MD Glasgow 1833. Practised in Cuba
1833−43 and in New York 1843−9. Married grand-daughter of President Thomas Jefferson.
                                                                                                   Addison

MEIKLEHAM, William, 1802−52   Ch 2
ed Glasgow University. Professor of Physics, Member of the Faculty of Procurators, Glasgow
1828. Writer. Clerk of the College 1831−44, Clerk of Senate 1831−45. Bankrupt 1845.
Emigrated to America. Died in Milwaukee.   Addison

MELISH, John 1771−1822
Geographer and traveller: b Perthshire, ed Glasgow University 1806; established cotton house,
Savannah Georgia. Settled in Philadelphia 1811. Wrote book of travels, associated with
William Maclure (qv) published maps.   DAmB

MELVILLE, Herman 1819−91   Ch 1
Novelist; b New York; served on whaling vessels and began writing on his travels; Typee
(1846), Omoo (1847), White Jacket (1851) and Moby Dick (1851) among others. Visited
Scotland.   DAmB

MELVIN, David 1810−94   Ch 4
At Glasgow University 1827. A Loom card manufacturer. After 1863 papermaker and
merchant in Oxford, England. Temperance pioneer and at death the longest abstainer in UK.
                                                                                                   Addison

MENZIE, William Crawford
Manager City Improvement Dept, Glasgow: b Glasgow 1853. Emigrated to New Zealand 1879.
Returned. Emigrated to Cleveland, Ohio, then spent four years in Chicago; superintendent
W E Frost Co, timber furnishings 1887; returned to Glasgow, 1892.   Glasgow 1909

MERCER, Hugh c1725-77
Revolutionary soldier: b Aberdeenshire, ed medicine Aberdeen University. Emigrated after 1745 Rising. Served in Revolutionary Army. Killed in War.   DAmB

METHVEN, James
(Stewarton) Associate Burgher Class 1822 son of minister there: emigrated to USA.   MacKelvie

MICHIE, Peter Smith 1839-1901
Soldier, educator: b Forfar. Emigrated 1843 to Cincinnati. Served with distincton in the Civil War. Studied in Europe. Became professor at the Military Academy.   DAmB

MIDDLEMAS, Jasper
(Yetholm) 1825 UP Class. Emigrated as minister to Bethlehem, Albany NY.   MacKelvie

MIDDLESWARTH, Ner
b Glasgow 1783 Emigrated with parents to New Jersey, 1792 then to Pennsylvania: served in War in 1812 State House of Representatives 1815-41. State Senator 1853-5. Representative in Congress Whig 1853-5. President Beaver Furnace Co.   Congress

MILLAR, John 1735-1801   Chs 1, 2
Professor Glasgow University: b Shotts: wrote influential work on origin of ranks. By family, intellect and politics closely associated with the radicals of the day.   DNB

MILLAR, John   Ch 1
Son of the above, involved in radical Scottish politics; fled to America 1794, settled in Princeton and died 1795.   DNB

MILLAR, Alfred Jacob 1810-74
Artist: b Baltimore. Studied in USA and in Europe. Established studio in New Orleans where Sir William Drummond Stewart persuaded him to join his 1837 expedition to the west. He produced a magnificent collection of the declining Indian life on the plains. Came to Scotland and painted two studies for the restored chapel of St Anthony, Murthly Castle. Returned to USA.   M C Ross, The West of Alfred Jacob Miller (Norman Oklahoma 1950)

MILLER, James
b London, matriculated Glasgow University 1820: emigrated to America as a preacher. Died at St Charles, Iowa 1867.   Addison

MILLER, James
(Arbroath 1789-1819). Emigrated to America; died there.   Small

MILLER, James
(Falkirk-East) UP Class 1811: joined Independents and emigrated to USA.   MacKelvie

MILLER, James
(Newmilns) 1823 UP Class withdrew. Emigrated to USA.   MacKelvie

MILLER, William
(Falkirk) UP Class 1814. Emigrated to USA immediately after licensed.   MacKelvie

MILLIGAN, James
b 1785. Minister and radical abortionist: b Dalmellington, Ayrshire. Emigrated 1802; ed Jefferson College, settled in Vermont. Wrote several religious tracts and vigorously opposed slavery until 1830s.   R A Roth in New England Quarterly 55, 1982 540-63

MINTO, Walter, 1753-96
Mathematician: b Cowdenham, Scotland, ed Edinburgh University. Emigrated 1786. Became Professor of Mathematics under John Wutherspoon at the College of New Jersey.   DAmB

MITCHELL, Alexander 1817-87
Banker, financier, railroad builder, congressman: b Ellon, Aberdeenshire. Emigrated at 22 as secretary of Wisconsin Insurance Company which became a state bank under his presidency. He put the Milwaukee and St Paul Railroad on a sound base and expanded its lines to 5000 miles. Republican. 1870-4 Congress.   DAmB: Congress

MITCHELL, Andrew 1799–1876
b Anderston, ed Glasgow University. Became a merchant in Glasgow and New York. Addison

MITCHELL, David
Presbyterian minister: b Glasgow, ed Glasgow University. At St Luke's Glasgow 1858–62 and
Forfar 1862–5 before going to the Scotch Church, Jersey, USA.   Addison

MITCHELL, David Brydie, 1766–1837
Governor of Georgia: b Muthill Perth. Emigrated 1783 to estate in Savannah. Governor
1809–13, 1815–17: supported popular education and internal improvements.   DAmB

MITCHELL, James Ure 1833–1905   Ch 1
Universalist minister. Served in Glasgow and Dundee. Visited America on a number of
occasions.   Seaburg

MITCHELL, John
(Wellington Street Glasgow). DD from Princeton and Glasgow—no date. Died.   MacKelvie

MITCHELL, John
b 1810. Dundee weaver founder member of the Dundee Democratic Society; believed to have
written Chartist poetry; friend of William Thom, poet; leader of the Chartist march on Forfar;
left for New York 1842 a 'wanted' man.   Boston and Wright

MITCHELL, Moncrieff, 1818–89
New York merchant: b Glasgow, ed Glasgow University. Died Tremont House, Sea Girt, New
Jersey.   Addison

MITCHILL, Samuel Latham 1764–1831
b Hempstead NY. Graduated in medicine Edinburgh University 1786. Lawyer, Land
Commissioner, State Assemblyman 1791–2. Professor of Chemistry and Natural History,
Columbia College. Editor NY Medical Repository 1797–1813 Representative-Democrat
1801–4, 1810–13 Senate. 1804–9 Professor of Natural History in NY. College of physicians
and Surgeons 1808–20. Professor of Botany and Materia Medica 1820–26. Vice-President
Rutgers Medical School 1826–30.   Congress

MOFFATT, James
b 1870 Glasgow; ed Glasgow and Oxford; Chair of Church History Glasgow College 1895: to
Union Theological 1927. LL D Dickinson College Pa 1928.   Lamb

MOFFAT, James Clement 1811–90
Church Historian: b Glencree, Scotland. Emigrated 1833; ed Princeton. Professor at Lafayette
College 1839. Eventually 1861 Professor of Church History, Princeton.   DAmB

MONCRIEFF, William Glen
(Hamilton) 1834 UP Class: served Musselburgh; emigrated to USA.   MacKelvie

MONIE, J
(Airdrie). DD Ithuriel College USA.   CYUB 1903–04

MONTEITH, Robert 1812–84   Chs 1, 5
Catholic philanthropist, Literateur and Patron. Friend of Tennyson and Newman.
Corresponded with O A Brownson. Largely responsible for the Scottish Catholic revival after
his conversion to Catholicism in 1846.   Bernard Aspinwall, Innes Review 33 (1982) 75–76

MONTGOMERY, Edmund Duncan 1835–1911
Philosopher: b Edinburgh. Studied in Germany. Practised medicine. Emigrated 1870 trying to
aid freed slaves in Georgia. Moved to Texas 1872 and wrote numerous studies of philosophy.
                                                                                DAmB

MONTRESOR, James Gabriel 1702–76
Military Commander: b Fort William. Served in British Army with considerable distinction in
colonial wars. Returned to England 1760.   DAmB

MOODY, Dwight L 1837–99
Evangelist: b Northfield Mass. Worked in retailing in Chicago. Became involved in YMCA.

Visited Britain 1867 and 1870. Built up Sunday school and worked as city missionary. Mounted very successful evangelistic campaigns in Britain in 1873–5, 1881, 1891–2. Invited Professor Henry Drummond to his summer gathering 1887.   DAmB

MOONLIGHT, Thomas 1833–99
b Forfarshire. Territorial Governor of Wyoming 1887–90.   Black

MOORE, John Bishop 1835–1901
b Westneath, Ireland. Emigrated to Charleston SC 1848. Ordained 1860. Bishop of St Augustine. Interested in immigration schemes. Friend of Revd Edward McGlynn.   DAmB

MORAN, Benjamin, 1820–86
Diplomat and author. Son of mill manager. Established cloth mill in Pennsylvania. Wrote travel books. Secretary in US Embassy London. Visited Glasgow.   DAmB

MORAN, Mary Nimmo 1842–99
Painter and etcher: b Strathaven, Lanarkshire. Emigrated with father 1847. Married Thomas Moran, artist, 1862. Exhibitions in America. They studied and worked in Paris; acquainted with Corot. Began successful careers on return. Because of her failing health her husband encouraged her to become an etcher, with marked success. In 1882 she toured Great Britain. Exhibited at 1893 Worlds Columbian Exposition, Chicago.   NAW

MORAN, Thomas 1837–1926
Painter: b Bolton Lancs. Emigrated to USA in 1844. Married Mary Nimmo of Strathaven, a painter. Congress bought his 'The Grand Canyon' of the Yellowstone for $10,000. Settled in Philadelphia, 1872.   DAmB

MORISON, John
b Glasgow; matriculated Glasgow University 1847. Drowned New York Bay 1853, aged 22.
                                                                                             Addison

MORRIS, George
(Glasgow-Regent Place) Ass Burgher Hall Class of 1826. Emigrated to America, settled in Silverspring, Pennsylvania.   MacKelvie

MORRISON, James
(Campbell Street, Glasgow) (Keith 1829–39). Emigrated to Lawrence County New York. Son became Bishop of Duluth, Minn.   Small

MOTT, James 1788–1868   Chs 1, 2, 3
Reformer abolitionist: b Long Island New York. Quaker. Engaged in business. Became deeply involved in the anti-slavery campaign., Attended 1840 World Anti-Slavery Convention in London with his wife (qv): wrote Three Months in Great Britain (1841). Firm supporter of women's equality, and presided at 1848 Seneca Falls Women's Rights Convention. Partly responsible for the formation of Swathmore College, 1864.   DAmB

MOTT, John R 1865–1955   Ch 1
YMCA leader. Frequently visited Glasgow, 1890 to 1914, to promote activities and attend conferences.   C H Hopkins, Life, (Geneva 1979)

MOTT, Lucretia Ceffin 1793–1880   Chs 1, 2, 3
Reformer abolitionist: b Nantucket. Quaker; married James Mott 1811. Became a liberal Hicksite Quaker in 1820s and became active in Women's rights and abolition of slavery. Attended organising convention 1833 American Anti-Slavery Convention in London. Visited Glasgow; amid much controversy she eventually spoke in the Glasgow Unitarian Chapel.
                                                                                             DAmB

MOULTON R G 1849–1924
Professor, lecturer, author: b Preston Lancashire, ed London and Cambridge. Associated with extra-mural education. Visited USA 1890. Became Professor of Literature Chicago University 1892–1919. Wrote many books but best known for his Reader's Bible 1896–8.   DAmB

MUIR, Adam Stuart
Free Church Minister: ed Glasgow and Toronto Universities. Congregational Minister 1845–7; joined Free Church. 1849 went to Boston, USA. Returned 1855. At Leith 1859.   Ewing

MUIR, James
Minister son of Revd George Muir of Old Cumnock and High Kirk, Paisley. Emigrated to
USA. Minister at Alexandria, Virginia.   Sprague 3 516

MUIR, Sir James
Merchant, senior partner in Findlay and Co. With interests in New York, New Orleans,
Charleston. Provost 1889–92.   POG

MUIR, John
b 1828. Lord Provost of Glasgow University. Partner in James Finlay and Co, East India
merchants. Made 7 visits to India. Also mill owner in Deanston and Catrine. American
interests in teas and cotton.   LPOG

MUIR, John 1838–1914
Naturalist: b Dunbar. Emigrated to Wisconsin 1849. ed University of Wisconsin. Walked
thousands of miles through the USA and Canada. Wrote several books on his experiences.
Awakened the conservationist movement in America.   DAmB: Ewan

MUIR, Thomas 1765–98
ed Glasgow University. Deeply interested in Scottish political association in French
Revolutionary Era. Tried for treason. Defended by Robert Graham (qv supra). Transported
West Australia. American friends fitted out ship in New York to rescue him. En route to USA
the ship was wrecked. Captured by Indians. Eventually died in France 1798.
                    Peter MacKenzie, The Life of Thomas Muir (Glasgow 1831)

MUIRHEAD, James Fullarton 1853–1934
Traveller and author: b Glasgow, ed Edinburgh University. Married Helen, daughter of Josiah
Quincy, Boston, great-granddaughter of Josiah Quincy, President of Harvard. English editor
of Baedeker's handbooks for 35 years; he wrote the volume on USA. Worked in Leipzig and
USA. Wrote America The Land of Contrasts (1898).   Who Was Who 1929–40

MUIRHEAD, John Henry 1855–1940   Ch 5
Philosopher: ed Glasgow and Oxford University. Professor of Philosophy Birmingham
University 1896–1922. A founder of the Ethical Society 1891. Idealist and friend of Edward
Caird.   DNB

MULLINER, Samuel   Ch 1
Scottish Mormon missionary from Haddington. Returned from America to labour in Scotland
1839.   Mormon Archives, Salt Lake City, Utah

MUNNIS, Robert c1817–1866
American Presbyterian Board missionary to India: b Antrim, ed Glasgow University. Died in
Himalayas.   Addison

MUNRO, Henry 1730–1801
Clergyman, loyalist: b Scotland, ed St Andrews University. Chaplain to North American
troops 1757. Became missionary for Society for the Propagation in the Gospel. Returned to
England 1778, to Scotland 1783.   DAmB

MURDOCH, David c1801–1873
b Dunbartonshire, ed Glasgow University. Died Elmira New York.   Addison

MURDOCH, James E 1811–93
Actor, lecturer and elocutionist: b Philadelphia, wrote Orthophony with William Russell (qv).
Enjoyed great success in London 1865.   DAmB

MURDOCH, John
Class of 1805: went to America.   MacKelvie

MURDOCH, John 1709–76
Merchant. Provost 1746–7, 1750–1, 1758–9. Engaged in Virginia trade.   POG

MURDOCH, William Anderson
b 1885. Indian Missionary 1911–21: ed Glasgow University 1907. Minister later in St Louis
USA.   Lamb

MURPHY, Francis 1836-1907   Ch 4
Founder of the temperance Blue Ribbon Society: b Wexford. Emigrated at 16. Temperance activist after early drink problems. Promoted by John Wanamaker (qv infra) Toured Scotland.
                                                                                         DAmB

MURPHY, James 1835-91   Ch 6
Fenian organiser, formerly served in 20th Massachusetts regiment in the American Civil War. Operated from Glasgow. Involved in the attack on Clerkenwell prison 1867. Went to Paris and then returned to New York as superintendent of national cemeteries and then as a New York tax collector.   P Quinlivan and P Rose, The Fenians in England 1865-72 (London 1982)

MURRAY, Albert 1812-1878
Naturalist: b Edinburgh. President Edinburgh Botanical Society: contributed to Transactions. In London 1860 Secretary of the Royal Horticultural Society. In 1873 Utah collecting specimens   Ewan

MURRAY, Alexander
Chartered accountant: b Rogart, Sutherland. On Glasgow Town Council from 1891. Delegate to Presbyterian Council in 1889. Washington DC Travelled widely in USA. Temperance activist.   Glasgow 1909

MURRAY, John
Associate Presbytery Class 1742. Emigrated to America.   MacKelvie

MURRAY, John
Secretary Glasgow Emancipation Society. Landowner and religious activist. Associated with James McCune Smith (qv). Died 1849.
                                      Duncan Rice The Scots Abolitionists (Baton Rouge 1981)

MURRAY, John 1742-93
Minister: b Scotland; ed Edinburgh University. Emigrated to Pennsylvania 1763, at Second Presbyterian Church, Philadelphia. Then settled in Maine. Member of the Provincial Congress.   Alan Heimert, Religion and the American Mind (Cambridge Mass 1966) 560

MURRAY, Philip 1886-1952
Labour leader to New Glasgow Scotland; of Irish Catholic parents. Emigrated to Pennsylvania 1902. Joined United Mine Workers. By 1920 vice-president. Largely responsible for massive union recruiting drives among coal and steel workers in 1930s. President of Committee for Industrial Organisation 1940. Active in National Association for Advancement of Coloured People. Strongly anti-communist.   DAmB

MURRAY, Robert 1835-74
b Glasgow; ed Glasgow University. Studied law 1856-7. Drowned in Passaic River, New Jersey.   Addison

MUTER, Robert
(Glasgow-Duke Street) DD from USA. Died 1842.   Fasti

NAISMITH, Christopher
Presbyterian minister: ed Glasgow University. Served in Liverpool, Helensburgh and in Boston 1870-7. Later minister of Free Church in Arbroath.   Addison

NAPIER, Thomas Macready
b 1872 Uddingston, ed in Philadelphia Schools. Glasgow University 1909-11. Served as assistant Minister in several charges before accepting St Mark's Glasgow in 1925.   Lamb

NASMITH, David 1799-1839   Ch 1
b Glasgow. Originated City Mission Movement. Toured USA and Canada visiting numerous towns and cities to spread his ideas.   Chambers Eminent Scotsmen

NATION, Carry Amelia Moore 1846-1911   Chs 3, 4
Temperance reformer: b Kentucky. After an unhappy childhood and marriage she enthusiastically took up temperance reform in Kansas. She began to take direct action,

smashing up bars to force compliance with state laws. Became a national figure. Lectured in
Glasgow.   NAW

NEILSON, Peter 1795–1861   Ch 1
Textile Entrepreneur. Spent many years in USA on business. Established mills in the south and
elsewhere for his father. Wrote his Six Years in America (Glasgow 1830).   Shepperson

NETTLETON, Asahel 1783–1844
Congregational Minister: b Connecticut; ed Yale. Never held a pastorate, never married and
never asked for remuneration. Very successful preacher. Health broke 1820. Opposed W G
Finney's sensationalist methods 1831–2. Founded college which subsequently became
Hartford Theological, 1834. In Glasgow 1830s.   DAmB: Carwardine

NEWLANDS, James B
(Campbell Street Glasgow) 1824 UP Class; abandoned course for medicine in Crieff, Forfar,
then to USA.   MacKelvie

NEWLANDS, John
Glasgow (Perth 1823–61). DD from Lafayette College Pennsylvania 1848.   Small

NEWLANDS, R W
(Eglinton Street Glasgow) BD Chicago. Ordained 1892. Held charge 1906–12.   CUYB 1909, 13

NICHOL, John, 1833–94   Chs 1, 3
Professor of English Literature Glasgow University: b Montrose, son of JP Nichol; ed
Glasgow and Oxford Universities. Founded Old Mortality Club which included T H Green.
Became Professor 1862. Wrote plays, poems and regularly contributed to the Glasgow Herald
and Guardian. Wrote the first academic history of American literature.   DNB

NICHOL, John Pringle 1804–59   Chs 1, 3
Astronomer: b near Brechin, ed Aberdeen. Became Professor of Astronomy, Glasgow
University, 1836. Friend of John Stuart Mill and Nassau Senior. In USA 1848–9. His second
wife,Elizabeth Pease of Darlington; Quaker family. A prolific writer on astronomy. Died at
Glenburn, Rothesay.   DNB

NICHOLS, Mary Gove 1810–84   Ch 3
Reformer: b New Hampshire. After an unhappy marriage she became an enthusiastic health
reformer. Lectured on anatomy to women in public, probably the first to do so. Involved in
health, temperance, dress reforms as well as spiritualism. Married T L Nichols 1848 (qv). Like
her husband became a Roman Catholic but still retained her spiritualist interests. Wrote several
novels including her autobiographical Mary Lyndon. Settled in Britain.   DAmB

NICHOLS, Thomas Low 1815–1901
Reformer: b New Hampshire. At Dartmouth but left before completing his medical course.
Deeply influenced by Sylvester Graham (qv). Became a newspaper editor in Lowell, New York
and then Buffalo. Associated with health reformers, the hydropathy, 'water cure' movement.
Married Mary S Neal Gove 1848 (qv). Qualified as a doctor New York University. Wrote
frequently for health journals, Esoteric Anthropology (1853) and, with his wife, Marriage
(1854). Moved to Ohio 1855. Became Roman Catholic. Removed to London 1861. Ran
hydropathic institution at Malvern 1867–75; a vegetarian centre in London. Strong
associations with Glasgow.   DAmB

NICHOLSON, David 1814–80   Ch 1
St Louis Department Store Operator: b Fowlis Wester. Worked in Glasgow and Oban.
Emigrated via Canada to USA to St Louis 1835. Began own business 1843. Soon had a massive
quality store of some five storeys.   St Louis Public Library

NICOL, George
Carpenter. Emigrated from Glasgow to Chicago then to Colorado.
        H Rider Haggard, Report on the Salvation Army Colonies in the United States and
                                                   Great Britain, CD 2562 (1905) p 42

NIXON, William, 1803–1900
Minister of the Free Church: b Camlachie; ed Glasgow University. Minister in Hexham 1831,
Montrose 1833–43. Joined Free Church. Minister Free St John's Montrose 1843–1900
Moderator of the FC General Assembly 1868. DD from an American college.   Addison

OGILVIE, James
Teacher: b Aberdeen. Emigrated at 19 to Virginia. Opened academy. Promoted elocution and
rhetoric. Had claim to title of Earl of Findlater. Failed, committed suicide. Died 1820.
                                                                                    DAmB

OGILIVIE, James
b Forfar; at Glasgow University 1826; merchant in New York; died in Dundee.   Addison

O'DONNELL, J J
Journalist; reporter on the Brooklyn Standard; travelled extensively in Scotland and Ireland
promoting emigration 1880. Prominent in Irish Land League in USA.
                                                          Minnesota Historical Society MSS

OLIPHANT, Laurence, 1829–88   Ch 1
Author, traveller and commune dweller: b Cape Town, South Africa. Travelled extensively in
Ceylon, Europe, Russia, North America. Secretary to Lord Elgin in Canadian treaty
negotiations with USA. In Circassia 1855, USA. 1856, China 1857–9, Italy 1860, Poland 1863,
MP Stirling Burghs 1865–7. Fell under the influence of Thomas Lake Harris and joined his
American community. In Paris as Times correspondent during the Commune. Returned to
Harris's community 1873. Began scheme for the colonisation of the Jews in Palestine. Fell out
with Harris. Married Rosamund Dale Owen, Robert Owen's daughter, 1888.   DNB

OLIVER, James 1823–1908
Inventor, manufacturer: b Roxburghshire. Emigrated 1835. Settled in New York then Indiana.
Began foundry business in South Bend Ind, specialised in innovative ploughs. Factory covered
62 acres and employed 2000.   DAmB

O'NEILL, Arthur 1814–96   Ch 3
b Chelmsford, entered Glasgow University 1835 to study medicine, converted to the ministry
and Chartism. Became a Baptist minister in Birmingham. Imprisoned for his Chartist
activities. Active in temperance, popular education, the abolition of slavery, capital punishment and war. Associated with Elihu Burritt.
                                             Herald of Peace. 1 January, 1 September 1896

ORD, George 1781–1866   Ch 2
Naturalist and Philogist. Philadelphian friend of Alexander Wilson. Went with him and
William Maclure to South in 1818. Close friend of Charles Waterton (qv).   DAmB

ORMISTON, William 1821–99
b Scotland. Minister in New York 1869–90. Returned to California.
                John T McNeill History of Presbyterianism in Canada (Toronto 1925) 33

ORR, Hugh, 1715–98
b and ed Lochwinnoch. Emigrated 1740. Built first trip hammer in colonies. Produced guns
and cannon for patriots in the Revolutionary war. With Robert and Alexander Barr introduced
carding and spinning machinery for textile industry. Aided by another Scot, Maclure built new
fly shuttle machine.   DAmB

ORR, James 1844–1913   Ch 5
Presbyterian clergyman: b Glasgow, ed Glasgow University. Became Professor of Church
History UP College 1891 and then Professor of Apologetics and Systematic Theology in the
Glasgow College 1900. Visited USA on several occasions 1895, 1897, 1905. Contributed to The
Fundamentals, 1909.
                                                                Lamb: Glasgow 1909

ORR, John S   Ch 5
b 1802 Demerara of Scottish father from Campbeltown, Argyll and a mother of Scottish

ancestry. In Greenock 1805–28. In London where he attended Edward Irving's Church. In America in 1850s. Prominent in American nativist disturbances and attacks upon Catholic churches 1854. In Greenock precipitated riots.

Temperance Journal 30 Septembr 1854 and 15 July 1855

OWEN, David Dale 1807–60
Geologist: b Braxfield House near New Lanark; ed London University; qualified as doctor. Emigrated 1827. Became state geologist of several states. DAmB

OWEN, Robert Dale 1800–77 Chs 1, 2, 3
b Glasgow, ed at Hofwyl, Switzerland. Emigrated to New Harvey 1825. Founder and editor of Free Inquirer 1828–32; Indiana State representative 1835–8. Representative Congress-Democrat 1843–7. Served as resident minister to Kingdom of Two Suites 1853–8.

R W Leopold, R D Owen (Cambridge Mass 1940): Congress

PAGE, Walter Hines 1855–1918 Ch 5
Journalist and diplomat: ed Johns Hopkins 1876–8. Returned to the South a reformer. 1898 became editor of the Atlantic Monthly, friend of Woodrow Wilson. Became ambassador in Great Britain 1913. Strongly pro-British in the First World War. DAmB

PAINE, Robert Treat 1835–1910 Ch 5
Philanthropist: ed Harvard. Spent two years in Europe before taking up law. Began cheap workman's housing in Boston area 1870, saving and loans, and educational centre. Active in charity, prison and peace movements. Episcopalian friend of Phillips Brooks. DAmB

PANTON, William, 1742–1801
Indian trader: b Aberdeenshire. Emigrated to S Carolina. Loyalist. Built successful farm in Spanish possessions of N America. DAmB

PARKHURST, Charles Henry 1842–1933
Presbyterian clergyman: b Mass; ed Amherst. In Europe 1869, 1870, 1872–3. Called to Madison Square Presbyterian Church 1880. Reformer. His sensational exposure in sermons of city vice gave rise to Lexow Investigation 1894. Retired 1918. DAmB

PARKMAN, Francis 1823–93 Ch 2
Historian: b Boston. Taught by William Russell (qv); ed Harvard. Wrote a series of major histories 1849–92 particularly concerned with Anglo-French rivalry in N America in the 17th and 18th centuries. DAmB

PARSELL, John 1820–85
b Glasgow, ed Glasgow University. Associated with various theatres as actor, player, manager. Went to the USA with Wyndham's Theatre, 1873. Manager Union Square Theatre, New York 1873–85. Addison

PARSONS, Frank 1854–1908 Chs 5, 6
Political scientist: b New Jersey; ed Cornell University, Civil Engineer; qualified as a lawyer 1887. Ran for mayor of Boston 1895 supported by socialists, prohibitionists and populists. Taught at Manhattan College, Kansas 1897. Involved in Boston settlement work. Enthusiastic admirer of Glasgow which he visited. DAmB

PARSONS, Lucy née Gonzalez
Wife of the Haymarket 'Martyr' Albert Parsons, executed in 1887. Lectured in Scotland in 1888. P Avrich, V De Cleyre (Princeton 1978)

PARTON, John
Businessman; b Morayshire, emigrated to Duluth 1886 and established the Glass Block department store, later partner with William White, a Scot from 1892. Macrae

PATERSON, Mary M
H M Inspector of Factories. One of the first women inspectors from 1893. Previously went on tour of USA with uncle, Dr Henry Muirhead. Became interested in social work especially industrial questions affecting girls. Glasgow 1909

PATERSON, William
(Wallacetown, Ayr) (Banff-Secession 1826–29). Emigrated to America 1829.   Small

PATILLO, Henry 1726–1801
Presbyterian clergyman: b Scotland. Emigrated to Virginia at 9. ed under Revd Samuel Davies.
Delegate to 1775 provincial congress of N Carolina.   DAmB

PATON, Isaac
(Ireland) 1743 Class. Emigrated to America.   MacKelvie

PATON, John Brown 1830–1911   Ch 5
Clergyman and philanthropist: b Ayrshire. First principal Congregational Institute
Nottingham, 1863–98; DD Glasgow 1882. Associated with the beginnings of Nottingham
University, the foundation of the National Home Reading Union 1889, the Bible Reading and
Prayer Union 1889, the English Land Colonisation Society 1892, with Herbert Baxter Adams
and Revd David Watson (qv). Editor and writer on reform matters.   DNB

PATRICK, William
Native of Kilsyth. Emigrated to Merigomish, Nova Scotia 1815. Died 1844.   MacKelvie: Small

PATTERSON, James Kennedy 1823–1922
Educator: b Glasgow. Emigrated 1842 to Indiana Became principal of several academies and
eventually president of the Agricultural and Mechanical College of Kentucky 1869. Visited
Scotland 1875. Won state financial support to build up his sturdy institution.   DAmB

PATTESON, Edward 1830–73
Free Church Minister. Licensed by Salem, Presbytery USA. Came to Scotland 1845.   Ewing

PATTISON, Granville Sharp 1791–1851
Anatomist: ed Glasgow University. Professor in the Andersonian Institution. Emigrated 1819
to Pennyslvania. Professor in University of Maryland, 1820–26. Returned to London
University 1831. Returned to America same year. Built up Jefferson Medical College,
Philadelphia and New York City University. Edited for several years medical journals.
Renowned as a teacher. Promoted grand opera in New York City.
                                        DAmB. T Kelly Birkbeck (1957) pp 282–83

PAXTON, Thomas
Hotelier: b Cupar, Fife 1860. Manager of City Improvement Trust Lodging House Gorbals
1886 after serving as police detective. Reputation built up. Lord Rowton, General Booth and
others discussed schemes with him. 1895 founded three model lodgings of his own. Associated
with Lawrence Veiller, Secretary of the Tenement House Committee; Charity Organisation
Society; Town Councillor 1905 onwards; exhibited housing plans at New York. Health
Exhibition, 1900.   Glasgow 1909

PEABODY, Elizabeth 1804–94   Ch 2
Educator: b Massachusetts. Began a school in 1820. Associated with W E Channing (qv) for
almost a decade as amanuensis. Wrote Record of a School (1935) on her experiences.
Established first American kindergarten 1860. Member of Alcott's Concord School 1879–84.
                                                                                    DAmB

PEARCE, C W and Bella   Ch 1
Radical figures involved in Spiritualism and social reform around 1900. Played host to Thomas
Lake Harris and his wife.   T L Harris Papers

PEDDIE, Thomas Baldwin 1808–1889
b Edinburgh. Emigrated to Newark NJ 1833. Luggage Manufacturer. State assemblyman
1864–5. Mayor of Newart 1866–9 Representative-Republican 1877–9. Vice-president Essex
County National Bank.   Congress

PEDDIE, William
(Edinburgh-Bristo Street): b Perth. DD Jefferson College, Pennsylvania 1843.   Small

PEDEN, Robert
U Secession minister: b Kilmaurs; ed Glasgow University. Emigrated to USA. Preacher and
edited a periodical.   Addison

PHELAN, James D 1861−1930
Reform. Mayor of S Francisco and ed San Francisco. Successful banker. Elected mayor, eliminated considerable civic graft, built parks and playgrounds. In Glasgow 1901. Later visited Europe 1913. Opposed oriental immigration. Art collector and poet.   DAmB

PHILLIPS, William Addison 1824−93
b Paisley. Emigrated 1838 with parents to Randolph County, Illinois. Radical abolitionist. Newspaper correspondent 1845−62. Lawyer 1855 in Kansas. Founded city of Salina, Kansas 1858. Commander of Cherokee Indian Regiment in Civil War Representative-Republican 1873−9. President of Kansas Historical Society. Elected to Congress 1872, 1874, 1876.
Congress

PHYFE, Duncan 1768−1854
Cabinet Maker: b Loch Fannich. Emigrated to Albany, NY 1783/4. Built up successful business in New York. Strict Calvinist renowned for his craftsmanship.   DAmB

PILLANS, James 1778−1864   Ch 2
Educator: ed Edinburgh University. Rector of Edinburgh High School 1810−20, then professor at Edinburgh University 1820−63. Wrote extensively on educational matters. Contributed to the Edinburgh Review.   DNB

PILLSBURY, Parker 1809−98
Reformer: b Mass, ed Andover and entered the Congregational ministry. From 1840 became a full time reformer with interests in abolitionism, temperance, woman suffrage and peace. Joint editor with Elizabeth Cady Stanton (qv) of Revolution 1868−9.   DAmB

PINGREE, Hazen 1840−1901   Ch 5
Manufacturer, referring mayor of Detroit: b Maine. Served in the Civil War. Won mayoralty election as a Republican on reform ticket. Civic improvements in street lighting, railways etc. Travelled extensively in Africa and Europe. Died in England.   DAmB

PINKERTON, Allan 1819−84   Ch 1
Glasgow son of a policeman; powerloom dresser and physical force Chartist; founder Glasgow Democratic Club, and O'Connorite club; Rockford Illinois; Chicago in 1842; began detective agency. Author, The Molly Maguires and the Detectives 1877.
S A Lavine and J D Horan (1965): H Swiggett (1952)

PITCAIRN, John 1722−75
British Officer: b Dysart, Scotland. Served in Boston during Revolutionary disturbances. Killed at Bunker Hill.   DAmB

PITCAIRN, John 1841−1916
Manufacturer: b Johnstone, Renfrew, Scotland. Emigrated 1850 to Pennsylvania. Railway executive. Turned to civil interests 1883. One of the organisers of the Pittsburgh Plate Glass Company. Staunch Swedenborgian.   DAmB

POE, Edgar Allan 1809−49
Author: b Boston. Left an orphan. Fostered by Scottish Virginia merchant, Joseph Allan 1780−1834; related to John Galt. Brought to Irvine, Scotland. 1815−16. Returned to America with guardian: ed University of Virginia. Began his writing career.   DAmB

POLLOCK, Robert 1795−1879
Minister: b Neilston, ed Glasgow University, LL D University of Philadelphia 1868. Utd Ass Church Buckhaven 1826−45 and Kingston, Glasgow 1846−79.   Addison

POLLOCK, Thomas 1654−1722
Colonial Governor of N Carolina, 1712−14, 1722: b Glasgow. In Carolina 1683. Served as member of the General Court and of the Governors' Council.
Biographical Directory of American Colonial and Revolutionary Governors 1607−1789

PORTER, Robert Percival 1852−1917   Ch 5
Journalist: b Norwich, England. Emigrated to USA. Worked in Chicago. Director of the Eleventh US Census 1890−4. A protectionist. Vigorously opposed to municipal ownership. Invariably in conflict with Robert Donald (qv). Also wrote on Japan.
Who Was Who in America 1897−1942

PORTEOUS, James Moir 1822–91
Free Church Minister. Served in Wanlockhead and Edinburgh. DD from USA.   Ewing

POST, Louis 1849–1928   Ch 5
Reformer, newspaper editor, government official; b New Jersey. Member of Howard Cusby's New York Church; abandoned that and eventually became Swedenborgian. Worked in S Carolina during Reconstruction. Lawyer. Editor Chicago Public with support of Tom L Johnson and J Fels. Appointed to Chicago schoolboard by E F Dunne. Visited Scotland 1908 and 1910. Asst Secretary of Labour under Woodrow Wilson.   DAmB

POTTS, James Faulkner   Ch 1, 4
Minister of Glasgow New Church, Swedenborgian. Spent several months on exchange in USA. 1877.   See his Letters From America (1880)

PRIESTLY, Joseph 1733–1804   Ch 1
b Yorkshire. Became renowned Unitarian clergyman; wrote on Scottish philosophy; won a reputation as a scientist; associated with Whig and radical political movements to such an extent his house was destroyed by a Birmingham mob in 1791. He emigrated to Pennsylvania in 1794 and died there.   DNB

PRIMROSE, Archibald Philip, 5th Earl Rosebery 1847–1929
Statesman and author: ed Oxford. Distinguished political career. Prime Minister 1894. Successful race horse owner. Visited USA 1873.   DNB

PRINGLE, Francis
(Ireland) Class of 1767. Emigrated to America 1772. Settled in Pennsylvania 1799.   MacKelvie

PRINGLE, William
(Perth-N) Associate Presbytery Class of 1818. Emigrated to America as probabioner.
                                                                                 MacKelvie

PROUDFOOT, James
1748 Class. Associate Presbytery 1754 missionary to America.   MacKelvie

PROUDFOOT, James
b 1812. Glasgow grain dealer; friend of O'Conner, president of the Chartist Universal Suffrage Assoc; helped from Glasgow Charter Association 1842; left for Boston 1844.   Boston

RAE, John
b Lanarkshire; evangelical preacher and miner; emigrated to West Virginia; master workman in Knights of Labour. President of United Mineworkers of America.   Yearley

REDFORD, George 1785–1860
Congregational minister: b London, ed Glasgow University. DD Amherst. At Uxbridge 1812–26 and Worcester 1826–52. President of the Congregational Union of England and Wales 1834.   Addison

REGAN, John   Ch 1
Ayrshire teacher emigrated to Illinois; wrote The Emigrants Guide To the Western States of America (1852).   Emigrants Guide

REID Hugo   Ch 2
Entrepreneur, early Scottish settler in California: b Cardross, Dumbarton. Developed thriving trading post and lands. Defender of Indians.
                                Susan Bryant Dakin, A Scotch Paisano Berkeley 1978

REID, Robert 1816–1908   Ch 4
First Secretary Scottish Temperance Union. Emigrated to USA 1864. Returned 1871. Established Vegetarian Restaurant in London 1880.   Temperance League Journal 8 Feb 1908

REITH, Revd George   Ch 4
Minister UF Church: b Aberdeen 1842. Widely travelled in USA   Glasgow 1909

REITH, Sir John 1889–1971   Ch 5
b Glasgow. Public man, army officer, in Washington DC during World War I. Presiding genius over the founding of the BBC. Rector Glasgow University.   DNB

REMOND, Revd Charles Lenox 1810−73   Ch 1
Black American preacher who visited Glasgow in the campaign against slavery and the
American Colonisation Society.   DAmB

REMOND, Sarah Parker c1826−87   Ch 1
Anti-slavery lecturer and physician: b. Salem, Mass of freed parents. Her brother became well
known as a lecturer in Britain. In 1859 travelled to Britain to lecture with Revd Samuel Jay
May. In Scotland. Attended London University 1859−61. After the Civil War lectured on
behalf of the Freedman's Aid Association of London. Studied medicine in Italy.   DAmB

RENTOUL, Lawrence
(Perth-N) Associate, Presbytery. Emigrated to USA as probationer. Class 1812.   MacKelvie

RESTON, John
(Greenhead) 1808−9 deposed: emigrated to USA.   MacKelvie

RICHARDSON, Sir Benjamin Ward 1828−96   Ch 4
Physician and sanitary reformer: ed Glasgow and St Andrews. FRS 1867. Promoted health
reform, total abstinence and healthy recreation like bicycling and soccer.   DNB

RICHMOND, May Ellen 1861−1928   Ch 5
Pioneer social worker: b Belleville, Illinois. Lost both parents by age of 7. Took up social work
with Baltimore Charity Organisation 1888; became its treasurer 1889, general secretary 1891.
Drawn into contact with D C Gilman, Amos G Warner. 1900 moved to Philadelphia as COS
Secretary. 1909 Director Charity Organisation Dept Russell Sage Foundation. Editor 1905−9
Charities and the Commons. Visited Glasgow.
                              M E Richmond, The Long View: DAmB: NAW

RITCHIE, John c1781−1861
(Edinburgh, Hope Park) DD Rutgers 1829.   Small

ROBERTSON, Agnes Kelly 1833−1916
Actress and wife of Don Boucicault, playwright: b Edinburgh. Went on the Scottish stage at an
early age. Emigrated 1853 and won an American reputation 1853−60. Returned to USA in
1872−3. Divorced her husband.   NAW

RODGER, Robert
Lord Provost 1707−8, 1711−12. Merchant in the American Colonial Trade   POG

RODGERS, Moses
b Down, Ireland; Matriculated Glasgow University 1818. Trained for the Irish Presbyterian
ministry but never licensed. Emigrated to America and died there in the 1860s.   Addison

ROGER, John
1765 Class. Missionary in Pennsylvania 1770.   MacKelvie

ROGERS, Henry Darwin 1808−66
b Philadelphia. Professor of Natural History Glasgow University 1857−66. Former Professor
in Dickinson College and University of Pennsylvania.   Addison: Glasgow Graduates

ROWE, Leo Stanton 1871−1946   Ch 5
Political Scientist and Diplomat. German parents; ed University of Pennsylvania. Studied in
Germany 1892. Instructor in Municipal Government, University of Pennsylvania 1895.
Published Problems of City Government (1908). President of the American Academy of
Political and Social Sciences 1902−30. Became an expert of S America.   DAmB

ROY, Andrew
Scottish miner; Ohio state mines inspector; inspired first state safety law.   Berthoff

ROY, David
b Muthill; ed Glasgow University, studied for the ministry and emigrated as a probationer to
America. Settled in Nova Scotia.   Addison

RUSH, Benjamin
Doctor and educator. Admirer of Scottish Education at all levels. Held John Maclean in high
regard. Prominent in improving American medicine.   DAmB

RUSSELL, Bertrand Arthur William, 3rd Earl Russell 1872–1970
Philosopher and social reformer: ed Cambridge University. Paid first of many visits to USA 1896. In World War I he was forbidden to address Glasgow meeting chaired by Sir Daniel M Stevenson but speech read by labour leader, W Smillie. Later imprisoned for his pacifist stance. Renowned for his philosophical work, social comment and pacifism.   DNB

RUSSELL, Charles Edward 1860–1941   Ch 5
Journalist, author, reformer and socialist: b Davenport, Iowa. A newspaper man he became a regular contributor to the muckraking journals, Everybody's, Hamptons and Cosmopolitan. Wrote 27 books. Joined the American Socialist Party 1908. Unsuccessful candidate in serveral elections 1910–14. Broke with the party in World War I. On US government mission to Russia 1917. A founder member of the National Association for the Advancement of Coloured People 1909. His articles gave rise to practical prison and housing reforms.   DAmB

RUSSELL, James
(Dunblane) Associate Presbytery Class of 1816. Emigrated to America as probationer.
                                                                                    MacKelvie

RUSSELL, John
(Milnathort) Associate Presbytery. Class of 1818. Emigrated to America as probationer.
                                                                                    MacKelvie

RUSSELL, William 1798–1873
Educator: b Glasgow, ed Glasgow University. Emigrated to Georgia 1817 where he conducted a private academy connected with Chatham Academy; moved to New Haven 1822; Boston 1825; editor American Journal of Education 1826; joined A Bronson Alcott (qv supra) 1830 near Philadelphia; in Boston 1838, conducted school of speech with J E Murdoch (qv). Associated with Andover, Phillips Academy, Abbot Academy and Harvard for elocution. Pre-eminent in promoting the professionalisation of teaching new techniques and better schools.
                                                                                    DAmB

RUTHERFORD, Robert 1728–1803
b Scotland, ed Royal College, Edinburgh. Emigrated to Tennessee, then Virginia State Senator 1776–90. Representative Congress 1793–97   Congress

ST CLAIR, Andrew 1734–1818
b Thurso, Caithness. Studied at Edinburgh University and medicine under Dr John Hunter, Army Officer. Settled in Virginia 1764. Served with patriots in Revolutionary wars. Congress 1785–87. One of the founders of the iron industry in Pittsburgh. Gov of NW Territory 1789–1802.   Congress

SADLER, Herbert Charles 1872–1948
b London, ed Glasgow University, BSc 1893. Spent three years in shipbuilding. Assistant Professor of Naval Architecture, Glasgow University 1896–1900. Professor at Michigan University 1900–28. Dean of College of Engineering 1928–37. Married to R M Wenley's daughter. Retired 1940.   Roll of Glasgow Graduates: University of Michigan

SALMOND, Charles Adamson
b Arbroath 1853; ed Edinburgh University. DD Princeton 1902.   Lamb

SANDEMAN, David T
b Dundee 1838. Newspaperman. Retired from Glasgow Herald 1907. Toured extensively in USA   Glasgow 1909

SANGER, Margaret 1879–1966   Chs 1, 3
Birth control advocate: b New York state, of Catholic family. Trained as a nurse. Married William Sanger an architect. A member of the IWW union. Associated with Emma Goldman and other radical feminists. Contributor to the socialist Call. Prosecuted for disseminating contraceptive information through the mails. Her second husband oil millionaire though she enjoyed an open marriage. Visited Glasgow on several occasions.   NAW

SANKEY, Ira D 1840–1908   Chs 1, 4
Singing evangelist. From his Sunday school he developed his choir and YMCA associations
with Dwight L Moody (qv). They were in Scotland together on an evangelising campaign
1873–5. Published his Sacred Songs and Solo 1873. His gospel Hymns became popular
throughout the world.   DAmB

SAWYER, Thomas Jefferson
American Universalist leader in correspondence with the Glasgow Congregation in the 1830s.
                                                                          R E Miller

SCHAW, William
(Ayr-Darlington Place) DD Jefferson College, Pennsylvania 1837. Died 1847.   Small

SCOTT, Ernest Findlay 1868–1954
b Co Durham, ed Glasgow University, Oxford; Professor of Church History: 1908 New
Testament: 1910 in Queen's University, Kingston, Canada. Professor of New Testament
Union Theological NY 1919.   Lamb

SCOTT, Gustavus 1753–1800
b Virginia; studied at Aberdeen University with mother and at Middle Temple, London
1765–71. Member of Continental Congress 1784–5. A Commissioner to superintend the
erection of public buildings in Washington DC 1794–1800.   Congress

SCOTT, James
(Inverness-Pitcumgreen) DD Monmouth College Illinois 1871.   Fasti

SCOTT, Joseph
(Lochgelly 1824–33). Emigrated to America. Died 1857.   Small

SCOTT, William
Banker and entrepreneur: ed Robert Gordon's Aberdeen; accountant in the Aberdeen Fire and
Life Insurance Co; became accountant of Illinois Investment Co in America; numerous
successful investments enabled him to retire about 1858 from New York to Aberdeen. His
estate was estimated at £250,000 at his death in 1872.   Smith

SCOULAR, William 1814–72
b Kilbarchan. Edited Lowell Courier 1841–7 and wrote a history of Massachusetts and the
Civil War.   Black

SCUDDER, Vida Dutton 1861–1954   Ch 5
Christian Socialist, writer, professor. One of first two American women to study at Oxford.
Settlement house worker.   DAmB

SENIOR, Richard
Merchant's son: b Glasgow ed Glasgow University. Died New York 1854.   Addison

SHAW, Albert 1857–1947   Ch 5
Journalist and reformer: b Ohio, ed Grinnell College, Iowa, and Johns Hopkins. Began
serious studies of European city government 1888. Wrote Municipal Government in Great
Britain and Municipal Government in Continental Europe 1895. Member of the Southern
Education Board, supported black disfranchisement, editor of the American Review of
Reviews. A millionaire. Several times in Glasgow the last time on 3 September 1939.   DAmB

SHAW, Anna Howard 1847–1912   Chs 1, 3, 5
Minister, lecturer and suffragist. b Newcastle-on-Tyne, England of Scots ancestry. Emigrated
1857. Eventually settled in Michigan frontier: ed Albion College and Boston University. She
began to preach in Methodist Churches 1870. Later MD 1886. Became a lecturer for the
Women Suffrage Movement. Became a Vice-president National American Suffrage Ass, then
president 1904.   NAW: DAmB

SHAW, James
Surgeon: b near Kilmarnock; ed Glasgow University, LFPSG 1846. Served on the Allan Line
for many years. Died aged 78 1892.   Addison

SHAW, Joesph
(Alyth) Associate Presbytery, Missionary to USA Philadelphia. Became Professor of Languages, Albany College, Died 1825 Philadelphia.   MacKelvie

SHEARER, Sir John 1843–1908
Dry Dock Company. Town Councillor 1883–1903. Widely travelled in USA   Glasgow 1909

SHELDON, Charles Monroe 1857–1946   Chs 1, 4, 5
Clergyman and best selling author: b New York State, ed Boston University and Andover. Congregational minister in Topeka Kansas 1889–1919. Wrote the successful In His Steps (1897). Toured Britain in support of prohibition cause, 1900 and 1917–18. Visited Glasgow.
                                                                                                                              DAmB

SHINWELL, Rt Hon Emanuel   Ch 4
b 1884 London, Glasgow Councillor, MP 1922–24, 1928–31 Linlithgow, 1935–50 Seaham, 1950–70 Easington. Cabinet Minister.   Stenton and Lees

SHIRLAW, Walter, 1838–1909
Artist: b Paisley. First President Society of American Artists.   Black

SHORTRED, John
UP Class 1771. Went to America as a probationer.   MacKelvie

SILLIMAN, Benjamin 1779–1864   Chs 1, 2
Chemistry and Natural History professor at Yale: b Connecticut, ed Yale. John Maclean greatly influenced him (qv). In Britain 1805 to secure scientific equipment. In Edinburgh and Glasgow. Yale Medical School established 1813 through his pressure. Editor, proprietor and founder of the American Journal of Science and Art 1818. Associated with Lowell Institute 1838. Again in Europe 1851. Deeply religious figure. Wrote A Journal of Travels in England, Holland and Scotland and of two passages over the Atlantic in years 1805 and 1806, 2 vols (New York 1910).   DAmB

SIMON, Michael, DL JP
b 1842 London. Fruit Importer. Town Councillor 1884. Travelled widely in USA also visited America as delegate on behalf of the Glasgow Exhibition 1900: business connection in Boston and Canada.   Glasgow 1909

SIMPSON, Sir George 1792–1860
b Ross. Emigrated via London to New York 1820. Then entered Hudson's Bay Co Service. Frequently in Britain. Knighted 1841. Traveller. Wrote Narrative of a Tour Round the World 1841–2, (1847).   DNB

SIMPSON, James
Minister: b Falkirk, ed Glasgow University. Minister at Kirkcaldy 1857–60, Dysart 1860–1900. LL D from USA.   Addison

SINCLAIR, John
b 1847. Free Church Minister: ed Edinburgh University and FC College. Ordained 1879 Bowden. 1890 went to 1st Presbyterian Church St Paul, Minnesota. DD (USA).   Ewing

SKINNER, John
Minister: b Auchtermuchty, ed Glasgow University. Secession Church Partick 1827–39. DD Washington College Pa 1846. Served in Lexington Virginia, Harmony and Easton NJ. Then went to Canada.   Addison

SLATER, Oscar   Ch 1
Centre of the famous Glasgow murder trial 1909. Convicted of murdering Miss Marion Gilchrist and released 18 years later. A German Jew, real name Oscar Leschzeiner. Came to Britain living with a Frenchwoman in New York. Glasgow and on the continent, they ran social clubs. Gambler, arrested in New York. Tried, found guilty and sentenced to death. Committed to life imprisonment. Slater eventually released in 1927 on a technicality. Incidentally, Miss Lambie, Gilchrist's maid, had married and removed to America and so could not be brought forward to help clear Slater.   Glasgow Herald Obituary 2 February 1948

SMART, William 1853–1915   Chs 3, 5
Professor: b Renfrewshire, ed Glasgow University. Engaged in manufacturing. Lecturer at
Dundee 1886–7, Queen Margaret College, Glasgow 1886–96, Glasgow University 1892–6 and
thereafter professor. Associated with Workmen's Dwelling Company. Served on Royal
Commission on Poor Laws and wrote several economic works.   Who Was Who

SMITH, Alexander 1813–61
Roman Catholic bishop; b Rathven, Banff, ed Aquhorties, Blairs and Rome. Consecrated
bishop 1847. In USA in 1848–9 seeking funds for the Irish immigrants into Scotland.
                          P F Anson The Catholic Church in Modern Scotland (London 1937)

SMITH, David c1793–1867
Minister: b Perthshire; DD from Dartmouth College 1850; ed Glasgow University. Secession
minister Biggar 1823–67. Moderator UP. Synod 1867.   Addison

SMITH, George Adam
b 1856 Calcutta, ed Edinburgh and Germany. 1892 Professor Free Church College Glasgow.
Three lecturing visits to USA. 1896 Johns Chicago: 1899 Yale and Chicago. 1903 social
unionist.   Glasgow 1909

SMITH, George 1808–99
Banker: b Old Deer, Aberdeen ed Marischal College, Aberdeen 1823–25; after unsuccessful
efforts in medicine and farming emigrated to America in 1833. With a relative, William Smith
made successful speculative investments in Chicago and Wisconsin lands. Returned to
Scotland 1836. With Alexander Anderson, a cousin in Aberdeen (qv), established an American
investment company and on return effectively established the Wisconsin Marine and Fire
Insurance Company as a Bank in the face of legal restrictions. His enormously successful
banking, railway and land investments allowed him to retire finally to London in 1861, where
he passed the rest of his life as a multimillionaire resident of a London club. His estate was
estimated at $52 millions at his death.   Smith

SMITH, Hoke 1855–1931
Secretary of the Interior, Gov of Georgia, US Senator: b N Carolina. Lawyer and newspaper
editor. He entered politics eventually becoming Governor in 1907–9, 1911, US Senate
1911–21. Involved in inspiring rural life.   DAmB

SMITH, Revd James 'Shepherd' 1801–57   Ch 2
Preacher and social reformer: ed Glasgow University. Influenced by various millenarian
figures developed his own utopian views. Became closely associated with the Owenite
movement.   DNB

SMITH, James
(Glasgow) Erskine. Emigrated to USA 1839, Washington, Pennsylvania, Returned. Died 1845.
                                                                            MacKelvie

SMITH, James McCune 1813–65   Ch 4
Black physician and writer: b New York, ed Glasgow University in arts and medicine. 1832–7,
Paris and then practised medicine in New York, allegedly with first pharmacy in USA operated
by a black. Active in abolitionism.   DAmB

SMITH, John
1767 Class. Sent as missionary to America 1770.   MacKelvie

SMITH, Madeline   Ch 1
Perhaps the most famous or notorious accused in a Victorian murder trial. Charged with
murdering her lover, acquitted by the Scottish 'not proven' verdict. Later married George
Wardle 1861. He later worked as a manager for William Morris. In London they were drawn
into the literary and artistic world of George Bernard Shaw, Rossetti and Henry James as well
as socialist circles. Parted from her husband who went to Italy 1889. He died 1910. She
emigrated to America c1890 according to her death certificate. Married a Mr Sheehy. She died
1926.   Newspaper clippings in the Mitchell Library Glasgow

SMITH, Nathan 1762–1829
5th medical graduate of Harvard, further medical education at Glasgow, Edinburgh, London
1796–7. Started Bowdoin Medical School; 1821 began developing Yale Medical School.
DAmB: Jeanette Mirsky and Allan Nevins,
The World of Eli Whitney (New York 1952) p 294

SMITH, Robert 1722–77
Colonial architect and builder: b Glasgow. Emigrated to Philadelphia. Built Naussau Hall,
Princeton University, which served as a model for smiliar buildings in other universities. Built
several churches as well as dwelling houses. Prominent in the colonial movement against the
British. Member of the American Philosophical Society.   DAmB

SMITH, Robert
Presbyterian minister: b Kilmaurs, ed Glasgow University. Minister 1815–43 Church of
Scotland. Joined the Free Church 1843–65. DD from an American College 1845.   Addison

SMITH, Russell 1812–96
Painter: b Glasgow. His father a Glasgow doctor emigrated on account of political views, to
Pennsylvania 1819 and established cutlery business in Pittsburgh. Smith began painting
theatrical scenery and portraits in Europe 1851–2.   DAmB

SMITH, Thomas 1745–1809
b Cruden, Aberdeen, ed Edinburgh University. Emigrated to Pennsylvania 1769 lawyer.
Continental Congress 1780–82. Judge of Pennsylvania, Supreme Court.   Congress

SMITH, Thomas
(URR) Associate Presbytery Class of 1778. Missionary to America.   MacKelvie

SMITH, William 1727–1803
Educator, Clergyman. First Provost of the College, Academy and Charitable School of
Philadelphia. b Aberdeen, ed Aberdeen University. Emigrated 1751; active in education.
1762–4 collected funds for his college in Europe. Staunch patriot.   DAmB

SMITH, William c1754–1821
Episcopal clergyman: b, Aberdeen, ed (probably) Aberdeen. Emigrated to America. Active in
building up Episcopalianism in America. Opened grammar school in New York. Also
composed hymns and devotions.   DAmB

SMITH, William A   Chs 3, 4
Founder Boys Brigade. Spread his organisation in USA which he visited in 1907.
F P Gibbon, William Smith (Glasgow, 1934.)

SMITH, William Alexander   Ch 5
Glasgow businessman. Built first telephone in Scotland. Director of Natural Telephone Co.
Interests in motor manufacturers. Business connections with USA. Interviewed for Chicago
Tribune 1905 debate on municipal ownership.   Chicago Tribune

SOMERVILLE, Andrew
(Dunbarton-High Street 1830–47). DD Princeton 1845–55. Sympathised with working class
and Anti-Corn Law League. Died 1877.   Small

SOULE, Caroline Augusta 1824–1903   Chs 1, 4
Universalist missionary to Scotland: b Albany New York; wrote numerous popular novels,
articles and edited several journals. In Scotland as missionary 1875, 1878–82, 1886–92.
Retired, lived in Glasgow to her death.
A Seaburg in Transactions Unitarian. Historical Society 14, 1967, 28–41

SPEEDIE, William
(Abernethy). Gave up course 1828 UP class and emigrated to America.   MacKelvie

SPENCE, James
A Liverpool born writer on American affairs who lectured in Glasgow on behalf of the
Confederacy. Organiser of the Southern Independence Association with a Glasgow branch.
Brian Jenkin, Britain and the War for the Union 2 vols (Montreal 1974–80)

SPENCER, Marcus Acheson
b 1892 Pittsburgh Pa, ed Princeton University, Union Theological and Edinburgh University. Served in various New York and New Jersey churches. Later Washington DC and Ohio; to Scotland 1925. Shettleston-Sandyhills 1927.   Lamb

STALKER, Duncan
(Comrie 1807-30). Emigrated to Argyle, New York 1830.   MacKelvie

STANTON, Elizabeth Cady 1815-1902   Chs 1, 2, 3
Reformer, woman's rights activist: b Johnston, NY; strongly influenced by Scottish presbyterian minister. Attended 1840 World Anti-Slavery Convention. 1848 Woman's Rights Convention New York. President of the National Woman's Suffrage Association 1869-90 and its successor National American Woman's Suffrage Association. Produced the controversial Woman's Bible 1895-1898. Visited Glasgow. 1840 and 1882.   DAmB

STARK, Andrew
Minister: b Slammanan, ed Glasgow University. Minister at South Shields 1818-22 and Grand St New York 1822-49.   Addison: Fasti

STARK, James c1775-1850
(Dennyloanhead). Ordained 1797. DD Princeton.   MacKelvie: Small

STARR, Ellen Gates 1859-1940   Ch 3
Social reformer: b Laona, Illinois, ed Rockford. Visited Europe. Visited Toynbee House, London. Founder Hull House settlement. Active in reform efforts in Women's Trades Union League. Trained in bookbinding under Cobden-Sanderson. Became Roman Catholic 1930. Entered convent 1935.   DAmB

STEAD, F H 1857-1928   Ch 3
Social reformer and congregationalist minister: ed Manchester, Bradford and Glasgow University. Germany. Served in Leicester. Editor Independent and Nonconformist 1890-92, Assistant editor Review of Reviews 1894-1912. Prominent in the campaign for old age pension.   Glasgow Herald 16 January 1928

STEAD, William Thomas 1849-1912   Chs 3, 5
Journalist and author. Renowned as the editor of the Pall Mall Gazette 1883-90 for his exposés of Victorian society. Began Review of Reviews 1890. Visited America and wrote If Christ Came To Chicago (1894). Promoted civic reform. Spiritualist interests. Many Glasgow associations. Drowned on the Titanic.   DNB

STEARNS, John H 1829-95   Ch 4
President New York Temperance League and editor of the National Temperance Advocate. Visited Glasgow 1891.   League Journal 18 May 1895

STEVENS, Lillian Norton Ames 1844-1914
Temperance reformer: b Dover Me. Helped found Maine Women's Christian Temperance Union 1874. President of State WCTU 1878. Ardent suffragist and social reformer. President of national SCTU 1898. Visited Glasgow.   NAW

STEVENSON, Sir Daniel Macaulay 1857-1944   Chs 4, 5, 6
Chancellor of Glasgow University, 1934-44; Lord Provost of Glasgow 1911-14; extremely successful coal exporter, his grandfather edited The Liberator and Free Trade Advocate. His father a prominent social crusader. Early Fabian, became Liberal. He met Hitler, Mussolini and Hindenburg. Served on Glasgow Town Council 22 years. Advocate of local public libraries (Municipal Libraries, Glasgow 1894). Strong local patriotism and international brotherhood; peace advocate. Endowed chairs of Italian and Spanish, Glasgow University, as well as scholarships for Spanish, French and German studies; Stevenson Citizenship Fund £21,000, 1920; chairs at Liverpool and International Relations, London University; founded director-ship Chalham House; generous benefactor to drama, music and art, like the Franco-Scottish Society and the British Institute, Florence. His brothers, R Macaulay Stevenson, the artist, and John, manufacturer of ordnance in Pennsylvania. Failed in efforts to win a seat in Parliament 1922, Chairman Glasgow Workmens Dwelling Company.
          Times 12 July 1944: Glasgow Herald 12 July 1944: Who Was Who

STEVENSON, John 1848–1938
Entrepreneur: b Glasgow brother of Sir Daniel Macaulay Stevenson above. Studied chemistry in Glasgow University. Seven years apprenticeship as machinist. Emigrated 1872. Worked at Carnegie Steel Works, Pittsburgh. Became partner in a firm, Mackintosh, Hemphill & Co to 1878; moved to Newcastle Pa; partnership in iron firm taken over by US Steel. Established ordnance plant in 1905. Republican and Presbyterian.
J G White, A Twentieth Century History of Mercer County Pa (1909) v 2 573–4

STEWART, A, MD, LL D
(USA) Aberdeen EU Hall 1864   CUYB 1903–4

STEWART, Eliza Daniel 1816–1908   Ch 3, 4
Temperance reformer: b Piketon, Ohio. Active in Good Templars and Band of Hope. Organised first woman suffrage body in Springfield, Ohio 1866. Notable in Woman's Crusade against Whisky 1874. In Scotland 1876 and 1892. Later joined John Alexander Dowie (qv) Church.   NAW

STEWART, James
1758 Class, Missionary to Pennsylvania.   MacKelvie

STEWART, James 1775–1821
b Scotland. Emigrated to N Carolina. In business State assembly 1798–9. State Senate 1802–4, 1811–13. Representative 1818–19   Congress

STEWART, John Erskine
b 1895 (Edinburgh-N Richmond Street) b Bishopton, ed Glasgow University 1920. Union Theological New York 1924.   Lamb

STEWART, Sir William Drummond   Ch 1
Adventurer, patron and gentleman of Murthly Castle, Perthshire. Travelled extensively in the west. Took the artist Alfred Jacob Miller to paint the Indian civilisation.   M C Ross (1968)

STIRLING, John 1677–1736
Provost 1728–9. Merchant with brother Walter in American trade.   POG

STODDARD, A F
Carpet manufacturer: b Northampton Mass, 1810; worked as clerk for the Tappan brothers, the evangelical abolitionist businessmen; married their elder sister; associated with William Lloyd Garrison; established a carpet plant at Elderslie, Scotland; lived at Bloomfield, Port Glasgow; became a British Subject.   The Letters of W L Garrison, eds W M Merrill and Louis Ruchames, 6 vols (Cambridge Mass 1971–81) v 5 1861–67 515–6:
J Neville Bartlett, Carpeting the Millions:
The Growth of the British Carpeting Industry (Edinburgh 1978)

STRACHAN, Patrick Copland 1805–72
Banker: b Tillioch, Aberdeen, ed Marischal College Aberdeen. A farmer he was selected as manager of the Illinois Co in America 1836; became a director of numerous insurance and banking companies; leading figure in St Andrews Society New York. Retired about 1858 to London.   Smith

STRANG, Alexander
b 1870 East Kilbride, ed Beliot Academy, Wisconsin USA, Glasgow University. Shettleston-Sandyhills 1902.   Lamb

STRANG, John
b Kippen, ed Glasgow University; emigrated as a probationer to America. Matriculated 1816.
Addison

STRATON, Henry Douglas
b Bannockburn, ed Glasgow University and UP theological college. Killed in the American Civil War.   Addison

STRONG, Josiah 1847–1916   Ch 5
Clergyman, social reformer, author. Congregationalist minister. Wrote Our Country 1886,

best seller. Likewise the New Era 1893. Founded League for Social Service 1898, reorganised 1902 as American Institute for Social Service. To Britain 1904; organised British counterpart.
DAmB

STUART, John
(Pathhead-Kirkcaldy) 1757 Class; served for a time in USA.   MacKelvie

SWAIN, John
(Jedburgh) UP Class 1806; turned to medicine; emigrated to USA   MacKelvie

SWAN, John,
Associate Burgher Hall, Class of 1806 (Jedburgh-Blackfriars). Took up medicine and emigrated to America.   MacKelvie

SWANSON, W S 1861–1919   Ch 4
Minister U F Church; b Amoy, China; ed Thurso, George Watsons and Edinburgh University. Ordained 1888. Held several charges before being called to Paisley Road Glasgow 1900. Made visits to USA Temperance advocate.   Lamb

SYMINGTON, Andrew 1785–1853
b Paisley, ed Glasgow University. Minister Relief Presbyterian Church Paisley 1809–53. Professor of Divinity 1820–53. DD University of Western Pennsylvania 1831.   Addison

SYMINGTON, William 1824–79
At Glasgow Hamilton Street 1859. DD Washington College USA   Ewing

TAIT, James Selwin 1846–1917   Ch 1
Entrepreneur and speculator: b Scotland, promoter of various land cattle and colonisation schemes in the west and in Florida. Published The Cattlefields of the Far West (1884) and several novels. Also a publisher. Failed and died in obscurity.
    J Tebbel, A History of Book Publishing in the US 2 vols (New York 1972–75) v 2 377–79

TAPPAN, Arthur 1786–1865   Chs 1, 3
Merchant Reformer: b Northampton Mass. Entered dry goods business with great success. Driving force in the American Sunday School, Bible Society, Home Mission and evangelical activities. Leading abolitionist who broke with Garrison's extremism. Generous benefactor Broadway Tabernacle, New York, Keyon, Lane and Oberlin Colleges with his brother Lewis (qv).   DAmB

TAPPAN, Henry P 1805–81   Ch 2
Clergyman, philosopher; b New York state, ed Union College. Professor City University of New York; wrote on philosophy and theology. Visited Glasgow. President of Michigan University 1852–63. Spent most of the rest of his life in Europe.   DAmB

TAPPAN, Lewis 1788–1873   Chs 1, 3
Merchant abolitionist: b Mass. Treasurer in Channing Unitarian Church Became evangelical 1828 and joined business, moral partnership with brother Arthur. Active in abolitionism. Founded first credit rating company 1841.   DAmB

TAYLOR, W M 1829–95   Ch 4
(Bootle-Derby Road). DD from Yale and Amherst 1872. Accepted call and settled in New York.   DAmB: MacKelvie

TAYLOR, Revd Walter Ross, DD 1838–1907
b Thurso; 1868 Kelvinside FC Moderator Free Church 1900. Widely travelled in USA
Glasgow 1909

TAYLOR, William
(Stonehouse) 1798–1817). Emigrated to America. Died in Canada 1837.   MacKelvie

TELFER, David
(Bridge of Teith 1747–66). Emigrated to America 1770–71 to Pennsylvania. Died there.
MacKelvie

TENNANT, Sir Edward Priaulx, Bart, MP
Chemical industrialist's son. Barrister. Widely travelled in USA.   Glasgow 1909

THATCHER, Benjamin Bussey 1809–40   Ch 1
Unitarian, author, educator: ed Bowdoin; editor Colonisationist 1833–4; to Britain 1836.
                                                                                         DAmB

THOM, William   Ch 1
Minister of Govan 1748–90: ed Glasgow University. Wrote on emigration and social,
educational questions.   Fasti

THOMSON, Adam
(Coldstream West). DD Miami College, Oxford Ohio 1838, Died 1861.   MacKelvie

THOMSON, James
b Lockerbie (Auchtergavan 1806–16). Emigrated to America. Died 1830.   MacKelvie

THOMSON, Johnstone c1799–1882
b Ayrshire, attended Glasgow University 1821. Emigrated to Montreal Canada. Died Victoria,
Texas.   Addison

THOMSON, Sir William, Baron Kelvin 1824–1907   Chs 2, 5
Scientist: b Belfast, came to Glasgow in 1832 where his father was Professor of Mathematics in
the University; ed Glasgow and Cambridge Universities; Professor of Natural Philosophy at
Glasgow 1846–99; director Atlantic Telegraph Co 1856; demonstrated the potential use of
Niagara Falls for electrical generation 1881; developed manufacturers for his inventions;
adviser to Johns Hopkins in its early days.   DNB

THORBURN, Grant 1773–1863
Seedsman and author: b Dalkeith, Scotland. After being imprisoned for his radicalism, fled to
New York 1794. Became the first major American seedsman, with the first American seed
catalogue. Wrote various memoirs. A model for John Galt tale.   DAmB

TOLMIE, William Fraser
Doctor; Glasgow graduate; emigrated to Far West 1833; founder and chief trader of Fort
Nesqually; aided early American settlers in the Oregon country.   Winther.

TORRENS, Bailie James, 1811–84   Ch 4
Painter: b Edinburgh. Established his own business in Greenock. Briefly emigrated to
America. Returned to head new business, Torrens and Husband. Social reformer and active in
Scottish Permissive Bill and Temperance Association.   Social Reformer November 1884

TRAIN, George Francis 1829–1904   Ch 3
Made his fortune in shipping in USA and Australia. Became railroad and tramway
entrepreneur. Offered to operate services in Glasgow 1861. Vigorous supporter of militant
feminists.   DAmB

TRUEBLOOD, Benjamin Franklin 1847–1916   Ch 5
Educator, publicist and peace advocate: b Salem, Indiana. A Quaker, he became Professor of
Classics, Penn College, Iowa, subsequently President of Penn and Wilmington College, Ohio.
1890 became professional worker for peace, 1891 travelled in Europe. 1892–1915 editor
Advocate of Peace. Tireless worker in print, on state and at conferences. Visited Glasgow.
                                                                                         DAmB

TUCKERMAN, Joseph 1778–1840   Chs 1, 3, 4
Unitarian clergyman of old puritan ancestry; ed Harvard with W E Channing; minister in
Chelsea; growing concern for the poor he began his 'ministry at large'. Visited Britain and
Glasgow but back in USA his health broke in 1836; went to Cuba 1838 where he died.   DAmB

TUDHOPE, Archibald 1801–61
Clergyman: b Paisley, ed Glasgow University. Taught at Port Glasgow. At Annan 1834–38.
Emigrated to Philadelphia 1838. Resigned his charge 1849 and spent a year in Scotland and
elsewhere in Europe. Died Philadelphia.   St Andrew: Addison

TURNBULL, Frederick 1847–1909
b Glasgow. Introduced Turkey Red Dyeing to USA. Black

TURNBULL, W B
(Jedburgh) 1833 Up Class Emigrated to USA. MacKelvie

VAN DER HYDE, Revd Ch 1
Curate of St Mary's Glasgow. Emigrated to New Orleans 1889. Scottish Catholic Directory

VAUX, Robert Ch 2
Educator, Merchant. Quaker, promoter of infant schools. President of Board of Philadelphia
Schools 1818–31. Also deeply involved in temperance, savings banks and libraries public.
DAmB

VEBLEN, Thorsten Bunde 1857–1929
Economist and social theorist: ed Culeton College, Minn and Johns Hopkins Yale. Wrote The
Theory of the Leisure Class (1899). To Stanford at invitation of D S Jordan 1906. Then
various appointments until his death. DAmB

VINCENT, Henry 1810–78 Ch 4
b Cheltenham; Chartist lecturer in Bristol and South Wales; involved in Newport Rising 1839;
left UK for Philadelphia, Chicago; New York 1866 and again in 1868–70. Lectured often in
Scotland for temperance organisations. Died London. Boston

WADDELL, Peter Hateley 1817–91 Ch 1
b Slamannan; ed Glasgow University. Joined Free Church 1843 then founded the Church of
the Future, 1860 cd. Church built in Howard Street Glasgow for him 1870. Difficulties
followed and rejoined the Established Church 1888. DD From an American University. Died
1891 in Glasgow. John C Gibson, Life and Letters of Peter Hatley Waddell

WALD, Lillian 1867–1940 Ch 5
Public health reformer and settlement worker: b Cincinnati. Began to organise home nursing
for immigrants and professional public nursing training. Active with child problems, peace and
civil liberties. NAW

WALKER, George
(Falkirk). Emigrated 1835 to Dobbsferry, New York. MacKelvie

WALKER, John Hunter
b Binnie Hill Stirling: leader of Illinois State Federation of Labour; emigrated to USA at 9;
joined Knights of Labour at 11. Yearley

WALKER, Robert
General Superintendent of Glasgow Corporation Markets. b Stewarton, Ayrshire 1848.
Emigrated at 22 to USA for two years. Returned 1872 entered corporation scene.
Glasgow 1909

WALLACE, Alexander 1816–93
UP minister and vigorous temperance advocate and author. DD Westminster College, USA.
1864. After several charges he was minister at East Campbell Street Glasgow 1857–93.
Addison

WALLACE, John S 1851–1916
Judge and mineowner; b Coatbridge served apprenticeship as engineer and worked on North
British Railway. Father encouraged him to emigrate to Ohio 1874. Rose to be mine manager
then opened workings on his own account; owned largest wholesale retail coal co in South
Dakota; surveyed and laid out Burlington township. North Dakota Historical Society

WALLACE, Wilfred c1824–93
Merchant in New York city: b Dumfries; ed Glasgow University. Died Jersey City. Addison

WALLING, William English 1877–1936
Socialist and reformer: b Louisville, ed Louisville and Edinburgh where his father was a physician on the American Council. Studied at Chicago University; worked as a factory inspector and in a settlement house. Promoted Women's Trade Union League 1903, National Association for the Advancement of Coloured People, 1908; Russia 1905, met Lenin. Left Socialist Party in 1917. Died Amsterdam.   DAmB

WARD, Nahum
Ohio landowner of 12,000 acres from Marietta, Ohio who sought to induce Glaswegians to emigrate in 1822.   N Ward, A Brief Sketch of the State of Ohio (1822)

WARDLAW, Ralph 1779–1853   Ch 1
Congregational minister, antislavery, temperance campaigner: b Dalkeith, ed Glasgow University. Ministered in Glasgow to his death. Supporter of the British and Foreign Bible Society. DD Yale 1818.   DNB

WARNER, Amos Griswold 1861–1900   Ch 5
Sociologist: ed Johns Hopkins. Became Secretary Baltimore Charity Organisation Society 1888. Author of American Charities. To Stanford University 1893 but dogged by ill health.
                                                                                          DAmB

WATERTON, Charles   Ch 1
Naturalist. Travelled through the United States on one of his South American trips. Retained links with George Orr (qv) Married into the Edmonstone family of Cardross.   DNB

WATSON, Alex
(Perth) 1832 UP Class: teacher emigrated to USA.   MacKelvie

WATSON, Revd David 1869–1943   Ch 5
Social reformer and Minister: b Alva. Held St Clements, Glasgow 52 years to retirement from charge 1938. Supporter of Glasgow Workmen's Dwelling Company. Steeped in American Social Gospel Writers. Convener, Church of Scotland Social Work Committee for 8 years. DD 1913. Founder Chairman Scottish Christian Social Union 36 years.
                                  Glasgow Herald 6 November 1943 and Scottish Biography 1938

WATSON, George
Professor of Medicine: b Glasgow 1791, ed Glasgow University. MD Jefferson College, Philadelphia. FRCS London. Taught College St Medical School. Acquitted in body-snatching case 1814. Surgeon at the Royal Infirmary, Glasgow c1816. Private teacher of anatomy 1818. At University of Maryland 1820–5, London University 1827–31, Jefferson College, Philadelphia 1831–40 and University of New York 1840–51. His career has remarkable similarities to that of Granville Sharp Pattison in the same source.   Addison

WATSON, Hugh
b Ireland, ed Dublin and Lebanon University USA. Princeton University and Theological College. Served two charges in USA and two in Canada. To Britain 1923. To Methven Perth 1929.   Lamb

WATT, David Gilkinson c1818–1897
Ayrshire, ed Glasgow University. Minister served in several English towns and finally in St Petersburg Fla. Died London.   Addison

WEBSTER, Daniel 1782–1852
Statesman Lawyer: b New Hampshire; ed Dartmouth. A Federalist, he entered Congress in 1813–7, 1823–7. In Senate 1827–41, 1845–50. Secretary of State 1841–3 and 1850–2. Negotiated the Webster-Ashburton Treaty which settled the north eastern boundary of Canada and USA. Supported the 1850 Compromise which lost him abolitionist support. Visited Scotland 1839.   DAmB

WELLS, James Revd
b Castleyards, Dumfries 1838, ed Edinburgh University and Germany. 1867 delegate to Presbyterian Churches of America, instrumental in bringing Moody to Glasgow.
                                                                                  Glasgow 1909

WHITAKER, Thomas 1813–1899
Veteran temperance lecturer. Spent 8 months in USA 1874. Ofen lectured in Glasgow.
Boase: Scottish Reformer 25 November 1899

WHITE, James Bain, 1835–97   Ch 1
b Stirlingshire. Emigrated to Fort Wayne, Indiana 1854. Calico printer and tailor. Served and
wounded in Civil War 1861–2. Ran department store, wheel manufacturer and banker.
Representative Republican 1887–9.   Congress

WHITE, Robert
b 1837. Harbour Master of Glasgow. b Southampton. Served with navy twenty years. Became
Harbourmaster 1878. Travelled in USA 1908.   Glasgow 1909.

WHITEFIELD, George 1714–70   Ch 1
Evangelist in Scotland, England and S Colonies of America: b Gloucester, England, ed
Oxford. Frequently crossed the Atlantic on evangelical campaigns with immense success.
Worked in Scotland. His Life and Works, 6 vols written and edited by Revd John Gillies of
Cambuslang.   DNB

WHITLOCK, Brand 1869–1934   Ch 5
Reform Mayor of Toledo, novelist: b Ohio; worked in journalism and law. Worked for the
Liberal Governor Altgeld of Illinois. Strongly opposed to capital punishment. Mayor 1905–13.
Ambassador to Belgium 1913–22. Won great esteem through his relief work and sympathy for
Belgium in the First World War.   DAmB

WHYTE, James
(Kinkell) Associate Presbytery, Class of 1815. Emigrated to Salem, New York 1825. MacKelvie

WIER, William
Minister: b Ireland, ed Glasgow University. Irish Presbyterian church 1817. Ordained for New
Orleans 1819.   Addison

WILCOX, Delos F 1873–1928   Ch 5
Franchise and public utility expert. Served on various reform organisations and public
investigative commissions on municipal utilities. His conclusions were favourable to public
ownership.   DAmB

WILLARD, Frances 1839–1898   Chs 3, 4
Temperance advocate, womans suffrage and social reformer. Visited Glasgow twice.   DAmB

WILLARD, Josiah Flynt 1869–1907   Ch 3
Writer on vagrancy. His aunt was Frances E Willard. Son of Professor in Chicago Biblical
Institute. Travelled widely. Worked on Tolstoy's estate. Health deteriorated through drink.
DAmB

WILLIAMSON, David
(Whitehaven) 1787–1820. Emigrated to New York 1820. Died 1821.   Small

WILLIAMSON, John
b 1903 Glasgow. Radical agitator. Emigrated at 10. In Virginia, Philadelphia, Seattle,
Chicago. Through a Mr Harris from Glasgow turned to De Leon views. Joined the Communist
party. In Russia 1924. Active in numerous labour disputes. Eventually deported back to
Scotland 1955 under the Smith Act.
See his Dangerous Scot: The Life and Work of An American Undesirable (New York 1969).

WILLIAMSON, Mary 1839–1925   Ch 1
Universalist minister, served in Dundee 1866–1925 after returning from USA. Revisited several
times. Preached in Glasgow. Close friend of Caroline A Doule, the American Universalist
missionary.   Seaburg

WILSHIRE, (Henry) Gaylord 1861–1927   Ch 5
Editor and socialist: b Cincinnati, ed Harvard. Editor Wilshire's Magazine 1900. Unsuccessful
candidate for Congress 1890 and 1909, Parliament, in Manchester England 1894, and for the
Canadian parliament 1906. Visited Glasgow.   Who Was Who in America

WILSON, J Stitt
Ex-minister of religion, California Christian Socialist who became Mayor of Berkeley. Visited
Glasgow.   Stow and Persons

WILSON, James 1742–98
b Carskedo, near St Andrews, ed St Andrews, Glasgow and Edinburgh Universities. Emigrated
1765. Lawyer. Continental Congress. Signed Declaration of Independence. Associate Justice
US Supreme Court 1798–99. First Professor of Law College of Pennsylvania 1790.   Congress

WILSON, James 1836–1920
b Ayrshire; emigrated 1851, Connecticut; 1855 Iowa; ed Grinnell College; state legislature
1867–71; elected to Congress 1872–6; Secretary of Agriculture 1896–1912 longest term;
appointed by Woodrow Wilson to investigate British agriculture.   DAmB

WILSON, John MP 1828–1905
Represented Govan 1889–1900. Iron tube manufacturer. Home ruler, temperance advocate.
Business and reform interests in USA.   Stenton

WILSON, Sir John, DL
Wilsons and Clyde Coal Co: b 1844. Served on Glasgow Town Council 1894. MP 1895.
Temperance active in Workmen's Compensation interest. Toured widely in USA.
                                                                                          Glasgow 1909

WILSON, Walter   Ch 1
Glagow Colosseum drapers and chain of shops: b Gorbals. Town Councillor 1887. Toured
USA 1878 and 1903.   Glasgow 1909

WILSON, William Bauchop 1862–1934
b Blantyre. Emigrated with parents to Arnot, Pennsylvania 1870. Coal miner 1871–98
International Secretary Treasurer United Mineworkers Union 1900–1908. Secretary of Labour
under Woodrow Wilson 1913–21. Representative Democrat 1907–13.   Congress

WILSON, William
b Scotland: rose through UMW to become first Secretary of Labour under Woodrow Wilson.
                                                                                          Berthoff

WILSON, Woodrow 1856–1924
28th President of the USA. Son of Presbyterian minister: ed Johns Hopkins under H B
Adams. Appointed to Princeton. In Glasgow 1896. Became President of Princeton 1902;
Governor of New Jersey 1910. President USA 1912–20. Took America into World War I and
failed to win approval for American entry into the League of Nations.   DAmB

WINES, E C 1806–79   Ch 3
Prison reformer, educator, minister: b New Jersey. Editor American Journal of Education for
a spell. Gave monumental report on prisons 1867. Toured Europe 1871. International
Revolutionary Congress 1872.   DAmB

WINES, F C 1838–1912
Son of above. Social reformer 1869 in charge of Illinois public charities. Toured Europe 1878.
                                                                                          DAmB

WINTON, Alexander 1860–1932   Ch 1
b Grangemouth, ed Common school; served his time in Clyde engineering; emigrated to New
York 1878; Delameter Iron Works Engineer on New York S American ships. Married 1883
moved to Cleveland; began cycle business 1895; built early motorcycle, 1897; founded Winton
Motor Carriage Co; began marine engine business 1911, introduced diesel engines 1917: rail
cars builder; sold out his business in 1927.   W S McKinstry Alexander Winton (Cleveland nd)

WITHERSPOON, John 1723–94   Ch 2
b Gifford, Haddingtonshire, ed Edinburgh University. Ministry of Beith 1745. Paisley 1757
Resident of the College of New Jersey 1768. Member of Continental Congress. Signed
Declaration of Independence.   Congress: Collins Witherspoon 2 vols

WOODS, Leonard 1774–1854   Chs 2, 4
Congregational minister and professor of theology; b Princeton, a moderate Calvinist; founder member of the Board of Commissioners for Foreign Missions 1810; the American Tract Society 1814; the Education Society 1815; the American Temperance Society 1826. Wrote numerous tracts and pamphlets. In close touch with Glasgow religious reformers.
DAmB

WOODS, Robert A 1865–1925   Ch 5
Settlement worker, sociologist and reformer: b Pittsburg, of Scotch-Irish parents; ed Amherst and Andover. In London and Glasgow 1890–91. Wrote English Social Movements (1891) The City Wilderness (1898); Americans in Process (1902) etc as well as a campaign biography of Calvin Coolidge (1924).   DAmB

WRIGHT, Frances 1795–1852   Chs 1, 2, 3
Reformer: b Dundee, Scotland. Brought up in Glasgow and London. Daughter of a Dundee radical printer. Wrote play Altorf perfomed in New York (1819). A Few Days in Athens (1822) and later her Views of American Society. Associated with Robert Dale Owen in schemes for the reordering of society and education. Tried to liberate slaves in her model colony Nashoba, Tennessee. A popular lecturer she injoyed considerable notoriety for her feminist views. DAmB

YOUNG, William
Student minister (1781 Class). Emigrated to America and became a teacher in New York.
MacKelvie

YOUNG, William 1825–96
Deputy chief of Lloyd's. b Surrey, ed Glasgow University. Insurance broker 1856–96. Governor of Dulwich College 1872–96. Died in New York.   Addison